The
LITIGATION
PARALEGAL

A Systems Approach

Sixth Edition

Options.

We understand that affordable options are important. Visit us at cengage.com to take advantage of our new textbook rental program, which can be bundled with our MindTap products!

Over 300 products in every area of the law: MindTap, textbooks, online courses, reference books, companion websites, and more – Cengage Learning helps you succeed in the classroom and on the job.

Support.

We offer unparalleled course support and customer service: robust instructor and student supplements to ensure the best learning experience, custom publishing to meet your unique needs, and other benefits such as Cengage Learning's Student Achievement Award. And our sales representatives are always ready to provide you with dependable service.

Feedback.

As always, we want to hear from you! Your feedback is our best resource for improving the quality of our products. Contact your sales representative or write us at the address below if you have any comments about our materials or if you have a product proposal.

Accounting and Financials for the Law Office • Administrative Law • Alternative Dispute Resolution • Bankruptcy Business Organizations/Corporations • Careers and Employment • Civil Litigation and Procedure • CP Exam Preparation • Computer Applications in the Law Office • Constitutional Law • Contract Law • Criminal Law and Procedure • Document Preparation • Elder Law • Employment Law • Environmental Law • Ethics • Evidence Law • Family Law • Health Care Law • Immigration Law • Intellectual Property • Internships • Interviewing and Investigation • Introduction to Law • Introduction to Paralegalism • Juvenile Law • Law Office Management • Law Office Procedures • Legal Research, Writing, and Analysis • Legal Terminology • Legal Transcription • Media and Entertainment Law • Medical Malpractice Law • Product Liability • Real Estate Law • Reference Materials • Social Security • Torts and Personal Injury Law • Wills, Trusts, and Estate Administration • Workers' Compensation Law

---

CENGAGE
Learning®

5 Maxwell Drive
Clifton Park, New York 12065-2919

For additional information, find us online at: **cengage.com**

The
LITIGATION
PARALEGAL

A Systems Approach

Sixth Edition

James W.H. McCord, J.D.
Pamela R. Tepper

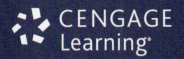
CENGAGE
Learning®

Australia • Brazil • Mexico • Singapore • United Kingdom • United States

The Litigation Paralegal: A Systems Approach, Sixth Edition
James W.H. McCord, J.D. and
Pamela R. Tepper

SVP, GM Skills & Global Product
  Management: Dawn Gerrain

Product Director: Matthew Seeley

Product Manager: Katie McGuire

Senior Director, Development:
  Marah Bellegarde

Senior Product Development Manager:
  Larry Main

Senior Content Developer: Melissa Riveglia

Senior Product Assistant: Diane Chrysler

Vice President, Marketing Services:
  Jennifer Ann Baker

Marketing Manager: Scott Chrysler

Senior Production Director: Wendy Troeger

Production Director: Andrew Crouth

Senior Content Project Manager:
  Betty L. Dickson

Managing Art Director: Jack Pendleton

Software Development Manager: Joe Pliss

Cover image: iStockPhoto.com/mevans

For product information and technology assistance, contact us at
Cengage Learning Customer & Sales Support, 1-800-354-9706

For permission to use material from this text or product,
submit all requests online at **www.cengage.com/permissions**.
Further permissions questions can be e-mailed to
permissionrequest@cengage.com

Library of Congress Control Number: 2015948381

ISBN: 978-1-285-85715-2

Cengage Learning
20 Channel Center Street
Boston, MA 02210
USA

Cengage Learning is a leading provider of customized learning solutions with office locations around the globe, including Singapore, the United Kingdom, Australia, Mexico, Brazil, and Japan. Locate your local office at: **www.cengage.com/global**

Cengage Learning products are represented in Canada by Nelson Education, Ltd.

To learn more about Cengage Learning, visit **www.cengage.com**

Purchase any of our products at your local college store or at our preferred online store **www.cengagebrain.com**

Printed in Mexico
Print Number: 04   Print Year: 2020

To Sandy,

*the love of my life, and
in loving memory of my parents*

Marks W. and Hazel C. McCord

J. McCord

AND

*To my family, the Teppers, and my St. Thomas family,
the Van Beverhoudts, all your support does not go unnoticed.*

Thank you is never enough.

Pamela

BRIEF CONTENTS

CONTENTS

CHAPTER 4
Drafting the Complaint   165

CHAPTER 5
Filing the Lawsuit, Service of Process, and Obtaining a Default Judgment 201

CHAPTER 6
Defending and Testing the Lawsuit: Motions, Answers, and Other Responsive Pleadings   238

CHAPTER 7
Discovery and Electronic Discovery: Overview and Interrogatories   291

CHAPTER 8
Discovery: Depositions   352

CHAPTER 9
Discovery: Document Production and Control, Medical Exams, Admissions, and Compelling Discovery   396

CHAPTER 10
Settlement and Other Alternative Dispute Resolutions   452

CHAPTER 11
Trial Preparation and Trial   503

CHAPTER 12
Post-Trial Practice from Motions to Appeal   548

PREFACE

Litigation is a vital and often dramatic component of our system of dispute resolution. *The Litigation Paralegal: A Systems Approach*, Sixth Edition provides students and faculty with learning resources written specifically for them—resources combining the theories and principles of law with practical paralegal skills, paralegal ethics, and a sensitivity toward the goals and needs of the paralegal profession, all in the context of the law office.

Like the *Fifth Edition* of this text, the *Sixth Edition* is a comprehensive revision impacting every chapter. Although the changes are numerous, the most significant changes are the additions of new features, which include Technology Update, Trade Secrets, Ethical Considerations, and Case Study: Understanding the Law. Each new feature provides important information that can be used in the paralegal's daily practice.

The "Technology Update" focuses on advances in technology relating to the civil litigation arena. Such areas as cloud computing and predictive coding are highlighted in this section.

The feature titled "Trade Secrets" includes practical tips and suggestions that will help paralegals in their day-to-day job assignments. How to use social media in civil litigation is just one of the areas discussed in the Trade Secrets feature.

The "Ethical Considerations" feature concentrates on the many ethical issues paralegals encounter. These sections are intended to offer some guidance on the distinction between the role of the attorney and the role of the paralegal in the legal profession.

Previous editions discussed important cases throughout the text. In the *Sixth Edition*, important or precedential cases are analyzed in Case Study: Understanding the Law. For some, this may be their first introduction to case analysis and review. In this section, cases are summarized and digested with review questions posed at the end for critical review of the concepts discussed in the featured case.

Additionally, the *Sixth Edition* continues exploring the ever changing area of *electronic discovery* and the associated ethical and practical responsibilities of the lawyer and the paralegal in that area. Since the *Fifth Edition*, more revisions to the *Federal Rules of Evidence and Civil and Appellate Procedure* have occurred and are examined further, as are the practice requirements of the *Health Insurance Portability and Accountability Act*. Relevant new forms have been added or substituted and others revised to reflect current practice.

Similarly, new features have been added to assist the student in applying and understanding the information discussed in the chapter. These features are "Apply Your Knowledge" and "Internet Exercises." Both features assist the student in reinforcing the concepts addressed in the chapter as well as learning how to locate information on the Internet. Many of the exercises encourage the student to understand the differences in the federal and state systems, including forms and rules of court.

There are also new exercise and assignment features at the end of each chapter. The newest addition is the Case Assignments. This feature assists the student in following one case—the *Forrester* case—from interview to appeal. Drafting all the key litigation documents is the mainstay of this exercise and will assist the student in building a portfolio that can be used as future examples of how to draft a particular document, or to be used as a sample of the student's abilities when interviewing for prospective jobs. The Case Assignment is intended as a skill builder and a practical way for the student to see the development of the concepts in the course of study and, in turn, real life. Additionally, many of the Systems Folder Assignments and Application Assignments from the *Fifth Edition* Workbook have been updated and incorporated into the end-of-chapter questions.

Finally, the attention to the application of state rules and practice is continued in the *Sixth Edition*. The *Sixth Edition* encourages students through many of the exercises and features to review state rules and practice and note the differences and similarities to federal practice.

This text is suited to several types of litigation students: the traditional college classroom student, the student in an online course, and the paralegal being trained in the law office as a litigation paralegal.

ORGANIZATION OF TEXT

The Litigation Paralegal: A Systems Approach, Sixth Edition remains true to its origins. It continues to introduce students to the law office and takes them chronologically through the steps and tasks involved in litigation, from the facts of the cases they will be working on to judgment enforcement and appeal. Chapter by chapter they build proficiency in the specific tasks or competencies that are required of them as paralegals. The text places the student in a law office setting where the instructor assumes the role of the paralegal's supervising attorney. This office training procedure uses a systems approach in which the student develops a litigation systems folder complete with forms, documents, checklists, rules, relevant websites, and practice tips. The folder, completed by the end of the course, provides the student with a valuable resource.

Use of the systems approach enhances the process of both teaching and learning litigation paralegal skills. Because a good systems folder helps the student on the job and maybe even in securing a job, the systems folder provides an extra incentive to do the accompanying assignments at the end of each chapter thoroughly and accurately. It teaches the benefits of being organized and develops the confidence to create a system in any area of law. Utilization of the systems approach also reinforces the skills presented in the text. The text, its exercises, and instructor's manual, however, are flexible and designed to accommodate approaches other than a systems approach.

FEATURES OF THE TEXT

In each chapter the student is given the following:

1. Learning objectives

2. One or more specific litigation tasks

3. Substantive and procedural background on the task.

4. Guidelines and directions on how to perform the task

5. Examples from a sample case on how to perform the task

6. Practical application of concepts discussed

7. Helpful websites

8. Study questions to review and reinforce learning

9. Key terms for vocabulary building

10. Case Assignments for drafting and skill building

Application of Knowledge

Each chapter, according to its focus, contains a varying balance of exercises for in-class or out-of-class assignments and discussions.

Systems Folder Assignments structure the building of an impressive practice system of topically arranged forms, legal principles, rules, checklists, and other material. An outline of the systems folder contents is in Appendix A.

Application Assignments require the application of legal principles to new fact situations or to practice skills. They test the student's understanding of the concepts presented within the chapter.

Internet Exercises encourage familiarity with electronic research on relevant websites.

Other features of the text include:

- **Professional Associations and Resources**
  References to numerous relevant professional organizations, associations, and related websites, publications, standards, and other resources are provided.

- **Case Law and Other Authority**
  Citations refer to pertinent case law, statutes, rules, and American Bar Association standards. The Case Study: Understanding the Law feature provides the student with precedential or relevant cases on the topics covered in the chapter. Questions for Review test the student's understanding of the legal precepts presented in the case identified.

- **Sample Practice Forms**
  Many practice forms, pleadings, motions, and other documents are included to provide familiarity with forms and to give a basis from which to work with state forms or to draft forms.

- **Checklists**
  Checklists give step-by-step guidance in specific practice situations and provide examples for developing additional checklists as needed.

- **Diagrams, Tables, and Charts**
  Visual aids facilitate learning, stimulate interest, and summarize and organize important information. Space is provided in exhibits for the addition of state-specific information.

- **Legal Terminology**
  Key legal terms are highlighted in bold and defined in the text as well as in the margins for quick access. They are also listed at the end of each chapter and in the Glossary at the end of the text.

- **End-of-Chapter Exercises and Assignments**
  New exercises are included at the end of each chapter, including Systems Folder and Application Assignments as well as Case Assignments that follow a case from the beginning of the litigation process to the final stages on appeal, providing students with a portfolio for future reference and use.

NEW FEATURES AND CHANGES TO THE SIXTH EDITION

- **Most Significant Additions**
  The most significant additions include updated information on e-discovery (including the duty to protect and preserve evidence) and related forms, courtroom decorum for paralegals, and the latest in courtroom presentation technology and practice. Practical tips and important cases highlight the new edition's features as well as new exercises and assignments emphasizing Internet skills and drafting.

- **General Resource Guide for Investigation on the Web**
  Chapter 3 contains an updated guide to law-related and other resources on the web. Used as is or as a resource to be periodically updated in the law office, the guide is a valuable, categorized resource.

- **Updated Internet and Application Exercises**

- **Case Examples**
  Recent case examples, including Supreme Court cases, are included throughout the text. Relevant and significant cases are now summarized with review questions added for critical thinking and understanding of the legal precepts addressed in the chapter.

- **Systems Folder Assignments and Application Assignments**
  Many of the Systems Folder Assignments and Application Assignments from the *Fifth Edition* Workbook have been updated and added to the end of each chapter.

- **Updated Pleadings, Motions, and Time Limits Chart**
  This chart, located at the end of Chapter 6, has been expanded and updated to reflect recent changes in the Federal Rules of Civil and Appellate Procedure.

- **Changes to the Federal Rules**

  The text identifies and explains important changes in the federal rules on civil procedure, evidence, and appeal. Those impacting e-service and filing, e-discovery, attorney/client privilege and trial preparation materials (work product), subpoenas, and citation of unpublished court opinions are most important.

- **American Bar Association Standards**

  Expanded discussions of ABA standards on e-discovery, Ethics 2000, and ABA Principles for Juries and Jury Trials (2005) are presented.

- **Other Changes**

  Other changes have been made in every chapter of the book to see that forms and checklists are current and that text and concepts are both current and clear. Additions include jurisdiction, class actions, federal tort claims practice, metadata, high-low agreements, offer of judgment, types of verdict, practice tips, and other topics and procedures.

SUPPLEMENTAL TEACHING AND LEARNING MATERIALS

Instructor Companion Site

The online Instructor Companion Site provides the following resources:

Instructor's Manual and Test Bank

The **Instructor's Manual** and Test Bank have been greatly expanded to incorporate changes in the text and to provide comprehensive teaching support. The Instructor's Manual contains instructional tips, suggested class activities, and answers to the text questions.

PowerPoint Presentations

Customizable Microsoft PowerPoint® Presentations focus on key points for each chapter. (Microsoft PowerPoint® is a registered trademark of the Microsoft Corporation.)

Cengage Learning Testing Powered by Cognero is a flexible, online system that allows you to:

- author, edit, and manage test bank content from multiple Cengage Learning solutions

- create multiple test versions in an instant

- deliver tests from your LMS, your classroom, or wherever you want

Start Right Away!

Cengage Learning Testing Powered by Cognero works on any operating system or browser.

- No special installs or downloads needed

- Create tests from school, home, the coffee shop—anywhere with Internet access

What Will You Find?

- **Simplicity at every step.** A desktop-inspired interface features drop-down menus and familiar, intuitive tools that take you through content creation and management with ease.
- **Full-featured test generator.** Create ideal assessments with your choice of 15 question types (including true/false, multiple choice, opinion scale/Likert, and essay). Multi-language support, an equation editor, and unlimited metadata help ensure your tests are complete and compliant.
- **Cross-compatible capability.** Import and export content into other systems.

To access additional course materials, please go to login.cengage.com, then use your SSO (single sign-on) login to access the materials.

> Please note the Internet resources are of a time-sensitive nature and URL addresses may often change or be deleted.

ABOUT THE AUTHORS

James W. H. McCord earned his law degree at the University of Wisconsin-Madison and practiced civil and criminal law before becoming the first director of the Paralegal Program at Eastern Kentucky University. He has served as president of the American Association for Paralegal Education and as a member of the American Bar Association Commission on Approval of Legal Assistant Programs. He has published articles and other books on paralegals and paralegal education, including the coauthored *Criminal Law and Procedure for the Paralegal: A Systems Approach*.

Pamela R. Tepper is presently the Solicitor General of the Virgin Islands Department of Justice, in St. Thomas, Virgin Islands. She presently manages the Solicitor General Division which focuses on appeals, contract review, administrative representation of the executive branch departments and the preparation of legal advice to those departments. She formerly was an Assistant Attorney General and the Deputy Solicitor General of that Department, managing the divisions contracts, appeals, and special projects. From 2000 to 2008, Ms. Tepper was the Vice President of Legal Affairs and General Counsel at the Governor Juan F. Luis Hospital and Medical Center, St. Croix, Virgin Islands. For over 20 years, Ms. Tepper has taught at a number of paralegal programs, including the Southeastern Paralegal Institute and Southern Methodist University in Dallas, Texas; The University of Texas, Arlington campus; and the University of the Virgin Islands. Along with this textbook, Ms. Tepper is the author of *The Law of Contracts and the Uniform Commercial Code, Third Edition, Basic Legal Writing for Paralegals, Second Edition, Legal Research and Writing*, and *Texas Legal Research, Second Edition*.

ACKNOWLEDGMENTS

As is true with previous editions of this text, this edition would not have been possible without the invaluable contributions of so many people. As always the Cengage Learning family has supported this endeavor unconditionally. But this book would not have seen the light of day had it not been for the efforts of Melissa Riveglia, our Content Developer. She is our sounding board, our guiding light, and, above all, our rock. We don't know what we would do without her. Her quiet strength is never underestimated and we are grateful to have worked with her on this book as well as others. THANK YOU, Melissa.

Family is integral to a project of this magnitude. Thanks go out to Marc Tepper for being there when needed and to the Tepper family for being supportive. A special thanks goes out to Sandy McCord for her contributions to this text. And many thanks go to Eastern Kentucky University for setting the stage for the *Sixth Edition* of this book. All the tools and resources used, such as the use of the impressive under-graduate law library and resources of the Department of Government and the Paralegal Program, created the backbone for this edition and previous ones.

We also are grateful for the valuable contributions of the Cengage Learning team for this sixth edition: Katie McGuire, Product Manager; Diane Chrysler, Senior Product Assistant; and Betty Dickson, Senior Content Project Manager.

Finally, we are indebted for the many hours spent by the individuals reviewing drafts of this edition and giving us valuable suggestions. Thank you so much.

James W.H. McCord, J.D.

Pamela R. Tepper

Reviewers

Sally B. Bisson
College of Saint Mary
Omaha, NE

Beverly Woodall Browman
Everest Institute
Pittsburgh, PA

Reginia Judge
Montclair State University
Montclair, NJ

Elizabeth Mann
Greenville Technical College
Greenville, SC

Scott Sean
St. Petersburg College
Clearwater, FL

WELCOME TO THE LAW OFFICE: FOUNDATIONS FOR LITIGATION

OUTLINE

OBJECTIVES

AFTER READING THIS CHAPTER, YOU WILL BE ABLE TO:

- Understand the role of the paralegal in the law office
- Recognize the importance of law office procedures in the practice of law
- Explain the ethical obligations of the paralegal in the legal arena
- Distinguish between the federal and state court systems
- Identify the different types of jurisdiction and in which court cases should be filed

INTRODUCTION

civil litigation
The process whereby one person sues another person in a court of law to enforce a right or to seek a remedy such as financial compensation.

Civil litigation is the process whereby one person sues another person in a court of law to enforce a right or to seek a remedy such as financial compensation. Established procedures facilitate the fair resolution of conflicts that might not otherwise be peacefully resolved. Our focus is civil litigation, suits between private citizens for wrongs such as the carelessness leading to an auto accident or the failure to follow the terms of a contract. We will not address criminal litigation, which is the government suing a person for specific violation of the criminal code such as murder and robbery.

The following cases are typical of the kinds of circumstances that spawn litigation. They are real in the sense that there are hundreds of cases just like these, involving human pain and deeply felt emotions.

In the chapters to come, paralegal tasks will be presented in the context of one or more of these cases. Case I, the *Forrester* case, will be the text's main reference. Some of the other cases will be used for task assignments. The remaining cases illustrate other kinds of litigation. The cases will also be used to place you in as realistic a law office setting as a textbook can create.

☐ CASE I
Negligence or Not: The Case of the Out-of-Control Van
Forrester v. Hart and Mercury Parcel Service, Inc.

On her way to work Tuesday, February 26, Ann Forrester ducked her head against the cold wind and stepped gingerly across the ice patches on Highway 328 to put a letter in the mailbox. Her husband, William Forrester, and children, Sara, age four, and Michael, age eight, waited in the car in the Forrester driveway, ready to be dropped off at work, day care, and school. They live in a small town called Statesville in Middleton County.

Michael yawned and drew pictures on the frosty car window with his fingernail. Sara banged her new pink snowboots against the seat. "Cut that out, Sara!" William warned, then opened the car door to yell, "Hurry up, Ann, or we'll be late!" She didn't seem to hear.

Richard Hart, married and father of three teenage children, sang along with the radio as he drove his Mercury Parcel Service van the morning of February 26. After delivering this express package, he would take a breakfast break. It hadn't been fun driving in the wind and patchy ice from Dayton, Ohio into the state of Columbia.

As the van topped a sharp crest in the road, Mr. Hart saw a woman on the right side of the road stepping out onto the highway. He pressed down hard on the brake pedal, but the van didn't stop.

The woman, Ann Forrester, looked up at the approaching van. She saw it skidding toward her. Ann Forrester scrambled frantically, in vain. Mr. Hart could not bring the vehicle under control, and it struck Ms. Forrester, then smashed into a tree. ■

☐ CASE II
Knowledge of a Preexisting Problem: The Smoldering Electrical Connection
Ameche v. Congden

Margie and Leroy Congden, owners of Maple Meadows Campground, were told that electrical outlets at some of the campsites weren't working. The Congdens groaned. It was the middle of the busiest season of the year.

Leroy confirmed that the problem included all sites from 30 to 39 and found that repair would necessitate digging a trench across the ten campsites to excavate the faulty wiring.

"We have to keep those sites available, at least until after Labor Day," Margie told Leroy. "There's no way we can notify all the people who have made reservations that we won't have a place for them, and there isn't another campground within one hundred miles."

Leroy made an appointment with an electrician to do the repairs after September 7, then ran a connecting line of extension cords from the outlet at site 40 to the affected sites. He was careful to string the cords along the gravel edge of the campsites away from traffic areas. The rubber casing on one of the cords was broken in several places, he noticed, but concluded it would not be a problem.

On the afternoon of August 21, Carl and Zoe Ameche set up their camper on site 36 of Maple Meadows Campground. Meanwhile, their six-year-old son, Zach, collected bugs and sticks and gathered gravel into piles.

When Carl finished with the camper, he noticed an extension cord connection lying on the ground near where his son was playing. He pulled the cord away from the campsite into a grassy area.

Mr. and Mrs. Ameche unpacked and relaxed in their camper, occasionally noticing a flickering of the camper light. Emerging later, they found the grassy area behind their campsite in flames. Carl found Zach unharmed, trapped on the other side of the fire, and was able to carry him to safety, but received severe burns on his own arms and legs in the process. Since most campers had not yet checked in, there were no other injuries, but several campsites, some recreation facilities, and many of the venerable maple trees for which the camp was named, were destroyed. ∎

☐ CASE III
Negligence or Product Defect: The Daredevil versus the Motorbike Design
Coleman v. Make Tracks, Inc.

Harold James, an executive at Make Tracks, Inc., propped his feet on his desk and looked out over the skyline of Legalville. He had finally brought his successful bicycle company into the motor age with the new three-wheeled all-terrain vehicle, Big Track, now being shipped to markets across the region.

James had pushed diversification to capture a more modern image for the company in a speed-conscious society. The positive reaction to television ads featuring the Big Track over bold computer graphics and rock music seemed to bear him out.

His friends had urged him to take the safer route, to stay with bicycles. After all, he had three kids to educate. He was glad he had not listened.

At the Coleman farm on Labor Day, September 4, laughter and wisecracks focused on Sean Coleman, the only child of Sam and Emma Coleman. His effervescent personality and athletic skills had made him a leader at Lafayette County High. His intelligence and academic record convinced adults in the community that he would go far. In two years he would be off to Columbia State University, where he planned to major in agriculture in preparation for managing the family farm.

Now Sean was celebrating with his friends—trading stories, eating hot dogs, and taking turns riding the new Big Track three-wheeled all-terrain vehicle that he had received for his recent sixteenth birthday.

"So, Hotshot," called Sean's best friend, Jason Hackett, "Let's see you ride that thing like they do on TV!"

Sean gave him a thumbs-up signal, and was off, riding up a nearby hill. Rapidly increasing speed, he hit full throttle at the steepest incline before the crest of the hill. The front wheel lifted off the ground, flipping the vehicle backward onto Sean. The county rescue squad rushed him to the hospital, unconscious. ∎

□ CASE IV
Contractual Obligations: The Effect of The Inexperienced Partner—Christmas Humbug
Briar Patch Dolls, Inc. v. Teeny Tiny Clothing Manufacturing Co.

Pandemonium broke out in the aisles of toy departments across the country. There were fewer than forty shopping days until Christmas, and the stock of popular Briar Patch Dolls was 30 to 60 percent short.

Briar Patch Dolls seemed to be an overnight craze, but it had taken Paul and Judy Heinz twelve years to build up from the cottage industry production of a few hand sewn rag dolls for a local gift shop. The business had grown slowly and gradually from a fledgling storefront in Asheville, North Carolina, until last year, when the Heinzes decided on a major expansion. They invested their last dollars in new equipment, employees, and a national advertising campaign that produced Christmas orders for 100,000 dolls—ten times last year's number. Production of the dolls proceeded on schedule.

Paul and Judy Heinz obtained clothing for the dolls from the Teeny Tiny Clothing Manufacturing Company, Inc., which made the trademark denim overalls worn by all Briar Patch Dolls. Three friends owned and operated Teeny Tiny Clothing and had expanded it to keep pace with Briar Patch. Although not all past contracts for the denim overalls had been filled on time, sales of the dolls had not been substantially hurt.

The general manager and primary force in the enterprise was Ethel Meyers, an energetic, creative woman. Her partners, Harriet Smith and Alice McGinnis, were mostly interested in supplementing their families' incomes while their children were in college.

In January of the prior year, a contract had been signed between Briar Patch Dolls, a Vermont Corporation, and Teeny Tiny Clothing, a Massachusetts Corporation, for 100,000 pairs of doll overalls, sewn to specification, to be delivered in increments of 25,000 on March 15, May 15, July 15, and September 15. Within thirty days of delivery, Briar Patch was to pay two dollars for each pair of overalls delivered in satisfactory condition.

On March 11, Ethel Meyers died. Teeny Tiny Clothing tried to meet the contract anyway. On March 15, 24,000 overalls were delivered, of which 5,000 were unsatisfactory. The other delivery dates were met as follows:

May 15:	15,000 pieces, 5,000 unsatisfactory
July 15:	10,000 pieces, 5,000 unsatisfactory
September 15:	7,000 pieces, 3,000 unsatisfactory
October 15:	3,000 pieces, 2,000 unsatisfactory

As a result of the delays, inadequate shipments, and defects, Briar Patch was able to fill only 40 percent of its orders. At a profit of ten dollars per doll, Briar Patch lost $600,000.

The next year, children's television programming became saturated with colorful ads for Jolly Lolly clown dolls, which replaced Briar Patch Dolls as number one on children's Christmas lists. ∎

☐ CASE V
Incompetence or Sexual Harassment: Workplace Discrimination
Rakowski v. Montez Construction Co.

Darlene Rakowski was proud to be the first woman to be hired for a nonsecretarial position by Montez Construction Company. Adam Stroud, the foreman who hired her, said he really didn't think a woman was tough enough for the job, but she was determined to try.

As she arrived the first day, catcalls and whistles erupted from the crew. A couple of the men followed her, doing an exaggerated bump and grind. The sexual behavior ended after Ms. Rakowski complained to the foreman. Thereafter, however, Ms. Rakowski was assigned menial tasks, primarily fetch and carry orders on the ground. Rarely was she allowed to work with equipment on actual construction, although her vocational school training had prepared her to do so. Her usually competent work on these simple tasks elicited loud mocking from her co-workers and almost weekly profane outbursts from the foreman. His complaints never included instructions on how to do a better job, but rather references to Ms. Rakowski's stupidity and worthlessness, and were always made in front of other workers. When a male worker made mistakes, Mr. Stroud called him into his office for a quiet conference. Ms. Rakowski went to Mr. Stroud to complain about her treatment, and he responded that she was taking it too seriously.

As the incidents continued, Ms. Rakowski became more distraught, occasionally bursting into tears, which only intensified the mocking and jeering from her fellow workers. In desperation she went to Carlos Montez, owner of the company. He promised to look into the problem, and advised her to "loosen up."

Conditions did not change. Complaints about the quality of her work and her inability to lift certain items, follow directions, and operate tools safely were filed in her personnel record. She was not given the normal opportunity to rebut such charges. Very upset, Ms. Rakowski missed more and more work.

Having made her decision to look for another job, Ms. Rakowski travels from employment agency to employment agency with no success. She feels trapped, wondering, "What am I going to do?" ■

OFFICE MANUAL

Successful litigation requires skill and efficiency. One tool for efficiency is the office manual or handbook. These books, in loose-leaf or electronic format, consist of information, policies, and procedures that help employees work more effectively from the first day forward. Paralegals may be assigned the task of writing an office manual.

The following section is an example of a manual designed to orient a new paralegal to the firm. This manual describes the structure and personnel of the law office and some of the essential procedures, such as timekeeping and billing, employed by most law firms. Thriving in a law office environment is crucial to your well-being and is addressed here as well. Learning processes employed in your training are introduced in the manual, as are the ethical and professional responsibilities that you must assume from the start. In short, the *Paralegal Handbook* addresses fundamentals essential to becoming an effective litigation paralegal. Following the handbook is a review of the U.S. court system and the somewhat complex issues of jurisdiction, venue, and related concepts.

THE PARALEGAL HANDBOOK

White, Wilson & McDuff

Attorneys at Law

Federal Plaza Building, Suite 700

Third and Market Streets

Legalville, Columbia 00000

(111) 555-0000

THE PARALEGAL HANDBOOK: OFFICE ORIENTATION AND ETHICS

THE LAW FIRM'S STRUCTURE AND PERSONNEL ORGANIZATION

Titles/Diversity

Partners

Attorney owners of the law firm who share in profits.

Associates

Attorneys who are salaried in a law firm.

This firm is structured like many other law firms in the United States. **Partners** are the attorney-owners of the law firm and share in its profits. *Senior partners* are the partners who have been with the firm the longest and often have the greatest ownership share. Attorneys who have not yet become partners and are salaried are **associates**. More experienced associates are sometimes given the title *senior associate. Staff attorneys* are hired for economic reasons and, unlike associates, have no expectation of becoming partners. *Temporary or contract attorneys* may be hired for a limited period of time to address a brief expansion of the firm's workload. Some attorneys may have the designation *of counsel,* which means they maintain an advisory capacity or refer clients to the law firm (or do both).

Personnel other than lawyers include paralegals, paralegal managers, law clerks, and legal secretaries. *Paralegals* (also called legal assistants) are educated in legal skills and provide legal services under the supervision of an attorney, or as otherwise permitted by law. *Paralegal managers* (often experienced paralegals) administer paralegal hiring, training, and productivity. *Law clerks* work in the law office while completing their law degrees. Clerical, administrative, and computer services for the office are provided by *legal secretaries or administrative assistants.* Small law offices may have fewer levels of employees, and large firms can have legal administrators, litigation managers, investigators, errand runners, and receptionists. A relatively new addition to some law firms is the *nonlawyer manager/executive.* Akin to corporate chief operating officers, these employees often have executive authority for the firm's business policies and strategies, within the professional and ethical constraints of our state bar association. Our office structure is typical of the small or medium-sized firm and is illustrated in the office organization chart in Exhibit 1.1.

Diversity in our office personnel at all levels enriches our work environment, improves communication with an increasingly diverse clientele, and is good for business. A rapidly growing list of businesses and major corporations look to hire law firms with diverse personnel, including women and minority partners. Developing corresponding policies and benefits, such as better access for the physically challenged in accordance with the American with Disabilities Act ("ADA") plus child care, flex time, and family leave programs, is our goal.

The Changing Law Office: Our Practice and Future Goals

New technology and a global economy are offering both pressures and incentives for law offices to change their ways of doing business. Office executives face the challenge of keeping their firms competitive not only with firms across the courthouse square, but also with firms across the nation and world.

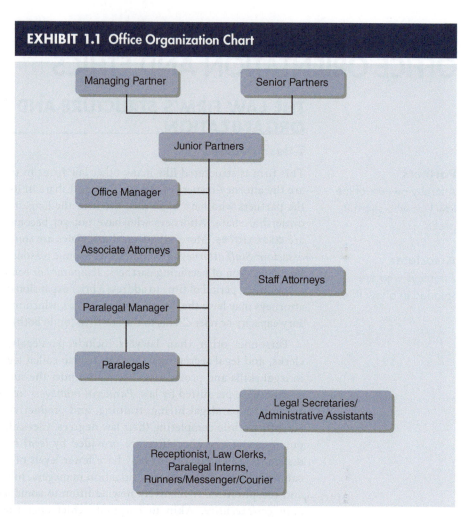

EXHIBIT 1.1 Office Organization Chart

- Managing Partner
- Senior Partners
- Junior Partners
- Office Manager
- Associate Attorneys
- Staff Attorneys
- Paralegal Manager
- Paralegals
- Legal Secretaries/Administrative Assistants
- Receptionist, Law Clerks, Paralegal Interns, Runners/Messenger/Courier

multijurisdictional practices

The provision of legal services in states other than the one for which the attorney is licensed.

pro hace vice

Application by licensed attorneys to practice for a limited purpose in another jurisdiction where they are not licensed.

Seeking efficiency in both time and cost, increasingly sophisticated clients expect to access legal services through the Internet and even to bid online to set the cost of those services. **Multijurisdictional practices**, the provision of legal services in states other than the one for which the attorney is licensed, is fast becoming the norm. Predictors envision *multidisciplinary businesses* housing, for example, legal, accounting, real estate, engineering, or other departments in one firm. Although multidisciplinary practice is currently not permitted in most states, the realities of the e-world may force that change. The e-world also has led to law firm use of Web pages and informative *blogs* (Web logs—topical chronological journals) to serve clients and market legal services. As a member of this office, you will become an important part of our efforts to compete on a new and broader scale. Thus, one of your jobs as a paralegal will be to assist in determining the rules for practicing in a multijurisdictional world. Identifying the requirements, such as learning the steps for **pro hace vice** status in a state, will be important in your job responsibilities. Petitioning a court for *pro hace vice* status permits an attorney to practice law in a jurisdiction for which he or she is not licensed. Usually this status is limited on a case-by-case basis. Understanding the *pro hace vice* requirements in a particular state will assist the firm in fulfilling its ethical obligations and avoid the unauthorized practice of law.

The Work of the Firm: Our Specialties

This firm is primarily engaged in civil litigation. Our cases include the following:

Personal injury cases arise when an individual has been physically injured from the negligence (carelessness) of another—for example, an automobile accident or a slip-and-fall case. This type of case accounts for most of the litigation work we do.

Malpractice cases involve alleged acts of negligence on the part of physicians, counselors, lawyers, or other professionals.

Product liability cases belong to a special type of personal injury case in which the individual has been physically injured by a defective product, such as an exploding beverage bottle, adulterated food, or unsafe machinery.

Contracts cases involve one party having suffered a loss from the failure of another party to meet the terms of an agreement between them. A typical contract case could involve the failure to complete construction of a house, or the failure to pay once construction is complete.

Corporation cases are brought by one corporation against another for such incidents as trademark violation or industrial espionage.

Antitrust cases deal with individuals, government, or a business suing another business for harmful trade practices, such as price discrimination, unfair competition, or monopolization of a market.

Securities cases arise from disputes regarding the ownership, value, or other issues regarding stocks, bonds, certificates, and other documentation of financial property.

Civil rights cases involve an individual or the government suing another party for violation of rights guaranteed by federal and state law. A typical civil rights litigation might involve race, sex, disability, or age discrimination.

Intellectual property cases primarily encompass disputes over patents, copyrights, and trademarks.

The Role of the Paralegal: An Indispensable Team Member

The paralegal is an essential component in our delivery of legal services. You will spend the largest share of your time gathering and organizing factual information and drafting legal documents. You also will conduct legal research and investigation, assist at hearings and trials, oversee the timely scheduling and filing of matters, and help the office keep our clients informed as to the status of their cases. Unresponsiveness is among the most significant reasons a firm loses clients. Recently, our paralegals have begun to participate in case planning, client meetings, and firm marketing. Their familiarity with technology and the Internet makes them valuable to this firm's aggressive efforts to adapt to the e-world.

The firm bills clients directly for your services in the same manner we bill for the time of our attorneys. Court decisions, including the Supreme Court decision in *Missouri v. Jenkins,* 491 U.S. 274 (1989), confirm the legality and advantages of billing for paralegal time.

CASE STUDY: UNDERSTANDING THE LAW

The leading case on what a law firm is permitted to bill for a paralegal's time was decided in the precedential case of *Missouri v. Jenkins*, 491 U.S. 274 (1989). In that case, this issue before the U.S. Supreme Court was what constituted billable time for a paralegal and at what market rate should a paralegal's time be billed as part of an award for attorney's fees. The Court held that a paralegal's time could be included in an attorney's fee award and that rate should be at market rate and not the cost to the firm. The court reasoned that the use of paralegals "encourage[s] cost-effective delivery of legal services and, by reducing the spiraling cost

of ... litigation." *Id.* at 288. The Court looked to community practices for billing paralegals and noted that separate billing for their services was the usual and customary practice. Thus, the Court agreed that paralegal services were a separate billable fee, recognizing the importance of paralegals in the legal setting.

Questions for Review: Read *Missouri v. Jenkins*. What was the main issue in the case? What was the position of the state of Missouri on the payment of paralegal fees? What was the reasoning of the dissent in *Jenkins*?

A growing body of federal and state authority, plus Guideline 8 of the revised *ABA Model Guidelines for the Utilization of Paralegal Services (2004)*, either sanction or strongly encourage such billing. A lower court's capping of paralegal fees at an amount lower than that paid attorneys in indigent cases was held by the Iowa Supreme Court to be an abuse of discretion [*Greatamerica Leasing Corp. v. Cool Comfort Air Conditioning and Refrigeration, Inc.*, 691 N.W.2d 730 (Iowa 2005)]. The basis, according to the court, should be what is reasonable in light of current market rates for paralegal fees and similar factors. Several federal and state statutes specifically authorize billing paralegal time. We are not allowed to bill for the time of a legal secretary or clerk. The paralegal, therefore, is an important source of income and profit for the firm. Because you will be performing tasks often done by an attorney, but billed to the client at a lower rate, the client, too, will benefit from your work. *As long as you work efficiently, you will help this firm provide legal services to more people at a more reasonable cost. Therein lies the heart of the paralegal profession.*

The paralegal manager coordinates the paralegal staff and is the liaison between the partners and the paralegals. She allocates tasks to the paralegals. Should you have any questions or concerns about your position, please direct them to her. Any questions concerning a particular task should be directed to the attorney for whom the task is being completed. All paralegals are expected to be proficient in the use of computers and their operating systems, such as Word, Excel, and other standard programs required to efficiently perform their jobs.

Paralegals at our firm are paid overtime, consistent with the Department of Labor's revised Fair Pay regulations of the Fair Labor Standards Act. Some paralegals, because of their level of education and administrative responsibility, may be considered exempt from the overtime provisions, such exemption making them viewed more as professionals and eligible for flexible hours and pay bonuses. Other paralegals have set hours and may be entitled to overtime pay. The Fair Labor Standards Act protects them from not being compensated for after-hours work. Because the paralegal profession continues to evolve, requiring more specialized knowledge and higher levels of responsibility, the overtime issue will need to be revisited both for individual employees and for the profession as a whole.

INTERNET EXERCISE

Determine the types of legal activities in your jurisdiction for which a paralegal can be billed by a law firm and which activities cannot be billed. Explain the distinction for what is considered billable time in your jurisdiction.

IMPORTANT LAW OFFICE PROCEDURES: WHAT YOU NEED TO KNOW

Introduction

Every office has a variety of established procedures each new employee must learn. Procedures are necessary for the sake of efficiency, uniformity, and quality. Learning the required procedures will save you time and help you to survive and thrive in the law office. One of the first things you should do, therefore, is to locate and read the office procedures manual. It will provide information ranging from pay periods and sick leave to cash receipts and conference calls. Three procedures of particular importance are timekeeping, disbursement entry, and deadline control.

Timekeeping and Billing: The Requirement of Managing Your Time

billable hours

The time spent on a client's case that can be billed to the client.

Timekeeping is a procedure whereby attorneys and paralegals regularly record how much time they spend on a client's case or on other matters. A law firm is compensated for its work and analyzes its productivity (including that of each paralegal) on the basis of such records. The time spent on a client's case that can be billed to the client is called **billable hours**. The lawyer's fee, and hence the firm's income, is often based on billable hours. Some types of billing and fees are:

Hourly rate billing—a price based on the total number of hours worked at a specified per-hour charge

Task-based billing—set prices for different types of tasks that may vary depending on the nature or difficulty of the task (phone call, travel, document drafting, etc.)

Flat fee billing—an overall, preset price to handle a matter from start to finish (frequently used for routine, high volume matters)

Contingency fee—an amount to be paid only if the client wins the case, usually a percentage of the money awarded to the client and common in personal injury cases

Retainer fee—upfront payment to secure legal services and to cover anticipated costs and attorney fees

Value billing—a pricing method (increasingly demanded by many businesses and corporations) that requires the law firm to estimate what the legal representation will cost and what services, specifically, the client will pay for (used to bid for a prospective client's business and to help the client budget the cost of legal services)

Regardless of the type of billing, it is essential to keep accurate time and task records from the start. This process is computerized in most firms. A typical window is seen in Exhibit 1.2.

Guidelines for Entering Your Time

1. Enter the client's name, the related file or account number, and the date of entry.

2. Enter your identification code.

EXHIBIT 1.2 Permanent Time Log

Time/Bill			
I.D. Code	KS	↓	**Related Expense**
Client	Ann Forrester		**Type**
File No.	02-3010		**Amount**
Date			
Service	Phone Conference ↓ NC		

Start 1255   **Total Time** .25   **Bill** $25.00

Stop 1310   **Rate/Hr** 75

Flat Rate

Description Regarding her upcoming deposition: time, place, materials to review.

3. Enter or click the type of service provided, such as telephone calls, meetings or research.

4. Click the NC box if time was spent on a nonbillable item such as a professional meeting or public service activity.

5. Enter the number of whole hours worked on the service plus any partial hours, usually measured in tenth or quarter of an hour increments (six minutes equals one tenth of an hour; 15 minutes equals one quarter of an hour).

6. If the software permits, enter a description of the task that accurately conveys to the client the work performed.

7. Enter information on any out-of-pocket expenses incurred that are to be reimbursed by the client, such as long-distance phone calls, mileage traveled, and online fees.

From time to time, our billing systems will be updated. When this occurs, training will be provided on the system.

Timekeeping software can generate a bill to the client, provide billing reports for each attorney and paralegal, and produce financial summaries for the firm as a whole. Cutting-edge programs allow data entry by cellular phone and satellite, and let clients receive and review their bills online. There are numerous types of time and billing software. You will be trained on the current time and billing system used by the firm.

electronic billing
The posting of billing information by the law office to a secure electronic host site for instant client access.

Electronic billing (e-billing) is the posting of billing information by the law office to a secure electronic host site for instant client access. Although attaching a bill to an e-mail is technically e-billing, the more important trend involves the use of vendor systems that permit the online sharing of billing information. E-billing's speed and flexibility provides customized financial information to the client efficiently.

Learning to produce accurate time and billing data is essential. Start by getting a few typical client bills and review them with an experienced paralegal or attorney. Consult, as well, on what is an appropriate balance of billable and nonbillable time.

You should familiarize yourself with proper billing practices and standards. Consult your supervising attorney or paralegal manager if you have questions. Important ethical guidelines limit billing practices such as double billing. This is the practice of billing several clients the full amount for time spent on behalf of all the clients. It is unethical to bill one client for three hours of flight time if two hours of that in-flight time is spent working on a brief for another client. Formerly, some law firms billed the first client for three hours at the full rate and the second client two hours at the full rate, creating unfair income for five hours of work instead of the real total time of three hours. You cannot do this and should consult one of your supervisors on how to bill multiple clients for a common task.

Other ethical concerns arise when a paralegal is encouraged to misrepresent clerical work (nonbillable) to a client as nonclerical and billable or some similar deception. Such practices are highly improper and can lead to serious consequences for both the attorney and the law office. Another current ethical issue is the unbundling of legal services.

unbundling legal services
The mutually agreed limitation of legal representation to one distinct step in a legal matter or process that may have numerous steps.

Unbundling legal services is the mutually agreed limitation of legal representation to one distinct step in a legal matter or process that may have numerous steps. For example, an attorney and a client may contract for the attorney to handle a trial but not the appeal, or draft a legal document but not file it or present it in court. Unbundling's rationale is to make legal services more affordable by allowing clients to do some things on their own or to contract for just what services they can afford. Because this flies in the face of traditional ethical standards that require lawyers to be responsible for the entire representation process, many states are revising their codes to permit reasonable, segmented representation.

Disbursement (Expense) Entry: Charges Billed to the Client

Disbursements are expenses incurred on behalf of the client and can be directly attributed to that client's case. Disbursements include such things as phone calls, faxes, postage, photocopies, online research service, travel, filing fees, and others; record these expenditures on disbursement forms or computerized equivalents. Many time and billing software programs also have a disbursement feature. Exhibit 1.3 is an example of the format and data needed.

Guidelines for Recording Disbursements

1. Enter the client's name, file number, the date, and your initials or code.

2. Enter the expense type (photocopies, lodging, travel, etc.).

3. Enter the amount of the expense.

4. Enter comments to provide specific information.

The disbursement entries are collected manually or electronically for billing. This kind of recordkeeping leads to well-documented bills and reduces disputes over fees.

EXHIBIT 1.3 Permanent Disbursement Record

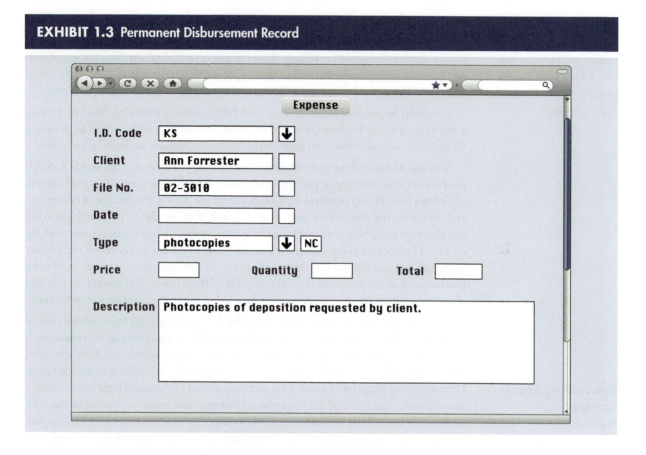

Deadline (Docket) Control

Hovering over every attorney and paralegal is the fear of making a mistake costing the client a significant sum of money or, even worse, the client's one lifetime opportunity to sue for just compensation or to challenge an unjust suit. Mistakes lead to malpractice claims that, if not settled, lead to costly malpractice lawsuits. Such claims raise the firm's insurance costs, damage reputations, and can result in disciplinary action by the state bar. One misconception, however, is that good attorneys and good paralegals do not make mistakes. The reality is that even the best make mistakes. Keep in mind, however, that a good paralegal knows that errors are likely and takes every precaution.

Some of the errors most often leading to malpractice claims include calendaring and deadline control errors, failure to know or properly apply the law, failure to do adequate research and investigation, faulty drafting of legal documents, failure to inform clients, incorrect or inadequate advice, conflicts of interest, and acts and omissions of associates and employees.

Office procedures and systems, such as those for timekeeping and disbursements, reduce errors. One critical system is deadline control. Missed deadlines are the primary reason law offices are sued for professional malpractice. Every office must have a system ensuring that important deadlines are met. These systems, often called **tickler systems**, involve a regular calendaring (docketing) process. When the attorney or a paralegal in the office becomes aware of a deadline, it is entered onto a deadline control slip or computer equivalent. If every member of the legal team is responsible for recording

tickler systems
Calendaring system for deadlines used in a law office.

EXHIBIT 1.4 Deadline Slip

Docket Entry

I.D. Code			
Client		Time	
File No.		Place	
Date Entered		Start	
Deadline for	⬇	Due	6/15/16
Priority level	3	Reminder 1	6/08/16
		2	6/13/16
Remarks	First interview of Ann Forrester	3	6/16/16

or "noticing" a deadline, then the chance of an omission is greatly reduced. Most systems are electronic. These systems automatically calculate and calendar deadlines required by any relevant state or federal rules of procedure, for example, when an important document must be filed in court within a specified number of days from a triggering event. If the trigger event changes, the program can recalculate and reenter the needed dates. Exhibit 1.4 indicates what data is needed.

Guidelines for Entering Deadline Data

1. Enter the name of the client and the file number of the case to which the deadline applies.

2. Enter the task that must be completed. Some tasks require other related tasks to be done by other people in the firm, or software facilitates the assignment of deadlines to more than one employee. Enter this information.

3. Enter the deadline date and reminder dates for the particular task in the designated boxes.

4. Enter the start date (the day the task should be started) in the designated box.

5. Enter under "Remarks" any specific direction to assist in completing the task.

6. If done electronically, the data is automatically recorded in the firm's master calendar. If done manually, see that the required form is delivered to the person in charge of recording deadlines.

On each start date, the person responsible for the designated task will receive an electronic or other reminder and will receive increasingly urgent reminders until the task is done. The person charged with the task indicates its completion by initialing after "Done" on the form or as required by the deadline software. The deadline system also should include a post-deadline reminder that the target date was missed and some corrective action should be taken.

Notebook computers, tablets, iPads, smartphones, and other electronic devices facilitate the exchange of deadlines and other information between the office and other locations.

Technology Management

Our office increasingly expects our paralegals to function as technology managers. It is important for you not only to master technological procedures, but also to inform yourself of the latest software for carrying out procedures. Your knowledge of software, e-mail procedures and security, video conferencing, instant messaging, PIMs, and other means for us to communicate with each other and our clients makes you a much more valuable employee.

E-Mail

Our office relies heavily on communication through our office computer network and the Internet. E-mail is a primary means of sending information, including many kinds of documents. Our office, like many others, requires its employees to sign an agreement with the following essentials:

1. We encourage the use of computers and electronic communication for the business of the firm.

2. Use e-mail for office business only and in an appropriate manner.

3. The firm reserves the right to monitor the use of e-mail by each employee.

4. Your e-mail passwords shall not be shared with any unauthorized person.

5. Inappropriate and offensive e-mail is prohibited.

6. Unauthorized use of e-mail and the Internet includes accessing or downloading pornography, hacking into computers, playing games, and compromising the security of the firm's confidential and other information.

Smartphones

The firm may issue you a smartphone or cellular telephone for use in your job. This telephone shall only be used for office related and business purposes. All information communicated on the firm-issued telephone is not considered private. Do not access social media on your firm telephone unless it is for a business purpose. Firm-issued telephones cannot be used for personal e-mailing, texting, or instant-messaging. You should consider having a smartphone or cellular device for your personal use. A personal telephone should not be used to conduct firm business. The firm may, from time to time, issue updated policies on the use of cellular telephones. Be mindful that information stored on your cellular telephone may be subject to discovery in the course of litigation or in the course of firm business. **You do not own this information nor do you have an expectation of privacy.**

Texting

Like e-mail, texting often is a method of communicating with the firm and clients. Limit your texting to work-related activities on your work-issued cellular telephone. As with any data or information on your smartphone or cellular telephone, it may be subject to discovery in the course of litigation or furtherance of firm business. The firm reserves the right to monitor the use of texting by any of its employees.

Technology Security

The security of our firm's records and our communication processes, including all electronic communication, is paramount. It is every employee's duty to protect client confidentiality, prevent identity theft, and ensure the integrity of our network and operating systems. Here are a few cautionary tips regarding security in general:

- When e-mailing confidential documents, use encryption or, at the very least, use the office's standard confidentiality disclaimer with intended recipient information and subject as the e-mail message and enclose the confidential document as an attachment only.
- Use a metadata removal program for documents being sent out of the office (metadata is invisible but retrievable electronic information about the preparation and history of a document that can be harmful in the hands of opponents or others).
- In addition to virus protection, use programs that prevent others from invading your computer system with spyware, password crackers, network scanners, and the like.
- When out of the office, avoid the use of shared wireless or Internet café services except for routine, non-confidential communication.
- Confirm that your computer work is backed up regularly.
- If working at home on office business, be sure your home computer is also protected by a firewall and other needed security devices.
- Take great care to prevent the theft of portable electronic devices used for office business.

Chapter 9 on document management contains an additional discussion of security.

TECHNIQUES FOR THRIVING IN THE LAW OFFICE: BECOMING A TEAM PLAYER

In addition to learning office procedures and following them closely, practicing the following techniques will help you thrive in the law office:

- Become acquainted with your fellow employees. Respect for others can foster better working relationships.
- Review your ethical responsibilities and those of the firm on a regular basis.
- Learn the chain of command in the office and the roles of your supervising attorney or paralegal manager, the secretaries and others to whom you will give assignments, and other members of the firm. Know where authority rests and who is responsible for what.

- Understand that you are a part of a team whose members are likely to have conflicting deadlines and schedules. The team's success requires appreciation for cooperation, mutual consultation, compromise, and the contributions of all its members.

- Know how to assign work. Decide to whom the work should be assigned and submitted, how much advance notice is normally required before the expected completion date, what procedure is appropriate in last-minute rushes, whether completion dates should be given, and whether special forms for delegating tasks are used. Compliance with these procedures will enhance your relationship with those to whom you assign work and will contribute to office efficiency.

- Submit work as error-free as possible. Take the time to check grammar, spelling, citations, form, accuracy, and clarity. Do not rely on computer programs exclusively for these types of checks. When time permits, study the rules of good writing to improve your communications skills. Attention to detail is essential.

- Keep careful track of client files. Misplaced case files lead to frustration and can adversely affect our representation of a client. Follow strictly the office policy on checking out and returning files.

- When addressing clients, use Mr., Ms., Dr., or other appropriate titles. Avoid first names unless there is no doubt the situation makes it acceptable.

- Be sensible when using the telephone. How you conduct yourself when using the phone is a direct reflection on this firm. Exercise good common sense and be polite, businesslike, and brief. Ethically, it is important that everyone you speak with on the phone understand that you are not an attorney. Make this clear at the outset of the conversation whenever there might be any doubt. Plan ahead for phone calls; knowing what information you need helps keep conversations brief. Incomplete messages and misunderstandings on the phone can be a problem; it is a good idea to have people repeat addresses and phone numbers that you have given them and for you to repeat information that you receive.

- In addition, some phone conversations are important enough to confirm in writing the terms, dates, or arrangements discussed on the phone. If possible, do this immediately following the phone call. The letter serves as an important record of the conversation. In some instances, if a letter of confirmation seems inappropriate, a brief memorandum to the file may be useful.

- Learn to complete assignments efficiently. Each time you receive an assignment, be sure you thoroughly understand it and the time frame in which it must be completed. Obtain the facts underlying the task—know why you are doing the task. Ask questions to determine exactly what is required of you, especially if you have never done such an assignment before. Prioritize your assignments according to deadline, how much time they will take, and other factors.

- Once you have the assignment in mind, decide the best way to complete the task. Use the guides and examples provided during your training. Ask the attorney for additional guidance. Do not try to reinvent the wheel on each assignment. If the information supplied to you is insufficient, seek examples in our legal form files, in the numerous form books, in the statutes, and in the state and federal rules. Ask the advice of others who have done similar work and would be glad to give you some suggestions. Keep a log of each of your assignments, indicating when the task was given and when it was completed. Such a log will help you build a systems folder, described later in this handbook. It will also help you list specific skills on your resume should you decide to apply for an advanced position in this firm or elsewhere. It will be used in an annual evaluation of your work.

- Remember the importance of your work to our clients. On any job there will be times when you are tired or simply bored. These are times rife with the potential for error. Remind yourself that our clients rely heavily on us, and what we do has considerable impact on their lives and businesses.

- Reduce stress and its debilitating effects by learning not to take curtness and gruffness personally, understanding that this is a symptom of the pressure felt by others. Set your limits and stick to them. Use the firm's policies when necessary to defend yourself tactfully. Notify others well in advance of doctor's appointments and other personal business, then keep your personal appointments. Stay healthy by getting regular exercise, taking necessary breaks, anticipating crunch times and pacing yourself, getting adequate sleep, and avoiding those things that contribute to long-term debilitation such as abuse of alcohol and prescription and other drugs.

- Dress professionally.

- Learn the criteria in your office for a job well done and those for advancement.

- Keep a sense of humor. While you need to regard your work seriously, it is equally important to be able to laugh, to see the humor in your own follies as well as in the situations in which you find yourself.

TRADE SECRETS: LOOKING PROFESSIONAL COUNTS!

Just like law firms have dress codes, courts do as well. Suits normally are expected for men and women with professional variations. Courts react adversely to extreme deviations from that professional dress code, sometimes imposing sanctions to those who disregard those codes. In Indiana, an attorney deviated from the accepted dress code and was admonished by the Court. In a case entitled *In Re Proper Courtroom Attire*, Case No. 05C01-1408-CB-000005, a Blackford County Circuit Court Judge ordered an attorney to wear socks in court. The attorney responded by telling the Judge that he hated wearing socks and that unless he was shown orders or other authority he would continue the practice. As you might guess, the judge responded by ordering the attorney to wear socks as part of proper court attire otherwise he would be sanctioned, fined, or possibly held in contempt. Included in the order was a provision that a copy of the order be circulated to members of that bar. What that means for you, as a paralegal, is that proper professional attire is required of you at all times. You are a reflection of your own professionalism and dressing appropriately is simply part of the image you want to project—you do not want to bring on the wrath of your law firm, or worse a court, because of your attire. What attorneys and paralegals do is serious business and, thus, respect for the formality of the courtroom and those that are represented is implicit in how we present ourselves. Always dress appropriately when you are in a professional setting.

THE TRAINING PROCEDURE: WHAT TO EXPECT

Procedure, Task Information, Assignments

You will begin your training with several cases currently being handled by this firm. You will work through the cases at a relatively slow pace, concentrating on the paralegal tasks one step at a time as they arise chronologically. For each assigned task, you will be given the following:

1. Information on the nature and purpose of the task to be performed

2. Directions or guidelines as to how to perform the task

3. Examples of the completed tasks

4. Opportunities to perform the task yourself

5. Evaluation of your work

During this training period, you will be performing the following duties:

1. Researching

2. Investigating

3. Interviewing

4. Organizing materials

5. Summarizing materials

6. Drafting documents, forms, and correspondence

7. Responding to questions on concepts, principles, and procedures

Developing a Litigation System

litigation system
A detailed procedure manual that is a chronological collection of the guidelines, forms, correspondence, checklists, procedures, and pertinent law for all steps in the litigation process.

A **litigation system** is a detailed procedure manual that is a chronological collection of the guidelines, forms, correspondence, checklists, procedures, and pertinent law for all steps in the litigation process. It also can be known as a systems folder. As a personal resource it provides advantages in efficiency, uniformity, accuracy, and quality. It will help you learn the benefits of being organized and can be easily updated. Because a good systems folder will help you on the job, and perhaps in securing a job, the systems folder should provide an extra incentive to do your assignments thoroughly and accurately. (Regular use of the system approach will help reinforce the individual litigation skills presented in this text and will help develop confidence in your ability to create a system in any area of law.)

Should your supervisor (instructor) choose to use the system development approach to your training, one of your continuous assignments will be to construct a paralegal's litigation systems folder. Either use a three-ring binder or create one electronically. If you use a three-ring binder, it should have enough tabbed dividers to accommodate the following divisions:

1. Quick reference information
   a. Pertinent office procedure
   b. General information (courts, names, addresses, deadlines, and so on)

2. Interview

3. Investigation

4. Pleadings and service of process

5. Discovery

6. Settlement

7. Pretrial

8. Trial

9. Post-trial

10. Appeal

You may choose to computerize the systems folder. Create similar divisions as listed above; add appropriate sections to accommodate the needs of a particular case.

As you are asked to do certain tasks, place the necessary information into the appropriate section of the system in chronological order. Your system will gradually take shape and should be complete by the conclusion of the training period.

As you begin your employment with the firm (and as this course of study progresses), you will be given numerous paralegal assignments. Some assignments are located at the end of each chapter and will be assigned by your supervising attorney (instructor). They will help you apply and learn the material you have read. When doing the assignments, assume that you are in the state of Columbia, whose laws are the same as the laws of your state. Because most of your future work will be in *your state,* pay particular attention to the applications of this text and assignments to the practice of law in *your state.*

ETHICAL AND OTHER PROFESSIONAL RESPONSIBILITIES

Introduction

professional ethics
For attorneys, the rules of conduct that govern the practice of law.

Soon you will be working with cases and the people involved in those cases. In dealing with others, be ever mindful of the high standard of **professional ethics** to which your actions must conform. Professional ethics, as applied to attorneys, are the rules of conduct that govern the practice of law. Each person working for this firm is responsible for knowing what is expected and is to act accordingly. A breach of ethical standards will reflect badly upon this firm and may also lead to the disbarment of one or more of our attorneys. It may cost you your job and subject you to prosecution for the unauthorized practice of law.

Valuable resources relevant to your ethical responsibilities include your state's rules of professional conduct for lawyers, the *ABA's Model Rules of Professional Conduct,* the *ABA's Model Guidelines for the Utilization of Paralegal Services,* the *Code of Ethics and Professional Responsibility of the National Association of Legal Assistants, Inc.,* the National Federation of Paralegal Association's *Affirmation of Responsibility,* and the ethics code of your state paralegal association. The guidance provided by these documents is quite consistent.

INTERNET EXERCISE

Locate a copy of your state's code of professional responsibility on the Internet. Determine whether your state addresses the professional responsibility of paralegals and what those entail. If your state does not specifically address the professional responsibility of paralegals, determine what code your state follows and how it is applied.

legal advice

Independent professional judgment based on knowledge of the law and given for the benefit of a particular client.

What a Paralegal May Not Do

Except as specifically permitted by law, paralegals *may not* perform any of the following functions:

1. Provide legal services directly to the public without the supervision of an attorney. More states and the federal system are permitting paralegals to represent the public in limited controlled settings, such as landlord/tenant matters, immigration, and Social Security cases. Check your state and federal jurisdictions for the applicable rules for a particular matter.

2. Give **legal advice** or counsel a client. Legal advice is independent professional judgment based on knowledge of the law and given for the benefit of a particular client.

3. Represent a client in court or other tribunal or otherwise act as an advocate for a client unless specifically permitted to do so by law or rule of court. (See #1 above for further clarification.)

4. Accept or reject cases for the firm.

5. Set any fee for representation of a client.

6. Split legal fees with an attorney (bonuses and profit-sharing plans not tied to a specific case are permissible).

7. Be a partner with a lawyer if any of the activities of the partnership include the practice of law [exception: the District of Columbia ethics Rule 5.4(b)]. The American Bar Association rejected a proposal to relax the prohibition against fee sharing and multidisciplinary practice.

8. Solicit cases for a lawyer.

9. Perform tasks that are the unauthorized practice of law as defined in the pertinent state. One state supreme court has stated that prior to any attempt on its part to better define and regulate the unauthorized practice of law, the state bar association must provide the court with demonstrable, quantifiable evidence of the extent of and harm caused by the unauthorized practice of law. Note, as well, that the unauthorized practice of law is now a felony in Florida [Fla. Stat. § 454.23 (2004)], and other states are considering enacting such laws. *Doe v. Condon,* 341 S.C. 22; 532 S.E.2d 879 (2000) is a case where a paralegal's action was scrutinized by a court where the issue of what is considered the unauthorized practice of law was front and center.

CASE STUDY: UNDERSTANDING THE LAW

The South Carolina Supreme Court in *Doe v. Condon,* 341 S.C. 22; 532 S.E.2d 879 (2000), was faced with determining whether certain actions of a paralegal were considered the unauthorized practice of law. The court was asked to answer three questions: "(1) whether it is the unauthorized practice of law for a paralegal employed by an attorney to conduct informational seminars for the general public on wills and trusts without the attorney being present; (2) whether it is the unauthorized practice of law for a paralegal employed

(continued)

CASE STUDY: UNDERSTANDING THE LAW

by an attorney to meet with clients privately at the attorney's office, answer general questions about wills and trusts, and gather basic information from clients; and (3) whether a paralegal can receive compensation from the paralegal's law firm/employer through a profit-sharing arrangement based upon the volume and type of cases the paralegal handles." *Id* at 880. Based on the recommendations by a court-appointed referee, the court held that all three situations constituted the unauthorized practice of law. Focusing on a 1980 case as their precedent, the Court stated that "preparatory work" by a paralegal for an attorney did not constitute the unauthorized practice of law. Such activities as legal research, investigation, or the composition of legal documents, which an attorney reviews and reaches an independent judgment, were proper. Because in this case, the paralegal was acting independently and taking a lead rather than a subordinate role in both

conducting the seminar and meeting with clients, the Court found that these acts constituted the unauthorized practice of law. This violated the South Carolina rules of ethics and professional responsibility. Similarly, it was against the South Carolina code of ethics to profit share with a nonlawyer. The end result was that, given the facts, each activity constituted the unauthorized practice of law.

Questions for Review: Read *Doe v. Condon*. What rules of ethics did the Court use to support its conclusion? Would the Court have reached the same result if the attorney (1) had been a presenter along with the paralegal at the seminar and (2) had participated in the meeting and interview process with clients? Are there any circumstances where the rules of ethics permit a paralegal to share in the profits from a law firm?

What a Paralegal May Do

Paralegals may perform a wide array of tasks and be confident their work will not create a breach of ethics if it meets certain criteria:

1. The task must be delegated by an attorney.

2. It must be performed under an attorney's supervision.

3. Paralegals must clearly designate their status as a paralegal.

4. The lawyer must retain a direct relationship with the client (the attorney must retain control over the relationship).

5. The task must involve information gathering or be ministerial and cannot involve the rendering of legal advice or judgment (unless the legal advice or judgment is provided by the paralegal directly to the attorney).

6. The work must be given final approval or be examined by the attorney.

7. The work must not have a separate identity but merge with the attorney's final work product.

In addition, the name of a paralegal may appear on a firm's business card and letterhead if the person is designated a paralegal.

Paralegals may represent clients at federal administrative hearings. This includes hearings of matters such as supplemental Social Security or black lung benefits. Some states have passed administrative procedure acts similar to that of the federal government permitting paralegal representation without attorney supervision.

APPLY YOUR KNOWLEDGE

Under what circumstances, if any, in your jurisdiction may a paralegal practice law unsupervised? Determine under what legal authority this practice is governed, such as a statute, court rule, or bar association opinion. Is there a distinction between paralegal practice in state court practice and federal practice? If so, under what circumstances can a paralegal represent the public?

Expanding the range and responsibility of what paralegals are permitted to do under the supervision of an attorney should help meet the needs of millions of U.S. citizens. Various state legislatures or supreme courts continue to consider proposals to license or register paralegals. Whether paralegals should be licensed as a profession and be permitted to provide legal services beyond what they do now will continue to be hotly debated, especially in those states that reexamine the availability of legal services to their respective citizens.

California became the first state to enact legislation that not only defines a paralegal/legal assistant, but also requires a paralegal to have specific educational and experience qualifications, coupled with mandatory continuing legal education requirements. No one other than a qualified paralegal may use the paralegal/legal assistant title. The legislation does not, however, expand what paralegals can legally do for clients.

Along with California, Washington has created an expanded role for nonlawyers calling them Limited License Legal Technicians ("LLLT"). Passed in 2012, the limited license legal technician can represent and advise individuals in specific areas of the law. Similar to California, the LLLT must meet certain minimum educational requirements and pass a state-regulated exam. This distinction is new and will develop, no doubt, over time.

Confidentiality, Honesty, Conflict of Interest, and Other Ethical Considerations

Paralegal ethical standards, for all practical purposes, are the same as those for attorneys. Attorneys, not paralegals, are disciplined by the bar for ethical breaches. Paralegals, however, are bound by the nature of their jobs to uphold each rule as if they were the attorneys.

Attorneys are bound by the ethical standards set by their state's highest court. Most states have adopted the American Bar Association's *Model Rules of Professional Conduct* with some local amendments. Studying the *Model Rules of Professional Conduct* provides a paralegal with an understanding of most of the ethical standards in effect in any particular state. Because some states have deleted or amended some of the ABA's rules, however, you should obtain a copy of your state's version of the ethical standards. These are available through state bar associations. Place these in the ethics section of your systems folder, if you are keeping one, or retain a copy in your office. As a paralegal you must always maintain the confidentiality of clients, be honest, and avoid conflicts of interest. Each of these ethical considerations encompasses your practice in the following manner.

Confidentiality: A paralegal shall hold inviolate the confidences of a client. Nothing the client tells you or that you learn about the client may be revealed to anyone outside the office, not even to a spouse or parent. ABA Model Rule 1.6 states that a client's confidences shall not be revealed unless the client gives "informed consent" or the disclosure is "impliedly authorized to carry out the representation." An attorney *may* reveal confidential information to prevent "reasonably certain death or substantial bodily harm," to prevent a client's crime or fraud reasonably certain to cause substantial financial injury and furthered by the attorney's legitimate services (or to mitigate or rectify such injury), to get advice to assure ethical compliance, to defend an action or complaint against the attorney arising out of representation of the client, or to comply with "other law or court order."

Parallel state ethics rules regarding disclosure of confidential information may vary. Generally, to preserve confidentiality, a client's statement to you or other employees of the firm should not be made in the presence of outsiders. Exceptions to this rule of thumb will be discussed in Chapter 3 and subsequent discussions of attorney/client privilege. Further, the duty to protect confidentiality extends beyond the conclusion of the representation and even after the death of the client [Rule 1.9(c)(2)].

Today law office technology raises added concern about preserving confidential information. E-mail can be copied accidentally or forwarded to unintended recipients, so it must be used with great care. Nevertheless, the use of e-mail carries an expectation of privacy parallel to that of regular mail and standard phone-line conversations. Therefore, e-mail use does not violate Model Rule 1.6. Cellular phone transmissions are not as secure as e-mail, and their use for confidential conversations is risky. Although some protection against intentional interception and recording of wire, oral, and electronic communications is provided by the federal wiretap statute (18 U.S.C.A. 2510, *et seq.*), neither e-mail nor cellular phones or other wireless devices should be used for transmitting especially sensitive material. Giving third parties (often vendors) access to a law office's computers to remedy technology problems or to assist in electronic aspects of litigation requires great caution to protect client confidentiality.

The disposal of outdated hardware, often containing sensitive files, can lead to breaches of confidentiality. Offices should have procedures in place that truly erase or destroy residual computer files. Simply deleting files is not adequate.

Honesty: A paralegal must maintain the highest standards of professional integrity and avoid any dishonesty, fraud, deceit, or misrepresentation. This rule applies to all dealings with the client, judges, court employees, opposing attorneys, and the public.

Conflict of Interest: A paralegal should avoid and reveal any conflicts of interest. This requirement rests on the rationale that citizens must have faith in the legal system to seek the peaceful resolution of their disputes. Since conflicts of interest can dilute an attorney's

TECHNOLOGY UPDATE: CLOUD COMPUTING

One of the new, and somewhat controversial, topics in the practice of law is cloud computing. Cloud computing is generally defined as the practice of storing data remotely on servers that are accessed through the Internet. Information such as client files, billing, and any information relating to the practice of law places the data on remote servers out of the immediate control of the lawyer. Unlike storing data directly on the computer as has been the practice in the past, with cloud computing, lawyers subscribe to the service, which is called "software as a service" (SaaS), and access their information through the use of an Internet browser, such as Internet Explorer, Safari, or Firefox. Think of it as storing all your data in a remote warehouse, except this warehouse is in cyberspace. Accessing data is through the Internet with the use of a computer or other electronic device, such as an iPad

or smartphone. It seems that cloud computing adds mobility and flexibility when accessing data, but the issue in the practice of law is confidentiality, security and privacy. Is client information sufficiently protected in the cloud? Because the information is stored remotely, access and security issues abound, it is incumbent upon the lawyer to be sure that the service purchased is secure and that the information stored is protected from both physical and technical destruction. Serious issues arise when using cloud computing, with the most critical the safeguarding of the stored information of clients. How the confidentiality, security and privacy issues will be treated by courts and bar associations is developing. Cloud computing appears to be the present trend for storing information. The technology will continue to be refined and updated as the needs of lawyers and the public grow.

allegiance to the client and damage independent professional judgment, they are barred by Model Rules of Professional Responsibility. A paralegal must also be loyal to the client and avoid such conflicts. A conflict of interest would occur if this firm accepted a case to sue Mr. Hart, and then was hired by Mr. Hart to sue someone else. In this situation, confidential information learned from Mr. Hart in the second case could be used against him in the first case. In such circumstances, the second case should not be accepted.

In another example, if a client represented by the firm sued the O.K. Manufacturing Company, a conflict of interest would arise if the paralegal assigned to the case owned stock in the company. It is obvious that the paralegal may hesitate to do the best job possible when the outcome of the case could have an adverse effect on the paralegal's income. In such a situation, the paralegal should inform the supervising attorney of the conflict. A remedy for the conflict would be to take the paralegal off that case.

Law offices must be extremely sensitive to actual and potential conflicts of interest. Not only can violations lead to serious ethics sanctions, but also to costly and embarrassing disqualification from otherwise lucrative cases and the long-term representation of valued clients.

Hiring new personnel who have worked at another law firm is fraught with potential conflict problems. For example, if a paralegal worked on behalf of Mr. Hart at the first firm, but now must handle cases against Mr. Hart at the second firm, a paralegal might be likely to use such confidential information gained from Mr. Hart while working for the first firm against him at the second firm. Remedies for this situation are to disqualify the law office because of the conflict or not to hire the transferring paralegal. These remedies are harsh and pose an unfair restraint on the freedom of employment. The preferred method to deal with such real or potential conflicts is to surround the new employee with an "ethical wall" that screens the employee from any contact with the case that causes the conflict. This approach is recommended by the ABA and has been adopted in most jurisdictions. In *Leibowitz v. the Eighth Judicial District Court of the State of Nevada*, 78 P. 3d 515 (Nev. 2003), the Nevada Supreme Court reversed a former decision that prohibited such screens for nonlawyer personnel, and reiterated the recommended criteria for a proper conflict of interest screen:

1. The new nonlawyer employee must be warned not to reveal any information relating to the representation of the former employer's client.

2. The employee must be told not to work on any matter the employee worked on for the former employer or on which the employee has information gained during the former employment.

3. The new firm should implement safeguards beyond the above warnings to see to it that the new employee does not work with matters worked on during the prior employment (such as notifying all office lawyers and paralegals that the relevant employee must not work on the specifically identified matter).

4. The new firm must inform the adverse party (or counsel) that their former employee has been hired and of the screening methods used.

Even in the few jurisdictions where screening is not yet permitted or in circumstances when screening is not likely to be effective (for example, where the information has already been disclosed), disqualification of the law firm in the new case may still be avoided if the client from the new employee's previous office gives informed, written consent to the otherwise disqualified firm to go ahead with the representation despite the existing conflict. A client can even waive future conflicts of interest if the proper procedures are followed.

If a paralegal, subsequent to working for one law firm, has been hired by another law firm, it is paramount for that paralegal not only to confirm the absence of conflicts in a new case with the current firm's clients and cases but also the absence of conflicts with any cases the paralegal worked on or clients worked for at the previous law firm. As discussed above, failure to make such checks or to report such information can have serious consequences. If a paralegal is given the responsibility to interview a prospective employee, any potential conflicts arising from the employment of the interviewee must be identified.

Other Professional Considerations

Some professional ethics are not found in the codes but are nevertheless quite important. In professional working relationships, mutual respect and loyalty between employer and employees is especially important. Publicly criticizing one's fellow workers or one's clients, who deserve the utmost courtesy, respect, and every effort on our part to preserve their dignity, is not consistent with professional loyalty. Relationships with clients must always be kept on a professional level. If a relationship becomes too personal, it threatens objectivity, confidentiality, and one's loyalty to the firm.

Professional loyalty to the firm extends to the practice of law, which supersedes loyalty to any specific individual. Attorneys are directed to call attention to the unethical practices of other attorneys, or in some instances, of the illegal conduct of their own clients to avoid assisting in fraud or crime [Rule 4.1 (truthfulness in statements to others) subject to Rule 1.6 on revealing confidentiality] or perjury [Rule 3.3 (candor toward the tribunal)]. Similarly, a paralegal must be prepared to report unethical behavior to the appropriate person within the firm. In *Brown v. Hammond,* 810 F. Supp. 644 (E. D. Pa 1993), a paralegal who was fired for refusing to be involved in wrongful billing practices was allowed to sue for wrongful discharge.

Advertising Legal Services: Advertising of legal services in various forms raises ethical questions. For example, a law firm ad that featured a pit bulldog and displayed an 800-pit-bull phone number was sanctioned as unprofessional and unethical in *The Florida Bar v. Pape,* 918 So.2d 240 (Fla. 2005). Paralegals may be asked to draft proposals for firm advertisements or brochures. The various state bars have attempted to review such advertising with mixed success. The Supreme Court of the United States strengthened bar efforts to control advertising. In *Florida Bar v. Went For It, Inc.,* 115 S. Ct. 2371 (1995), the court upheld the constitutionality of a bar association rule prohibiting lawyers from sending direct-mail solicitation to victims or their families within thirty days of an accident. Some law firms are utilizing paralegals to place advertising on the Internet in the form of Web sites. It is best to check state bar ethics guidelines, including those on how to avoid creating inadvertent attorney/client relationships, prior to using the information highway for this purpose.

Malpractice: Avoiding **malpractice** is a top priority that requires the attention of the entire law office staff. Carelessness by paralegals or others in the office can be costly. You can help prevent malpractice by paying close attention to details, double checking deadlines and other aspects of your work, employing standardized practice systems,

malpractice
Legal negligence that causes harm to a client for which an attorney or law firm may be sued.

adhering to ethical practices, avoiding the unauthorized practice of law, identifying troublesome cases and clients, keeping current on relevant changes in the law and procedure, asking questions, reporting concerns, and following other good employment practices.

Pro Bono Work: Firms appreciate assistance in efforts to provide free legal services to the poor, called **pro bono** work. The National Association of Legal Assistants, the National Federation of Paralegal Associations, and state and local paralegal associations encourage paralegals to participate in pro bono work. Doing pro bono work with the bar is beneficial to the law firm, the paralegal, and the person served.

pro bono
Free legal services provided to those unable to afford representation.

It is helpful for each of us to be mindful that our actions reflect upon this firm and the professions we each represent. We encourage you to go beyond this brief word of caution on ethics. Study ethics in more detail as you learn other litigation tasks. The more you know about the ethical responsibilities of the attorney and paralegal, the more likely you will be able to spot and avoid trouble. Additional ethical considerations will be highlighted as they arise in the chapters ahead.

YOUR PROFESSIONAL DEVELOPMENT

White, Wilson & McDuff has always encouraged its employees to improve themselves professionally. For that reason, our firm will support you in your efforts toward personal professional development. Keep informed of what is going on in your field; attend continuing education seminars; participate in paralegal associations; and subscribe to literature that will benefit your career. Here is a brief list of some organizations, their addresses, and pertinent literature. Seek information as well from the local affiliates of these national organizations and from your local and state association:

- Your local paralegal association
- American Association for Paralegal Education

  19 Mantua Road

  Mt. Royal, NJ 08061

  (856) 423-2829

  Fax: (856) 423-3420

  E-mail: info@aafpe.org

  Web: http://www.aafpe.org

  Publications: *The Paralegal Educator; The Journal of Paralegal Education and Practice*

- American Bar Association

  321 North Clark Street

  Chicago, IL 60610

  (312) 988-5000

  E-mail: askaba@abanet.org

  Web: http://www.abanet.org

- ABA Standing Committee on Legal Assistants

  E-mail: legalassts@abanet.org

  Web: http://www.abanet.org/legalservices
- International Practice Management Association (f/k/a) International Paralegal Management Association

  980 N. Michigan Ave., Suite 1400

  Chicago, Illinois 60611

  (312) 214-4992

  Fax: (888) 662-9155

  E-mail: info@paralegalmanagement.org

  Web: http://www.paralegalmanagement.org
- National Association of Legal Assistants

  1516 South Boston, #200

  Tulsa, OK 74119

  (918) 587-6828

  Fax: (918) 582-6772

  Web: http://www.nala.org

  Publication: *Facts and Findings*
- National Federation of Paralegal Associations

  23607 Highway 99, Suite 2-C

  Edmonds, WA 98026

  (425) 967-0045

  Fax: (425)771-9588

  E-mail: info@paralegals.org

  Web: http://www.paralegals.org

  Publication: *National Paralegal Reporter*
- *Paralegal Assistant Today*

  Conexion International Media, Inc.

  6030 Marshalee Drive, Suite 455

  Elkridge, MD 21075-5935

  (443) 445-3057

  Fax: (443) 445-3257

  Web: http://www.paralegaltoday.com

COURTS AND JURISDICTION

INTRODUCTION

Moving beyond the foundations discussed in the office handbook, this section discusses the function, structure, and jurisdiction of both the federal and state court systems. Then it explains the relationship between jurisdiction and venue, and how these distinct concepts determine the choice of a proper court for a lawsuit.

BASIC COMPONENTS OF A COURT SYSTEM

The federal and state court systems have at least two types of courts in common: the trial court and the appellate court.

The Trial Court

trial court
Court where initial lawsuit is filed.

The **trial court** is the real workhorse of the court system. This is where most **lawsuits** are filed. Trial courts decide questions of law and questions of fact. Questions of fact focus on what happened: How fast was Mr. Hart driving? Was the road wet? Was the traffic light red? The jury, if there is one, or judge decides the questions of fact. Questions of law focus on the law or proper procedure to be applied to a particular case: Is the evidence admissible? Was the hearing conducted in a fair and impartial manner? Is the statute constitutional? Questions of law are always decided by the judge. Beyond deciding questions of law, the judge sees to it that the rules of evidence and procedure are applied fairly, that order and decorum are maintained, and that the trial progresses expeditiously. In addition to deciding questions of fact, juries or judges decide whether the party bringing the lawsuit has met its burden of proof. Following that decision, the judge enters a formal finding called a **judgment**.

lawsuits
Formal complaint filed by a wronged party.

judgment
Formal finding by judge.

Most cases are resolved in the trial court. Trial courts have a variety of names: county, district, superior, common pleas, traffic, circuit, city, justice of the peace, or even supreme court in New York state. The trial courts may also be divided into branches or specialized courts: criminal, juvenile, probate, or family court.

The Appellate Court

If a trial court judge commits an error, the losing party has the right to appeal the case to an appellate court. Grounds for appeal include incorrect application of the law, a verdict not supported by the weight of the evidence, and errors in procedural or other rulings. The appellate court considers questions of law only and does not retry the facts of the case. It decides cases by reading the legal arguments of the parties, listening to oral arguments, and reviewing the written transcript or video record of the trial.

The federal and state court systems each have a final court of appeal. This court is called the supreme court in most systems. Others call it the court of appeals, supreme judicial court, or supreme court of appeals. The published opinion of an appellate court becomes the rule of law (precedent) in the particular geographical jurisdiction of that court.

The Intermediate Appellate Court

Thirty-seven states and the federal system have an intermediate appellate court. Where it exists, this court stands between the trial court and the court of final review. Most appeals from the trial courts must go to the intermediate appellate court and are resolved there. Some cases, usually of considerable significance, are appealed from the intermediate appellate court and are accepted by the supreme court or court of final appeal for review. See Exhibit 1.8 for an illustration of a typical state court system.

JURISDICTION: THE POWER OF A COURT TO HEAR A CASE

jurisdiction
The power or authority of a court to hear and decide the questions of law or fact (or both) presented by a lawsuit.

personal (in personam) jurisdiction
Courts' power to hear a case against a person.

summons
Notice of a lawsuit to a party.

long-arm statutes
Statutes which identify circumstances where a person from another jurisdiction can be held accountable in that jurisdiction.

in rem (property) jurisdiction
Jurisdiction over property.

subject matter jurisdiction
Jurisdiction defined by nature or subject of the type of lawsuit handled by a court.

general jurisdiction
Ability of court to hear all types of cases.

Jurisdiction is the power or authority of a court to hear and decide the questions of law or fact (or both) presented by a lawsuit. Most courts have a *geographical jurisdiction*, meaning that they hear cases that arise within specific geographical boundaries. The boundaries may encompass the city limits for municipal courts or the entire nation for the U.S. Supreme Court. Court decisions become law only within the specific geographical boundaries in which the court has jurisdiction.

The court also has **personal (in personam) jurisdiction**. This means the court must have the power over the particular person named in the lawsuit to enter a judgment against that person. This is usually accomplished by serving a **summons** and a copy of the complaint on the person being sued (the defendant). Traditionally, state courts had personal jurisdiction only over defendants located in the state. Today more states are passing **long-arm statutes** that permit service in other states under prescribed circumstances. In federal courts, personal jurisdiction is gained by serving the necessary documents within the geographical district of the court. The Internet's worldwide reach has raised new questions regarding personal jurisdiction. Electronic contacts alone can be sufficient to establish personal jurisdiction. Personal jurisdiction and what types of minimum contacts are sufficient to establish it are discussed in more detail in Chapter 5.

In rem (property) jurisdiction is the authority of the court to attach (seize) property (real estate, jewelry, bank deposits, or other property) within its geographical jurisdiction to resolve claims to the property. *Quasi in rem jurisdiction* is the authority of a court to seize and use property (within its jurisdiction) of a defendant over whom it does not have personal jurisdiction to pay a judgment against the defendant entered in an action indirectly related or unrelated to the property. For example, a court may use a defendant's small piece of land located in state to satisfy a bank's judgment against the defendant who has moved out of state and who has failed to make car payments legally owed to the bank. Quasi in rem jurisdiction is normally used when a state does not have the needed long-arm statute to gain personal jurisdiction.

Relevant to personal jurisdiction is the concept of sovereign immunity. *Sovereign immunity* protects governments and people in government positions from being sued for conducting legitimate (even if injurious) government business. Although the federal and state governments have passed laws waiving this protection in some types of cases, the doctrine can deprive a court of the authority to adjudicate some matters.

Each court has some form of **subject matter jurisdiction**. This jurisdiction is defined by the nature or subject of the lawsuits handled by that court—for example, criminal, juvenile, civil, or appellate cases.

If a court has **general jurisdiction**, it can hear all types of cases. Most states have trial courts of general jurisdiction where subject matter jurisdiction is assumed unless one party can demonstrate that the court does not have the necessary subject matter jurisdiction.

Original jurisdiction indicates that cases first enter the system at this court level— they "originate" here. Therefore, a court having original jurisdiction over criminal cases is the first to hear and try criminal cases. Most trial courts are courts of original jurisdiction.

A court has *limited jurisdiction* if its authority to hear and decide cases is limited to specific types of cases. A court specifically labeled a traffic court can hear only traffic cases; criminal court, only criminal cases; and so forth. Limited jurisdiction becomes *exclusive jurisdiction* if a court is the only court permitted to handle a specific type of case.

jurisdictional amount
Specific dollar amount that must be claimed in an action to meet jurisdictional minimum of a given court.

Frequently the jurisdiction of a court is limited by the amount of money claimed in the lawsuit. For example, a state's lower court may have jurisdiction over all civil cases up to $5,000, with the higher trial court having jurisdiction over all civil cases involving more than that amount. Frequently this monetary value is referred to as the **jurisdictional amount** or amount in controversy.

supplemental jurisdiction
The power of federal courts already having jurisdiction over a federal claim to hear a state claim and add parties if that claim is based on essentially the same facts as the federal claim.

Supplemental jurisdiction (28 U.S.C. § 1367) permits federal courts already having jurisdiction over a federal claim to hear a state claim if that claim is based on essentially the same facts as the federal claim. The federal court, under the same circumstances, may also add parties over which it would not otherwise have jurisdiction. Supplemental jurisdiction includes what has previously been called *pendent, pendent party,* and *ancillary jurisdiction.*

Another type of jurisdiction is *removal jurisdiction.* Most often this refers to the ability of federal district courts to remove cases from state courts to federal court if the federal court has jurisdiction to hear the case. Removal jurisdiction and procedure are discussed further in Chapter 6.

concurrent jurisdiction
Two courts having the ability to hear the same type of case.

When two courts have jurisdiction on the same type of case, the courts are said to have **concurrent jurisdiction**.

The jurisdiction of each court is legally defined by the constitution and statutes of the governmental entity that creates the court. Other aspects of jurisdiction will be addressed later in this text. For an overview of jurisdiction, review Exhibit 1.5.

EXHIBIT 1.5 Summary of Jurisdiction

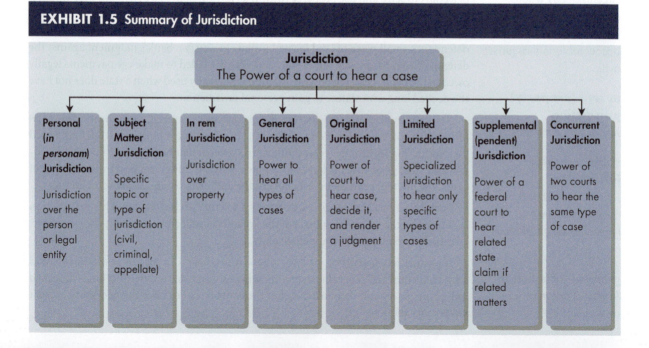

Jurisdiction — The Power of a court to hear a case							
Personal (in personam) Jurisdiction	**Subject Matter Jurisdiction**	**In rem Jurisdiction**	**General Jurisdiction**	**Original Jurisdiction**	**Limited Jurisdiction**	**Supplemental (pendent) Jurisdiction**	**Concurrent Jurisdiction**
Jurisdiction over the person or legal entity	Specific topic or type of jurisdiction (civil, criminal, appellate)	Jurisdiction over property	Power to hear all types of cases	Power of court to hear case, decide it, and render a judgment	Specialized jurisdiction to hear only specific types of cases	Power of a federal court to hear related state claim if related matters	Power of two courts to hear the same type of case

Jurisdiction and the Internet: The Courts Divided

With the advent of the Internet and the world of cyberspace, the basics of jurisdiction and how it is applied have been turned upside down. What was considered a relatively settled area of the law is now fraught with upheaval, creating different standards for asserting jurisdiction over persons, places, and things. Because the Internet encompasses cyberspace and avoids the typical brick and mortar type of analysis, courts have struggled to find a common definition to use when asserting jurisdiction. To understand this dilemma, we must examine the landmark case of *International Shoe v. Washington,* 326 U.S. 310, 316 (1945) where the U.S. Supreme Court determined the test for a court asserting jurisdiction over a person. In that case, the Court stated that justice required that a court may only assert jurisdiction over a defendant if it had such "minimum contacts" to not offend notions of fair play and justice. *Id.* at 316.

Later precedential cases from the U.S. Supreme Court refined that definition. Cases such as *Hanson v. Denckla,* 357 U.S. 235, 253, 78 S. Ct. 1228, 2 L. Ed. 2d 1283 (1958), *Burger King Corp. v. Rudzewicz,* 471 U.S. 462, 474, 105 S. Ct. 2174, 85 L. Ed. 2d 528 (1985), and *World-Wide Volkswagen Corp. v. Woodson,* 444 U.S. 286, 297, 100 S. Ct. 559, 62 L. Ed. 2d 490 (1980) added clarification to *International Shoe* by stating that a defendant must "purposefully avail themselves of the privilege of conducting activities in a forum state" to invoke the benefits of that state's laws and protections. One more case, *Helicopteros Nacionales de Colombia, S.A. v. Hall,* 466 U.S. 408, 104 S. Ct. 1868, 80 L. Ed. 2d 404 (1984), added another criteria in the test for personal jurisdiction. The *Helicopteros* case added that "continuous and systematic general business contacts" are required to satisfy due process minimum contacts for jurisdiction.

More current U.S. Supreme Court cases have clarified and narrowed some of the basic definitions of general jurisdiction, at least in the corporate setting. A 2011 case, *Goodyear Dunlop Tires Operations, S.A. v. Brown,* __ U.S. __, 131 S.Ct. 2846 (2011) narrowed the definition of general jurisdiction. In that case the U.S. Supreme Court stated that jurisdiction over a foreign corporation is proper "to hear any and all claims against [it]" only when that corporation's affiliations are so constant and pervasive "as to render [it] essentially at home in the forum State." This includes such areas as a corporation's place of business or place of incorporation. Home in this context is equivalent to an individual's **domicile**. Thus the new standard under *Goodyear* is that the corporation's affiliations must be so continuous and systematic as to render it "home" in that forum state. This is a major deviation from the minimum contacts standard of *International Shoe.* Following the *Goodyear* case is *Daimler AG v. Bauman,* __U.S. __ 134 S.Ct. 746 (2014). In *Daimler,* the U.S. Supreme Court focused its decision on general and not specific jurisdiction, further clarifying *Goodyear.* Rejecting the past jurisdictional test that made substantial, continuous, and systematic business contacts the touchstone for asserting jurisdiction, now a plaintiff must show that a defendant either has its principal place of business or is incorporated in a state so that the contacts are so "continuous and systematic" as to render it essentially home in the forum state. Thus, with this test, where a corporate defendant can be sued is substantially narrowed to only those forums where due process determines it is fair to sue the defendant. Basically, these landmark cases set the benchmark for deciding personal jurisdiction in cases and what is needed to assert jurisdiction over a party.

domicile
A person's true, permanent home.

The bar was moved with the introduction of the Internet. Now, courts are faced with examining what contacts or activities constitute sufficient contacts over which a court can assert personal jurisdiction. Because of the often circuitous contacts the Internet presents, the courts have been faced with modifying the previous standards for personal jurisdiction. Similarly, with the introduction of *Goodyear* and *Daimler,* what constitutes jurisdiction through the Internet may change in the future. However, one standard that has been adopted by some courts originates from a Pennsylvania federal district court case, *Zippo Mfg. Co. v. Zippo Dot Com, Inc.*, 952 F. Supp. 1119 (W.D. Pa. 1997). The *Zippo* case created a new test that focused on Internet cases—a sliding scale test based on the quality and nature of the Internet activity. Was the defendant actively doing business through the Internet or was the defendant simply posting information, which the court referred to as "passive." Where the activity is passive, the court will not assert jurisdiction. However, the real problem arises with those cases that fall in between. The test must be applied on a case-by-case basis examining the level and nature of the activity of the Internet business involved. Although a majority of federal courts has adopted the *Zippo* analysis, there is no commonly accepted test for Internet cases. As of the publication of this text, the U.S. Supreme Court has not had an opportunity to weigh in on this issue. What is important to understand is that cases involving personal jurisdiction on the Internet are developing and until the U.S. Supreme Court decides a case, there is no uniformity in how courts approach the subject.

A recent case, *Caiazzio v. American Royal Arts Corp*, 73 So. 3d 245 (Fla. 2011), dealt with Internet personal jurisdiction. In an unusual move, the Court rendered a decision in the case after the parties submitted voluntary dismissals based upon a settlement. (Normally courts will not render a decision after the parties file a voluntary motion to dismiss, but the Court stated that the issues were too important and wanted to issue a decision to guide future litigants on Internet jurisdictional issues.)

CASE STUDY: UNDERSTANDING THE LAW

Caiazzio v. American Royal Arts Corp involves the purchase of a supposedly originally signed Beatles Revolver album. The basic facts are, Frank Caiazzo operates a business known as "Beatles Autographs." He specializes in buying, selling, and authenticating Beatles memorabilia. He's the defendant who resides in New Jersey and (sometimes) resides in Florida and whose business is on the Internet. American Royal Arts Corp (ARA) sells rock-n-roll memorabilia—the Plaintiff. One of ARA's customers wanted to buy the signed Beatles Revolver album for $14,900. Before ARA's customer would do that, he wanted the signatures authenticated. The customer sends a scanned copy of the album cover to a company in England who in turn sends it to Caiazzo for evaluation. Caiazzo believed the signatures to be forged and thus ARA lost the sale. Because of Caiazzo's conclusions, ARA believed its reputation, among other issues, was damaged and sued him. The issue before the court was whether the Florida court had jurisdiction over Caiazzo.

Performing an extensive jurisdictional analysis, starting with *International Shoe*, its progeny and the Florida long-arm statute, the Court analyzed the quality of the contacts of Caiazzo and his company and whether it was reasonable and foreseeable that he could be required to answer a lawsuit in Florida. Did Caiazzo's actions comport with the notions of fair play and justice as established by the due process clause of the U.S. Constitution? In its decision, the Court ultimately followed a strict "minimum contacts" analysis. Rejecting the sliding scale approach of *Zippo Mfg. Co. v. Zippo Dot Com, Inc.*, 952 F. Supp. 1119 (W.D. Pa. 1997) where a court considers how "active" or "passive" the actual Internet contacts are, the Florida appeals court in this case held that the *Zippo* test may be part of a jurisdictional analysis when the Internet is involved. Additionally, the Court distinguished between the concept of specific and general jurisdiction. For specific jurisdiction, the Court focused on the Florida long-arm statute and Caiazzo's contacts with the state.

(continued)

CASE STUDY: UNDERSTANDING THE LAW

The Court found specific jurisdiction, which means that the Court had personal jurisdiction over him. As for general jurisdiction, the Court performed a different analysis focusing on whether Caiazzo had "substantial, continuous, and systematic" minimum contacts. In this instance, the Court found that the contacts were almost exclusively on the Internet and those contacts were not substantial and continuous enough to warrant general (personal) jurisdiction over Caiazzo. The end result was that the Court did find personal jurisdiction, but under specific and not general jurisdiction.

Questions for Review: Examine *Caiazzio v. American Royal Arts Corp*, 73 So. 3d 245 (Fla. 2011) and determine the test the Court used for specific jurisdiction. What is the test for general jurisdiction? How do the tests differ? How did the Court analyze the Internet contacts and what case precedent did they apply in reaching their decision?

FEDERAL COURTS AND THEIR JURISDICTION

Introduction

Article III of the Constitution establishes the main federal courts and their jurisdictions. These courts are called constitutional courts and their judges are tenured for life. The constitutional courts consist of the United States Supreme Court, the United States Court of Appeals, and the United States District Court.

Legislative courts are established by act of Congress under Article I of the Constitution. Their judges have set terms. These are the specialized courts such as the United States Claims Court and the United States Tax Court.

All federal courts have limited subject matter jurisdiction and can exercise their power only with specific authorization. This authorization requires a constitutional source (Article III or Article I) and an act of Congress (found as United States Code provisions).

United States District Court

federal question
"[A]ll civil actions arising under the Constitution, laws, or treaties of the United States" (28 U.S.C. § 1331).

diversity of citizenship
Jurisdictional requirement for U.S. District Court that parties of a lawsuit be citizens of different states.

The United States District Court is the trial court in the federal system. There are ninety-four district courts, with at least one in each state and territory. These courts have original jurisdiction in a number of areas, the two most important being **federal question** cases and diversity of citizenship cases. Federal question cases are "all civil actions arising under the Constitution, laws, or treaties of the United States" (28 U.S.C. § 1331). These cases require the determination of rights under federal law and interpretation of its provisions. For example, a statute that unduly restricts freedom of the press would raise a federal question under the First Amendment, or a person suing to challenge a denial to that person of certain Social Security benefits would be raising a question about federal law (i.e., the Social Security regulations). The U.S. Supreme Court recently expanded the reach of federal question jurisdiction to even the most traditionally exclusive state law actions when, embedded in the state case, there is a substantial, disputed question of federal law [*Grable & Sons Metal Products Inc. v. Darue Engineering & Mfg.*, 125 S. Ct. 2363 (2005].

The second most important area of original subject matter jurisdiction for the district court is **diversity of citizenship** cases. "The district courts shall have original jurisdiction of all civil actions where the matter in controversy exceeds the sum or value of $75,000, exclusive of interest and costs, and is between … citizens of different states" [28 U.S.C. § 1332(a)(2)]. The rationale for federal diversity jurisdiction is to provide a party in the case with access to a neutral federal court, rather than having to litigate in a state court that might be biased in favor of an opponent who is a resident of the state in which the state court is located.

Several issues arise under this provision. The district court does not have jurisdiction unless diversity is complete. Each defendant must be a citizen of a different state from each plaintiff. For example, three plaintiffs, two from Kansas and one from Wisconsin, could sue four defendants, two from Missouri and two from Nebraska, assuming $75,000 in dispute; but the same plaintiffs could not sue in federal district court if just one defendant was from the same state as any of the plaintiffs. For the purpose of determining diversity jurisdiction, citizens of the District of Columbia are treated as if they were citizens of a state.

A citizen's state is defined as the state of domicile. The domicile is the true permanent home—the place to which one intends to return after being away—and is frequently determined by looking at a person's place of employment, site of voting or automobile registration, site of property, and the like.

For purposes of diversity, a corporation is considered a citizen of both the state in which it is incorporated and the state where it has its principal place of business [28 U.S.C. § 1332(c)]. If a company is incorporated in several states, the modern view (though not accepted in all jurisdictions) is to treat it as a citizen of each of those states. The "principal place of business" is the center of most of the corporation's activities, and if that isn't determinative, the site of the corporation's headquarters is. A national bank is a citizen in the state "designated in its articles of association as its main office" [*Wachovia Bank, National Association v. Schmidt*, 126 S.Ct. 941 (2006)].

If a party is an insurance company, that company is a citizen not only of the state of incorporation and the state of its principal place of business, but also of the state of the insured [28 U.S.C. § 1332(c)]. The insured is the person protected under the policy.

Determining diversity in other situations can present other problems. If the organization is an unincorporated association, it is a citizen of each state where each of its members is domiciled. For partnerships, it is unclear whether limited partners are included in diversity questions [*Carden v. Arkoma Associates*, 494 U.S. 185 (1990)]. Limited liability corporations (LLCs) are increasingly being treated as partnerships for diversity determinations [*Cosgrove v. Bartolotta*, 150 F.3d 729 (7th Cir. 1998)]. Where all of the parties in a business case are otherwise diverse, the fact that two of the opposing parties actually reside in the same foreign country is irrelevant to potential state court bias and, therefore, diversity is not defeated. **Class action** (numerous individuals with a common legal interest, i.e., all users of a certain product) citizenship is generally in the state of the named representative. Under the Class Action Fairness Act (CAFA) [Pub. L. No. 109–2, 119 Stat. 4 (2005)], however, federal diversity jurisdiction is satisfied in class action cases filed on or after February 18, 2005 if the case meets the special jurisdictional amount (see below) and at least one plaintiff is diverse from at least one defendant [28 U.S.C. § 1332 (d)(2), (6), (8)].

Here are other points on diversity jurisdiction. Diversity of citizenship must be alleged in the complaint (the document that states the claim) (28 U.S.C. § 1653). Once it is established, it cannot be altered by the parties' moving from state to state. It must exist, however, at the time a case is removed to federal court. Diversity jurisdiction is not defeated because the defendant claiming diversity fails to negate the existence of

class action

Lawsuit filed by individuals with a common interest.

an unnamed potential defendant, who, if included, would defeat diversity jurisdiction [*Lincoln Property Co. v. Roche,* 126 S. Ct. 606 (2005)]. Diversity does not give federal district courts jurisdiction in domestic relations or probate matters.

In addition to diversity being complete, the "amount in controversy" must meet the $75,000 requirement. Normally the district court will accept jurisdiction based on the allegation of amount in the complaint unless it is legally clear that the plaintiff cannot recover the required amount. Federal jurisdiction is not lost if recovery is eventually less than the requirement, but costs may be assessed [28 U.S.C. § 1332(b)].

Here is how the "amount in controversy" is determined in several contexts:

1. If the suit is for a declaratory judgment or an injunction, it is most often the value or cost to the plaintiff if relief were denied.

2. In most actions, it is the amount of plaintiff's harm or the defendant's costs to comply.

3. If suing under a federal statute that permits recovery of attorney's fees, that amount can be added to make $75,000.

4. If the case is an installment contract case and it is the entire contract that is in dispute, it is the value of the entire contract; otherwise, it is just the amount that has accrued in the installments to date.

5. If the case involves one plaintiff against one defendant, it is the value of all claims against the defendant (i.e., a combination of tort and contract claims).

6. If there are multiple plaintiffs, each plaintiff's claim must be $75,000 or more. The claims cannot be combined to make the amount. If one plaintiff meets the jurisdictional amount, however, other plaintiffs may be added whose claims are less than the requisite amount through the district court's application of supplemental jurisdiction [*Exxon Mobil Corp. v. Allapattah Servs.,* 125 S.Ct. 2611(2005)].

7. If multiple parties own property in common, it is the value of the property that is determinative (for three plaintiffs owning property in common, the value would not have to be $225,000).

8. In a class action, each person's claim must be in excess of the $75,000 amount. This requirement has been significantly modified in *Exxon Mobil v. Allapattah* and by CAFA. CAFA extends diversity jurisdiction in class actions where there is at least one plaintiff and one defendant that are diverse *and* where the combined monetary claims of all plaintiffs exceed five million dollars [28 U.S.C. § 1332(d)(2), (6), (8)].

9. If there is a counterclaim, determination under current law is not clear.

In addition to the federal question cases and diversity cases involving more than $75,000, federal district courts have original subject matter jurisdiction over the following:

1. Exclusive jurisdiction over all admiralty, maritime, and prize cases (28 U.S.C. § 1333).

2. All suits brought by the United States, its agencies, or officers (28 U.S.C. § 1345).

3. Suits against the United States or its officers (concurrent with U.S. Claims Court up to $10,000) (28 U.S.C. § 1346).

4. Suits to compel officers of the United States to perform their duty (28 U.S.C. §1361).

5. Removal of suits against federal officers in state courts (28 U.S.C. § 1442).

6. Suits in bankruptcy (28 U.S.C. § 1334).

7. Suits in patents, plant variety protection, copyrights, trademarks, and unfair competition (28 U.S.C. § 1338).

8. Suits involving internal revenue and customs duties (28 U.S.C. § 1340).

9. Suits in civil rights (28 U.S.C. § 1343).

10. Suits affecting ambassadors and other public ministers and consuls (28 U.S.C. § 1351).

State courts have concurrent jurisdiction with federal courts in all matters within federal jurisdiction, except if federal jurisdiction is exclusive, as in the case of copyright and patent law.

The district courts have subject matter, diversity jurisdiction over suits between citizens of a state and citizens or subjects of a foreign state [28 U.S.C. § 1332(a)(2)], where citizens or subjects of foreign states are "additional parties" on either side of the suit, and where a foreign state sues "citizens of a state or of different states" [28 U.S.C. § 1332(a)(3) and (4)]. This type of diversity jurisdiction involving foreign states and their citizens or subjects is called **alienage jurisdiction**.

alienage jurisdiction
A diversity jurisdiction involving foreign states and their citizens or subjects.

United States Court of Appeals

The United States Court of Appeals is the intermediate appellate court in the federal system. It is divided into thirteen courts consisting of eleven regional circuits, a Court of Appeals for the District of Columbia, and the U.S. Court of Appeals for the Federal Circuit. The courts of appeals have appellate jurisdiction over all appeals taken from final decisions of the United States District Court (28 U.S.C. § 1291). Each court of appeals hears appeals from the federal district courts in their respective circuits. The Court of Appeals for the Federal Circuit has exclusive subject matter jurisdiction over appeals in patent, trademark, and plant variety protection cases, plus appeals from the U.S. Claims Court and those involving government employment and international trade (28 U.S.C. § 1295). It reviews decisions of the U.S. Court of International Trade, the U.S. Claims Court, the U.S. Court of Veterans Appeals, and the decisions of the Board of Appeals or the Board of Patent Interferences of the Patent and Trademark Office, the Commission of Patents and Trademarks, and the Trademark Trial and Appeals Board.

The map in Exhibit 1.6 shows the geographical arrangement of the circuits for the U.S. Court of Appeals and their respective federal district courts.

APPLY YOUR KNOWLEDGE

Determine from the map in Exhibit 1.6 the federal circuit and district courts that serve your state. Place that information in your systems folder.

United States Supreme Court

The United States Supreme Court is the highest-level appellate court in the federal system. Its one chief justice and eight associate justices function as the authority on the Constitution and ensure the supremacy of federal law. Supreme Court jurisdiction is defined in Article III of the Constitution and cannot be increased or decreased by Congress. It has appellate jurisdiction over appeals from the United States Court of

EXHIBIT 1.6 U.S. Courts of Appeals and U.S. District Courts

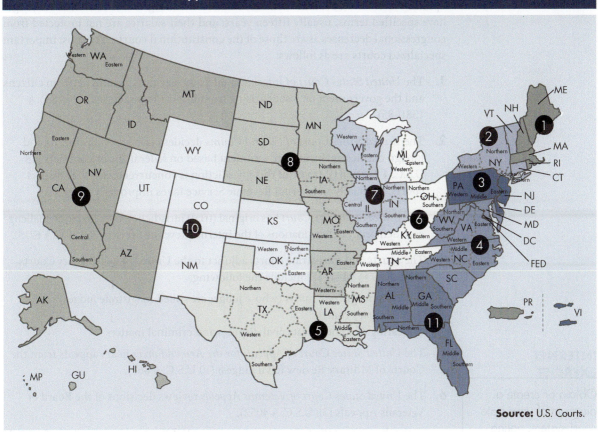

Source: U.S. Courts.

writ of certiorari

A discretionary writ that allows the Supreme Court to take only cases that, in its opinion, have sufficient national significance to warrant its attention.

Appeals (28 U.S.C. § 1254) and from the highest-level appellate courts in each state if the appeal raises a question of federal law (28 U.S.C. § 1257). Since 1988, cases reach the Supreme Court almost exclusively by **writ of certiorari**. This is a discretionary procedure that allows the Court to take only the cases that, in its opinion, have sufficient national significance to warrant its attention. The Court also uses the writ to resolve issues in which the courts of appeals are in serious conflict. Some constitutional matters come to the Court through a certification process distinct from the writ of certiorari.

The Supreme Court also has original jurisdiction in the following matters:

1. Controversies between two or more states (exclusive).

2. All actions or proceedings to which ambassadors, public ministers, and consuls of foreign states are a party.

3. All controversies between the United States and a state.

4. All actions or proceedings by a state against citizens of another state or against aliens.

Items 2–4 are subject matter jurisdictions held concurrently with lower federal courts.

SPECIALIZED FEDERAL COURTS

Specialized federal courts are established as Article I legislative courts. Their judges have specified terms, usually fifteen years, and their salaries are not protected from congressional decreases as are those of the constitutional courts. The most important specialized courts are as follows:

1. The *United States Court of International Trade* decides disputes between citizens and the government on issues arising from import transactions (28 U.S.C. § 1581–85).

2. The *United States Court of Federal Claims* decides claims of U.S. citizens and foreign entities against the government based on federal law or contracts [28 U.S.C. § 1491(a)(1)] (some of this jurisdiction is concurrent with U.S. district courts, especially in Internal Revenue Service taxes improperly collected).

3. The *United States Tax Court* has original (trial) jurisdiction over taxpayer challenges to deficiency determinations of the Internal Revenue Service (26 U.S.C. § 6213).

4. The courts and magistrate courts adjunct to the United States District Courts (28 U.S.C. §§ 7441–87) include the following:
   a. *federal magistrate courts* (whose judges are called magistrate judges)
   b. *bankruptcy courts*
   c. hearing of some private civil disputes and criminal matters

5. The *United States Court of Appeals for the Armed Forces* hears appeals from the Courts of Military Review (civil judges) (10 U.S.C. § 867).

6. The *United States Court of Veterans Appeals* reviews decisions of the Board of Veterans Appeals (38 U.S.C. § 4052).

See the diagram of the federal court system in Exhibit 1.7. Note the flow of appeals in the system.

STATE COURTS AND THEIR JURISDICTION

State courts are considered courts of general jurisdiction. All legitimate claims, including most of those that can go into the federal courts, can be filed in the state courts of original jurisdiction. State court judges are elected, appointed, or some combination of the two. Note how your state's judges come to office and for what length of term.

An increasing number of state court systems have or are developing specialized courts such as family, drug, community crime, medical malpractice, and business/technology courts. These courts are designed to expedite specific types of cases and to develop judges with pertinent expertise. The diagram in Exhibit 1.8 illustrates the structure of many state court systems. Note the flow of appeals in this diagram.

VENUE: WHERE CAN THE CASE BE HEARD?

Venue, literally "neighborhood," is the concept that determines where a case should be heard. Generally it means the defendant's neighborhood and/or the neighborhood where the incident occurred giving rise to the legal claim in the

---

INTERNET EXERCISE

Obtain or create a diagram of your state court system, noting which courts function as trial courts (original jurisdiction) and as intermediate or final level courts of appeal (appellate jurisdiction). Be able to identify the subject matter jurisdiction of each of your state courts. This is important because most of your work will be done in state court.

venue

"Neighborhood"; the geographical area in which a court with jurisdiction can hear a case; distinct from jurisdiction.

EXHIBIT 1.7 The Federal Court System

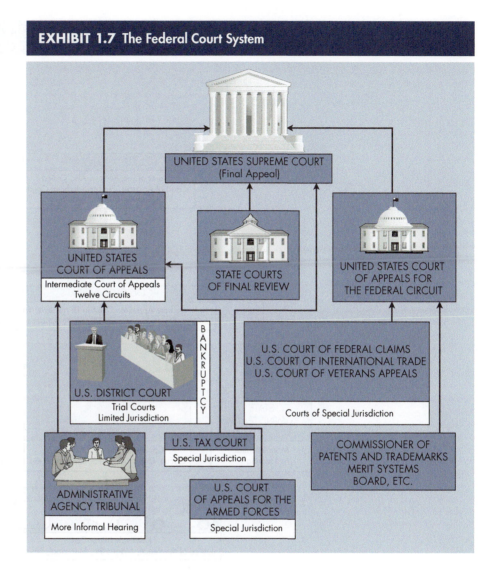

lawsuit. In most states this means the county where the defendant resides and the county where the incident happened. Some states have passed statutes or rules of procedure that define what court has venue generally and in specific kinds of situations such as in probate or property matters. Learn the venue requirements for your state.

The venue requirements for the United States District Court, 28 U.S.C. § 1391, are as follows:

(a) A civil action wherein jurisdiction is founded only on diversity of citizenship may, except as otherwise provided by law, be brought only in

    (1) a judicial district where any defendant resides, if all defendants reside in the same State

    (2) a judicial district in which a substantial part of the events or omissions giving rise to the claim occurred, or a substantial part of property that is the subject of the action is situated, or

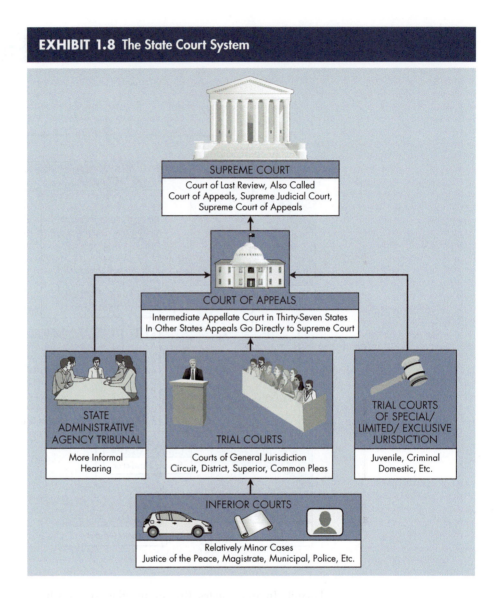

EXHIBIT 1.8 The State Court System

(3)	a judicial district in which any defendant is subject to personal jurisdiction at the time the action is commenced, if there is no district in which the action may otherwise be brought.

(b)	A civil action wherein jurisdiction is not founded solely on diversity of citizenship may, except as otherwise provided by law, be brought only in

(1)	a judicial district where any defendant resides, if all defendants reside in the same State

(2)	a judicial district in which a substantial part of the events or omissions giving rise to the claim occurred, or a substantial part of property that is the subject of the action is situated, or

(3)	a judicial district in which any defendant may be found, if there is no district in which the action may otherwise be brought.

(c) For purposes of venue under this chapter, a defendant that is a corporation shall be deemed to reside in any judicial district in which it is subject to personal jurisdiction at the time the action is commenced. In a State which has more than one judicial district and in which a defendant that is a corporation is subject to personal jurisdiction at the time an action is commenced, such corporation shall be deemed to reside in any district in that State within which its contacts would be sufficient to subject it to personal jurisdiction if that district were a separate State, and, if there is no such district, the corporation shall be deemed to reside in the district within which it has the most significant contacts.

(d) An alien may be sued in any district.

(e) A civil action in which a defendant is an officer or employee of the United States or any agency thereof acting in his official capacity or under color of legal authority, or an agency of the United States, or the United States, may, except as otherwise provided by law, be brought in any judicial district in which

    (1) a defendant in the action resides

    (2) a substantial part of the events or omissions giving rise to the claim occurred, or a substantial part of property that is involved in the action is situated, or

    (3) the plaintiff resides if no real property is involved in the action. Additional persons may be joined as parties to any such action in accordance with the Federal Rules of Civil Procedure and with such other venue requirements as would be applicable if the United States or one of its officers, employees, or agencies were not a party.

The summons and complaint in such an action shall be served as provided by the Federal Rules of Civil Procedure except that the delivery of the summons and complaint to the officer or agency as required by the rules may be made by certified mail beyond the territorial limits of the district in which the action is brought.

(f) civil action against a foreign state as defined in section 1603(a) of this title may be brought

    (1) in any judicial district in which a substantial part of the events or omissions giving rise to the claim occurred, or a substantial part of property that is the subject of the action is situated

    (2) in any judicial district in which the vessel or cargo of a foreign state is situated, if the claim is asserted under section 1605(b) of this title

    (3) in any judicial district in which the agency or instrumentality is licensed to do business or is doing business, if the action is brought against an agency or instrumentality of a foreign state as defined in section 1603(b) of this title, or

    (4) in the United States District Court for the District of Columbia if the action is brought against a foreign state or political subdivision thereof.

Venue is distinct from jurisdiction. It does not address which court has personal or subject matter jurisdiction. Rather, it addresses a location that should be fair to the parties and is likely to be close to witnesses, evidence, or the property in question. It might help to think that subject matter jurisdiction presents the question of *which court* handles this kind of case. Personal jurisdiction asks against *whom* can this court enforce a judgment, and venue asks *where*, in relationship to the parties, the event, or the property, can this case be heard.

As in the case of jurisdictional requirements, the general venue requirements at both the state and federal levels are further defined by statutes specific to a particular type of case or circumstance. In probate matters, state court venue is typically where the estate is located. Similarly, in disputes over property, venue is proper where the property is located, also known as the "situs" of the property.

TRANSFER OF CASES, FORUM NON CONVENIENS

Under 28 U.S.C. § 1404 and similar state laws, courts have the discretion to transfer a case to a more convenient court if the current court is inconvenient, even though the plaintiff may have met all the jurisdiction and venue requirements. This is a legal concept known as *forum non conveniens*. If a defendant demonstrates that the current forum is truly inconvenient (unfair, too costly, too far from evidence, and so on) and that another court exists with all the requisite jurisdiction and venues, then the court may transfer the case to the better forum.

If venue is improper, the court can dismiss the case or transfer it to a court that has venue [28 U.S.C. § 1406(a)]. Objection to venue, if not made early in the suit, will be waived, unlike objections to subject matter or personal jurisdiction.

Accurate determinations of jurisdiction and venue can range from being quite simple to exceptionally complex. Thorough research relevant to the parties and facts of each particular case is critical. Because you may be asked to participate in that process, your understanding of these fundamentals is important knowledge for the rest of this course and, eventually, for the law office. The next section will help you derive a better understanding of the application of jurisdiction and venue to choosing an appropriate court.

ETHICAL CONSIDERATIONS

Choosing where to file a lawsuit seems like an easy, unencumbered process. You determine where the parties reside, develop your legal theories and causes of action, and then file your lawsuit. Simple? Maybe not. If an attorney attempts to circumvent the rules of court and gain an unfair legal advantage, that conduct may be considered unethical. Forum shopping is when an attorney looks for the most advantageous or friendly court to file his lawsuit. Is this illegal or unethical? As a general rule, the answer is "no." Attorneys do it all the time. For example, an attorney who files a negligence lawsuit or product liability case wants to file in a place where jury awards tend to be higher. Or, attorneys seek courts that may favor or lean toward a particular point of view, such as a court that has a history of being more liberal or conservative on social issues. That is considered often times simply part of an attorney's strategy. But if the filing of a lawsuit harasses a potential party, is that ethical? A fine line is drawn. There are ethical rules that require attorneys to have a good faith basis for filing a lawsuit and not file lawsuits in bad faith or for purposes of harassment. (Some would argue that filing a lawsuit is harassment but most of us would acknowledge that most lawsuits have a legitimate legal basis.) ABA Model Rule of Professional Conduct 3.1 establishes the benchmark that lawyers must follow. Rule 3.1 reiterates the principle that attorneys must have a good faith belief that the claims that they filed are meritorious and have a basis in law. Thus, the legal process cannot and should not be abused. As we delve into the civil litigation process, this concept coupled with other ethical standards will set the tone for how we conduct ourselves and how others respond in the complex setting of litigation.

CHOOSING A COURT: THE RELATIONSHIP BETWEEN JURISDICTION AND VENUE

Here is a review of the factors that must be taken into consideration in deciding which court can hear a matter. First, the court must have subject matter jurisdiction. Most state courts, unless they are specialized courts, are courts of general jurisdiction and can hear most matters. The federal courts have limited jurisdiction and can hear only those matters defined by law for them to hear.

Once it is determined which courts have subject matter jurisdiction, it must be determined which courts have venue. Keep in mind that in most states, venue rests with the court in the county where the defendant resides and in the county where the incident occurred giving rise to the lawsuit. Some state statutes define the venue for specific matters. Federal venue is defined in 28 U.S.C. § 1391 and subsequent sections as delineated on the section on venue. Recall that for venue purposes, corporations, insurance companies, national banks, aliens, foreign states, and actions in which a defendant is the United States or one of its officials or agencies, are treated specially, and the specific statute should be consulted.

Of the courts that have both subject matter jurisdiction and venue, it must be determined which, if any, of these courts have personal jurisdiction (or in the case of property such as real estate, which has *in rem* jurisdiction over the property). To gain personal jurisdiction over the defendant, the defendant must be served with a summons and complaint. The summons is generally valid only in the geographical area over which the court has authority. Generally, therefore, federal district courts can serve a summons on persons only in the district in which the court sits. State courts can get personal jurisdiction only over persons within the boundaries of the state in which that court sits. State statutes called long-arm statutes can extend personal jurisdiction beyond a state's borders to persons living in other states if those persons have had or do have sufficient contact with the state seeking personal jurisdiction. For example, if Florida has passed a long-arm law to reach across state boundaries, a motorist from New York driving in Florida generally is deemed to be subject to the personal jurisdiction of the Florida courts for wrongful acts (negligence) while operating a motor vehicle in Florida. This is true even if the motorist has returned to New York. In diversity cases, the law of the state in which the federal court sits determines the reach of the federal court. In addition, specific federal statutes may give the federal district courts personal jurisdiction beyond each court's district boundaries. Long-arm statutes will be discussed further in Chapter 5.

Corporations are subject to personal jurisdiction in any state where the law invokes personal jurisdiction if the cause of action arises out of the corporation's "doing business," "transacting business," or registration to do business in that state. Usually, if a corporation regularly does business in a state, it is subject to personal jurisdiction in the state. If the corporation is subject to personal jurisdiction in a state, it is also deemed subject to personal jurisdiction of the U.S. district court in that state.

Now, how good are you at applying these general rules to determine in which courts an action can be filed? Assume that X, a California resident, wants to sue Y, a resident of western New York, for $80,000 in damages stemming from an automobile accident in northern California. Which courts have subject matter jurisdiction? At least the state trial courts of California and New York have the original and general jurisdiction to hear the case. The federal district courts in the Northern District of California and the Western District of New York have the needed limited subject matter jurisdictions, that is, diversity jurisdiction involving more than $75,000.

Which courts have venue? One California state trial court has venue—the trial court located in the county where the accident occurred. A New York trial court has venue in the county where Defendant Y resides. Federal venue rests in the Northern District of California because this is a diversity of citizenship case and in such cases venue is located where a substantial part of the events or omissions arose. Federal venue also rests in the Western District of New York because, in diversity cases, venue exists where any defendant resides when all defendants reside in the same state.

Assuming there is no long-arm statute, which courts can get personal jurisdiction? Courts normally can get personal jurisdiction only in the state or federal district in which they sit. Only the New York state trial court and the federal district court for the Western District of New York have the defendant residing in their geographical boundaries. Therefore, X must bring suit in either the New York state court or the federal court for the Western District of New York. Exhibit 1.9 shows which courts can hear the case of *X v. Y.*

With this information, the attorney would have to consider the judges in each court, possible bias in state court, convenience to witnesses and evidence, and all other factors that would work either in X's favor or to X's disadvantage in deciding which of the two courts would be best.

If, in the prior action, Z is also a defendant and lives in Utah, where could X sue? Add the following to the previous breakdown (Exhibit 1.10).

Utah cannot qualify for joint federal venue because not all of the defendants reside in Utah, no personal jurisdiction exists over all the defendants, and the substantial events or omissions did not occur there. This is also true for the federal court in New York. Therefore, no federal court will work for suing both defendants simultaneously or individually, so X must sue Y and Z separately in their respective state or federal courts. Note that in federal actions with one defendant, all the defendants reside in one state. Therefore, venue exists in the district of the defendant's residence.

EXHIBIT 1.9 Example of Which Courts Can Hear the Case of X v. Y

	Subject Matter Jurisdiction	Venue	Personal Jurisdiction
California State Court	Yes	Yes	No
California Federal Court	Yes (Diversity)	Yes	No
New York State Court	Yes	Yes	Yes
New York Federal Court	Yes	Yes	Yes

EXHIBIT 1.10 Where Could X Sue?

	Subject Matter Jurisdiction	Venue	Personal Jurisdiction
Utah State Court	Yes	Yes (for Z only)	Yes (for Z only)
Utah Federal Court	Yes	Yes (for Z only)	Yes (for Z only)
N.Y. Federal Court	Yes	Yes (for Y only)	Yes (for Y only)

X could sue Y and Z in California state or federal court only if California had a long-arm guest motorist statute giving California courts personal jurisdiction over out-of-state residents involved in automobile accidents in California.

If the original X and Y example involved a federal question, such as a violation of a constitutional right, the federal venues would be the same as in the preceding diversity example. State venue would exist in the county in which the action arose and where the defendant resides (the proper county in New York). But again, without a long-arm statute, only the district court in New York and the state court in New York have personal jurisdiction.

This time, try to determine where A and B can sue under the following circumstances. A resides in Wyoming and B resides in Colorado. They wish to sue C, a corporation, for a contract violated in Colorado in the amount of $100,000. C is incorporated in Delaware and has its principal place of business in Colorado. Take a minute to work this out before reading on. Test your understanding.

If you sued in Delaware and Colorado state courts, you are correct. Here is why. Each state in question has subject matter jurisdiction. Diversity jurisdiction for a federal court action does not exist—diversity must be complete, and B is from Colorado and so is defendant C (principal place of business). Without diversity jurisdiction, the federal courts are out of the picture. Since state venue normally exists in the county of the defendant's residence as well as the county where the action arose, venue exists in Delaware and Colorado. The only state courts with personal jurisdiction are those where the defendant resides—in this case Delaware and Colorado, if Colorado state law holds that the principal place of business is sufficient for personal jurisdiction to exist. The action, therefore, can be heard in state courts in Colorado or Delaware.

But what if C's principal place of business is Chicago, Illinois, instead of Colorado? Then we have plaintiffs from Wyoming (A) and Colorado (B) and a defendant (C) from Delaware (state of corporation) and Illinois (principal place of business). Because of general jurisdiction, each of the named states has subject matter jurisdiction. Federal diversity jurisdiction exists in each of the district courts—the districts of Colorado, Wyoming, Northern Illinois, and Delaware. State venue exists in Delaware and Illinois (residence of defendant) and in Colorado (where case arose). Federal venue, under 28 U.S.C. § 1391(c), for a *defendant* corporation lies in any district in any state where under that state's law the corporation does enough business that the state has personal jurisdiction over the corporation. Personal jurisdiction can be obtained at least in Delaware and in Illinois and, if there is enough business, in Colorado and Wyoming. Federal venue, therefore, would exist in these states and double in Colorado because that is where the cause arose. Exhibit 1.11 shows the possibilities.

APPLY YOUR KNOWLEDGE

Using the facts from Case IV at the beginning of the chapter, determine what state and in what courts could Briar Patch file a lawsuit against Teeny Tiny Clothing.

Plaintiffs would definitely have four courts to choose from and possibly as many as eight because of the defendant corporation venue rule and the expanded personal jurisdiction through corporate contacts in the state.

Once jurisdiction and venue are determined, the final choice of which state or federal court to file the action in is based on several additional factors: which of the courts in question tend to award the highest or lowest monetary amounts, which courts move cases along the fastest or slowest, which court is closest to or has personal jurisdiction over key witnesses, how do the judges compare, will the law applied be different and, if so, which law will best benefit the client. Paralegals are occasionally asked to research such comparative factors.

EXHIBIT 1.11 Example of Possibilities

	Subject Matter Jurisdiction	**Venue**	**Personal Jurisdiction**
Colorado State Court	Yes	Yes	? (depends on contacts)
Wyoming State Court	Yes	No	? (depends on contacts)
Delaware State Court	Yes	Yes	Yes
Illinois State Court	Yes	Yes	Yes
Colorado Federal Court	Yes	Yes	? (depends on contacts)
Wyoming Federal Court	Yes	?	? (depends on contacts)
Delaware Federal Court	Yes	Yes	Yes
Illinois Federal Court	Yes	Yes	Yes

A CASE ROADMAP

Exhibit 1.12 sets out the various steps in handling a case from start to finish. Although you will be learning the process in more detail later, this case roadmap will help you to know where you are headed when working on a case. Photocopy this diagram and place it in your systems folder.

EXHIBIT 1.12 Case Roadmap

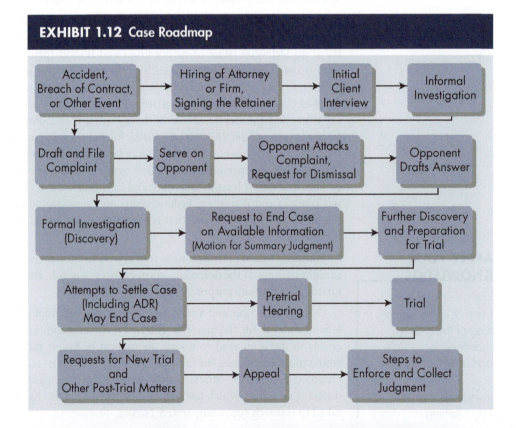

SUMMARY

The *Paralegal Handbook* introduced you to the law firm, its structure, the kinds of cases it handles, the role of the paralegal, office procedures, ethical considerations, and the methods to be employed in your training. In addition, the handbook has emphasized techniques for thriving in the law office and your professional development.

You have also reviewed courts, jurisdictions, and venue. Cases originate in either a state or federal court. Both have trial level courts and appeals courts. Some states have a two-tiered system while others have a three-tiered system. The highest court for all cases is the U.S. Supreme Court. Case decisions from that court apply to all state and federal jurisdictions.

Personal jurisdiction requires a court to have jurisdiction over the person. In some cases, a court will examine the contacts through long-arm statutes. Constitutional tests, such as the minimum contacts and the reasonableness of those contacts, must occur before a court will find jurisdiction over a defendant. Not only must a court have personal jurisdiction over a party, but the court must have subject matter jurisdiction as well. In rem jurisdiction provides jurisdiction over property. Federal jurisdiction occurs when there is a federal question, such as a federal statute or issues arising from the U.S. Constitution. Diversity jurisdiction occurs when parties from different states or a foreign country are involved and where the sum in controversy is over $75,000. Concurrent jurisdiction arises when two courts are proper to file a lawsuit. Usually when this occurs, an attorney will determine the best place to file the lawsuit.

And finally, venue is the place where a case is filed. Venue can be in the county where the parties reside or the federal district where the parties are located, for example. Venue could be proper in a number of places, depending on the issues involved in a case. These fundamentals are essential to a good beginning to your career.

KEY TERMS

alienage jurisdiction

associate

billable hours

civil litigation

class action

concurrent jurisdiction

diversity of citizenship

domicile

electronic billing
    (e-billing)

federal questions

general jurisdiction

in rem (property) jurisdiction

judgment

jurisdiction

jurisdictional amount
    (amount in controversy)

lawsuit

legal advice

litigation system

long-arm statutes

malpractice

multijurisdictional practice

partner

personal jurisdiction

pro bono

pro hace vice

professional ethics

subject matter jurisdiction

summons

supplemental jurisdiction

tickler system

trial court

unbundling legal services

venue

writ of certiorari

QUESTIONS FOR STUDY AND REVIEW

Use the following study questions as a summary of the terms, definitions, concepts, and procedures in this chapter, and to prepare for an exam on these materials

1. Define *paralegal*.

2. Why is a paralegal valuable to a law firm? Identify significant legal authority on billing for paralegal time.

3. Why are timekeeping and deadline control important?

4. What are some ethical concerns regarding timekeeping and billing?

5. What is a litigation system and why is it beneficial?

6. Define *professional ethics* in the context of the practice of law.

7. Why are professional ethics so important to a law firm?

8. What are the things a paralegal may not do?

9. What are the seven criteria that assure a paralegal's actions will not be or cause a breach of ethics?

10. What is a conflict of interest and the rationale for the relevant ethical standards?

11. What is meant by the term *professional loyalty* as applied to your fellow workers? The client? The practice of law?

12. What are the characteristics of the common components of court systems in the United States?

13. What is jurisdiction? Define the various kinds of jurisdiction: geographical, personal, general, and so on.

14. What are the personal jurisdictional considerations regarding a defendant when the Internet is involved?

15. What three things must a court have in order to hear a case and bind a party to the court's decision? Be able to apply these concepts to determine what court or courts can hear a lawsuit depending on domiciles of the parties and other factors.

SYSTEMS FOLDER ASSIGNMENTS

1. Set up a three-ring binder (or electronic equivalent) with the tab dividers arranged as described in the litigation system section of the text. Copies of the office structure and forms previously discussed should be placed in the systems folder as indicated in Appendix A. Begin a table of contents for your systems folder and add any information assigned by your instructor.

2. Look up your state's ethical rules that govern confidentiality, conflict of interest, attorney supervision of lay persons and legal assistants, professional integrity, and others.

Record the rule numbers in an ethics section of your systems folder. Look up your state's unauthorized practice of law statute; note the wording and the possible penalties. You might want to add this to your folder. As you read further in this text and in other sources, insert in your folder the citations for key ethical rules and guidelines.

3. Locate the names, addresses, and phone numbers of your local and state paralegal associations. If you need help obtaining this information, try the Internet or a director of a local paralegal program or any

experienced paralegal. The headquarters of the state bar association might also have such information. For future reference, you may choose to place your expanded lists of sources for professional development in your systems folder.

State Paralegal Association	Local Paralegal Association
Name:	Name:
Address:	Address:
Phone:	Phone:
E-Mail:	E-Mail:
Web Site:	Web Site:
Contact Person:	Contact Person:
Meeting Dates and Times:	Meeting Dates and Times:

4. Make a copy of the federal court structure diagram found in the text and add any explanatory notes you feel will be useful to you in the future. Include in your diagram the names of U.S. district courts that sit in your state and the U.S. Court of Appeals that covers the circuit in which your state is situated.

Make a similar explanatory diagram for the court system of your state. Research the material to be placed in the diagram, including any jurisdictional amounts, by looking under courts, judiciary, and jurisdiction in the index of your state statutes or constitution, usually located in the law library, or search your State Court Web site. Some states have an administrative office of the courts at the capitol, which may provide preprinted state court diagrams.

Place both diagrams and the State Court Web site address in the court section of your litigation systems folder.

5. Consult the state's legal directory in the library or online sites to obtain all court addresses, names of clerks of court, important telephone numbers, and so on. Research state statutes for the subject matter jurisdiction of your state's highest, intermediate, and trial courts. Place this data in the court structure portion of your systems folder.

Federal Court System	Address:
Highest Court	Clerk:
Name:	Phone:
Jurisdiction:	
Intermediate Appellate Court	Address:
Name:	Clerk:
Jurisdiction:	Phone:
Trial Courts	Address:
Name:	Clerk:
Jurisdiction:	Phone:
State Court System	
Highest Court	Address:
Name:	Clerk:
Jurisdiction:	Phone:
Intermediate Appellate Court	Address:
Name:	Clerk:
Jurisdiction:	Phone:
Trial Courts	Address:
Name:	Clerk:
Jurisdiction:	Phone:

APPLICATION ASSIGNMENTS

1. Using the ethical standards and rules cited in the text, answer the following questions on ethics:

   a. You have just researched an issue and have found that inattentive driving is a breach of the duty of care that a driver owes to others. In a phone conversation, the client asks you, "If the driver of the vehicle that struck me was inattentive, is he in the wrong?" How should you answer?

  b. Ms. Pearlman asks you to draft a release of medical information form for a client. This form is drafted and signed by the client and given to the hospital. Under what conditions can you do this and avoid the unauthorized practice of law?

  c. You are working on a client's case for Ms. Pearlman. She is gone, so you want to consult with Mr. White, another attorney in our firm. To do so, however, you must reveal to Mr. White some confidential information about the client. Would this be a breach of confidentiality?

2. You are a paralegal working for an attorney who has represented Safe Bet Insurance Company. A potential client wants to sue Safe Bet. Is there a potential conflict of interest, and if so, may your attorney represent the new client?

3. In interviewing a client, you and your attorney are convinced that some information provided by the client is false. What consequences can result from the presentation of such information to the court? What model rule of professional conduct applies?

4. Determine in which courts subject matter jurisdiction, personal jurisdiction, and venue exist in the following problems:

  a. M, a resident of Wisconsin, and O, a resident of Minnesota, sue Corporations X and Y for industrial injuries amounting to $40,000 for each plaintiff resulting from an accident that occurred in Illinois. X is incorporated in Delaware and Ohio, and Y is incorporated in North Carolina with its principal place of business in Ohio.

  b. J and K reside in Oregon and sue R, who resides in Kentucky, and S, who resides in Washington, for a tort (libel) amounting to injuries exceeding $75,000 each, which occurred in Washington.

5. Glitter is a corporation that rents expensive jewelry to businesses and individuals. It is incorporated in Delaware and has its principal place of business in Northern Indiana. It is licensed to do business in every state except Alaska and Hawaii. Flick, Inc., is a movie company incorporated in Idaho with its principal place of business in Utah. It does no business to speak of in any other state.

  During Flick's filming in Nevada, an expensive necklace rented from Glitter falls into a piece of machinery on the set and is destroyed. Glitter wants to sue Flick for negligently destroying the jewelry (worth $700,000). Flick decides to sue Glitter, blaming the loss of a week's filming on the loss of the necklace, which they claim was caused by a faulty clasp made by Glitter. Answer the following and provide a explanation for your response:

  a. If Glitter sues Flick, is there subject matter jurisdiction in federal district court?

  b. What, if any, kind of subject matter jurisdiction exists in federal district court?

  c. What issue concerning personal jurisdiction exists when considering the suit by Glitter against Flick in Nevada state and federal court?

  d. Aside from Nevada, in what state and federal courts can Glitter sue Flick?

  e. If Flick sues Glitter, does venue exist in the state courts of Idaho and Utah? Why or why not?

CASE ASSIGNMENTS

1. Your law firm has been hired to represent Ann Forrester in her lawsuit against Mercury Parcel Services, Inc. and its driver Richard Hart. Determine in what court any future lawsuit would be filed and explain the basis for your decision.

2. As Mrs. Forrester's attorneys, what ethical obligations do you have regarding any communications you have with her regarding her potential lawsuit? What ethical obligations does your law firm have with regard to Mrs. Forrester's husband William?

2

THE INITIAL INTERVIEW

OBJECTIVES

AFTER READING THIS CHAPTER, YOU WILL BE ABLE TO:

- Understand the importance of the initial client interview
- Develop a plan for preparing, conducting and summarizing the interview
- Determine the types of questions to ask in an interview for the most effective results
- Recognize how to handle challenging clients in a professional manner
- Define the term statute of limitations and identify its significance in the litigation process

INTRODUCTION

Today, you have the opportunity to begin working on a case. (Please reread Case I.) Mr. White has met with Ann Forrester, who will be coming to the office for her initial interview for a personal injury negligence case. It may not always fall to the paralegal to do the interview alone. Sometimes the paralegal assists the attorney, sometimes the attorney and paralegal interview jointly, and sometimes the attorney conducts the interview alone. Increasingly, however, offices place this responsibility on the paralegal. It is your job to prepare and conduct the interview with Mrs. Forrester.

The client interview is a significant step. First, it sets the tone for the entire relationship between the prospective client and the law firm. The client should leave feeling comfortable with the relationship and confident that matters will be handled competently. Second, it sets the tone for the critical relationship between the client and the paralegal that may last months or even years. Third, it is the important beginning of investigation, a fact-gathering process requiring other interviews and techniques that will be discussed in the chapters to follow. The initial client interview and subsequent interviews determine the basis of the lawsuit (or its defense), the firm's acceptance of the case, and the fee.

THE INTERVIEW PLAN

You will need to set up an interview plan in order to derive maximum benefit from the time spent with the client. Use the following Interview Plan Checklist in developing your interview plan.

THE INTERVIEW PLAN: A CHECKLIST

Step 1	Review all available information on the case.
Step 2	Locate or develop an appropriate interview form.
Step 3	Select a location for the interview.
Step 4	Determine what information the client should bring.
Step 5	Schedule the interview (tentatively); check with attorney.
Step 6	Anticipate and arrange for any special needs.
Step 7	Review pertinent ethical and tactical considerations.
Step 8	Review recommended interview techniques.
Step 9	Prepare orientation and instruction materials for the client.
Step 10	Prepare any forms for the client's signature.
Step 11	Prepare the interview site.

THE INTERVIEW PLAN: THE NUTS AND BOLTS

Step 1

REVIEW ALL AVAILABLE INFORMATION ON THE CASE. Check the file for news clippings, police reports, and any other readily available information. Any background you gain about the incident will direct you in researching additional information.

Further, attorneys have learned to be cautious about what cases they accept and what clients they represent. The case's potential for a successful outcome, likely profitability, and compatibility with the attorney's expertise are all important considerations. Important, as well, are the potential client's character, honesty in business dealings, caliber as a witness, and ability to work easily and cooperatively with others. Information that you can gather that enables your attorney to screen out bad clients and cases can save a lot of expense, time, and headache down the line. Gathering information about persons and businesses is discussed in Chapter 3.

Step 2

LOCATE OR DEVELOP AN APPROPRIATE INTERVIEW FORM. An interviewer needs to identify what information is needed from the client and what questions will best elicit that information. A form questionnaire can save preparation time and serve as a guide for the interviewer. Such forms can usually be found in the firm's form files, or in trial practice manuals readily available at the firm or local library. Our firm has an interview form for personal injury–automobile negligence cases. See Exhibit 2.1 and Exhibit 2.2. Read the form carefully; it will raise your awareness of what needs to be covered in this type of case.

EXHIBIT 2.1 Checklist Form: Client Background Information

Please type or print. If using the paper version of this form please use back or extra sheets if more space is needed. (Please note that forms should be adjusted according to the type of case and facts that the client may have.)

Name _____ Soc. Sec. No. (last 4 digits) _____

Have you hired any other attorney on this matter? _____

Address (including county) _____

Zip Code _____ Years at this address _____

Home Phone _____ Work Phone _____

Date of Birth _____ Age _____ Sex _____

If minor, guardian's name and address _____

Marital Status: S ____ M ____ D ____ W ____ Other ____

Spouse's Name _____ Date of Birth _____

Home Phone _____ Work Phone _____

_____

Spouse's Place of Employment (if applicable) _____

Spouse's Job Title _____

Children's Names   Ages   Addresses

_____

_____

_____

(continued)

EXHIBIT 2.1 Checklist Form: Client Background Information (*continued*)

Date of Marriage/Divorce _____ If other marriages, list date, spouse, and children on back.

If self-employed, nature of business, address, phone, partners, salary or approximate income.

_____

If you have been involved in any prior litigation, please give details, type of action, plaintiff-defendant, attorney, court, year, result.

_____

_____

Depending on the type of case, the following questions may be appropriate:

Gross Income _____ Attach tax returns from the last three years.

Property: List all real estate owned/if held solely, jointly, etc./value, mortgage, etc.

_____

If requested, attach a list of personal property (bank accounts, stocks and bonds, autos, furniture, etc.).

Source: Adapted from Elliott & Elliott, *A Tort Resume for Use in Prosecution and Defense of All Damage Claims*, with permission.

EXHIBIT 2.2 Checklist Form: Automobile Accident

PARTIES—GENERAL INFORMATION

( ) Plaintiff _____ Age _____ Sex _____ Phone _____

( ) Address _____ City _____ County _____ State _____ Zip _____

( ) Bus. Address _____ City _____ County _____ State _____ Phone _____

( ) Ins. Carrier _____ Address _____ Phone _____

   Amt. Ins. Liab. _____ P.D. _____ Med. _____ Collision _____

   Uninsured Motorist _____ Any Coverage Deductible? Which? _____

_____

Request copy of policy from client.

(Ask questions about the potential defendant(s). Information may not be known at the time of the initial interview. Later research may be required.)

( ) Defendant 1. _____ Age _____ Sex _____ Phone _____

( ) Address _____ City _____ County _____ State _____ Phone _____

( ) Bus. Address _____ City _____ County _____ State _____ Phone _____

(continued)

EXHIBIT 2.2 Checklist Form: Automobile Accident (*continued*)

( ) Ins. Carrier _____ Address _____ Phone _____

   Amt. Ins. Liab. _____ P.D. _____ Med. _____ Collision _____

   Uninsured Motorist _____ Any Coverage Deductible? Which? _____

_____

Request copy of insurance policy.

( ) Other Defendants. _____ Age _____ Sex _____ Phone _____

( ) Address. _____ City _____ County _____ State _____ Phone _____

( ) Bus. Address. _____ City _____ County _____ State _____ Phone _____

If additional insurance, the following questions should be asked:

Ins. Carrier. _____ Address _____ Phone _____

Amt. Ins. Liab. _____ P.D. _____ Med. _____ Collision _____

Uninsured Motorist. _____ Any Coverage Deductible? Which? _____

FACTS OF ACCIDENT

( ) Date of Accident _____ Time _____ Material Facts _____

_____

_____

( ) Type of Case (Check Applicable Subject Matter)

   ( ) Employer, Employee, & Independent Contractor   ( ) Invitees & Licensees Product Liability
   ( ) Transportation—Airplane, Automobile, or Train   ( ) Wrongful Death
   ( ) Workers' Compensation   ( ) Other

( ) Diagram accident scene if physical facts are important

_____

_____

( ) Indicate & note on diagram the following information:

   ( ) Width of streets or roads measured _____

   ( ) Number of lanes _____ Any peculiar curves or hills _____

   ( ) Yellow lines _____ Stop signs or traffic devices _____

   ( ) Skid marks _____ Position of vehicles after accident _____

   ( ) Type of road surface— _____

   ( ) Dry or wet _____ Weather—fog, rain, drizzle, sleet, or snow _____

   ( ) Visibility—good or bad _____ Day, night, dusk, or dawn _____

_____

   ( ) Clear or cloudy _____ Other _____

EXHIBIT 2.2 Checklist Form: Automobile Accident (*continued*)

( ) Ascertain. if pictures were taken of accident scene _____

( ) When _____ By whom _____

( ) Address _____ Phone _____

( ) If not, take pictures of accident scene immediately (be sure the date is noted on the back of the picture and who took pictures.)

( ) Place pictures obtained or taken in evidence file

( ) Comments _____
_____

( ) Automobile information

   ( ) Plaintiff Vehicle

      ( ) Year _____ Make _____ Model _____ Color_____

      ( ) Manuf. I.D. _____

      ( ) Tag No. _____ Type of steering _____

      ( ) Defects of vehicle—Brakes _____ Lights _____ Motor _____

         Steering _____ Tires _____ Other _____

         Comments as to condition _____
_____

( ) Location of Vehicle—Identify where the vehicle, which is the subject of the accident, is presently located.
_____

   Address _____ Phone _____

   Were Pictures Taken of Automobile _____

   When _____ By Whom _____

   Address _____ Phone _____

( ) If not, take pictures at garage & place in evidence file

   Taken by _____ When _____ Address _____

( ) Note alleged speed prior to collision

( ) Indicate impact points on vehicle diagram & note interior damage

   Right Side Length _____ ft.   Front Width _____ ft.   Rear   Left Side

( ) Owner of plaintiff vehicle _____ Age _____ Sex _____

( ) Address _____ City _____ State _____ Phone _____

( ) Business Address _____ City _____ State _____ Phone _____

( ) Ins. Carrier _____ Address _____ Phone _____

(continued)

EXHIBIT 2.2 Checklist Form: Automobile Accident (*continued*)

Amt. Ins.—Liab. _____ P.D. _____

Med. _____ Collision _____

Uninsured Motorist _____ Any coverage deductible? Which? _____

_____

( ) Driver plaintiff vehicle _____

( ) If the person driving vehicle different from the owner identify: Relationship to owner _____

Driving with permission _____

( ) Destination & purpose _____

( ) Impediments of driver—Intoxication _____ Glasses _____

Hearing _____ Other physical defects _____

If passengers in the vehicle with driver determine: (1) Seat location in vehicle (2) Seat belt
(3) Distractions (4) Other _____ .

_____

_____

( ) Defendant Vehicle

( ) Year _____ Make _____ Model _____ Color _____

( ) Manuf. I.D. _____

( ) Tag No. _____ Power or regular steering _____

( ) Defects of vehicle—Brakes _____ Lights _____ Motor _____

Steering _____ Tires _____ Other _____

Comments as to condition _____

( ) Location of vehicle: Identify where the vehicle, which is the subject of the accident, is presently located

_____

_____

Were pictures taken of automobile? _____

When _____ By whom _____

Address _____ Phone _____

( ) If not, take pictures at garage & place in evidence file

Taken by _____ When _____ Address _____

( ) Note alleged speed prior to collision _____

( ) Indicate impact points on vehicle diagram & note interior damage

Right Side Length   Front Width   Rear   Left Side
_____ ft.   _____ ft.

( ) Owner of defendant vehicle, if different from driver. _____ Age _____ Sex _____

( ) Address _____ City _____ State _____ Phone _____

( ) Business Address _____ City _____ State _____ Phone _____

EXHIBIT 2.2 Checklist Form: Automobile Accident (*continued*)

( ) Ins. Carrier _____ Address _____ Phone _____

    Amt. Ins.—Liab. _____ P.D. _____

    Med. _____ Collision _____

    Uninsured Motorist _____ Any coverage deductible? Which? _____

_____

( ) Driver defendant vehicle _____

( ) Relationship to owner_____

    Driving with permission _____

( ) Destination & purpose _____

( ) Impediments of driver—Intoxication _____ Glasses _____

    Hearing _____ Other physical defects _____

    Passengers—Seat location in vehicle

_____

_____

( ) Identify any traffic violations by plaintiff & defendant

    Charges against   Court   Hearing date   Result

_____

_____

( ) Get copy of traffic court testimony if recorded & place in evidence file

( ) Possible witnesses to accident including parties

    Witnesses   Address   State   Age   Phone (Cell)

_____

_____

_____

( ) Witness Statements Record (Use checklist in taking statements)

Last Name	Taken by	Given to	Written, Recorded,	Copy
Witness	Plaintiff	Defendant	When? or Oral	Retained
Witness for				

    General Description of Statement information:

_____

_____

_____

( ) Statement taken by police _____ Police Reports _____

    Get copy of any police reports from the accident. (Be sure it is signed.)

( ) Place all statements in evidence file

( ) Impeachment of parties & witnesses (note unfavorable military record)

    Name   Crime Conviction   Date   Good or Bad Character

_____

_____

_____

(continued)

EXHIBIT 2.2 Checklist Form: Automobile Accident (*continued*)

( ) Parties' prior accidents

Plaintiff _____

_____

Defendant _____

_____

MEDICAL

( ) Plaintiff—Summary of Injuries? (Indicate degree of disability—Restriction of activities in work, sports, etc.)

_____

_____

_____

( ) Note Injuries on Diagram

( ) <u>Indicate Plaintiff's Area of Pain (prepare a summary and note on diagram, if necessary)</u>

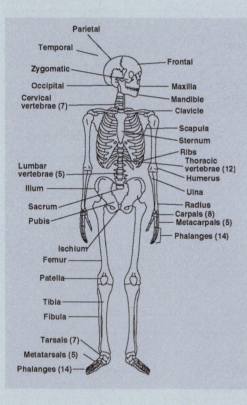

( ) Symptoms
  ( ) Headaches (indicate any explanation next to symptom)
  ( ) Dizziness
  ( ) Nausea
  ( ) Nervousness
  ( ) Insomnia
  ( ) Appetite
( ) Head
  ( ) Brain
  ( ) Forehead
  ( ) Ears
  ( ) Eyes
  ( ) Nose
  ( ) Mouth
  ( ) Teeth
( ) Neck
  ( ) Muscles
  ( ) Spine
  ( ) Throat
( ) Chest
  ( ) Heart
  ( ) Lungs
  ( ) Ribs
( ) Abdomen
( ) Internal Injuries
( ) _____
_____

( ) Arms (Rt. or Left)
  ( ) Upper
  ( ) Forearm
  ( ) Elbows
  ( ) Wrist
  ( ) Hands
  ( ) Fingers
( ) Trunk
  ( ) Shoulders
  ( ) Spine
  ( ) Thoracic
  ( ) Scapula
  ( ) Lumbar
  ( ) Sacrum
  ( ) Coccyx
  ( ) Pelvis
  ( ) Hips
( ) Legs (Rt. or Left)
  ( ) Thighs
  ( ) Upper
  ( ) Lower
  ( ) Knees
  ( ) Ankles
  ( ) Feet
  ( ) Toes
( ) Indicate Radiations of Pain
( ) Note Cuts, Bruises, Burns, Bumps, Sutures, Fractures, Missing Teeth, Swelling, Contusions, Points of Bleeding, Unconsciousness, etc.

EXHIBIT 2.2 Checklist Form: Automobile Accident (*continued*)

PLAINTIFF MEDICAL & PAIN AREAS

( ) Same information for defendant's injuries (if any)

( ) Ambulance, hospital, & doctor service, findings & treatment

( ) Ambulance service—By whom? _____ Other _____

Any first aid administered? If so, what? _____

Note time ambulance arrived at accident scene _____

( ) Hospitals   Address   Phone   Period of treatment   Surgery.

Treatment _____

_____ X-Rays taken? When? _____

( ) Doctors   Address   Phone   Period of Treatment   Surgery

1. Diagnosis, Treatment, & Prognosis _____

_____ X-Rays taken? When? _____

2. Diagnosis, Treatment, & Prognosis _____

_____ X-Rays taken? When? _____

(Repeat inquiry for additional treating physicians as necessary for particular case.)

( ) Summary comments as to percentage of disability & patient prognosis (This information should be obtained from the healthcare professionals and treatment centers, such as hospitals.)

_____

_____

_____

PRIOR MEDICAL TREATMENT—PLAINTIFF & DEFENDANT

( ) Plaintiff—Prior Medical Treatment

Doctors & Hospitals   Address   Phone   Period of Treatment

1. _____

2. _____

3. _____

Treatment _____

_____

( ) Note relationship of prior (preexisting) to present injuries _____

_____

_____

( ) Prior claims of any nature? When? Where?

_____

_____

( ) Defendant—prior medical treatment

Doctors & Hospitals   Address   Phone   Period of Treatment

1. _____

2. _____

(continued)

EXHIBIT 2.2 Checklist Form: Automobile Accident (*continued*)

3. _____
Treatment _____

( ) Note relationship of prior (preexisting) to present injuries _____
_____
_____
_____
_____

( ) Prior claims of any nature? When? Where?
_____
_____
_____
_____

( ) Summary degree of prior disability
( ) Plaintiff _____
( ) Defendant _____

DAMAGES—PLAINTIFF

( ) Plaintiff employment subsequent & prior to accident

Subsequent to	Dates	Position	Annual Earnings

Prior to (last 2 yrs.)	Dates	Position	Annual Earnings

( ) Education & Job Training _____
_____

( ) Family Situation

Spouse & Children	Relationship	Age

EXHIBIT 2.2 Checklist Form: Automobile Accident (*continued*)

( ) Computation of General Damages—Note age of injured party _____

    ( ) Pain & suffering (past, present, & future) estimate of party—value assessed per day

    $ _____ × _____ Days = $ _____ × Life Expectancy _____ = $ _____

( ) Diminution capacity to labor as element of pain & suffering

    (past, present, & future) estimate of party-value assessed per day

    $ _____ × _____ Days = $ _____ × Life Expectancy _____ =$ _____

    ( ) Loss of consortium (estimate of party) value assessed per day

( ) Computation of special damages (Date accident) _____

    $ _____ × _____ Days = $ _____ × Life Expectancy _____ =$ _____)

    ( ) Loss of Earnings

        ( ) Past & present to date of trial—days in hospital _____

        ( ) Past & present continued (At home _____ Returned to work—Date _____)

        ( ) Total Days _____ × Per Diem Wages $ _____ = $ _____

    ( ) Annual Average Earnings $ _____ Capacity Reduced _____ %

    Disability $ _____ × _____ Use Annuity Table _____ %

    Column to reduce to present cash value or × _____ Life Expectancy

    (for gross when reduction not required) $ _____

( ) Hospitals, Nurses, Doctors, Drugs (Supports & Braces), & Ambulance Expenses

Hospitals	Period	Amount
_____	_____	$ _____
_____	_____	
_____	_____	
_____	_____	
_____	_____	
_____	_____	$ _____ $ _____

Nurses	Period	Amount
_____	_____	$ _____
_____	_____	$ _____ $ _____

Doctors	Period	Amount
_____	_____	$ _____
_____	_____	
_____	_____	
_____	_____	
_____	_____	$ _____ $ _____

(continued)

EXHIBIT 2.2 Checklist Form: Automobile Accident (*continued*)

Pharmacy   Period   Amount

_____ $ _____

_____

$ _____ $ _____

Ambulance   Period   Amount

_____ $ _____

$ _____ $ _____

( ) If death, request information on funeral expenses and related costs—Mortician's Name & Address

_____ $ _____

( ) Property Damage

     ( ) Automobile—fair market value before $ _____ $ _____

         Less fair market value after accident $ _____ $ _____

         Diminution in value $ _____ $ _____

     ( ) Reasonable Hire Days × Rental Value $ _____ $ _____

Source: Adapted from Elliott & Elliott, *A Tort Resume for Use in Prosecution and Defense of All Damage Claims*, with permission.

Use the interview form as an aid; *do not rely on it entirely*. Each case is unique, and you will need to add or delete questions as appropriate.

Some cases will require you or the attorney (or both of you) to develop a special interview form or set of questions to cover in the interview. Until you become more experienced, this should be done in close consultation with the attorney working on the case. In order to develop your own questionnaire, you will need to review the file to identify the cause of action. If necessary, ask the attorney to identify the cause of action: negligence, breach of contract, sexual harassment, or other.

Research the cause of action and identify the elements that need to be proven to establish a case or its defense. Jury instruction books and legal encyclopedias will provide a quick overview of the key elements for a particular cause of action and its defenses. In regard to the *Forrester* case (Case I), assume that your research has produced the following information:

A BRIEF LOOK AT THE SUBSTANTIVE LAW OF NEGLIGENCE. Law is divided into two major areas: substantive law and procedural law. **Substantive law** defines the duties owed by one person to another. **Procedural law** defines the rules and steps that must be followed in a lawsuit. The substantive law of negligence states that all individuals have a duty to conduct themselves in their activities so as not to create an

substantive law

Law that defines the duties owed by one person to another.

procedural law

Law that defines the rules and steps that must be followed in a lawsuit.

unreasonable risk of harm to others. The elements that must be proven to show that negligence exists include the following:

duty

In tort law, due care owed by one person to another.

1. *Duty:* the existence of a **duty** of due care owed by one person to another. For example, in Case I, Mr. Hart had a duty to drive the van without creating an unreasonable risk of harm to any other drivers or pedestrians, such as Mrs. Forrester.

2. *A breach of that duty:* failure to conform to the required standard of care. The required standard of care is that which is reasonable under the circumstances. What is reasonable is a matter of experience and common sense. For example, if Mr. Hart were speeding, especially on icy roads, and/or was not paying close attention to the road, his conduct would fall short of what is reasonable under the circumstances to protect others.

proximate cause

In tort law, the cause-and-effect relationship that must be established to prove that the conduct in question was the substantial cause of the injury in question.

3. *The cause of the injury:* that the conduct in question was the natural and **proximate** (probable) **cause** of the resulting harm. Some states define it as a substantial cause of the injury. If Mrs. Forrester could have crossed the road safely had it not been for Mr. Hart's excessive speed, then Mr. Hart's speed would be the natural and proximate cause of Mrs. Forrester's injuries.

4. *Injury in fact:* an actual injury or loss must have resulted from the incident. If Mrs. Forrester, for example, suffers a broken hip as a result of the negligent act, then that is sufficient to provide this fourth element of negligence. It is also important that the injury be a foreseeable consequence of the negligence and not some quirk.

The defenses to negligence include the following:

1. *Comparative negligence* is the law in the majority of states and in Columbia (unless your instructor indicates otherwise). The doctrine of comparative negligence permits a plaintiff who is contributorily negligent to recover, but the award is reduced proportionately by the percentage of the plaintiff's negligence. For example, if Mrs. Forrester stepped onto the highway without looking, then slipped as she tried to retreat, a jury might find her 30 percent negligent. If Mr. Hart was driving too fast to stop, a jury might find him 70 percent negligent. If Mrs. Forrester's damages came to $100,000, the award would be reduced by 30 percent to $70,000. In some states, Mrs. Forrester would be barred from any recovery if her comparative negligence was found to exceed 50 percent. Some states still use the term *contributory negligence* for this doctrine, although it is a modified version of contributory negligence (see number 3).

2. *Assumption of risk* states that plaintiffs may not recover for damages if they knowingly place themselves in danger. For example, if Mrs. Forrester had decided to stay in the middle of the road and thumb her nose at any oncoming vehicle, she would be assuming the risk of injury, and Mr. Hart would have a defense to Mrs. Forrester's action for negligence.

3. *Contributory negligence* is an important concept even though most states have abolished it as a defense. If the action of the plaintiff, the person suing for injuries, was a contributing factor in the accident, the plaintiff cannot recover her losses from the defendant, the person being sued. For example, if a jury found that plaintiff Mrs. Forrester had contributed to her own injuries by failing to look both ways before crossing the highway, she would be barred from any recovery, even if defendant Mr. Hart was found to be primarily responsible for the accident. The harshness of this rule explains why it has been abolished in many states. Assume that contributory negligence is not the law in Columbia unless your instructor indicates otherwise.

4. *Last clear chance* is a doctrine that permits parties to recover damages who normally could not because of their contributory negligence. In that sense, it is a defense to the defense of contributory negligence. It applies when the plaintiff, through her own negligence, is placed in the defendant's path so that the defendant has the last clear chance to avoid an accident. If the defendant does not react as a reasonable person should (and therefore is negligent), causing injury to the plaintiff, the plaintiff may recover regardless of her initial contributing negligence. For example, assume that Mrs. Forrester carelessly ran across the ice on the road, slipped, and fell, leaving her directly in the path of Mr. Hart's van. Also assume that Mr. Hart had a last clear chance to avoid the accident. If he was inattentive and did not avoid the accident, Mrs. Forrester could still recover damages in spite of her own negligence.

After identifying the elements of the action, draft questions that elicit information that will help prove or disprove the elements or defenses. Forming questions to elicit information is a matter of applying common sense to the elements that must be proved. For example, to determine whether the defendant has created an unreasonable risk of harm to the plaintiff under the circumstances, the interviewer would need to find out what the circumstances were. The question should be asked, "What are all the possible circumstances that might have a bearing on the accident?" Each factor that comes to mind should be listed.

Circumstances possibly affecting an accident include the following:

- time (such as rush hour, dusk, night)
- weather (such as cold, rainy, foggy)
- lighting (such as bright, dim, dark)
- road conditions (such as slippery, dry, oily, rough)
- road structure (such as lanes, narrow shoulders, curve, straight, level)
- location of parties (including specific measurements in feet, inches)
- dress of parties (as pertinent to cause of accident)
- condition of parties (such as intoxicated, drugged, tired)

- disabilities of parties (such as poor eyesight, poor mobility, poor hearing)
- obstructions (such as limitations on view of parties, bushes, trees, terrain, sun glare)
- traffic (such as heavy, light)
- caution signs (including all traffic signals, barricades, posted signs, etc.)
- relevant ordinances (such as speed limit, school zone, crosswalk)
- helplessness of parties (facts indicating parties' inability to avoid or extract themselves from the peril)

The next question is, "Is there any evidence that an unreasonable risk of harm was created [carelessness]?"

Evidence of creating an unreasonable risk of harm includes the following factors:

speed of vehicle(s)
    plaintiff's opinion
    underlying basis for opinion (observability)
    skid marks (length and location)
    time intervals and distances to estimate speed
    police report information

attentiveness of defendant
    plaintiff's view of defendant
    witness's view of defendant
    direction driver was looking
    distractions at point in road
    time interval between when driver should have observed plaintiff and first attempt to brake or take evasive action
    distance between point where driver should have first seen plaintiff and start of skid marks
    lack of skid marks
    sounding of horn

obstructions under the control of defendant
    broken windshield
    frost, condensation, ice on windshield
    stickers
    car ornaments

unsafe vehicle
    immediate loss of control (brakes, steering, bald tires)
    lack of skid marks (brakes)
    high engine roar (stuck accelerator)
    dipped down on one side (springs, shock absorbers, overload)

Creating questions or areas for inquiry is a brainstorming process that raises a variety of possibilities. This process should be repeated for each of the

APPLY YOUR KNOWLEDGE

Using one of the fact scenarios from Case II, III, IV or V in Chapter 1, create an interview form that can be the basis of an interview for the case you have chosen.

elements as well as the defenses. Complete your interview form with the following information:

- Add the standard general information questions (name, address, phone) found on most interview forms to complete the new interview form.

- Have the attorney review the draft interview form and make suggestions for other questions.

- Amend the form where appropriate.

Once you understand this method of creating an interview form, you should be able to create a form or expand an existing one in any area of law.

Step 3

SELECT A LOCATION FOR THE INTERVIEW. Most interviews will take place in the convenience of the office. This gives the interviewer control over outside interruptions and assures privacy, which is a paramount consideration. A disabled, elderly, or ill client, however, may require a personal visit. Sometimes it is advantageous to conduct all or part of an interview at the scene of the accident or where a view of some evidence would be particularly helpful. Before conducting an outside interview, however, obtain approval from the supervising attorney. This is important not only for reasons of cost, but also because outside interviews, depending on the circumstances, heighten safety concerns and expose the interviewer to accusations of misconduct. When the client is contacted to schedule the appointment, determine whether the site you have chosen is convenient.

Step 4

DETERMINE WHAT INFORMATION THE CLIENT SHOULD BRING. Before calling the client, review the interview form and make a list of those items the client should bring to the interview. Typically in a personal injury case the client should bring all medical bills and dates of treatment; accident reports; pertinent names, addresses, and phone numbers; a diagram of the accident; and any other relevant documents. Even if a client does not have access to some of these items, it is important to tell the client to obtain as much of the needed information as possible prior to the interview.

In contract cases, the client should bring key dates surrounding the contract; the time, place, and nature of negotiations preceding the contract; the names, addresses, and phone numbers of people present during the negotiation or during discussion if it was an oral contract (lawyers, all parties, accountants, and so on); points of disagreement and how they were resolved; all drafts of the contract and the contract as signed by the parties; all papers, correspondence, memoranda, and so on, relating to the contract; anything indicating an attempt to modify the contract; and any documentation relating to actual damages or attempts to minimize damages.

Step 5

SCHEDULE THE INTERVIEW. When scheduling an interview, provide for some flexibility in its length. This allows for a more relaxed atmosphere for the client, and provides the opportunity for the interviewer to take more time should circumstances warrant it.

When telephoning the client to set the time for the interview, schedule the appointment as soon as possible because of case filing deadlines, the need to establish an attorney-client relationship to the exclusion of other interested firms, and to provide an opportunity to demonstrate a sincere interest in the client and the case. Use the phone conversation to assess whether the client has any special disabilities or needs that could affect the interview and for which arrangements need to be made. Inform the client about the availability of interpreters and ADA accessibility to your office, including parking, ramps, doorways, office space, proximity of properly equipped restrooms, and other considerations. The time of the interview should be coordinated with the supervising attorney to allow the attorney to meet with the client prior to the interview. This meeting helps establish the attorney-client relationship and may be used to answer the client's questions about the firm's fees. Occasionally this meeting with the attorney is not possible and the paralegal is directed to proceed accordingly.

Following the phone conversation, fill out a deadline control slip noting any tasks, such as preparation of a letter confirming the appointment or preparation of any documents to be signed by the client at the interview. Note the date on your calendar as well as Mr. White's calendar, and that of the administrative assistant or receptionist who will greet Mrs. Forrester. Then prepare a letter confirming the appointment. You may choose to draft your own letter or copy a similar letter from another file. Have your supervising attorney review the letter and send it. Send the letter through the mail or e-mail a copy of the letter, if the client agrees to conducting communications through that medium. With electronic communications ever-changing, check with your firm as to the accepted modes of communicating with clients. An example of such a letter is shown in Exhibit 2.3. This letter can be easily adapted for a contract dispute or other type of case.

Step 6

ANTICIPATE AND ARRANGE FOR ANY SPECIAL NEEDS. These might include arranging for an interpreter, having a diagram board ready, preparing for unique ethnic or occupational jargon, or reviewing special medical terminology. If a child is to be interviewed, a few toys might be helpful. Some evidence suggests that young children talk more freely in a play setting and describe what happened to them more easily when using a doll or other props for demonstration purposes.

Step 7

REVIEW PERTINENT ETHICAL AND TACTICAL CONSIDERATIONS. The paralegal handbook has already set out for you some of the significant ethical considerations you must keep in mind while interviewing any client. It might be useful to review those prior to each interview until you have such considerations firmly in mind.

The interview is a time when clients want to ask you questions: What does my case look like? Will I be liable? What is your fee? Don't you think I ought to sue? Anticipate such questions and prepare a response. Use the opportunity to make clear your status as a paralegal and your ethical limitations. Your response to the previous questions could be the following:

> I am sorry, but I am not permitted to answer that question because it calls for legal advice. Paralegals are not permitted to give legal advice, but Mr. White will be glad to respond to that question. I will pass your questions on to him.

Avoid tape-recording or having the client sign a written statement, unless otherwise directed by your supervising attorney. The opponent may be able to acquire the

INTERNET EXERCISE

Go to http://www.atanet.org, click on *find a translator*, and locate the name of an ATA translation from (1) Spanish to English; (2) Haitian (patois) to English; and (3) Japanese to English.

EXHIBIT 2.3 Confirmation of Appointment Letter

WHITE, WILSON & MCDUFF
ATTORNEYS AT LAW
FEDERAL PLAZA BUILDING, SUITE 700
THIRD AND MARKET STREETS
LEGALVILLE, COLUMBIA 00000
(111) 555 - 0000

June 24, _____

Mrs. Ann Forrester
1533 Capitol Drive
Legalville, Columbia 00000

Your Case File No. Pl 3750

This is to remind you of your appointment on Wednesday, June 29, at 2:30 p.m. at our office. The purpose of the appointment is to discuss in detail the accident you were involved in on February 26 of this year. The appointment is for an hour, or more if necessary.

Please bring the items checked in the following list, if they are available:

(X) A copy of your Social Security card
(X) Insurance carrier, policy limits, address, and phone number
(X) Copy of insurance policy
(X) Name(s) of the other party or parties and any information you have about them, including insurance carrier
(X) Police reports
(X) Photos of accident, injuries, or other damage
(X) Photos of accident scene
(X) Diagram of accident and location
(X) News clippings regarding accident
(X) Names, ages, birth dates of spouse and dependents
(X) Description of vehicle(s) in accident, license number, owner, damage
(X) Medical bills, attending physicians, medical insurance, medical history
(X) Occupation and salary information, time lost
(X) Accident or injuries subsequent to this incident
(X) Any correspondence regarding accident
(X) Names, addresses, and phone numbers of other witnesses
(X) Be prepared to describe accident
( ) Other _____

We appreciate your gathering as much of the information as you can. I look forward to meeting you. In the meantime, I can be reached at 555 - 0000.

Sincerely,

Terry Salyer

Litigation Paralegal

client's recorded statement under some state rules of civil procedure and would try to use that statement against the client. You may take notes of the interview and record your impressions of the facts and the client's demeanor and truthfulness. Such records are normally protected under the attorney-client privilege.

Ethical and practical considerations require that you run a conflict-of-interest check on the potential or recently accepted client or verify that one has been completed. Do not assume that a check has been done. Law offices maintain paper or electronic conflict check sheets that include, but are not limited to, the office's personnel and close relatives; current, potential, and former clients; the adversarial parties; the type of case; names and information relevant to any business transactions facilitated by the firm; and other relevant conflict information. To avoid disqualification of the entire firm or other problems as a result of information obtained during a consultation or an initial interview, the following practices may be helpful, *if approved in advance by your attorney*:

1. Make a pre-interview call to the prospective client to determine what the nature of the case is and the names of persons or entities involved, while also stressing to the person not to reveal any confidential information in the process.

2. Have the potential or new client sign a form consenting that no information disclosed during this preliminary stage will prevent the firm from representing a different client in the matter (ABA Model Rules of Prof'l Conduct R. 1.18, cmt. 5).

If a conflict is uncovered, report it immediately. Normally, the office will decline or withdraw from the representation.

Step 8

REVIEW RECOMMENDED INTERVIEW TECHNIQUES. The following techniques have proven useful:

1. Have the client meet with the attorney first, giving the attorney the opportunity to explain the role of the paralegal and what that means to the client in reduced cost. The attorney can then introduce the paralegal. This sequence should help develop client confidence in the firm's professionalism and in the paralegal.

2. Make the client comfortable. Offer refreshments and break the ice with light, pleasant conversation.

3. Be friendly and respectful. Address the client as Mr., Mrs., Ms., or Dr., as appropriate.

4. Create a private environment free of interruptions. Have your calls held. If necessary, place an Interview in Progress sign on the office door.

5. Explain the purpose of the interview and let client know you need their help.

6. Inform the client that you, the attorney, and any employees of the law office are required to protect the information provided by the client and that such information is held in the strictest confidence. Explain that honesty is essential and that it can be disastrous to hold back any information, no matter how personal or embarrassing it might be. On the other hand, explain that it is human to forget, and it is not unusual that something forgotten now can be recalled

later. Discuss, also, that it is normal for people to want to fill in gaps in their memory; that they need to be careful about presenting information they do not remember clearly.

7. Express confidence about what you are doing. Thorough preparation and planning will help you be more confident. It is equally important to avoid trying to impress the interviewee with all of your legal knowledge and vocabulary.

8. Avoid being condescending. Try to put yourself in the client's position and think how you would like to be addressed.

9. Take accurate, detailed, and legible notes.

10. Be a good listener. Silences during the interview process are inevitable and can be productive periods of thought and recall. Avoid the temptation to end the silence quickly. Be patient, supportive, and accepting. Encourage the expression of feelings, and avoid making value judgments.

11. Be mindful of the client's body language or idiosyncratic mannerisms and note them for the attorney. Body language is important because of the jury's potential reaction to it. Be cautious, however, in interpreting body language; such interpretation is not a precise science.

12. Let clients tell their stories. It is important to them. Come back later to pick up significant details.

13. Use open narrative questions such as "What happened? What happened next?" This allows clients to proceed at their own pace and encourages a freer flow of information, which is more conducive to fact gathering.

leading question
Question phrased in such a manner as to suggest the desired answer (e.g., "It was raining that night, wasn't it?").

14. Avoid questions that suggest an answer. For example, "Mrs. Forrester, you did look both ways before you stepped onto the highway, didn't you?" This is a **leading question** and encourages clients to respond as they perceive you want them to respond, and not necessarily with the truth. This type of question restricts the flow of information.

15. Avoid "why" questions, which are often viewed by the interviewee as a sign of disapproval. A less confrontational approach might be "Try to help me understand this," or "Would you please elaborate on your reasons for doing that?"

16. Probe the accuracy of judgments regarding items such as speed, distance, color, time, or size. Determine, if possible, the basis of the judgment or test its accuracy through example or comparison to some similar item or distance.

17. Be mentally prepared to deal with sensitive or personal matters in a forthright yet empathetic manner. Avoid skirting the issue or using euphemisms. Such shyness or hesitancy on the part of the interviewer can encourage dishonesty.

18. Deal tactfully but directly with suspected dishonesty. Do not be afraid to indicate that a response doesn't seem to stand up or to follow from the other evidence.

19. Restate the client's information when necessary to make sure you understand: "Now let me see if I have this right. You said you stepped out … ?"

20. Be thorough in asking about the accident or other alleged wrongs and any damages. Cover how the injury or loss affected the family's life or, in a business or contract case, how the action affected the business, its customers, and other factors. The more details you can obtain, the better.

An important interview of a young child or a mentally challenged person requires special techniques. Review pertinent resource material on how to proceed or use a specially trained interviewer.

Interviewing is an art that requires practice and experience. Techniques that work well for some people do not work well for others. Experiment and develop your own style.

Step 9

PREPARE ORIENTATION AND INSTRUCTION MATERIALS FOR THE CLIENT. Clients will normally have a variety of questions concerning the litigation process as well as what will be expected of them. Some firms have developed a videotape that the client views either before or after the initial interview to provide guidance and information to the client. If the client hires the firm, make sure the client leaves with information on the following matters. It is best to have this information in a brochure previously approved by the attorney to avoid any questions about giving legal advice.

1. The attorney is your legal advocate whose function is to assume responsibility for your case and represent you to the best of the attorney's ability.

2. The paralegal assists your attorney in handling your case, providing you with a more thorough preparation at a lower cost.

3. You will need to provide your attorney with *all* the information you can gather and recall about the incident, your injuries and losses, and any statements you have made to others.

4. It may be necessary to provide your attorney with intimate personal information. Expect that the information you give will be held in the strictest of confidence consistent with the highest standards of professional loyalty.

5. Refrain from making any statements to others about the incident or about your injuries or losses. Such statements may be used against you in court and could weaken your case. Refer any inquiries or requests to your attorney.

6. Do not sign any documents releasing others from liability or accepting payments for injuries. Do not file an accident report without first checking with your attorney.

7. Begin a daily medical journal in which you will record the condition of your injuries and medical treatment. Daily references to pain, suffering, sleeplessness, limitations on normal activity, changes in condition, and trips to the hospital or physician should be noted. Keep a record of your expenses: mileage, prescriptions, drugs, crutches, wheelchair, private nurse, and so on.

8. Record all employment losses: days missed; lost pay and benefits; and missed raises, promotions, merit pay, and bonuses. Also note the date of your return to work and any subsequent effects your injuries have on your ability to do your job.

9. Make a record of all damages to property and estimates for repair. Do not discard, give away, or sell such property without consulting your attorney.

10. List your expenses in hiring others to perform domestic work and maintenance or child care needed as a result of your injuries.

11. Apprise your attorney or paralegal of your medical, property, and disability insurance coverage in order that steps may be taken to inform the companies of the incident and claims may be made. You do not want to waive your right to a claim; such claims may provide necessary cash for living expenses. Money paid by your insurance company will be reimbursed to the insurance company if it is awarded to you in the lawsuit for the same damages previously paid for by the insurance.

12. You should be aware that most cases are settled before trial; your case may be settled through negotiation prior to trial.

13. The filing of a case is important because it keeps the case moving, provides access to the opponent's information, and encourages a more timely resolution of the matter. Once a case is filed, it may take from one year to several years before it comes to trial. No settlement will be agreed upon without your full knowledge and acceptance.

14. Keep the paralegal informed of any new information that arises or that you recall. Inform us of any change in address, extended vacation plans, and so on. Refrain from asking others questions about your case. This frequently leads to confusion and incorrect information. If you have questions about your case, please ask us. We will be glad to help.

15. Prior to trial you will be called to the office to review information and to prepare for trial. You may be asked to provide sworn testimony about the incident at a deposition. This is required by law. You will be given time to prepare for this deposition. You may also be asked to undergo an examination by a physician chosen by the opponent in order to verify your injuries. This is permitted by law.

16. Your case may not end following a decision by the court. Frequently appeals are filed before a case is final. This can take a long time.

Step 10

PREPARE ANY FORMS FOR THE CLIENT'S SIGNATURE. The interview is a good time to have the client sign several documents, including the fee arrangement, which the attorney and the client should have discussed. Remember, it is the unauthorized practice of law for a paralegal to negotiate or set legal fees. There are two typical fee agreements. The first is for representation based on an hourly rate. Prepare an explanation for the client concerning how the hourly rate will be broken down for billing purposes, such as by one-quarter, one-sixth, or one-tenth of an hour. The second is for representation based on a percentage of the award won by the plaintiff, allowing for no fee if the plaintiff does not win. This is called a **contingent fee**.

contingent fee
Legal fee for representation based on a percentage of the award won by the plaintiff and allowing for no fee if the plaintiff does not win.

Many client-attorney fee disputes arise because the nature of the fee was not made clear to the client from the beginning and because the fee arrangement was not put in writing. Be prepared to explain the fee contract and have the client sign the written fee agreement. In some firms only the attorney will take this responsibility, but even then the paralegal may be responsible for drafting the fee agreement (see Exhibit 2.4 and Exhibit 2.5). Some flexibility in the fee agreement is preferable. For example, the following language was held appropriate:

> Your ultimate fee may vary depending on the time limitations imposed by you, the questions involved, the skill requisite to perform the legal service properly, or the amount involved and the results obtained. [*Silva v. Buckley*, not reported in S.W.3d, WL 23099681 (Tenn.Ct.App. 2003)]

Court rules dictate the nature and limits of contingent fee agreements in some states. A recent example of how a court interpreted a contingent fee agreement was in *Siraco v. Astrue*, 806 F. Supp. 2d 272 (D.Me. 2011).

CASE STUDY: UNDERSTANDING THE LAW

Siraco v. Astrue, 806 F. Supp. 2d 272 (D.Me. 2011) involves the interpretation of a statute permitting the award of contingency fees in Social Security cases. The focal point of the case was whether a law firm was entitled to its 25% contingent fee when the paralegal performed most of the work on the case. Good news, the Court allowed the law firm to recover the full contingency fee. Here are the facts. The claimant, Ms. Siraco, filed a claim for Social Security benefits and lost. She hired a law firm to appeal her case to the Commissioner of Social Security (Astrue). The law firm required Siraco to sign a contingent fee agreement where the firm would retain 25% of the recovery if she won and nothing if she lost. Siraco won her appeal and was awarded $45,455.50. Of that award, the firm was entitled to $11,366.62. ($6,000.00 had already been awarded to the firm, leaving $5366.88 in dispute.) Simple, right? The problem arose because the paralegal did most of the work on the case and therefore, most of the fee earned was from the paralegal's work and not the attorneys. The paralegal worked 25.2 hours and the attorney worked 4.7 hours on the case. The Commissioner believed that the award was therefore unreasonable. The Court held otherwise. Basing its decision on the U.S. Supreme Court Case *Gisbrecht v. Barnhart*, 535 U.S. 789, 122 S. Ct. 1817, 152 L. Ed. 2d 996 (2002), the Court found (1) that a contingent fee was permissible and (2) that it was reasonable for the services rendered.

The Court looked to the time spent and the results, and not a fixed-type calculation used under other types of fee arrangements. The focus is on the contingent fee agreement. In this case, the problem, at least for the Commissioner, was that most of the time was the paralegal's, creating, in his eyes, a windfall for the law firm. Was this proper and was the law firm entitled to compensation? The Court said "yes" and focused on the efficiency of the use of staff, results, and time spent on the case. The Court did not find the total contingent fee unreasonable given competitive rates. As stated by the Court, "if a firm can organize its practice efficiently by using less of its lawyers' time, yet still produce high quality legal work, it should not be penalized in the fee it can recover. A different conclusion would lead this and other lawyers to do more of the work themselves and delegate less to paralegals, to no apparent gain" for anyone. *Id.* at 278. The court determined the fee to be reasonable and permitted the paralegal's time to be included as billed.

Questions for Review: Examine the *Siraco* case. What was the basis of the Commissioner's challenge to the award? Why did the Court disregard the lodestar formula? Would the Court's reasoning have changed if the amount of the award to Ms. Siraco would have been higher with a higher attorney's fee? Why or why not?

EXHIBIT 2.4 Fee Agreement

LEGAL REPRESENTATION AGREEMENT

I hereby employ the firm of _____, with the understanding that the law firm, through its attorneys,

_____ will represent me and provide legal services for me in:

_____

_____

and I authorize the firm to commence an action in this matter as may be advisable in the judgment of the firm, subject to my approval. I also understand that the law firm may assign other or additional attorneys to represent me, with my approval, as may be required from time to time.

I understand that as part of this representation I must be truthful with the law firm, cooperate and assist in the preparation of my case as required. I will appear for depositions, court appearances or any other meetings as required by the law firm. In turn, the law firm will keep me informed of developments in my case. If any personal information changes, such as address, telephone number, e-mail or whereabouts, I will immediately advise the law firm. **I agree not to compromise the claim for which the law firm was hired without discussing it in advance and the law firm is not authorized to compromise any claims on my behalf without my consent and authorization.**

Attorney's fees and expenses
I agree that the following method is to be used for determining the proper amount of legal fees:

1. FEES:

The attorney's fees for services performed under this agreement shall be based upon a rate of $ ___ per hour. Hourly billing will be to the [tenth (.1)] or [quarter (.25)] of an hour and rounded to the nearest such increment. (If more than one attorney, or paralegal, at differing rates, then so specify.)*

I understand that all time expended by personnel in the law firm on my behalf should be expected to be billed at the rate of those personnel. Rates for other firm personnel are as follows:

Partner:

Associate:

Paralegal:

I agree that the fees are reasonable based upon the law firm's ability, training, experience, skill and education.

2. RETAINER: (Choose one):

A. In order to secure the time and services of the attorney for this matter, I agree to make an initial, nonrefundable payment in the amount of $ ___ toward my attorney's fees and expenses. The funds will be held in my Lawyers' Trust Account. I understand this is the minimum fee I will be charged for services and expenses.

B. In order to secure the time and services of the attorney for this matter, I agree to make an initial payment in the amount of $ ___ toward my attorney's fees and expenses. This retainer fee shall be a credit against hourly attorney's fees and costs advancements. The funds will be held in my Lawyers' Trust Account. It will be refunded to the extent it has not been utilized for this purpose.

3. COSTS:

A. I authorize my attorney to retain any individual and entities to perform services necessary for investigation or completion of legal services. I agree to pay the fees or charges of every person or entity hired by the attorney to perform necessary services.

B. I acknowledge that my attorney may incur various expenses in providing services to me. I agree to reimburse the attorney for all out-of-pocket expenses paid. If I am billed directly for these expenses, I agree to make prompt

EXHIBIT 2.4 Fee Agreement (*continued*)

direct payments to the originators of the bills. Such expenses may include, but are not limited to, service and filing fees, courier or messenger services, recording and certifying documents, depositions, transcripts, investigations, witnesses' fees, long-distance telephone calls, copying materials, overtime clerical assistance, travel expenses, postage, notary attestations, and computer research.

Should a payment be remitted by way of check and is returned for insufficient funds or stop payment, a $25.00 returned check fee will be assessed and any associated fees incurred by the law firm.

Billing

I agree to the following schedule of billing:

1. Fees, charges, and expenses will be billed on at least a monthly basis as they accrue.

2. The retainer shall be paid in full upon the execution of this agreement. The retainer shall be a credit against monthly bills.

3. I agree to make payments promptly. I understand that failure to make payments is sufficient reason for the attorney to withdraw from representing me in this matter, whether or not litigation has been commenced. I will be notified in writing prior to any withdrawal. I agree that a letter to my last known address is sufficient notice.

Consultations

I understand that personal and telephone consultations with my attorney shall be part of my representation and I will be billed by the attorney for the time spent on such consultation.

Discharge of attorney

I may, if unsatisfied with the services for any reason, discharge the attorney at any time; however, it is understood that the attorney will be paid or arrangements will be made for the payment of all fees and costs.

Representation

It is expressly agreed and understood by me that no promises, assurances, or guarantees as to the outcome of this matter have been made by the attorney. Payment is not contingent upon the outcome of this matter.

I will send you copies of pleadings, documents, correspondences and other information filed or prepared on your behalf throughout the case. These copies will be your file copies and should be retained by you. When the case is completed, I will close my file and return all original documents to you and will maintain a copy of your file for the number of years required by (insert your state's statutory requirement) statute. After that time, your file will be destroyed unless you advise me otherwise in writing prior to (insert your state's statutory requirement) statutory deadline.

Applicable Law

This agreement is governed by the laws of [state] and any questions relating to the meaning or enforceability of any provisions of this agreement shall be interpreted by [state] law.

THIS AGREEMENT WILL NOT TAKE EFFECT AND THE LAW FIRM WILL HAVE NO OBLIGATION TO PROVIDE LEGAL SERVICES, UNLESS AND UNTIL A SIGNED COPY OF AGREEMENT IS RECEIVED AND RETAINER FEE IS PAID UNDER PARAGRAPH 2.

(continued)

EXHIBIT 2.4 Fee Agreement (*continued*)

I have read this fee agreement, and have had opportunity to discuss it with my attorney or any other attorney. I understand, agree and accept all of the terms within this agreement.

Dated this _____ day of _____, _____

Attorney _____ Client _____

_____

*Note that any additional reservation of right to increase the fee in the future for increased hourly rates must be specifically stated.

Source: Adapted from Katzman, "Using Written Fee Agreements," Wis. Law., Dec. 1990, 15, 16; with permission of the Wisconsin Bar Association.

EXHIBIT 2.5 Contingent Fee Agreement

1. I, _____, having been injured on _____, hereby agree to retain, _____, of the law firm of _____ as my attorney to make claims or bring suit against anyone necessary.

2. My attorney is to receive _____% of the gross settlement or judgment for legal services. This percentage will increase to _____% of the gross settlement or judgment in the event of an appeal of the final judgment to the court of appeals or supreme court.

3. I UNDERSTAND THAT I COULD RETAIN THE ATTORNEY TO REPRESENT ME IN THIS ACTION AND COMPENSATE HIM/HER ON AN HOURLY BASIS, BUT I EXPRESSLY DECLINE TO DO SO, SUBJECT TO PARA. 12.

4. I also have been informed that I am responsible to pay for costs and disbursements including, but not limited to:

_____

_____

_____

My attorney may, but is not obligated to, advance these and other costs he or she believes are reasonable and necessary for preparing and presenting any claim. Any costs advanced by the attorney for which he or she was not reimbursed shall be paid to the attorney for costs within 30 days of receiving a written statement thereof.

-OR-

I agree to pay costs of investigation. out-of-pocket costs and expenses [on a monthly or quarterly basis/as they are billed] by remitting the billed amount monthly [or as agreed].

I agree to keep my medical billings up-to-date, if applicable.

5. I agree to cooperate with my attorney and assist in the preparation of the case as requested.

6. I AGREE NOT TO SPEAK WITH OTHERS OR CONSULT OTHER LAWYERS ABOUT THIS CASE.

EXHIBIT 2.5 Contingent Fee Agreement (*continued*)

7. I understand that as part of this representation I must be truthful with the law firm, cooperate and assist in the preparation of my case as required. I will appear for depositions, court appearances or any other meetings as required by the law firm. In turn, the law firm will keep me informed of developments in my case. If any personal information changes, such as address, telephone number, e-mail or whereabouts, I will immediately advise the law firm. **I agree not to compromise the claim for which the law firm was hired without discussing it in advance and the law firm is not authorized to compromise any claims on my behalf without my consent and authorization.**

8. I understand that if no recovery is obtained for me, no attorneys' fees shall be due; however, I will remain responsible for costs and disbursements. I also understand that settlement shall not be made without my approval or the approval of my guardian.

9. I understand that by signing this agreement, I am promising not to release the names of any experts and/or consultants hired in regard to my case. I further understand that the names of any experts and/or consultants hired in regard to my case are the property of the attorney and law firm and are not my property. I expressly agree that my attorney may promise experts/consultants that their names and/or reports will not be revealed to anyone, including me.

10. I understand that my attorneys may withdraw if they believe my case lacks merit or is not fiscally responsible to pursue.

11. I understand that the Attorney cannot promise or guarantee a particular result in this matter and has not done so.

12. I understand that in the event that, contrary to the advice of my attorneys, I instruct my attorneys to discontinue the matter, the matter shall be discontinued and I shall pay the law firm a reasonable hourly rate, plus expenses, for the time they have expended on my behalf.

13. If any changes to the terms of this agreement are made, those changes must be in writing and signed by both parties.

14. This agreement is governed by the laws of [state] and any questions relating to the meaning or enforceability of any provisions of this agreement shall be interpreted by [state] law.

15. THIS AGREEMENT WILL NOT TAKE EFFECT AND THE ATTORNEY WILL HAVE NO OBLIGATION TO PROVIDE LEGAL SERVICES, UNLESS AND UNTIL A SIGNED COPY OF THIS AGREEMENT IS RECEIVED BY THE ATTORNEY.

16. I have read and my attorney has explained the agreement and I understand the same.

Dated: _____ Client _____

Witness: _____

(Law Firm) _____

Attorney _____

Source: Adapted from Katzman, "Using Written Fee Agreements," Wis. Law., Dec. 1990, 15, 16; with permission of the Wisconsin Bar Association.

ETHICAL CONSIDERATIONS

In Chapter 1, there was considerable discussion about client confidentiality. It is clear that client confidentiality exists when representation is accepted by the client and the firm. However, what are the ethical and professional responsibilities when either party declines the representation. Are the matters that were discussed in the initial interview or conference considered confidential? Has an attorney/client relationship formed? The answer is "yes." If for any reason either the attorney or the client decides not to pursue the representation, the matters discussed in the initial interview are deemed confidential. This means that neither the attorney nor paralegal can disclose the information gained during that interview. Sometimes things just do not work out; sometimes personalities do not mesh. The reasons behind the decision to decline representation or the hiring of a firm or attorney is of no consequence. The ethical responsibility of maintaining a client's confidences remains. In the movie *Something to Talk About,* Julia Roberts' character, Grace, contemplates divorcing her cheating husband Eddie (Dennis Quaid). In an exchange between Roberts' character and a friend, the friend suggests that Roberts contact a particular divorce lawyer first before her husband gets a chance. If Roberts visits the lawyer and declines to hire him, anything disclosed during that interview is confidential. If her husband decides to speak to the same lawyer, the lawyer must decline the representation because Roberts already spoke with him, even though she did not ultimately hire him. Client confidentiality is a continuing one arising from the duty of loyalty between the parties. Therefore, the interview process not only seeks information but establishes the important confidential relationship between lawyer and client. Think of client confidentiality like some vows in the marriage ceremony—until death do us part.

While addressing fee agreements, a cautionary word regarding law office Web sites is in order. Because you may become responsible for the office's Web site, note that such sites can, intentionally or unintentionally, create an attorney/client relationship. If the firm's intent is not to create such a relationship via the Web site, the site should contain a clear statement that any initial information conveyed to the firm will not be treated as confidential. Conversely, if the intent is to facilitate the creation of an attorney/client relationship via this electronic format, it is best to set out a clear agreement that requires the prospective client to acknowledge having read and agreed to the language by clicking an acceptance button. The agreement should include language that protects the firm if there is a conflict of interest or other reasons for declining the representation.

Signed documents are of considerable assistance to the paralegal in subsequent investigative work. Among these forms are authorizations signed by the client permitting those holding confidential information, such as doctors and employers, to release that information to the lawyer. Exhibit 2.6 is a standardized release form designed to cover a variety of needed information. It can be used when one is not yet sure of the entire range of items that will be needed.

Medical records and other highly private health care information are now protected under the Health Insurance Portability and Accountability Act (HIPAA), 45 CFR §§ 164.501, et. seq. Therefore, any authorization to release medical information that you might need your client to sign must comply with federal requirements and any provisions of parallel state law that are more protective than HIPAA. See Chapter 3 for an example of an authorization to disclose protected health care information form. Some health care providers insist that you use their release forms. If you deal regularly with

EXHIBIT 2.6 Standardized Release Form (not medical)

WHITE, WILSON & MCDUFF
ATTORNEYS AT LAW
FEDERAL PLAZA BUILDING, SUITE 700
THIRD AND MARKET STREETS
LEGALVILLE, COLUMBIA 00000
(111) 555 - 0000

Address

Date

RE: (Name of client, date of birth)

This form authorizes _____ to release to my attorney, White, Wilson & McDuff, or their designated representative, all of the following information about me as indicated (X), and to discuss it, send it, make it available for inspection, or photocopy it as they may request.

( ) Employment records: description of position, length of employment, pay, benefits, absences, performance, accumulated sick leave, etc.

( ) Academic and school records: attendance dates; evaluations; grade performance; psychological, aptitude, and achievement tests; class ranking; teachers, etc.

( ) Military records

( ) All state and federal tax returns for the years _____

( ) Other: _____

_____   _____
Client   Date

_____
Address

certain providers, consider getting a supply of their forms (or preferably an electronic copy) to have readily available.

In the following chapters, other specialized authorization forms are presented and discussed. For a particular situation, these may be preferable to a form that attempts to meet all needs.

Step 11

PREPARE THE INTERVIEW SITE. Use your office or a conference room, if preferable. You will need to make sure the site is neat and clear of all other files so confidentiality of other clients is preserved. A clean, neat area and desk suggest to clients that you have everything under control. In addition, the clients will realize that you have set

TRADE SECRETS: THE ART OF LISTENING

In the movie *Pulp Fiction*, there's an exchange between John Travolta and Uma Thurman's characters Vincent Vega and Mia Wallace where Mia asks: "Do you listen or wait to talk?" Vince's response is "I wait to talk…" Unfortunately, that is what most people do, and when interviewing clients or witnesses that approach could cost you valuable time and information. One of the keys to being an effective interviewer and in turn an effective paralegal is learning how to actively listen and not just hear. When a client speaks, they are providing valuable information and you should be listening intently. You should be listening to what they say and what they don't say. This kind of listening is involved and exhausting, but is a skill that needs to be learned and perfected. Simply throwing questions at a client without listening to the responses is not productive; you could miss valuable information if your interview style is too rigid or regimented. Being prepared is one thing, but being inflexible can lead to miscommunication. Think before you speak. Think about what the client said and ask meaningful follow-up questions to elicit the kind of information you need. Gain a client's trust by showing that you care about their problem and their circumstance. That is the reason they came to see the firm in the first place. So, don't wait to talk, listen. And this means to try not to interrupt the client when they are telling you

their story or providing information. When you interrupt it gives the impression that you are not listening—that you are simply waiting to talk. Listening takes a lot of self-restraint and energy. You have to be constantly paying attention to the conversation and exchange. While you are listening, learn to move the conversation along. Ask questions that will elicit information and get a client to open up. For example, "Can you be more specific about what happened?" will open up the possibility of a more detailed discussion of the situation. Compare that to posing the question "Why did you let that happen?", which sounds accusatory and shows no empathy toward the client. It seems cold and impersonal—like you do not care and are not listening.

A good listening technique is repeating what the client said and posing a follow-up question. For example, "let me make sure I understand the facts then, are you saying …." This shows the client you are listening. If you misstate the facts, the client will, no doubt, correct you. What is important as you begin to understand the interview process is that you will learn through each interview what techniques work for you. But, remember that no matter what technique you use, master the fine art of listening and don't just hear what the client has to say.

aside this time especially for them. We all like to feel important, and clients are no exception. If your office and your manner convey to clients that they are important, your interview will be that much more productive.

Make sure the office is arranged in a way you feel will be most comfortable for the client (facing each other across a desk, side by side at a table, or seated in chairs set in a conversational arrangement) and is equipped with everything you and the client will need. You should have paper for taking notes and drawing diagrams, extra pens or sharpened pencils, tissues, and ice water, coffee, and tea. Paralegals also use portable electronic keypads with small display screens for note taking, such as tablets and iPads. Some software provides simultaneous audio recording while taking notes. Be sure to have your own diagram present if you intend to work from that, and any photographs or other items you will be using or referring to. All the forms you drafted should be at hand for the client's signature.

In addition, you will want to remind the administrative assistant or receptionist to hold your calls and to help head off other interruptions.

As a part of your preparation, be sure you know the procedure to follow in the event of an emergency. It does happen, though rarely, that the interviewee will faint, have a heart attack or seizure, or otherwise experience a medical emergency. The office should have a regular procedure that you should know so that you can react quickly and confidently to such a situation.

You have now gone through a fairly thorough preparation process for the interview. The interview, whether it is your first or one hundred and first, will go more smoothly, and the client will have more confidence in you because of it. With this kind of preparation, little can go wrong.

THE INTERVIEW

You are now prepared to conduct the initial interview with Mrs. Forrester. The following are some examples of how you might conduct the interview. Assume that Mrs. Forrester has already met with Mr. White and that he brings the client to your office. (Mrs. Forrester is in a wheelchair.)

THE INTRODUCTION

MR. WHITE: *Mrs. Forrester, I would like you to meet Terry Salyer, the paralegal who will be assisting me with your case. Terry, this is Mrs. Ann Forrester, who, as you know, suffered injuries in a car-pedestrian accident this past year and is seeking our firm's assistance.*

PARALEGAL: *How do you do, Mrs. Forrester? We have spoken on the phone, and I have looked forward to meeting you.*

MR. WHITE: *I'll leave you with Terry, who will be asking you some important questions. We will meet again later. It was good to see you.*

Another frequent scenario for an introduction occurs when the secretary or receptionist informs you that your appointment has arrived. Clear your desk and go out to meet the client, letting her know that you are eager to meet and work with her.

PARALEGAL: *Please come into my office. I would be happy to fix a cup of coffee or tea for you. We also have some soft drinks. Would you care for anything?*

MRS. FORRESTER: *Not now, thank you, maybe later.*

Close the office door, return to your chair, and speak briefly about the weather, ask about her family, or about how she is doing with the wheelchair. Explain your role as a paralegal and the purpose of the interview. Ask for the information that Mrs. Forrester was requested to bring.

PARALEGAL: *Thank you for taking the time to gather this material. It will be very helpful. I have some questions I need to cover with you. You can start by telling me your full name.*

MRS. FORRESTER: *Ann Brooke Forrester.*

> PARALEGAL: *Your home address is 1533 Capitol Drive, Legalville, Columbia, Zip 00000?*

> **MRS. FORRESTER**   *Yes.*

You can now proceed to work through the questions on the form you have prepared, listening carefully, recording all pertinent information, and drawing from the information brought in by the client as needed.

Assume that Mrs. Forrester goes on to describe the accident summarized as follows. It was a partly sunny, windy, cold morning. There was ice on the road in front of the Forrester house. Mrs. Forrester crossed the highway to mail a letter. The point of crossing sits in a depression in the road with knolls rising to the east and west, obscuring some vision. A van came over the east knoll, slid and hit Mrs. Forrester, who was seriously injured.

QUESTIONS ON CIRCUMSTANCES OF THE ACCIDENT

Now you need to focus on specific details. The following questions demonstrate the level of detail necessary to see whether evidence establishes the required elements of proof of breach of duty. (*P* stands for paralegal and *F* stands for Mrs. Forrester.)

> **P:**   *Mrs. Forrester, you mentioned in your description of the accident that the road was icy. I'd like to go back to that. Did you personally observe that the road was icy?*

> **F:**   *Yes, when I walked across the road.*

> **P:**   *Was it icy enough for you to alter your normal walk?*

> **F:**   *Yes, I kind of shuffled over the icy patches.*

> **P:**   *The ice did not cover the entire road?*

> **F:**   *That's right.*

> **P:**   *Was the ice thick?*

> **F:**   *No, just a thin layer, like heavy frost. Some had already begun to melt in the sun and other areas were completely dry.*

> **P:**   *Did you notice the condition of the road on the downslope from where the van approached?*

> **F:**   *Not really. It was in the early morning shadows, however, and what ice was there probably did not melt.*

> **P:**   *On what do you base that opinion?*

> **F:**   *Several days before the accident we had similar weather. That slope remained icier because of the shadows.*

> **P:**   *Is there anyone besides yourself and the defendant who might have observed the ice on the road?*

F: Yes.

P: Their names and addresses, please.

The questioning must be detailed. Listen carefully and take advantage of the opportunity to get witnesses' names on this particular point. It is a good idea when receiving such names to use a local phone directory immediately to confirm the spelling of the names as well as addresses and phone numbers.

P: Mrs. Forrester, I would like to go back to what you said about the van seeming to keep coming at you. Did the defendant see you first, or did you see the defendant first?

F: I am not sure; however, when I looked up, the van was already coming down the slope, so the defendant should have seen me first.

P: When you first saw the van, was there any indication that the driver was taking evasive action?

F: No, in fact, the van just kept coming for what must have been at least four seconds, it felt that long. Before it hit me I heard a skidding sound and the van began to fishtail.

P: Describe what you mean by "fishtail."

F: The rear of the van began to move sideways—back and forth.

It is important that you call attention to words that might not be clear (in this case, *fishtail*) and ask for further explanation. It is also a good idea to clarify the meaning of all words you do not understand or that may be misused by the client.

THE ISSUE OF COMPARATIVE OR CONTRIBUTORY NEGLIGENCE

P: Earlier, you mentioned wearing a warm winter coat with a high, furry collar. Was the collar high enough to go over your ears?

F: Yes, it was.

P: Do you always wear it that way?

F: No, but I did on this day. The wind was cold, and I pulled my collar up and tucked my head into it.

P: Did you tuck your head into it far enough that your vision was obscured?

F: It was not obscured looking forward, but, yes, it was, I guess, on the sides.

P: By "sides" do you mean your peripheral vision?

F: Yes.

P: Help me on this. You said "I guess," referring to the coat's obstruction of your vision. Was your side vision obscured?

F: *Yes, it was.*

P: *Would you have seen the van sooner had you not pulled the coat up around your head?*

F: *I don't know. It's possible. I did look to the left and then the right before stepping onto the road.*

P: *What were you looking at once you stepped onto the road?*

F: *The road immediately in front of me. I did not want to slip on the ice.*

Note several things. First, a high collar might be a hearing obstruction. Second, the client said she tucked her head into the collar, raising the possibility of a sight obstruction. And third, responses such as "I guess" are insufficient. Tactfully press the client for a more precise response.

THE EXTENT OF INJURY AND SENSITIVE INQUIRY

The following questions come after a fairly extensive description by the client of severe injuries to the left hip, pelvic region, lower back, and left leg. The client has stated that she is nearly paralyzed on her left side from the waist down. At this point in the interview, the client begins to weep. The paralegal gets up from behind the desk, comes over to the client, and offers tissues.

P: *Mrs. Forrester, I know these must be very difficult times for you. Let's take a short break. How about a glass of water or maybe some soda?*

(Mrs. Forrester nods. Leave the room to give the client a few moments of privacy and time to regain her composure. Bring her a glass of water.)

P: *May I get you anything else?*

F: *No, but thank you. I feel better now.*

P: *I realize it must be difficult to talk about your injuries. The more you can help me with information, however, the better job we can do for you.*

F: *I understand. Let's go on.*

P: *Mrs. Forrester, have you had any problems as a result of the injuries regarding normal bodily functions?*

F: *Yes, I have some difficulty controlling my bladder.*

P: *I need to make sure I understand this correctly. You urinate regardless of any effort to control the urination process on your part?*

F: *That is correct.*

P: *Now, it is important for me to determine how this inconvenience and anxiety affect you.*

APPLY YOUR KNOWLEDGE

What additional questions would you ask Mrs. Forrester? Based upon the interview presented, what would be your next steps? Detail your plan of action for the Forrester case.

Go on to explore the details, including any sense of humiliation, frustration, or degradation. Do not let the sensitivity of the issue stop the detailed inquiry. In most cases, sensitive issues must be dealt with forthrightly, using straightforward vocabulary. Avoid euphemisms.

One thing to be observed in reading through these interview segments is the need to ad-lib questions. Such questions will follow naturally if you listen carefully and keep in mind the elements of the action as well as the defenses.

DEALING WITH DIFFICULT CLIENTS

Every law office has its difficult clients. Learning to deal with them is an important skill that allows you to remain in control. Psychologists recommend a method for defusing angry clients, called "pace and lead." Instead of becoming defensive or telling a client to calm down, acknowledge a client's anger with words and body language (pacing). For example, a client stands up and angrily responds to the need to sign more documents. Using "pacing," the paralegal stands up and says in a similarly angry tone of voice something like, "Isn't it awful, form after form. You would think it could be simpler." Then the paralegal "leads" the client toward less anger and more productivity by saying in a less angry tone, "We eliminate forms whenever we can, but we must use these forms currently required by the court. We're working on simplifying this process." Then, pointing to the document, the paralegal says in a calm but sympathetic voice, "Please start reading here and sign down here." "Pace and lead" keeps you and the client on the same side.

Another type of angry client is the abusive one who rants, demeans, and gives orders. Allowing this person to vent may diminish the anger. Above all, stay calm and realize this is not personal. If the anger persists, a prearranged interruption such as a phone call from the secretary or a colleague who needs to see you immediately can provide a brief cooling down period. Irate telephone callers should be told to calm down or be disconnected. Documenting such calls to your supervising attorney could diffuse the situation and alert the attorney to the propensities of the client.

Techniques for dealing with the compulsive drop-in or frequent telephone caller include keeping him or her focused on what, if anything, is new and pertinent information. Lengthy social chit-chat can be derailed by asking, "How can I help you?" It is perfectly proper to indicate that you have another matter that you must attend to or, if the client is in your office, combine that approach with getting up and ushering him or her to the door.

The "I-can't-be-bothered-executive" may require direct contact from your supervising attorney or the plying of a high ranking assistant to that executive. Do not be afraid to ask for assistance when you need it.

Some clients are seductively dependent and feed your ego, while others can be sexually aggressive. Resolute and objective professional conduct soon deflects these attentions. There are times, however, when even the most professional individual is vulnerable to such attention. Such times require awareness and disciplined professionalism. Seeking assistance from experienced colleagues can be helpful, as can some of the available resource books on working with difficult people and on violence in the workplace.

TECHNOLOGY UPDATE: THE AGE OF VIDEOCONFERENCING

Travel is expensive and time consuming. Waiting for flights or trains is valuable time wasted and money ill spent. A more expeditious and cost effective method of conducting client interviews and meetings is videoconferencing. Videoconferencing is a method of communicating between two or more locations simultaneously through two-way video and audio. This technology uses telephone or Internet access to connect people in different locations to a common meeting. With clients dispersed all over the country, and the world for that matter, videoconferencing offers an affordable solution. Videoconferencing also can assist those who have challenges traveling. Some individuals who are ill or elderly cannot or prefer not to travel long distances, or to new places for that matter. Videoconferencing offers an alternative solution; however, finding a suitable location for the client to access the technology is an important consideration.

With videoconferencing, the parties can see and observe demeanor and other important characteristics similar to being in person. One of the drawbacks to using this technology is the audio delay in the transmission. That means you should wait before you speak when using videoconferencing. Since everything can be seen and observed, proper business attire should always be worn. For those of us who have the messy desks and offices, using videoconferencing may be a welcome excuse to clean up!

Drawbacks also exist with videoconferencing. You should always be aware when the microphone is on and off. Be careful with the paper shuffling, laptop use, and telephone ringing. Stay away from noisy areas, such as air conditioners or street areas, if possible. Videoconferencing works best with more broadband width—the more kilobits per second (kbps) the better the quality of the transmission. Sometimes the amount of kbps cannot be increased, which detracts from the quality of the interaction of the parties.

Videoconferencing is not an exclusive substitute to the personal face-to-face interview, but offers a viable alternative when the face-to-face interview, conference, or meeting is not available.

CONCLUDING THE INTERVIEW

statute of limitations
Law stating the time limit in which an action must be filed. If the time limit is not met, the defendant has a defense to the action, and the case will be dismissed.

In concluding the interview, give the client a list of all the information that remains for the client to gather. Also remind the client to notify you of any new information regarding the accident, witnesses, injuries, and so on. Provide the client with the client information brochure. It might be helpful to give the client her own file folder in which to keep records and documents over the course of the lawsuit. Attach your business card to the folder. Then explain the documents that need to be executed and have them signed. After one last reminder to the client not to make any statements about the case and not to discuss the case with others, the interview can be concluded. Some interviewers choose at this time to turn off the billing clock and visit informally with the client to show their interest in the client. This is an effective technique, especially if used sincerely. Tell clients that you will keep them informed periodically of the progress in their case.

CONFIRMING THE STATUTE OF LIMITATIONS

Once you have found out the date of the occurrence and the nature of the action, it is important to check the **statute of limitations**. This may have been done already, but if not, it should be done now. The statute of limitations is the date by which an action must be filed. If it is not filed by the required time, the defendant has a defense to the action, and the case will be dismissed. Rarely is there an excuse of sufficient degree for a judge to permit an action to be filed after the required date. Therefore, the paralegal must unfailingly check the statute of limitations for the particular type of action involved. The time periods vary depending on the type of action and the state. Usually someone in the office will have previously made a quick-reference list of the common time limits. If not, statute books will list the time limits under the topic Statute of Limitations or by the type of case: negligence, contract, product liability, and so on.

The time period involved in the statute of limitations is a specified time such as one year or two years. When claims are based on federal laws with unspecified statutes of limitations, federal courts must look to parallel limits in the law of the state in which they are located. Title 28 U.S.C. § 1658 sets a uniform four-year limit in all such actions based on federal laws enacted after December 30, 1990. Normally the statute of limitations starts with the date of the injury, accident, breach of contract, and so on. In such circumstances, the lawsuit must be filed before one year elapses if it is a one-year statute of limitations or before two years elapse if it is a two-year statute, and so forth. If the precise origin of the injury is not apparent or the symptoms of the injury are not likely to manifest themselves for some time after the event that caused them (for example, in black lung cases in coal mining or in cancer cases caused by exposure to toxic substances), then the statute begins to run at the time the symptoms were first noticeable or at a time a reasonable person should have noticed the symptoms or problem. This may not occur until many years later. Information that places a person on notice that a problem exists, however, cannot simply be ignored. For example, in *Winters v. Diamond Shamrock Chemical Co.*, 149 F.3d 387 (5th Cir. 1998), *cert. denied* 526 U.S. 1034 (1999), extensive media coverage caused the statutory time to run because it "notified" the plaintiff to the extent that she should have investigated any link between her cancer and exposure to Agent Orange. The action must be started before the statute runs; it does not have to be concluded in that time. The statute of limitations is so significant that it should be conspicuously noted on the front of the case file and placed in the deadline calendaring system.

Paying attention to the statute of limitations is critical to any case. One court in California was faced with a statute of limitations dealing with different time zones. *Papenthien v. Papenthien*, 16 F.Supp. 2d 1235 (S.D. Cal. 1998) illustrates what a difference a day makes.

CASE STUDY: UNDERSTANDING THE LAW

Papenthien v. Papenthien is a domestic violence case. This case had a number of procedural challenges regarding venue and statute of limitations, but our focus are the facts surrounding the statute of limitations issues. In this case, the wife alleges that her husband physically abused her in a hotel in Hong Kong on February 25, 1993 at 1:30 am. The wife filed a complaint against her husband in a California court on February 24, 1994, although they had moved to other states. (California was the state where the couple resided during the marriage. The 9th Circuit Federal Court of Appeals found that California did have jurisdiction to hear the case.) When the case was refiled in the federal district court again, there was clear evidence from the wife's deposition that the incident took place at 1:30 am Hong Kong time. No one disputes this. What the husband now argues is that since Hong Kong time was a day ahead, Mrs. Papenthien had to file her lawsuit by February 24, 1994 and not February 25, 1994. They held that time zones do make a difference and are considered in determining a statute of limitations. Because of that, the Court held that the original complaint should have been

(continued)

filed by February 24, 1994, thus missing the statute of limitations. The lawsuit for domestic violence was dismissed because the statute of limitations was missed by one day. Whether other courts will follow the Southern District of California's reasoning remains to be seen, but it illustrates the importance of knowing when your statute of limitations begins in a client's case.

Questions for Review: Read the *Papenthien* case. What other issues did the court consider in dismissing the case? What is the doctrine of the "law-of-the-case" and why did it apply to this case? Was the result in *Papenthien* a fair result? Defend your answer.

INTERNET EXERCISE

Determine the statute of limitations in your jurisdiction for a (1) negligence case, (2) medical malpractice case, and (3) breach of contract case.

If, after careful calculation, it appears the statute of limitations has run, notify your supervising attorney immediately. There may still be life in the lawsuit. For instance, the defendants' ten-day out-of-state vacation during the two-year statutory limit allowed the personal injury plaintiff to file a lawsuit two days late [*Johnson v. Rhodes*, 733 N.E.2d 1132 (Ohio 2000)]. A defendant's misleading and false statements, which were relied on by the plaintiffs and resulted in delay in the filing of the plaintiffs' suit, were sufficient to extend the time limit in *Wall v. Construction and General Laborers' Union Local 230*, 224 F.3d 168 (2d Cir. 2000). If a lawsuit is filed within the prescribed time limit but is dismissed, it is treated as if no action had been filed.

SUMMARIZING THE INTERVIEW

From the notes and the interview form, prepare a summary of the interview. A summary sheet appears in Exhibit 2.7; the completed version is in Exhibit 2.8. Enter one copy of the summary into the file and give another copy to the supervising attorney.

EXHIBIT 2.7 Summary Sheet: Initial Interview of Client

File no.:   Date opened: Interviewer:
Client: (M) Spouse: (C) Children, ages: (P)Phone:
Party opponent(s):
Date of incident:
Type of Action: Statute of limitations:
Summary of facts of action:
Noteworthy facts related to elements of action:
Noteworthy facts related to possible defenses:
Witnesses:
Summary of injury and treatment to date:
Total medical bills to date:
Summary of business or wage loss:
Total business or wage loss to date:
Evaluation of client as witness:
Other comments:
Things to do:

Try not to allow too much time between the interview and your summary. The summary should be prepared as close to the interview as possible. Memories fade and recollections change, even the paralegal's. Therefore, do not procrastinate or put off this task.

EXHIBIT 2.8 Summary Sheet: Initial Interview of Client (completed)

File No.: Pl 3750   **Date opened:** 6/23/____   **Interviewer:** T.S. 6/29/____
Client: (P) Ann Forrester   (M) William Forrester   (C) Michael, 8;   (Phone) 555 - 1111
                                                                Sara, 4

Party opponent(s): (D) Richard Hart (Ohio resident)
                Mercury Parcel Service (Ohio resident, Hart's employer)

Date of incident: 2/26/____

Type of action: P.I. negligence, auto-pedestrian

Statute of limitations: 2/26/____

Summary of facts of action:
    P walked across Highway 328 three miles west of Legalville, Columbia, to mail letter. Coming back, P was struck by van owned by Mercury Parcel Service. Crossing point was in depression in road obscuring long-range vision of both pedestrian and driver. Road had patchy ice. D was driving about 40 mph in 35-mph zone. P was struck on left side and thrown to side of road. Van went off and struck tree.

Noteworthy facts related to elements of action:

Breach of duty: P states D going too fast for icy conditions, slid on ice. Also P states D delayed evasive action and may have been inattentive. P says her husband felt D looked quite tired. According to P's husband, van windshield partially fogged over.

Noteworthy facts related to possible defenses:

Comparative negligence: P was in hurry to mail letter to leave for work, had head tucked into coat and vision to side obscured. Thinks she looked left, not sure; did look to right. Didn't see van until it was headed down slope toward her. Didn't hear van coming.

Witnesses:
    Ms. Freda Schnabel saw accident from crest of opposite hill while driving her car toward accident. Her address is 1625 Capitol Dr.
P's husband, William Forrester, also saw some of accident.
Officer Jeremy Burton was first police officer on scene.

Summary of injury and treatment to date:
    Several fractures to left hip, pelvis, and left leg. Partial paralysis on left side from waist down. Loss of bladder control. Considerable pain in injured area. Permanent disability likely, currently confined to wheelchair. Emergency treatment: 2/26/____ Good Samaritan Hospital, 4600 Church St., Legalville, Columbia.

Treating physician(s): Albert Meyer, M.D., orthopedic surgeon
                Medical Arts Building, 4650 Church St.

Consultant: Robert S. Ward, M.D., urology

Total medical bills to date: $40,000

Summary of business or wage loss:
    Full-time teacher, Legalville Board of Education, $34,000 annually.
    Unable to work since accident. Note: Wage loss could be substantial if injury permanent.

Total business or wage loss to date: $ 17,000

Evaluation of client as witness: Client is pleasant, intelligent, and should be good witness.

Other comments: Client wanted to know if she should file a lawsuit. I explained she needed to discuss this with Mr. White, who would be meeting with her.

Things to do: Gather medical records, interview witnesses, locate van.

KEEPING THE CLIENT INFORMED

A significant improvement paralegals have brought to the law office is increased communication with clients. Lack of communication from the law office is a frequent complaint of clients. Therefore, with the attorney's approval, the paralegal should assume the primary responsibility of keeping the client well informed. Schedule a report letter to be sent to the client at least once a month. Try to respond to all the client's inquiries as soon as possible and acknowledge receipt of any information sent to you by the client. This personal attention assures clients that they are not merely a case file number.

In this regard, knowing how to design a letter with good news or bad news is important. Here are a few tips. Your letter should be brief, polite, and, above all, easily understood. Good news is best stated first with any necessary explanation to follow.

Dear Ms. Rakowski:

I am pleased to inform you that the Montez Construction Company has agreed to meet to discuss a settlement of your lawsuit.

To take the best advantage of this opportunity, Ms. Wilson needs you to be present ....

Bad news requires the greatest tact and, if possible, should be sandwiched between more positive language that conveys a positive attitude toward the client and the case.

Dear Ms. Rakowski:

Ms. Wilson and I enjoyed our chance to meet with you last Friday in preparation for the settlement conference with the Montez Construction Company. Unfortunately, the company representatives have cancelled that meeting.

Although Ms. Wilson is tied up in a trial this week, she wants you to know she will continue to pursue the matter vigorously on your behalf and will call you to discuss the latest developments.

Communication is also critical at the start of the case to document and make it absolutely clear to a person seeking legal representation by the law office that either the firm is accepting or rejecting the case. Ethical, malpractice, and other concerns make this essential. Normally, the office has copies of such letters. You may be asked to draft a version of the letter. Wording for a disengagement (or nonengagement) letter might appear as follows.

Dear Mr. Beckley,

Thank you for coming to our law office on (specific date) and meeting with me to discuss your legal concern. We understand the importance of this matter to you. Upon further review, however, our office must decline representing you in the matter.

(Language can be added about having not formed a legal opinion in the matter and the importance to the person of seeking the advice of another attorney as soon as possible because of any applicable statute of limitations).

Again, this letter is to notify you that we will not represent you in this matter. Enclosed are the documents that you left with us.

SUMMARY

The initial interview forms the basis for the client/law firm relationship and provides information essential to determining a cause of action or defense. The importance of the interview and its interactive nature cause some paralegals to feel intimidated or uneasy about this process. Take comfort from knowing, however, that experience and thoughtful planning can ease your anxiety and greatly increase your effectiveness. A good interview plan checklist, well-designed and thorough interview forms, and knowledge of the applicable area of law facilitate a smooth interview.

Interpersonal skills such as a sensitivity to the needs of the client and being able to anticipate and deal with difficult personalities will bring a human quality to your work that will be appreciated by both clients and supervisors. If you add to this your understanding of the significance of client screening, conflict of interest checks, HIPAA compliant medical releases, the statute of limitations, and an ability to capture critical information in a concise summary, your service to the client and the law office at this stage will be truly professional.

KEY TERMS

contingent fee

duty

leading question

procedural law

proximate cause

statute of limitations

substantive law

QUESTIONS FOR STUDY AND REVIEW

1. For what reasons is the initial interview with the client important? What should be considered when screening a potential client?

2. What are the eleven steps in the interview plan? Explain how each step is accomplished.

3. Identify and define the four legal elements that must be proved by the plaintiff in a negligence case.

4. How does one develop pertinent questions for an interview?

5. What are some of the considerations in selecting a location for the interview? Why is scheduling a flexible time for the interview important?

6. What types of things should the client bring to the interview?

7. Identify the special needs one should anticipate in planning an interview.

8. What special ethical and tactical concerns must a paralegal be aware of when interviewing a client?

9. What is a fee agreement and why do so many client v. attorney fee disputes occur? What is good practice regarding law office Web sites and fee agreements?

10. What federal law governs a medical facility's release of a client's medical information to a paralegal?

11. What is a statute of limitations? When should it be checked? When does a statute of limitations begin tolling in various circumstances?

12. How do you use "pace and lead" and other techniques to deal with a difficult client?

13. How should you summarize or evaluate an interview?

14. How can the paralegal play a key role in keeping the client informed of the status of the client's case?

15. What is a disengagement letter and why is it important?

SYSTEM FOLDER ASSIGNMENTS

1. List the interview tasks and the purposes of the tasks at the beginning of the interview section in your systems folder. Place a copy of the Interview Plan Checklist in your systems folder. Add to this section any forms, techniques, examples, or other material that you or your instructor deem useful.

2. Review the interview forms in Exhibits 2.1 and 2.2 and compile a list of the names, addresses, phone numbers, medical records, insurance information, and so on, that you would like Mrs. Forrester to bring to the interview. Make a copy of the list and place it in the systems folder. This list will be useful when you call or write the client and will serve as a checklist for future cases.

3. Make the letter in Exhibit 2.3 into a form letter for your systems folder. Redraft the letter to suit your style and needs, leaving blank those areas of the letter that will contain the variable information (names, addresses, date, and so on) for each new client. Once your form is set up, it can be placed in your systems folder requiring the entry of only the variable information for each repeated use. Throughout this

training period, follow this form-making procedure for letters and other documents that will be used repeatedly from one case to the next.

Note: Keep track of your time by filling out the time log.

White, Wilson & McDuff
Attorneys at Law
Federal Plaza Building Suite 700
Third and Market Streets
Legalville, Columbia 00000

4. Your supervising attorney has asked you to develop a draft of a brochure for clients with information the client should receive at the initial interview. Include any additions to the brochure suggested by your instructor. Place the brochure in your systems folder.

5. Note in your systems folder what forms you should have ready for the client at the initial interview. Include samples of those forms or references to where they can be located quickly, such as the page number in the textbook, the form number in a form file, or in computer files.

APPLICATION ASSIGNMENTS

1. Test your research skills and learn about your state law by researching the terms *negligence*, *contributory negligence*, and *comparative negligence* in your state's jury instruction book, statutes, or digest. For additional understanding of these concepts, look in a legal encyclopedia, *Am Jur's Proof of Facts*, or other national reference sources. Note what must be proved. Research may be conducted either electronically or through books.

2. Adapting the methods you have learned to a variety of circumstances is an important process and an invaluable ability in the law office. Test your understanding of the methodology described in step 2 of planning the interview by creating an interview form for a breach of implied warranty case. Assume that you are representing one of the defendants in the Forrester case. The theory is that the brakes of the van were defective and that is why the accident occurred. Research the legal requirements for a breach of warranty case and prepare the interview form.

3. Your firm is handling a wrongful death case for the plaintiff. Since the deceased is not available to testify, how can you introduce the human factor into the case? Who would you interview and what information would you want to gather? What information would you gather in other ways?

    Now assume you work for the defense. What information would you gather and how would you gather it?

4. Since the Forrester case involves patient medical information, review your state's (and federal) requirements for the release of medical records and other medical information and prepare the document for Mrs. Forrester's signature.

5. Locate the common statutes of limitations through the index to your state's statutes. Compile a list of the statute numbers and time limits for cases involving personal injury, property damage, wrongful death, contracts (oral and written), and products liability.

    a. Personal injury _____ years

        statute number _____.

    b. Property damage _____ years

        statute number _____.

    c. Wrongful death _____ years

        statute number _____.

    d. Contracts

        oral _____ years

        statute number _____.

        written _____ years

        statute number _____.

    e. Products liability

        _____ years

        statute number _____.

        _____ years

        statute number _____.

CASE ASSIGNMENTS

1. Mrs. Forrester has decided to hire your law firm to represent her in the personal injury lawsuit she intends to file against Richard Hart and Mercury Parcel Service, Inc. Your attorney has asked you to prepare the fee agreement between the firm and Mrs. Forrester. Draft the document in accordance with the legal requirements in your jurisdiction.

2. Prepare a letter to Mrs. Forrester summarizing both the firm's and her responsibilities in the course of her representation. Remember to consider including information, such as who to contact if questions arise, the need for cooperation in gathering information for the case, and confirmation of best methods of contacting the client, for example. Be creative and locate sample letters from the Internet, law firms, and formbooks.

3

EVIDENCE AND INVESTIGATION

OBJECTIVES

AFTER READING THIS CHAPTER, YOU WILL BE ABLE TO:

- Conduct a sound investigation of a case
- Understand the general rules that apply to evidence in the courtroom
- Identify the different types of evidence
- Determine the sources of information that will assist in proving the elements of a client's case
- Know how to gather evidence, such as reports and documents, and learn how to preserve that evidence in preparation for trial

INTRODUCTION

For your next assignment, Mr. White wants you to do the investigation of the *Forrester* case.

Investigation is the formal and informal process of gathering information to determine what the facts are in a case. Formal investigation involving exchanges of information between opposing attorneys as governed by court rules and sanctions is called **discovery**. This is the focus of Chapters 7 through 9. Chapter 3, however, focuses on informal investigation. Fact gathering in informal investigation is achieved by interviewing the client (Chapter 2), interviewing witnesses, and reviewing documents, records, physical evidence, and test results. The purposes of the investigation are numerous and include the following:

discovery

Formal investigation involving exchanges of information between opposing attorneys as governed by the rules of court.

1. To identify and locate the factual evidence that may be used by both sides to support or defeat each element of a cause of action

2. To locate persons and property

3. To establish expert opinion evidence

4. To develop evidence to discredit (impeach) a witness or opponent

5. To determine if there is sufficient factual evidence to support or defend the cause of action at trial or to form the basis for a settlement

6. To find additional evidence if necessary

7. To preserve evidence for trial

8. To organize the evidence for trial

Investigation requires the search of all the evidence, pro and con, and is so important a process that cases are won or lost on the degree of diligence devoted to investigation.

THE RELATIONSHIP OF EVIDENCE LAW TO INVESTIGATION

INTRODUCTION

The primary purpose of investigation is to accumulate evidence for trial. That evidence must be evaluated to determine if it is admissible—whether it can be used in a court of law. Although investigative decisions should be made in close consultation with the supervising attorney, the more the paralegal knows about the rules of evidence, the more assistance the paralegal can provide. An efficient investigator uses a fundamental knowledge of the rules of evidence to evaluate the usefulness and admissibility of the evidence as it is gathered. Knowledge of the rules also guides the investigator to the most valuable evidence, thus saving time and money. Job satisfaction is enhanced if the paralegal understands the underlying reasons for investigative tasks.

testimonial evidence
Spoken or signed, evidence elicited from a witness.

documentary evidence
Paper evidence such as letters, contracts, or medical records.

real evidence
The thing itself, physically present as opposed to being described, such as a scar, implement, or live view of the accident scene.

demonstrative evidence
Depiction or representation of something such as a photo of a scar or a diagram of the accident scene.

EVIDENCE IN GENERAL: WHAT IS IT?

Evidence is a distinct body of law that defines and regulates what information may be presented at trial. It is the information that the trier (jury or judge) uses to decide whether the plaintiff has proved the case. The rules of evidence help to ensure the fairest possible trial through the efficient presentation of reliable and understandable evidence. Truth and justice are the rules' ultimate goals. The rules of evidence for the federal system are the Federal Rules of Evidence, cited as FED. R. EVID. Many state systems have adopted the Federal Rules of Evidence, and the rules of most other states have much in common with the Federal Rules. This section focuses on the Federal Rules of Evidence. Compare it with your state rules of evidence.

Evidence is broadly classified into four types: Testimonial, documentary, real, and demonstrative. **Testimonial evidence** is spoken or signed, and has been elicited from a witness. **Documentary evidence** is paper evidence such as letters, contracts, and medical records. **Real evidence** is the thing itself, physically present as opposed to being described, such as a scar, weapon, or live view of the accident scene. **Demonstrative evidence** is a depiction or representation of something, such as a photo of a scar or a diagram of the accident scene. See Exhibit 3-1.

Evidence within each of these categories is either direct or circumstantial. **Direct evidence** is directly observable and proves the truth asserted. In Case I, for example, if the neighbor saw the van hit Mrs. Forrester, a statement to that effect in court by the neighbor would be direct evidence that the van did hit Mrs. Forrester. On the other hand, if the neighbor saw a damaged van and Mrs. Forrester lying near it, a statement to the effect by the neighbor would be circumstantial evidence that the van

EXHIBIT 3.1 Classification of Evidence

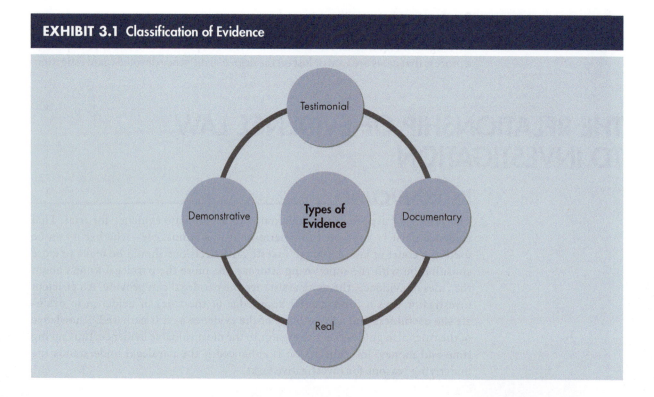

direct evidence
Evidence that is directly observable and proves the truth asserted.

circumstantial evidence
Evidence that suggests the existence of some other occurrence or thing.

admissible evidence
Evidence that may be presented in court because it complies with the rules of evidence that it must be relevant.

relevant
Admissible in court, of consequence to the determination of the action, and tending to prove or refute a fact of consequence.

material
Of consequence to the determination of the action.

probative value of evidence
The degree to which evidence tends to prove or actually proves something.

hit Mrs. Forrester. **Circumstantial evidence** suggests the existence of some other occurrence or thing. Both types of evidence may be valuable to a case. See Exhibit 3.1.

ADMISSIBLE EVIDENCE: THE RELEVANCY FACTOR

Admissible evidence may be presented in court because it complies with the rules of evidence. To be admissible, evidence must be **relevant**. Relevance has two components: the evidence must be **material**—of consequence to the determination of the action—and it must tend to prove or refute a fact of consequence (FED. R. EVID. 401). Being of consequence to the determination of the action (materiality) means that it bears a meaningful relationship to the determination of the issues at hand. For example, if the issue is whether Mr. Hart was careless when operating his van, would the color of his hair be of consequence to the determination of the issue? No. Would Mr. Hart's testimony that he was driving at thirty miles per hour be of consequence to the action? Yes. Speed in conjunction with the circumstances can be an indication of carelessness or carefulness; therefore, the testimony is material.

To be relevant, however, evidence must also tend to prove or refute a fact of consequence. If the fact of consequence is that Mr. Hart was traveling at thirty miles per hour, would his testimony that he was driving about thirty miles per hour tend to prove or refute this fact? Yes, it helps prove he was going thirty miles per hour (a fact of consequence). Therefore, the testimony meets both tests and is relevant and generally admissible. Among the most frequently heard objections are those asserting that the evidence is immaterial or irrelevant.

INADMISSIBILITY OF RELEVANT EVIDENCE: THE EXCEPTIONS

Evidence Based on Prejudice, Confusion, or Delay

Even relevant evidence is not always admissible. The evidence is inadmissible if the **probative value of evidence**—its strength to prove what it purports to prove—is outweighed by other factors deemed harmful to the trial process. These factors are identified in Rule 403 of the Federal Rules of Evidence and similar provisions in state rules of evidence.

The danger of unfair prejudice means that relevant evidence can be excluded if it is likely to cause a jury to decide an issue because it evokes undue sympathy, contempt, horror, or strong emotion. If a judge, for example, believed that a photograph showing Mrs. Forrester's little girl crying over her injured mother would so evoke the jurors' sympathy that it would distract them from the actual injury portrayed in the photograph, the judge could exclude the photograph despite its relevance. The key is whether the danger of unfair prejudice substantially outweighs the probative value of the evidence.

If the evidence is likely to create confusion—that is, create unnecessary side issues or simply be too complex for most jurors—it may be excluded under this rule. Or if the evidence is too misleading and likely to cause jurors to place more weight on the evidence than fairness dictates, it may be excluded. For example, a jury may put too much credence on the results of a lie detector test or an unscaled model of the scene of an accident.

The remaining concerns under Rule 403 are directed at saving time and money in the trial. Thus, if the probative value of evidence is substantially outweighed by its consumption of court time, it can be excluded. Similarly, if it wastes time or is merely a repetitious accumulation of evidence already adequately presented, the court may exclude it. Another consideration here is if repeated or extended presentations on a certain point would cause jurors to unduly emphasize its importance, such evidence may be limited or excluded if its probative value is substantially outweighed by its detrimental effect.

Character Evidence

Evidence of a person's character or a particular trait offered as proof that a person's conduct conformed to that trait on a particular occasion is inadmissible (FED. R. EVID. 404). One major exception to this rule occurs when character, or a trait of character, is an element of a claim. To illustrate, a defense to an action for making false and damaging statements about another would be to prove that the statements are true. Hence, evidence of truthfulness and specific instances of such conduct would be admissible [FED. R. EVID. 405(b)]. When evidence of character is admissible, a witness may testify to the reputation of the person or render an opinion on the person's character [FED. R. EVID. 405(a)]. In these situations, inquiry into specific instances of relevant conduct is permissible on cross-examination of the witness. Any permissible testimony on reputation or opinions on a person's character focuses on reputation in the subject's neighborhood (residence) or among associates.

Evidence of Habit or Routine Practice

habit
The semiautomatic, repeated response to a specific situation.

Evidence of habit or routine to prove that conduct on a specific occasion conformed to the habit or routine is generally admissible (FED. R. EVID. 406). **Habit** is the semiautomatic, repeated response to a specific situation. Brushing one's teeth each morning or automatically fastening the seat belt every time one rides in a car are examples of habit. **Routine (custom)** is the equivalent of habit for organizations. Products may be routinely inspected for defects, accounts routinely inspected for improper expenditures, and prospective employee references routinely checked. It is the nearly invariable regularity of habit and routine that makes them valid as evidence. Acts similar to the act in question, however, are not generally admissible as evidence because they may be remote in time to the occurrence in question or may lack the reliability of the invariable frequency of actions characterized as habit or routine.

routine (custom)
The equivalent of "habit" for organizations.

Evidence of Offers to Compromise, Insurance, and Remedial Measures

Evidence of offers to compromise or statements or conduct pursuant to compromise are inadmissible, as are evidence of insurance coverage and subsequent repairs to correct a defect that caused damages (FED. R. EVID. 408).

Evidence of Past Sexual Conduct, Past Sexual Crimes

Generally, evidence of a victim's past sexual conduct is not admissible. Evidence of a defendant's past sexual crimes is admissible in a civil case alleging sexual assault or molestation. Because of the significant exceptions to these general rules, the specific rule must be consulted when working with such cases (FED. R. EVID. 412–415).

Illegally Obtained Evidence

Courts can exclude evidence in civil cases, as well as in criminal cases, if it was illegally obtained. For example, since Georgia prohibits unauthorized interception of cordless telephone conversations, evidence from such an interception by a neighbor could not be used by a husband against his wife. The evidence was ruled inadmissible in *Barlow v. Barlow*, 526 S.E.2d 857 (Ga. 2000).

PRIVILEGED CONFIDENTIAL COMMUNICATIONS AND THEIR IMPORTANCE IN THE INVESTIGATIVE PROCESS

Privilege makes inadmissible certain communications of a confidential nature because of their social utility. The main privileges are: attorney-client, priest-penitent, physician-patient, social worker-client, husband-wife, and journalist-confidential source (Exhibit 3.2).

<u>The Attorney-Client Privilege</u>. The attorney-client privilege protects confidential communication made by the client to the attorney in the course of legal representation. Its rationale lies within the very foundations of the legal system, that the peaceful prevention and resolution of disputes begins with individuals confidently and, necessarily, confidentially seeking professional legal advice. The privilege is the client's, but it may also be invoked by the attorney. The privilege can be waived either voluntarily by the client or by an accidental revelation of the communication caused by the attorney's or paralegal's carelessness. Such involuntary revelation by the law firm is a serious breach of confidentiality and may result in legal action against the firm, not to mention loss of the client's lawsuit. Because of the serious consequences of such carelessness, paralegals must guard against such slips as mixing protected information with other information sent to an opponent, discussing confidential information where third parties might overhear it, asking the client questions in the presence of a third party, and leaving files (both physical and electronic) in places accessible to third parties.

In *State v. Ingraham*, 966 P.2d 103 (Mont. 1998), the defendant was charged with several felony counts related to a traffic accident. After the accident, the defendant was driven home by his friend, a paralegal who worked as an independent contractor for the defendant's father, who was an attorney. The defendant told the paralegal that the accident was caused by his dogs' trying to jump into the driver's seat of his vehicle. The court ruled that the incriminating statement was not protected by the attorney-client privilege because such a relationship had not been established and the statement was made to a friend, not a person acting in a legal capacity, which was further proved by the fact that the paralegal was not paid for this time.

EXHIBIT 3.2 Summation of Privileges

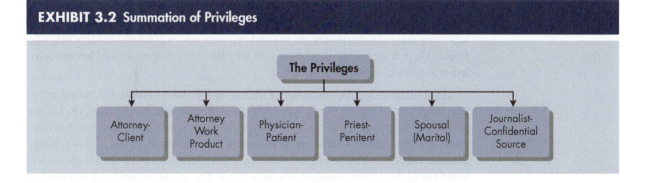

Third party consultants, such as accountants, language translators, scientists, and others hired to assist in furthering a client's legal matter are, as a general rule, encompassed by the privilege. When the purpose of the consultation is less clearly tied to acquiring knowledge needed for the planning and strategy of the litigation, however, the application of the privilege is less clear. Also in such circumstances when confidential information is mixed with other information, the purpose of the consultation may be unclear, and the attorney-client privilege deemed waived. For example, the use of a media or a public relations expert in a high profile case might create such a problem. Therefore, prior to participating in third party consultations, seek guidance from your supervising attorney on what, if any, confidential information can be shared.

The attorney-client privilege does not apply if the client sues the attorney and the attorney needs the privileged information to defend against the suit. Furthermore, most jurisdictions do not extend the privilege to cover a client's requests for information on how to commit a fraud or other crime.

Despite the fundamental value of the attorney-client privilege, it has come under significant erosive pressures. The perceived importance of successfully prosecuting large corporate fraud, controlling terrorism, and addressing other wrongdoing has, in the view of some, necessitated the subordination of the privilege. The obvious concern is whether such subordination will undermine client confidence and forthrightness when disclosing information to the client's attorney and paralegal. A discussion of the related concept of attorney work product, which has also come under such pressure, is discussed in the ethics section of this chapter.

The Physician-Patient Privilege. The physician-patient privilege protects confidential information about a patient's medical condition and treatment. The information may not be revealed by the physician unless the privilege is waived by the patient or unless the patient puts his or her medical condition in issue, such as in a medical malpractice suit or a personal injury suit.

The Priest-Penitent Privilege. Similar protections and exceptions apply to the priest-penitent relationship. Also known as the clergy privilege, this privilege protects communications between a religious advisor and the confessor. Issues have arisen as to who is considered clergy. Determining who is considered clergy is usually dictated by state law and often is determined by the intent of the confessor. Having a general conversation with a member of the clergy does not constitute a privileged conversation.

The Marital Privilege. Husband-wife (spousal, marital) privilege protects communications between married persons. Where recognized, one spouse can invoke the privilege to prevent the other from revealing this information. A spouse may also refuse to testify against a spouse. With the landmark decision by the U.S. Supreme Court in *Obergefell v. Hodges*, __ U.S. __, 135 S. Ct. 2584, 192 L. Ed 2d 609 (2015), legalizing same sex marriages, the marital privilege now will extend to same sex marriages. There is a growing legal debate on whether this privilege should be expanded to partners in a long-term relationship.

The Journalist-Confidential Source Privilege. A journalist-confidential source privilege, known as the reporter's privilege, exists in most states and Washington, DC but not in the federal system. This privilege protects a reporter's confidential sources when reporting or researching a news story. Perhaps the most famous example of this privilege is in the Watergate scandal of the 1970s where Carl Bernstein and Bob Woodward followed the leads of their confidential source "Deep Throat" in the downfall of President

CASE STUDY: UNDERSTANDING THE LAW

The facts in *New York Times v. Gonzales* center on a government investigation of organizations funding and raising of money for terrorist organizations in the United States. The government was focusing on two organizations whose assets they intended to freeze as well as conduct a search of both organizations. Somehow two *New York Times* reporters found out about the government's plan and contacted the two targeted organizations asking for comment on the intended searches and asset freezes. When the government found out about the reporters' information, a grand jury investigation was commenced to find out who leaked the information about the searches and asset freezes. The government wanted access to the Times' telephone records. which they refused to relinquish claiming privilege. The Times brought an action for declaratory judgment claiming that the government could not access the phone records from a third party stating

that those records are shielded from the grand jury investigation and privileged. In its court opinion the Second Circuit did find that a privilege existed protecting the phone records of the Times, even though those records were in the hands of a third party. The Court continued to acknowledge the privileges, but held that given the set of facts, which involved national security issues, the privilege was not absolute. The Court ordered that the Times cooperate and disclose the information requested.

Questions for Review: Closely examine *New York Times v. Gonzales*. What was the pivotal issue in the case that the court relied upon to reach its holding? What case did the Court rely upon to reach its result and why? Does the case abolish the reporter privilege? Support your response based upon the case decision.

Richard Nixon. In a more recent exercise of the reporter privilege, *New York Times v. Gonzales*, 459 F.3d 160 (2nd Cir. 2006), the New York Times was claiming the journalist privilege against the U.S. government in a case involving the attacks of September 11, 2001.

Social Worker-Client Privilege. In addition to the more established privileges listed above, a relatively new privilege between the social worker and client has been recognized by a number of jurisdictions. This privilege is based upon court's recognition of the mental health services provided by social workers, especially those of modest means as the U.S. Supreme Court acknowledged in *Jaffe v. Redmond*, 518 U.S. 1, 116 S.Ct. 1923, 135 L.Ed. 2d 337 (1996).

All of these privileges can be invoked after termination of the relationship if the communication in question occurred during the existence of the privileged relationship.

Privilege against Self-Incrimination. Another privilege that can be invoked in civil litigation is the privilege against self-incrimination. The Fifth Amendment to the U.S. Constitution allows a person to refuse to reveal information or to testify when such information is evidence of a crime committed by the person or may lead to such evidence. The privilege does not apply if the person has been convicted of the crime or has been granted immunity from prosecution of the crime.

The law of the local jurisdiction must be consulted for unique rules on privileged communications.

EVIDENCE ADMISSIBLE FROM A PARTY

The relevant admission of an opposing party (party-opponent) is admissible. It may be oral, written, or nonverbal conduct. The admission is generally damaging to the party making the admission and suggests a belief or position inconsistent with

INTERNET EXERCISE

Examine your state's privileges. Does your state permit additional privileges? If so, identify those privileges. Place the list of privileges from your jurisdiction in your systems folder, if you are keeping one.

the one the admitting party is taking at trial. This damaging nature, however, is not a requirement for admission. Therefore, the often-used designation of "admission against interest" is a misnomer under the federal rule and similar state rules.

RULES REGARDING THE TESTIMONY OF A WITNESS: WHAT'S ALLOWED AND WHAT'S NOT

Requirement of Firsthand Knowledge

The testimony of witnesses must be based on firsthand knowledge. In other words, the witnesses must have seen, heard, smelled, touched, or otherwise directly observed the subject of their testimony (FED. R. EVID. 602).

Opinion

Federal courts (FED. R. EVID. 701) and those of many states allow laypersons to give opinions. One such type of opinion is based on perceived facts leading to opinions on speed, weight, height, distance, and so on. A second type of opinion is that of a skilled lay observer. This opinion is based on repeated observations permitting identification of a specific signature or voice, or an assessment of the sanity of a person the observer knows.

Language was added to Rule 701 to prevent experts in specialized or scientific fields (FED. R. EVID. 702) from giving expert opinion disguised as lay opinion.

Expert Opinion

Highly specialized experts are permitted to give their opinions on matters at issue that relate to their field (FED. R. EVID. 702). Doctors, for example, are permitted to give their opinion regarding an injury, the cause of an injury, and the prognosis (outlook). Typically, engineers and scientists are among those experts permitted to give opinions.

The court will permit expert opinion if the "scientific, technical, or other specialized knowledge will assist the trier of fact to understand the evidence or to determine a fact in issue" (relevance) and if the witness is "qualified as an expert by knowledge, skill, experience, training, or education" (reliability). This test was confirmed as the appropriate standard for expert opinion in *Daubert v. Merrell Dow Pharmaceuticals, Inc.*, 113 S. Ct. 2786 (1993). The Supreme Court said the expert's reasoning or methodology must be scientifically valid and able to be applied to the facts in issue. Factors such as the method's rate of error, whether the method lends itself to testing and peer review, and whether it has gained general acceptance in the scientific community should be considered.

In 1999 the Supreme Court ruled that these reliability tests are not limited to the testimony of scientific experts [*Kumho Tire Co. Inc. v. Carmichael*, 526 U.S. 137 (1999)]. Federal Rule of Evidence 702 was subsequently amended to require the same level of court examination for all types of expert testimony. The resulting standard for determining the admissibility of expert opinion evidence in the federal system and states with parallel provisions is that (1) the testimony must be relevant and helpful, (2) the expert must be specially qualified, (3) the methodology used by the expert must be reliable, and (4) the evidence must be capable of being applied and actually be applied reliably to the facts of the case. Once expert testimony is found admissible, the opponent can still cross-examine the witness to test the opinion. Despite *Daubert*, *Kumho*, and the subsequent revision of Rule 702, a significant minority of states still

APPLY YOUR KNOWLEDGE

Determine in your jurisdiction what rules of evidence apply for lay opinion and expert opinion. Are your state's rules different than the Federal Rules of Evidence and if so what are those differences?

rely on an earlier standard of admissibility set out in *Frye v. U.S.*, 293 F. 1013 (D.C. Cir. 1923). The *Frye* (general acceptance test) permits admissibility if the scientific method used or principle relied on is generally accepted in the relevant field.

Should you be assigned a task that requires you to better understand the language of a rule of evidence, consult the advisory committee's notes, which explain each rule and any changes in the rule in more detail. For example, the advisory committee's notes for Rule 702 explain not only the rationale behind the rule, but also that an expert may not base an opinion on the principles of astrology, necromancy, or clinical ecology, because these "junk sciences" are unfounded.

The importance of Rule 702 cannot be overstated, particularly for the plaintiff. If the plaintiff's expert's testimony is key to the case, but later on appeal is found to have been improperly admitted by the trial court, the appellate court can enter judgment for the defendant. The plaintiff loses, therefore, and there is no second chance [*Weisgram v. Marley Co.*, 120 S. Ct. 1011 (2000)]. One useful fee-based resource for finding court opinions and other information on admissibility of expert opinion is http://www.dauberttracker.com.

Evidence of Character and Conduct of a Witness

A paralegal needs to remember that the jury's perception of a witness's truthfulness (credibility) may make the difference between winning and losing a case. Therefore, any evidence that bears on the truthfulness of a witness should be noted.

Under the Federal Rules of Evidence, it is permissible for others to enter an opinion on a witness's truthfulness or reputation for truthfulness. Specific conduct that bears on a witness's truthfulness may be inquired into by the attorneys but cannot be proved by independent evidence. Criminal convictions less than ten years old also are significant if the possible punishment was for more than one year in prison or the crime reflected dishonesty or untruthfulness [FED. R. EVID. 609(a)]. Religious beliefs are not admissible to show credibility. Rules 607 and 610 of the Federal Rules of Evidence apply to evidence of a witness's character and conduct.

Prior Statements of a Witness

A paralegal should take note of any statements of a witness on matters likely to be important at trial that may be used to challenge or support a witness's truthfulness. For example, if a witness testifies that Mr. Hart's van was going forty-five miles per hour at the time of the accident, and the same witness told a police officer that the van was going about twenty-five miles per hour, the prior inconsistent statement could be damaging to the witness's credibility.

Capacity to Observe, Record, Recollect, or Narrate

Any witness may be examined for the ability to observe, record, recollect, or narrate in order to demonstrate any weaknesses. Extrinsic evidence—evidence other than the testimony of the witness in question—may be used to prove such weaknesses. Mental capacity, intelligence, distractions, distance from the event observed, lighting conditions, influence of drugs or alcohol, and a multitude of other matters that affect reliability may be inquired into or proved by other evidence. Children are permitted to testify if the judge is satisfied that the child has a basic understanding of the importance of telling the truth and is able to observe, recall, and convey information.

Hearsay and the Exceptions: It's Not What You Think!

Hearsay is evidence that relies on the firsthand observation of another person rather than the person testifying. For example, Ms. Schnabel, the neighbor, might testify that Mr. Forrester told her that Mr. Hart's van was going forty-five miles per hour. Since that statement is based on Mr. Forrester's observation and not on the firsthand observation of Ms. Schnabel, it is hearsay as to the speed of the van. Hearsay is considered unreliable and is generally inadmissible. The paralegal, therefore, must not rely on hearsay but should seek out the original firsthand source for needed evidence.

There are, however, some important exceptions to the hearsay rule. These are found in the Federal Rules of Evidence, beginning with Rule 801(d), and in similar state rules. The key to the exceptions to the prohibition against hearsay in a case is their reliability. The exceptions are:

Prior statement of a witness: A statement previously made by a witness is admissible at trial if the witness is subject to cross-examination and any of the following elements are present:

1. The statement is inconsistent with the witness's trial testimony and given under oath.

2. The prior statement is consistent with the witness's testimony and is offered to meet an attack on the declarant's honesty or motives.

3. The statement was one identifying a person after seeing the person.

Admission by party opponent: A previous statement made by a party may be admitted against that person by the opponent. See the preceding section, "Evidence Admissible from a Party."

Present sense impression: A statement made during or immediately after an event is observed or a condition is described is admissible. (Example: Mr. Johnson said, "That car is going too fast to make that curve!")

Excited utterance: An excited utterance is admissible. (Example: "My husband said, 'Look out! That car is coming into our lane!'")

Then-existing mental, emotional, or physical conditions: This exception is designed to admit some evidence other than conduct to reveal a person's state of mind regarding intent, plan, motive, emotion, and pain. (Example: "Mrs. Forrester said, 'My hip hurts so much I can barely stand it.'" Example: "Mr. Hart said, 'I'll get those brakes fixed next month.'") Statements that are present sense impressions, excited utterances, or about then-existing mental, emotional, or physical conditions are called **res gestae statements**.

res gestae statements

Statements that are present sense impressions, excited utterances, or about then-existing mental, emotional, or physical conditions.

Statement made to receive a medical diagnosis: (Example: "Mrs. Forrester said to me [doctor], 'My left hip is very painful.'") Such a statement is admissible.

Recorded recollection: A statement recorded when a witness's memory was fresh is admissible when the witness cannot recall the contents of the statement.

Records: Records kept in the regular course of business, such as motel registration or time cards, are admissible.

Statement of reputation: If it concerns family history, boundaries, or a person's character, such a statement is admissible.

Court judgment: A conviction of fraud, for example, would be admissible if offered to prove any fact essential to the case.

declarant

The person making the statement.

Unavailability of witness: Some hearsay evidence is admissible only if the **declarant** is unavailable to testify (Fed. R. Evid. 804). Unavailability means the witness is dead, is unavailable through reasonable efforts, refuses to testify or is protected from testifying, or can't remember.

Former testimony: If a witness is unavailable at trial, the witness's former testimony is admissible as long as it was subject to cross-examination at the time by one having a similar interest to the opponent's.

Statements under belief of impending death (dying declarations): A statement made by a person who believed his or her death was imminent is admissible when offered to show the person's belief regarding the cause or circumstances of death. Under common law, the person must have died; in the Federal Rules, the person must be unavailable.

Statements against interest: The law has assumed that a person would not make a statement against his or her financial, business, or legal interest unless it were true. Therefore, when a witness is unavailable, that witness's previous statement against his or her interest is admissible.

Computer data must be scrutinized to determine whether it is hearsay and whether it meets one of the hearsay exceptions. For example, if a person enters data such as accounting records, a graph, or summaries into a computer, this data is hearsay. The fact that a person enters into a computer checkbook that a bill was paid on a specified date does not prove it was paid on that date. But purely computer-generated data, such as that generated by an automated phone number recording system, is not entered by a person, and therefore, is not hearsay. The latter is inherently more reliable than the former.

physical evidence

Tangible articles; evidence that can be seen, touched, or heard.

RULES REGARDING PHYSICAL EVIDENCE AND AUTHENTICATION

Physical evidence is evidence that one can see, hear, touch, or otherwise perceive firsthand: the scene of an accident, a contract or other written instrument, an x-ray, the viewed injuries or scars of the plaintiff, or a photograph. Because such evidence is perceived firsthand by the trier of fact and not through the description of a witness, it can be very persuasive. Physical evidence needs to be authenticated in order to be admissible. In other words, it must be shown to be what it purports to be. Therefore, the paralegal also must determine what is necessary to have that evidence authenticated. Rule 901(b) of the Federal Rules of Evidence suggests several ways that evidence can be authenticated:

INTERNET EXERCISE

Determine in your jurisdiction under what statute the hearsay exceptions are found and whether there are additional hearsay exceptions. If so, list those additional exceptions.

1. Testimony of a witness who has knowledge that a matter is what it is claimed to be. (Example: "I made the entries in the log describing which deliveries Mr. Hart was to make the day of the accident, and that is the log.")

2. Testimony of a nonexpert on someone's handwriting. (Example: "I have seen Mr. Hart's signature many times, and that is his signature.") This method can apply to voice identification as well.

3. Testimony of an expert witness based on adequate comparison. (Example: "I have examined exhibit A and several samples of handwriting known to be Mr. Brown's; it is my opinion that exhibit A is Mr. Brown's handwriting.")

4. Testimony about distinctive characteristics. (Example: "My wife's coat was all handsewn, and the aunt who made it sewed her initials, B.J., into the lining. Yes, that is my wife's coat.")

5. Testimony about a telephone conversation determining whether the other person was the person in question. (Example: "I called Richard Hart at the extension number listed for him at Mercury Parcel Service, and he answered and said, 'This is Richard Hart.'")

chain of custody
The chronological record tracing a piece of evidence to the event that has resulted in the action, proving that it is the item in question.

If an item of evidence is not unique, such as an automobile tire, it can be shown to be the tire in question by establishing a **chain of custody**. A chain of custody is a chronological history of the storage or use (or both) of an item since the event in question. Testimony demonstrating a complete chain should remove reasonable doubt as to the authenticity of the item.

Scientific evidence resulting from blood, breathalyzer, and other scientific analyses requires testimony that the theory underlying the test is valid and the equipment used is reliable. Failure to prove these points may result in the evidence's admissibility being challenged or deemed inadmissible altogether. In preparing a case, always consider who will testify as to the validity of tests given and the reliability of the process and equipment used.

Some evidence is self-authenticating, requiring only a government seal, official attestation, or the signature of an official in charge of such documents. Federal and state documents and public records come under this category. Official publications, such as books and pamphlets, are self-authenticating, as are newspapers and periodicals, trade inscriptions, notarized documents, commercial paper, or any other signature or document declared so by act of Congress.

best evidence rule
Rule that allows only the original document or item to be admitted (exceptions are allowed for practical reasons).

The content of writings, recordings (including mechanical recordings), and photographs (including x-rays, motion pictures, and videotapes) also require authentication. These things fall under the **best evidence rule** (FED. R. EVID. 1002). By this rule, only the original document or item is admissible. This is to prevent admission of altered or fraudulent copies. Therefore, an investigator must strive to secure the original item. In some circumstances, however, copies may be substituted. This is so when the authenticity of the original is not in question, when use of a duplicate will not be unfair to the other party, or when the original is lost or destroyed (unless in bad faith by the proponent). Writings, recordings, or photographs too voluminous for practical court use may be summarized.

In the past, business records were authenticated by a witness. Now United States and foreign business records can be authenticated in federal court by affidavit [FED. R. EVID. 902(11) and 902(12)] as long as the opponent is given proper notice [FED. R. EVID. 903(11)].

COMPUTER EVIDENCE: THE NEW AGE

The age of digital technology has made once reliable documents, photographs, audiotapes and videotapes, and other evidence susceptible to undetectable alteration. Authentication of such evidence today may require proof of a chain of custody.

Courts are increasingly applying the authentication requirements of Rule 901 to computer evidence. This evidence could consist of a variety of business or other records, or models for recreating data or simulating an event. If the computerized evidence is (1) a complete record of data rather than an attempt to fill in gaps in the data, (2) based on simple rather than complex manipulation of data, (3) a routine process, and (4) easily verifiable, that is, testable, then the computer evidence is likely to be admissible. The more computer evidence departs from each of these four criteria, the more difficult authentication becomes. More detailed authentication requires an examination of the data input process, how the data is processed by the computer, and whether the output is what it is represented to be.

Official government Web sites are self-authenticating. Occasionally, however, information on the site may be successfully challenged [*State v. Davis*, 10 P.3d 977 (Wash. 2000)]. In *Davis*, population statistics on the state's Web site were ruled to be hearsay.

OTHER EVIDENTIARY CONCEPTS

Judicial Notice

judicial notice
Admission of evidence without authentication, either a fact commonly known in the territorial jurisdiction of the court or a fact readily verifiable through undisputed sources.

Judicial notice permits a judge to admit certain evidence without authentication. Such evidence can be judicially noticed if it is a fact not subject to reasonable dispute and meets one of two criteria: (1) the fact must be commonly known in the territorial jurisdiction of the court or (2) the fact is readily verifiable through undisputed sources (FED. R. EVID. 201). By eliminating the need for authentication, judicial notice saves time and expense. A court might take judicial notice of acts and records of the court, geographic and historical facts, matters of public record, or the viability of the underlying basis for a scientific test, such as for the presence of alcohol in the blood.

APPLY YOUR KNOWLEDGE

Using your jurisdictional law, find three examples of cases where the court refused to use judicial notice. Explain why the court did not recognize judicial notice.

Stipulations

stipulation
Formal agreement between opposing parties to a lawsuit regarding matters pertinent to the lawsuit, such as to admit certain evidence without testimony.

A **stipulation** is an agreement between the parties that permits evidence to be admitted as true without authentication. Stipulations are formally received by most courts because they save time and often reduce the need for witnesses. For example, in a contract dispute, the parties might stipulate that the signatures are authentic or that the contract is the original, eliminating the need of proof of these facts.

In other than an evidentiary context, a stipulation is a specific condition parties agree to in a contract or other legal document or in an agreement on procedural matters, such as where to depose (examine) a witness (FED. R. CIV. P. 29).

Burden of Proof

burden of proof
The obligation to prove the allegations; usually falls to the accuser.

Even in the earliest stages of investigation, understanding which party has the **burden of proof** and on which points will allow the paralegal to be of more assistance in ferreting out evidence useful to the client's case. Since the plaintiff is the accuser and the one seeking a remedy, the law places the burden on the plaintiff to plead and prove the allegations set out in the complaint. Only when the plaintiff has satisfied the minimum burden does it become necessary for the defendant to rebut the plaintiff's evidence with evidence of his or her own. The defendant, however,

affirmative defense

Defense showing that the defendant is not liable even if the plaintiff's claim is assumed to be true and for which the defendant bears the burden of proof.

preponderance of the evidence

Evidence that is more convincing to the trier than the opposing evidence; meets the requirement for the burden of proof in civil cases.

clear and convincing evidence

A higher standard of proof than preponderance of the evidence; requires that the matter be shown to be highly probable.

proof beyond a reasonable doubt

Proof that is so strong it excludes any other reasonable hypothesis or explanation—almost a certainty.

presumption

A mechanism that allows a jury to presume a fact is true based on indirect evidence if it might be awkward or difficult to prove by direct evidence. For example, mailing a letter creates the presumption it was received. A presumption stands unless it is rebutted.

bears the burden of proving affirmative defenses. An **affirmative defense** shows that the defendant is not liable even if the plaintiff's claim is assumed to be true. Self-defense, payment of debt, and assumption of risk are examples of affirmative defenses. If a party is in a position to have the only knowledge of a fact, that party bears the burden on the fact.

In civil cases, the person who bears the burden of proof must meet that burden by a **preponderance of the evidence**. "Evidence preponderates when it is more convincing to the trier than the opposing evidence," and the burden is met by "proof which leads the jury to find that the existence of the contested fact is more probable than its nonexistence."

In some types of civil cases (citizenship, fraud, mutual mistake, and content of lost deeds), the standard is proof by clear and convincing evidence. **Clear and convincing evidence** is a higher standard of proof than "preponderance of evidence" and requires that the matter be shown to be highly probable.

Criminal cases require the highest burden of proof: proof beyond a reasonable doubt. **Proof beyond a reasonable doubt** is proof that is so strong it excludes any other reasonable hypothesis or explanation—almost a certainty. See Exhibit 3.3.

Presumption

An evidentiary **presumption** is a mechanism created by rule of law that presumes a specific fact to be true when certain other preliminary evidence is established. Thus, if it is proved that Ann Forrester mailed a letter to Richard Hart, and the letter was never returned to Ann Forrester as unclaimed, it is presumed that Richard Hart received the letter. The presumption of an unestablished fact, that Hart received the letter, avoids difficult, time-consuming, or awkward proofs. Unless Hart comes forth with evidence to rebut the presumption, such as, "I never received the letter," the jury will be instructed that the delivery has been established.

SOURCES FOR RESEARCHING EVIDENCE LAW

Keep in mind that rules of evidence are more complex than can be covered here, and occasions arise in the law office when you will need more information on a particular rule of evidence. When you do, there are several sources to consider: *Wigmore on Evidence*, the hornbook *McCormick on Evidence*, and the legal encyclopedias. The Federal Rules of Evidence with Advisory Committee Notes and the evidentiary statutes and rules of each state should not be overlooked. Imwinkelried's book, *Evidentiary Foundations*, can be useful as a quick guide to what evidence is necessary to establish proper foundation. An evidentiary foundation is that testimony necessary to establish that a person was in a position to have observed or have knowledge of the facts to which he or she will be testifying. It establishes firsthand knowledge. Some of the sources mentioned above, including the Federal Rules of Evidence, can be found on Westlaw® or Lexis®. A Web site that provides links to the rules is http://www.uscourts.gov/rules/index.html. You can get to some state rules through www.state.[state abbreviation].us.

EXHIBIT 3.3 Burdens of Proof

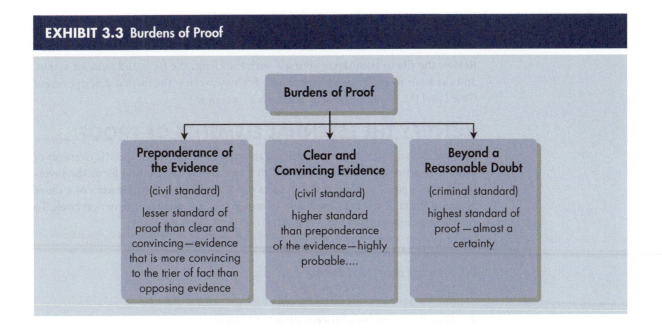

THE INVESTIGATION PROCESS

INTRODUCTION

With some of these evidentiary concepts and principles in mind, you can begin the investigation. The three stages in the investigation procedure include planning the investigation, gathering the evidence, and preserving the evidence.

Thorough planning is extremely important to a good and efficient investigation. Some cases can be characterized as bottomless pits that sap the energy and time of the paralegal and the financial resources of the client. Proper planning allows for a thorough yet sensible approach that works to the benefit of paralegal and client alike.

PLANNING THE INVESTIGATION: HOW TO START

A sound approach to planning an investigation should include the following steps:

1. Review the file and other available information.

2. Identify the essential elements of proof as defined by the appropriate substantive law.

3. Identify what facts will be needed to prove each of these elements.

4. Determine what sources, including witnesses, may provide those facts.

5. Record the investigation plan.

6. Consult with the attorney in selecting the most appropriate sources and methods of investigation to be followed.

REVIEW THE FILE AND OTHER AVAILABLE INFORMATION

Review the file to familiarize yourself with the client, the facts, the cause of action, and the leads to evidence and witnesses. For now, review the factual descriptions of Case I and the summary of Mrs. Forrester's interview.

IDENTIFY THE ESSENTIAL ELEMENTS OF PROOF

The realization that evidence is gathered to prove or disprove the specific elements of a cause of action permits the paralegal to immediately narrow and focus the investigation. Chapter 2 explained the process of identifying the key elements of a cause of action through research, particularly research in a good jury instruction book. To review, the elements that our client, Mrs. Forrester, must prove are:

1. Duty of care (as dictated by conditions)

2. Breach of duty (carelessness)

3. Injury

4. Causal relationships between breach and injury

5. Damages

In addition, Mrs. Forrester must disprove comparative negligence.

IDENTIFY WHAT FACTS WILL BE NEEDED

Drawing from practical experience and common sense, list facts that need to be gathered to prove the elements in the case. Typical facts for several key elements are listed in Exhibit 3.4.

DETERMINE WHAT SOURCES, INCLUDING WITNESSES, MAY PROVIDE FACTS

Sources of Information and Evidence

Identifying possible sources for information and evidence is a process of applying the information already gathered in the file, as well as a knowledge of investigative sources of information and common sense. Some typical sources of information and evidence for a personal injury investigation are included in Exhibit 3.5.

EXHIBIT 3.4 Facts for Several Key Elements

Breach of Duty	Injuries	Comparative Negligence
Carelessness	Fractures	Attentiveness
Road conditions	Pain	Obstructions to sight and sound (coat)
Mechanical defects	Disabilities	Haste (carelessness)
Speed of van	Insomnia	
Driver's condition		

EXHIBIT 3.5 Checklist of Evidentiary Source

For Negligence Cases

Source	Likely Information
Client	Occurrence, other witnesses, damages, etc.
Witnesses	Occurrence, other witnesses, injuries, etc.
Scene of accident	Obstructions, distances, special circumstances, surveillance tapes
Police reports	Details of accident, witnesses, officer at scene, photos, sobriety tests
Event data recorder ("black box," if available)	Digitally preserved information at time of accident on engine speed, braking, air bag deployment, malfunctions
Department of Motor Vehicles	Accident reports, driving records
News accounts (newspapers, microfilm, videotapes)	Details, witnesses, reporters
Reporters (notes)	Details, photos, witnesses
Emergency personnel (ambulance crew, paramedic, tow truck operator)	Details, injuries
Fire marshal (reports)	Causes of fire, witnesses
Transcripts of related trials or hearings (criminal, traffic)	Statements of witnesses and parties, admission
U.S. Weather Bureau	Official weather reports
Licensing and inspection authorities	Code and licensing violations
Police agencies (local police, FBI)	Criminal records for impeachment
Internet and public or university library	General reference information Directories for scholarly and professional associations Experts in pertinent field, consultants Business information Corporate information Federal and state agencies Census reports
Hospital	Names of nurses, doctors, technicians; x-rays, medications, related medical records, pain and suffering, bills
Physicians	Consulting physicians, treatment history, diagnosis, prognosis, disabilities, pain and suffering, bills
Physical therapists	Disabilities, necessary treatment, likelihood of success
Close relatives, friends, and neighbors	Effects of the injury, disabilities
Medical literature	Injuries, medication, side effects, prognosis

(continued)

EXHIBIT 3.5 Checklist of Evidentiary Source (*continued*)

Department of Vocational Rehabilitation	Expert witnesses, statistics on job rehabilitation and earning potential
Injured party's employer	Performance records, wages, firings, promotion potential

Federal Agencies

Federal Aviation Administration (FAA), www.faa.gov	Airline accidents, safety standards
Department of Transportation, www.dot.gov	Vehicle and driver safety standards
National Highway Traffic Safety Administration, www.nhtsa.gov	Vehicle complaints, investigations, recalls
National Oceanic and Atmospheric Administration, www.noaa.gov	Certified weather reports
National Climatic Data Center, Asheville, NC, www.ncdc.noaa.gov	Certified weather information by state
Department of Agriculture, www.usda.gov	Aerial photos, plants, wildlife
Department of Interior (Geologic Survey), www.doi.gov	Maps
Internal Revenue Service, www.irs.gov	Former tax rates and schedules
Census Bureau, www.census.gov	Demographic statistics
Occupational Safety and Health Administration, (OSHA), www.osha.gov	Job safety standards
Agency for Toxic Substances and Disease Registry, www.atsdr.cdc.gov (See also the medical and other sites listed in this exhibit.)	Toxicity, sites, advisories

State Agencies

www.state.[your state's two-letter abbreviation].us

Department of Transportation	Traffic flow, highways, bridges, signals, signs
Department of Labor and Industry	Industrial safety rules and regulations, statistics
Department of Geology	Geological surveys
Office of Secretary of State (corporations)	Corporate addresses, officers
Department of Insurance	Auto liability coverage, insurance company requirements
Department of Business and Professions	Licensing requirements of trades and businesses
Bureau of Vital Statistics	Certified records of birth, death, divorce, etc.
Department of Revenue	Personal property licenses, taxes, ownership, transactions
Wright and Allen, *The National Directory of State Agencies*, Information Resource Press	Directory of state agencies

Electronic Investigation and the Internet: Law and General Topic Research

Obtaining the best information most efficiently lies at the heart of successful litigation. Researching information is easier and yet more complex today than ever before

EXHIBIT 3.5 Checklist of Evidentiary Source (*continued*)

County and Local Agencies

Check county (parish), city, or town Web sites for local agencies.

Courthouse (clerk's offices)	Lawsuits, criminal cases, property ownership, liens, UCC filings (also see Exhibit 3.2)
Tax Assessor's Office	Ownership, location, taxes, and assessed value of property
Voter Registration	Voter's address, age, sex, race, and voting precinct
District, County, or City Attorney's Office	Criminal records, location of person
Coroner's Office	Cause of death and related hearings, records
Chamber of Commerce	Local businesses, services, literature
Department of Public Works and Traffic	Street blueprints, timing of traffic lights, expert witnesses, statistics
Universities and colleges	Experts in a variety of fields

because of computer or electronic research. Inexperienced electronic researchers can waste expensive billable hours "surfing" the numerous electronic sources trying to find something helpful. Knowledgeable electronic researchers first locate the specific sources most pertinent to the investigation of their case through general guides to electronic research. Networking with colleagues in the office or through electronic bulletin boards (e-mail lists) may produce more specialized sources.

Exhibit 3.6 is a general resource guide for investigation on the Web to help you make more efficient use of the information highway. Update it frequently.

EXHIBIT 3.6 General Resource Guide for Investigation on the Web

Common search engines

www.yahoo.com

www.google.com

www.altavista.com

www.bing.com

Blog directories:

www.blogsearchengine.com

www.bloglines.com

www.technorati.com

Law Search Engines

www.findlaw.com

   free service owned by Westlaw

www.lawcrawler.com

www.law.com

www.ilrg.com

Internet Legal Resource Guide

www.law.cornell.edu

   federal and state statutes, decisions, rules, etc.

www.westlaw.com

www.lexis.com

   free service at www.lexisone.com

www.loislaw.com

(Verdicts)

www.verdictsearch.com

(continued)

EXHIBIT 3.6 General Resource Guide for Investigation on the Web (*continued*)

Government Resources

www.uscourts.gov

www.firstgov.gov
   official links to U.S. and some state sites

www.governmentguide.com

www.fedworld.gov
   list of government resources

www.fedstats.gov
   links to federal statistics

www.census.gov
   Census Bureau

www.whitehouse.gov

www.house.gov

www.senate.gov

http://thomas.loc.gov
   pending and passed legislative bills by topic or title

www.gpoaccess.gov

federal documents from the U.S. Government Printing Office

www.nfoic.org
   federal and state freedom of information requests

www.forms.gov
   official U.S. forms

www.loc.gov
   Library of Congress

Investigative Resources

www.merlindata.com
   index of investigative research sites

www.militarysearch.org
   military status of any person

Consumer and Product Information

www.cpsc.gov
   Consumer Product Safety Commission

www.pueblo.gsa.gov
   Consumer Information Center

www.consumer.gov
   U.S. Consumer Gateway (resources by subject)

www.nhtsa.gov
   National Highway Traffic Safety Administration
   (vehicle complaints, investigations, recalls)

Environmental/Occupational Safety

www.epa.gov
   Environmental Protection Agency

www.osha.gov
   Occupational Safety and Health Administration

www.cdc.gov/niosh/about.html
   National Institute for Occupational Safety and Health

www.atsdr.cdc.gov
   Agency for Toxic Substances and Disease Registry

Business, Labor, and Employment

www.doc.gov
   U.S. Department of Commerce

www.dol.gov
   Department of Labor

www.sba.gov
   Department of Commerce, Small Business Administration

www.bbb.org
   Better Business Bureau

www.companylink.com
   data on companies

www.corporateinformation.com

www.incspot.com
   U.C.C./corporate filings

EXHIBIT 3.6 General Resource Guide for Investigation on the Web (*continued*)

People/Business Locators

www.anywho.com
www.google.com
www.facebook.com
www.linkedin.com
www.beenverified.com
www.switchboard.com
http://people.yahoo.com
www.ancestry.com
   Social Security death index
www.bop.gov
Bureau of Prisons, find prison inmates

(Assets)
www.searchsystems.net
   registered assets such as real estate, cars, boats, planes, etc.; also criminal records, bankruptcies, and liens
www.carfax.com
   a car's history
(Credit Reports)
Note: personal credit checks are illegal except those authorized by Fair Credit Reporting Act

Climate Reports

www.noaa.gov
   National Oceanic and Atmospheric Administration

www.ncdc.noaa.gov
   National Climatic Data Center

Maps/Aerial Photos

www.usda.gov
   Department of Agriculture (also plants and wildlife)

www.doi.gov
   Department of the Interior (Coastal and Geologic Survey)

Experts/Prior Testimony

www.dauberttracker.com
   expert evidence cases
www.expertpages.com
   organized by topic and state

News and Media

www.newspaperlinks.com
http://newslink.org/menu.html
www.newspapers.com

(For a local newspaper, use a general search engine and type in the name of the newspaper to see if articles are online.)

Public Records (birth, death, marriage, etc.)

(See Investigative Resources, this exhibit)
www.knowx.com
   background public information about businesses, persons, assets

http://vitalrec.com/index.html
   birth, death, marriage, and divorce records

(continued)

EXHIBIT 3.6 General Resource Guide for Investigation on the Web (*continued*)

Medical/Pharmacy

www.cdc.gov
   U.S. Center for Disease Control
www.fda.gov
   U.S. Food and Drug Administration
www.ama-assn.org/laps/amahg.htm
   doctor finder

www.merck.com
   Merck Manual of Diagnosis and Therapies
www.nlm.nih.gov
   National Library of Medicine (access Medline
   free by choosing PubMed)
www.jdmd.com
   medical abbreviations, medical and dental mal
   practice consultants, glossary

Statistical Resources

www.fedstats.gov
http://tracfed.syr.edu
www.nces.ed.gov
   National Center for Education Statistics

Vehicle Value

www.kbb.com

METHODS FOR GATHERING INFORMATION OR EVIDENCE

Once the potential sources of information have been identified, choose the method most suitable to obtain that information. Consider efficiency as well as expense; spending a great amount of money and time may not be justified if the amount in controversy is small. Use the following resources:

- **The scene of the incident.** In many cases, not just personal injury cases, a specific location may offer significant evidence. A visit to the location (office, scene of accident, factory) is essential. Remember to check for business or traffic control surveillance tapes.

- **The telephone.** Pinpointing the best source of information, especially if it involves leaving the office, interviewing people, going through files, and so on, can be a costly and time-consuming process. A preliminary assessment of these sources by telephone can reduce the amount of time and money spent. For example, if several people witnessed a particular occurrence, it might be wise to call each of them for a preliminary interview to determine whether an in-person visit is warranted.

- **Mailed or emailed requests.** Some information is obtainable through a relatively inexpensive request by correspondence or email. Medical, school, employment, and agency records can frequently be obtained in this manner if the request includes the proper authorization to release the information. Examples of particular requests by correspondence or email will be covered later in this chapter.

- **The Internet.** An increasing amount of information is available on the Internet for free. Although some of the private databases charge monthly or usage fees, the cost can be relatively inexpensive compared with more cumbersome and traditional methods of gathering information. Any office having a personal computer, an Internet connection, and the necessary software can access a database. Should you find yourself without access to the Internet, many public and university libraries provide such services to the public. The average search takes about ten to twenty minutes, and costs are reasonable.

- **Personal interview.** In most circumstances involving key witnesses, there is no substitute for a personal interview. Personal interviews take time, careful planning, and skill. Because of costs, it may not be feasible to interview less important witnesses in person. The phone can be a big help in this case. It is better, however, to err on the side of too much interviewing than on too little. Interviews produce good evidence as well as the opportunity to assess the ability of the witness to testify.

- **Professional research and search services.** At times, it pays to hire professional search services. These companies provide a highly experienced and well-trained staff who have access to information unavailable to you. Although these services are often expensive, they should be employed when the information sought is critical or needs to be gathered quickly. A variety of professional search services are available: PARASEC (www.parasec.com, 800-533-7272) provides document retrieval from anywhere in the country, including county services. It will also conduct searches of records and statements filed with secretaries of state. Corporation Service Company (www.incspot.com, 800-872-4636) offers a wide array of corporate information search services.

- **Private investigators.** Some firms use private investigators to do their factual investigation. Others use investigators only in certain situations. Investigators are not overly expensive, and using one may make it unnecessary for the office's paralegal to testify about the evidence-gathering process. A list of 14,000 independent investigative agencies with ratings is available through Investigators Anywhere (www.investigatorsanywhere.com).

- **Legal and topical research.** An important part of any investigation involves going to the Internet, CD-ROM library, law library, or general library to locate pertinent statutes, rules, and regulations; news articles; scholarly articles on particular points of law, investigation, and use of evidence; medical information; commercial information; sources for expert witnesses; and other sources. A local library's copy of the city directory is useful for tracking individuals. An older directory may list a phone number that is now unlisted. Also note that Westlaw, Lexis, and other subscription legal research services now offer nonsubscription, single search services for a reasonable flat fee.

- **Photos and video.** Photography and videotaping not only preserve evidence but may also be the only way to effectively gather and demonstrate evidence. A relatively inexpensive digital camcorder with basic editing capabilities can help you create a compelling settlement request. If the photo or video is critical for trial, a professional photographer may be employed.

- **Scientific tests.** Re-creations, chemical analysis, and other forms of testing may be the only way to support the theory of the plaintiff or defense. The employment of state and private laboratories is normally essential in such circumstances.

- **Experts.** Related to testing, the use of scientists, professors, engineers, mechanics, medical personnel, and other experts in the relevant field is increasingly essential to win cases. Sometimes victory hinges on which side has the best expert. Associations of experts such as TASA (Technical Advisory Service for Attorneys) offer American and foreign experts in thousands of fields, as well as in alternative methods of resolving disputes (www.tasanet.com, 800-523-2319).

- **Freedom of Information Act ("FOIA") requests.** FOIA requests are inexpensive and can provide valuable information from federal and state agencies. It is best to consider such requests early in the litigation process. A more detailed discussion of FOIA requests is addressed in the context of discovery in Chapter 9.

RECORD THE INVESTIGATION PLAN

Keeping in mind evidentiary considerations, the elements of the cause of action or its defenses, the potential sources of information, and the methods and costs of gathering that evidence, write out the detailed investigation plan as demonstrated in Exhibit 3.7.

EXHIBIT 3.7 Investigative Plan

Possible to Prove or Acquire	Possible Source of Information	Method Cost
Defendant	Dun's Market Identifiers	Internet search
Mercury Express—financial status, service agent, home office, etc.	Corporation Service Co.	Professional search service
Breach of Duty		
Weather conditions	Certified copy of weather conditions from National Climatic Data Center	Mail/Internet
Mechanical defect	Inspection of vehicle	Hire mechanic
	Police report	Mail
	Vehicle maintenance records	Mail request
	Mechanic who services vehicle	Phone/interview (deposition)
Condition of driver	Police report	Mail/email
	Police officer	Phone/personal interview
	Copy of breathalyzer report	Mail/email
		Clerk of court file
	Ms. Schnabel (witness)	Personal interview
Conditions at scene	Scene of accident	Visit scene (photograph)

EXHIBIT 3.7 Investigative Plan (*continued*)

Plaintiff's injuries

Immediate injuries, broken bones, etc.	Doctors' reports	Mail/email
	Emergency room records	Mail/email
	Hospital records	Mail/email
	X-rays	Mail/email
	Doctors' testimony	Interview, letter, reports evaluated
Immediate and long-term disabilities	Doctors' reports (follow-up visits)	Mail/email
	Doctors' testimony	Interview (after reports evaluated)
	Mrs. Forrester	Initial interview
	Mr. Forrester	Interview
	Nurse	Phone (followed by interview)
	Friends	Phone (followed by interview)
Pain	Mrs. Forrester's testimony (pain log)	Initial and follow-up interviews
	Mr. Forrester	Interview
	Nurse	Phone (follow-up interview)
	Hospital and doctors' reports	Mail/email
	Doctors' testimony	Interview
	Ambulance assistants	Phone
	Ms. Schnabel (witness)	Interview

Comparative Negligence

Attentiveness of plaintiff (haste of plaintiff)	Police report	Mail/email/in person
	Insurance and Mercury accident reports	Mail/email (discovery)
	Mrs. Forrester	Interview
	Mr. Forrester	Interview
	Ms. Schnabel	Interview
	Mr. Hart	Deposition
Obstruction of sight and sound by coat worn by plaintiff	Coat itself	Obtain from Mrs. Forrester
	Possible re-creation tests with coat at scene	(Suggestions from supervising attorney)
	University consultant	Phone (follow-up by email and interview)

Note: This table is for illustrative purposes. It is not complete as to possible facts to prove, sources, or methods.

CONSULT WITH THE SUPERVISING ATTORNEY

Take the completed investigation plan to the attorney. A brief discussion should be held to determine the most feasible approach regarding sources, methods, and available time and money. You will be better able to assist in making decisions about sources and methods as you gain experience. The investigation plan should be amended as indicated by the attorney. At this time it should be made clear who is responsible for carrying out each step of the investigation, especially if the attorney regularly assumes some of this responsibility or if the office employs investigators.

ETHICAL AND RELATED CONSIDERATIONS

ETHICS: YOUR MORAL COMPASS

Investigation brings the paralegal into more contact with the public than at any other stage of litigation. The manner in which the paralegal approaches and conducts these contacts will reflect upon the reputation of the client, the firm, the paralegal, and the paralegal profession. If the contacts are thoughtful and ethical, the process will benefit the firm and help establish a responsive network of individuals who will be willing to help in future cases. Conversely, if the contacts are tactless and unethical, the consequences will be uncooperative witnesses, unsatisfactory information, a loss of confidence in the paralegal and the firm, and possible disciplinary action. Therefore, when investigating a case, keep in mind the following ethical considerations.

Be thorough in preparing and investigating a case, an important aspect of "competency" required in Rule 1.1 of the Model Rules of Professional Conduct. Similarly, be diligent and prompt to avoid the loss of important evidence (Rule 1.3). Exercise independent judgment so as not to become unduly influenced by the client or the client's directives to engage in unlawful or even unethical conduct. Know the limits to the scope of representation (Rule 1.2). Good investigation is essential for you to keep your client informed and able to make knowledgeable decisions (Rule 1.4). Seek all the evidence, both pro and con, and report your findings so the attorney can adequately advise the client—even if this includes information the client does not want to hear (Rule 2.1).

While investigating and researching, be aware of the attorney's as well as your own obligation to be candid with the court. Inform the attorney of any relevant evidence that is false or appears false; record all legal authority so the attorney can inform the court of clear opposing authority if the other side fails to present it; avoid inflating the importance of any evidence that might make the attorney appear to be presenting false statements to the court; correct false evidence presented to the court by informing the attorney; and in cases where there is only one side (ex parte), see to it that the attorney can present all material facts, both pro and con, to the court [Rules 3.3(a) and 3.3(d)].

Fairness to the opposition also is essential. Avoid any act that obstructs others' access to evidence or unlawfully alters, destroys, or conceals evidence [Rule 3.4(a)(b)]. It is also unethical to instruct a third person to refrain from speaking to or from giving information to the opposition unless the person is an employee or agent of the client [Rule 3.4(f)]. Paralegals can be involved in cases that attract public attention; in such circumstances and as a general rule, make no comments to the press. Attorneys may do so, but under strict guidelines (Rule 3.6). False statements to others on important facts are violations of the code [Rule 4.1(a)]. In some circumstances, there is a duty to speak up to prevent a client from committing fraud or a crime [Rule 4.4(b)]. If you are aware that your client is planning a fraudulent contract or agreement, the supervising attorney should be informed so remedial measures can be taken.

ETHICAL CONSIDERATIONS

We already know that attorneys have ethical responsibilities. Some of those responsibilities encompass truthfulness, candor, and honesty when dealing with clients and the public. How an attorney presents him- or herself is important. Most times clients seek attorneys with an expertise and reputation for skill in certain types of cases. Sometimes an attorney's connections can play a role in developing client relations. But, as we all know, holding oneself out as an expert in a field or having connections in an industry must be real. That minor point escaped an attorney in California who Photoshopped herself into pictures with numerous celebrities. Falsely advertising yourself by Photoshopping your image is sanctionable conduct—consider it evidence manipulation in the lowest form. In an opinion issued by the state bar of California in September 2014, the lawyer was sanctioned with a suspension for six months for misrepresenting herself on her firm's Facebook publicity page. Apparently, the attorney took photos of celebrities and overlayed her image into the photo. This act was deceptive and misleading to the public. Attorneys have ethical responsibilities to be honest and forthright in advertising themselves. Here, the attorney manipulated photographs through Photoshop; this act is akin to manipulating evidence by giving the public an impression of the attorney which is not so. Like evidence, advertising cannot be manipulative to give a false impression. Both situations present ethical issues and violations that are sanctionable conduct. The conduct of this attorney is a reminder of your ethical responsibilities and the repercussions of thinking that what you do, and how you do it, will not get noticed.

When speaking with others, always identify yourself as a paralegal from your firm or office so there can be no misunderstanding of your title or purpose. If the need arises to speak with a person who is represented by an attorney, speak with that person only with the permission of or through that person's attorney (Rule 4.2). If the person is not represented by an attorney, avoid implying your neutrality and correct any misunderstanding about whom you represent (Rule 4.3). Remember that you may not violate the rights of others (stealing a key document or harassing a potential witness, for example) or do anything for the purpose of embarrassment, delay, or to burden another (Rule 4.4). Keep in mind that to breach any of these ethical standards could subject your supervising attorney to disciplinary action, since the attorney is responsible for the ethical conformance of each employee (Rule 5.3).

Also, be aware of provisions of federal and state law that may come into play when conducting investigations. For example, the Fair Credit Reporting Act strictly governs and penalizes the request for and the unauthorized use of personal credit reports. Equally restrictive prohibitions are found in the Electronic Communications Privacy Act, the Health Insurance Portability and Accountability Act ("HIPAA"), and other federal and parallel state laws. Carefully reviewing the investigation plan with your attorney often flags such concerns.

ATTORNEY'S WORK PRODUCT (TRIAL PREPARATION MATERIALS): KNOWING WHEN IT APPLIES

Further, be aware of the law regarding an attorney's work product. Under Rule 26 of the Federal Rules of Civil Procedure and the rules of most states, a party may obtain from another party information that is relevant to the subject matter involved in the action. This information includes the existence, description, nature, custody, condition and location of any books, documents, or other tangible things, and the identity and whereabouts of persons having knowledge of disclosable matter. This exchange of information is called discovery.

attorney's work product (trial preparation materials)
The attorney's mental impressions, conclusions, opinions, or legal theories concerning a case; not discoverable.

Excepted from discovery under Rule 26(b)(3) are the mental impressions, conclusions, opinions, or legal theories of the attorney or the attorney's agent. Typically, this includes written or recorded notes, memoranda, interviews, and investigative and other reports. This exception is called the **attorney's work product (trial preparation materials)**. As a tactical measure, each party will try to protect as much material as possible from discovery while trying to discover as much as they can from the opponent. This concept was never more real than in *Rico v. Mitsubishi Motors, Inc.*, 42 Cal. 4th 807, 171 P.3d 1092, 68 Cal. Rptr. 3d 758 (2007).

CASE STUDY: UNDERSTANDING THE LAW

Rico deals with the inadvertent disclosure of an attorney's notes (considered attorney work-product) to opposing counsel and what the opposing counsel did with those notes. This case involves a fatal SUV rollover. At a deposition, the plaintiff's counsel (Rico) accidentally received a privileged document of the defense counsel's strategy and expert witness analysis. Although not marked as attorney work product, it was quite obvious that the document was not meant for opposing counsel and discoverable. However, believing that they had hit the jackpot, the plaintiff's counsel failed to disclose the receipt of the document and used its contents against the defense in a subsequent deposition. One of the members of the defense counsel team realized what had happened. Quick to react, the defense filed a motion to disqualify the plaintiff's counsel for failure to disclose to the defense counsel the receipt of the "obvious" privileged document. California has an ethical rule and procedure when mistakes like these occur. When an attorney inadvertently receives a document that upon closer examination is the attorney's work product, the receiving attorney must notify opposing counsel and return the document. Here, since the plaintiff's counsel wrongfully used the document, the court granted the defense counsel's motion to disqualify the plaintiff's attorneys from representing the plaintiff in the case.

Questions for Review: Read the *Rico* case. What was the basis of plaintiff's counsel's argument for using the document as part of discovery? In the court's reasoning, what case law did the court rely upon to reach its decision and why? Was the result in *Rico* fair and just? Support your response.

The primary concern is to recognize that the work product exception exists to prevent divulging information that should not or need not be disclosed. Attorney work product is further discussed in the context of discovery in Chapter 7.

REVEALING INFORMATION TO A WITNESS

It is possible for a witness or other source of information to turn the tables on the investigator by finding out more from the investigator than the investigator does from the source. Some investigators, especially novices, seem to feel that if they generously answer the questions of the other person, the other person will in turn generously answer their questions. This approach is unproductive and can lead to the revealing of confidential or undiscoverable information. Avoid this situation by stating that you are bound to preserve confidentiality and may not discuss what you know about the case. The majority of witnesses will accept this explanation with no effect on their willingness to participate.

GATHERING THE EVIDENCE

INTRODUCTION

When you have in mind an investigation plan as well as an awareness of ethical, evidentiary, and other considerations, it is time to gather the actual information. The three significant investigative procedures that will be emphasized in this section include gathering reports, records, and other documents; investigating the scene of the accident; and taking the statements of witnesses. Remember your investigative plan needs to be flexible as your needs change depending upon the type of case you are preparing. The focus of our investigative plan is the Forrester case—a negligence/personal injury case.

GATHERING REPORTS, RECORDS, AND OTHER DOCUMENTS

Medical Records

The investigation plan indicates that evidence needs to be gathered regarding the injuries of the plaintiff, including pain and suffering. A complete plan also would call for evidence of doctor and hospital bills. The task at hand is to gather that information. The most common method of verifying the plaintiff's injuries and bills is to request the medical records and doctors' reports describing the treatment rendered. Such records will not only help prove the plaintiff's case but also provide a well-documented record that will be useful in settling the case.

Records regarding the treatment of the plaintiff in Case I, Mrs. Forrester, can be obtained, typically, by writing to the medical records clerk or custodian of the hospital, in this case the Good Samaritan Hospital in Legalville, Columbia. As long as such requests are accompanied by the HIPAA-compliant authorization to release medical information executed by Mrs. Forrester at the time of her initial interview, there should be no difficulty in obtaining the desired information. The medical authorization must be current. If the authorization is not current, it will have to be reexecuted. If the patient about whom information is requested is dead, a minor, or otherwise incapacitated, the authorization must be signed by the executor or administrator of the patient's estate, the child's parent or guardian, or the incapacitated person's guardian or other legal representative. The defendant's paralegal can get these records, pursuant to HIPAA, in four ways: by obtaining (1) the patient's signed authorization through the plaintiff's attorney, (2) a judicial or administrative order, (3) a subpoena signed by a judge, or (4) a subpoena or discovery request with (a) assurances of notice to the patient with time to object, or (b) assurances that reasonable efforts have been made to get a qualified protective order (an order indicating how the records, once disclosed, will be protected). The methods for the defense to obtain medical records are discussed further in the context of discovery in Chapters 8 and 9. The state statutes on medical records should be consulted as well. HIPAA preempts relevant state law unless the state's provisions are more protective. Beyond the one set of records the patient is entitled to without cost, the hospital will charge a per page fee for the reports. In many jurisdictions, the medical records clerk or custodian is not required to send the records unless the fee is paid in advance. Most record requests are phrased as "any and all records" pertaining to the treatment for an injury occurring on a specific date; but it is preferable to mention specifically emergency room reports, outpatient reports, and the face sheet of the patient's chart (which contains good background information plus a physician diagnosis in some cases), since these records will not necessarily be automatically included in the response. The available records include:

- Physician's discharge summary
- Emergency room and outpatient reports
- Patient's chart
- History and physical information
- Reports from operating room
- Pathology reports
- X-ray reports (summary plus film impression)
- Lab reports (summary)
- Progress notes by physician or interns
- Doctors' orders to nurses regarding medication and other care
- Consulting physicians' reports
- Nurses' notes

The following records are not usually requested; however, they can prove useful in specific situations or in malpractice cases. Because these records technically belong to the hospital, a subpoena may be needed to obtain them.

- Incident reports (if previous records reflect a fall or other accident)
- Statistical reports (by physician, disease, type of patient, etc.)
- Departmental records (radiology, physical therapy, etc.)
- Committee minutes and reports (problems and solutions)
- Peer review (licensing and accreditation reports)

Prior to making a request for records, contact the records clerk or custodian (or designated privacy officer) to find out the fee and any particular rules or procedures that should be followed. The institution may insist that you use its authorization form. Draft a letter to the medical records clerk or custodian of the hospital, giving the full name, address, and date of birth of the person whose records are requested. The use of full Social Security numbers is now widely discouraged. Enclose the authorization for release of protected health information (HIPAA). Special authorization forms for release of psychotherapy notes and records for treatment and diagnosis of HIV and chemical dependency may be required. An example of a form letter adapted to Mrs. Forrester's case is included in Exhibit 3.8. An example of an Authorization to Release Protected Health Information form is shown in Exhibit 3.9.

EXHIBIT 3.8 Request for Medical Records (Cover Letter)

WHITE, WILSON & MCDUFF
ATTORNEYS AT LAW
FEDERAL PLAZA BUILDING, SUITE 700
THIRD AND MARKET STREETS
LEGALVILLE, COLUMBIA 00000
(111) 555-0000

Ms. Betty Noble
Director of Medical Records
Good Samaritan Hospital
4600 Church Street
Legalville, Columbia 00000

Re: Medical Records of Mrs. Ann Forrester
1533 Capitol Dr., Legalville, Columbia 00000
Birth date: 4/23/

Dear Ms. Noble:

The firm of White, Wilson, and McDuff has been retained to represent the above-named individual.

Enclosed is a current Authorization to Release Protected Health Information executed by our client. I request a copy of all of your medical records on Mrs. Forrester. The enclosed authorization includes all Health Insurance Portability and Accountability Act requirements (45 CFR §164.508) as indicated below.

Core Elements:
(i)   A specific and meaningful description of the information to be used or disclosed;
(ii)   Your name (or facility's name) identifying you as the person(s), or class of persons, authorized to make the requested disclosure;
(iii) The name of the attorney and law office identifying us as the person(s), or class of persons, to whom the covered entity may make the disclosure;
(iv)   A description of the purpose of the requested disclosure;
(v)   An expiration date or event (with statement that neither has occurred); and
(vi)   Signature of the patient and date (or signature of patient's personal representative and description of representative's authority to act for the individual).

Required Statements:
(i)   The patient's right to revoke the authorization in writing plus any exceptions to the right to revoke and how to revoke the authorization;
(ii)   The inability of you or your facility to condition treatment, payment, enrollment, or eligibility for benefits on the signing of this authorization; and
(iii) The potential for information disclosed pursuant to the authorization to be subject to redisclosure by the recipient and no longer be protected by the privacy regulations.

Miscellaneous Elements:
(i)   The authorization may not contain any material information that is false, and
(ii)   An authorization for psychotherapy notes may not be combined with other types of authorization.

[Add any other state-specific requirements, e.g. some state statutes or regulations require medical records (or one complete copy) to be provided free.]

On receipt of the records, our firm will submit reasonable payment for any preparation fee.
Thank you for your assistance.

Sincerely,

Terry Salyer
Paralegal

Enclosure: Authorization to Release Protected Health Information

EXHIBIT 3.9 Authorization to Disclose Protected Health Information: Plaintiff (HIPAA Compliant)

AUTHORIZATION TO DISCLOSE PROTECTED HEALTH INFORMATION

TO: (Health Care Provider/Address)
RE: (Client/DOB)

AUTHORIZED RECIPIENT: (Law Firm/Address) or its representatives.

RECORDS TO DISCLOSE [Pursuant to the Health Insurance Portability and Accountability Act, 45 CFR § 164.508 (and, where appropriate, cite any relevant state statute)]: ALL medical records including but not limited to: history, physical, dental, outpatient, inpatient, medication, laboratory, pathology, physical therapy and other rehabilitation, mental health, psychiatric (psychotherapy notes excepted), chemical dependency, HIV, billing, health insurance, Medicaid, and Medicare records; physician, nurse, progress, emergency and operating room orders, notes, and reports; discharge summary; and summary reports and films of X-rays, MRIs, and other scanning devices regarding my medical treatment rendered by you and all such information maintained in my medical file. [Although psychotherapy notes are not included in this request, please inform authorized recipient if such notes exist.]

PURPOSE: To authorize you to release all my medical information to my attorney for the purpose of civil litigation. You may rely on a photocopy of this authorization as if it were the original.

EXPIRATION: This authorization expires in [three years (or state date or event)] from the date of signature.

REVOCATION: I know I may revoke this authorization at any time by submitting a signed, written notice of revocation to the health care provider listed above and to my attorney.

REDISCLOSURE: I know the information disclosed pursuant to this authorization is subject to redisclosure by the authorized recipient and no longer protected under the Federal Privacy Rule.

FURTHER AUTHORIZATION: You are also authorized to speak confidentially with my law firm or any of its representatives and provide deposition and trial testimony.

CONDITIONS: I know treatment, payment, and enrollment or eligibility for benefits cannot be conditioned on whether I sign this authorization.

_____
[client signature]
[If personal representative,
sign and describe authority]

_____
[date]

Another source of valuable medical information is a narrative medical report prepared by the treating physician or physicians. A request for such a narrative is a simple matter, but not without pitfalls. Doctors may charge a substantial fee for such summaries, which frequently contain unneeded information. The better practice is to obtain the hospital records first, review them, and then request from the physician the specific information needed. Since the paralegal and the firm are likely to be working periodically with the physician and nurse or assistant, it is a good idea to develop a cordial relationship with them. Noting the name of the physician's nurse for

INTERNET EXERCISE

Using your jurisdiction, find out how to request medical records and draft the medical authorization form that conforms to your jurisdiction's legal requirements.

your file, for example, will expedite future contacts. Such connections can be helpful when gathering information.

When requesting information from a doctor, many paralegals use a standardized letter. Unfortunately, such a letter is likely to lead to a rather general or incomplete response. A letter to the doctor needs to be as specific as possible and based on detailed information gathered from the medical records and the complaints identified by the client. It is a good idea to confirm with the client each matter complained of to the doctor so the report will be complete. An example of such a letter appears in Exhibit 3.10. Occasionally a doctor needs a follow-up letter such as in Exhibit 3.11.

If the plaintiff has died, another report of value is the autopsy report, which represents the findings of the medical examiner or coroner on the cause of death and the medical evidence to support the conclusion. Such reports may be obtained through the office of the coroner or medical examiner. Funeral costs and related records should also be obtained.

Employment Records

Another area of importance to Mrs. Forrester's case is her loss in gross wages as a result of the accident. Such losses are recoverable and can make up an important part of a damage claim. That is why Mrs. Forrester was asked to execute the authorization for release of employment information at the initial interview. Send a copy of the authorization along with a request letter to the personnel office where Mrs. Forrester is employed. Remember that a person may have more than one employer or source of income. The letter should request a brief history of annual earnings, current salary or hourly wage, days of work missed since the accident, and overtime and bonuses missed. Request information on disability insurance to assist the client in meeting expenses.

If the client is self-employed, an average weekly gross income would have to be determined from the client's tax records or from the client's accountant. Keep in mind the following formula: average gross weekly income, less normal costs not incurred because of injury (such as the purchase or sale of goods, phone bills, and mileage), equals weekly amount claimed.

In serious injuries, or in the case of death, loss of future earnings is also an important component of damages. Inquiry should be made about labor contracts that dictate pay into the next several years; possible loss or reduction in fringe benefits; any schedule of eligibility for promotion, bonuses, overtime, stock options, and profit sharing; and other special considerations. In addition, it is wise to seek the assistance of a qualified vocational expert or economist (or both) to form a sound claim for future loss of earnings or to challenge such a claim. One source of assistance is the American Board of Vocational Experts.

Other Records

Other records or documents may be obtained on behalf of the client as long as the proper authorizations have been signed. Information from the federal as well as some state governments may be obtained through forms and procedures described in the particular Freedom of Information Act.

Check Documents

Check documents immediately. Regardless of what information is requested, you will need to ensure that the information received is correct and clear. Requests for

EXHIBIT 3.10 Request for Physician's Narrative Medical Summary

WHITE, WILSON & MCDUFF
ATTORNEYS AT LAW
FEDERAL PLAZA BUILDING, SUITE 700
THIRD AND MARKET STREETS
LEGALVILLE, COLUMBIA 00000
(111) 555-0000

Albert Meyer, M.D.
Medical Arts Building
4650 Church St.
Legalville, Columbia 00000

Re: Mrs. Ann Forrester, 1533 Capitol Drive, Legalville, Columbia 00000
Birthdate: 4/23/____

Dear Dr. Meyer:

Mrs. Forrester has retained this office to represent her regarding injuries sustained from being struck by a van on February 26, _____. Mrs. Forrester suffered multiple fractures of the pelvis and left leg, and also had spinal and internal injuries. As a result of these injuries, Mrs. Forrester is currently bound to a wheelchair and may not be able to return to work for some time.

To assist Mrs. Forrester, we would appreciate it if you would send us a report on the following:

1. Your diagnosis of Mrs. Forrester's mental, emotional, and physical injuries
2. Your opinion as to the cause of Mrs. Forrester's injuries
3. A description of the treatment given Mrs. Forrester
4. Likely degree of pain and discomfort related to such injuries
5. Mental, physical, and emotional limitations as they relate to employment, recreational activities, and enjoyment of life
6. Future treatment needed
7. Prognosis
8. Likelihood of Mrs. Forrester being able to return to work. If so, when?

In addition, please send an itemized bill for all your services related to these injuries.

The necessary authorization is enclosed. Upon receipt of your report, this office will promptly pay any preparation fee.

Please keep us informed regarding Mrs. Forrester's future visits to your office and any change in condition or prognosis.

Thank you for your cooperation.

Terry Salyer
Paralegal

Enclosed: Authorization to Release Protected Health Information

cc: Mrs. Ann Forrester

EXHIBIT 3.11 Request for Medical Update

WHITE, WILSON & McDUFF
ATTORNEYS AT LAW
FEDERAL PLAZA BUILDING, SUITE 700
THIRD AND MARKET STREETS
LEGALVILLE, COLUMBIA 00000
(111) 555-0000

Albert Meyer, M.D.
Medical Arts Building
4650 Church St.
Legalville, Columbia 00000

Re: Mrs. Ann Forrester, 1533 Capitol Drive, Legalville, Columbia 00000
Birthdate: 4/23/

Dear Dr. Meyer:

Your report of September 9, _____ on Mrs. Forrester was very helpful. Six months have passed since that report, and we need an update. Please provide us with detailed information on the following:

[List those points where specific elaboration is needed beyond the first request. Add a catchall question asking for information on any new or otherwise significant developments.]

Please include copies of itemized bills for your services to Mrs. Forrester since September 9. A copy of the appropriate authorization should be in your files.

Thank you again for your assistance.

Terry Salyer
Paralegal

cc: Mrs. Forrester

corrections or explanations should be made immediately where errors exist or information is unclear. It is also important to have a guide to reading medical records, a medical dictionary, or a guide to the vernacular of the particular subject area. Do not assume that these words are correctly used or that someone else in the office, particularly the attorney, will be able to decipher the language.

INVESTIGATING THE SCENE OF THE ACCIDENT

Viewing the scene of the accident or source of the claim at the time of the injury (or as soon thereafter as possible) is essential to sound investigation. Secondhand reports and photos are certainly useful, but they do not substitute for a personal visit to the scene.

Advance planning helps you spend your time at the scene more efficiently. A quick review of the information in the file including the summary of the client's interview and the elements of proof critical to the case helps focus attention on the most important facts. It also helps to anticipate the need of any special investigative tools.

Some typical tools are necessary for investigating the scene. A tablet is helpful for sketching out the scene and saving it electronically. Of course, standard tape measures and other measuring devices are helpful in evaluating the scene. For others who prefer a more traditional approach, a quad-ruled tracing paper pad and clipboard are useful for diagramming the scene of the accident. Tape measures of varying length and a walk-along, wheeled measuring device for longer distances are essential. A digital camera provides instant photo review and retakes, and easy importability into documents such as a settlement proposal. They also can be downloaded into a computer, iPad, or other electronic devices for easy future access. Modern smartphones offer an alternative to a digital camera, including videoing capabilities. Some still prefer video cameras, but the key point is to use what gets the job done. Your law firm will provide you with the tools and training to effectively master examination of an accident scene.

Other useful tools that conjure up visions of Sherlock Holmes include a flashlight, magnifying glass, stopwatch, protractor (for measuring angles), labeling tags, and various sizes of plastic bags (for storing evidence). Occasionally a specific type of case may require some other useful instruments.

A checklist form of things to note and record at the scene appears in Exhibit 3.12.

ACQUIRING THE STATEMENTS OF WITNESSES

Locating the Witnesses: Being a Detective

Locating witnesses as soon as possible is important to investigation. Memories fade quickly, making it difficult for witnesses to recall important details. Witnesses also tend to develop an attachment to the side that contacts them first, creating an impediment for the opposing investigator. Being first to the witness gives you an advantage. The following list contains ideas for locating witnesses:

- Ask the client, other known witnesses, the reporting police officer, emergency personnel, and so on.
- Review photographs for bystanders, license numbers, and other leads.
- Locate news reporters, camera operators, and freelance photographers.
- Visit the scene at the same time of day and week to locate persons who might routinely frequent the area (joggers, walkers, delivery personnel, school crossing guards).
- Canvass the immediate area for local residents and businesses, or farm workers in rural areas.
- Place an ad in the local newspaper with a photo of the accident, asking witnesses or people with information to call.

If only a photo of the person is available,

- Canvass the area asking people who are likely to know many people, such as local politicians and officials, police, bankers, or school officials.
- Place an ad with the photo requesting information.

EXHIBIT 3.12 Accident Scene Checklist

1. Nature of area: urban, rural, intersection, highway, school zone, other _____

2. Weather (if at scene soon enough to observe) _____

3. Other conditions: visibility _____

   road surface _____

   lanes _____

   curves _____

   grade _____

   speed limit _____

   other _____

4. Witness   Position to view accident   View, obstructions

   _____   _____   _____

   _____   _____   _____

   _____   _____   _____

5. Possible distractions that might cause inattention _____

6. Measurements of critical distances[a]

   skid marks _____

   road width _____

   distance vehicle traveled after impact _____

   distance from witness position to scene _____

   other _____

7. Traffic control

   signs _____

   lane markings _____

   other _____

8. Sun or other lighting conditions at time of day accident occurred

   from plaintiff's position _____

   from defendant's position _____

   from witness's position _____

   other _____

9. Temporary conditions

   construction _____

   parked vehicles _____

   other _____

10. Flow of traffic, same time of day, same day of week _____

[a] A handy formula for converting speed to distance (and vice versa) is mph $\times$ 1.5 = ft. per sec.

(continued)

EXHIBIT 3.12 Accident Scene Checklist (*continued*)

11. All possible causes of accident _____
    _____

12. Evidence of damage
    vehicles _____
    signs _____
    trees _____
    buildings _____
    other _____

13. Photograph and videotape important items noted above from different angles to show relevant conditions or defects such as a pothole in the street, uneven sidewalk, slippery spots, etc.

14. Carefully note pertinent directions (N, NE, E, SE, S, SW, W, NW) _____

15. Locations of other possible witnesses regularly at the scene
    homes _____
    businesses _____
    joggers _____
    dog walkers _____
    farm workers _____
    maintenance or public works people _____
    other _____

16. Other physical evidence relevant to case _____

17. Special needs
    expert to view scene _____
    professional photographer to capture lighting, angles (good source: International Council of Evidence Photographers) _____
    _____
    _____
    aerial photograph _____
    other _____

18. Carefully preserve evidence.

If only a name is available,

- Do a Google search or other search on the Internet.
- Use the telephone book, voter registration lists, or the city directory.
- Consult postal officials (you may need to use post office Freedom of Information form 1478 for forwarding address).
- Call contacts at utility companies and public service offices.

TRADE SECRETS: SOCIAL MEDIA, SOCIAL MEDIA, SOCIAL MEDIA

Who remembers a world without Facebook, Twitter, Instagram, and other forms of social media networking? Most people have Facebook pages, Twitter accounts, or visit or have posted videos on YouTube. Where does everyone post their personal information in some form on another—on social media Web sites. Therefore, when searching for information about someone, check social media. If you have a person's name or company, use a search engine, such as Google to do a search on that person or company. Chances are the person or company has a Facebook page that you can access for information. LinkedIn also is another great networking site for information about people and companies. The amount of information that can be discovered in a "click" is limitless and, often times, mind boggling. Stay abreast of the newest and current social media and networking trends, as the next "big thing" will provide you with your connection to valuable information.

- Check with local credit bureaus (you may find restrictions or conditions).
- Check with the motor vehicle and licensing bureau.

If only the name and occupation are available,

- Perform a Google search or other Internet engine search.
- Check social media sites for information about the person.
- Contact the personnel office of a likely employer (possible restrictions).
- Speak with coworkers.
- Seek information from the licensing agency if it is a regulated profession.
- Contact unions or trade associations.

If only the avocation or school is known,

- Contact sports leagues or hobby societies.
- Consult alumni groups.

See Exhibit 3.6 for good person and business locator Web sites.

If a witness is particularly critical and hard to locate, the office may have no choice but to hire a private investigation firm to locate the person.

Locating Expert Witnesses

Sometimes a case may involve the highly complex and technical principles of medicine, mechanics, engineering, electronics, or other fields. In such cases it may be necessary to locate an expert witness, not only to interpret information but also to translate it to a jury and to give an opinion relevant to the issues. The supervising attorney or the senior member of the firm will make the decision to hire an expert. The decision is an important one because hiring an expert can be expensive.

Nevertheless, it may fall to the paralegal to locate an expert. Some ways to locate an expert are as follows:

- Check with colleagues about experts used in previous cases and the office's list of experts.
- Ask the client about experts in the client's field, if relevant.

- Locate pertinent articles in professional journals or books on the topic and contact the authors (frequently considered experts in the field).

- Ask other firms who have had similar cases to recommend an expert they have used.

- Contact local or state bar associations for assistance through some of their specialized bar committees.

- Contact professional societies.

- Contact the applicable department or research facility at a college or university.

- Contact pertinent government agencies (local, state, and national) that often employ experts in a particular field.

- Check national legal newspapers, bar associations, and paralegal publications for advertisements by experts. Request references and names of former clients

- Check the expert Web sites in Exhibit 3.6.

Planning the Interview

Once the potential witness is located, it may be best to call the witness to see what information can be obtained. This step should be bypassed if the witness is evasive or seems likely to be so. If a personal visit is necessary to have the witness sign a written statement, the interview should be planned. The planning process and techniques are essentially the same as those for planning and conducting an interview with the client (see Chapter 2).

Determine the purpose of the interview. Determining the purpose of the interview is absolutely necessary. Some witnesses are interviewed to provide a broad look at events—the witness to the accident, for example. Other witnesses, such as the mechanic who checked the brakes on Mr. Hart's truck, will be interviewed to explore entirely different information, possibly with a narrow focus. Each witness is therefore sought out for a purpose, and that purpose should clearly dictate the extent and nature of preparation.

As an initial step in planning the interview, locate or develop any helpful forms and checklists. The law firm often has copies of such forms. These forms are designed to make sure the interviewer covers the essentials. Exhibit 3.13 is the Witness Information Cover Sheet to be filled out at the interview and used later for quick reference.

Exhibit 3.14, Checklist for Witness Interview, is easily adaptable to any personal injury case. It can be used as a guide during questioning and as a check to see that all significant items have been covered in the interview prior to drafting the written statement.

Develop the questionnaire. In addition to using this general questionnaire, the paralegal needs to take the planning stage further by developing questions that focus on the key issues of the case as they relate to elements and defenses in the case. For example, in Mrs. Forrester's case, some initial questions must be probed in detail with one key witness, Ms. Schnabel. Some of these questions for each of the key elements in negligence are as follows:

Element. *Duty (defined by conditions at the time).*

Issue. *Was ice a factor in determining degree of caution required?*

EXHIBIT 3.13 Witness Information Cover Sheet

1. _____ 2. _____ 3. _____
   Date   Interviewer   Place

4. _____ 5. _____ 6. _____
   Client   File No.   Type of Case

7. _____ 8. For Def._____ Plt. _____
   Full Name of Witness

Photo

9. Summary of Statement _____
   _____
   _____
   _____

10. Availability _____

BACKGROUND

11. _____ (_____)
    Address, City, County, State, Zip Code   Years at

12. _____ - _____ 13. Citizen (____) (____) 14. _____
    Home Phone   Work Phone   Yes   No   Nationality/Race

15. _____ 16. _____ 17. _____ 18. _____
    Date of Birth   Age   Sex   If Minor, Guardian's Name

19. _____ 20. _____
    Close Relative or Friend (Not Immediate Family)   Address/Phone

21. S ____ M ____ D ____ W ____ Other ____ 22. _____
                                                    Spouse's Full Name

23. _____ 24. _____ 25. _____
    Spouse's Address If Other Than 11.   Spouse's Place of Employment   Phone

EMPLOYMENT

26. _____
    Witness's Employer   Address   Job Title

27. Education: School/Address/Degree or Diploma/Date

    a. H.S _____

    b. Voc. _____

    c. Coll. _____

    d. Grad. _____

    e. Other _____

28. Experience as Witness (____) (____) _____ _____ _____
                           Yes   No   Date   Location   Type of Case

29. Ever been convicted of fraud, theft, or other dishonesty? Give details.

    _____
    _____

EXHIBIT 3.14 Checklist for Witness Interview

☐ 1. Complete Witness Information Cover Sheet.
☐ 2. Identify taker of statement, time, date, place.
☐ 3. Witness's activity just prior to accident: ☐ location ☐ time ☐ date
    ☐ witness's activity ☐ view of scene ☐ distance from scene
    ☐ obstruction ☐ location of plaintiff and defendant
    ☐ activity of plaintiff ☐ activity of defendant ☐ others present
    ☐ names ☐ their location ☐ activities
    ☐ other possible witnesses ☐ others in vehicle
    ☐ key issue questions
☐ 4. Setting at time of accident:
    ☐ time ☐ weather ☐ lighting conditions ☐ road conditions
    ☐ wind ☐ unforeseen obstructions (repair work, children, animals, fallen trees or rocks, etc.)
    ☐ dangerous conditions
    ☐ traffic flow ☐ speed limits ☐ traffic signs
    ☐ school zone ☐ intersection ☐ type of road ☐ hills
    ☐ curves ☐ shoulders ☐ any unusual or particularly notable activity of parties or others
    (recklessness, inattentiveness, evidence of influence of alcohol or drugs, etc.)
    ☐ speed of vehicles ☐ distance between plaintiff and defendant
    ☐ vehicle window obstructions ☐ other conditions of importance
    ☐ when witness's attention first drawn to plaintiff and defendant
    ☐ other key issue questions
☐ 5. The accident:
    ☐ time ☐ general description of sequence
    ☐ attempt to evade (sound horn, brake, head for shoulder, etc.)
    ☐ skidding ☐ sounds of contact
    ☐ detailed description of what happened to plaintiff and defendant (thrown from car, hit windshield, fell, etc.)
    ☐ detailed description of what happened to vehicles
    ☐ exact point of contact ☐ exact position of parties at time of contact ☐ position of other people ☐ opinion
    as to cause of accident
    ☐ diagram ☐ other key issue questions
☐ 6. Setting after accident:
    ☐ witness's description of scene (diagram)
    ☐ position of plaintiff and defendant ☐ position of vehicles
    ☐ injuries and damage (persons and property)
    ☐ description of sequence of events after accident
    ☐ time of arrival and activity of all emergency personnel
    ☐ care rendered at scene to injured ☐ other persons and witnesses present after accident, including reporters,
    photographers, investigators ☐ cleanup activities (name of tow truck)
    ☐ who, if anyone, made or recorded statements ☐ conversations overheard (parties, witnesses, emergency
    personnel, etc.)
    ☐ opinion as to truthfulness and character of parties and witnesses
    ☐ witness's record of character and honesty ☐ any conversation with any of the parties since accident about
    accident or injuries
    ☐ other key issue questions
☐ 7. Record statement and have witness read, sign, and date it.
☐ 8. Check to see if witness made statements about the accident to anyone else. If so, to whom and what kind (oral,
    written, recorded)?
☐ 9. Assess witness's abilities
    ☐ voice ☐ sincerity ☐ power of observation ☐ confidence
    ☐ appearance ☐ appreciation of importance of truthfulness
    ☐ recognition of evidence, persons, photos, etc. ☐ objectivity
    ☐ truthfulness ☐ vulnerability to impeachment
    ☐ willingness to testify ☐ availability for trial

Questions. Was ice on the road the morning of the accident? How much of the road near the scene and at the scene of the accident was covered by ice? Where was the ice? Had you experienced any difficulty on the ice yourself? Did your tires slip? Did you have control problems?

Element. Breach of duty.

Issue. Was Mr. Hart driving too fast under the icy conditions?

Questions. How fast were you driving? How fast do you normally drive at that point? How fast was Mr. Hart driving? From your observations, how did the ice affect or enter into the accident? In your opinion, was Mr. Hart driving too fast for the icy conditions? Explain the basis for your answer.

Element. Breach was proximate cause of injury.

Issue. Was Mr. Hart's speed under the icy conditions the cause of Mrs. Forrester's injuries?

Questions. In your opinion, what was the primary cause of the accident? Explain. Do you feel there were any other contributing causes? If so, what were they? Explain. Which cause was most significant? Explain.

This question-planning process should be followed for any issues that might prove pivotal in the success of the case. Other key factors in the *Forrester* case include speed related to obstructions caused by the hills, inattentiveness of pedestrian, position of pedestrian, reaction time of the driver, evidence of mechanical defects, and so on. Questions need to be planned to gather information on the key points of contention for each of the elements. This requires thorough preparation. Such preparation will help clarify the objectives of the particular interview and will make the interview much more valuable to the outcome of the case.

Determine the place of the interview. Another part of the planning process is deciding where the interview should take place. Occasionally a witness will agree to come to your office, but more than likely the interview will take place in the home, at the witness's place of employment, in a restaurant, in a car, or at the scene of the accident. Whenever possible the location should offer as much freedom from outside interruption and influence as possible. Witnesses should not be interviewed together, because one witness can influence or taint the statements of the other(s).

Assess other considerations. As in the initial interview, special problems or needs should be anticipated. Will you need a translator? Will you need a special setting for an interview with a child? Should you arrange for someone else to be present if the witness is likely to be hostile or accuse you of unethical behavior? Will the witness expect to be paid? (Expert witnesses expect to be paid.) Check the office for the local practice and appropriate fee. Be sure that the fee is approved before incurring the expense.

Conducting the Witness Interview

Because the personality and attitude of each witness can be quite different, there is probably no standard method of approaching a particular witness. You will have to draw upon experience, intuition, and common sense as the situation dictates. Some pointers are worth remembering, however. Courtesy should be of the first order. Calling ahead to arrange the interview is an important consideration. In circumstances such as in the case of a hostile witness when it may be better not to call, you should choose a time likely to be convenient to the witness. Make it clear to the witness who you are, your status, which party you represent, and your purpose. If the witness is a friend of your client, or simply neutral, introducing some information about your client that will evoke sympathy may encourage the witness to help you. Keep in mind, however, the ethical responsibility not to be misleading or deliberately dishonest and to preserve client confidentiality.

If witnesses are unwilling or hesitant to grant the interview, emphasize that you need their help and that it could be instrumental in bringing this matter to a quick, just, and less costly resolution. Cooperation now might reduce the time they would have to spend in the future. Also, delaying the interview may cause memory to fade, and valuable evidence will be lost. If this doesn't work, tell the witness that your firm can subpoena them to testify under oath, and it would be easier and more convenient to go ahead now than to do so under the subpoena. If this strategy fails, there is probably little choice but to withdraw and consider having them formally deposed, as discussed in Chapter 8.

A Witness Information Cover Sheet (see Exhibit 3.13) should be completed at the outset either in electronic or paper form depending on your preferences. This should be kept with the witness's statement. When organizing items for settlement or trial, you may refer to the cover sheet for a quick review of the witness and what he or she had to say.

The investigator's approach to the interview will depend on the witness. Some will want to tell you the entire story, while others will need regular questioning to focus their thoughts and to keep them on relevant information. Take notes, but listen carefully; do not be so concerned about your next question that you do not listen carefully to the answer to your last one. When you are not clear on a point, restate what the witness has said and ask if you have understood correctly. Be ready to employ the variety of interview techniques designed for the initial interview in Chapter 2. Do not try to compose a statement for the witness until you are sure that you know the information well.

The following are sections of an interview with Mrs. Forrester's neighbor, Ms. Schnabel. The purpose of this example is to illustrate an approach to setting up an interview, a sequence to follow, a way to elicit detailed facts instead of beliefs, and a method to implement aspects of the interview plan (most particularly the key issue questions).

Illustrative Interview: Case I

Setting Up the Interview

Setting: The doorstep of the witness's home (*I* stands for interviewer; *W* stands for witness).

I: *Good afternoon, Ms. Schnabel. I'm Terry Salyer, a paralegal with the law firm of White, Wilson and McDuff. I'm the one who spoke with you on the phone earlier this week. I appreciate your willingness to talk with us. As you know, we are trying to help Mrs. Forrester recover compensation for the terrible injuries inflicted on her in an accident last February.*

W: Well, I have been thinking about this, and my husband feels that I shouldn't get involved. We are terribly busy and I just don't have the time to be going to court. I'm really not sure how helpful I can be anyway. I'd like to help Mrs. Forrester, but I think I'd better stay out of it.

I: I can understand your concern, Ms. Schnabel, but one of the things we hope to accomplish in interviewing you is to get a better picture of what happened. It is likely that what you tell me could actually shorten this case, possibly make your testimony at a trial unnecessary, and allow for an early and just settlement of this matter. Frankly, it may be better for everyone involved in this incident, especially Ann Forrester, for you to tell us what you observed now, than to wait until months down the road when you might have to testify in court and you have forgotten much of what happened. I ask you to put yourself in Mrs. Forrester's place—if you were she, not only would you want the help, but you would need it. I'll make every effort to be as brief as my job will permit. May I come in?

W: Well, I guess so. My husband won't like it, but I'll do what I can.

I: Thank you. You have a lovely home.

W: Thank you. Please sit down.

I: I'll be asking you several questions about what you observed at the accident and then ask you to reconfirm what you said in a written statement. I have several background questions to ask you. [Follow the Checklist for Witness Interview, or use the checklist to make sure you have covered everything at the conclusion of the interview.]

Questions Regarding Witness's Activity Prior to Accident

I: Ms. Schnabel, do you remember the date on which the accident involving Mrs. Forrester occurred?

W: Yes, it was February 26, the day after my husband's birthday.

I: What were you doing that morning immediately prior to the accident?

W: I was driving my grandchildren to school.

I: What way did you go that morning?

W: I turned onto Highway 328 and headed toward town.

I: What direction would that be?

W: East.

I: What was the weather like that morning?

W: It was a cold, windy morning. I recall that the road was slippery. [It might be best to finish questions about the weather, and then go on to questions about it being slippery.]

Questions Regarding the Conditions at the Time of the Accident

I: Could you describe in more detail what you mean by "slippery"?

W: Yes, there were patches of ice on the road. I remember that my wheels spun when I turned onto the highway. I noticed several more slippery spots, so I drove quite slowly.

I: How far did you drive before you came to where you observed the accident?

W: Oh, about a quarter of a mile.

I: Were there other slippery spots on that quarter mile of road?

W: Yes, there were several.

I: What percentage of the road was slippery?

W: Oh, I'd say about 20 percent.

I: Was there ice on both sides of the road?

W: Yes.

Questions Regarding the Accident

I: Ms. Schnabel, would you please draw me a diagram of the accident location?

W: Yes.

I: Using the diagram, describe the sequence of events of the accident itself.

W: Ann Forrester was walking on the road toward her house. The van was coming down the hill in her direction. Suddenly, the back of the van began to swerve from side to side. Mrs. Forrester tried to get out of the way, but the van kept sliding into the middle of the road and hit her. Mrs. Forrester was thrown to the side of the road.

Using Follow-up Questions to Gain Greater Factual Detail

I: How close was the van to Mrs. Forrester when it started to skid and turn?

W: Pretty close.

I: Please state the distance in feet.

W: About thirty-five to forty feet.

I: What would you estimate to be the distance between your front window and your mailbox? [This gives an indication of the witness's judgment of distance. The actual distance can be measured later.]

W: *Around sixty to seventy feet.*

I: *Was there any observable attempt by the driver of the van to warn Mrs. Forrester or to avoid the accident?*

W: *Not that I recall.*

I: *Not even a sounding of the horn?*

W: *No.*

I: *Not any braking?*

W: *Well, yes. It sounded like the wheels locked on the van. There was some sliding and some skidding.*

I: *Describe those sounds, please.*

Probing Further for Details

I: *Could you see the driver of the van just before the accident?*

W: *Not really.*

I: *Were the windows of the van fogged over?*

W: *I really didn't notice.*

I: *How fast was the van going when you first saw it?*

W: *He seemed to be going pretty fast.*

I: *How fast was that?*

W: *Oh, I'd say about forty to forty-five miles per hour.*

I: *Help me understand how you arrived at that estimate.*

W: *Well, thirty years of driving for one thing, but also because the van came over the hill so quickly and seemed to cover the ground between it and Ann so fast, even after the driver tried to brake the van.*

I: *What was the distance between the van when you first saw it crest the hill and Mrs. Forrester?*

W *I'd say about one hundred feet—maybe a little more.*

I: *Did you see if Mrs. Forrester looked before she stepped onto the road?*

W: *No, she was already on the road when I came over the hill.*

I: *Where was Mrs. Forrester's attention directed when you first saw her?*

W: *I can't be certain, but she seemed to be looking at the road.*

I: *Please describe that in more detail.*

W: *She was looking down and straight ahead.*

I: *Was her head tucked into her coat collar?*

W: *I kind of recall her collar being up around her neck and ears—but I'm really not sure.*

(Note the absence of expressions such as "poor Mrs. Forrester" or "poor Ann," which might suggest a strong bias held by Ms. Schnabel, thus weakening the possible effectiveness of her testimony at trial.)

The remaining part of the interview concerns the witness's impression of the situation immediately after the accident. Here, a good investigator would concentrate on the witness's observation of injuries to either party, especially on any overt indications of pain and suffering endured by Mrs. Forrester. Prior to writing the statement, review the checklist to make sure all areas of the planned inquiry have been covered.

I: *Ms. Schnabel, is there anything else you would like to add? [This avoids accusations of restricting what the witness was allowed to say.]*

W: *Not that I can think of.*

I: *Ms. Schnabel, I will take what you have told me and draft a written statement for you to review and sign. This will take me a few minutes, so if you have something to do in the meantime, please go ahead and I will let you know when we are ready to resume.*

Drafting the Statement

The statement of a witness is taken for several reasons, as we have seen in other contexts. It tells the attorney what facts can be corroborated or refuted, which determines what the issues in the case will be and how good the evidence will be on those issues. More directly, the statement serves as a record of the witness's recollection of the facts, which can be used months and even years later to refresh the memory of the witness. It commits the witness to his or her story. It can also be used in cross-examination to impeach the testimony of a witness who later contradicts the earlier statement. Statements of opposing parties also can serve as admissions that can be used against them in court. In addition, if a statement is sufficiently convincing and corroborates key facts, it may help bring about an early settlement of the case.

APPLY YOUR KNOWLEDGE

What additional questions would you ask Ms. Schnabel? What pitfalls or concerns do you see from Ms. Schnabel's statement or observations?

There are several different ways to record a statement. One method is to have witnesses write their own statements and sign them. This process is inexpensive, but few witnesses are willing to do this, and if they are, the information often lacks factual detail. Another method is to have a court reporter (stenographer) accompany the paralegal and record the statement. This approach may be particularly helpful when interviewing an adverse party or witnesses partial to the opposition. It is not, however, recommended for witnesses favorable or partial to the client because any initial inaccuracies or misjudgments of the witness will be recorded prior to any corrections, making the witness appear uncertain. This method is also more expensive. Another method is to bring a neutral third party to hear the interview and sign the statement as a verification witness, or to record in a memorandum what the witness said, especially if the witness refuses to sign a statement. The advantage to these last two methods is that they provide a neutral third party to refute any statements by the witnesses that they did not read the statements, that the words in the statements are not their words, or that improprieties occurred. Without the neutral third party, the paralegal might have to testify to refute such an allegation. Unfortunately, the paralegal has a specific interest in the case and would probably not be viewed by the jury as a neutral witness. Sometimes it is best to have a reluctant or adverse witness sign a statement in the form of a sworn affidavit. These are harder to refute later.

The most common method involves interviewing the witness and drafting a statement for the witness to read and sign. In addition to these methods, statements may be taken by audio or video recorder or recorded over the telephone. Tape recordings or phone recordings should be conducted only with the full knowledge and permission of the witness and should be done so as to guarantee that the recordings are not subsequently tampered with or altered.

Tips for Taking and Drafting an Effective Statement

1. Visit the scene of the accident first to gain insights that will aid in taking a statement.

2. Note facts as opposed to beliefs ("twenty feet" as opposed to "too close").

3. Avoid references to automobile insurance; they can make the statement inadmissible.

4. Take statements from likely witnesses who say they didn't see anything; a change in their stories will subject them to impeachment.

5. Note, but do not include in the statement, the names of other witnesses. (The jury may wonder why some of these people are not called later at trial.)

6. Do not pay a witness for a statement without the attorney's approval. Fees for a statement are viewed skeptically by jurors, but reimbursement for expenses actually incurred by a witness, such as travel or missed work, is typical.

7. Do not probe further when you receive a favorable answer to a question, especially if the interview is witnessed by a court reporter or other third party. Further inquiry often reveals weaknesses or qualifications, which may impede a favorable settlement. (There are two schools of thought here. One says if you get what you need for settlement, stop. If you need more information later for trial, go back. The other school says get all the information you can at this point— even if it hurts. Ask your supervising attorney for guidance on this one.)

8. Do not give the witness a copy of the statement unless told to do so by the attorney. (It could fall into the opponent's hands.)

9. Use diagrams to aid the witness's explanations.

10. Avoid a witness's tendency to use qualifiers such as "I think," "maybe," and "could have," which weaken a favorable statement.

11. Draft the statement in the best light for the client without being misleading or inaccurate, or substituting the interviewer's vocabulary and grammar for that of the witness.

The statement should be drafted in the following sequence:

1. Begin with a background paragraph to identify the witness, address, date, time, marital status, occupation, and so on. If you use a form such as the Witness Information Cover Sheet, more detailed background is not necessary in the statement.

2. A second section should state the date of the accident, the setting prior to the accident, the witness's purpose in being there, and so on.

3. A third section should describe the sequence of events as observed by the witness (the accident or other occurrence).

4. A fourth section describes what happened following the accident.

5. Conclude with a brief statement to be signed: "I, _____, have read the above statement comprising _____ pages, and it is true to the best of my knowledge. I have initialed each page and sign this in the presence of _____ this _____ day of _____, _____."

If the witness is partial to the client and really wants to help, the statement could be drafted at the office and returned for signature at some later time. Otherwise, it is best to complete the process at the interview. Exhibit 3.15 is an example of a witness statement based upon the Forrester case.

The witness should then read the statement. Corrections should be made where needed, and the witness should indicate approval of the correction by initialing the correction. If a major change is required, or one that suggests uncertainty where you do not want uncertainty, the statement may need to be redrafted. This is where a laptop computer, tablet, or other portable electronic equipment is helpful; having a portable printer could be useful when taking a statement outside of the office. The witness should initial each page to verify that he or she has read each page, and then sign at the end of the statement. A third party also might sign to indicate that this is the witness's statement and was read and signed in the third party's presence.

Concluding the Interview

You might ask to take a photograph of the witness, which can be helpful in assessing the witness's impact on the jury and in recognizing the witness at a later time. Get a second phone number in case the witness moves or changes jobs. Most individuals have a cell phone number that normally does not change, so attempt to get that if possible and a personal e-mail address as well. Thank the witness for the assistance and leave a business card. Remind the witness to call you if he or she will be moving or will be gone for any extended period of time, or if additional information is recalled.

After the interview, review your interview notes and check the witness's statement for inaccuracies, typos, and leads that should be followed immediately. Make

EXHIBIT 3.15 Illustrative Statement

I am Freda C. Schnabel and I reside at Box 20, Route 328, Legalville, Columbia. I was born on May 16, _____, and am fifty-eight years of age. I am married, have three grown children, and am a housewife. I worked as a department store clerk for eight years.

On February 26, _____, about 7:35 a.m., I was driving my grandchildren to school. We went east on Highway 328. It was a cold, windy day and there were patches of ice along the road. About 20 percent of the highway was covered with ice. Because of the ice, I was driving twenty-five to thirty miles per hour. As we got to Forrester's house, I saw Mrs. Forrester crossing the road at a low spot in the highway. We were at a rise in the highway about 250 feet west of the spot where Mrs. Forrester was crossing. There is another rise in the highway a little more than 100 feet east from the same low spot. Until the car reaches the top of either rise, the driver cannot see the bottom of the low spot. There are other hills and low spots and some tricky curves on Highway 328 east of the point where the accident took place.

I started to slow down for Mrs. Forrester. A white van on the downslope east of Mrs. Forrester came on down the hill a ways. I'd estimate its speed to be about forty to forty-five miles per hour. It started to swerve from side to side. Mrs. Forrester hesitated, not knowing which way to go. She then headed for my lane, which was the south side of the road. I heard a few squeals of tires as the van veered toward the middle of the road. I heard a thud and saw Mrs. Forrester thrown to the side of the road where she landed like a sack of potatoes—very still and limp. The van kept veering left, crossed over my lane and hit a tree.

I pulled my car over to the side of the road near the van. The driver got out of the van. He was limping and had a cut on his forehead. Mrs. Forrester was lying face up. She kept screaming, "God help me, it hurts, oh, God, I'm dying, please help me." I told Mr. Forrester to call an ambulance and that I'd stay with his wife. Soon my grandchildren got some blankets to cover Mrs. Forrester. She was bleeding at her left side and leg. I remember her left foot pointing inward at an odd angle. The ambulance eventually arrived and took Mrs. Forrester and her husband. I offered to stay with the children.

I did get a chance to see the driver of the van a little later at the scene. He appeared tired—his face was pale; he had a five o'clock shadow; his voice was hoarse; and I noticed his clothes were wrinkled.

I, _____ have read the above statement comprising _____ pages and it is true to the best of my knowledge. I have initialed each page and sign this in the presence of Terry Salyer, this 3rd of September, _____.

note of the leads and enter them on your deadline calendar. Unpursued leads can be damaging to the case and embarrassing to the paralegal and the firm, especially if a settlement negotiation or trial is imminent and you realize that the lead should have been followed up months ago.

After reviewing your notes and the witness's statement, summarize the essence of the witness's statement in the appropriate place on the Witness Information Cover Sheet. Place the completed sheet and statement in the client's folder.

PRESERVING EVIDENCE

Learning to preserve evidence is essential for a good paralegal. Techniques for preserving evidence are examined in the following material.

PRESERVING ELECTRONIC EVIDENCE

Electronically stored evidence and, thus, its preservation are extremely important in many types of litigation. The unique nature of such evidence, including the ease with which it is generated, altered, erased, or otherwise corrupted, has created problems for the courts in determining what is good evidence and what should be done to sanction litigants who fail to preserve or, worse, deliberately destroy such evidence. Although the preservation of electronic evidence will be addressed further in discovery, a few words about it here are in order. Even at the initial investigative stage, the paralegal should know that a growing body of case law indicates:

- the duty to preserve electronic evidence commences when
    a. dictated by a specific statute, e.g. Internal Revenue Service and Occupational Safety and Health Administration requirements; or
    b. the party first knew or should have known that the evidence is potentially relevant to pending or future litigation; and
- once commenced, the duty requires a party to prevent the destruction or corruption of that evidence, e.g. implementing strict e-mail policies, suspending routine e-document destruction or alteration procedures, notifying all relevant employees of such a "freeze," and designating a party's employee to coordinate preservation procedures with counsel.

Further, be mindful that simply booting up and accessing data can alter electronic evidence. Therefore, an electronic data preservation (e-discovery) expert may need to be hired. Such a person can make uncorrupted copies of e-mails or other relevant evidence. Once the relevant data is copied, the computers can be put back into daily use. Subsequent to retrieval, the key to preserving the copied evidence is having a chain of custody of the evidence to assure a court and a jury that it is authentic and free from intentional or unintentional tampering. E-discovery experts often offer such chain of custody preservation services. Emerging federal and state rules of civil procedure increasingly govern the preservation of electronic information, particularly in regard to discovery.

IDENTIFICATION OF EVIDENCE: WHERE TO FIND IT AND HOW TO GET IT

Determining where to find and how to gather potential evidence in a case can be a challenge. Often times the type of incident will dictate when and how you receive evidence. For example in the Forrester case, investigators, from the police or even the fire department, normally would be called to the scene to document and investigate the circumstances of the incident. The police, for example, will probably question the parties involved and identify any potential witnesses of the accident. In this instance, timing is crucial for the police officer investigating the accident, especially when weather changes and cleanup of the site begins. Similarly, when injuries occur, such as in the Forrester case, memories are hazy and emotions run high. This may cause confusion and impact how evidence is preserved. Therefore, one of the most important steps for a police officer or investigator arriving at the scene of an accident or incident is to preserve the scene as quickly and completely as possible.

One method of preserving the scene is to cordon off the scene or set barriers to the scene. Having photographs and sketches of the scene assists in documenting the incident as it appears at the time of the occurrence. Usually, police will make diagrams of a car accident, for example, and take statements of the parties involved, if possible, or potential witnesses. In those situations where the police determine that the incident does not involve criminal activity, the scene will be released allowing investigators, such as insurance investigators, to examine and review the scene as needed.

Remember, it is highly likely that either the paralegal or private investigator will be viewing the scene after the occurrence of the incident. That means the scenes will have changed, items moved, and evidence removed or destroyed. Ultimately, the evidence from the initial investigating agency, such as the police or fire department, will be important to your preparation of the case. Reports, diagrams, and photographs can be obtained from the investigating agency. These documents are helpful in building the case and verifying the accuracy of the information received from the client and other sources. Note that documents, whether from a government or private agency, usually have charges associated with their production. Be sure the expenses, if any, are noted in the client's case file as discussed in Chapter 1. When challenges in acquiring documentation occur, **subpoenas** may be an alternative, but usually are through a legal process.

subpoenas

A document that commands or orders a person to appear in court or a designated place, which may include a request for documents.

Sketches of the scene may be a helpful tool. These assist in identifying the details of the place where the incident or accident occurred. Sketches can be hand drawn or electronically developed, such as on a tablet. Keeping abreast of new technological advances is important for the most current and up-to-date methods of investigation and identification.

Identification of potential evidence, whether physical, documentary, or otherwise, should take place at the earliest possible time. This will assist the paralegal or investigator in assessing known information relatively quickly. Obtaining information from public safety, fire departments, or emergency medical services and hospitals lead to important information about a case. These records can usually be obtained through authorization from the client or subpoena. Note that charges and fees are normally associated with these requests. Identifying evidence will invariably direct the paralegal or investigator to other information which will expand and advance your investigation.

PHYSICAL EVIDENCE: HOW TO PROPERLY ACQUIRE IT

Physical evidence is the tangible objects that are related to the case being investigated, whether in a civil or criminal context. Evidence such as a tire or a nail located in the tire is physical evidence. In any investigative context, taking physical custody of a piece of physical evidence often poses challenges and problems. The key to acquiring physical evidence is identifying a chain of custody.

CHAIN OF CUSTODY: ESTABLISHING A PROCESS

Civil cases generally have protocols covering preservation, collection, and possession of physical evidence, especially when there is potential for destruction, spoilage, or dissipation. Showing a process or link from discovering a physical piece of evidence to its introduction in court requires a chain of custody. Chain of custody is a continual link showing how evidence is acquired and transferred from person to person. If, for example in the Forrester case, the driver's glasses were found on the side of the road, the person investigating the case would show where the evidence was found, how it was preserved, by whom it was found and preserved, the methodology of the preservation, the identification of the evidence, and the process of safekeeping that evidence. This continuum shows the protocols, and more importantly shows that the evidence was not changed from the time it was discovered to the time it is, for example, introduced in a court case. What the chain of custody follows is the transfer of a piece of evidence from person to person in a specific form, which is recorded or embedded in a formal procedure.

Coupled with the chain of custody process is the collection process for the evidence. Evidence may be available, but deciding who is entitled to custody of the evidence may be a different issue altogether. Title of physical evidence may be questioned and taking possession of an object may not be proper or legal. Investigators should use proper judgment when determining whether to take possession of a piece of evidence. Although entertaining, this is not an episode of the "Good Wife" where Kalinda, the firm's ace investigator, manages to seize that critical piece of evidence surreptitiously finding the smoking gun and helping her team of lawyers win yet another case. Collection of evidence has a process and must be followed based on your law firm's protocols.

When searching for evidence from a scene, seek permission to enter the premises if private, or even public property. Check to see if the property is still subject to investigation or any other restrictions. And, above all, do not disturb the scene where the investigation is taking place.

The extent of your investigative tasks as a paralegal depend entirely on your law firm or employer. More often than not, training will be required to teach the proper procedures and protocols for identification, collection, and storage of evidence. Cases can be won or lost on how investigations are conducted. A sloppy investigation or careless handling of a client's case may result not only in a loss but may have ethical and professional responsibilities.

STORAGE AND THE SPOILAGE PROBLEM

Storing a physical object properly is critical once it is in the attorney's or investigator's possession. Similar to chain of custody, protocols for review of stored evidence are essential to preserving the integrity of the object as well as the process. Often times, law firms have policies, similar to those introduced in Chapter 1, for the review of physical evidence in a case. Learn the procedures your firm requires and follow them.

One of the issues that arises when storing evidence revolves around its physical integrity. Over time objects deteriorate and change character. Sometimes these changes can be controlled by environment, other times not. The point for evidentiary preservation is to take all precautions to preserve physical evidence in the form it was received. When changes or alterations occur, intentional or not, this is referred to as "spoilage or spoliation." Spoilage of evidence can occur when evidence is not properly stored, negligently handled, or materially altered. Courts do not look favorably when evidence is spoiled resulting in sanctions, ranging from fines to exclusion of the evidence at trial. Therefore, care should be taken when storing and preserving evidence to minimize any possibility of spoilage in a case (Exhibit 3.16).

EXHIBIT 3.16 Evidence Log

Evidence Log		
Case:	Event:	
Evidence:		
How Acquired:	Date:	
	By:	
Identifying Marks:		
By: _____ Date: _____		
Storage Location:		

Custodian	Date	Released To	Date/Purpose

CONTROL AND RETRIEVAL OF THE EVIDENCE

Once evidence is identified and acquired in a case, there should be a system of assurance that the item is the item that was obtained in the investigation. To assure integrity in the system, the investigator often places on the physical evidence unique markings or identification to show that the object is the same object that was retrieved and taken into custody. Together with the object's markings, the investigator will document through a record the process and procedures followed when logging in and taking custody of the evidence. The reasoning behind this process is that it is important to show who had control of the evidence from its receipt until its ultimate presentation at trial. Just like you see on television or when streaming your favorite episodes of CSI, investigators carry forensic kits which provide tools for preserving and identifying evidence for later use. Common components in evidence kits are paper tags, plastic or opaque bags, marking pens, and other objects that assist investigators in identifying and preserving the integrity of the evidence. The key to preservation of evidence is the control procedures and the retrieval process used. If the process is properly performed, it will link evidence to critical facts which will lead to relevant and admissible evidence in a client's case.

As a paralegal, you should be mindful of the processes discussed in this chapter and the importance of your role. When trial dates approach, you should have a plan as to your preparation, which will include checking the evidence that will be used in the case. Do not wait until the last minute to check on the evidence. Any issues that may need attention should be addressed well in advance of trial. You do not want to check evidence a few days before trial only to learn that it has disappeared or is in a substantially different state than when it was originally received. Part of your plan for control and retrieval of physical evidence is to periodically check on its condition. This strategy will mimimize last-minute problems or, at least, provide sufficient time to address them.

Original documents should always be preserved. A common method of preservation is to place the document in an envelope, then label it with a description of the contents and its source, the date of the document, and any other pertinent information. Be sure you sufficiently identify the document on the outer portion of the envelope to avoid confusion later. Most cases present a lot of documents, so staying organized and differentiating documents is important. DO NOT WRITE ON OR ALTER AN ORIGINAL DOCUMENT. This could cause the document to be inadmissible in the case. Therefore, you should always make a working copy of a document to make notes and comments on. Stamping the document as a copy is the prudent course of action and avoids confusion between the original and copy.

TESTING AND EXAMINATION

Often times legal theories are tested through the examination of evidence. It is not unusual in a case for evidence to be examined or tested, which could destroy the original evidence. In those types of situations, the testing of the evidence is in a controlled setting where all parties to the case have representatives present or are in agreement with the process for testing the evidence. For example, evidence may be sent to a laboratory for determination of chemical components in a fire, or fluid samples can be sent to a laboratory to determine whether someone was under the influence of a drug when an accident occurred. There are many reasons to test evidence, but the critical element is the process and that it is free from taint.

In a case, the investigator, attorneys, or paralegals could be responsible for testing of evidence. No matter who is responsible, steps will be taken to preserve the chain of custody and the integrity of the process.

To ensure the process remains reliable, it may be documented through video or other recording devices. All persons who participate in the process of testing or examining the evidence should be identified by name and representation in the process. If experts are involved, they should be included in the identification process as well. Documenting the process of testing or examination, especially when evidence is disassembled or its components destroyed, is important as failure to do so could result in the exclusion of the evidence or the results of the testing at trial—or if done in violation of the rules of procedure could result in sanctions by the court.

A WORD ABOUT SURVEILLANCE AND ACTIVITY CHECKS

Recall the movie *Unfaithful*, where Diane Lane's character, Connie Sumner, begins an affair with Olivier Martinez's character, Paul Martel. Eventually, Richard Gere's character, Edward Sumner, suspects his wife's infidelities and hires a private investigator to verify his suspicions. Just as in the movies, verifying a person's activities and whereabouts may be necessary in the course of litigation. Surveillance becomes necessary when a claimant in a lawsuit "claims" injuries, but in reality it is a ruse. For example, a person in a car accident claims severe back injuries and cannot lift objects over 10 lbs. or has difficulty walking. An investigator doing surveillance can document the activities of the claimant to determine the truthfulness of the claim. If the investigator catches the claimant lifting his or her children and playing with them, then the surveillance, and in turn, your law firm, will expose their case. Surveillance should be conducted by the trained professional. They have the proper equipment, know the rules of law, and know how to preserve the information.

In addition to personal injury cases, domestic disputes, such as divorce and custody cases, present situations where surveillance may be required. Surveillance may result in discovering a cheating spouse or the fitness of a parent. Again, the use of a trained professional is critical.

Another type of surveillance is activity checks on individuals. These types of checks are a bit less formal and often are conducted by physically visiting places where a claimant or potential plaintiff frequents. These checks can be done in the place where the claimant or plaintiff lives or works. These activity checks aid in learning more about others' observations of the individuals making claims. Such checks can result in valuable information that will assist in developing a case.

DOCUMENTARY AND DEMONSTRATIVE EVIDENCE

Documentary evidence generally includes written or recorded information. Typically documentary evidence consists of letters, contracts, deeds, photographs, and virtually any piece of paper that is related to a case. It is one of the most common and important pieces of evidence when preparing and investigating a case. Identifying and preserving any documentary evidence that is located is critical in the development of any case. As will be discussed in later chapters, understanding the rules of evidence is important when documentary evidence is located as those rules will determine whether evidence is admissible or relevant. Issues such as preserving the original for trial and using copies are important considerations in the investigative process. Know how your document was acquired and who can authenticate the document. Do not underestimate the power of documentary evidence as it can be the centerpiece of many case disputes. Think of a case involving a contract dispute. Probably the most critical piece of information is the contract document itself. Or, in a dispute between family members over a will or trust, the central piece of evidence involves a document. Be sure you follow your procedures to preserve and identify documentary evidence, as loss or destruction of documents could adversely affect a case.

As important as documentary evidence is demonstrative evidence. Think of it as a visual aide—an illustration. Demonstrative evidence takes many forms and can be sketches, drawings, diagrams, simulations, models, or other formulations. The form must be a fair and accurate representation of what is being depicted. For example, in a personal injury case, a model may be created of a part of the human body to assist the jury or judge in understanding complex medical information. As part of creating demonstrative evidence, the person or firm that created the model should be present at trial so that they can testify as to how the model or evidence was created. No matter the form of the demonstrative evidence, authentication of how it was created and by whom is critical to its admissibility. That does not mean that all demonstrative evidence will go unchallenged by opposing counsel, however.

APPLY YOUR KNOWLEDGE

Find examples of demonstrative evidence from your favorite movies. Examples of movies are *My Cousin Vinny*, *Erin Brockovich*, and *Reversal of Fortune*.

More and more demonstrative evidence is computer generated. However, this often poses authentication issues and challenges by opposing counsel of their usage. Verify in your jurisdiction the rules for using computer generated demonstrative evidence. Admissibility varies from state to state.

Photography

Gone are the days of traditional film cameras. Today we are in the digital age where photographs are taken from digital cameras. Sure, some still use the traditional 35 mm camera, but this is now uncommon. Consequently, as you may guess, use of digital photography is both a blessing and a curse. Immediate view of a photograph is possible, but with that comes potentially immediate alteration of the photograph as well.

To ensure accuracy and credibility to photographs, law firms often employ experts or experienced investigators to photograph scenes or information for a case. The professionals know what is needed for a photograph to be admissible and therefore have strict methodologies for the taking of photographs. These methodologies include preparing a detailed photo log identifying the procedures used in shooting the photograph. Such information about the photograph includes the date, time, place, type of camera, and whether any enhancements, such as lightening, were used. The photo log not only assists the photographer in remembering the details of the shoot but also sets the foundation for any testimony that may be required at trial for the photograph's admissibility.

Consideration of the purpose of the photographs is important. What are you trying to convey or accomplish? Are the pictures for the purpose of showing the accident scene, such as tire marks, signage, and general conditions? Are the pictures showing the injuries sustained and the extent of those injuries? Will photographs of the blood from a scene or bruises convey the pain and suffering of a party? These considerations are important in determining the evidentiary value of photographs and who should be taking the photographs. Note that it is best as a paralegal to refrain from taking pictures, as then you may be called as a witness in a case. Better to leave the photography to the professionals.

Another consideration for photographs are the various sources that take pictures as part of their job responsibilities. Police and fire departments capture scenes they are called to investigate. The coroner's office preserves evidence by taking pictures as well. Don't forget to consider newspaper and freelance photographers when gathering pictures; the bigger and highly publicized the event the higher likelihood there are photographs of the incident. Sometimes neighbors will snap shots of an incident that produce valuable photographs for a case.

Google Earth and Other Independent Sources

Sometimes aerial views of a scene are necessary and helpful in preparing a case. Professional photographers can be hired, but one Internet source that provides geographical imagery is Google Earth. This site provides maps and other geographical information for virtually anywhere on earth through satellite imagery. Through Google Earth, accessing a street or intersection is possible, which can illustrate important information for a case. Other sources for geographical images are the U.S. Coast Guard, U.S. Geological Survey, U.S. Department of Agriculture, and the U.S. Department of Interior. These agencies map areas and have ground and aerial photographs which may be helpful. Do not forget local agencies from cities and counties. Zoning and planning boards can be an excellent source of area photographs. Although acquiring photographs from agencies is not free, the cost is nominal and is well worth exploring as an alternative to hiring a private photographer. Regardless of whether a government agency or private photographer is used, always consult your supervising attorney for guidance as to how to proceed on a case.

Destroying Photographs: Think before You Act

Preserving photographs prior to commencing a lawsuit is both an ethical and statutory obligation. When a incident occurs, there is a high likelihood that litigation will ensue. Any photograph resulting from the incident is potentially discoverable and should be preserved. This includes photographs that are favorable or unfavorable to your case. Those photographs taken either in anticipation of litigation or taken to memorialize the incident which one knew or should have known would be relevant to a case must be preserved. The result of destroying photographs could range from sanctions by the court to grievances filed to a bar association for ethical violations. The question is when does the duty to preserve photographs arise and under what circumstances. There are various signs or events that trigger the obligation. The obvious one is when a client hires your firm to represent them, the obligation to preserve attaches. When a letter is received by an opposing party of an intention to file litigation, the obligation generally exists. But, most importantly, whether to preserve or destroy photographs is a judgment for your supervising attorney. Always consult the attorney before making decisions that could be permanent in a case.

Chin v. Port Authority of New York & New Jersey, 685 F. 3d 135 (2nd Cir. 2012), is a recent illustration of what is required under the duty to preserve evidence, overruling a much cited 2010 New York District Court case, *The Pension Committee of the University of Montreal Pension Plan v. Banc of America Securities*, 685 F. Supp. 2d 456 (S.D.N.Y. 2010).

CASE STUDY: UNDERSTANDING THE LAW

Howard Chin was among 11 plaintiffs that filed a race discrimination action against the Port Authority of New York and New Jersey claiming that they were denied promotions because they were Asian. Relying on *The Pension Committee of the University of Montreal Pension Plan v. Banc of America Securities*, Chin and other plaintiffs wanted an adverse instruction to the jury in his case as a discovery sanction because the Port Authority failed to implement a document retention policy resulting in the destruction of approximately 32 promotion folders and evaluations containing information about his and the others' cases. Documents were apparently destroyed in the wake of the 9/11 attacks. The district court (lower court) denied Chin's motion, which he appealed to the Second Circuit Court of Appeals. Citing the decision in *Pension Committee*, Chin argued that Port Authority's failure to issue a litigation hold was gross negligence as it caused the destruction of potentially relevant evidence requiring the adverse instruction. The Second Circuit disagreed and declined to follow the decision in *Pension Committee*. (Remember a higher court does not have to follow the decision of a lower court.) In rendering its decision, the Second Circuit held that the failure to institute a "litigation hold" is not considered gross negligence by itself but is just one of the factors a court should consider in determining whether to issue discovery sanctions. The Court did not want to find that the failure to issue a litigation hold was "automatically" gross negligence as it considered it

(continued)

too inflexible a policy, especially in complex litigation cases. Also, the Court did not agree that a court *must* issue an adverse jury instruction when a finding of gross negligence is found. Rather, the Court determined that a court *may* find such an inference and was not required to do so. The final and most important result of the *Chin* case was that the Court did not want to set forth a hard and fast rule regarding litigation holds and evidence destruction, but opined that the district courts should evaluate such violations on a case-by-case basis giving the trial court judge discretion in determining the best course of action in a case. Although the *Chin* decision appears to be a relaxation of the absolute need to issue litigation holds in cases, it does not negate the obligation to preserve evidence in a case and issue litigation holds in cases.

Questions for Review: Review the pertinent sections of the *Chin* decision (focus your review on the document retention issue). What factors did the court consider in reaching its decision on whether to issue sanctions? Why did the Court rule that the district court did not abuse its discretion in denying sanctions? Under what circumstances would the *Chin* decision have a different result? Explain your response.

THE TREND: VIDEOGRAPHY

Videography is a useful method of investigation as well as surveillance. Video cameras come in all shapes and sizes, making it easier to document information about a client's case. They are useful in all type of cases showing, for example, scenes of any accident, the extent of injuries, or witness statements. As with any other type of evidence, the videographer must be able to authenticate the video process such as how the video was acquired, the type of equipment used and date and time of filming. This is important for evidentiary and admissibility purposes at trial.

Videography also is helpful to illustrate a person's daily routine, especially in personal injury cases. These videos are known as "day-in-the-life" videos. The video can illustrate what the plaintiff's life is like since sustaining injuries and show the changes in the daily routine, for example. This is a good method for showing the pain and suffering of a plaintiff which relates directly to the damages aspect of a case. Day-in-the-life videos are effective courtroom tools for the jury and often can lead to settlement discussions as they show the real-life effects, as painful and difficult as they may be to view, of the injuries and changes in a person's life. As suggested throughout this chapter, videoing a scene, incident, or person is best reserved for the professional videographer who has the equipment and know-how to present the situation. You do not want to have a shaky or misdirected video, which can detract from the objective of the video itself. Professionals also understand the importance of authentication of the process used in procuring the video. Therefore, leave the videoing to the professional for the most effective results.

PRESERVATION OF ELECTRONIC AND TRADITIONAL EVIDENCE

Gathering and preserving evidence can be tricky business. Knowing how to preserve and maintain the integrity of the evidence gathered is an important element in the investigation and discovery process. Each piece of evidence collected requires preservation—some having unique characteristics that are beyond sliding a document in an envelope.

Electronic Evidence

Electronic evidence is critical to save when a case is started or when one "reasonably anticipates" litigation. Most firms or businesses have e-mail deletion policies and document destruction policies. When litigation commences or is anticipated, any electronic device which may have potential evidence must be preserved. This preservation is usually accomplished by the firm or business issuing a notice to place a hold on any destruction or deletion activities. Any electronic device is subject to the destruction hold, including such electronic communications as e-mails, texts, voice mails, computers, tablets, smartphones, or any other type of communication device where electronic information may be stored. Usually, most businesses or law firms will follow up this hold procedure with a litigation hold letter. This letter places all on notice that any evidence related to the relevant case should not be destroyed or deleted and any related policies will be automatically suspended. When transmitting the litigation hold letter the best practice is to have (1) verification that the letter was sent out, (2) a list to whom the letter was sent, and (3) a form of receipt from the recipient of the notice letter, such as e-mail verification or certified mail delivery. Additionally, any electronic evidence should be properly stored in cool safe places. Computer disks and video-audiotapes can be damaged from environmental factors. Watch out for destruction of information from exposure to magnetic fields and simple everyday actions such as spilling coffee or drinks.

Physical, Photographic, and Documentary Evidence

Safeguarding physical and documentary evidence can be achieved in a number of ways. Place physical evidence in dry, cool places where there is a consistent temperature. Segregate the physical evidence in a case from other cases when possible. Mixing evidence with other cases is possible if an organized procedure is not followed. Remember that chain of custody issues are important as previously discussed in the chapter; that means keeping a log of who views evidence, with the time and date clearly marked on the log. Similarly, preserve photographic and documentary evidence in either an envelope or transparent slip. Photographs and documents tend to fade in time and care should be taken in their preservation. As with physical evidence, photographs should be stored individually in cool dry places. Humidity could damage pictures such as causing them to fade or get sticky, affecting the integrity of the photograph. Paralegals often are the "keepers" of the evidence and knowing how to properly store different types of evidence is essential. When in doubt as to firm policy on storing evidence or how to store particular types of evidence, ask your supervising attorney; if evidence is particularly unique or sensitive, check manuals or the Internet on how to store and guard against deterioration of particular types of evidence.

CONTINUING OBLIGATION TO INVESTIGATE AND DISCOVER

The investigative process and evidence gathering does not stop when a case is filed. As the case facts unfold, new facts and information develop which will involve further examination by the paralegal and attorney. The obligation to investigate is a continuing one in the litigation process requiring the paralegal and attorney to delve deeper into the case, gathering information that not only benefits or exposes weaknesses in a client's case but also requires providing information to the opposing party in a

TECHNOLOGY UPDATE: THE BLESSING AND CURSE OF PHOTOSHOP

Most of us have heard about Photoshop™. It is a software program that allows the manipulation and editing of photographs—usually with positive results. Its uses range from restoring old or damaged photographs to changing color and composition. Sounds like a great thing and it is. The question is, how does Photoshop affect evidence and how do you know what is real and what is artificially created? The rules of evidence require that photographic evidence must be authenticated as real. With today's technology, that process becomes increasingly more difficult. Photoshop and similar software are so advanced that most people cannot detect changes in a photograph. There are those that can determine a digitally altered photograph from the real thing. Trained experts look for obvious changes such as shadows, halos, and reflections in the photograph. But that is stating the obvious. Experts can examine a photograph more deeply for hints of manipulation through metadata, image cloning, and pixel repetition contained within photographs. Some irregularities the naked eye can spot; others must be identified through software programs that detect the changes. In today's digital world, authentication of photographs is a real issue—one that you will face as a paralegal. Stay current on the technology developments in photo-manipulation software and be aware of photographic deception. A picture evidences the person, place, or thing photographed, but this notion is being challenged in the digital age.

case under the rules of civil procedure. Investigation and evidence gathering assists the attorney in evaluating a client's case and prepares for more formal types of discovery such as depositions and other discovery requests, which are discussed in later chapters. A thorough plan of investigation eliminates the guess work in a case with preparation being the key to representing the client in the best possible way. If you are properly doing your work, you will know all the intimate facts and legal issues of a client's case and know best how to assist the client, along with your law firm, in navigating the complex litigation process. Remember, surprises should only occur in television and movies.

Once the initial investigation and gathering of evidence has commenced, reporting back to your supervising attorney is advised. Preparing a memorandum memorializing your findings and progress is appropriate. Affix the memorandum to the client's file with the pertinent documentary evidence included. This will give your attorney an opportunity to evaluate the client's case and determine the next steps in the process. The next steps could range from filing a lawsuit to pursuing settlement options (discussed in Chapter 10). Your hard work is invaluable to both the client and supervising attorney in determining the best course of action on behalf of the client's case.

SUMMARY

Because a lot of material is covered in this chapter, note the material that is clearly reference material so you can find it in the future as needed. Focus on those concepts and terms that are significant and will be helpful when you are not next to your office computer nor in a law library—when you are talking with a client or out in the field gathering evidence, for example. The study questions at the end of this chapter will help identify most, but not all, of this material.

The purposes of investigation can be summed up as the need to provide your client with the knowledge to make informed decisions and to provide your attorney with the best available evidence to assess and hopefully win the case. Investigation of any type is not likely to be effective, however, without a good grasp of the rules of evidence, what is admissible and what is not, as set out in both the state and federal rules. Generally, evidence must be relevant, which means it must be material and tend to prove or refute a fact of consequence. But even relevant evidence may not be admissible because of its prejudicial or detrimental nature. Unreliable evidence such as hearsay is excluded except when its source or nature suggests reliability.

Understanding the rules of evidence helps you develop a plan for investigation, from understanding the elements of the law that must be proved or refuted to developing a list of likely sources for obtaining information. Learning your ethical responsibilities is extremely important in giving you a mooring in safe harbor at troubling moments. In investigation, a paralegal needs to be thorough, prompt, objective, and honest; must avoid falsehoods, misrepresentations, and the revealing of attorney-client privileged information; and must remain independent in professional responsibility. To do otherwise can jeopardize the case and the attorney's and paralegal's reputations. Consult your supervising attorney before conducting any investigation.

Gathering the evidence requires a knowledge of where to look, the most efficient methods and technologies, and the relationship between the economics of the case and the cost of the investigation. Interviewing witnesses is a critical part of this process and requires diligence, planning, and tact. Drafting a good statement that is an accurate reflection of the witness's point of view is an art that improves with practice.

Finding all the evidence in the world is of little value if you do not know how to preserve it. This can be done by diagramming, photographing, storing, testing, and properly inventorying all evidence. Evaluate the evidence and report to the attorney on what has been gathered so decisions about filing or defending a lawsuit can be made.

KEY TERMS

admissible evidence	demonstrative evidence	probative value of evidence
affirmative defense	direct evidence	proof beyond reasonable doubt
attorney's work product (trial preparation materials)	discovery	
	documentary evidence	real evidence
best evidence rule	habit	relevant
burden of proof	judicial notice	res gestae statement
chain of custody	material	routine
circumstantial evidence	physical evidence	stipulation
clear and convincing evidence	preponderance of the evidence	subpoena
declarant	presumption	testimonial evidence

QUESTIONS FOR STUDY AND REVIEW

1. Why does an investigator need to understand the relationship between investigation and evidence law?

2. Define and give examples of testimonial, documentary, real, and demonstrative evidence.

3. What is relevant evidence and when will relevant evidence not be admissible?

4. What are the rules of evidence (for federal and for your state) governing the following areas?

Character	Hearsay
Habit or routine	Physical evidence
Privilege	Authentications
Requirement of witness to testify	Best evidence
Admission of party opponent	Judicial notice
Lay opinions	Reputation for truthfulness
Expert opinion	Past sexual conduct and past sexual crimes

5. Define *preponderance of evidence* and *clear and convincing evidence.*

6. What are the six stages in planning an investigation?

7. What information should go into a written investigation plan?

8. Discuss the major ethical and related concerns (including attorney's work product) that are particularly applicable to investigation.

9. What procedures should be followed in investigating the scene of an accident?

10. List some good techniques for finding a witness and for finding an expert witness.

11. Why is it important to interview a witness as soon as possible after the accident?

12. Why are the elements of a cause of action important to planning an interview?

13. Describe useful techniques in interviewing a witness (review the appropriate section of Chapter 2). How does an interviewer gain the cooperation of a witness?

14. What are the purposes of taking a statement and why should a paralegal review a statement immediately after it has been taken?

15. Describe the purpose of preserving evidence and some good techniques for preserving evidence.

SYSTEMS FOLDER ASSIGNMENTS

1. Place a reference note in your systems folder, including page numbers, to the techniques for conducting a witness interview stated in this chapter; draft your own list of tips for taking and drafting an effective witness statement and place it in your systems folder.

2. Identify in your systems folder some of the techniques for locating witnesses and experts listed in this chapter.

3. Draft a detailed checklist for preserving evidence and file it in your systems folder.

4. Sketch the Forrester accident scene from the viewpoint of Ms. Schnabel.

5. Summarize Ms. Schnabel's statement to be included on the Witness Information Cover Sheet for the case file.

APPLICATION ASSIGNMENTS

1. The following is a list of possible evidence in Case I, the Forrester case. Based on your understanding of the necessary elements in a negligence case from Chapter 2, the information in this chapter, and the rules of evidence for both the federal (F) and your state courts (S), indicate whether the listed items of evidence are admissible (A) or inadmissible (I). State any applicable reason and rule number.

Evidence	Fed	State	Reason	Rule(s)
Witness: "Mr. Hart is a good baseball player."	I	I	irrelevant	F401 S
1. Witness: "Mr. Hart smelled of beer."				
2. Bloody video of Mrs. Forrester's hip repair				
3. Routine practice of Mercury to check all brakes of vehicles				
4. Forrester's offer to Mercury to settle for $50,000				
5. Hart told wife he was too tired to be driving				
6. Forrester's letter to friend stating she didn't look for traffic				
7. Doctor's testimony that van caused Forrester's injuries				
8. Testimony from Hart's minister that Hart is honest				
9. Witness at scene: "That van driver didn't even try to stop."				
10. Mercury vehicle service log				

2. Citing the relevant Model Rules of Professional Conduct, what should you do under the following circumstances?

   a. Your firm is representing a federal judge in a civil suit. You have come to admire this judge and know that the firm believes he is a very valuable client. One night you are working with the judge on his case. There is a letter in the file that the judge received from a third party. The judge asks you to change one word in the letter because he knows that is what the party said he meant in the first place. The judge has offered you a terrific federal job at the close of this case. What would you do?

   b. As you are preparing a legal memo on a case for your supervising attorney, your fellow paralegal tells you not to deal with or cite two of the strongest cases against you because that is likely to help the other side—especially if they failed to find these cases. What should you do?

3. Draft a document retention policy that could be used by your law firm. Remember to include e-mail and texts in your policy.

4. Prepare a sample template for a litigation hold letter that can be used by your law firm in civil litigation cases. Be sure to research your jurisdiction's case law on the issue prior to finalizing your template.

5. Identify the types of demonstrative evidence that may assist in the presentation of the Forrester case and what evidentiary value it would have for a jury.

CASE ASSIGNMENTS

1. Draft the litigation plan for the Forrester case. Include in the plan the following:

    a. Potential causes of actions and defenses;

    b. List of potential evidence in the case;

    c. Methodology to acquire evidence listed in section (b) above;

    d. Ways to ensure that the evidence acquired is preserved;

    e. List of potential witnesses and summary of possible testimony

    Be complete and creative in preparing the litigation plan.

2. Prepare a litigation hold letter for the Forrester case. Identify those individuals or entities that should be included as recipients of your letter.

DRAFTING THE COMPLAINT

OUTLINE

Introduction

The Complaint in Detail

Exhibits and
Appendixes

Systems Checklist for
Drafting a Complaint

Injunctions

Summary

OBJECTIVES

AFTER READING THIS CHAPTER, YOU WILL BE ABLE TO:

- Draft a complaint and delineate its components
- Differentiate between fact pleading and notice pleading
- Understand how to draft the allegations and causes of action paragraphs in the complaint
- Prepare the prayer for relief
- Distinguish between the requirements for requesting a temporary restraining order and temporary injunction

INTRODUCTION

DRAFTING A COMPLAINT: THE BASICS

Learning to draft effective complaints and similar pleadings is an art; like other arts it takes time and, above all, practice. This art is an important one. If done well, the complaint is succinct, adequate, and permits the action to proceed. If done poorly, the complaint will lead to costly delay, negative impressions of the advocate's ability, and worst of all, dismissal and possible loss of the client's cause of action. Like other skills addressed in this text, learn this one well and your value to the firm and the client increases significantly.

Before you draft the complaints for these cases, you will learn the purposes for the complaints, the structure and components of both state and federal complaints of various kinds, how to ensure each complaint states a cause of action, and how to properly include exhibits and appendices. Further, you will practice drafting complaints according to a checklist, learn about pleading for an injunction (another form of action), and continue to expand your litigation system.

DEFINITION AND PURPOSE

due process of law
Fair, prescribed judicial proceedings that must be followed before a person may be deprived of life, liberty, or property; guaranteed by the Constitution.

The Fifth Amendment and the Fourteenth Amendment to the Constitution of the United States guarantee that a person shall not be deprived of "life, liberty, or property, without **due process of law**." Most civil lawsuits attempt to deprive the defendant of money or other property. Therefore, the procedure used in deciding whether that person will be deprived of that property must meet the requirement of due process. In other words, the procedure must be fair. One way to ensure fairness is to require that all parties be informed of the basis of the lawsuit, initially accomplished through formal documents called pleadings that must be filed in court.

pleadings
Formal documents filed in a lawsuit that inform all parties of the basis for and defenses to the lawsuit; normally include the complaint, answer, counterclaim and reply, answer to cross-claim, and third-party complaint and answer.

Pleadings are formal documents that state and clarify the issues in a case by setting out the claims and defenses of the parties. A variety of state and federal pleadings are allowed by the respective rules of each jurisdiction. Some pleadings are claim pleadings; they state a claim against the other party. These pleadings include the complaint, counterclaim, cross-claim, and third-party complaint. Other pleadings are defense pleadings that respond to the claim and may state defenses. They include the answer, reply to counterclaim, answer to cross-claim, and a third-party answer. Most of these pleadings are discussed in subsequent chapters.

complaint
The formal document used to commence a lawsuit; tolls the statute of limitations, identifies parties, and states the cause of action the plaintiff alleges against the defendant.

The first of the pleadings, and the focus of this chapter, is the **complaint**. The purpose of the complaint is to: (1) commence the lawsuit and toll the statute of limitations, (2) introduce the cause of action, (3) invoke the court's jurisdiction, and (4) present the facts, thus (5) informing the defendant about who is suing him or her, for what reason, and for how much money or other award. This gives the defendant "notice" and the opportunity to respond to the allegations and to prepare adequately for trial. Thus, the complaint helps ensure fairness and compliance with procedural due process.

AN EXAMPLE

In preparing to draft a complaint, it is useful to obtain a copy of a previously filed complaint. One can be obtained from another case file, the firm's form file, a previously compiled systems folder, the Internet, or form books in the law library. Most state rules of civil procedure and the Federal Rules of Civil Procedure provide examples of complaints. Some states and local courts require the use of a specific complaint form.

A sample complaint, with sections labeled for illustrative purposes only, appears in Exhibit 4.1.

EXHIBIT 4.1 Sample Complaint (State)

	STATE OF COLUMBIA CAPITOL COUNTY CIRCUIT COURT
(caption)	MARY E. JOHNSON, Plaintiff
	v. Civil Action, File No. <u>00000</u>
	ARTHUR HENDRICKS, Defendant JURY TRIAL DEMANDED
	COMPLAINT FOR NEGLIGENCE
(body)	The Plaintiff states that:
	1. The court has jurisdiction in this matter under Section 403A, Title 23 of the Columbia Revised Statutes.
	2. Plaintiff is a paralegal and resides at 43 South Senate Avenue, Legalville, in Capitol County, Columbia.
	3. Defendant is a baker and lives at 500 Maple Street, Legalville, in Capitol County, Columbia.
	4. Defendant owns and operates the Deli Bakery at 508 Maple Street, Legalville, in Capitol County, Columbia.
	5. On August 23, _____, at the bakery, Defendant sold Plaintiff a chocolate éclair, which was negligently prepared containing pieces of glass.
	6. Plaintiff ate the pastry, receiving the following damage:
	a. Great pain and suffering
	b. Internal injuries
	c. Medical and hospital bills
	d. Loss of income
(prayer for relief)	WHEREFORE, Plaintiff demands judgment in the amount of ten thousand dollars ($10,000), together with the costs and disbursements of this action.
	Plaintiff demands trial by jury.
	————————————— Plaintiff's Attorney 407 E. Second Avenue Legalville, Columbia 00000 (303) 555-1111 Fax number e-mail address Bar Number (if required)

(continued)

EXHIBIT 4.1 Sample Complaint (State) (*continued*)

(verification)	State of Columbia
	County of Capitol
	Mary Johnson, on oath, deposes and states that she has read the foregoing complaint and that the matters stated therein are true to the best of her knowledge, information, and belief.

Mary Johnson
Subscribed and sworn to before me
this 12th day of October, _____

Notary Public
My commission expires: _____

THE COMPLAINT IN DETAIL

CAPTION

The caption of the complaint is the heading that identifies the location of the action, the court, the docket or file number, and the title of the action. The title includes the parties and sometimes the nature of the action (e.g., complaint for negligence). Although the paralegal may be of considerable assistance in determining the court, the parties, and other specifics for the caption, the attorney must make the final decision on such matters.

Rule 10 of the Federal Rules of Civil Procedure designates what must be included in a pleading filed in federal court. Form 1 and subsequent forms in the Federal Rules appendix of forms give recommended examples. Likewise, parallel state and local practice rules and forms should be consulted. If the complaint is to be filed electronically (discussed in Chapter 5), the caption should state "Electronically Filed."

Parties

The caption of the complaint must designate the parties to the lawsuit. The parties include the **plaintiff**, the party bringing the lawsuit (suing the other party), and the **defendant**, the party being sued for an alleged wrong. Parties can include individuals, corporations, unincorporated associations, partnerships, government entities, representatives of a person or an estate, and others. A potential defendant whose identity will be learned later in an action can be identified as "John or Jane Doe." Some potential parties may be immune from suit because of sovereign immunity; others might be reachable only through a required administrative procedure, such as in workers' compensation claims; and still others, particularly government agencies, may require notification of a claim or intent to sue before an action can be brought. Strategy issues regarding jurisdiction, venue, who can

plaintiff
The party bringing the lawsuit.

defendant
The party being sued for an alleged wrong.

afford to pay damages, and other matters make the choice of defendant important and occasionally complex.

Real Party in Interest

The plaintiff must be a real party in interest [Rule 17(a)]. A **real party in interest** is the one who has the right to sue by law. For example, Columbia state negligence law gives those injured in negligence cases the right to sue to be compensated for their injuries. Therefore, Mrs. Forrester is a real party in interest and has the right to sue. In some circumstances the injured party may be unable to sue—for example, a child, or a deceased person. When this situation occurs, the law allows a parent of the child or administrator for the deceased to be the plaintiff. Since these legal representatives have the right to sue by law, they are the real party in interest and can sue in their own names [Rule 17(a)]. The real party in interest requirement simply determines who is the right person or persons to bring a particular lawsuit.

Standing to Sue

Standing to sue is a legal concept that allows a plaintiff to pursue a lawsuit only if that plaintiff has suffered or will suffer a direct or actual injury. Our adversarial system of justice requires a party to have such a significant interest in the case that the party will pursue the interest aggressively. This requirement meets the constitutional demand of Article III, Section 2 that courts decide real controversies, not hypothetical ones. For example, Mrs. Forrester's sister may suffer anxiety over her sister's injury, but her concern will not normally reach the degree needed to have standing to sue either for her sister's injuries or her own anxiety over the injuries.

Capacity to Sue or Be Sued

A party must have the **capacity** to sue or be sued. Persons have such capacity unless they are under the age of majority (eighteen in most states), are incompetent, insane, or dead. Although minors and incompetent persons may lack capacity to sue, they can be named as defendants. The law of each state determines whether a person has the capacity to sue. Capacity in the federal courts is determined by the law of the state in which the person resides (domicile). In those cases in which persons do not have legal capacity, they may sue or be sued through a legal representative such as a parent for a minor or a spouse as the representative for the estate of the deceased. If the person does not have a legal representative or needs an independent representative just for the action such as in a child custody case, then a **guardian ad litem** (or "next friend") is appointed by the court. When a party dies or becomes incompetent during a lawsuit, another party may be substituted as long as it is done within ninety days of notice of the death to the court.

Corporations are considered "persons" under the law, and therefore have the capacity to sue and be sued. Consequently, because Mercury Parcel Service corporately owns the van that caused Ann Forrester's injuries and is also the employer of Richard Hart, it can be sued as a codefendant.

A recent Supreme Court of Nebraska case, *Carlos H. v. Lindsay M.*, 238 Neb. 1004, 815 N.W. 2d 168 (2012), addressed a minor's ability to sue and be sued. The case involved an adoption.

CASE STUDY: UNDERSTANDING THE LAW

Carlos H., a minor, wanted to challenge the adoption of his child and seek custody. He sued directly in his name and, in turn, sued the child's mother, Lindsey M., a minor, in her name directly as well. The lower court found that the father did not timely file his objection to the adoption and that the father was not a proper party to bring the action under a Nebraska statute. Since the father was a minor at the time he filed his suit, he lacked capacity to bring the case. In turn, since the mother was a minor as well, she lacked the capacity to defend herself. Both parties should have been represented by either a guardian ad litem or "next friend," such as a parent. Therefore, the lower court dismissed the case and Carlos appealed. The Nebraska Supreme Court agreed with the lower court. However, in analyzing the appeal, the court first had to determine whether it had jurisdiction. The question the court had to decide was whether either Carlos or Lindsey had the capacity to sue or be sued. Capacity to sue is based on the right of a party to come into court. Without capacity—the legal authority to act—a party cannot sue or be sued. If a minor may have suffered an injury or have a claim, the law provides for other persons to appear for the minor on their behalf. Therefore, since Carlos was a minor and did not have capacity to sue, he was not a proper party to bring the lawsuit. The case was dismissed by the Nebraska Supreme Court.

Questions for Review: Read *Carlos H. v. Lindsey M.* What statute addressed the capacity issue? If the proper party brought the case, what would the caption look like? Draft the caption. Was the result of the court fair and just? Support your response.

Joinder of Parties

joinder of parties

The uniting of parties making claims or defending against an action as co-plaintiffs or co-defendants.

In setting up a complaint, be aware of who should and can be added as parties to a lawsuit, which is governed by federal and state rules. You should consult both while studying this section. The federal rules on **joinder of parties** aim to reduce litigation and protect people's legal rights by including all the parties in one lawsuit who have a legal interest arising out of the same event. If a matter is going to be resolved, it should be resolved in a manner that is just for all concerned; no party of significance should be left out.

Federal Rule of Civil Procedure 19(a) requires joinder when a person is subject to service of process (discussed in Chapter 5) and whose joinder will not deprive the court of jurisdiction, such as where the new party will defeat diversity jurisdiction. Further, joinder is required when it is necessary to grant complete relief to the existing parties, or the party to be joined claims an interest in the action that, if left unaddressed, will leave the interest completely or partially unprotected or is likely to cause any existing party to bear unjust multiple or inconsistent obligations.

If a required party cannot be joined, such as when the party cannot be served or when joinder would defeat diversity jurisdiction, the court must consider whether to dismiss the suit and how dismissal will impact all of the interested parties. For example, failure to dismiss the action may subject the defendant to multiple lawsuits from different plaintiffs in different jurisdictions.

Federal and state rules also allow the joinder of multiple plaintiffs and defendants on a permissive (voluntary) basis. Federal Rule of Civil Procedure 20(a) permits the joinder of any plaintiffs and any defendants when claims for or against the potential parties arise out of the same occurrence and stem from any common questions of law or fact. This rule does not require those joined to have the exact same interest in the lawsuit. For example, Mr. Forrester may join Mrs. Forrester's lawsuit, not because he suffered the injuries to his wife, but because he was deprived of his wife's affection and consortium.

Joinder is encouraged, and the rules are broadly interpreted to permit it. When joining parties, however, you must consider how adding the new party will impact on jurisdictional matters. When joinder is voluntary, the action will not be dismissed if a party elects not to join a potential party (Rule 21).

As a practical matter, plaintiffs will join defendants to increase the chances of gaining more compensation. Mrs. Forrester is much more likely to gain a large sum of compensation from Mercury Parcel, Mr. Hart's employer, than from Mr. Hart himself. The defendant best able to pay damages is frequently called the "deep pocket." Some states, such as Wisconsin, have enacted laws that limit the liability of "deep pockets" according to a threshold percentage of liability or their degree of fault. The U.S. Congress has looked hard at this issue as well. Therefore, check your state and federal law regarding joint and several liability to determine if any limits have been imposed.

Defendants can join other parties as well. This issue is discussed in Chapter 6, which deals with defending a lawsuit.

A 1990 law, 28 U.S.C. §1367, reinforces the authority of federal courts to join cases or parties that have no federal jurisdiction independent of the original federal case. When considering adding such claims or parties, consult this statute and the pertinent Federal Rules of Civil Procedure.

Interpleader

interpleader

The joining of those parties that have the same claim against a third party; done to limit the liability of the third party.

Rule 22, the **interpleader** rule, permits a plaintiff to join as defendants those parties who have claims against the plaintiff when the plaintiff is exposed to multiple liability. For example, if defendant A has a claim to the plaintiff's property as does B, the plaintiff may interplead B as a defendant and let the court decide who gets the property. If done in separate suits, the plaintiff could be found liable to both parties.

In addition to Rule 22, a similar interpleader mechanism is available under 28 U.S.C.A. §1335 (statutory interpleader). If interpleader is being considered, consult this statute for its more liberal diversity amount ($500 instead of $75,000), different venue requirements, and other differences.

Class Actions

class actions

A suit by or against an entire class—whose members are too numerous for a joinder—represented by one or a few individuals.

Class actions are permitted under Rule 23. For such actions, one or more members of a class may sue or be sued as representative of the entire class, rather than joinder of all members of the class, if the following elements are present:

- The members of the class are too numerous for joinder.
- There are common questions of law and fact.
- The claims of the representative are typical of those of the class.
- The representative will protect the interests of the class.
- Separate actions would be likely to bring inconsistent results.
- Separate actions might hinder or preclude the action of the other members of the class.

APPLY YOUR KNOWLEDGE

Locate a copy of the complaints in one of the following class action lawsuits: (1) Skechers toning sneakers; (2) GM ignition recall; (3) Dow Corning breast implant removal; (4) Yaz contraception pills; (5) Any other case of interest. Identify who filed the lawsuit and where it was filed. Summarize the basis for the class action and determine the causes of action.

- The adverse party has acted or failed to act in a manner applicable to the entire class.

- A class action is the superior action under the circumstances.

If the elements are met, the court will certify the class and order that the action proceed as a class action. Class actions provide a unique legal mechanism whereby a citizen's relatively small and financially impractical claim can be combined with the claims of similarly wronged parties to make the lawsuit not only practical but also potent. This type of lawsuit has been particularly useful in cases involving securities fraud, antitrust, product liability, and deceptive marketing practices. Class actions also have been used to design workable settlements for large companies facing potentially countless individual lawsuits, particularly in mass product liability cases of national scope. For example, a recent class action involved Skechers sneakers. Skechers advertised that its Shape-Ups brand, a uniquely soled sneaker, would shape up legs and buttocks and assist consumers in losing weight. Those claims appear to have been questionable. Those who purchased the Skechers sneaker could participate in a $40 million settlement by way of the class action lawsuit. A district court's order granting or denying class action certification can be appealed immediately (interlocutory appeal) rather than having to wait until the trial is concluded [FED. R. CIV. P. 23(f)]. Conflicting court approaches to class action cases and congressional perceptions of abuse led to revisions of Rule 23 (2003) and the passage of the Class Action Fairness Act, which expanded federal jurisdiction (see Chapter 1). See the forms of various types of complaints at the end of this chapter for an example of a complaint for a class action suit.

Intervention

Rule 24 permits a party to intervene in an action either as a plaintiff or as a defendant when specifically permitted by U.S. law; when the action may impede or impair the intervenor's interest, which is otherwise unrepresented by the existing parties; or when the applicant's claim or defense raises the same question of law or fact as the existing claim. Intervention is accomplished by a *motion to intervene* [Rule 24(c)]. If an intervenor can show the requisite interest in the litigation [Rule 24(a)(2)], there is no separate need for the intervenor to establish standing [*San Juan County, Utah v. U.S.*, 420 F.3d 1197 (10th Cir. 2005)].

"Et al."

"Et al." is an abbreviation for the Latin *et alia*, meaning "and others." Rule 10(a) of the Federal Rules of Civil Procedure and parallel state rules require that all parties to an action be listed in the caption. Pleadings that come after the complaint, however, may state the name of the first party on each side followed by the *et al.* abbreviation. This can save paper and time in actions involving numerous parties.

Sample Captions

Here are examples of caption formats for a variety of circumstances and parties. Note that some states require the caption of the complaint to include the addresses of the parties. Consult current local practice, because privacy concerns may limit addresses to city, county, and state only. Add these examples of captions to your systems folder (Exhibit 4.2).

EXHIBIT 4.2 Example of Captions

Example of Caption: State Court

STATE OF COLUMBIA   CAPITOL COUNTY   CIRCUIT COURT

ANN FORRESTER, Plaintiff

      v.   Civil Action, File No. 1000

RICHARD HART and
MERCURY PARCEL SERVICE, INC., Defendants

COMPLAINT FOR NEGLIGENCE

Example of Caption: Federal Court

UNITED STATES DISTRICT COURT FOR THE EASTERN DISTRICT
OF COLUMBIA Civil Action,   Case No. 1001

ANN FORRESTER,

                Plaintiff

     v.

RICHARD HART and   COMPLAINT
MERCURY PARCEL SERVICE, INC.,

                Defendants

Party Caption for Suit by Minor or Person Under Disability

BARRY SMITH,
a minor by his parents and guardians,
SAMUEL and EDNA SMITH,

                Plaintiff

     v.

JOHNSON MOTORS, INC.,

                Defendant

Party Caption for Suit by Deceased Person

HAROLD WEBER
Executor of the estate of
[(or) Personal Representative for the Estate of]
MARY WEBER,

                Plaintiff

     v.

FRANCIS LONG,

                Defendant

(continued)

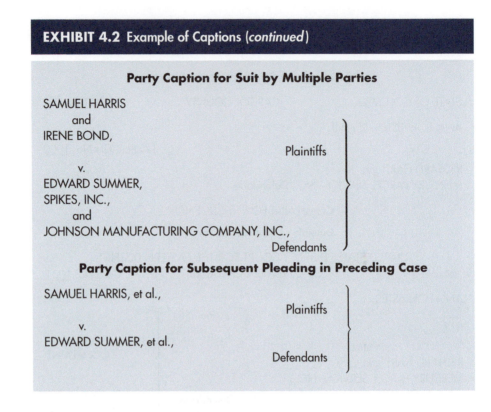

EXHIBIT 4.2 Example of Captions (*continued*)

Party Caption for Suit by Multiple Parties

SAMUEL HARRIS
   and
IRENE BOND,

                           Plaintiffs

   v.
EDWARD SUMMER,
SPIKES, INC.,
   and
JOHNSON MANUFACTURING COMPANY, INC.,
                           Defendants

Party Caption for Subsequent Pleading in Preceding Case

SAMUEL HARRIS, et al.,
                           Plaintiffs

   v.
EDWARD SUMMER, et al.,

                           Defendants

THE BODY OF THE COMPLAINT

Jurisdictional Allegations

As discussed in Chapter 1, jurisdiction is the authority of a court to decide a case and enforce its decisions. Subject matter jurisdiction is the court's authority to hear certain types (subjects) of cases. An allegation of jurisdiction must be included in complaints filed in federal courts, because those are courts of limited subject matter jurisdiction. A plaintiff must demonstrate to a federal court through the jurisdictional allegation that the court has the subject matter jurisdiction to hear the case.

Although the trial courts of most states are courts of general jurisdiction, it is best to allege jurisdiction unless you are absolutely positive that your state rules do not require such an allegation. More than likely, you will need the names and domiciles of the parties, the cause of action and its location, a reference to any controlling jurisdictional state statute, and any jurisdictional amount. This information is stated in the first paragraphs of the complaint.

Since paralegals are often responsible for drafting complaints, they must know the jurisdictional requirements for the pertinent court and take care that the amount or other jurisdictional requirements are properly alleged. The final determination of whether the client's case meets the jurisdictional requirement, and what court the case should be filed in, will be left to the attorney. Nevertheless, it is important to know the jurisdictional fundamentals needed for drafting jurisdictional allegations and for understanding the attorney's choices. A review of these fundamentals as discussed in Chapter 1 may be useful at this time.

Typical formats for allegations of subject matter jurisdiction for a complaint to be filed in federal district court appear in Exhibits 4.3, 4.4, and 4.5.

EXHIBIT 4.3 Jurisdictional Allegation of Diversity

Sample 1

1. Jurisdiction of this court is based on diversity of citizenship and the amount in controversy exceeds the sum of $75,000, exclusive of interest and costs.

Sample 2

1. Plaintiff is a [citizen of the State of Columbia] [corporation incorporated under the laws of the State of Columbia having its principal place of business in the state of Columbia] and defendant is a corporation incorporated under the laws of the State of [Ohio] having its principal place of business in [Ohio] [a state other than the State of Columbia]. The matter in controversy exceeds, exclusive of interest and costs, the sum of $75,000.

Note that diversity for a corporation is based on two locations: the state of incorporation and the state where the corporation has its principal place of business. If either of those locations is the same as that of the opposing party, diversity does not exist.

EXHIBIT 4.4 Jurisdictional Allegation for Federal Question Cases

1. The action arises under [the Constitution of the United States, Article _____, Section _____]; [the _____Amendment to the Constitution of the United States, Section _____], [the Act of _____, Stat. _____; U.S.C., Title _____ § _____]; [the Treaty of the United States (here describe the treaty)].

EXHIBIT 4.5 Jurisdictional Allegation for Cases Arising under Federal Statute

Sample 1

1. The action arises under the Act of _____, Stat. _____, U.S.C., Title _____, § _____.

Sample 2

1. The action arises under the National Environmental Policy Act of 1969, § 102; _____ Stat. 852; 42 U.S.C. § 4332 (1970).

In those states where jurisdictional allegations are required, the following format in Exhibit 4.6 may be appropriate:

EXHIBIT 4.6 Jurisdictional Allegation for Cases Arising under State Statute Where Jurisdictional Amount Is Necessary

1. The jurisdiction of this court arises under Section 335, Title 17, of the State Code of Columbia. The amount in controversy exceeds $2,500, exclusive of interest and costs.

Note: In Exhibit 4.6, it was necessary to allege the $2,500 in order to get into the state circuit court, in this case the highest-level trial court in the state. The sample complaint at the beginning of this chapter contains an example of a jurisdictional allegation for cases arising under state statutes not requiring a jurisdictional amount.

Identification of the Parties

The complaint should state the domicile of the plaintiff and the defendant. Jurisdictions and form books vary on whether "domicile" requires you to include the complete address of the parties or simply the city, county, and state. Exhibit 4.7 include addresses.

EXHIBIT 4.7 Examples of Addresses

2. Plaintiff resides at 301 South Short Street, in the City of Legalville in the County of Capitol in the State of Columbia.
3. Defendant resides at 5130 West North Avenue, in the City of Lancaster in the County of Capitol in the State of Columbia.

---

cause of action
Statement of the claim upon which relief may be granted in an action.

In some jurisdictions it is necessary to state the names and addresses of the parties in the complaint to demonstrate that the court has proper venue. This is true if venue is to be based on the convenience of the parties. If venue is to be based on the location of the incident precipitating the lawsuit, then that location (state, city, and county) must be made clear in the body of the complaint. In the federal system, proper venue does not have to be alleged in the complaint; it is considered a matter for the defendant to raise. Venue may be waived by the defendant; jurisdiction may not be.

Allegations (Cause of Action)

INTRODUCTION. The allegation section is the heart of the complaint. It states the *claim upon which relief may be granted*, often called the **cause of action**. The writing of this section of the complaint is critical to the initial success of the plaintiff's lawsuit, for if it is not done correctly or completely, either the action will be dismissed or the complaint will have to be amended.

WHAT MUST BE ALLEGED. The specific answer to what must be alleged lies in the law of each jurisdiction. It would be comforting to all of us if drafting an adequate

ETHICAL CONSIDERATIONS

Review. That is what your attorney is required to do whenever you draft a complaint or any legal document for that matter Monitor. The attorney must always oversee your work. This concept goes hand in hand with the attorney's requirement to review your work. Supervise. You always are under the supervision of a licensed attorney, plain and simple. Never forget that. Under the rules of professional responsibility, it is an attorney's ethical duty to review, monitor, and supervise all work prepared by a paralegal. You will be delegated work by your attorney to prepare. However, that attorney must use independent professional judgment in determining whether a document is legally sufficient and encompasses the undertaking of that client's representation. This supervision is something you should welcome. Ultimately, it is the attorney who is responsible for the work product produced and filed with the court. His or her signature is affixed to that document, not yours. Mistakes, although technically shared—and there will be mistakes—are the responsibility of the attorney. What this means for you is that when you have documents reviewed, have the attorney initial and date the document indicating review. Even having them use words such as "reviewed" or "approved" is a good indication of their affirmative act of supervision. Legal opinions from most state bar associations who have weighed in on the topic are virtually unanimous in their adherence to these ethical principles. It is always the responsibility of the attorney to supervise the paralegal, no matter how experienced or skilled. Do not place yourself in a compromising situation where because of your competence you are blamed for tasks whose responsibility is the attorney's. Court case after court case find that even when an attorney attempts to "pass the buck" of responsibility, courts consistently hold the attorney liable for any errors committed. The duty to supervise is absolute in the legal profession.

APPLY YOUR KNOWLEDGE

Go to your state bar association's Web site and find opinions on the attorney's duty to supervise paralegals or other non-lawyer professionals. Review the opinions and determine the ethical rules cited and the outcome and recommendation of the state bar association.

body of a complaint were an exact science. Unfortunately, an adequate complaint often depends on the history of pleadings in a particular jurisdiction, that is, the case law on adequate pleading and the rules of civil procedure for the pertinent court. Therefore, regardless of the specific points to be covered here, it is absolutely essential that you become familiar with what is acceptable in the court in which the action will be filed. Reviewing copies of successful pleadings previously filed in that court can be helpful, but researching the rules of procedure and the case law applicable to that particular court is preferable. Regardless of the differences among jurisdictions, some factors are applicable to most complaints.

Think of the claim as a syllogism. A syllogism is a logical formula for an argument based on three parts: a major premise, a minor premise, and a conclusion. The major premise is the rule of law. It is stated like this: if A, B, and C exist, then the plaintiff is entitled to relief X. The minor premise consists of the facts to support the rule of law: that A, B, and C exist. Then the conclusion is: since A, B, and C exist, the plaintiff is entitled to X. Let us look at this from the perspective of a negligence case.

The rule of law or major premise in a negligence case would develop this way: if (A) there is a duty to the plaintiff, (B) a breach of that duty occurred, (C) injury or damage to the plaintiff resulted, and (D) the breach of duty was the substantial cause of injury, the plaintiff is entitled to compensation for the resulting damages.

In order to have in mind the major premise underlying a successful complaint, *you must know the applicable rule of law for the claim and each element of that rule of law* (duty, breach, injury, etc.). Chapter 2 discussed how you can research the elements of the rule of law in jury instruction books, legal encyclopedias, and the particular statute involved.

The minor premise in the syllogism is that A, B, and C exist. In terms of a negligence action, it is stated as follows: (A) the defendant was operating a motor vehicle on the highway and had a duty to drive safely; (B) the defendant drove negligently by speeding, failing to keep proper lookout, and failing to keep his vehicle under control; (C) the plaintiff suffered several broken bones, internal injuries, and considerable pain; and (D) the plaintiff's injuries were substantially caused by the defendant's breach of duty (allowing his vehicle to strike her). In brief, these facts support the allegation that A, B, C, and D exist. In other words, *you must state facts to satisfy each element of the rule of law.* These facts must be alleged in the body of the complaint, for if the alleged facts can be proven to exist through evidence presented by the plaintiff at trial, then the minor premise is established, bringing the syllogism to its conclusion (the designated relief to the plaintiff). Should the drafter carelessly omit facts needed to support one of the required elements of the rule of law, the syllogism is incomplete, and the complaint is defective and subject to dismissal.

Keep in mind that the major premise—the rule of law and each of its elements—is not stated in the body of the complaint. Its function is to determine what facts must be alleged in the complaint and what remedy is available. The complaint drafted with an understanding of these logical and necessary relationships will be a superior complaint.

GUIDELINES AND TECHNIQUES FOR DRAFTING THE BODY OF THE COMPLAINT. In addition to thinking through the legal syllogism, there are several other guidelines and techniques that you should have in mind before drafting the body of the complaint.

- <u>Privacy Concerns.</u> Be aware of any applicable court rules that because of privacy concerns restrict the personal identification information that can be stated in a complaint, pleading, or other court document. Federal and parallel state and local practice impose the use of only the last four digits of a Social Security number; the initials of minors; the year of birth (no specific date); and city, county, and state of the home address. Federal court policy on privacy is at http://www.privacy.uscourts.gov. Proposed Federal Rule of Civil Procedure 5.2 incorporates the policy on privacy (Dec. 2007).

- <u>Write in Plain English.</u> Be clear and concise. Get to the point quickly, state it simply, and eliminate all unnecessary words and phrases. Avoid archaic, redundant, and obscure legalese. Do not get caught in the trap of perpetuating the obscure language found on many legal forms and documents. Judges, juries, and others will read the complaint or hear it being read. If it is unnecessarily wordy or obscure, it will waste time and be a source of irritation for those people you want on your client's side.

Which of the following would you rather read?

Complaint Example 1

Comes now the above named plaintiff, by his attorney, Albert Grey, for his complaint, respectfully shows to the court and alleges as follows: At all times hereinafter mentioned, Plaintiff was and still is a resident of Legalville, Columbia, residing at 201 Short Street.

Complaint Example 2

Plaintiff resides and has resided in the City of Legalville in the County of Capitol in the State of Columbia.

(Example 2, of course)

Several good books on plain English and effective legal writing are: Wydick's *Plain English for Lawyers*, Good's *Mightier Than the Sword*, Goldfarb and Raymond's *Clear Understandings*, Stark's *Writing to Win: The Legal Writer*, and Garner's *Elements of Legal Style*.

- <u>Paragraph Identification and Content.</u> Use brief, numbered paragraphs. Short paragraphs are best for the sake of clarity, and the numbers provide easy reference. Avoid complex, run-on paragraphs by limiting each paragraph to a single idea.

- <u>Advocate and Write in the Active Voice.</u> Be an advocate when drafting. Strive for language that is assertive and persuasive, evokes sympathy for the client, and conveys a confident attitude toward the claim. "The Plaintiff was hit by the van" is colorless and evokes little emotion. "The van struck the Plaintiff, throwing her to the side of the road" would be a more assertive statement. On the other hand, do not overdo it. You do not want to sound phony or theatrical.

- <u>Good Faith Requirements.</u> Avoid impertinent, scandalous, or immaterial language. A complaint is not to be used for harassment or any other improper purpose (Rule 11). If language is improper, it subjects the complaint to attack and the inappropriate language will be stricken [Rule 12(f)]. Furthermore, the use of such language makes suspect the motive of the plaintiff and the judgment of the law firm.

- <u>Organization of the Complaint.</u> Organize the paragraphs of the complaint so that they flow logically. A complaint should tell an interesting, chronological story. One paragraph should lead into the next. This order not only makes the complaint read more smoothly, but also enhances clarity and effectiveness.

- <u>Keep It Simple.</u> Reveal no more of the facts than necessary. Your client gains no advantage by having the complaint reveal too much. To do so may simply show weaknesses or contradictions in the case, or even suggest defenses to the opposition.

- <u>Do Not State Evidence or Conclusions.</u> It is not the purpose of the complaint to prove the case. Allegations such as "The Defendant had 300 feet in which to avoid the accident, according to skid marks, but did not apply his brake until only 100 feet were left" do not belong. A conclusion such as "Defendant breached his duty of care" is excluded because it serves no useful function other than possibly to prejudice a jury. Some conclusions such as "Defendant negligently operated the vehicle" have been accepted as useful to a general understanding of the specific cause of action. Regardless, including evidence or conclusions will make the body of the complaint intolerably long-winded as well as subject to attack. Stick to alleging the facts.

- <u>Be Truthful.</u> Keep in mind at all times when drafting pleadings that the supervising lawyer is under a serious ethical responsibility of truthfulness and can be severely disciplined for pleadings that reflect a disregard for the truth. Model Rule 3.3(a)(1) of the American Bar Association's Model Rules of Professional Conduct, which has been adopted by most states, requires truthfulness in pleadings.

- <u>Permissible Alternative Language.</u> When the truth of the matter is uncertain but there is some basis for a statement, make the statement on the basis of information and belief. For example: "On information and belief, Defendant Hart was an employee of the Mercury Parcel Service at the time of the accident."

- <u>Do Not Anticipate Defenses.</u> When the facts of a case may raise defensive issues, such as contributory negligence, payment of the debt, or self-defense, the complaint should not include any direct attempt to address those concerns. An allegation that "Plaintiff did not fail to keep a lookout prior to crossing the street" or "Plaintiff was exercising due care for her safety at all times prior to the accident" are subjects to be raised by the defendant and not the plaintiff.

- <u>Alleging Alternative Parties or Theories.</u> When there is uncertainty or alternative parties or causes, that uncertainty is permissible in the complaint. Suppose a piece of rodent was found in some corn served to a customer at a restaurant. The culprit could be the packager of the corn or the server of the corn. An acceptable allegation in the complaint would be: "Defendant City Cafe or Defendant Green Grower Canning Company negligently or willfully allowed animal remains to be mixed with corn served to the Plaintiff at said cafe, causing Plaintiff to become violently ill."

- <u>Do Not State the Law.</u> It is not the function of the complaint to serve as a vehicle to argue the law or to cite cases in support of the client's case. The law, however, should appear in the complaint in the following instances: if the action is brought pursuant to the specific provisions of a particular statute, administrative rule, or ordinance; and if the action is brought in one state and the plaintiff is relying on the law of another state.

- <u>Damage Allegations.</u> It is better to state the various types of damages incurred by the plaintiff in one concise paragraph as opposed to several wordy paragraphs when permitted by the rules of the particular jurisdiction.

  > As a consequence of Defendant's negligence and the aforesaid resulting injuries, the Plaintiff has incurred, and will incur, substantial monetary losses for hospital and medical care, loss of income and benefits, and property damage.

  The law in some jurisdictions, however, requires that each type of damage be stated separately and in detail, including the specific part of the body that was injured. The rules on damages do differ and need to be consulted. One must be careful as well to allege damages in an amount sufficient to meet any jurisdictional amount.

- <u>Stating Different Legal Theories.</u> State separate claims or theories for claims in separate counts: Count One for negligence, Count Two for breach of warranty, and Count Three for battery. Each count will have its own separate body of allegations, damages, and demand for judgment. Information alleged

APPLY YOUR KNOWLEDGE

Research whether your jurisdiction requires damages to be pleaded in separate paragraphs or in one collective paragraph. Are there differences between your state and federal jurisdictions' requirements for pleading damages?

fact pleading

The requirement that the body of a pleading state in detail the facts in support of each element of the rule of law or claim.

in the introductory paragraphs or that would be repeated from Count One, may be incorporated in the other counts. For example:

COUNT THREE

Plaintiff hereby incorporates by reference the allegations contained in paragraphs 1 through 7 of Count One.

FACT (CODE) PLEADING. Columbia, as is true of a number of other states, requires **fact pleading**. The body of the complaint must state the ultimate facts (the minor premise) in support of each element of the rule of law or claim (the major premise). In other words, sufficient detail must be alleged to tell the defendant the basis of the complaint. The difficulty in this type of complaint is knowing what is enough without unnecessarily revealing too much. The answer to this dilemma lies in the experience, rules, cases, and statutes of the particular jurisdiction in which the claim will be filed. An example of an adequately alleged claim for Columbia is shown in Exhibit 4.8. The labels on the left side of the page are for your guidance and are not part of the complaint. **Note:** Some jurisdictions use Roman numerals to number the paragraphs in the complaint.

NOTICE PLEADING. The Federal Rules of Civil Procedure, which have been adopted by many state jurisdictions, require a briefer form of pleading called

---

EXHIBIT 4.8 Sample Allegation Section of a Negligence Complaint for a Fact Pleading State

date/time duty/conditions venue connection to other defendants	**4.** On February 26, _____, at approximately 7:30 A.M., Defendant Hart was operating a motor vehicle on a hilly and partially icy section of Highway 328 about three miles west of the City of Legalville, County of Capitol, in the State of Columbia. Defendant Hart was driving a vehicle owned by Defendant Mercury Parcel Service for whom Hart is an employee and for whom he was working at all times in the course and scope of his employment.
breach of duty alternative theories	**5.** Defendant Hart operated his vehicle in a negligent manner and without regard for Plaintiff by: (a) operating the vehicle at an excessive rate of speed under the circumstances; (b) failing to exercise a proper lookout and attentiveness; (c) failing to exercise adequate control of the vehicle; and (d) otherwise failing to exercise due and adequate care under the circumstances.
substantial cause of injury	**6.** As a direct consequence of Defendants' negligence, Plaintiff was struck down and seriously injured by Defendants' vehicle as she was walking south across Highway 328.
injuries	**7.** As a result of said negligence, Plaintiff suffered fractures of the left leg and hip; damage to the lower spine; torn muscles, tendons, tissue, and nerves; insomnia; inability to walk; confinement to a wheelchair; intense depression; and other maladies; all of which, now and in the future, will cause her intense pain, great suffering, and considerable inconvenience.
damages	**8.** As a consequence of Defendants' negligence and the aforesaid injuries, the Plaintiff has incurred and will incur the loss of considerable sums of money for hospital and medical care, loss of income and benefits, property damage, and domestic expenses.

(continued)

EXHIBIT 4.8 Sample Allegation Section of a Negligence Complaint for a Fact Pleading State (*continued*)

[Compare to the traditional allegation of damages in paragraphs 8–10]

Alternative

Medical
expenses
(damages)
other
damages
other
damages—
loss of income

8. As a further consequence of the injuries, Plaintiff has been and will continue to be obligated to pay large sums of money for medical and hospital bills.
9. As a result of these injuries, Plaintiff has and will continue to be unable to fulfill her daily duties and will be unable to do so for an indefinite time, to her loss.
10. As a further consequence of Defendants' negligence, Plaintiff has been unable to pursue her regular or any other employment and will be unable to do so for an indefinite period of time causing her considerable loss of income and benefits.

[The allegations above are for illustrative purposes only and do not exhaust other possible causes of action against the defendants.]

---

notice pleading

Abbreviated form of pleading authorized by the Federal Rules of Civil Procedure and parallel state rules.

notice pleading. One purpose of notice pleading is to eliminate some of the uncertainty and resulting litigation concerning what factual allegations are sufficient. Notice pleading simply informs the defendant of the claim and the general basis for the claim (notice). Rule 8(a) of the Federal Rules of Civil Procedure states that the body of the complaint must contain "a short and plain statement of the claim showing that the pleader is entitled to relief." Rule 8(d)(1) states: "Each averment of a pleading shall be simple, concise, and direct. No technical forms of pleadings or motions are required." Forms in the Federal Rules set out the necessary allegations. Exhibit 4.9 is based on one of those forms:

EXHIBIT 4.9 Sample Allegation Section of Negligence Complaint for Federal or Other Notice Pleading Jurisdiction

2. On February 26, _____, on Highway 328 in Capitol County, Columbia, Defendant negligently drove a motor vehicle striking down Plaintiff who was then crossing Highway 328.

3. As a result, Plaintiff fractured her left leg and hip bones and was otherwise seriously injured. She has been prevented from transacting her business, and has suffered and will continue to suffer great physical and emotional pain. In addition, she has incurred and will continue to incur expenses for medical attention and hospitalization in the sum of $750,000.

Note: Despite the brevity of the body of the complaint, there are effective allegations on each essential element of the syllogism.

Some specialized rules on pleading are found in parts of Rules 8, 9, and 10. Most notably, Rule 9 on "pleading special matters" requires the equivalent of fact pleading (pleading specifically and with particularity) in cases of fraud or mistake. Failure to do so may result in the opponent asking the court to dismiss the case. Two recent U.S.

Supreme Court cases, *Bell Atlantic v. Twombly*, 550 U.S. 544 (2007) and *Ashcroft v. Iqbal*, 556 U.S. 662 (2009), have examined the extent to which a plaintiff must plead facts in order overcome a defendant's motion to dismiss for failure to state a cause of action. (Motions to dismiss will be discussed in more detail in Chapter 5.)

CASE STUDY: UNDERSTANDING THE LAW

Twombly and *Iqbal* changed the way attorneys plead their complaints rendering long standing principles cited in the landmark case, *Conley v. Gibson*, 355 U.S. 41 (1957), obsolete. The basic facts for *Twombly* and *Iqbal* are as follows:

Twombly

Twombly arises out of a complaint filed for antitrust violations. That complaint, according to the U.S. Supreme Court, did not allege facts that would lead to a "plausible" claim for relief rather than the previous standard under *Conley*—that "no set of facts in support of his claim . . . would entitle him to relief." Essentially, the *Twombly* court required more facts to sustain a challenge for insufficiency or failure to state a claim, in antitrust claims and complex litigation cases. As the Court stated, the pleader must allege "enough facts to state a claim to relief that is plausible on its face."

Iqbal

Iqbal was a complaint filed against then Attorney General John Ashcroft and FBI Director Robert Mueller that allege that after the 9/11 attacks the AG and Director ordered the detention of Arab Muslims in violation of the U.S. Constitution. Following the foundation laid in *Twombly*, the U.S. Supreme Court held that Iqbal did not allege a "plausible" cause of action against the AG and Director. In doing so, the Court reinforced the principles set forth in *Twombly* now holding that the "plausibility" standard applied to all civil cases. In *Iqbal*, the Court applied the analysis one step further by stating the pleader must "plead factual content that allows the court to draw the reasonable inference that the defendant is liable for the misconduct alleged."

In both cases, the standard for notice pleading was heightened, requiring attorneys to plead more factual allegations to withstand defensive motions to dismiss the complaint.

Questions for Review: Review the *Twombly* and *Iqbal* decisions. What causes of action did the U.S. Supreme Court find were not sufficiently pled in each case? What are the holdings in each case? What practical effect do *Twombly* and *Iqbal* have on complaints filed in federal courts?

REMEDIES AND THE PRAYER FOR RELIEF (DEMAND FOR JUDGMENT)

INTERNET EXERCISE

Determine whether your state is a fact pleading or notice pleading jurisdiction and determine what effect the *Twombly* and *Iqbal* decisions have had on your state's pleading requirements.

Following the allegation section, the complaint should contain a prayer for relief (demand for judgment), which is commonly referred to as the "wherefore" clause. This clause demands that judgment be entered for the plaintiff and that relief be granted accordingly. Some of the typical remedies that the plaintiff may demand are damages, recovery of property, injunctions, and specific performance.

Damages are sums of money awarded to compensate the plaintiff for a variety of injuries and losses. **General damages** are those damages that are a natural and direct result of the defendant's wrong and the resulting injury—for example, pain and suffering or emotional trauma. General damages do not have to be pleaded in the complaint in order to prove them at trial. Pain and suffering, emotional distress, and loss of consortium are frequently grouped under the term *noneconomic damages*. About half of the states now have caps (upward limits) on the monetary

general damages
Damages that are a natural and direct result of the defendant's wrong, such as pain and suffering, humiliation, and loss of enjoyment of life.

special damages
Damages that are incurred because of the defendant's wrong and the actual result of the injury, but not the necessary result, such as medical bills, lost wages, or property loss.

exemplary (punitive) damages
Damages awarded to a plaintiff beyond actual loss as punishment for conduct of the defendant that is particularly aggravated; also called punitive damages.

prohibitory injunctions
Order that informs a defendant to refrain from a specific course of conduct.

mandatory injunctions
Requirement that the defendant perform conduct specified by the court.

specific performance
In breach of contract cases, the requirement of the offending party to fulfill specific terms of the contract regarding a unique piece of property.

amount that can be awarded a plaintiff. A few state high courts have declared such caps unconstitutional.

Special damages are damages that are incurred but do not necessarily follow from the defendant's wrong. For example, pain is the natural and direct consequence of being struck (general damage), but one does not necessarily incur hospital bills for being struck, so the hospital bill would be a special damage. It is the result of the injury but not necessarily the natural result. Other special damages could be doctors' fees, loss of income, loss of profits in a contract situation, and property damage. Special damages must be specifically alleged in most jurisdictions, including the federal courts.

Exemplary (punitive) damages are damages awarded to the plaintiff when the defendant's conduct is particularly aggravated, malicious, or reckless. Such damages are designed to punish the wrongdoer and to deter similar conduct. For example, if a manufacturer sold a product which it knew could cause serious injury because of a defect, an injured party could receive exemplary damages. The award is in addition to all other damages. Some states have enacted laws placing caps on punitive damages, as well as noneconomic damages.

Because some punitive damage awards have been excessive, questions regarding the fundamental fairness of punitive damages have attracted considerable legislative and judicial attention. In *State Farm Mutual Auto Ins. Co. v. Campbell*, 123 S.Ct. 1513 (2003), the Court reiterated that, as a matter of due process, punitive damages are constitutional if they are reasonable. The key factors include the degree of reprehensibility of the relevant conduct, the ratio of punitive to compensatory damages (usually should be a single digit ratio), and sanctions (such as criminal penalties) for comparable misconduct.

Recovery of property is a remedy available to a plaintiff when property has been wrongfully taken, transferred, sold, or otherwise kept from its rightful owner. In such cases, the property may be seized (attached) by the court and returned to the rightful owner. The eviction of a tenant is an example of a recovery of property remedy.

Injunctions are remedies designed to prevent future harm and, in some cases, correct past harm. **Prohibitory injunctions** order the defendant to refrain from a specific course of conduct, and **mandatory injunctions** require the defendant to continue or take some course of conduct. For example, an ornate fence divides the property of two new residents of a subdivision. Neighbor A wants the fence torn down, claiming it to be his fence. Neighbor B loves the fence and wants it to remain. Owner B can get an injunction against A ordering A not to tear the fence down until it can be determined who owns it. Injunctions are discussed in more detail at the end of this chapter.

Specific performance is a remedy unique to contract law. Instead of granting damages when a breach of contract occurs, the court can require the offending party to live up to the specific terms of the contract regarding a unique piece of property. If one party agrees to sell an original painting and then reneges, damages are of little value to the party who wanted the painting. In this case, the court may require the seller to surrender the painting called for by the contract (see Exhibit 4.10).

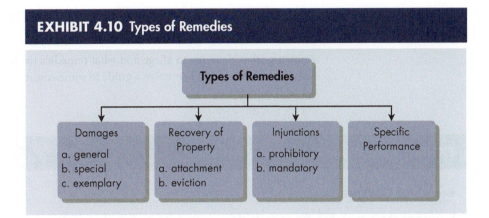

EXHIBIT 4.10 Types of Remedies

Rule 8(a) of the Federal Rules of Civil Procedure requires a demand (wherefore) clause. Should a complaint contain more than one claim or count, each count needs to have a separate "wherefore" clause. The plaintiff is not bound by the relief requested if it is inappropriate or inaccurate as revealed later in trial. The court, however, may not grant the plaintiff more than that requested in the complaint if the defendant defaults (fails to oppose the action) according to Rule 54(c). It is good practice to add a catchall phrase such as the one at the end of the following sample prayer for relief (Exhibit 4.11).

EXHIBIT 4.11 Sample Prayer for Relief (Demand)

WHEREFORE Plaintiff demands judgment against Defendant in the sum of seven hundred and fifty thousand dollars ($750,000), together with the costs and disbursements of this action and for such other relief as the court deems just and equitable.

TECHNOLOGY UPDATE: PREDICTIVE ANALYTICS

Predictive analytics is the science of predicting outcomes by using available data. Think of the movie *Moneyball*, where Brad Pitt's character, Billy Beane, hired Peter Brand, played by Jonah Hill, to accumulate statistics about a baseball player's averages to determine whom to draft for their baseball team. At the time, and perhaps even now, it was a novel idea. The concept changed the way the Oakland A's chose their team. Fast forward to now where attorneys are using data and software to predict outcomes in their cases. There is software that will assist attorneys in analyzing information and predicting outcomes in clients' cases. By acquiring data, such as how a judge rules on certain types of motions or the amount of jury awards in particular cases, attorneys can better determine the likelihood of success in a case. Such data gathering will limit some of the uncertainty and provide attorneys with better predictors, which in turn will provide better guidance for clients. This technology could assist attorneys in determining whether to take a particular type of case, whether to select a person for a jury for a trial, and possibly whether to pursue settlement and the amount of that settlement. The possibilities are endless in the legal profession and should be considered not only in the litigation process, but also in law office management as well. This is the future of practicing law.

A BRIEF GUIDE TO CAUSES OF ACTION AND REMEDIES

Knowing what elements to allege and what remedies to claim is essential to drafting complaints. Exhibit 4.12 contains a guide to some common causes of action and their respective remedies.

EXHIBIT 4.12 Causes of Action and Remedies

Breach of Contract

In any type of contract action, the existence of the contract and the type of contract must be proven. The law recognizes three types of contracts.

1. Oral contracts

   In the complaint, the plaintiff must allege the terms of the contract including the consideration for the contract.

2. Written contracts

   The plaintiff must allege the terms of the contract or attach a copy of the contract to the complaint as an exhibit.

3. Implied contracts

   An implied contract may exist when, despite no formal agreement, the actions of the parties cause the court to find that a contract exists. For example, a person operating a restaurant may be found by the court to have an implied contract to provide the public with healthy, wholesome food. If the patrons in the establishment are suddenly struck with hepatitis, a suit for breach of this implied contract may result.

In a suit of breach of implied contract, the following facts must be alleged in the complaint:

— The performance by the plaintiff of the contract terms or the excuse for his [or her] nonperformance;
— The facts which caused the defendant to fail to fulfill his [or her] part of the contract; and
— The damages suffered by the plaintiff as the result of the defendant's nonperformance.

Remedies available

- *General damages*: Compensation for the injuries suffered by the plaintiff directly stemming from the defendant's breach.
- *Special damages*: Compensation for the "out-of-pocket" expenses suffered by the plaintiff due to the breach, such as loss of earnings, medical expenses, and injury to property.
- *Attorney's fees*: Attorney's fees are available in any contractual action if called for under the terms of the contract.
- *Costs of suit*: Costs of suit are available in any action at the discretion of the court.
- *Liquidated damages*: Some contracts include in their terms a "liquidated damages" provision, spelling out specific sums payable by a party upon breach of the contract. These provisions may have an effect on the damages awarded to the plaintiff.
- *Exemplary damages*: Recently, some state courts have recognized and approved the award of exemplary or punitive damages in a breach of contract case, if the breach is found by the court to have been "willful or malicious." Exemplary damages are awarded by the court to punish the defendant because of the particularly reprehensible nature of his actions.
- *Prejudgment interest*: Some contracts have provisions for the payment of interest by the defendant on any sums which are to be found due and owing to the plaintiff.

EXHIBIT 4.12 Causes of Action and Remedies (*continued*)

Negligent Torts Causes of Action

The types of torts in this classification include the following:

- Personal injury
- Wrongful death
- Attorney malpractice
- Medical malpractice
- Infliction of emotional trauma
- Wrongful termination

In any negligent tort, the following elements must be pled:

- The existence of a duty owed by the defendant to the plaintiff

There is no hard and fast rule for determining the existence of a duty. The general rule is the question: how would a "reasonable" person have acted in the role of the defendant? If this reasonable person would have performed differently than the defendant and would have taken steps to prevent or lessen the injury suffered by the plaintiff, then a duty exists for the defendant to act in the same manner.

- Breach of the duty
- Plaintiff suffered an injury caused by defendant's breach of duty

Remedies Available in a Negligent Tort Action

In any negligent tort action, the plaintiff may recover the following:

- *Compensatory damages*: The plaintiff may recover damages for the detriment suffered as a result of the defendant's negligent conduct.
- *Lost earnings*: Plaintiff may recover any wages lost because of the defendant's negligent conduct. The amount of lost earnings to be awarded to the plaintiff is based upon the plaintiff's possible future earnings, not past income.
- *Lost profits*: This remedy is available when it can be proven that the plaintiff had a reasonable expectation of earning profits based upon prior earnings.
- *Injury to personal property*: The plaintiff can be awarded damages based upon the damage and the loss of use of personal property.
- *Personal injuries*: The plaintiff can recover damages to compensate for the injuries incurred because of defendant's negligent actions and any injuries the plaintiff can reasonably expect to incur in the future.
- *Pain and suffering*: Plaintiff can recover for past pain and suffering, and if [the] injury is permanent, for the pain and suffering expected to occur in the future.
- *Emotional distress*: Recoverable by the plaintiff in most states only if he [or she] has suffered a physical injury.
- *Loss of consortium*: Recoverable by spouse of the plaintiff for loss of the love and affection of a spouse.
- *Exemplary damages*: Exemplary or punitive damages are available where it can be shown that the defendant acted with malice or criminal indifference.

Relief Available in a Wrongful Death Action

The damages available in wrongful death actions differ from those available in other negligent torts as follows:

- *General damages*: In most states, the monetary damages awarded in a wrongful death action are based upon a formula which takes into account the future monetary contributions and the value of any personal service, training, or advice that may have been given by the decedent to heirs.
- *Spousal damages*: A surviving spouse may recover for the loss of the defendant's love and affection and the value of future earnings.

(continued)

EXHIBIT 4.12 Causes of Action and Remedies (*continued*)

- *Parental damages*: The parents of a deceased child may recover for loss of the child's comfort and society. The parent's future costs for the child's support and education may be discounted in the award.
- *Emotional and mental distress*: Damages for these factors are available when death is not instantaneous.
- *Exemplary damages*: The laws of most states disallow the awarding of exemplary damages in a wrongful death action.
- *Funeral expenses*: The decedent's survivors are entitled to the reasonable cost of all funeral expenses.
- *Damages otherwise available to the decedent*: The administrator of the decedent's estate is permitted to maintain any action on behalf of the decedent that would have accrued had the decedent survived, such as an action for damage to personal property. Such actions are usually joined in the wrongful death complaint.

Source: Adapted from Litigation Paralegal, by Phillip J signay, 1991 by James Publishing, Inc., with permission of the publisher.

SEPARATE COUNTS

Rule 18 of the Federal Rules of Civil Procedure states that a "party asserting a claim . . . may join . . . as many claims . . . as he has against an opposing party." Rule 8 also permits claims to be set out in separate statements or counts.

A single occurrence may result in several claims for relief. In the rodent-in-the-corn example mentioned earlier, the victim had at least two claims against each of the defendants. One claim was for willful or negligent conduct stated in the alternative. The other was for a breach of warranty that the food was edible and safe. The negligence claim could be alleged as Count One and the breach of warranty claim as Count Two. It is also possible, as in our contract case (Case IV, in which the doll clothing company was unable to fulfill its obligation to the dollmaker), that instead of one contract, there could be several contracts, each with a specific delivery date: May 15, July 15, September 15, and October 15. Each of these contracts could be joined in one complaint and alleged in four individual counts. Another possibility exists in the *Forrester* case. If Ann's husband had been joined as one of the parties, the complaint could also allege that William Forrester has suffered and will continue to suffer the loss of consortium (marital affection) of his wife due to the negligence of the defendant. The form of the second count is demonstrated in Exhibit 4.13.

EXHIBIT 4.13 Sample Separate Count

Count Two

1. Plaintiffs hereby incorporate by reference paragraphs 1 through 6 of Count One.
2. Because of Defendants' negligence, Plaintiff William Forrester has suffered loss of the consortium of his wife, Ann Forrester, in the amount of twenty thousand dollars ($20,000).

WHEREFORE, Plaintiff William Forrester demands judgment against Defendant in the sum of twenty thousand dollars ($20,000) and costs and for such other relief as this court may deem just and proper.

Note: The phrase "incorporate by reference" is item one of the sample separate count. This phrase is a drafting mechanism that saves time and space by integrating previous material as if it were restated in its entirety but without having to restate it.

Note: Each separate count should have a separate "wherefore" clause.

DEMAND FOR JURY TRIAL

Rule 38(b) of the Federal Rules indicates that a demand for a jury may be placed in the complaint. This demand is advisable in both federal and state courts. Verify with the attorney the desirability of making a demand for a jury trial before including it in the complaint. The demand can be made later (ten days after service of the last pleading), but by putting the demand in the complaint, a strategic and embarrassing oversight can be avoided. The demand should be in a conspicuous place, such as in the lower right corner of the caption or at the end of the "wherefore" clause above the attorney's signature, as shown in the next sample. State rules and local practice may vary (Exhibit 4.14).

EXHIBIT 4.14 Sample Signature Block (Subscription) and Demand for Jury Trial

> Plaintiff demands trial by jury.
> October,
>
> _____
>
> Arthur White
> White, Wilson & McDuff
> Attorneys at Law
> Federal Plaza Building
> Suite 700
> Third and Market Streets
> Legalville, Columbia 00000
> Telephone: (111) 555-0000
> Bar No: (Required in many states)

THE SIGNATURE BLOCK (RULE 11)

Federal Rule of Civil Procedure 11(a) and parallel state rules require that the complaint (and other pleadings and motions) be signed by the attorney or, if the party is not represented by an attorney, by the party. The address and phone number must be included. Some states require that an e-mail address and, if an attorney, the bar number of that attorney be part of the signature block. Unsigned papers are subject to being stricken if the defect is not corrected immediately after notice of the problem [Rule 11(a)]. As electronic filing of case documents increases (see Chapter 5), electronic signatures are increasingly considered valid. The attorney's assigned electronic identification name and password are sufficient in some courts. Confirm local practice.

The signing of the complaint or other pleading has serious implications. The paralegal should not present the document to the attorney for signature unless it is the product of thoughtful deliberation and investigation. Although it is the attorney who signs the document, the paralegal is often relied on to make some initial judgment as to whether the pleading meets the rules. If it does not, and the attorney signs it, the attorney and the law firm are subject to serious sanctions for ethical violations, in addition to penalties. Rule 3.1 of the Model Rules of Professional Conduct prohibits frivolous pleadings and motions, and Rule 4.4 forbids conduct with no substantial purpose other than to embarrass, delay, or burden another. Courts take Rule 11 requirements very seriously. The plaintiff in *Nieves v. City of Cleveland*, 153 Fed. Appx. 349 (6th Cir. 2005) found out just how seriously a judge takes the filing of frivolous complaints.

CASE STUDY: UNDERSTANDING THE LAW

In *Nieves v. City of Cleveland*, 153 Fed. Appx. 349 (6th Cir. 2005), Jennie Nieves was evicted from a property owned by Martin Fano. Angry about the eviction, Nieves attempted to reenter the property. Not willing to leave quietly, she harassed tenants by making racial slurs, broke a door, and threw a brick through a window. Because of her conduct, a criminal indictment was issued, but ultimately dismissed. Nieves filed a complaint under 42 U.S.C. section 1983 against Fano and a number of city officials. Various motions were filed by the parties. One filed by Fano, a motion for sanctions, placed Nieves and her attorney on notice that the filing of the 1983 action was in bad faith. A 1983 action cannot be filed against a private citizen. The motion for sanctions was granted. The matter was initially appealed and remanded because the district court judge did not follow the proper procedures when awarding sanctions. After a hearing, the district court judge again granted the motion for sanctions and awarded legal fees. In its opinion, the Sixth Circuit Court of Appeals found that Nieves's attorney failed to investigate the claims of his client and that any reasonable attorney would have known with a modicum of legal research that a 1983 action cannot be filed against a private citizen. The court stated that there was little if no evidentiary support for Nieves's claims and that the filing of a 1983 claim against Fano was particularly egregious. Nieves, through her attorney, filed baseless claims. The appeals court found the motion for sanctions for violation of Rule 11 was proper, although the court did reverse the award of attorney's fees for that portion that awarded fees for the prosecution of the first appeal.

Questions for Review: Read the *Nieves* case and determine what other issues were decided in the case. What was the basis for not following the district court's award of attorney's fees to Fano? What lessons are learned from the *Nieves* case regarding the filing of complaints?

Be acutely aware of the following Federal Rule 11(b) provisions:

(b) Representations to Court. By presenting to the court (whether by signing, filing, submitting, or later advocating) a pleading, written motion, or other paper, an attorney or unrepresented party is certifying that to the best of the person's knowledge, information, and belief, formed after an inquiry reasonable under the circumstances,—

(1) it is not being presented for any improper purpose, such as to harass or to cause unnecessary delay or needless increase in the cost of litigation;

(2) the claims, defenses, and other legal contentions therein are warranted by existing law or by a nonfrivolous argument for the extension, modification, or reversal of existing law or the establishment of new law;

(3) the allegations and other factual contentions have evidentiary support or, if specifically so identified, are likely to have evidentiary support after a reasonable opportunity for further investigation or discovery; and

(4) the denials of factual contentions are warranted on the evidence or, if specifically so identified, are reasonably based on a lack of information or belief.

VERIFICATION

The certification method used in the federal system and many states makes verification unnecessary in those jurisdictions. Where verification is required, it consists of a brief affidavit sworn to by the party stating that the party has read the pleading, and it is true except for statements made on information and belief. The purpose of the verification is to deter the filing of false claims by imposing the threat of criminal prosecution for false swearing. Check your state practice on whether notarization is required for the verification (see Exhibit 4.15).

As already mentioned, the filing of a pleading, especially a complaint, is a serious matter that can have a serious impact on the lives of others. When the pleading is sworn to and signed by the client, special care should be given to see that the client reads it carefully; is given the opportunity to ask questions; is asked to raise the right hand and repeat the oath; and is asked to sign the pleading. Above all, if you act as notary, you must witness the client's signature to affirm that the oath was sworn and signed in your presence (Exhibit 4.16).

EXHIBIT 4.15 Sample Pleading Verification

State of Columbia
County of Capitol

Ann Forrester, being first duly sworn on oath according to law, deposes and says that she has read the foregoing complaint and that the matters stated therein are true to the best of her knowledge, information, and belief.

_____
Ann Forrester

Subscribed and sworn to before me this 1st day of October, _____

_____
Notary Public

My commission expires January 1, _____.

TRADE SECRETS: THE FORM OF ELECTRONIC SIGNATURES

Here is the scenario. A complaint is prepared for electronic filing. You assisted in the drafting. Your supervising attorney logs in to the electronic filing system, pays the filing fee, and files the complaint. Soon thereafter, an electronic e-mail message is received indicating that the filing was rejected. Why was the filing rejected? The rules of that court were reviewed thoroughly, so you thought. Everyone is baffled. A telephone call is made to the clerk's office to determine why the complaint was rejected. To your amazement, the clerk communicates that the electronic signature was incorrect. The rules of that court require the signature to appear as follows: /s/ John Jones. The complaint had: s/ John Jones. One small deviation of a singular back slash and the document was rejected. According to the clerk, without both back slashes, the signature was defective. Of course, your supervising attorney is shaking her head in amazement, but in order to perfect the filing, the signature line must be changed. Although this example may seem extreme and picayune, it illustrates the importance of reviewing the rules of each court before filing a document. Some courts follow the posture that s/ followed by the attorney's name is the correct way to electronically sign a document; others follow /s/ with the attorney's name as the correct form. As inconsequential as this may seem, courts want documents the way they want them and reviewing and keeping up with the ever changing rules is critical for any paralegal or attorney. Court Web sites are an excellent place to review court rules. Each court Web site normally has the rules of that court posted, including any special requirements of a particular judge. Simply make it a habit to verify a court's rules prior to filing a document to assure yourself and your supervising attorney of the current status of the rules. Courts identify the most recent updates or amendments of the rules, such as "these rules were amended as of (date)." Unfortunately, generally they do not indicate *what* rules were changed and where those changes were made. Suffice it to say, if court rules have been amended, verify the applicable rule related to your filing for any amendments. This may seem tedious, but better to be safe than sorry rather than having your document rejected by a court for failure to comply with its rules and format requirements.

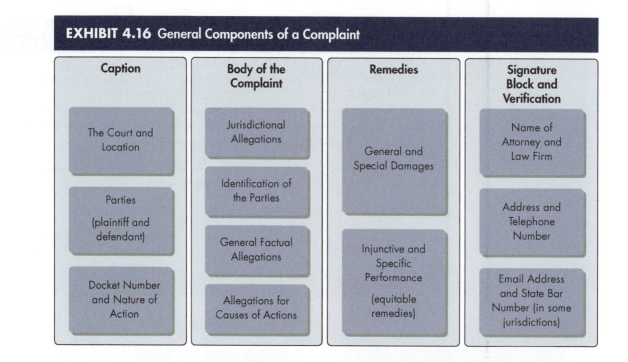

EXHIBIT 4.16 General Components of a Complaint

Caption
- The Court and Location
- Parties (plaintiff and defendant)
- Docket Number and Nature of Action

Body of the Complaint
- Jurisdictional Allegations
- Identification of the Parties
- General Factual Allegations
- Allegations for Causes of Actions

Remedies
- General and Special Damages
- Injunctive and Specific Performance (equitable remedies)

Signature Block and Verification
- Name of Attorney and Law Firm
- Address and Telephone Number
- Email Address and State Bar Number (in some jurisdictions)

EXHIBITS AND APPENDICES

At times, exhibits or an appendix attached to the complaint can be helpful. It is required in some jurisdictions, most commonly in contract cases where the contract or a copy of the contract is included. Exhibits normally include contracts, promissory notes, bills of lading, correspondence, and other documents at issue. An appendix often is used to further explain technical language used in the documents. Exhibits and appendices can be helpful to the parties, but especially to the judge and jury.

Exhibits or appendices are attached following the verification or certification, and essentially become a part of the complaint. The drafter includes references to the attachments in the body of the complaint, as shown in the following example.

6.   That the Defendant prepared a contract that was entered into with the Plaintiff on June 15, _____, a copy of which is attached and marked "Exhibit A," and incorporated into this complaint.

The exhibits and appendix could appear as follows (first page after verification or certification):

Agreement between Plaintiff and Defendant.

EXHIBIT A

[here insert language of contract]

APPENDIX A

[here insert explanatory note or term defined]

"Extraordinary Whole Life 13" refers to a special insurance policy that . . . "

A cost bond must be included with civil complaints in some states. This assures the court that the plaintiff is able to pay court costs if awarded to the other side.

When all aspects of the complaint are ready, they should be placed in their proper order. The paralegal sees to it that the necessary copies are prepared by the legal secretary or copy clerk, including one for the file, one for each defendant, and the original for the court.

SYSTEM CHECKLIST FOR DRAFTING A COMPLAINT

PREPARATION

- [ ] If the complaint is to be filed in state court, consult state rules for differences from the federal rules. Remember that each court may also have its local rules.
- [ ] Review the file for the names and addresses of the parties, the type of claim, and so on.
- [ ] Confirm in what court the action should be filed.
- [ ] Confirm the existence of venue, subject matter jurisdiction, and personal jurisdiction.
- [ ] Research the necessary elements for each cause of action to be alleged.
- [ ] Formulate those elements into a legal syllogism to form the body of each count of the complaint. (If A, B, and C exist, then plaintiff is entitled to X.)
- [ ] Identify the facts needed to support each element of the syllogism.

- [ ] Identify the appropriate remedies.
- [ ] Consult with the supervising attorney to confirm all of the preceding points.
- [ ] Make corrections as the attorney indicates, and do further research or investigation as needed.
- [ ] Check your systems folder for appropriate samples of both federal and state complaints or sections thereof.
- [ ] Obtain one good copy of a recent complaint for the type of claim or claims to be alleged and for the specific court in which the action is to be filed.
- [ ] Check local court rules for size of paper, backing sheets, color, and any other requirements.
- [ ] Check court rules for electronic filing requirements.

DRAFTING

- [ ] Draft the caption.
  - [ ] Indicate the court (branch, if several branches) and its location.
  - [ ] Indicate the parties, the joinder thereof; check spelling and the addresses if included; capacity, real party in interest, and so on. Federal Rule 17, 19, 20; State rule _____; systems folder page _____.
  - [ ] Apply pertinent rules on redaction (editing) to protect personal identity information.
  - [ ] Indicate the docket or court file number of the action if available, or leave an appropriate space.
  - [ ] Indicate the type of complaint (negligence, breach of contract, etc.).
  - [ ] Include the references to federal and state rules and forms on drafting. Federal Rule 10(a); State Rule _____, Form _____; systems folder page _____.
  - [ ] Include a demand for jury trial if so instructed.
- [ ] Draft simple, concise, and direct statements. Avoid repetition and legalese.
- [ ] Use double spacing; quoted matter should be single spaced.
- [ ] Draft the jurisdictional allegation, if required, including any monetary amount. Federal Rule 8(a)(1); State Rule _____; systems folder page _____.
- [ ] Make sure all allegations regarding venue, if required, are included (not necessary in the federal system): location of incident and addresses of parties. State Rule _____; systems folder page _____.
- [ ] Draft the body of the complaint.
  - [ ] Include facts to support each element of the claim.
  - [ ] Use brief, numbered paragraphs limited to one idea. Federal Rule 10(b); State Rule _____; systems folder page _____.
  - [ ] Add just enough detail to meet the minimum requirement for fact pleading or for notice pleading, depending on applicable rules. Federal Rule 8; State Rule _____; systems folder page _____.

☐ Do not state evidence or conclusions.

☐ Avoid impertinent, scandalous, or immaterial language. Federal Rule 11, 12; State Rule _____.

☐ Be truthful; make sure there are provable facts to support a good-faith allegation. Model Rule 3.3(a)(1).

☐ State those allegations that are uncertain but have some basis on information and belief.

☐ Do not anticipate defenses.

☐ Plead hypothetically, in the alternative, and state uncertainty when necessary. Federal Rule 8; State Rule _____; systems folder page _____.

☐ Do not plead the law, except (1) when the action is under a specific statute or administrative rule, or (2) when the action is in one state but relies on the law of another state.

☐ List various damages in one paragraph, unless local rules or practice dictate otherwise.

☐ Check to see that all separate claims are alleged and all separate counts included. Federal Rule 8, 18; State Rule _____; systems folder page _____.

☐ Check to see that paragraphs flow logically and tell an interesting and easy-to-read story.

☐ Choose assertive, persuasive words to evoke sympathy and convey confidence.

☐ Check that all incorporations by reference (including exhibits and appendixes) have been accurately stated where needed.

☐ Draft special matters as they arise.

☐ Aver the capacity of the parties unless not required by local rules. It is not required in the federal system [Rule 9].

☐ Aver the circumstances supporting the allegation of fraud or mistake with particularity [Rule 9].

☐ Aver malice, intent, knowledge, or other condition of the mind generally [Rule 9].

☐ Aver the performance of all conditions precedent generally [Rule 9]; aver the denial of performance with particularity.

☐ Aver that an official document was issued or act done in compliance with the law [Rule 9].

☐ Aver a judgment or decision of domestic or foreign court, administrative tribunal, or of a board of officers without alleging facts showing jurisdiction to render it.

☐ Aver time and place [Rule 9].

☐ Aver specifically any special damages [Rule 9].

☐ Draft the prayer for relief (demand for judgment).

    ☐ State relief in the alternative when necessary. Federal Rule 8; State Rule _____; systems folder page _____.

        ☐ Damages   ☐ Recovery of property

        ☐ Injuries   ☐ Specific performance   ☐ Other

☐ Draft the signature block and see to it that the attorney's address and phone number are included. Federal Rule 11; State Rule _____; systems folder page _____.

☐ Draft verification if required (not required in federal pleadings). Federal Rule 11; State Rule _____; systems folder page _____.

☐ Have the client swear to the truthfulness of the complaint and sign it in your presence if you are a notary.

☐ Attach exhibits and appendices.

☐ See that the complaint is typed and prepared with sufficient copies.

INJUNCTIONS

At times the attorney will instruct the paralegal to draft a request for an injunction or temporary restraining order to accompany the complaint. This is necessary in some circumstances to prevent further deterioration in the subject of the lawsuit, or some other violation of a party's rights. For example, if a defendant is sued over a boundary dispute, a preliminary injunction may be in order to prevent the defendant from cutting down trees on the disputed property until the suit is resolved.

Rule 65 sets out the difference between a preliminary injunction and a temporary restraining order. The important thing to remember, however, is that these documents are filed to require the other party either to do or refrain from doing some act. Without such action, the plaintiff could possibly suffer irreparable harm.

The injunction or temporary restraining order should be filed with the complaint along with a proposed order prohibiting or demanding the action in question. The request is often supported by a memorandum of law. A surety bond must also be filed with the court.

INTERNET EXERCISE

Locate examples of requests for temporary restraining order and preliminary injunction and determine the common threads that are in each type of request. What is the common language that appears in these motions?

CONVENTIONAL AND ELECTRONIC FILINGS: IS THERE A CHOICE?

Now that you have mastered how to draft a complaint, the next task that must be performed is the filing of that complaint. With filing, you are giving notice that a lawsuit has been filed. There are two ways to file a complaint: directly with the clerk's office or electronically. Some states permit a complaint to be filed either way; other states require complaints to be filed electronically only. As a paralegal, you must check your jurisdiction's rules to determine what procedure is available. Remember that the federal and state court systems are different. The requirements for the filing of a federal complaint in your jurisdiction may be different from filing a complaint in a state court.

Conventional Filing

Before electronically filing, all complaints and court documents were filed directly with the clerk's office. What this meant is that either you would physically file your complaint with the clerk's office or mail it in. After payment of the filing fee, the clerk's office would assign a docket number to the case and manually write it on the complaint. Once this was done, the document was ready for service. Some courts, even the federal courts, allow conventional filing. In the federal system, the complaint is generally the only document that can be filed conventionally or in person. Of course, there are exceptions to this, but they are few. State courts that do not have electronic filing systems still require conventional filing of complaints and require conventional filing of all documents directly with the clerk. Conventional filing is becoming less common, but still exists. Know what the process is in your state and federal courts.

Electronic Filing

CM/ECF (case management/ electronic case filing)
Electronic filing system used in the federal court system.

Electronic filing is the accepted practice in most federal courts and with few exceptions is the only method of filing documents. Filing a complaint electronically requires that the attorney register with the court's electronic filing system. In the federal courts, it is known as the **CM/ECF (Case Management/Electronic Case Filing)** system. For states, the electronic filing system varies requiring the paralegals to familiarize themselves with each system used in the jurisdiction where the complaint is being filed. By registering with the court's electronic filing system, the attorney is given a user name and password. With the user name and password, the attorney logs in and follows the prompts for filing of the complaint. Note that many of the courts have tutorials to assist in determining the procedure for filing a complaint. It is prudent to review the process to save time and headaches. For example, let us assume that when filing the complaint, the attorney wants to review a previous screen and hits the "back" button. In some instances, this may cause the transaction to be cancelled requiring the process to begin again. Or, let's assume that the attorney is ready to pay the filing fee, inputs all the credit card information, and wants to check a previous screen for something. The act of hitting the back button may cause the credit card to be charged twice resulting in double billing. When this happens, contact the clerk's office of the court that the complaint was filed in. At some point in the near future, electronic filing will be the only means of filing court documents. Mastering the process is an important skill.

Part of mastering the process is mastering the nuances of what is required by the courts and judges. Often individual judges have individual requirements regarding electronic filing. Some judges require that copies of all electronically filed documents be transmitted to the judge's chambers, the clerk's office, or through e-mail. It may seem like a duplication of efforts, but that simply may be what a particular judge requires. Check the local rules of the courts in which documents may be filed. There may be special rules that go beyond the Federal Rules of Civil Procedure or local rules for that matter. Review the court's Web site for special rules pertaining to a court or judge in that jurisdiction.

SUMMARY

Drafting good pleadings is an important art that increases your value to the law firm. The first pleading to be drafted in litigation is the complaint. It introduces the cause of action, invokes the court's jurisdiction, presents the facts of the case, and provides due process notice to the defendant. A complaint consists of three main parts: the caption, the body, and the prayer for relief. What must be stated in these sections is established by court rules, the nature of the action, remedies available, and techniques of drafting. Sample forms and a checklist for drafting complaints are provided in the chapter as guides to be adapted for state or federal court. The assignments for the chapter emphasize your need to practice applying the techniques and procedures outlined in the chapter.

In addition, you have learned about the pleadings needed to file for an injunction. An injunction may be sought as a lone action or as a remedy in conjunction with another action. Its purpose is to request a court to prohibit the action of another or to command that the other party take some action. Injunctions are an important tool in our legal system to prevent damage before it occurs. Sample motions for an injunction have been provided for your use. Familiarity with and practice at each of the tasks presented in this chapter will increase your ability and confidence as a paralegal. This includes mastering the requirements for filing documents electronically, both in the federal or state court systems.

KEY TERMS

capacity	exemplary (punitive) damages	plaintiff
cause of action	fact pleading	pleadings
class action	general damages	prohibitory injunction
CM/ECF (case management/ electronic case filing)	guardian ad litem	real party in interest
complaint	interpleader	special damages
defendant	joinder of parties	specific performance
due process of law	mandatory injunction	standing to sue
	notice pleading	

QUESTIONS FOR STUDY AND REVIEW

1. Describe the various sections of a complaint, their contents, and the functions of each section.

2. What are the minimum requirements in order for a person to be eligible to sue or be sued? What happens when a person has grounds for a lawsuit but does not have the legal capacity to sue?

3. What is the federal and your state rule on joinder of parties in a lawsuit?

4. What are class actions and in what ways can they be beneficial?

5. What role do jurisdictional amounts play in both federal and state courts?

6. What are the necessary components of an adequate jurisdictional allegation?

7. Why is venue important to the drafter of a complaint? When venue must be alleged, what specifically needs to be included?

8. What is a syllogism? A major and minor premise? How can it be useful to the drafter of a complaint?

9. What ethical consideration must a paralegal keep in mind when drafting a complaint? Cite the disciplinary rule.

10. What is the difference between fact pleading and notice pleading? What federal and state rules set out guidelines for pleading?

11. What is the difference, if any, between a prayer for relief, a demand for judgment, and the "wherefore" clause?

12. What are damages and what is the difference between general and special damages? What are noneconomic damages?

13. What does it mean to have multiple counts in a complaint? Should there be a "wherefore" clause in each count? What is the proper method of incorporating paragraphs of one count into another?

14. What does an attorney certify in signing a complaint where verification is not required?

15. What is the purpose of an appendix to a complaint? What is the proper way to reference either an exhibit or an appendix?

SYSTEMS FOLDER ASSIGNMENTS

1. Research the rules of civil procedure for your state for the recommended caption form. If the rules of your state do not have sample forms, go to a book on forms or the Internet for civil action in your state. Place a copy of the state caption form with copies of the captions from the text at the beginning of the complaint section of your systems folder. Also list the applicable rules and forms. Note any state rules or policy regarding the redaction of privacy information.

2. Following class discussion on drafting complaints, especially regarding state court rules, complete the state and systems folder reference blanks in the System Checklist for Drafting a Complaint, and place it in your systems folder.

3. Check the pleading rules of your own state. Gather examples of local complaints by researching recent editions of legal forms and pleading books, or obtain them from your instructor. Try to locate a full range of examples of complaints that include pleading in the alternative, pleading in the hypothetical, joined parties, and joined claims and counts. Place them in your systems folder. Add references to the page numbers in this text where samples of specific types of complaints can be located. Add references to or copies of injunction and restraining order forms.

4. Review the federal rule on class action lawsuits. Prepare a general outline of the required allegations for a class action suit.

5. For your systems folder, research the elements of the following causes of action for reference in preparing complaints for your supervising attorney:

   a. Anticipatory breach of contract

   b. Specific performance (Construction case)

   c. Unfair competition

   d. Discrimination case (racial, age, and religion)

   e. Wrongful termination of employment

   f. Medical malpractice

   g. Legal malpractice

APPLICATION ASSIGNMENTS

1. Your boss is an avid baseball fan and cannot believe his luck. In walks Johnny Vance who was injured when he was at the Kansas City Royals game. He tells your boss, Bernard Roberts, that while watching a Royals game, the mascot, Sluggerr, tossed a hotdog at him and injured him. He wants to sue the Kansas City Royals organization and your attorney has asked you to prepare the complaint. Refer to *Coomer v. Kansas City Royals Baseball Organization*, 437 S.W. 3d 184 (Mo. 2014) for a synopsis of the facts and create your own complaint with possible causes of actions.

2. While attending a football game, Harry Crane was filmed by the network television cameras sleeping during the game. This broadcast was watched by millions of people as it was one of the play-off games. During the broadcast, the commentators focused on Harry and said that he was a slovenly character who was in a stupor during one of the biggest games of the year. The commentators continued to broadcast that Harry was so bored that he had nothing better to do than sleep through the game. They said that he looked like he had "way too much beer and pizza" based on appearance. Harry is furious and says his reputation has been ruined. He was tired from some medication he was taking and did not appreciate the national attention he received. He wants to sue the National Football League for defamation, intentional infliction of emotional distress, damages, and exemplary damages for the intentional acts of the League's announcers. Research the elements of the causes of action that Harry wants to advance and determine whether Harry has a legitimate claim against the NFL. Prepare a memorandum with your findings to your supervising attorney. (Based on *Rector v. MLB*, ESPN New York.)

3. Micky Speer has contracted with hall of fame trainer Eddie Fast to train Mr. Fix, a racehorse, for the Kentucky Derby. Fast resigns on April 6, a month before the race, in a dispute over fringe benefits. To force Fast to train his horse through the race of a lifetime, Speer sues for specific performance. What are the elements of a cause of action for specific performance? Prepare a complaint that Mr. Speer intends to file against Eddie Fast. (Be creative.)

4. List and give examples of four types of remedies typically sought by plaintiffs in civil litigation.

5. Using the facts from the *Ameche* case (Case II in Chapter 1), draft a complaint using notice pleading.

CASE ASSIGNMENTS

1. Prepare the complaint that your law firm will file on behalf of Mrs. Ann Forrester from Case I.

2. Your attorney is not sure whether she wants to file the Forrester matter in state court or federal court. Prepare a memorandum using your state and federal case law to determine what options are available in deciding in which court to file the complaint.

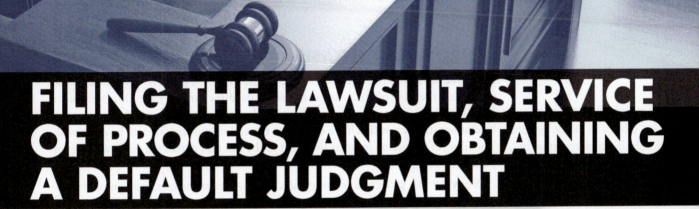

FILING THE LAWSUIT, SERVICE OF PROCESS, AND OBTAINING A DEFAULT JUDGMENT

OBJECTIVES

AFTER READING THIS CHAPTER, YOU WILL BE ABLE TO:

- Prepare the documents needed to serve a defendant in a lawsuit
- Determine the different requirements for service of process in the federal and state court systems
- Serve a defendant under a state's long arm statute
- Draft a default judgment for a state or federal case
- Identify the circumstances under which a default judgment may be set aside

INTRODUCTION

THE TASKS: FILING THE LAWSUIT, SERVING THE SUMMONS, OBTAINING A DEFAULT JUDGMENT

Mr. White has met with Mrs. Forrester and reviewed her case. She has decided to go forward with her lawsuit. You have been assigned the following tasks:

1. Prepare the necessary documents to file the action.

2. File the documents with the court clerk.

3. Serve each defendant with the summons and complaint.

4. If the defendant does not respond, prepare the necessary documents to obtain a default judgment.

PURPOSE OF THE TASKS

service of process
Delivery to the defendant of official notification of the lawsuit and of his or her need to respond; delivery of a copy of the summons, complaint, writs, and other documents to another party.

Filing the lawsuit is the first formal step in the litigation process. It establishes the date when the case officially begins, and all deadlines in the case ultimately stem from that date. If the claim has not been filed prior to the running of the statute of limitations, the opposition has a defense to the action and the case will be dismissed. The filing of the action informs the court of the suit and makes the claim a matter of public record.

Service of process (delivery of a copy of the summons and complaint) officially notifies the defendant of the lawsuit and the defendant's need to respond (answer). Service also gives the court personal jurisdiction over the defendant, which is necessary for the court to impose a binding judgment on the defendant. Discussion of the default judgment is reserved for later in this chapter.

PREPARING DOCUMENTS FOR FILING AN ACTION AND FOR SERVICE OF PROCESS

DETERMINE WHAT DOCUMENTS ARE NEEDED

There are several ways to determine what is needed to file an action. One method is to ask an experienced paralegal or attorney in your law firm. Another method, until you are familiar with the requirements, is to visit the clerk of the court in which the action will be filed. The clerk will explain to you what is needed and will probably give you copies of some of the forms you will need. Do not be afraid of appearing uninformed. The clerks are there to help you and want you to have a good start.

This visit will acquaint you with the clerk's personnel, who will be of considerable help to you in the years to come. If you treat these individuals with courtesy and respect, remembering that they also are under pressure and time constraints, your relationship with the clerk's office should develop on a cordial and productive basis.

INTERNET EXERCISE

Determine the statutory authority in your state which identifies the service of process requirements for filing a lawsuit in your state court.

Consult the court filing and service requirements in the Federal Rules of Civil Procedure (FED. R. CIV. P.) and parallel state rules. An excellent Web site for the rules, their latest and proposed revisions, and committee commentary is http://www .uscourts.gov. State rules may be available through the Web sites of your state courts, a state law library, a state law school library, or a commercial site such as Westlaw or Lexis. Frequently, courts have their own local rules in addition to the standard rules that dictate what documents must be prepared and filed. Confirm with the attorney the method of service of process to be used.

GATHER AND PREPARE THE DOCUMENTS NECESSARY FOR FILING AND SERVICE

Introduction

Once the required documents are identified, draft the necessary information into the forms, or, in some cases, draft the entire document. Note that the latest edition of federal court forms can be found at uscourts.gov. Your state court site may have forms as well.

Complaint

The complaint has been prepared, but this is a good time to check its accuracy and to see that it has been signed by the attorney or verified by the client as required by the jurisdiction and that the necessary copies have been prepared. Blue backings may be required by the state if filed through the conventional (in person) method; they are not required in federal court, and are impractical if the document will be delivered electronically.

Summons

summons

A document issued by the court that informs the defendant of the action and requires the defendant to respond or appear by or at a designated time; when served, gives the court personal jurisdiction over the defendant.

A **summons** is a document issued by the court that informs the defendant of the action and requires the defendant to respond or appear by or at a designated time. When served on the defendant, it gives the court personal jurisdiction over the defendant. Federal Rule of Civil Procedure 4(a) provides the requirements for a valid summons in federal court. All states have similar requirements. The summons is signed by the clerk of court, bears the seal of the court, identifies the court and the parties, is directed to the defendant, states the name and address of the plaintiff's attorney, states the time within which the defendant must appear and defend, and provides notice that failure to respond will result in a default judgment being entered for the plaintiff in the amount demanded.

Most clerks have preprinted copies of the summons. Obtain a copy of the summons, and see that it is properly and accurately filled out. Exhibit 5.1 is a federal summons which can be used for the Ann Forrester case. Rule 4(b) permits the listing of multiple defendants on the summons. Copies must be prepared for each defendant.

Civil Cover Sheet

A Civil Cover Sheet should be prepared for each civil case filed in federal district court. Some states require the completion of a similar form. Exhibit 5.2 is an example of the federal Civil Cover Sheet. Always make sure that this cover sheet is signed by the attorney.

APPLY YOUR KNOWLEDGE

Using the form in Exhibit 5.1, note any differences in your state summons from the federal form.

EXHIBIT 5.1 Summons in a Civil Action

AO 440 (Rev. 06/12) Summons in a Civil Action

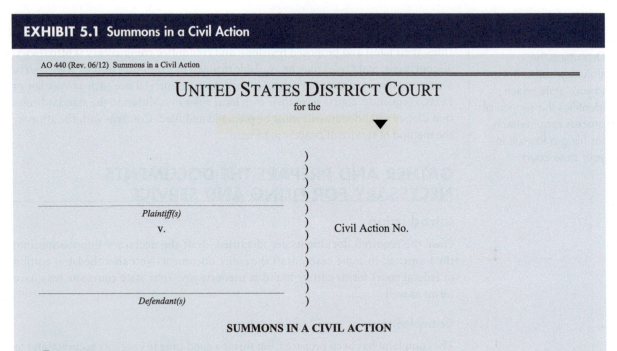

UNITED STATES DISTRICT COURT
for the

▼

<table>
<tr><td></td><td>)</td><td></td></tr>
<tr><td></td><td>)</td><td></td></tr>
<tr><td></td><td>)</td><td></td></tr>
<tr><td></td><td>)</td><td></td></tr>
<tr><td>_____
Plaintiff(s)</td><td>)</td><td></td></tr>
<tr><td>v.</td><td>)</td><td>Civil Action No.</td></tr>
<tr><td></td><td>)</td><td></td></tr>
<tr><td></td><td>)</td><td></td></tr>
<tr><td></td><td>)</td><td></td></tr>
<tr><td>_____
Defendant(s)</td><td>)</td><td></td></tr>
</table>

SUMMONS IN A CIVIL ACTION

To: *(Defendant's name and address)*

A lawsuit has been filed against you.

Within 21 days after service of this summons on you (not counting the day you received it) — or 60 days if you are the United States or a United States agency, or an officer or employee of the United States described in Fed. R. Civ. P. 12 (a)(2) or (3) — you must serve on the plaintiff an answer to the attached complaint or a motion under Rule 12 of the Federal Rules of Civil Procedure. The answer or motion must be served on the plaintiff or plaintiff's attorney, whose name and address are:

If you fail to respond, judgment by default will be entered against you for the relief demanded in the complaint. You also must file your answer or motion with the court.

CLERK OF COURT

Date: _____   _____

Signature of Clerk or Deputy Clerk

EXHIBIT 5.1 Summons in a Civil Action (*continued*)

AO 440 (Rev. 06/12) Summons in a Civil Action (Page 2)

Civil Action No.

PROOF OF SERVICE
(This section should not be filed with the court unless required by Fed. R. Civ. P. 4 (l))

This summons for *(name of individual and title, if any)* _____

was received by me on *(date)* _____ .

❏ I personally served the summons on the individual at *(place)* _____

_____ on *(date)* _____ ; or

❏ I left the summons at the individual's residence or usual place of abode with *(name)* _____

_____ , a person of suitable age and discretion who resides there,

on *(date)* _____ , and mailed a copy to the individual's last known address; or

❏ I served the summons on *(name of individual)* _____ , who is

designated by law to accept service of process on behalf of *(name of organization)* _____

_____ on *(date)* _____ ; or

❏ I returned the summons unexecuted because _____ ; or

❏ Other *(specify):*

My fees are $ _____ for travel and $ _____ for services, for a total of $ 0.00   .

I declare under penalty of perjury that this information is true.

Date: _____

_____
Server's signature

_____
Printed name and title

_____
Server's address

Additional information regarding attempted service, etc:

[Print]   [Save As...]   [Reset]

Source: U.S. Courts.

EXHIBIT 5.2 Civil Cover Sheet (Completed Form)

JS 44   (Rev. 12/12)

CIVIL COVER SHEET

The JS 44 civil cover sheet and the information contained herein neither replace nor supplement the filing and service of pleadings or other papers as required by law, except as provided by local rules of court. This form, approved by the Judicial Conference of the United States in September 1974, is required for the use of the Clerk of Court for the purpose of initiating the civil docket sheet. *(SEE INSTRUCTIONS ON NEXT PAGE OF THIS FORM.)*

I. (a) PLAINTIFFS

(b) County of Residence of First Listed Plaintiff _____
(EXCEPT IN U.S. PLAINTIFF CASES)

(c) Attorneys *(Firm Name, Address, and Telephone Number)*

DEFENDANTS

County of Residence of First Listed Defendant _____
(IN U.S. PLAINTIFF CASES ONLY)

NOTE: IN LAND CONDEMNATION CASES, USE THE LOCATION OF
THE TRACT OF LAND INVOLVED.

Attorneys *(If Known)*

II. BASIS OF JURISDICTION *(Place an "X" in One Box Only)*

- ❏ 1 U.S. Government
       Plaintiff
- ❏ 2 U.S. Government
       Defendant
- ❏ 3 Federal Question
       (U.S. Government Not a Party)
- ❏ 4 Diversity
       (Indicate Citizenship of Parties in Item III)

III. CITIZENSHIP OF PRINCIPAL PARTIES *(Place an "X" in One Box for Plaintiff*
(For Diversity Cases Only)   *and One Box for Defendant)*

	PTF	DEF		PTF	DEF
Citizen of This State	❏ 1	❏ 1	Incorporated *or* Principal Place of Business In This State	❏ 4	❏ 4
Citizen of Another State	❏ 2	❏ 2	Incorporated *and* Principal Place of Business In Another State	❏ 5	❏ 5
Citizen or Subject of a Foreign Country	❏ 3	❏ 3	Foreign Nation	❏ 6	❏ 6

IV. NATURE OF SUIT *(Place an "X" in One Box Only)*

CONTRACT	TORTS		FORFEITURE/PENALTY	BANKRUPTCY	OTHER STATUTES

❏ 110 Insurance
❏ 120 Marine
❏ 130 Miller Act
❏ 140 Negotiable Instrument
❏ 150 Recovery of Overpayment
    & Enforcement of Judgment
❏ 151 Medicare Act
❏ 152 Recovery of Defaulted
    Student Loans
    (Excludes Veterans)
❏ 153 Recovery of Overpayment
    of Veteran's Benefits
❏ 160 Stockholders' Suits
❏ 190 Other Contract
❏ 195 Contract Product Liability
❏ 196 Franchise
	PERSONAL INJURY
	❏ 310 Airplane
	❏ 315 Airplane Product
	    Liability
	❏ 320 Assault, Libel &
	    Slander
	❏ 330 Federal Employers'
	    Liability
	❏ 340 Marine
	❏ 345 Marine Product
	    Liability
	❏ 350 Motor Vehicle
	❏ 355 Motor Vehicle
	    Product Liability
	❏ 360 Other Personal
	    Injury
	❏ 362 Personal Injury -
	    Medical Malpractice
		PERSONAL INJURY
		❏ 365 Personal Injury -
		    Product Liability
		❏ 367 Health Care/
		    Pharmaceutical
		    Personal Injury
		    Product Liability
		❏ 368 Asbestos Personal
		    Injury Product
		    Liability
		PERSONAL PROPERTY
		❏ 370 Other Fraud
		❏ 371 Truth in Lending
		❏ 380 Other Personal
		    Property Damage
		❏ 385 Property Damage
		    Product Liability
			❏ 625 Drug Related Seizure
			    of Property 21 USC 881
			❏ 690 Other
			
			LABOR
			❏ 710 Fair Labor Standards
			    Act
			❏ 720 Labor/Management
			    Relations
			❏ 740 Railway Labor Act
			❏ 751 Family and Medical
			    Leave Act
			❏ 790 Other Labor Litigation
			❏ 791 Employee Retirement
			    Income Security Act
				❏ 422 Appeal 28 USC 158
				❏ 423 Withdrawal
				    28 USC 157
				
				PROPERTY RIGHTS
				❏ 820 Copyrights
				❏ 830 Patent
				❏ 840 Trademark
				
				SOCIAL SECURITY
				❏ 861 HIA (1395ff)
				❏ 862 Black Lung (923)
				❏ 863 DIWC/DIWW (405(g))
				❏ 864 SSID Title XVI
				❏ 865 RSI (405(g))
					❏ 375 False Claims Act
					❏ 400 State Reapportionment
					❏ 410 Antitrust
					❏ 430 Banks and Banking
					❏ 450 Commerce
					❏ 460 Deportation
					❏ 470 Racketeer Influenced and
					    Corrupt Organizations
					❏ 480 Consumer Credit
					❏ 490 Cable/Sat TV
					❏ 850 Securities/Commodities/
					    Exchange
					❏ 890 Other Statutory Actions
					❏ 891 Agricultural Acts
					❏ 893 Environmental Matters
					❏ 895 Freedom of Information
					    Act
					❏ 896 Arbitration

REAL PROPERTY
❏ 210 Land Condemnation
❏ 220 Foreclosure
❏ 230 Rent Lease & Ejectment
❏ 240 Torts to Land
❏ 245 Tort Product Liability
❏ 290 All Other Real Property
	CIVIL RIGHTS
	❏ 440 Other Civil Rights
	❏ 441 Voting
	❏ 442 Employment
	❏ 443 Housing/
	    Accommodations
	❏ 445 Amer. w/Disabilities -
	    Employment
	❏ 446 Amer. w/Disabilities -
	    Other
	❏ 448 Education
		PRISONER PETITIONS
		Habeas Corpus:
		❏ 463 Alien Detainee
		❏ 510 Motions to Vacate
		    Sentence
		❏ 530 General
		❏ 535 Death Penalty
		Other:
		❏ 540 Mandamus & Other
		❏ 550 Civil Rights
		❏ 555 Prison Condition
		❏ 560 Civil Detainee -
		    Conditions of
		    Confinement
			IMMIGRATION
			❏ 462 Naturalization Application
			❏ 465 Other Immigration
			    Actions
				FEDERAL TAX SUITS
				❏ 870 Taxes (U.S. Plaintiff
				    or Defendant)
				❏ 871 IRS—Third Party
				    26 USC 7609
					❏ 899 Administrative Procedure
					    Act/Review or Appeal of
					    Agency Decision
					❏ 950 Constitutionality of
					    State Statutes

V. ORIGIN *(Place an "X" in One Box Only)*

- ❏ 1 Original
       Proceeding
- ❏ 2 Removed from
       State Court
- ❏ 3 Remanded from
       Appellate Court
- ❏ 4 Reinstated or
       Reopened
- ❏ 5 Transferred from
       Another District
       (specify)
- ❏ 6 Multidistrict
       Litigation

VI. CAUSE OF ACTION

Cite the U.S. Civil Statute under which you are filing *(Do not cite jurisdictional statutes unless diversity)*:
_____

Brief description of cause:
_____

**VII. REQUESTED IN
COMPLAINT:**

❏ CHECK IF THIS IS A CLASS ACTION
   UNDER RULE 23, F.R.Cv.P.

DEMAND $ _____

CHECK YES only if demanded in complaint:
JURY DEMAND: ❏ Yes   ❏ No

**VIII. RELATED CASE(S)
IF ANY**

(See instructions):

JUDGE _____

DOCKET NUMBER _____

DATE _____

SIGNATURE OF ATTORNEY OF RECORD _____

FOR OFFICE USE ONLY

RECEIPT # _____   AMOUNT _____   APPLYING IFP _____   JUDGE _____   MAG. JUDGE _____

Print	Save As...		Reset

Source: U.S. Courts.

INTERNET EXERCISE

Check your state and local rules to see if a parallel waiver of service of summons has been adopted. Identify the applicable state and local rules and list their requirements for waiver of service of summons. Also, confirm whether the Notice of Lawsuit and Request for Waiver of Service of Summons and the Waiver of Service of Summons can be delivered and executed electronically in your jurisdiction.

Notice of Lawsuit and Request for Waiver of Service of Summons; Waiver of Service of Summons

Rule 4(d) allows plaintiffs in actions filed in federal court to reduce the cost and time involved in serving the summons by placing a duty on the defendant to waive service of the summons. This process requires two documents to be provided and prepared by the plaintiff. The first is the Notice of Lawsuit and Request for Waiver of Service of Summons. It is addressed directly to the defendant, if an individual, or else to an officer or agent authorized to receive service. It identifies the court in which the action has been filed and the docket number, informs the defendant of the consequences of compliance and failure to comply with the request, sets forth the date the request is sent, and states that the defendant has thirty days (sixty if located in a foreign country) in which to return the waiver. The notice and request must be sent to each defendant. Exhibit 5.3 is the Notice of Lawsuit and Request for Waiver of Service of Summons.

The second document is the Waiver of Service of the Summons (see Exhibit 5.4). It includes the case caption, docket number, court, and date the request was sent. The plaintiff sends to the defendant two copies of this waiver to be signed, along with means of return (self-addressed, stamped envelope). If the defendant returns the signed waiver, the period in which to answer the complaint is extended from the usual twenty days to sixty days (ninety, if out of the country).

A defendant who fails to waive service of the summons must bear the cost of service, including the plaintiff's related attorney fees, unless good cause is shown. Good cause does not include a belief that the complaint is unfounded. A defendant who returns the waiver retains all defenses and objections to the complaint, including those regarding jurisdiction and venue.

The plaintiff's attorney may elect not to use the notice and waiver process, especially if the statute of limitations is about to expire, and no time remains to send and receive a waiver.

Request for Service of Process

Although most federal service is by waiver or effected by any person over eighteen not a party, the U.S. marshal located in each federal district may be requested through the court to make service. The marshal must serve process when the plaintiff is indigent (**in forma pauperis**) or a seaman [Rule 4(c)(3)]. The U.S. government is no longer required to use the marshal or appointed server.

When the marshal does serve process, Form Process Receipt and Return must be completed by the law firm and filed with the action. An example of this form is shown in Exhibit 5.5. This form is available through the marshal's office or at http://www.usmarshals.gov. The fee for the marshal's service is minimal, but must be included when filing the Process Receipt and Return.

Many state courts also require the filing of a request for service of process. Filed with the clerk of the state court, this request is then given to the local sheriff or constable with the summons and complaint.

Motion for Special Appointment to Serve Process

In some circumstances your attorney may decide that service should be made by a process server specially appointed by the court [Rule 4(c)(3)]. If so, prepare the motion. Exhibit 5.6 is an example of the motion.

in forma pauperis
"In the manner of a pauper"; permission given to a indigent person to sue without liability for costs.

APPLY YOUR KNOWLEDGE

Determine whether a request for service is required in your state and identify the legal authority for the request. Place a copy of the request form in your systems folder.

EXHIBIT 5.3 Notice of Lawsuit and Request for Waiver of Service of Summons

AO 398 (Rev. 01/09) Notice of a Lawsuit and Request to Waive Service of a Summons

UNITED STATES DISTRICT COURT
for the

▼

_____   )
_____Plaintiff_____   )
            v.   )   Civil Action No. _____
_____   )
_____Defendant_____   )

NOTICE OF A LAWSUIT AND REQUEST TO WAIVE SERVICE OF A SUMMONS

To: _____
(Name of the defendant or - if the defendant is a corporation, partnership, or association - an officer or agent authorized to receive service)

Why are you getting this?

A lawsuit has been filed against you, or the entity you represent, in this court under the number shown above. A copy of the complaint is attached.

This is not a summons, or an official notice from the court. It is a request that, to avoid expenses, you waive formal service of a summons by signing and returning the enclosed waiver. To avoid these expenses, you must return the signed waiver within _____ days *(give at least 30 days, or at least 60 days if the defendant is outside any judicial district of the United States)* from the date shown below, which is the date this notice was sent. Two copies of the waiver form are enclosed, along with a stamped, self-addressed envelope or other prepaid means for returning one copy. You may keep the other copy.

What happens next?

If you return the signed waiver, I will file it with the court. The action will then proceed as if you had been served on the date the waiver is filed, but no summons will be served on you and you will have 60 days from the date this notice is sent (see the date below) to answer the complaint (or 90 days if this notice is sent to you outside any judicial district of the United States).

If you do not return the signed waiver within the time indicated, I will arrange to have the summons and complaint served on you. And I will ask the court to require you, or the entity you represent, to pay the expenses of making service.

Please read the enclosed statement about the duty to avoid unnecessary expenses.

I certify that this request is being sent to you on the date below.

Date: _____   _____
                              Signature of the attorney or unrepresented party

                              _____
                              Printed name

                              _____
                              Address

                              _____
                              E-mail address

                              _____
                              Telephone number

[Print]   [Save As...]   [Reset]

Source: U.S. Courts.

EXHIBIT 5.4 Waiver of Service of Summons

AO 399 (01/09) Waiver of the Service of Summons

UNITED STATES DISTRICT COURT
for the

▼

	)	
_____	)	
Plaintiff	)	Civil Action No.
v.	)	
_____	)	
Defendant	)	

WAIVER OF THE SERVICE OF SUMMONS

To: _____
         (Name of the plaintiff's attorney or unrepresented plaintiff)

    I have received your request to waive service of a summons in this action along with a copy of the complaint, two copies of this waiver form, and a prepaid means of returning one signed copy of the form to you.

    I, or the entity I represent, agree to save the expense of serving a summons and complaint in this case.

    I understand that I, or the entity I represent, will keep all defenses or objections to the lawsuit, the court's jurisdiction, and the venue of the action, but that I waive any objections to the absence of a summons or of service.

    I also understand that I, or the entity I represent, must file and serve an answer or a motion under Rule 12 within 60 days from _____, the date when this request was sent (or 90 days if it was sent outside the United States). If I fail to do so, a default judgment will be entered against me or the entity I represent.

Date: _____

                                                  _____
                                                  Signature of the attorney or unrepresented party

_____
Printed name of party waiving service of summons

                                                  _____
                                                     Printed name

                                                  _____
                                                        Address

                                                  _____
                                                   E-mail address

                                                  _____
                                                   Telephone number

---

Duty to Avoid Unnecessary Expenses of Serving a Summons

    Rule 4 of the Federal Rules of Civil Procedure requires certain defendants to cooperate in saving unnecessary expenses of serving a summons and complaint. A defendant who is located in the United States and who fails to return a signed waiver of service requested by a plaintiff located in the United States will be required to pay the expenses of service, unless the defendant shows good cause for the failure.

    "Good cause" does *not* include a belief that the lawsuit is groundless, or that it has been brought in an improper venue, or that the court has no jurisdiction over this matter or over the defendant or the defendant's property.

    If the waiver is signed and returned, you can still make these and all other defenses and objections, but you cannot object to the absence of a summons or of service.

    If you waive service, then you must, within the time specified on the waiver form, serve an answer or a motion under Rule 12 on the plaintiff and file a copy with the court. By signing and returning the waiver form, you are allowed more time to respond than if a summons had been served.

Print	Save As...		Reset

Source: U.S. Courts.

EXHIBIT 5.5 Process Receipt and Return

U.S. Department of Justice
United States Marshals Service

PROCESS RECEIPT AND RETURN
See *"Instructions for Service of Process by U.S. Marshal"*

PLAINTIFF	COURT CASE NUMBER
DEFENDANT	TYPE OF PROCESS

SERVE AT

NAME OF INDIVIDUAL, COMPANY, CORPORATION. ETC. TO SERVE OR DESCRIPTION OF PROPERTY TO SEIZE OR CONDEMN

ADDRESS *(Street or RFD, Apartment No., City, State and ZIP Code)*

SEND NOTICE OF SERVICE COPY TO REQUESTER AT NAME AND ADDRESS BELOW

	Number of process to be served with this Form 285
	Number of parties to be served in this case
	Check for service on U.S.A.

SPECIAL INSTRUCTIONS OR OTHER INFORMATION THAT WILL ASSIST IN EXPEDITING SERVICE *(Include Business and Alternate Addresses, All Telephone Numbers, and Estimated Times Available for Service)*:

Fold   Fold

Signature of Attorney other Originator requesting service on behalf of:

☐ PLAINTIFF
☐ DEFENDANT

TELEPHONE NUMBER	DATE

SPACE BELOW FOR USE OF U.S. MARSHAL ONLY-- DO NOT WRITE BELOW THIS LINE

I acknowledge receipt for the total number of process indicated. *(Sign only for USM 285 if more than one USM 285 is submitted)*	Total Process	District of Origin	District to Serve	Signature of Authorized USMS Deputy or Clerk	Date
		No.	No.		

I hereby certify and return that I ☐ have personally served , ☐ have legal evidence of service, ☐ have executed as shown in "Remarks", the process described on the individual , company, corporation, etc., at the address shown above on the on the individual , company, corporation, etc. shown at the address inserted below.

☐ I hereby certify and return that I am unable to locate the individual, company, corporation, etc. named above *(See remarks below)*

Name and title of individual served *(if not shown above)*

☐ A person of suitable age and discretion then residing in defendant's usual place of abode

Address *(complete only different than shown above)*

Date	Time	☐ am ☐ pm

Signature of U.S. Marshal or Deputy

Service Fee	Total Mileage Charges including *endeavors*	Forwarding Fee	Total Charges	Advance Deposits	Amount owed to U.S. Marshal* or (Amount of Refund*)
					$0.00

REMARKS:

DISTRIBUTE TO:
1. CLERK OF THE COURT
2. USMS RECORD
3. NOTICE OF SERVICE
4. BILLING STATEMENT*: To be returned to the U.S. Marshal with payment, if any amount is owed. Please remit promptly payable to U.S. Marshal.
5. ACKNOWLEDGMENT OF RECEIPT

PRIOR EDITIONS MAY BE USED

Form USM-285
Rev. 11/13

Source: U.S. Department of Justice.

EXHIBIT 5.6 Motion for Special Appointment to Serve Process

THE UNITED STATES DISTRICT COURT FOR THE CENTRAL DISTRICT OF COLUMBIA

Civil Action, File No. _____,

_____,
Plaintiff

v.

Motion for Special Appointment to Serve Process

_____,
Defendant

Pursuant to Rule 4(c)(2), Federal Rules of Civil Procedure, _____ moves this Court to specifically appoint _____ to serve the _____ on _____ in this action. Said person to be appointed is not less than eighteen years of age and is not a party to this action. Said appointment will bring a savings in costs to the United States Marshal.

_____
Attorney

Order

IT IS ORDERED this _____ day of _____, _____, that _____ be appointed to serve the _____ on _____ in this action. Proof of such service shall be made by affidavit in accordance with Rule 4(l), Federal Rules of Civil Procedure.

By the Court

_____
United States District Court Judge

Affidavit of Service of Summons and Complaint

When service is performed by a specially appointed process server, an affidavit of service must be completed pursuant to Rule 4(l). There are times when your state court may also require such an affidavit. An affidavit appropriate for federal court is shown in Exhibit 5.7.

Consent to Exercise of Jurisdiction by Magistrate Judge

This document is drafted only on the specific direction of the attorney. Its purpose is to inform the court that the parties agree to have the matter tried by a **federal magistrate judge** rather than the district court judge. If so directed, this document should be prepared and presented to the clerk at the same time the complaint is filed as dictated by local federal practice. It will then have to be signed by the defendant and returned to the clerk of court. Exhibit 5.8 is the form for consent to exercise of jurisdiction by a United States magistrate judge.

federal magistrate judge
Judge appointed under 28 U.S.C. §631 to assist U.S. District Court judges in conducting routine matters in the federal trial courts.

Nongovernmental Corporation Disclosure Statement

If your client is a nongovernmental corporation, Rule 7.1 now requires a disclosure statement to be filed with the court. Two copies must be filed on the party's first appearance or action in the case. The statement must disclose any parent corporation and any publicly held corporation owning 10 percent or more of the party's stock or state that there

EXHIBIT 5.7 Affidavit of Service of Summons and Complaint

**UNITED STATES DISTRICT COURT FOR
THE CENTRAL DISTRICT OF COLUMBIA CIVIL ACTION**

File No. _____

_____
Plaintiff

v.

_____
Defendant

Affidavit of Service of Summons and Complaint

I served a copy of the summons and complaint in the above matter by __[type of service]__ at [time] on the _____ day of _____, _____, on

Name _____

Address where served _____

____[signature of process server]_____

Name

Signed and sworn to before me on:

_____

_____

Notary Public

My commission expires on _____

EXHIBIT 5.8 Consent to Exercise of Jurisdiction by a United States Magistrate Judge, Election of Appeal to District Judge

UNITED STATES DISTRICT COURT
_____ **District of** _____

Plaintiff

v.

Defendant

NOTICE, CONSENT, AND ORDER OF REFERENCE—
EXERCISE OF JURISDICTION BY A UNITED STATES
MAGISTRATE JUDGE

Case Number:

NOTICE OF AVAILABILITY OF A UNITED STATES MAGISTRATE JUDGE
TO EXERCISE JURISDICTION

In accordance with the provisions of 28 U.S.C. §636(c), and Fed.R.Civ.P. 73, you are notified that a United States magistrate judge of this district court is available to conduct any or all proceedings in this case including a jury or nonjury trial, and to order the entry of a final judgment. Exercise of this jurisdiction by a magistrate judge is, however, permitted only if all parties voluntarily consent.

EXHIBIT 5.8 Consent to Exercise of Jurisdiction by a United States Magistrate Judge, Election of Appeal to District Judge (*continued*)

You may, without adverse substantive consequences, withhold your consent, but this will prevent the court's jurisdiction from being exercised by a magistrate judge. If any party withholds consent, the identity of the parties consenting or withholding consent will not be communicated to any magistrate judge or to the district judge to whom the case has been assigned.

An appeal from a judgment entered by a magistrate judge shall be taken directly to the United States court of appeals for this judicial circuit in the same manner as an appeal from any other judgment of this district court.

CONSENT TO THE EXERCISE OF JURISDICTION BY A UNITED STATES MAGISTRATE JUDGE

In accordance with provisions of 28 U.S.C. §636(c) and Fed.R.Civ.P. 73, the parties in this case consent to have a United States magistrate judge conduct any and all proceedings in this case, including the trial, order the entry of a final judgment, and conduct all post-judgment proceedings.

Party Represented	Signature	Date
_____	_____	_____
_____	_____	_____
_____	_____	_____

ORDER OF REFERENCE

IT IS ORDERED that this case be referred to _____
United States Magistrate Judge, to conduct all proceedings and order the entry of judgment in accordance with 28 U.S.C. §636(c) and Fed.R.Civ.P. 73.

_____   _____
Date   United States District Judge

NOTE: RETURN THIS FORM TO THE CLERK OF THE COURT <u>ONLY IF</u> ALL PARTIES HAVE CONSENTED <u>ON THIS FORM</u> TO THE EXERCISE OF JURISDICTION BY A UNITED STATES MAGISTRATE JUDGE.

is no such corporation. The reason for filing a corporate disclosure statement is to determine whether the sitting judge on a case has a potential conflict of interest in any of the corporate entities potentially involved in a case. Knowing this information will determine whether a judge may be disqualified from hearing the matter. If there is a potential conflict, the judge normally will **recuse** himself or herself from hearing the case.

recuse
To disqualify oneself from hearing a case to avoid a potential conflict of interest.

OBTAIN THE PAYMENT FOR THE FILING FEES

After the documents are prepared and checked for accuracy and necessary signatures, payment for the filing fee should be obtained. Each firm will have its own procedure in this regard depending on whether the case is filed in federal or state court. If the procedure is not in the office procedures manual, ask an experienced secretary, administrative assistant, or the office manager. If the action is to be filed in state court, include any necessary service of process fee, which is paid to the clerk in some states and directly to the sheriff or process server in others. If the summons is to be served in a foreign jurisdiction, the fee is generally paid directly and in advance for serving the documents. Exhibit 5.9 is a general summary of the needed documents for filing a lawsuit.

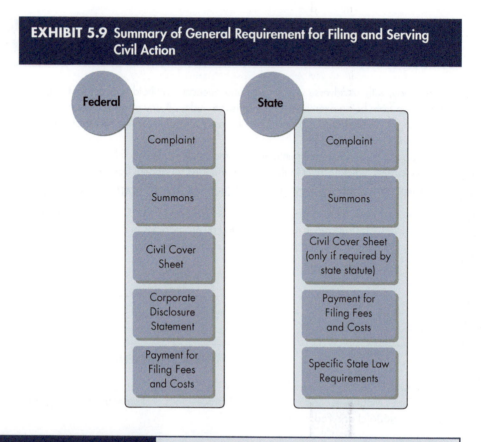

EXHIBIT 5.9 Summary of General Requirement for Filing and Serving Civil Action

Federal
- Complaint
- Summons
- Civil Cover Sheet
- Corporate Disclosure Statement
- Payment for Filing Fees and Costs

State
- Complaint
- Summons
- Civil Cover Sheet (only if required by state statute)
- Payment for Filing Fees and Costs
- Specific State Law Requirements

ETHICAL CONSIDERATIONS

Filing fees, expenses, and attorney's fees are paid by the client. As a paralegal you may be on the receiving end of a client's advance or retainer. The question for you is "where do I deposit the money received from a client?" The general response to that question is in a client trust account. Normally, a law firm has different accounts. There is a firm's operating account, which represents monies earned by the firm and deposited in that account after they are earned. There also is the client trust account, which is *always* separate from the law firm's operating account. Never shall the two be mixed or comingled. Therefore, when a client pays monies to the firm for services, those monies are deposited in the client's trust account and when monies are either expended on the client's behalf or fees earned and billed, then and only then can the fees be transferred and deposited into the law firm's operating account for use by the attorney. If unearned client funds are deposited in a firm's account, this is a violation of the code of ethics and professional responsibilities of the attorney. For the paralegal, payment of

filing fees should come from the operating account directly and then be reimbursed from the client's trust account or by having the funds transferred from the client's trust account into the attorney's operating account. Be careful when handling client funds for whatever purpose and be sure to document the use of client funds toward any type of expenses in a lawsuit. If you are presented with a situation where the attorney directly deposits a client's advance or retainer in an operating account, this should raise a "red flag" for you. Chances are the attorney committed an ethical violation and, even worse, a criminal act, such as conversion or embezzlement. Unfortunately, there are a myriad of cases where paralegals have been held accountable or liable for the transgressions of their employer. In the extreme cases, both attorney and paralegal have seen jail time. Know and understand that there is a line that should not be crossed when handling or using client monies. Keep it simple and avoid, if possible, direct dealings with the law firm's bank accounts. If you work in a small firm and you do deal with the firm bank accounts, be conscious of the ethical and professional rules for disbursement and receipt of client funds.

FILING THE LAWSUIT

TRADITIONAL METHODS OF FILING

When all the required documents have been prepared, checked for accuracy, and signed, it is time to file the action. Although filing the summons, complaint, and subsequent papers is occasionally done in a rush, it is a simple procedure. The prepared documents are taken to the clerk of the court in which the action is to be filed. Personal delivery of the papers to the clerk is the most common method of filing, but using certified mail to send the summons, complaint, and other necessary documents to the clerk is permitted.

The clerk stamps the date on the original complaint and, in the federal system, immediately assigns the action a civil case number and possibly a judge. The action commences in federal court upon the delivery of the complaint to the clerk (Rule 3). In some state courts, the action does not commence until a summons and a copy of the complaint are served upon the defendant.

The court clerk then issues a summons with the court seal and the clerk's signature. The clerk in federal court then asks what method of service will be used. This is done to see that all needed documents are presented. A summons for each defendant is then either returned to be served on the defendant (federal court) or delivered to the sheriff or process server for service (state court).

For all practical purposes, the procedure is the same in all federal district courts. State court procedures vary, but are similar. However, many federal courts now require all complaints to be filed electronically and it is incumbent upon the paralegal to learn what process applies in the jurisdiction in which a complaint is filed.

E-FILING

e-filing

A court-approved, Internet-based system for filing, serving, and accessing legal documents.

Electronic filing or **e-filing** is a court-approved, Internet-based system for filing, serving, and accessing legal documents. It eliminates trips from the law office to the court house, reduces paper and photocopying costs, provides twenty-four-hour access for attorneys and clients, and facilitates filing documents and viewing case files from locations other than the law office. Ideally, the e-filing system immediately confirms the filing of a document and its service on the opponent, and it calculates the required court fees and electronically transfers the funds. Savings to clients may be as much as seventy-five percent of traditional filing costs. Federal Rule of Civil Procedure 5(d)(3) and parallel state rules authorize the filing of documents by electronic means. Rule 77 authorizes the court to use electronic means to notify parties of the entry of a court order or judgment.

E-filing systems normally have a closely associated system that provides both the public and attorneys with access to electronic court documents. A number of states have e-filing and public access systems. The e-filing system for U.S. district courts, bankruptcy courts, the courts of appeals, the Court of International Trade, and the Court of Federal Claims is the Case Management/Electronic Case Filing system (CM/ECF). It provides electronic docket management with Internet filing of most case documents. In addition to twenty-four-hour access, its benefits include instant creation of docket entries, notification of any new entry to the parties in the case with hyperlinks to the new document and the pertinent case, and an instant filing confirmation receipt for the attorney's file. The automatic notification of the new entry is called Notice of Electronic Filing (NEF). It constitutes service of the document.

The federal court public access component is Public Access to Court Electronic Records (PACER). Anyone, including attorneys and their clients, with a PACER account and password can access PACER to locate and view federal court documents in specific cases. Only court-registered attorneys with a PACER account and a separate required login protocol and a password can access CM/ECF to file and view case documents. A PACER account is free, and parties receive one free, downloadable copy of a filed document with nominal fees for other documents. The court can order that some documents be sealed, which requires the documents to be filed in hard copy only and then sealed by the court. Sealed documents are unavailable through the e-system. The electronic docket will reflect that the sealed document has been filed.

Technical components needed to use the federal system include a recent computer operating system, a relatively fast Internet connection, a recent version of Firefox, Google Chrome or Internet Explorer, word processing software, a personal e-mail account, and both Adobe Acrobat Reader and Acrobat Writer (or similar software) to view and create documents in portable document format (PDF). A scanner is needed to image any documents not in electronic form so they can be converted to PDF for filing.

Many federal courts (and some state courts) now require cases to be filed electronically. Paralegals are likely to do the filing. Seek what training is available from your state or federal district court. A tutorial in e-filing is offered on the Web site of most federal district courts. The Web sites also offer the latest version of the CM/ECF User's Manual. Further, attorneys are permitted to bring paralegals to the hands-on training sessions offered by the federal district courts. Regardless of whether you are filing documents in a state or federal e-filing system, the process is reasonably uniform. See Exhibit 5.10 for a Checklist for E-Filing.

Although pleadings, motions, and other court documents can be filed electronically in the federal system, check your local system for what documents can be e-filed. Some federal district courts do not initiate cases electronically until the complaint is filed in the traditional manner. Many of these courts are not yet equipped to accept credit card payment of the filing fee, so check with the respective court clerk to be sure that e-filing of the complaint is acceptable and, if so, what payment procedure is required. Once a case is filed, the parties are designated, and the case is assigned a number, subsequent documents can be filed electronically.

INTERNET EXERCISE

Go to your jurisdiction's federal court Web site. Locate the tutorial for the e-filing of documents. Review the tutorial for future reference and e-filing guidance.

Note this important rule about serving e-filed documents. The initial summons, which notifies the defendant that a lawsuit has been filed, must be served according to the traditional procedures outlined in Rule 4 (see next section). Under Rule 5(b)(2)E), all other documents designated by the rules to be served on the parties may be served by electronic means, *if* the person served has given written consent. The pertinent note of the Committee on Rules of Practice and Procedure states that the consent may be electronic, it cannot be implied, and it should specify its scope and duration. E-service is complete on transmission, unless the party making service learns that the service failed.

EXHIBIT 5.10 Checklists for E-Filings

WORD DOCUMENT

1) "Electronically Filed" is stated in the caption of the pleading.
2) There is a completed certificate of service. (signature (/s/John Smith), dated etc.)
3) There is an "/s/(attorney's typed name)" with the attorney's name typed on the signature line.

PDF DOCUMENTS

1) If the main document is created with a word processing application, it must be **converted** to PDF format instead of printed and scanned to create the PDF. Note: Some state systems automatically convert Word files to PDF. If documents are filed electronically in a state court, check the rules and process for conversion of the document.
2) The main pleading is a **separate** PDF document from any attachments, and each exhibit is a separate PDF document and properly labeled.
3) There are no missing pages. All pages are in order and right side up.
4) Every page is legible. (The main document and all attachments).
5) Prior to conversion, be sure any personal information is redacted according to the rules of that jurisdiction.

ELECTRONICALLY FILING THE PLEADING

1) The attorney's name on the signature line **must** match the name of the attorney logged into ECF.
2) Choose the correct case. (There may be related cases; the system may ask you to click on the correct case.)
3) Check the case number and caption of the case on top of each screen.
4) Choose the most accurate/appropriate event. (If unsure, stop and contact a clerk of the court or case manager for assistance. If after court hours, file the document and contact the court at the earliest possible time for assistance.)
5) If this is a multi-part motion, multiple reliefs should be chosen.
6) All attachments must be filled individually and separately from one another, and named appropriately.
7) For each document filed or electronically attached, verify that you are filing the correct document by opening the PDF document at the "Browse" screen with Acrobat Reader before the document is uploaded into ECF. (If a document is uploaded and is incorrect, you can hit the back button and redo the transaction.)
8) A proposed order must be a separate document and accompany the motion as an electronic attachment, *not* as a separate entry.
9) When filing a "Motion for leave to file a document," the subject document is to be filed as an electronic attachment to the motion, *not* as a separate entry.
10) Describe all attachments completely and concisely.
11) If given the opportunity to create a link to an existing event, do so when appropriate.
12) Use the optional text box, when given the opportunity, to further describe your pleading. Rule of thumb: the docket text should accurately reflect the title of the pleading being filed.
13) If you use the optional text box, make certain that information added should not be a separate entry.
14) Note that e-filing systems are different in state courts. For e-filing requirements in your state, review the process from the respective state court through tutorials or in-person trainings, if available. DO NOT rely on the checklist for federal filings for your state filings. Prepare a separate checklist for your state court systems and place it in your systems folder for ready reference.

TRADE SECRETS: PRINTING A VERIFICATION OF FILING

Traditional methods of filing always produced a file stamp from a clerk verifying the date and time a document was filed in that court. This was and is evidence of the formal filing of a legal document with a court. With e-filing, the traditional methods of filing have changed, dispensing with the in-person file stamp and verification. Depending on the type of e-filing system, a notice of filing with the time and date is generated confirming the filing with the court. In the federal CM/ECF system, when the filing is successful, an automatic e-mail confirmation is generated allowing the user to print a copy of the confirmation and a copy of the document filed with the case number, court, time of filing and date affixed to the top of the document. Always print a copy of the e-mail confirmation and the electronically file-stamped document for your records so you have verification of its filing. If there is ever any question as to whether the document is filed, you have a record of the filing. Sometimes mistakes occur in the court's electronic filing system. By printing both the e-mail confirmation and the file-stamped document, you will have that record in case challenges occur regarding the filing. When questions arise as to whether a document was filed or not, you will be glad you have a copy of your filings in your office file. This practice should be applied for every document that is electronically filed in a case. Yes, that is every document. Serving the initial complaint is only the beginning of the litigation process, and developing good habits early on is critical.

Similarly, many court state systems have e-filing systems as well. They may have different confirmation procedures than the federal CM/ECF system. Some systems do not generate an automatic confirmation and require the clerk to approve the filing. If this is the case, print the confirmation of filing for evidence of the filing of the document for your records, even if the document has not been approved for filing by the court's clerk. The filing confirmation proves that a document was timely filed with the court for statute of limitations, statutory, or court order deadlines, for example. Some state e-filing systems parallel the federal system and have an automatic confirmation system.

This bears repeating. *Our best practice is to print the confirmation of the filing and the e-stamped document.* No matter the type of e-filing system, confirmation of filing for your files is essential. This practice should be automatic for any document you file with a court.

SERVICE OF PROCESS

Once the action is filed, it is essential to serve the summons and a copy of the complaint on the defendant in order for the court to gain personal jurisdiction over the defendant. In state court this is usually necessary to begin the action. The court's judgment is not binding against the defendant unless personal jurisdiction has been obtained by service of process. Consequently, it is an extremely important step.

Under Rule 4(c) the plaintiff must serve the summons and a copy of the complaint on each defendant within 120 days [Rule 4(m)] of filing the complaint. Failure to do so shall result in dismissal of the action unless good cause for failure to comply can be shown to the court. In some states, the responsibility for service of the summons rests with the clerk of court. If service is the clerk's responsibility, it is best to provide information on the best place(s) and time to find the defendant.

The methods of service vary depending on the court (state or federal), the type of defendant, and the location of the defendant (in state, out of state, or in another country).

In *Hall v. Haynes*, 319 S.W. 3d 564 (Tenn. 2010), the central issue before the Supreme Court of Tennessee was what constituted proper service of process on two defendants—one an individual and one a corporation. The *Hall* case illustrates the importance of knowing who the proper party is to serve and making sure that the proper party is actually served according to the law of the state where service of process is being attempted.

CASE STUDY: UNDERSTANDING THE LAW

Billy R. and Billie Gail Hall filed a lawsuit against Dr. Douglas Haynes, Jr., M.D. and MedSouth Healthcare, P.C. alleging medical malpractice in treating a medical condition of one of the Hall's. Summons were issued by the county clerk which directed service on Dr. Haynes and the registered agent for MedSouth Healthcare, Stevens Melton, M.D. According to the facts, various individuals at the front desk area accepted service of process from first a process server and then through certified mail. None of the defendants were ever served personally as required by Tennessee statute. Although under the facts, it was acknowledged that both Dr. Haynes and Dr. Melton as registered agent were aware of the lawsuit by the Halls, they were never personally served but received notice through various employees who did not have the legal authority to receive service of process. It was established in the case that the various employees of MedSouth did receive and sign for certified mail and subpoenas. The court found a significant difference, however. Focusing on the Tennessee Civil Rules of Procedure, the court analyzed Rule 4.04(1) which identified how a defendant must be served within the state. The statute required personal service on an individual defendant or an authorized agent. The court examined what constituted actual or apparent authority of an individual to accept service for another. Accepting documents in some instances in a business, for example, does not necessarily constitute an agency relationship for service of process. Here, Dr. Haynes did not authorize an employee of MedSouth to accept service on his behalf. And, the employee did not know that she was signing a summons acknowledging receipt of a lawsuit. Therefore, under Tennessee law, the service was invalid. (Note that this is the law in Tennessee

and may differ in other states.) As for service on the corporate defendant, the court applied similar reasoning. The question for the corporate defendant is whether the registered agent was served according to the rules of procedure. No employee of MedSouth was considered a subagent designated for service, which the facts of the case bore out. Thus, since Dr. Melton was not personally served and did not have anyone who was his appointed subagent, the service was void. The final issue the court had to decide was whether service by certified mail on these two defendants had been properly effectuated. Following similar reasoning, the court examined what constitutes an authorized agent for purposes of accepting certified mail of a lawsuit. Again, the court focused on the authority that was extended to various employees with the court ultimately finding that Rule 4.04 had not be followed, and determined that both attempts at service were invalid. The court noted that had the plaintiffs restricted the delivery of the certified mail to a particular person the service would have been valid. The end result, which also is important to understand about this case and service, is that because of the failed service, the one year statute of limitations for filing a medical malpractice case against the doctor and hospital had run. Therefore, this case illustrates the importance of verifying to whom documents are served and the time period in which they are served.

Questions for Review: Read *Hall v. Haynes*. What were the critical facts that the court relied upon in reaching its result for each defendant? How did the court distinguish between acceptance of a subpoena and acceptance of a summons? Why did the court differentiate the two situations?

REFERENCE GUIDE AND CHECKLIST FOR METHODS OF SERVICE

SERVICE ON INDIVIDUALS IN A STATE OR IN A JUDICIAL DISTRICT OF THE UNITED STATES

1. _Mail (State):_ Service on individuals by mail is permitted in a number of states. Check state practice carefully.

    a. Place a copy of the summons and complaint in an envelope addressed to the defendant or, if previously agreed to, to the defendant's attorney.

    b. Include a return-addressed envelope and two copies of an acknowledgment of service form, if your state requires it.

    c. Use first-class mail if an acknowledgment of service is used.

    d. When no acknowledgment is used, mail the documents to the defendant by registered or certified mail, return receipt requested. Mark the green certified mail card "Restricted Delivery Only" if you want only the named person to receive the envelope.

    e. The date the acknowledgment is signed is the date of service. If certified mail is used, the date of delivery marked on the return receipt is the date of service.

    f. Fill out the Return of Service on the original summons and file it (plus any signed acknowledgment) with the clerk.

2. _Waiver of Service of Summons, Federal Rule 4(d)_

    a. Dispatch by first class mail or other reliable means a Notice of Lawsuit and Request for Waiver of Service of Summons, two copies of the Waiver of Service of Summons, a copy of the complaint with the date of filing stamped on it, and a return-addressed, stamped envelope to each defendant.

    b. The defendant has thirty days from the date the request is sent (sixty days if the defendant is outside any judicial district of the United States) to return the waiver.

    c. On receipt of the signed waiver, place it in your case file. No return of service is filed.

3. _Other Federal Service:_ Rule 4(e) states that, unless otherwise provided by federal law, service on an individual (other than an infant or an incompetent person) may be made by the following means:

    a. Through the method of service used in the state within which the federal district court is located or that used in the state where service is made ("effected"); or

    b. Personal service

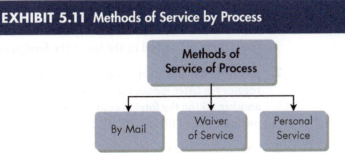

EXHIBIT 5.11 Methods of Service by Process

4. _Personal Service/Federal Rule 4(e)(2) and State:_ The rules governing personal service are similar among jurisdictions, but the pertinent rules should be checked for any unique features. Personal service is achieved in the following manner:

   a. Locate the defendant and personally hand a copy of the summons and complaint to the defendant or an agent authorized by appointment or law to receive service of process.

   b. If the defendant is not available, leave a copy of the summons and complaint at the individual's residence with a person of suitable _age_ (fourteen in many jurisdictions) and _discretion_ residing there. Leaving the complaint with another person is not permitted in some states.

   c. Serve the documents during reasonable hours, including Sundays and holidays, or during the night shift if that is when the defendant works.

   d. Fill out the return of service on the original summons, make a copy for your records, and file the summons with the clerk.

The general types of service of process are cited in Exhibit 5.11.

5. _Service on Infants or Incompetent Persons_

   a. Serve according to the state law where service is to be attempted [Rule 4(g)].

   b. If in a foreign country, follow the steps for service of individuals in a foreign country [Rule 4(f)].

   c. Normally, serve the legal guardian or appointed representative.

SERVICE ON INDIVIDUALS IN A FOREIGN COUNTRY [RULE 4(F)]

Unless a waiver of service of summons has been obtained, service on an individual in a foreign country should be effected in the following manner:

1. Determine whether the pertinent foreign country is a party to any international agreement or treaty governing service of process, such as the Hague Convention on the Service Abroad of Judicial and Extrajudicial Documents. For the terms and parties, see the last volume of _The Martindale Hubbell Law Directory_ or other international sources.

2. Follow the procedures outlined in the agreement [Rule 4(f)(1)].

APPLY YOUR KNOWLEDGE

Determine in your jurisdiction the process for serving a minor or incompetent person. Identify the statutory authority or rule.

If there is no applicable agreement, then follow Rule 4(f)(2).

1. Provided that service is "reasonably calculated to give notice," make service in the manner prescribed by the law of the foreign country; or

2. As directed by the foreign authority in response to a letter of request or a letter rogatory; a *letter rogatory* is a request from a court in one country to a court in another asking the foreign court to examine a witness according to that court's own rules (see FED. R. CIV. P. 28); or

3. Unless prohibited by the law of the foreign country,

   a. by actual delivery of a copy of the summons and complaint; or

   b. by signed receipt mail dispatched by the clerk of court; or

4. By other means directed by the court

SERVICE ON CORPORATIONS AND ASSOCIATIONS [RULE 4(h)]

1. If waiver of service has not been obtained, serve according to the law of the state in which the U.S. district court is located; or

2. Serve a copy of the summons and complaint to an officer, a managing or general agent, or any other agent authorized by appointment or by law to receive service [Rule 4(h)]. If the law authorizing the agent to receive service requires it, mail a copy of the summons and complaint to the defendant. In many states, the secretary of state is the statutorily designated official. Most secretary of state offices

TECHNOLOGY UPDATE: THE COMPUTERIZATION OF STATE INFORMATION

Because of budgetary constraints —lack of money—many states have lagged behind in the computerization of their secretary of state office's (or equivalent's) information on corporations. Most states now have information online relating to corporations, including registered agent listings and general corporate information, such as officers and addresses, which is helpful in preparing, filing, and serving lawsuits. It is helpful to check either your state corporations Web site or the state where your corporation is located for forms that are required when serving a corporate defendant. Unlike the past when government offices were only open 8 am to 5 pm, those states that have online services and information are available twenty-four hours a day, seven days a week. Many of these sites provide a guide in how to serve process and to whom process should be served. For example, in Louisiana, the Web site for its secretary of state explains how to serve process on not only registered agents but also foreign corporations and motorists involved in automobile accidents on Louisiana roads and highways. The site provides valuable information including a "frequently asked questions" section. Similarly, Missouri has a checklist for service of process of corporate entities along with the current fees. Along with information on service of process, Missouri has a treasure trove of forms for its business entities (which should be explored for other assignments from other classes). Some state Web sites are more helpful than others; however, regardless of the information you are researching, always check the applicable state corporations Web site for information relating to service of process for corporate defendants or other entities or individuals that require service through the secretary of state.

keep a current list of business officers or agents designated to receive service. This information also can be obtained through Westlaw and Lexis databanks.

SERVICE ON THE UNITED STATES [RULE 4(i)]

1. Serve the U.S. attorney for the district in which the action is brought, or an assistant U.S. attorney or clerical employee designated by the U.S. attorney in writing filed with the clerk of the court [Rule 4(i)], or

2. Send a copy of the summons and complaint by registered or certified mail to the civil process clerk at the office of the U.S. attorney and send a copy of the summons and complaint by registered or certified mail to the attorney general of the United States in Washington, D.C.; *and*

3. In any action attacking the validity of an order of an officer or agency of the United States not made a party, also send copies by registered or certified mail to the officer or agency.

4. Serve any U.S. officer, agency, or corporation in the manner previously described [Rule 4(i)(1)] and by also sending a copy of the summons and complaint by registered or certified mail to the officer, agency, or corporation.

Note that there are special practice considerations related to commencing an action for damages against the United States under the Federal Tort Claims Act (28 USC §§ 2671–80). The act's procedure can save time and litigation costs. The act has a *two year* statute of limitations. Prior to filing a court action, the injured party must file an administrative claim with the relevant agency, including the evidentiary documents to support the claim. Once the administrative claim is filed, there is a six-month waiting period before an action can be filed in federal court. If the administrative claim is denied, the plaintiff has six months from the date of notice of denial to file an action in U.S. district court.

SERVICE ON A FOREIGN, STATE, OR LOCAL GOVERNMENT

1. Serve a foreign government or entity pursuant to 28 U.S.C. § 1608.

2. Serve a state, municipal, or other government agency by effecting delivery on its chief executive officer or as prescribed by state law.

3. Note that some government entities require a person contemplating an action to file a demand by claim or other form with the entity before filing a lawsuit. This procedure can be found in the applicable laws.

SERVICE OUTSIDE THE GEOGRAPHICAL BOUNDARIES OF THE STATE OR FEDERAL DISTRICT COURT/LONG-ARM STATUTES

At one time it was difficult, if not impossible, to serve defendants who resided beyond the borders of a particular state or who had passed briefly through the state and had caused injury. This injustice has been corrected in most states with the passage of

long-arm statutes

Laws giving a court personal jurisdiction over nonresident persons or corporations in specified circumstances.

long-arm statutes. As previously discussed in Chapter 1, these laws give a court personal jurisdiction over nonresident persons or corporations in specified circumstances. The key to these statutes is whether the defendant has sufficient minimum contacts with the state to justify personal jurisdiction and whether the statute provides constitutionally based "fair play," which includes such due process concepts as adequate notice of the action and a fair opportunity for the defendant to be heard. As noted in Chapter 1, the principles of long-arm statutes applied by courts have now been extended to gain jurisdiction over a party's Internet contact with a state as discussed in *Zippo Manufacturing Co. v. Zippo Dot Com. Inc.*, 952 F. Supp. 1119 (W.D. Pa. 1997). Similar principles are being used for jurisdiction in international Internet lawsuits. Also, when a foreign defendant's contacts with a particular state are insufficient for personal jurisdiction, such jurisdiction may be gained by looking at its contacts with the United States [FED. R. CIV. P. 4(k)(2)]. Courts have upheld the validity of long-arm statutes on the logic that the cause of action should be remedied where the harm occurred as long as the minimum contacts are present and the nonresident is treated fairly (given due process).

The long-arm statute identifies which public official in the state must be served. For example, out-of-state corporations doing business in the state are typically served through the state's secretary of state, insurance companies through the commissioners of insurance, and out-of-state motorists through the commissioner of highways. Prior to filing an action using the long-arm statute, read the state's long-arm statute to determine which official should be served and with what documents.

The federal courts follow the long-arm procedure of the state in which the federal district court is located [Rule 4(k)(1)(A)]. A few federal long-arm provisions provide for nationwide personal jurisdiction in cases involving antitrust and securities laws as well as interpleader actions, which resolve a special type of property dispute. It pays to consult the specific statute under which a federal claim is brought to see if such extended jurisdiction exists. In addition, Rule 4(k)(1)(B) gives a federal district court jurisdiction over parties later added to an action (Rules 14 and 19) who reside within 100 miles of the district court in which the action was filed regardless of state boundaries. Even absent state court jurisdiction, in respect to claims arising under federal law, personal jurisdiction can be achieved by actual service of the summons or waiver if it is consistent with the Constitution and federal laws.

Here is a typical procedure for gaining service of process under a long-arm statute:

1. The original and two copies of the complaint are filed with the clerk of court.

2. The clerk issues the summons and mails two copies of the summons and complaint by certified mail to the secretary of state or other designated officer.

3. The secretary of state's office sends a copy of the summons and complaint to the nonresident defendant by certified mail, return receipt requested.

4. On return of the receipt, the secretary of state's office certifies to the clerk of court that service has been made.

5. If the secretary of state's office cannot gain service, the state statute normally sets out alternatives for service.

INTERNET EXERCISE

Find your state's long arm statute and identify how to serve (a) a state government, (b) a corporation, and (c) a partnership.

in rem action

An action involving the attachment of property to resolve claims to the property.

quasi in rem action

An action in which the court uses the property of a defendant over whom it does not have personal jurisdiction to pay a judgment against the defendant entered in an action unrelated to the property.

constructive service

Service of process other than direct service, such as through a newspaper of general circulation.

substituted service

Any type of service of process other than actual, personal service, such as through mail, waiver, publication, or legal representative.

Some secretary of state Web sites now provide computerized tracking of summonses served through that office.

SERVICE IN IN REM AND QUASI IN REM CASES

An **in rem action** is an action involving the attachment of property to resolve claims to the property, and is based in the state's sovereign authority over property within its borders. The property can include real estate; tangibles such as automobiles, jewelry, or art; and intangibles such as bank deposits, stocks, and promissory notes. If, for example, a man dies having a will that leaves his property to his wife but also leaves substantial evidence of his intent to leave a secret condominium to his mistress of many years, who should own the condominium? The mistress might sue in the court in the jurisdiction where the condominium is located, using an in rem action to determine who owns the property. The action is against the property and service is gained by the method outlined in the governing state or federal statute or by delivery of the summons and complaint to the person holding the property [Rule 4(n)(1)].

A **quasi in rem action** is one in which the court uses the property of a defendant over whom it does not have personal jurisdiction to pay a judgment against the defendant entered in an action indirectly related or unrelated to the property. For example, assume A has a court judgment against B for B's failure to pay A for an automobile A sold to B. B now lives out of state and the court cannot gain personal jurisdiction over B. B, however, owns a small piece of land in-state. A can sue B in a quasi in rem process to have the state court seize B's property and sell it to pay on the debt for the automobile. If A's action is successful but the land is worth less than the car debt, A can recover only the value of the land, because the court does not have personal jurisdiction over B or any of his other assets. An *in rem* action is against the property, a *quasi in rem* action is brought against the owner of the property. One might characterize *quasi in rem* statutes as "short-arm" statutes. *In rem* and *quasi in rem* jurisdiction can no longer be based simply on the state's traditional authority over the property within its borders. The constitutional prerequisites of jurisdiction set out in *International Shoe* must be applied in nonresident *in rem* and *quasi in rem* cases [*Shaffer v. Heitner*, 433 U.S. 186 (1977)]. On a showing that service cannot be made on a defendant by any method outlined in the rules, the court may seize the property according to the law of the state in which the district court is located [Rule 4(n)(2)].

In such cases, many jurisdictions authorize **constructive service**, which involves publication of the summons in a newspaper of general circulation in the area where the property is located. The newspaper will generally provide an affidavit of publication and the attorney will file an affidavit of compliance plus copies of the publication. Some publication statutes deem personal service of the defendant in another state to be adequate publication.

Substituted service is any type of service other than actual, personal service. Service by mail, waiver, publication, or through an attorney or other legal representative are all means of substituted service.

Setting up a quick-reference guide or checklist for the methods of service for your state may be helpful. Particularly note that the time allowed after filing the complaint within which to serve the summons may vary from the federal 120-day limit. Also, the sheriff may or may not be the person who effects personal service.

IMMUNITY FROM SERVICE OF PROCESS

In some instances, a person may not be legally served with a summons and complaint because of immunity from service of process. Commonly, defendants and witnesses attending a trial, or traveling to or from the trial, are immune from service. So too are defendants brought into a state by force or served in some fraudulent manner.

LOCATING "INVISIBLE" DEFENDANTS

In most instances, you will be asked to locate the defendant as early in the case as possible to determine how and where service can be made. Even a sheriff or process server will need directions. Therefore, it is helpful to know ways to locate people who are difficult to find. Chapter 3 sets out several methods, including Internet resources, to locate hard-to-find witnesses; many of those methods are applicable to locating hard-to-find defendants. Here are some of the better techniques for locating the "invisible" defendant:

Checklist for Locating Defendants

1. If you are trying to ascertain the registered agent for service of process on a corporation, either call or use the secretary of state's corporate division's Internet site for your state and the state in which the corporation is likely to be incorporated or have its principal place of business. Many of the techniques used to locate individuals are applicable to corporations and other business organizations.

2. Check telephone and city or county directories. Use Internet directories such as www.switchboard.com, www.whowhere.lycos.com, and locator services through Westlaw and Lexis, or try a fee service such as www.ussearch.com or www.gisusdata.com. The fees are reasonable, and some services do not charge if the search is unsuccessful.

3. Send an envelope addressed to the last known address of the defendant with the words "Forwarding Address Requested" written in the lower left-hand corner of the envelope. The envelope should have the firm's return address on it and the necessary return postage enclosed. The post office may require the submission of Form 1478 for a forwarding address under the Freedom of Information Act.

4. Send a plain envelope addressed to the defendant by registered mail marked "Return Receipt Requested" and check the box on the green card entitled "Show to whom, date, and address of delivery." The mail carrier will request the defendant to sign the card.

5. Contact the defendant's former landlord or neighbors to obtain a new address, the name of the moving company, or the names of relatives or friends who might know the new address or provide additional information. Sources providing such information include churches, schools, or colleges attended; former employers, present employer, co-workers; professional or trade associations; health insurance carriers; sports clubs, civic clubs, country clubs, and veterans' organizations; and banking institutions.

6. Check voter registration lists, tax rolls, land transfer records (for names of persons involved in recent property transfers who might know the defendant's whereabouts, such as a buyer, a real estate agent, or a bank employee), civil and criminal court records, and vital statistics records.

7. Check with utility, telephone, cable television, newspaper, and other community-based companies for the address.

8. Contact the pertinent state's auto registration and driver's licensing division.

9. Place an ad in the newspaper with a reward for information that leads to the location of the defendant.

10. Hire a private investigator. Consider having the investigator appointed to serve process under relevant state or federal [4(c)(2)] rules, especially where the sheriff or marshal cannot locate the defendant.

A word of caution is in order here. Prior to contacting employers, neighbors, relatives, and so on, review the consumer protection and collection laws for your jurisdiction, including the Fair Debt Collections Practices Act (15 U.S.C. § 1692). Note especially the section on what constitutes harassment or otherwise illegal collection practices. If you do not, you may find yourself in violation of the law and subject to serious penalty.

OTHER SERVICE OF PROCESS

Rule 4.1 covers methods for service of process other than a summons or a subpoena (Rule 45). Service shall be by U.S. marshal, deputy marshal, or an appointed person. Orders of contempt of a federal decree or injunction can be served nationwide, and other orders of civil contempt can be served in the state in which the district court is located or within 100 miles of that court. Check the appropriate rules for your state practice.

FILING AND SERVICE OF PLEADINGS AND PAPERS SUBSEQUENT TO THE COMPLAINT

certificate of service
Certification that a document has been served on the opposing party.

Once the lawsuit is started, pleadings, motions, notices, orders, and other documents must be served on the adverse party. Rule 5 of the Federal Rules of Civil Procedure sets out the procedure to follow for serving documents subsequent to the complaint. The original and supporting documents together with a **certificate of service** are filed with the clerk of court "within a reasonable time after service." Some courts permit the filing of documents by fax or other electronic means. Rule 5(b) has been amended to permit service by electronic or other specified means with the consent of the person being served. One copy of the documents should be served on each of the parties.

When it becomes clear that a party is represented by an attorney, service shall be on the attorney. Service is achieved by mailing a copy of the document to the attorney's last known address; if no address is available, then by delivering it to the clerk of court. Service is also achieved by handing it to the attorney, leaving it at the attorney's office with a clerk or other person in charge, leaving it in a conspicuous place, or leaving it at the attorney's usual place of abode with a person of suitable age and discretion. Further, service by fax is now common. The court, on its own motion, may alter some requirements of service if there are an unusually large number of defendants.

KEEP GOOD RECORDS OF SERVICE

Keep good records of the filing, service, and receipt of service of all the outgoing and incoming pleadings, notices, subpoenas, and motions in the entire case. Certified mail, Return Receipt Requested provides green receipts for the necessary documentation.

If an item is delivered by hand, a receipt that lists the delivered item, the date it was delivered, and the signature of the person acknowledging receipt should be used. These receipts should be attached to a file copy of the pertinent document. If you are acknowledging service on behalf of your firm (check to see when, if ever, your attorney wants you to do this), keep one copy of the acknowledgment or signed receipt in the client's file with the pertinent document.

OBTAINING A DEFAULT JUDGMENT

INTRODUCTION

default judgment

Judgment rendered against the defendant for the damages specified in the claim without the case going to trial, based on the defendant's failure to respond to the complaint within the time limit.

If the defendant does not file an answer to the complaint or a motion attacking the complaint or otherwise respond in the prescribed time period, the defendant is in default and a **default judgment** may be entered against the defendant without a trial. In other words, the plaintiff wins the action and is awarded the requested relief.

THE PROCEDURE AND NECESSARY FORMS

Default judgments help clear the court docket of cases that would otherwise languish for lack of a desire to defend or for some other reason. Their purpose is not to give the plaintiff an advantage, and for that reason they incorporate some due process safeguards for the defendant. These safeguards include satisfactory proof of service of the summons and complaint and the opportunity to have the default set aside if there is adequate justification.

Most states and the federal courts require a two-step process. The first step is the filing of a request to the clerk of court for entry of default. The request for entry of default normally requires an affidavit stating that the defendant has failed to respond to the summons or otherwise has failed to appear in the action within the required time period. This step is significant because the entry of default generally prevents the defendant from doing anything further to contest his or her liability. Therefore, it is advantageous to prepare the necessary request so it can be filed as soon as the twenty days or other applicable time period has elapsed or when directed to do so by your supervising attorney. See Exhibit 5.12 for examples of these forms.

Step two requires the filing of a request for entry of a default judgment. Note the distinct difference between the entry of default, which simply establishes the point in time of the default, and the judgment, which is a determination that the plaintiff has won the action and is entitled to a specific amount of money or other remedy. Step two is the request for this judgment.

In some jurisdictions both the request for entry and request for default judgment are done simultaneously with the filing of the request for entry of default. In other jurisdictions the filing of the request for entry of default has been eliminated. Some jurisdictions have a statutory waiting period before the judgment can be requested, and in others a default judgment may be lost if it is not pursued within a statutory period of time. Consult the specific rules of the court in which you have filed the action to determine the exact procedure and time limits. It is best to file for the judgment at the first possible opportunity.

EXHIBIT 5.12 Request for Entry of Default

REQUEST TO CLERK FOR ENTRY OF DEFAULT[1]

[Title of Court and Cause]

The plaintiff requests the clerk for the ___*[name of court]*___ to enter the Defendant's default in the above entitled action. The Defendant has failed to appear or otherwise answer the complaint, and is therefore in default as set out in the accompanying affidavit.

_____
Attorney for Plaintiff
(Address)
(Phone number)
FAX number
E-mail address
Bar number (if required)

AFFIDAVIT OF DEFAULT IN SUPPORT OF REQUEST FOR ENTRY OF DEFAULT

State of _____ ⎫
                                ⎬ ss.
County of _____ ⎭

_____, being duly sworn, deposes and says;

1. That s/he is Plaintiff's attorney and has personal knowledge of the facts set forth in this affidavit and all proceedings in the above matter.

2. That the Plaintiff, on the _____ day of _____, _____, filed this complaint against the Defendant.

3. The Defendant is not a minor and is not a mentally incapacitated person.

4. The Defendant's address is _____.

5. I am unaware that the Defendant in this matter _____ is or _____ is not on active military duty at the present time because _____.

6. The Defendant was served with a copy of the summons and the Plaintiff's complaint, on the _____ day of _____, _____.

7. More than 20 (or state your jurisdiction's requirements) days have elapsed since the Defendant was served with the summons and the complaint.

8. The Defendant has failed to answer or otherwise defend as to the Plaintiff's complaint, or serve a copy of any answer or other defense which it might have had, upon _____ and _____, attorneys of record for the said Plaintiff.

9. The Defendant owes the total amount of $_____. This amount is based upon the following, after all offsets and credits that may be due:

   A. _____

   B. Court costs of $_____.

10. This affidavit is executed in accordance with Rule No. 55(a) of the Federal Rules of Civil Procedure, for the purpose of enabling the Plaintiff to obtain an entry of default against the Defendant.

11. Additional statements (Check your jurisdiction for its statutory requirements.)

[Jurat]

[1]Note: The case caption should be included in all documents filed with the court. Or, see comment to exhibit 5.14.

_____
Attorney for Plaintiff

Adapted from West's Federal Forms, § 4663, v. 4 (1992), with permission of West Group.

Once the default is entered, the federal rules provide for two approaches to obtain the default judgment. If the suit is for a sum certain, meaning not readily challengeable nor subject to reasonable dispute, the request for judgment is submitted to the clerk with an accompanying affidavit attesting to the amount. Judgment is then entered by the clerk. Exhibit 5.13 is an example of a request for default judgment by the clerk with an accompanying affidavit.

Federal law and some states require submission of an affidavit of nonmilitary service, as shown in Exhibit 5.14. The Service Members Civil Relief Act (50 U.S.C. App. §§ 501–96) prohibits the entry of a default judgment against military personnel on active duty. Also draft a judgment for signature unless told not to do so. See an example in Exhibit 5.15.

If the claim is not for a sum certain, the request for default judgment is submitted to the court for determination [Rule 55(b)(2)]. Similar documents are required. The court may require a hearing in which evidence is required to prove the amount of the damages. If the defendant has appeared in the action or enters a special appearance to be heard

---

EXHIBIT 5.13 Request for Entry of Default Judgment by Clerk

REQUEST FOR ENTRY OF DEFAULT JUDGMENT BY CLERK WITH SUPPORTING AFFIDAVIT[1]

[Title of Court and Cause]

The Plaintiff in the above entitled action requests the clerk of *[name of court]* to enter judgment by default against the Defendant *[name of defendant]* in the amount of *[state sum]*, plus interest at the rate of *[state rate]*, and costs.

_____

Attorney for Plaintiff
(Address)
(Phone number)
Fax number
E-mail address
Bar Number, if required

AFFIDAVIT

State _____   ⎫
                              ⎬   ss.
County of _____   ⎭

[name of attorney], being duly sworn, deposes and states:
1. That s/he is the attorney for Plaintiff in the above entitled action.
2. That Defendant's default in this action was entered on *[date default entered]*.
3. That the amount due Plaintiff from Defendant is a sum certain in the amount of *[state amount]*.
4. That the Defendant is not an infant, incompetent person, or in military service.
5. That the amount indicated is justly owed Plaintiff, no part of which has been paid.

_____

Attorney for Plaintiff

[Jurat]
(A brief statement of amount due may be included.)

[1]Note: The case caption should be included in all documents filed with the court. Or, see comment to exhibit 5.14.

EXHIBIT 5.14 Affidavit of Nonmilitary Service of Defendant

[Fed. R. Civ. P. Rule 55(b)]
[Title of Court and Cause]

State of _____
County of _____

I, _____ being first duly sworn, on oath state:

1. My age is *[legal age]* years.
2. I reside at No. _____ , _____ Street in the City of _____ , State of _____.
3. My occupation is attorney at law and I am licensed to practice law in this jurisdiction.
4. I am the duly authorized agent for the plaintiff in the above entitled and numbered cause and as such have full knowledge of the facts in this case.
5. With reference to the matter in issue in the above cause, I have had representatives of this office call on defendant for the purpose of inducing him to comply with the demand set forth in the complaint filed herein; that from all of the facts, this affiant says that the defendant _____ is engaged in the business of _____ in the City of _____, and is not in the military service of the United States and is not entitled to the benefits of the Service members Civil Relief Act under 50 U.S.C. section 501 et.seq.).

_____

Subscribed and sworn to before me this _____ day of _____, _____.
Notary Public

_____

Adapted from West's Federal Forms, § 4672, v. 4 (1992), with permission of West Group.

EXHIBIT 5.15 Judgment of Default

[Title of Court and Cause]

JUDGMENT

Defendant _____ having failed to answer plaintiff's complaint or otherwise appear in this action and having his/her default entered, and on plaintiff's application and affidavit that defendant owes plaintiff the sum of _____ ($_____),

It is ORDERED and ADJUDGED
that plaintiff _____ recover from defendant _____ the sum of _____ ($_____), with _____ percent interest from (date) _____ and costs of the action.

_____
Clerk of Court
Dated _____

on the damage issue, or when the defendant is a minor or incompetent, notice of the application for judgment must be served on the defendant at least three days prior to the hearing on the application.

When the documents are completed, signed, and notarized, they should be filed with the clerk of court, and any required notice served on the defendant. If the court holds a hearing on the application, additional preparation on behalf of the attorney may be required.

Once the default judgment is entered, enforcement of the judgment is obtained in the same manner as for any other judgment (see Chapter 12). The plaintiff is limited to the amount of damages requested in the complaint and may not increase the amount.

DEFAULT AND MULTIPLE DEFENDANTS

Exercise special caution when seeking a default judgment when only one defendant is in default. Some jurisdictions permit only one judgment in an action, which might preclude proceeding against the other defendants. This situation is avoided in some jurisdictions by placing language in the judgment that states this judgment will be "joint and several" with any judgments granted against the remaining defendants. Seek the advice of your supervising attorney after checking the pertinent rules and cases.

CHECKLIST FOR DEFAULT JUDGMENT

Stage One

- Check calendar (deadline control system) for upcoming expiration of deadline to answer or otherwise defend case.
- Review case file and date and proof of service.
- If defendant defaults, take action to file request and affidavit with clerk as soon after default (twenty-first day in most jurisdictions) as possible or when directed to do so by your attorney.
- Draft entry of default and affidavit.
- Attach copies of proof of service of summons and complaint.
- Have the documents signed and notarized.
- File with clerk and obtain clerk's entry of default.

Stage Two

- As soon after entry of default as local rules and statutes permit or when directed to do so by your attorney, take action to request judgment of default. (Note: If there are multiple defendants and not all are in default, consult with attorney.)
- If the award is for a sum certain, draft a request for entry of default judgment by the clerk [Rule 55(b)(1) and your state rule].
- If the award requested is not for a sum certain, draft a request for entry of default judgment by the court [Rule 55(b)(2) and your state rule].
- Include the attorney's affidavit, the affidavit regarding military service, breakdown of debt, affidavit of costs, proof of service if required, and the judgment.
- Have appropriate documents signed and notarized.
- Deliver to clerk of court or electronically file.
- Obtain date for hearing if needed.
- If hearing is required, draft notice of hearing on application and have it signed and served on defendant at least three days prior to hearing.
- Notify all non-defaulting defendants of application for judgment or as directed by attorney.

SETTING ASIDE A DEFAULT JUDGMENT

Despite any excellent forms you may have drafted to obtain a default judgment, the defendant may be able to have a default judgment set aside. If so, the defendant can attack the complaint or file an answer as if the twenty-day period had not expired. The court will set aside the default judgment for *good cause*. Those things constituting *good cause* are enumerated in Rule 60(b):

> (1) mistake, inadvertence, surprise, or excusable neglect; (2) newly discovered evidence which by due diligence could not have been discovered in time to move for a new trial under Rule 59(b); (3) fraud . . ., misrepresentation, or other misconduct of adverse party; (4) the judgment is void; (5) the judgment has been satisfied, released, or discharged or a prior judgment upon which it is based has been reversed or otherwise vacated, or it is no longer equitable that the judgment should have prospective application; or (6) any other reason justifying relief from the operation of the judgment.

In more concrete terms, good cause might exist if a person has been incapacitated due to illness or injury, and is unable to attend to business; or if the attorney is ill or unavailable.

The motion must be made in reasonable time (up to one year from the date of judgment) for items 60(b)(1), (2), and (3). The form for a motion to set aside a default judgment appears in Exhibit 5.16. We will discuss motion practice in more detail in the next chapter.

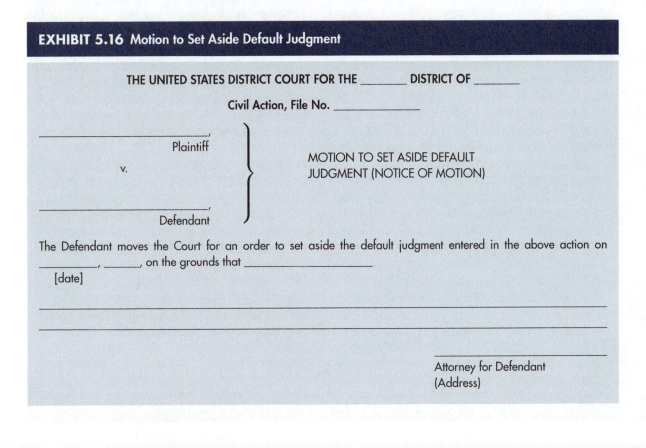

EXHIBIT 5.16 Motion to Set Aside Default Judgment

THE UNITED STATES DISTRICT COURT FOR THE _____ DISTRICT OF _____

Civil Action, File No. _____

_____,
Plaintiff

v.

_____,
Defendant

MOTION TO SET ASIDE DEFAULT JUDGMENT (NOTICE OF MOTION)

The Defendant moves the Court for an order to set aside the default judgment entered in the above action on _____, _____, on the grounds that _____
    [date]

_____

_____

_____
Attorney for Defendant
(Address)

Military personnel covered under the Service Members Relief Act have up to ninety days after release from active duty to reopen any default judgment entered against them while they were deployed.

How important is getting the address correct when requesting a default judgment from a court? As *Moghaddam v. Bone*, 142 Cal.App. 4th 283, 47 Cal.Rptr.3d 602 (2006) found, the typing of incorrect numbers in a zip code in an address can establish a basis for denying a default judgment.

CASE STUDY: UNDERSTANDING THE LAW

The facts in *Moghaddam v. Bone* involve the re-leasing of a car, where no one made the lease payments resulting in a lawsuit and default judgment. Kevin and Morgan Bone re-leased a cart to Houman Moghaddam. Neither party made lease payments on the car and ultimately Moghaddam received negative credit marks and sued the Bones for breach of contract and fraud. The Bones were supposedly served on July 28, 1999, at their residence in Aliso Viejo, California, which they deny. Having not answered the lawsuit, a hearing was scheduled to "prove up" the claim and damages for a default judgment. The Bones claim they did not receive notice of the hearing. Default judgment was formally entered on September 27, 2000, for $63,000 in compensatory damages and $50,000 in punitive damages. Judgments were filed by Moghaddam in two counties sometime in 2003. The Bones were mailed abstracts of the judgments by the Orange County clerk and received them at their Florida residence sometime late 2003 or early 2004. The Bones filed a motion to set aside the default judgment on November 8, 2004. Notice was mailed to Moghaddam at two different addresses—one in Irvine, California 92623 and Newport Beach, California 92626. Moghaddam claims he never received notice of the Bones' motion and somehow learned of it on January 13, 2005. The court granted the Bones' motion on December 7, 2004, as Moghaddam did not respond. The Bones' claim they mailed the order setting aside the default judgment to the Irvine, California address with a zip code of 92653. Moghaddam claims he never received notice of the order and moved to stay all proceeding. After hearing arguments, the court affirmed its orders setting aside the default and default judgment. Moghaddam appealed the orders entered by the court. The Bones attempted to dismiss the appeal as untimely, but the court examined the rule involving legal notice and the requirement that orders served by mail must be precise and are strictly construed by a court for

compliance. Any deviation in an address will affect proper notice. Thus, since the address was incorrect because the zip code was invalid, Moghaddam did not have proper notice of the order setting aside the default and default judgment. The zip code used was 92653 rather than 92623, which was written on Moghaddam original complaint. Therefore, the court also found that Moghaddam had appealed the court's December order within the 180 days required after the entry of judgment. Therefore, the court held that Moghaddam's appeal was timely and that the notice of the order setting the default judgment aside was invalid due to lack of proper notice. In turn, since Moghaddam never received proper notice of the order setting aside the default judgment, the default was improper. The court then considered whether the original default judgment against the Bones was proper. Both parties raised fraud issues against each other with the Bones relying on extrinsic fraud or mistake as the basis to set aside the default. The moving party must show: (1) a meritorious defense, (2) articulate excuse for not presenting a defense to the original case, and (3) diligence in seeking to set aside the default judgment after discovery. In this case, the court determined that the lower court improperly shifted the burden of proof to Moghaddam and ruled against him. As this court held, there is a strong policy of a party having "his day in court" and thus the court ordered a "do over" especially given the important factual issues that needed to be decided. The appeals court ordered the lower court to reconsider its motion to set aside the default and the default judgment.

Questions for Review: Locate a copy of *Moghaddam v. Bone*. What facts did the court deem disputed, requiring the remand to the trial court? What public policy did the court cite favoring its decision to remand the matter? What lessons are learned from *Moghaddam v. Bone* that a paralegal can apply in his or her daily practice?

SUMMARY

Chapter 5 focuses on the specific tasks you must perform to commence a lawsuit officially, serve the opponent properly, and get a judgment should the defendant default. The purpose of filing the lawsuit is to notify the court and the defendant of the action and to establish its official beginning date.

You determine what documents are needed to file the action and see that they are prepared, signed, and copied. A complaint is always needed, as is a summons unless the federal waiver of service of summons is used. The original documents are then filed with the clerk of the appropriate court, who stamps or otherwise verifies the filing of the complaint and assigns it a case number. A summons is issued for each defendant.

Subsequently, the plaintiff acquires personal jurisdiction over each defendant through service of a copy of the complaint and a summons or waiver. This can be accomplished by closely following the state or federal rules; the exact process is determined by whether the defendant is a person, a corporation, an out-of-state citizen, or a foreign citizen. Citizens and corporations of other states may be served under an applicable long-arm statute if adequate minimal contacts make the application of the statute constitutional. Constructive service requiring publication may be available to the plaintiff, especially in *in rem* actions.

If the defendant is properly served and fails to answer the complaint or otherwise defend the action, the plaintiff may seek a default judgment. Such a judgment ends the case and awards the plaintiff the sum or damages sought plus costs. No trial is held. Consult local rules of court and local form books to determine default procedure. Request the entry of default and judgment as soon as the law permits or as directed by your supervising attorney. If there is good cause for the defendant's default, the judgment may be set aside.

KEY TERMS

certificate of service	in forma pauperis	service of process
constructive service	in rem action	substituted service
default judgment	long-arm statute	summons
e-filing	quasi in rem action	
federal magistrate judge	recuse	

QUESTIONS FOR STUDY AND REVIEW

1. What event marks the commencement of a lawsuit in the federal court system? What usually commences the action in most state systems?

2. What is the purpose of the waiver of service of summons? What documents are needed for it? What documents are needed for service of process in your state?

3. The court cannot gain personal jurisdiction over the defendant until what happens?

4. What are the advantages of e-filing over traditional methods of filing?

5. Define CM/ECF and PACER; describe the benefits and procedures for both the e-filing and e-access processes.

   What are the federal rules and restrictions on electronic services of process?

6. What is the practical goal of service of process? What are the federal and your state time limits for service?

7. What are long-arm statutes? What injustice do they attempt to remedy?

8. What classes of persons and businesses will the long-arm statute reach in your state? What is (are) the method(s) of service required to comply with the long-arm statutes in your state?

9. Define *in rem* and *quasi in rem* jurisdiction. Who is served process in an *in rem* action?

10. How is service of process generally achieved in your state court system? What items are needed?

11. Define substituted and constructive service of process.

12. What are five techniques or sources for locating hard-to-find defendants?

13. How does a paralegal keep good records of service?

14. What is a default judgment? What is the benefit to the plaintiff of a default judgment?

15. What are the applicable rules and procedures for obtaining a default judgment? How and why may a default judgment be set aside?

SYSTEMS FOLDER ASSIGNMENTS

1. Obtain fee schedules for the federal, state, and local courts, including fees for service of process and the person to whom such service fees should be paid, as well as fees for the filing of subsequent pleadings and motions. If so directed by your instructor, contact the appropriate clerk of court for this information. Place the fee schedules in your systems folder with a reminder to update the information periodically.

2. Using an approach similar to the Reference Guide and Checklist for Methods of Service, draft a state service of process checklist for your systems folder. Look up any needed information in your state's rules of civil procedure or state statutes to complete your checklist.

3. After class discussion on locating difficult-to-find defendants, add additional techniques to the Checklist for Locating Defendants. Place the checklist in your systems folder.

4. Draft a brief Checklist for Filing and Service of Documents Subsequent to the Complaint—Federal and a similar one for your state. Note the applicable rules for future reference including any on e-filing and service. Place the checklists in your systems folder.

5. In your systems folder make a reference to the checklist for default judgment. Research the rules and forms applicable to obtaining a default judgment in your state courts, and draft a state checklist for default judgment. Add needed state forms to your systems folder.

APPLICATION ASSIGNMENTS

1. Prepare the necessary documents for filing Case II, the *Ameche* case, for both federal and your state courts. Use the sample forms provided in this chapter and the completed forms as a guide. Assume there is diversity jurisdiction. Check for accuracy.

2. Memo to: Terry Salyer, Paralegal

   From: Isadora Pearlman

   Subject: Research

   Completion Date: Three days from today

   Issue: What are the necessary minimum contacts required by our state statute to gain jurisdiction over a foreign corporation? Over a nonresident tortfeasor? Over an Internet marketer?

   Task: Prepare a short memorandum on the state and constitutional law on this subject. Guidelines: Check the annotated state statutes under "long-arm statutes," "foreign corporations," and "nonresident tortfeasors" for case law. Also try the state digest under similar key phrases. Since the state's long-arm statute affects both our federal and state court, decisions in both jurisdictions are helpful. See the section on researching and drafting a memorandum of law in Chapter 6.

3. Assume that you work for the firm that is representing Richard Hart and that for purposes of this problem, Mr. Hart is elderly and not well educated. He comes to your firm six months after a default judgment has been entered against him. Your attorney assigns you the task of determining if limited capacity brought on by aging and lack of education is sufficient good cause to have a default judgment set aside. Research the issue and prepare a brief outline on what facts are sufficient good cause to set aside a default judgment.

4. Go to the Web site for your state courts and determine if any levels of your state courts permit e-filing. If there is an e-filing system, what is its name? If not, are there plans to implement an e-system? Is there a tutorial for its use? How does an attorney access and use the system?

5. Research Section 804 of the Federal Debt Collections Practices Act. Which of the following practices would be unlawful in trying to locate a defendant?

   a. A paralegal contacts a neighbor of the defendant to locate the defendant.

   b. A paralegal informs a third person that the paralegal is a debt collector.

   c. A paralegal informs a third party that the defendant owes the plaintiff money after third party asks, "Does the defendant owe you money?"

   Does your state have similar rules? Research them and describe them here. Do you believe these restrictions are wise?

CASE ASSIGNMENTS

1. You want to serve Mercury Parcel Service, Inc. with a copy of the complaint in the *Forrester* matter. Using your state statute, identify the procedures for serving a corporation. Prepare the documents for serving Mercury Parcel Service.

2. Assume that Richard Hart, one of the defendants in the *Forrester* case, was served but did not respond. Prepare the documents for obtaining a default judgment according to the rules in your jurisdiction.

DEFENDING AND TESTING THE LAWSUIT: MOTIONS, ANSWERS, AND OTHER RESPONSIVE PLEADINGS

OUTLINE

OBJECTIVES

AFTER READING THIS CHAPTER, YOU WILL BE ABLE TO:

- Identify the different types of motions to dismiss under Federal Rule 12(b)
- Understand the purpose of removing a state action to federal court
- Draft an answer, affirmative defenses, counterclaim, and cross-claim
- Distinguish between amending and supplementing pleadings
- Prepare various responsive motions, including motions for judgment on the pleadings and summary judgment

INTRODUCTION

When the complaint is received, the defendant may do one or more of the following: do nothing and default, attack the complaint through appropriate motions, file a notice of removal to have the case removed from state court to federal court, or file an answer. The opponent may respond, amend, oppose, or reply as necessary.

Beyond this stage of the pleadings, both sides may test the lawsuit with the hope of ending it through a motion for judgment on the pleadings and a motion for summary judgment. We will look at motion practice through the chronology of tasks in the typical lawsuit, first through the defendant's motion to dismiss and other motions attacking the complaint.

MOTIONS IN GENERAL

INTRODUCTION

motion

A request for a court order granting relief to the moving party.

order

A directive from a judge requiring some act or restraint from some act in a lawsuit.

A **motion** is a request to the court for an order granting relief favorable to the moving party. An **order** is a directive from a judge requiring some act or restraint from some act in a lawsuit—for example, an order to dismiss the case. Motions may be made before, during, and after trial. It is frequently the task of the paralegal to draft motions and supporting documents and to research the law in support of the motion.

PURPOSE

Motions have many purposes; for example, to obtain judicial relief such as dismissal of the action, exclusion of evidence, new trial, and so on; to narrow the issues for trial; and to establish a record for appeal. The first of these purposes needs no explanation. The second, to narrow the issues for trial, reflects that motions are used for a variety of matters, some central to the cause of action that may eliminate the lawsuit altogether, and some of lesser impact to clarify and refine the lawsuit. The third purpose, to establish a record for appeal, indicates that motions raise questions of law that affect the outcome of the case and must be decided by the judge. The judge's decision on these questions is often appealed. The motion establishes that an issue was raised in a proper and timely manner, preserving the right to have the issue heard on appeal.

REQUIREMENTS AND COMPONENTS OF THE MOTION

The requirements and components of a motion set out in this section are common to many courts. Local practice may vary, however, so carefully check local rules and practice.

Federal Rule 7(b) and parallel state rules set out the basic requirements for a motion: It must be made in writing, unless it is made at trial or hearing; its grounds must be stated with particularity, setting forth the order sought; it should have the same caption as the complaint with the exception that *et al.* (meaning

memorandum of law (memorandum of points and authorities)

A document, normally shorter and less formal than a brief, stating the relevant legal authority and how it should be applied to the issues and facts of a case.

brief

A document stating the relevant legal authority and how it should be applied to the issues and facts of a case.

affidavit

A written, sworn statement.

affiant

The person who signs an affidavit.

"and others") may be used after the name of the first plaintiff or defendant rather than a list of all the other parties; and addresses are not necessary. Rules 7(b)(3) and 11 require that all motions be certified by the attorney's signature and include the attorney's address. It is good practice to include the attorney's phone number as well.

In addition to the motion, a notice of motion must be prepared. The purpose of the notice is to inform the opponent that a motion has been filed and will be heard by the court at a specified time and place. Due process requires that the adverse party be given notice and, therefore, a fair chance to prepare for the hearing and to refute the motion. The Federal Rules permit the motion and notice to be combined in one document called the notice of hearing on the motion [Rule 7(b)].

The motion is usually a single document that concisely states the nature of the request. A separate document, called a **memorandum of law (memorandum of points and authorities)** or a **brief**, is attached to the motion. This accompanying document is a statement of the relevant legal authority (such as statutes, rules, and case decisions) and how it should be applied to the issues and facts in the case. Generally, a brief is more formal and more complex than a memorandum of law, but some jurisdictions use the terms interchangeably in motion practice. Affidavits setting forth additional facts not in the complaint may also be appended to the motion or brief as exhibits. An **affidavit** is a written statement sworn to by the signer. The signer is called the **affiant**.

PROCEDURE: FILING, SERVICE, AND TIME LIMITS

When the documents are prepared and signed, the motion must be filed and served on the opponent's attorney consistent with the procedure set out in Rule 5 (including e-filing) and as discussed in "Filing and Service of Pleadings and Papers Subsequent to the Complaint" in Chapter 5.

A motion must be served not less than five days before the scheduled hearing on the motion [Rule 6(d)]. Three days must be added to the time limit if service is by mail or electronic means [Rule 6(e)]. State requirements may vary. Affidavits may be served no later than one day before a hearing on the motion [Rule 6(d)]. The adverse party may file a responsive affidavit or memorandum. Check local rules for the specific time limits.

MOTION TO DISMISS

TASK

Mr. McDuff has just received the complaint in a case similar to Mrs. Forrester's. In the new case, however, our firm represents the defendant, Allen Howard. Mr. McDuff would like you to look over the complaint to see if it can be attacked. After your review, Mr. McDuff will go over the complaint. If there are weaknesses in the complaint, your task will be to draft a motion to dismiss the opponent's complaint.

PURPOSE

The purpose of a motion to dismiss is to have the court dismiss the complaint and, thus, the lawsuit. Grounds for this motion include failure to state a claim for which relief can be granted, lack of jurisdiction, improper venue, defective service, and so on, to be discussed later. Filing the motion to dismiss or related objections to the complaint is also a common tactic to gain time to prepare the required answer to the complaint, because the time limit to answer is suspended until the motion is decided. This tactic is not ethically defensible when the basis for the motion is without substance (frivolous) and is submitted solely for delay.

If the complaint is dismissed, the plaintiff will probably respond by amending the complaint. Occasionally, however, the plaintiff is unable to correct the defect, and the case ends, much to the delight of the defendant. The savings in cost, time, and anxiety can be substantial. In other words, if the opponent can be kept out of court, our client cannot lose the lawsuit.

It is always best to check with your supervising attorney before drafting a motion to dismiss the complaint. Tactical reasons may exist for not filing the motion, especially if a defect can be easily corrected. The motion may alert the plaintiff to a weakness in the case that can be exploited to better advantage at a later stage in the case. A **demurrer** is the document used in some states to dispute the sufficiency of the complaint or other pleading. Its purpose is essentially the same as a motion to dismiss the complaint.

demurrer

A document used in some states to dispute the sufficiency of the complaint or other pleading.

DETERMINING WHAT TO ATTACK

If the motion to dismiss is for failure to state a claim, what weaknesses should you look for? If you will recall our discussion on drafting complaints (Chapter 4), the key to a successful complaint is a logical syllogism based on a rule of law, such as, if A, B, and C exist, then the plaintiff is entitled to remedy X. This rule is the major premise. The minor premise is stated in the complaint: A + B + C do in fact exist, therefore the plaintiff should receive remedy X. A syllogism opens two avenues for attack. The first is to determine whether a required element of the minor premise is missing in the complaint, that is, whether a required element—A, B, or C—in the rule of law has not been supported by alleged facts. If so, the minor premise is incomplete and the complaint fails to state a claim. The second avenue of attack is to look beyond the complaint to the major premise. The complaint may be based on an inaccurate or misconceived reading of the law. If so, there can be no claim. The court occasionally does, however, decide to accept a new rule of law.

Let us look at the body of the negligence complaint filed against Mr. Howard.

4. On September 2, _____, Defendant was operating a motor vehicle on South Maple Drive.

5. Defendant operated the vehicle in a negligent manner by failing to maintain a lookout and by failing to keep his automobile under control.

6. Plaintiff suffered great pain, broken ribs, and head injuries.

7. As a result of the injuries, plaintiff has incurred and will continue to incur doctor and hospital bills and loss of income and benefits.

Assume that you have researched the rule of law for a cause of action for negligence and find it to be: if A (duty) + B (breach) + C (injury) + D (breach is substantial cause of injury) exist, plaintiff is entitled to damages. Now apply the law to the complaint at hand to see if facts have been alleged to support each of the required elements of negligence. Paragraph four indicates that the defendant was operating a motor vehicle, which requires a duty of care toward others; therefore, a proper allegation of duty is present. Paragraph five alleges facts to show a breach of that duty. Paragraphs six and seven state facts in support of an injury to the plaintiff. So far, so good. But what is missing? The plaintiff has failed to allege facts to demonstrate D, that the defendant's breach of duty was a substantial cause of the plaintiff's injury. Because an entire element of the law is unalleged and unsupported, the complaint does not state a claim and is subject to a motion to dismiss. It is true that the omission may be easily corrected. On the other hand, there may not be a substantial connection between the defendant's negligence and the plaintiff's injuries, or the plaintiff may not have sufficient facts to demonstrate the connection. If the latter is true, the motion to dismiss will end the case against your client.

The body of the negligence complaint against Mr. Howard might read:

4. On September 2, _____, Defendant was operating a motor vehicle on South Maple Drive.

5. Defendant operated the vehicle in a negligent manner by failing to maintain a lookout and by failing to keep his automobile under control.

6. Plaintiff no longer feels safe operating a vehicle on South Maple Drive.

Here the complaint alleges that A + B + E (plaintiff's fear) exist, therefore the plaintiff is entitled to X damages. Research shows the underlying rule of law to be that A + B + C + D, not E, invoke the right to a remedy. The complaint does not match the law. Because it is based on an erroneous reading of the law, the major premise implied in the complaint does not hold up, and no cause of action is stated.

In the previous examples, the complaint is missing the proper allegations to state a claim on which relief can be granted. A third avenue of attack arises when the complaint alleges too much, revealing a defense to the action. Consider this premise: if A + B exist, and if W does not exist, then the plaintiff is entitled to relief. The existence of an element W, such as self-defense, would be a defense to the action. If in the factual allegation of the complaint, the plaintiff states that he was struck while lunging at the defendant, it might be sufficiently clear that W (self-defense) does exist. The motion to dismiss for failure to state a claim would be granted. Although oversimplified for purposes of illustration, these examples can be useful as a basic pattern in applying a syllogism to attack a complaint.

Prior to drafting the motion to dismiss the complaint, inform the supervising attorney of any apparent weaknesses in the opponent's complaint. This gives the attorney a chance to review the complaint, identify other weaknesses that need to be pursued, and assign any legal research needed to develop a basis for the motion founded in legal authority.

DRAFTING THE DOCUMENTS

Mr. McDuff agrees that the opponent's complaint is inadequate and assigns you the tasks of researching the legal basis for the motion to dismiss, writing a rough draft memorandum in support of the motion to dismiss, and drafting the motion to dismiss the complaint. You also are aware that the motion must be filed and served within the time permitted by the rules.

When any needed research is complete, draft the motion to dismiss the complaint. Exhibit 6.1 is an example of such a motion. Draft the notice of motion using the format demonstrated in Exhibit 5.16. In case a state uses the demurrer, it appears in Exhibit 6.2. In some states a demurrer must contain the supporting authority for the demurrer, often eliminating the need for a memorandum of law.

The remaining task is the writing of the rough draft memorandum of law in support of the motion. Although the memorandum should be drafted with the highest standards, it is useful to consider it a rough draft to emphasize to both yourself and the attorney that the memorandum needs to be reviewed and probably revised by the attorney before filing at the courthouse. Keep in mind that Rule 32.1 of the Federal Rules of Appellate Procedure now permits the citing in federal court of unpublished opinions issued after January 1, 2007. Exhibit 6.3 is a brief example of how a rough draft memorandum of law might look in Mr. Howard's case. Examples of the format for affidavits are found in Exhibit 5.14 and Exhibit 6.21.

In some jurisdictions the court requires that the motion be accompanied by a draft of the order for the judge to sign. Including this draft is a good idea even if it is not required. Exhibit 6.4 is an example of such an order. If your client is a nongovernmental corporate party, two copies of the parent and publicly held corporation disclosure statement must be prepared to accompany the defendant's first appearance in the case before the district court (Rule 7.1).

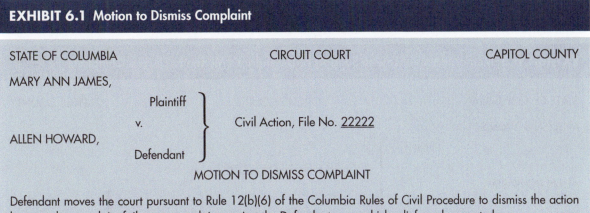

EXHIBIT 6.1 Motion to Dismiss Complaint

STATE OF COLUMBIA   CIRCUIT COURT   CAPITOL COUNTY

MARY ANN JAMES,

               Plaintiff

       v.   Civil Action, File No. 22222

ALLEN HOWARD,

               Defendant

MOTION TO DISMISS COMPLAINT

Defendant moves the court pursuant to Rule 12(b)(6) of the Columbia Rules of Civil Procedure to dismiss the action because the complaint fails to state a claim against the Defendant upon which relief can be granted.

                                           James McDuff
                                         Attorney for Defendant
                                         (Address)

Each of these documents should be proofed for accuracy, reviewed by the attorney, revised as needed, and then signed by the attorney. Obtain a hearing date from the clerk and, when possible, confirm the date with the plaintiff's attorney. Place the date on the notice of motion and serve one copy of it, the motion, and any accompanying documents, such as a memorandum of law and affidavits, on the plaintiff's attorney as previously indicated. Check local practice for any variations in procedure. Immediately after service on the other party, file the original documents and a certificate of service with the clerk. Have one set of the documents stamped by the clerk with the

---

EXHIBIT 6.2 General Demurrer

STATE OF COLUMBIA   CIRCUIT COURT   CAPITOL COUNTY

MARY ANN JAMES,

               Plaintiff

          v.   Civil Action, File No. <u>22222</u>

ALLEN HOWARD,

               Defendant

DEMURRER

Defendant demurs to Plaintiff's complaint, specifying:

  That the complaint does not state facts sufficient to constitute a cause of action against Defendant.

    WHEREFORE, Defendant prays that Plaintiff be awarded nothing by reason of her complaint and that he be dismissed with his costs of suit paid by Plaintiff.

                                                   _____

                                                   James McDuff
                                                   Attorney for Defendant
                                                   (Address)

EXHIBIT 6.3 Memorandum of Law in Support of Defendant's Motion to Dismiss Complaint

STATE OF COLUMBIA   CIRCUIT COURT   CAPITOL COUNTY

MARY ANN JAMES,

               Plaintiff

          V.   Civil Action, File No. <u>22222</u>

ALLEN HOWARD,

               Defendant

MEMORANDUM OF LAW
IN SUPPORT OF DEFENDANT'S MOTION TO DISMISS COMPLAINT

Defendant argues to the court that the Plaintiff's complaint should be dismissed on the grounds that it does not state a claim against the Defendant on which relief can be granted. In support of said motion, Defendant states the following:

EXHIBIT 6.3 Memorandum of Law in Support of Defendant's Motion to Dismiss Complaint (*continued*)

That Plaintiff's complaint does not allege facts in support of a critical element of a claim for negligence. A long-standing precedent in the state of Columbia is the case of *Winthrop v. Walters*, 200 Col. 392, 105 W.W. 63 (1934).*
That case established the rule of law that a civil complaint must allege and state facts in support of each element of the cause of action, and that failure to do so made the complaint defective and upheld the lower court's dismissal of the complaint for its failure to state a cause of action.

In the recent case of *Arnold v. Taggie*, 592 Col. 365, 354 S.W.2d 615 (1992)* where the plaintiff failed to allege that the defendant's negligent operation of a van was the cause of plaintiff's injuries, the court held the dismissal of the complaint for failure to state a cause of action was proper.

Plaintiff's complaint in this action does not allege that the Defendant's conduct caused her injuries, nor does it allege any facts to support such a conclusion.

Therefore, Plaintiff's complaint is defective and should be dismissed.

Date _____

_____
James McDuff
Attorney for Defendant
(Address)

*Citations in this memorandum are fictitious.

EXHIBIT 6.4 Order Granting Motion to Dismiss Complaint

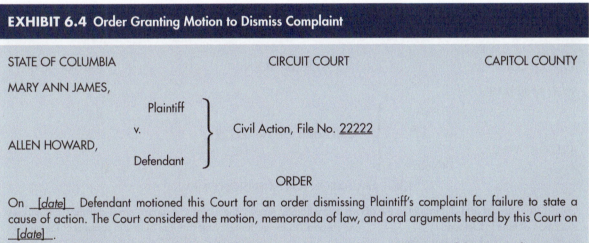

STATE OF COLUMBIA   CIRCUIT COURT   CAPITOL COUNTY

MARY ANN JAMES,

                    Plaintiff

            v.   Civil Action, File No. <u>22222</u>

ALLEN HOWARD,

                    Defendant

                            ORDER

On __[date]__ Defendant motioned this Court for an order dismissing Plaintiff's complaint for failure to state a cause of action. The Court considered the motion, memoranda of law, and oral arguments heard by this Court on __[date]__.

For GOOD CAUSE SHOWN, this Court finds that facts in support of several elements of the cause of action are insufficiently alleged failing to state a cause of action and that Defendant's motion to dismiss should be granted. SO ORDERED.

Date _____

_____
Signature of Judge

filing date for your firm's file. If e-filing, follow the procedures of the relevant court or jurisdiction.

Remember that in the Federal Rules and those of most states, the defendant must respond within 20 days of receipt of the complaint. This time limit may be extended to 60 or 90 days if the federal waiver process is used [Rule 12(a)(1)(A) and (B)]. Any motion must be served not later than five days before the time specified for the hearing on the motion, unless the rules or order of the court indicate otherwise [Rule 6(d)]. Local rules should always be checked. The opposing party may file a responsive memorandum of law to which the original moving party may reply.

Occasionally, one side or the other in a lawsuit may need an extension of time for some good reason. The paralegal may have the responsibility of drafting the necessary documents. Consult local practice for the proper procedure and forms. Many jurisdictions require a request to extend time to be made by motion. This motion is necessary if the other party will not agree to an extension. If the parties agree to the extension, one option is a joint application for an order extending the time. A joint application leads to a court order that eliminates any potential disputes regarding whether a request for extension was granted. Include an order extending the time for the court to sign. Exhibit 6.5 is an example of a joint application for an order extending the time.

OTHER MOTIONS TO DISMISS

The most common motions to dismiss are contained in Rule 12(b) of the Federal Rules of Civil Procedure:

1. Lack of jurisdiction over the subject matter

2. Lack of jurisdiction over the person

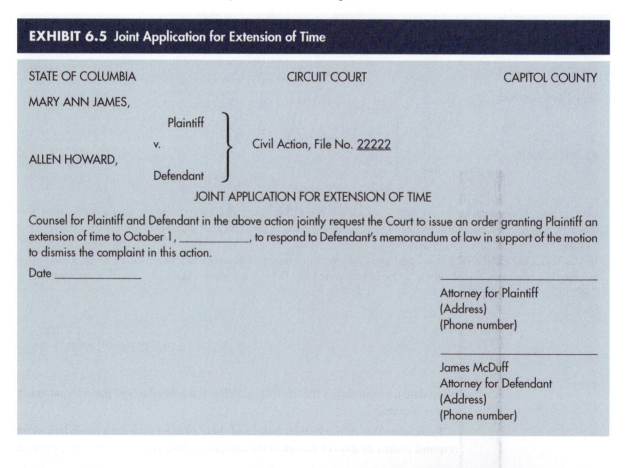

EXHIBIT 6.5 Joint Application for Extension of Time

STATE OF COLUMBIA   CIRCUIT COURT   CAPITOL COUNTY

MARY ANN JAMES,

                              Plaintiff

                    v.   Civil Action, File No. <u>22222</u>

ALLEN HOWARD,

                              Defendant

JOINT APPLICATION FOR EXTENSION OF TIME

Counsel for Plaintiff and Defendant in the above action jointly request the Court to issue an order granting Plaintiff an extension of time to October 1, _____, to respond to Defendant's memorandum of law in support of the motion to dismiss the complaint in this action.

Date _____

_____
Attorney for Plaintiff
(Address)
(Phone number)

_____
James McDuff
Attorney for Defendant
(Address)
(Phone number)

3. Improper venue

4. Insufficiency of process

5. Insufficiency of service of process

6. Failure to state a claim upon which relief can be granted (previously discussed in this chapter)

Note that Rule 12(b) and parallel state rules indicate that if a motion to dismiss for failure to state a claim is accompanied by affidavits or other supporting documents, the court shall treat the motion as a motion for summary judgment. A motion for summary judgment is, essentially, a request to decide the case on the basis of the documents without going to trial. In such circumstances, the plaintiff needs to respond with counter affidavits or other documents.

Although it is beyond the scope of this book to discuss separate examples of each of the 12(b) motions, the motion procedure previously discussed in this chapter applies to these motions as well as other motions presented in this text. Referral to a form manual, such as West Group's *Federal Legal Forms* or *American Jurisprudence Pleadings and Practice Forms* (rev. ed.), should provide you with any examples of the forms that you might need. Numerous forms, including some state-specific forms, are available on Westlaw and Lexis. Federal or state digests should provide leads to the case precedents needed to draft a memorandum in support of any of these 12(b) motions. High-powered commercial services such as Westlaw Litigator provide law offices with quick, electronic access to sample pleadings, motions and other forms, supporting briefs, and other litigation resources.

Form 19 of the Federal Rules gives an example of a motion to dismiss for failure to state a claim, for lack of service of process, for improper venue, and for lack of jurisdiction under Rule 12(b). Form 19 is duplicated in Exhibit 6.6.

EXHIBIT 6.6 Motion to Dismiss, Presenting Defenses of Failure to State a Claim, Lack of Service of Process, Improper Venue, and Lack of Jurisdiction Under Rule 12(b)

The caption of the case and court

The defendant moves the court as follows:

1. To dismiss the action because the complaint fails to state a claim against defendant upon which relief can be granted.

2. To dismiss the action or in lieu thereof to quash the return of service of summons on the grounds (a) that the defendant is a corporation organized under the laws of Delaware and was not and is not subject to service of process within the Southern District of New York, and (b) that the defendant has not been properly served with process in this action, all of which more clearly appears in the affidavits of M.N. and X.Y. hereto annexed as Exhibit A and Exhibit B, respectively.

3. To dismiss the action on the ground that it is in the wrong district because (a) the jurisdiction of this court is invoked solely on the ground that the action arises under the Constitution and laws of the United States and (b) the defendant is a corporation incorporated under the laws of the State of Delaware and is not licensed to do or doing business in the Southern District of New York, all of which more clearly appears in the affidavits of K.L. and V.W. here to annexed as Exhibit C and D, respectively.

(continued)

EXHIBIT 6.6 Motion to Dismiss, Presenting Defenses of Failure to State a Claim, Lack of Service of Process, Improper Venue, and Lack of Jurisdiction Under Rule 12(b) (*continued*)

4. To dismiss the action on the ground that the court lacks jurisdiction because the amount actually in controversy is less than seventy-five thousand dollars exclusive of interest and costs.

Signed: _____

Attorney for Defendant

Address: _____

Notice of Motion

To: _____

Attorney for Plaintiff

_____

Please take notice that the undersigned will bring the above motion on for hearing before this Court at Room _____, United States Court House, Foley Square, City of New York, on the _____ day of _____, _____, at 10 o'clock in the forenoon of that day or as soon thereafter as counsel can be heard.

Signed: _____

Attorney for Defendant

Address: _____

INTERNET EXERCISE

Under what state rule are motions to dismiss found? Compare Fed.R.Civ.P. 12 and your state rule. Identify the differences between the rules for future reference.

The Federal Rules and the rules of those states adopting the Federal Rules permit Rule 12(b) motions to be filed as part of the answer or other appropriate pleadings, or they may be filed separately as illustrated in this chapter.

OTHER MOTIONS ATTACKING THE COMPLAINT

The Motion to Strike

Two other motions are commonly used to attack the complaint: a motion to strike and a motion to make more definite and certain. Rule 12(f) states, "Upon motion . . . the court may order stricken from any pleading any insufficient defense or any redundant, immaterial, impertinent, or scandalous matter." Hence, the purpose of the motion to strike is to keep pleadings lean, to the point, and free of spurious and prejudicial language. The motion to strike can be an effective mechanism to keep pleadings sensible and fair.

In Chapter 4, the cases of *Twombly* and *Iqbal* were discussed relating to the detail that a plaintiff must allege to overcome a challenge to the sufficiency of the complaint. These principles have been applied relating to the detail a defendant must plead regarding its responses to the complaint, with a majority of the courts applying the *Twombly* and *Iqbal* standards. Although the issue has not reached the U.S. Supreme Court yet, *Racick v. Dominion Law Associates*, 270 F.R.D. 228 (E.D. N.C.2010) is an example of the majority viewpoint of most courts.

CASE STUDY: UNDERSTANDING THE LAW

This is a case of mistaken identity in a collection matter. In *Racick v. Dominion Law Associates*, the defendant's clients obtained a judgment against "Louis Racick" in New York for default on a credit card debt. The defendant filed a foreign judgment in Cumberland County, North Carolina where the plaintiff, Louis Racick, lives. Apparently, when the sheriff's department attempted to serve Racick, he showed then proof through his Social Security card that he was not the Louis Racick they were looking for. Racick attempted to contact the defendants on numerous occasions without success. During the time period while the judgment was still of record in Cumberland County, Racick applied for credit for a truck, which was denied, and applied to refinance his house, which was denied. Because of the defendant's failure to respond to the plaintiff's numerous attempts to rectify the situation, he filed this lawsuit alleging violations of the federal Fair Debt Collection Act. After served with the lawsuit, the defendant filed an answer which contained thirteen affirmative defenses. The plaintiff filed a motion to strike the affirmative defenses under Rule 12(f) and further stated that the plausibility standard articulated in *Twombly* and *Iqbal* should apply to the assertion of affirmative defenses. The defendant contended that *Twombly* and *Iqbal* standards do not apply to affirmative defenses. The court reviewed the *Twombly* and *Iqbal* cases, acknowledging that there is a split of authority as to whether they should apply to pleading affirmative defenses. However, the Racick court found that "fairness and common sense" dictate that the *Twombly* and *Iqbal* standards of having a plausible factual basis for an assertion, and not simply alleging a general assertion, should be the applicable standard. Applying this standard to the affirmative defenses alleged, the court reviewed individually the affirmative defenses asserted. The end result is that the court granted the plaintiff's motion to strike on most of the affirmative defenses pleaded, leaving the defendant to amend its answer and file sufficient detail to the remaining affirmative defenses to overcome another challenge from the plaintiff.

Questions for Review: Read *Racick v. Dominion Law Associates*. Why did the court follow the majority view and apply the *Twombly* and *Iqbal* standards? What affirmative defenses remained against the plaintiff and what instructions did the court give the defendant in amending their answer? What was the reasoning of the minority courts in not applying the *Twombly* and *Iqbal* standards?

The Motion for More Definite Statement

Rule 12(e) of the Federal Rules authorizes a motion when the complaint or other pleading is so vague or so devoid of facts that it is difficult to determine if a claim for relief or a defense to a claim has been stated. This motion is similar in function to a *special demurrer*, which is still used in some states to attack the complaint for insufficiency of facts. A request for a **bill of particulars**, which asks the opponent for more details, is used in some states. The purpose of the motion to make more definite and certain, the special demurrer, and the bill of particulars, however, is essentially the same: to provide the opponent with sufficient facts to determine the claim or defense and the opportunity to respond.

bill of particulars

A request for the opponent to make an ambiguous pleading more definite and certain.

You can assist the supervising attorney by reviewing outgoing or incoming pleadings for such defects, calling them to the attention of the attorney, and drafting the necessary motions and supporting documents. Rule 12(e) requires that the motion for more definite statement specify the defects complained of and the details desired.

In Exhibit 6.7, review the following excerpts from a complaint filed in federal district court. Do grounds exist for either a motion to strike or a motion to make more definite and certain?

EXHIBIT 6.7 Count One/Count Two

Count One

1. . . .
2. Defendant negligently drove a vehicle against Plaintiff who was crossing the highway.
3. As a result, Plaintiff was injured to the sum of twenty thousand dollars. WHEREFORE . . .

Count Two

4. . . .
5. Defendant negligently caused injury to Plaintiff.
6. As a result, Plaintiff has suffered serious emotional trauma to the sum of thirty thousand dollars. WHEREFORE . . .

This example demonstrates how problems may arise when a complaint is poorly drafted or without substance. Counts One and Two of this complaint could be subject to a motion to make more definite and certain for several reasons: There is no date specified in the complaint, no location is given, and no facts are presented to support the claim that the defendant was driving negligently. The defendant can only guess at the accusation. Without more detail, it may be impossible to determine if there is a defense. For example, the defendant may have been in South America at the time of the alleged accident. The motion to make more definite and certain eliminates guesswork for the defendant regarding the basis for the claim. It is not to be used to provide details to the defendant such as weather conditions, names of witnesses, and other facts that can be found out in discovery. The motion to make more definite and certain appears in Exhibit 6.8.

EXHIBIT 6.8 Motion for More Definite Statement

[*Caption omitted*]

MOTION FOR MORE DEFINITE STATEMENT

Defendant, pursuant to Rule 12(e) of the Federal Rules of Civil Procedure, moves this court for an order requiring Plaintiff to provide a more definite statement of the claim against the Defendant.

As grounds, Defendant states the Plaintiff's complaint is so vague and ambiguous that Defendant cannot reasonably frame a response thereto.

The complaint is defective for the reasons stated below:

1. In both Counts One and Two Plaintiff does not state on what date the alleged incident occurred.
2. Plaintiff failed to indicate the location of the occurrence, and
3. Insufficient facts are alleged in support of the claim of negligence or any other cause of action.

Defendant requests Plaintiff provide the following:

1. The date of the alleged incident.
2. The specific location of the incident, and
3. Facts describing how the Defendant was negligent.

(Attorney's signature block)
[*Notice of motion omitted*]

A motion to strike will not be allowed unless there is a clear reason to do so. In the preceding example it appears as if Count Two may be a restatement of Count One, but alleging a different injury, emotional trauma. The statement of two counts could make the jury think the defendant had committed two wrongs instead of one. Assuming that the motion for more definite statement revealed that Count Two simply repeated Count One, a motion to strike under Rule 12(f) for redundant material is in order. Emotional trauma would then be included in the damages clause to Count One. Exhibit 6.9 is such a motion.

Apply what you learn in reviewing pleadings for weaknesses to improve the drafting of your own complaints and other pleadings.

ETHICS REMINDER

Remember that the attorney's signature on a pleading, including a motion, certifies that the attorney has read the document, that it is well grounded in fact, that it is warranted by law or a good-faith argument to alter the law, and that it is not offered for any improper purpose (Rule 11). Keep this in mind while drafting and reviewing pleadings.

RESPONSE TO MOTIONS

When the plaintiff receives the defendant's motion, check to see if it was filed within the time limit provided by the applicable state or federal rule; that it contains the requisite information (in writing), particular grounds, relief sought, and any necessary affidavit [Rule 7(b)]; and that it contains the necessary signatures under Rule 11 or similar state rule.

To respond, you may need to research the matter (and brief it if the court has required it) and draft any opposing affidavit. After consulting with the attorney and obtaining needed signatures, serve the response to the motion before the hearing on the motion and according to the time limits set in local practice rules of the pertinent court. Any legal authority or supporting evidence that you have gathered becomes the basis for a possible oral argument before the judge. Some matters raised by motion are sufficiently routine that opposition and response are not necessary, or they may be resolved without a hearing, using a consent or agreed order signed by all parties. Check

---

EXHIBIT 6.9 Motion to Strike Redundant, Immaterial, Impertinent, or Scandalous Matter from Pleading

[Caption omitted]

MOTION TO STRIKE

Defendant, pursuant to Rule 12(f) of the Federal Rules of Civil Procedure, moves the court for an order striking Count Two of the Plaintiff's complaint on the grounds that it is redundant, repeating the same cause of action as Count One, causing confusion and prejudicing Defendant.

(Attorney's signature, address, and telephone number)

(Notice of motion omitted)

with your supervising attorney. If the motion to dismiss is denied, the defendant must proceed to file an answer; if successful, either the case will be dismissed with the possibility of a new start if the defect can be corrected, or the court may permit the plaintiff an opportunity to amend the complaint without dismissal.

REMOVAL OF STATE ACTION TO FEDERAL COURT

TASK

Mr. McDuff wants you to draft the necessary documents and follow the necessary procedure to have Alan Howard's case removed from the state court to the federal district court. This task can be important to the defendant's case, but the task itself is relatively simple.

PURPOSE

The objective of removal is to have the case transferred from state court to federal court jurisdiction. The defendant is given this privilege under 28 U.S.C. § 1441 *et seq.* It affords the defendant the same opportunity that the plaintiff has to choose either the state or federal court when their respective jurisdictions are concurrent. A case may not be removed unless the federal district court has original jurisdiction over the subject matter of the lawsuit. An attorney may choose federal court for a variety of strategic reasons:

1. A different judge, considering that federal judges have more control over the case and may comment on the evidence

2. A more competent jury (it is generally harder to get excused from federal jury duty) from a wider geographical area than a county or parish

3. A chance to have the case removed to an even more convenient federal court through the liberal transfer and venue rules within the federal system

4. A more liberal set of discovery, evidence, and pleading rules in federal court than in some state courts

5. A docket that may be less crowded in federal district court than in state court

Although some of these considerations can be quite complex, the end result can be an increased likelihood of winning the case.

CASES THAT MAY BE REMOVED

The United States Code Title 28 § 1441(a) states that

> any civil action brought in a state court of which the district courts of the United States have original jurisdiction, may be removed by the defendant or the defendants, to the district court of the United States for the district and division embracing the place where such action is pending.

Therefore, if federal original subject matter jurisdiction exists, as it does in diversity of citizenship and federal question cases, then the case may be removed. Note, however, that if a defendant is a citizen of the state where the action is brought, the purpose for diversity jurisdiction (avoiding bias against a nonresident) does not exist; therefore, removal is not permitted [1441 U.S.C. § 1441(b)]. Only defendants have the right of removal, and all defendants must agree to the removal. Removal is a statutory and not a constitutional right, so any close questions about the appropriateness of removal are to be decided against removal. The United States and its agencies and officers may remove an action to federal court [28 U.S.C. § 1442(a)]. Civil rights cases in which a person is denied the opportunity to have a federal right honored because of some unique aspects of state law can be removed to federal court (28 U.S.C. § 1443). Cases that may not be removed include workers' compensation cases, specified actions against railroads, some actions against interstate (common) carriers, and civil actions based on § 40302 of the Violence Against Women Act of 1994 [28 U.S.C. §1445(a–d)].

The right to remove a case must exist when the action is commenced and at the time of the notice of removal. Cases subject solely to state jurisdiction may be joined with a separate and independent federal question (not a diversity) case for removal [28 U.S.C. § 1441(c)]. Without this right, the defendant might be forced to stay in state court to avoid the extra cost of litigating related matters in both state and federal court. Finally, as mentioned in Chapter 1, the Class Action Fairness Act makes it easier to remove class action cases from state courts.

PROCEDURE

The procedure for removing a case to federal court is governed by 28 U.S.C. § 1446. This statute requires the following procedure:

1. File a "notice of removal" in the federal district court encompassing the area where the state action is pending. The notice must be signed in compliance with Rule 11 of the Federal Rules of Civil Procedure, and a copy of all "process, pleadings, and orders served on . . . defendants" must be attached to the notice [28 U.S.C. § 1446(a)].

2. The notice is a "short plain statement of the grounds for removal" [§ 1446(a)]. It should state:
   a. The statute conferring federal jurisdiction
   b. Facts in support of federal jurisdiction
   c. The date of receipt of the initial pleadings in the state action
   d. The applicable removal statute [28 U.S.C. § 1446(b)]
   e. That all defendants have joined in the removal action

3. The notice of removal must be served on all parties and filed within 30 days after commencement of the state action or, if the original action is not removable but becomes removable, 30 days after amendment or service of papers from which it can be determined that the action has become removable.

4. A copy of the notice must be "promptly" filed with the state court; the state court must proceed no further.

5. If the time limit for responding to the initial pleading has expired, the defendant has five days from the date the notice is filed to file any motion, objection, or answer to the plaintiff's complaint [Rule 81(c)].

APPLY YOUR KNOWLEDGE

Using your state's rules of civil procedure, prepare the necessary documents to remove the Forrester case from state court to federal court. Assume for purposes of this exercise that Mercury Parcel Service Inc.'s principal place of business is in Indianapolis, Indiana and Richard Hart resides in Chicago, Illinois.

The plaintiff can challenge the removal through a motion to remand the case back to the state court because of defects in the removal process. This motion must be filed within 30 days after the filing of the notice of removal [28 U.S.C. § 1447(c)]. With some exceptions, a U.S. district court's order to remand a case to state court is not appealable [28 U.S.C. § 1447(d)]. The district court's subject matter jurisdiction can be challenged any time up to the entry of judgment. If after removal the plaintiff joins additional defendants whose joinder defeats subject matter jurisdiction, the district court may deny joinder, or it may permit joinder and remand the case to state court [28 U.S.C. § 1447(e)]. Although attorney fees and costs incurred on removal may be awarded to the plaintiff if the case is subsequently remanded, the U.S. Supreme Court has ruled that such awards are not automatic, especially if there was an objectively reasonable basis for the removal [*Martin v. Franklin Capital Corp.*, 126 S.Ct. 704 (2005)]. Exhibit 6.10 is a suggested format for the notice of removal.

EXHIBIT 6.10 Notice of Removal

[28 U.S.C.A.§§] 1441, 1446]

[Title of Federal Court and Cause as in State Court]

To: The United States District Court for the _____ District of _____, _____ Division; and to: _____ Counsel for Plaintiff(s) from: _____, Counsel for Defendants. Pursuant to 28 U.S.C. §§ 1441 and 1446(b) files this Notice of Removal of this case from the [state court], to the United States District Court for the district of _____. In support of its Notice of Removal, Defendants would show as follows:

1. The above entitled action was commenced in the _____ Court of _____ county, State of _____ by Plaintiff on or about _____ and is now pending in that court. Process was served on the Defendants on the _____ day of _____, _____. A copy of the plaintiff's _____ (complaint, declaration, or other initial pleading) setting forth the claim for relief upon which the action is based was first received by the Defendants on the _____ day of _____, _____.

2. The action is a civil action for _____ [state briefly nature of case] and the United States District Court for the District of _____ has jurisdiction by reason of the diversity of citizenship of the parties. [Or, state other basis of federal jurisdiction. If other basis, paragraphs in this example should be modified accordingly.]

3. Plaintiff is a citizen of the State of _____ and Defendants are citizens of the State of _____. The matter in controversy exceeds, exclusive of costs and disbursements, the sum [or value] of $75,000. No change of citizenship of parties has occurred since the commencement of the action.

4. There is complete diversity of citizenship between the parties.

5. [State the basis for diversity of the Parties.]

6. All Defendants have joined in this removal action (if applicable).

7. Copies of all process, pleadings, and orders served upon petitioners are filed herewith.

8. Since this case involves complete diversity of the parties in interest and the amount in controversy is in excess of $75,000.00, this Court has jurisdiction over this case and claims asserted in the state court action under 28 U.S.C. section 1332 and therefore, this action is properly removable under 28 U.S.C. section 1441.

9. [Additional paragraphs, if necessary in your jurisdiction] The Notice of Removal is timely filed.

10. Notice was given to Plaintiff's counsel who stated that they [objected] [had no position] or [agreed to the removal action].

EXHIBIT 6.10 Notice of Removal (*continued*)

11. Notice of Removal has been served on Plaintiff and will subsequently be filed with the state court in which this action is presently filed.

12. Therefore, Defendants are entitled to removal from state court to this District Court.

Wherefore, Defendants request that the action presently pending before the [named state court], civil action _____ be removed to this Court.

Dated _____, _____

_____
Attorney for Petitioner

Address: _____

(Standard Signature Block)

Adapted from West's Federal Forms, § 1101, v. 2, with permission of West Group.

COMPUTATION OF TIME

In this chapter we have discussed a variety of procedures and responses that require one side or the other in the lawsuit to meet a deadline imposed by the rules: "within twenty days," "not less than five days before the hearing," or some other limit. You must be able to compute these time periods accurately, either to comply with the deadlines or to know when the adverse party is not in compliance. Federal Rule 6(a) states what days should be included or excluded in calculating the time period. The day the pleading is served or mailed, and the day the hearing is held, for example, are not counted. The last day of any time period may not fall on a Saturday, Sunday, or a legal holiday. When it does, the next regular business day is considered the final day of the period. When the period of time is *less than eleven days,* Saturdays, Sundays, and legal holidays shall not be counted. The legal holidays include New Year's Day, Martin Luther King, Jr.'s Birthday, Presidents' Day, Memorial Day, Independence Day, Labor Day, Columbus Day, Veterans' Day, Thanksgiving Day, Christmas Day, and any other days so designated by the president or Congress, or by the state in which the district court is held. When working in state court, the state's rule on time should be consulted.

Confusion arises if the rule or order states the time as "two months" rather than "sixty days" or "to" July 1 rather than "until" July 1. In these instances it is best to consult local rules. If they are unclear, consult the judge or a knowledgeable clerk. Generally speaking, however, "two months" means the specific number of calendar days in each of the next two months (28, 30, or 31 days). Two months from a specific date is that same numerical date—say the fourth—two months later (two months from June 4 = August 4). Sixty days is simply 60 calendar days starting with the first day after service or other required act. "To" a certain day usually means "up to" and does not include the designated day. "Until" normally means until the close of business on the specified day. An enlargement of time that has been granted by the court begins at the time the original time limit expires (i.e., if the answer was originally due on October 1, a 30-day extension would run through October 31). It bears no relationship to the date on which the court grants the motion to extend the time.

Here is a formula for computing the due date: date of service + the number of days in the prescribed time period − the number of days in the month if the days in the time limit exceed the number of days left in the month = due date. To calculate the due date for an answer to a complaint served on September 20, the formula would work as follows:

Date of Service: September	20
Plus prescribed time limit	20
Total	40
Minus days in September	30
Due Date	10th of October (unless Saturday, Sunday or holiday, then add days to next business day)

Remember that when service is by mail, electronic, or other means set out in Rule 5(b)(2)(B), (C), or (D), three days are added after the prescribed period would otherwise expire under subdivision (a) [Rule 6(e) as revised]. Saturdays, Sundays,

---

TRADE SECRETS: ELECTRONIC FILING DEADLINES

With traditional in-person filing deadlines, it was often easier to determine when a document was due for filing with the court. Clerks' offices closed at 5:00 pm, so documents generally could not be filed after that time requiring filing the next morning. Now, enter electronic filing. Any filing can be made up until 11:59 pm of the date a document is due to the court. A document that is filed before midnight, even though after 5:00 pm, will be considered filed within the deadline date and timely. The reality is with electronic filing, more time is afforded litigants to file documents without being late. The federal system of filing automatically accepts a document as filed at the time of filing with a corresponding confirmation. However, some state court systems have different electronic filing systems and do not automatically generate a confirmation e-mail until the document has been accepted by the court. Thus, if a document is filed after 5:00 pm, for example, and no one is there to approve the filing until the next day, you are faced with thinking the document was not filed and late. This may not be the case. But, where the real frustration comes in is that the document is effective for filing from the time of filing and not the date of acceptance. This technically means that you lost a day of response time. The e-mail confirmation is the next day even though it was filed the night before. This may seem inconsequential but when you may need every day given by statute to respond to a motion or brief, the loss of one day can be problematic. What that means for you as a paralegal is, when you are not sure of a deadline, it may be prudent to call the clerk's office and verify "their" due date for a pleading or brief. Take the guess work out of it. If additional time is needed, a motion for extension or enlargement of time can be requested. But, in those grey area situations, do not give way to chance; confirm the due date, even though there may be some disagreement. Additionally, when filing a document, especially after hours, and there are problems with filing or uploading a document—computer problems—immediately let the court know either through e-mail or telephone, even if you leave a voice mail for someone. This will alert the court staff of the problem early the next morning and will often avert deadline problems if challenged; or if challenged, there will be evidence of the technical difficulties and that there was an attempt to notify the court of the problem. Communication is key and verifying court deadlines when necessary is a good practice so you minimize the possibilities of missing critical deadlines.

and legal holidays are included in counting the three days. The new language that refers to when the prescribed period would otherwise expire is significant. For example, if the initial time limit is 20 days and ends on a Saturday, Rule 6(a) requires service on the next day that is not a Saturday, Sunday, or legal holiday. If the Monday is a legal holiday, then the "prescribed period" ends on Tuesday. The three-day mail extension after the prescribed period adds Wednesday, Thursday, and Friday. Friday is the final day to complete service of the document or other requirement. Failure to calculate time accurately can result in some serious consequences including default, loss of a claim or defense, payment of penalties or costs, and possible malpractice claims against the law firm. Always check local rules for any unique requirements.

DRAFTING THE ANSWER, COUNTERCLAIM, AND CROSS-CLAIM

TASK

For the purposes of this section, assume that you are a paralegal in the firm of Ott, Ott, and Knudsen, which is representing Mercury Parcel Service. You receive the following interoffice memo:

> Memo to: Chris Sorenson
>
> From: Lynn Ott
> Subject: Forrester v. Hart and Mercury Parcel
> Date: October 1, _____
>
> We have twenty days to file an answer to the complaint against our client, Mercury Parcel. Please draft the answer including a counterclaim against Mrs. Forrester for her negligence that resulted in injury to Mr. Hart, our need to replace him temporarily, and damage to our van. Please ask me if you need any assistance.

answer

A formal pleading filed in response to the complaint; identifies the issues to be contested and contains a statement of what the defendant admits and denies and what defenses to the claim, if any, will be presented.

The **answer** is a formal pleading filed in response to the complaint. It identifies the issues to be contested and contains a statement of what the defendant admits and denies and what defenses to the claim, if any, will be presented.

GENERAL REQUIREMENTS

Time

Prior to drafting the answer, the paralegal must note the deadline for filing the answer or a motion attacking the complaint. Federal Rule 12(a) requires a defendant to serve an answer or a motion attacking the complaint

- within 20 days after being served with the summons and complaint, or
- if service of process has been properly waived [Rule 4(d)], within 60 days after the date when the request for waiver was sent (90 days if the defendant was served beyond the jurisdiction of any federal district court), or
- within 60 days of service on the U.S. attorney if the defendant is the United States or an officer or agency of the United States.

If a motion attacking the complaint was filed by the defendant, then an answer must be served on the plaintiff within ten days of notice of the court's decision on the motion [Rule 12(a)(4)(A)] or, if the court grants a motion for a more definite statement, within ten days after service of the revised complaint. Consult your state rules for different requirements.

Style and Content of the Answer

The answer should be drafted similarly to the complaint:

- Be clear and concise [Rules 8(b) and (e)(1)].
- Use numbered paragraphs addressing, point by point, the elements of the complaint, each paragraph being a statement of a single set of facts [Rule 10(b)].
- Avoid impertinent, scandalous, or immaterial language [Rule 12(f)].
- Follow the complaint logically.
- Reveal no more facts than necessary.
- Avoid evidence and conclusions.
- Be truthful [Rule 11 and Disciplinary Rule 7–10(a)].
- State that the defendant lacks knowledge or information sufficient to form a belief as to the truth of the matter alleged, if that is the case [Rule 8(b)]. The court treats this as a denial.
- State separate defenses in separate paragraphs.

The difference between notice pleading and fact (code) pleading applies to answers as it does to complaints. An answer drafted for a code pleading jurisdiction requires more detail than an answer for a notice pleading jurisdiction. Check local procedure and forms for guidance.

STRUCTURE OF THE ANSWER

Introduction

The answer may have several components: legal defenses, admissions, denials, affirmative defenses, counterclaims, and cross-claims. After reviewing the complaint, the defendant's attorney indicates to the paralegal what needs to be done. This may be done electronically, or the attorney may scribble directions on a copy of the complaint. For complex complaints, use a color-coded system, for example: yellow highlight for facts admitted; blue for facts denied; and pink for allegations lacking knowledge to form a belief. The paralegal for the plaintiff would also find this method useful for keeping track of what has been admitted or denied by the defendant.

Defenses

Defenses using the Rule 12(b) motion to dismiss for failure to state a claim, lack of jurisdiction, insufficient process, and others are commonly filed as separate motions. They may also be a part of the answer [Rule 12(b)(1) and (2)], where they are set out following the caption. If these defenses have not been filed separately, the attorney should be consulted to see if they are to be added to the answer. This practice is important because a defense of lack of personal jurisdiction, improper venue, insufficiency of process, or insufficiency of service of process is waived unless raised in the first responsive pleading [Rule 12(h)(1)] or unless the court permits an amendment under Rule 15(a).

Denials

Rule 8(d) requires a party in a responsive pleading to deny the allegations of the other party or they will be deemed admitted. The answer, therefore, should contain a section where the opponent's allegations are denied, if the facts justify the denial. General denials, however, are discouraged by the rules of most jurisdictions. A general denial is a brief statement that denies all allegations and claims of the plaintiff. Because it fails to narrow the contested issues and encourages a sweeping, thoughtless response, it is not favored by the courts. Instead, Rule 8(b) requires the denials to be written in short, plain terms with a separate admission or denial for each of the plaintiff's allegations. The denial should make clear what language in what paragraph of the complaint is being denied.

Plaintiff's allegation:

4. Defendant's vehicle was traveling in excess of the speed limit at the time of the accident.

Defendant's corresponding answer would use the same paragraph number as the complaint and state a short, plain denial:

4. Defendant denies allegation of paragraph 4 of the complaint.

Or if the defendant agreed with the allegation, the response would be:

4. Defendant admits the allegation of paragraph 4 of the complaint.

It may be necessary to split a response and admit some and deny some of the allegation [Rule 8(b)].

Plaintiff's allegation:

5. Defendant is the owner of said van which struck Plaintiff.

Defendant's response:

5. Admitted in part and denied in part. It is admitted that Defendant owns said van. It is denied that said van struck the Plaintiff.

If the defendant has insufficient knowledge or information to form a belief as to the truth of the matter, then the response should so state [Rule 8(b)]. However, this type of denial should be made in good faith and not simply to avoid an admission, reveal a denial, or cover up an unwillingness to investigate the fact. The penalty assessed in such circumstances is a finding that the allegation is admitted [*Nieman v. Long*, 31 F. Supp. 30 (E.D. Pa. 1934)]. A response based on lack of knowledge follows.

Plaintiff's allegation:

6. As a result of Defendant's negligence plaintiff has suffered loss of employment.

Defendant's response:

6. Defendant lacks knowledge sufficient to form a belief as to the truth of the allegation in paragraph 6 of Plaintiff's complaint, and therefore denies same.

Denials should not be ambiguous. For example, if the plaintiff alleges that the defendant is the owner of the car that struck the plaintiff at the corner of Jefferson and Wells streets, and the defendant simply states "denied," it is impossible to know what is being denied—ownership of the car, location of the accident, or the fact that the car struck the plaintiff. The denial should be more specific. Denials that state facts suggesting a defense, but in fact are not really defenses, are called **argumentative denials**. For example, if the plaintiff alleges an accident occurred in Gary, Indiana on the evening of March third and the defendant replies, "Defendant was in Chicago on March 3," there is an implication that the defendant was elsewhere. However, that is not necessarily the case, since the person could travel to both places on the same day. This type of answer is only confusing and should be avoided.

Here are some other suggestions for drafting successful denials. If the defendant faces making a multitude of denials covering words as well as phrases, it might be easier to state the defendant's own version of the facts, using the following format:

> As to paragraph _____ of the complaint, [Defendant] alleges that [own version of facts]. Except as so alleged, Defendant denies the remaining allegations of paragraph _____.

When the term of a contract or other document is characterized in the pleading, it is best to deny the opponent's characterization and state that the documents speak for themselves.

When a co-defendant faces allegations or counts addressed to the other defendant, the language of Rule 8(b) does not excuse the defendant from denying claims asserted against a co-defendant. The following response is suggested:

> As to paragraph _____ of the complaint, [Defendant] denies having sufficient knowledge to form a belief.
>
> Paragraphs _____ to _____ [of Plaintiff's complaint] do not apply to this Defendant, but insofar as they do refer to, may refer to, or may apply to this Defendant, each allegation is denied.

If lack of capacity is alleged or performance of a condition precedent is denied, such must be done specifically and with particularity as required by Rule 9 on pleading special matters.

Exhibit 6.11 summarizes the denials available and their purposes.

Affirmative Defenses

An affirmative defense says, "There are facts present which defeat the plaintiff's claim." These facts are not denials; they are "new matters" and say, "Even if all of the plaintiff's allegations are true, the defendant has a defense to the claim and should prevail." Affirmative defenses are waived in federal court if not asserted in the answer.

Affirmative defenses are defined by substantive law. Each action or claim established by substantive law has one or more defenses that will defeat the claim. A civil action for battery can be defeated by proving self-defense; slander by proving the statement is true; negligence by proving contributory negligence (where it still exists as a defense) or assumption of risk; and so on.

argumentative denials

Denials that state facts suggesting a defense, but in fact are not really defenses.

INTERNET EXERCISE

Determine what your state rules are in answering a complaint. For example, does your state permit a general denial? When must affirmative defenses be pled? Must a motion to dismiss accompany an answer or can the motion be filed prior to the answer?

EXHIBIT 6.11 Forms of Denial in Pleadings

TYPE	FORM [each answer after "reasonable inquiry" must be accurate and submitted in good faith (Rule 11)]	EFFECT
Deny	Defendant denies the allegations of paragraph _____ of the complaint, or Denied (depending on jurisdiction).	Denies each allegation of that paragraph; any allegation not denied is admitted (Rule 8).
Without knowledge	Defendant is without knowledge or information sufficient to form a belief as to the allegation that (state specific allegation) of paragraph _____ of the complaint.	Works as denial but provides flexibility as more information comes to light. Defendant has burden to make "reasonable inquiry."
Admit in part	As to paragraph _____, defendant admits to operating the van on (date) but denies the balance of the allegations in the paragraph.	Makes the admission specific, but denial of remainder of paragraph avoids having to list and possibly omitting a response to some of the items.
Leave to proof	As to paragraph _____, defendant neither admits or denies but leaves plaintiff to his/her proof.	Works as denial by requiring plaintiff to prove facts at trial.
Own allegation	Defendant denies the allegation in paragraph _____ and alleges (own version of facts).	Gives defendant the opportunity to be free from certain implications of plaintiff's language and to state more accurately what happened.
No answer/ conclusion of law	The allegation in paragraph _____ of the complaint improperly states a conclusion of law.	Protects defendant but points out that pleadings are not to allege conclusions of law, just facts in support of the conclusions.
Denial on information and belief	Defendant, on information and belief, denies the allegation in paragraph _____ of the complaint.	Generally used by corporations to deny based on the best information they have at the time from their employees. Permits change if necessary.
Not applicable to defendant	Paragraphs _____ to _____ of the complaint do not apply to this defendant, but insofar as they do refer to, may refer to, or may apply to this defendant, each allegation is denied.	Provides notice that defendant feels the allegation does not apply to this defendant but protects defendant in case it is intended to apply.

It is the responsibility of the defendant's attorney to determine whether the substantive law provides a defense to the claim, and whether sufficient facts support a good allegation of that defense. Just as each element of a claim must be supported by facts in the complaint, so too must each element of an affirmative defense be supported by facts in the answer.

The attorney may tell you what defenses, if any, are to be drafted into the answer. Nevertheless, you need to know how to determine what defenses are available to the claim and what facts must be alleged to support the elements of the defense. The procedure for locating defenses is similar to the procedure for locating the elements of a claim as described in Chapter 4.

- Identify the descriptive word for the claim (negligence, contract, antitrust, etc.).

- In the index to the appropriate jury instruction book, look up the descriptive word for the claim and search for the subcategory on defenses or a separate section in the index on affirmative defenses. Turn to the designated instruction, which should define the affirmative defense and set out the elements that must be proven. *Am Jur Proof of Facts* is also a good source for this information.

- Go to a legal encyclopedia and look up the descriptive word for the claim and the subcategory under that topic on defenses. Here the defenses are defined and the elements set out.

- If the claim is defined by statute, consult the index of the annotated statutes to find the pertinent statute and defenses.

- Review the applicable digest of cases under the topic of the affirmative defense. These cases may shed light on what elements must be alleged and typical fact situations that invoke the defense.

Compare this information with the facts known about the case at hand, determining what defenses are applicable and what facts, if any, support an allegation of the defense.

Federal Rule 8(c) sets out the defenses that must be alleged affirmatively:

APPLY YOUR KNOWLEDGE

Mercury Parcel prepared an answer with affirmative defenses. The Second Affirmative Defense states: Plaintiff was contributorily negligent on the date of the accident. Mrs. Forrester does not believe that allegation is sufficient and wants to challenge it. Prepare the motion for more definite statement and motion to strike in accordance with your state rules of procedure.

accord and satisfaction	contributory negligence
arbitration and award	duress
assumption of risk	payment
estoppel	release
failure of consideration	res judicata
fraud	statute of frauds
illegality	statute of limitations
injury by fellow servant	waiver
laches	any other avoidance or affirmative defense
license	

Federal Rule 8(d)(2) indicates that affirmative defenses may be pleaded in the alternative, hypothetically, and even inconsistently. Therefore, in a negligence case a defendant might admit to the negligence but allege the running of the statute of limitations, or might allege that the plaintiff is comparatively negligent as well as having assumed the risk.

Affirmative defenses are placed immediately after the denials in the answer and appear in Exhibit 6.12.

In some states the affirmative defenses fall in a section on the answer titled "New Matter." The length and detail of the affirmative defense depend on the practice in a particular jurisdiction. In a notice pleading jurisdiction, the defenses may be stated quite briefly. In a code or "fact" pleading state, more detail may be required.

EXHIBIT 6.12 First Affirmative Defense/Second Affirmative Defense

FIRST AFFIRMATIVE DEFENSE

Plaintiff did not file this action before the one-year statute of limitations elapsed.

SECOND AFFIRMATIVE DEFENSE

Plaintiff signed a release on November 8, _____, relieving Defendant of all liability in this matter.

Under modern rules of pleading, the plaintiff is not required to plead responsively to the defenses. They are assumed to be controverted. The plaintiff, however, may choose to attack the defenses in the same manner as the defendant attacks the complaint: through a motion to strike or to dismiss, or through a demurrer in some jurisdictions.

Wherefore Clause: A Type of Conclusory Paragraph

The answer includes a "wherefore" clause:

WHEREFORE, Defendant demands a jury trial, requests that Plaintiff's complaint be dismissed, and that judgment be entered for the Defendant for his/her costs and disbursements.

A single "wherefore" clause is all that is necessary in most jurisdictions regardless of the inclusion of affirmative defenses or the number of affirmative defenses. Some attorneys prefer and some local practices require one "wherefore" clause after the denials and another after the affirmative defenses. Verify the local practice. The demand for a jury trial should be included in the answer; some drafters prefer to place it in the caption, while others place it in the "wherefore" clause. In some states, such as New York, a demand for a jury trial must be made in a separate document called a *notice of issue*.

Counterclaims

counterclaim

A claim asserted by the defendant against the plaintiff, often included in or with the answer.

The **counterclaim** is a claim asserted by the defendant against the plaintiff, which is often included in or with the answer. It may arise out of the same circumstances as the plaintiff's claim or from unrelated circumstances. It is a suit within a suit. For example, a bishop used tennis courts at the United States Naval Academy on a regular basis for a number of years. He was never charged for his use of the courts. When the bishop injured his leg playing tennis, he sued the Naval Academy for negligence. The Naval Academy in turn counterclaimed against the bishop for all the accumulated fees owed the academy for use of the court.

Rule 13 of the Federal Rules of Civil Procedure permits two basic types of counterclaims: compulsory and permissive.

COMPULSORY COUNTERCLAIMS. *Compulsory counterclaims* arise out of the original circumstances leading to the plaintiff's action against the defendant. For example, if Mercury Parcel thought Ann Forrester was responsible for the auto-pedestrian accident, it could counterclaim against Mrs. Forrester for the loss of business and damage to their van. Since this claim arose out of the same transaction as Mrs. Forrester's claim, Federal Rule 13(a) requires it to be brought in the answer. If not asserted, the claim could not be raised against the plaintiff in a separate lawsuit. The purpose of this rule is to have all claims related to a single occurrence resolved at one time. In some states where the Federal Rules have not been adopted, there are no compulsory counterclaims. With the filing of a counterclaim, statute of limitations must always be considered. In *Murray v. Mansheim*, 2010 SD 18, 779 N.W. 2d 379 (2010), the South Dakota Supreme Court was faced with deciding whether a defendant's counterclaim against the Plaintiff was timely.

CASE STUDY: UNDERSTANDING THE LAW

Murray v. Mansheim involves a two car accident where both the plaintiff and defendant were injured. A day before the statute of limitations ran, the plaintiff filed an action against the defendant, Mansheim. Mansheim timely filed an answer nearly a month later. Within the answer was a counterclaim. The question before the court was whether the counterclaim had been timely filed against the plaintiff, Murray. The general facts are straightforward. It is undisputed that both parties were injured on September 13, 2003. The statute of limitations in South Dakota is three years. The plaintiff filed the initial action on September 12, 2006 with the defendant's answer and counterclaim filed on October 6, 2006. Mansheim's claim was a compulsory counterclaim as it arose out of the same transaction and occurrence. Under South Dakota law, the court stated that since the counterclaim was compulsory, any statute of limitations was not tolled (stopped). The court analyzed when actions are commenced and whether there was a difference between compulsory and permissive counterclaims. Finding that actions are commenced when served on the opposing party, the real question the court had to answer was

whether the counterclaim relates back to the opposing party's initial filing of his complaint. Analyzing the split of authority among the various courts, the court answered "no" to this question. Counterclaims seeking affirmative relief are considered independent actions. Following this reasoning, the court found that statute of limitations should be strictly construed. What the court was saying was that Mansheim could have filed an independent action against Murray within the three year statute of limitations. Simply because Mansheim chose not to take this course, Murray should not be penalized. Mansheim made a decision and knew the possible consequences of that decision. Therefore, the action by Mansheim was time barred and the motion for summary judgment that the lower court granted was proper.

Questions for Review: Locate a copy of *Murray v. Mansheim* and review it. What facts would have changed the court's result? What secondary treatises did the court rely upon in reaching its decision? What viewpoint did the court follow and why?

PERMISSIVE COUNTERCLAIMS. Counterclaims may also be brought against the plaintiff for claims unrelated to the original action [Rule 13(b)]. Assume that Ann Forrester had owed money for services provided to her by Mercury Parcel. Mercury Parcel could assert a *permissive counterclaim* against Mrs. Forrester for the debt. The purpose of this rule is to use the one suit to resolve all outstanding matters between the parties rather than doing so through separate lawsuits. The defendant, however, may choose to assert the claim in a separate lawsuit and is not barred from doing so. If the claim is asserted in the answer, the traditional rule has been that an independent source of jurisdiction for the unrelated action must be asserted. Increasingly, however, federal courts hold that under 28 U.S.C. § 1367 (supplementary jurisdiction) an independent jurisdictional basis for a permissive counterclaim is not required [*Jones v. Ford Motor Credit Co.,* 358 F.3d 2005 (2nd Cir. 2004) and *Channell v. Citicorp National Services Inc.,* 89 F.3d 379 (7th Cir. 1996)]. In *Channell,* a "loose factual connection" to the original claim was constitutionally sufficient. A court will not permit the original action to be left in limbo for failure of the court to get jurisdiction over the counterclaim.

Counterclaims are added to the answer following the "wherefore" clause after the affirmative defenses. Appropriate portions of the complaint may be incorporated by reference. The claim must be drafted according to the same rules as the body of the complaint and assert facts necessary to support the elements of the claim.

The defendant may add other parties besides the plaintiff [Rule 13(h)], and the amount of the claim may exceed that of the original action [Rule 13(c)]. Should a counterclaim against the plaintiff arise after the answer has been filed, or if the defendant realizes that a counterclaim has been inadvertently missed, Rules 13(e) and (f), respectively, permit the subsequent filing of those claims by leave of the court. There is a filing fee for the counterclaim.

The counterclaim is subject to the same attack and motions as the complaint, and the plaintiff is required to reply to the counterclaim with denials and defenses in the same fashion that the defendant answers the complaint. The plaintiff's response to the counterclaim is called a reply and must be served on the defendant within 20 days after service of the answer and counterclaim [Rule 12(a)]. A counterclaim against the plaintiff does not give the plaintiff the right to remove a state action to a federal court [*Shamrock Oil & Gas Corp. v. Sheets,* 313 U.S. 100 (1941)].

Cross-Claims

When two or more persons are sued in an action, it is not unusual for one party to believe a co-party should bear the liability. For example, if a builder of an office building is sued over defects in the building, the builder may believe that any damages owed the plaintiff were caused by and should be the responsibility of his codefendant, the architect who designed the building. In such circumstances, the builder may file a cross-claim against the architect. Rule 13(g) permits a **cross-claim** to be filed against a co-party only if the cross-claim arises out of the original action or a counterclaim or relates to any property that is the subject matter of the original action. Cross-claims, therefore, do not require an independent source of jurisdiction. A party may choose to cross-claim or sue independently.

cross-claim

A claim by one party against a co-party in the same action.

A cross-claim must meet all the pleading requirements of any other claim. It is placed in the answer after the counterclaim or may be placed in a separate document. A cross-claim does not require a summons for service.

Should the original action be dismissed or otherwise disposed of, the court will still try a remaining cross-claim or counterclaim. If a cross-claim or counterclaim is made a part of the answer, the title of the document should be changed from "Answer" to "Answer, Counterclaim, and Cross-Claim."

If either a counterclaim or cross-claim or both are drafted into the answer, an additional "wherefore" clause is required in the answer, demanding judgment to be entered for the person bringing the claims for the sum requested, plus costs and interest. Generally, a party receiving a cross-claim has 20 days to answer.

Certification and Verification

All that is required to certify the answer under the federal rules of pleading is the signature, address, e-mail, and telephone number of the defendant's attorney [Rule 11(a)]. An electronic signature is valid for filing by electronic means. If the state rules require verification, the defendant must read the pleading, sign it, and have it notarized. As you may recall, a verification is the defendant's sworn statement that the defendant has read the pleading and that all the facts alleged are true or otherwise stated on information and belief. For this reason, it may be best not to plead inconsistent facts where verification is required. Local practice should be determined.

APPLYING YOUR KNOWLEDGE

Review your state's rules of civil procedure for answering a complaint and filing counterclaims and cross-claims. Prepare the answer for the Ameche case based on your state requirements.

SAMPLE ANSWER, COUNTERCLAIM, AND CROSS-CLAIM

The general requirements and components of an answer have been reviewed. The task assigned is to draft an answer for Mr. Hart to the complaint filed against him by Mrs. Forrester and her husband. The Forresters' complaint (notice and pleading examples) appear in Exhibit 6.13. Following the complaint is the corresponding answer (see Exhibit 6.14). Exhibit 6.15 is another example of a fact complaint using our facts from Case II—the Ameche case.

EXHIBIT 6.13 Forrester Complaint: Notice Pleading

UNITED STATES DISTRICT COURT FOR THE EASTERN DISTRICT OF COLUMBIA
Civil Action, File No. _____

ANN FORRESTER
and
WILLIAM FORRESTER,
                  Plaintiffs

v.

RICHARD HART
and
MERCURY PARCEL SERVICE, INC.,
                  Defendants

COMPLAINT FOR NEGLIGENCE
Jury Trial Demanded

COUNT I

1. Plaintiffs are citizens of the State of Columbia and Defendant Hart is a citizen of the State of Ohio; Defendant Mercury Parcel Service, Inc., is a corporation incorporated under the laws of the State of Delaware, having its principal place of business in the State of Ohio. The matter in controversy exceeds, exclusive of interest and costs, the sum of $75,000.

2. On February 26, _____, on Highway 328 in Capitol County, Columbia, Defendant Hart, an employee of Defendant Mercury Parcel, Inc., negligently drove a motor vehicle striking down Plaintiff who was crossing the highway.

3. As a result, Plaintiff fractured her left leg and hip bones and was otherwise seriously injured; has been prevented from transacting her business; has suffered, and continues to suffer, great pain of body and mind; has incurred, and will continue to incur, expenses for medical attention and hospitalization, all to the sum of $750,000.

WHEREFORE Plaintiff demands judgment against Defendant in the sum of $750,000.

EXHIBIT 6.13 Forrester Complaint: Notice Pleading (*continued*)

COUNT II

4. Plaintiff William Forrester hereby alleges and incorporates by reference paragraphs 1 through 3 of Count One.
5. Because of Defendant's negligence, Plaintiff has suffered loss of the consortium of his wife, Ann Forrester, in the amount of $20,000.

WHEREFORE, Plaintiff demands judgment against the Defendant in the sum of $20,000.

_____

Arthur White
Attorney for Plaintiffs
(Address)
(Phone number)

_____

EXHIBIT 6.14 Answer and Counterclaim to Forrester Complaint: Notice Pleading

UNITED STATES DISTRICT COURT FOR THE EASTERN DISTRICT OF COLUMBIA
Civil Action, File No. _____

ANN FORRESTER
    and
WILLIAM FORRESTER,
                    Plaintiffs

        v.

RICHARD HART
    and
MERCURY PARCEL SERVICE, INC.,
                    Defendants

DEFENDANTS' ANSWER
AND COUNTERCLAIM

COUNT I

1. Admitted.
2. Denied that Defendant drove vehicle negligently.
3. Defendant lacks knowledge sufficient to form a belief regarding the truth of the allegation in paragraph 3 of Plaintiff's complaint, and therefore denies same.

FIRST AFFIRMATIVE DEFENSE

Plaintiff was more than 50 percent negligent in causing the accident, and is therefore barred from recovery.

COUNT II

4. No answer required.
5. Denied.

(continued)

EXHIBIT 6.14 Answer and Counterclaim to Forrester Complaint: Notice Pleading (*continued*)

COUNTERCLAIM

On February 26, _____, on Highway 328 in Capitol County, Columbia, Plaintiff Ann Forrester negligently tried to cross the road in front of Defendant's vehicle, causing injury to Defendant Hart.

   As a result of plaintiff's negligence, Defendant Hart suffered lacerations and contusions and lost days of work all to the sum of $2,200.

SECOND COUNTERCLAIM

Defendant Mercury Parcel incorporates by reference the facts as alleged in the first counterclaim and alleges the Plaintiff's negligence caused damage to the defendant's vehicle and required the hiring of an extra employee for one week all to the sum of $4,250.

   WHEREFORE, Defendants request that Plaintiffs' action be dismissed and demand judgment against the Plaintiffs for $2,200 for Defendant Hart and $4,250 for Defendant Mercury Parcel Service, Inc., plus interest and costs.

_____
Attorney for Defendants
(Address)
(Phone number)

EXHIBIT 6.15 Fact Complaint Case II

STATE OF COLUMBIA   CAPITOL COUNTY   CIRCUIT COURT

CARL AMECHE
   and
ZOE AMECHE,
                        Plaintiffs
         v.
                                  Civil Action, File No. _____
MARGIE CONGDEN
   and
LEROY CONGDEN,

                        Defendants   Plaintiffs Demand Trial by Jury
                        COMPLAINT FOR NEGLIGENCE

Plaintiffs allege that:

1. The jurisdiction of this court is based on the amount in controversy in this action which is more than $2,500.
2. Plaintiff Carl Ameche is an accountant and resides at 222 2nd Street, Thorp, Ohio.
3. Plaintiff Zoe Ameche is the wife of Carl Ameche and resides with him.
4. Defendants Margie and Leroy Congden are the owners of the Maple Meadows Campground and reside at the campground which is located at Star Route 2, Highway 66, in the city limits of Legalville, Capitol County, Columbia.
5. On August 21, _____, Plaintiffs rented campsite 36 in the Maple Meadows Campground.
6. Defendants had negligently placed a worn extension cord running to campsite 36.
7. As a direct consequence of the Defendants' negligence, a fire was started that encircled the Plaintiffs' son, Zach, requiring Carl Ameche to place himself in peril in order to rescue his son.

EXHIBIT 6.15 Fact Complaint Case II (*continued*)

8. Because of the negligence, Carl Ameche suffered severe burns to his face, hands, and legs that have caused him intense pain, suffering, physical disability, considerable inconvenience, and permanent scarring.
9. As a consequence of the Defendants' negligence and the aforesaid injuries, Carl Ameche has incurred and will incur considerable expense for hospital and medical care, loss of income and benefits, and property damage to his clothing and camper.

WHEREFORE, Plaintiff demands judgment in the amount of three hundred and fifty thousand dollars ($350,000), together with the costs and disbursements of this action, and for such relief as this court may deem just and proper.

COUNT II

10. Plaintiffs hereby allege and incorporate by reference paragraphs 1 through 9 of Count I.
11. Because of the Defendants' negligence, Plaintiff Zoe Ameche has suffered loss of consortium of her husband, Carl Ameche, in the amount of fifteen thousand dollars ($15,000).

WHEREFORE, Plaintiff Zoe Ameche demands judgment against Defendants in the sum of fifteen thousand dollars ($15,000), together with costs, and for such relief as this court may deem just and proper.

Arthur White
White, Wilson, & McDuff
Attorneys at Law
Federal Plaza Building
Suite 700
Third and Market Streets
Legalville, Columbia 00000

(verification)

Assume for illustrative purposes that Richard Hart and Mercury Parcel Service are each represented by different attorneys and that Richard Hart has decided to cross-claim against Mercury Parcel. The cross-claim is placed in Hart's answer after the counterclaims, and the drafted language appears in Exhibit 6.16.

EXHIBIT 6.16 Cross-Claim

22. Defendant incorporates by reference paragraphs 1–21 of his answer.
23. Sometime during the week of February 20, Defendant Mercury Parcel Service negligently failed to check and maintain the van driven by Defendant Hart on February 26 as required by (state any applicable statutes or regulations).
24. Because of Defendant Mercury Parcel's negligence, the brakes on said vehicle were not functional, causing the wheels to lock and the vehicle to go out of control. The malfunctioning caused said vehicle to strike Plaintiff Ann Forrester, go off the highway, and strike a tree.
25. As a consequence of Defendant Mercury Parcel's negligence, Plaintiff and Defendant have both suffered the injuries and loss of income set out in the complaint and answer.

WHEREFORE, Defendant Hart demands judgment be entered against Defendant Mercury Parcel for him for $2,200 and for any liability Defendant Hart is required to pay Plaintiffs as a consequence of this lawsuit.

ETHICAL CONSIDERATIONS

Regardless as to whether a party is a plaintiff, defendant, or third-party litigant, Fed.R.Civ.P. 7.1 requires that a nongovernmental party file a disclosure statement. This concept was discussed in Chapter 5 in the context of a plaintiff filing a complaint. But, a plaintiff is not the only party that is required to file the disclosure statement. Any nongovernmental party to a lawsuit is required to file the disclosure statement when their first appearance is made before a court. As discussed previously, the disclosure statement identifies any parent corporation or publicly held entities that hold a 10 percent interest in the filing party's company or that none exists. The purpose of the rule is to permit judges, before a case commences, to disqualify their participation because of a conflict of interest. A conflict of interest exists when a judge, for example, has an interest in a corporation by holding its shares. This interest could influence the way a case is decided and thus by filing the Rule 7.1 statement, any conflicts of interest or the appearance of such are avoided. The 7.1 statement preserves the integrity of the judge and the judicial system by allowing judges to disqualify themselves from participating in a case because of an interest in a corporation. A Rule 7.1 disclosure is not the only situation where conflict of interests arise in the practice of law. Under the Model Rules of Professional Responsibility, a number of scenarios prohibit attorneys from engaging in situations which create conflicts of interest. These situations range from a lawyer's prohibition from representing a client where that representation will conflict with another client to using information about one client to the detriment of another. Lawyers may not receive gifts from clients or prepare a document where the lawyer will receive a substantial benefit, such as a will or a trust. The Model Rules identify numerous situations where lawyers can potentially create or be involved in conflicts of interest. For you as the paralegal, be aware of the conflict of interest requirement in the litigation process as well as those in the client representation process. The extensive body of law on conflicts of interests and their implications is beyond the scope of this text. Suffice is to say that being aware that the Model Rules prohibit certain types of conflicts of interests is important for paralegals. Your involvement in cases may create conflicts of interest for you and your firm and thus being aware of the rules is essential.

THIRD-PARTY PRACTICE (IMPLEADER)

INTRODUCTION

third-party practice (impleader)
The filing of a third-party complaint by the original defendant against a person not yet named a party to the lawsuit, alleging that the third party is or may be liable for all or a part of any damages won by the original plaintiff against the original defendant.

The pleadings discussed to this point, that is the complaint, answer, counterclaim, and cross-claim, occur between the original plaintiff(s) and defendant(s). **Third-party practice (impleader)** permits the original defendant to file a third-party complaint against a person not yet named a party to the lawsuit. This complaint alleges that the third party is or may be liable for all or part of any damages won by the original plaintiff against the original defendant. This process is like a cross-claim, except that it is against a previously unnamed party. The pleading filed by the original defendant against this new party is called a third-party complaint, and the original defendant becomes the third-party complainant. The newly named person becomes the third-party defendant.

PURPOSE

The purpose of third-party practice is to litigate all the claims arising from a single set of circumstances. Third-party practice is governed by Rule 14 of the Federal Rules of Civil Procedure and parallel state rules. Rule 14 gives the person who is defending against a claim the right to bring in a third party. A third-party complaint essentially says, "If I am going to be held liable in this action, then so are you because you are at fault." For example, Mrs. Forrester is suing Mercury Parcel for the injuries suffered in the pedestrian accident. Mercury Parcel may choose, in turn, to sue the van dealer or manufacturer for defects that contributed to or caused the accident. One of the advantages of such a suit is that one jury or one judge may hear all sides and render a more uniform decision. A third-party action may be based on *indemnification,* a theory that says if B is found liable, C owes B for the amount of the judgment. Or it may be based on *joint liability,* meaning B and C share the liability. Title 28 U.S.C. should be consulted to see what parties and claims may be heard by the federal court when the parties or claims do not have an independent source of federal jurisdiction.

PROCEDURE

The original defendant drafts a third-party complaint, files it with the clerk of court, and then serves a third-party summons and a copy of the complaint on the new party. A copy of the original complaint is attached to the third-party complaint.

Rule 14 gives the third-party plaintiff the right to implead another party without leave of court if the third-party complaint is filed within ten days after the answer. If it is filed after the ten days, a motion to implead must be filed to obtain the court's permission.

The third-party complainant must get personal jurisdiction over the other party, following the same procedure for service of process of the complaint outlined in Chapter 5 and Rule 4. A small filing fee may be required in some states. Independent subject matter jurisdiction is not required.

The third-party defendant may respond to the third-party complaint as any other defendant, including Rule 12 motions, counter- and cross-claims, and even a third-party action. Any claim against the original plaintiff may be asserted. The original plaintiff may implead as the respondent to any counterclaim [Rule 14(b)].

Follow these steps in preparing and filing a third-party action:

1. Obtain all necessary information on the third-party defendant.

2. Draft a motion for a third-party complaint unless the action is filed within ten days of the answer [Rule 14(a)]. Check state and local rules for variations in procedure.

3. Draft a third-party summons and third-party complaint.

4. File with the clerk of court using the summons and complaint as exhibit A.

5. On notice that the motion is approved, serve the third-party summons and a copy of the third-party complaint in the same manner that the original complaint is served (Rule 4). Attach a copy of the original complaint.

6. Note the calendar for the due date for the third party's answer.

Exhibits 6.17, 6.18, and 6.19 are examples of the third-party summons, complaint, and motion.

EXHIBIT 6.17 Summons Against Third-Party Defendant

[FED. R. CIV. P. Rule 14]

UNITED STATES DISTRICT COURT FOR THE SOUTHERN DISTRICT OF _____
Civil Action, File Number _____

A.B., Plaintiff

v.

C.D., Defendant and Third-Party Plaintiff   } Summons

v.

E.F., Third-Party Defendant

To the above-named Third-Party Defendant:

You are hereby summoned and required to serve upon _____, plaintiff's attorney whose address is _____ and upon _____, who is attorney for C.D., defendant and third-party plaintiff, and whose address is _____, an answer to the third-party complaint which is herewith served upon you within 21 days after the service of this summons upon you exclusive of the day of service. If you fail to do so, judgment by default will be taken against you for the relief demanded in the third-party complaint. There is also served upon you herewith a copy of the complaint of the plaintiff which you may but are not required to answer.

_____

Clerk of Court

[Seal of District Court]
Dated: _____

EXHIBIT 6.18 Third-Party Complaint

[FED. R. CIV. P. Rule 14]

[Title of Court and Cause]

1. Plaintiff A.B. has filed against defendant C.D. a complaint, a copy of which is hereto attached as "Exhibit A."
2. (Here state the grounds upon which C.D. is entitled to recover from E.F., all or part of what A.B. may recover from C.D. The statement should be framed as in an original complaint.)

WHEREFORE C.D. demands judgment against third-party defendant E.F. for all sums that may be adjusted against defendant C.D. in favor of plaintiff A.B.

Signed: _____
Attorney for C.D.,
Third-Party Plaintiff
Address: _____

EXHIBIT 6.19 Motion to Bring in Third-Party Defendant

[FED. R. CIV. P. Rule 14]

[Title of Court and Cause]

Defendant moves for leave, as third-party plaintiff, to cause to be served upon E.F. a summons and third-party complaint, copies of which are hereto attached as Exhibit X.

_____
Attorney for Defendant
C_____ D_____
Address: _____

AMENDING AND SUPPLEMENTING THE PLEADINGS

PURPOSE

The parties to the lawsuit are permitted by the Federal Rules and the rules of adopting states to amend and supplement their pleadings freely. Amendments are generally used to repair defective pleadings that may have omitted necessary elements of a cause of action, improperly or inadequately alleged subject matter jurisdiction, or used language that is too general or states evidence. An amendment might even be used to change a defense or other legal theory.

A supplemental pleading allows a party to add facts that have occurred since the original pleadings were filed. For example, Mrs. Forrester may want to supplement her pleadings if her injuries resulted in blindness or a stroke after the original pleading was filed; or a farmer who is suing a contractor for failure to complete a barn by winter may lose some cattle as a consequence after the complaint is filed. Federal Rule 15(d) authorizes supplemental pleadings.

Rule 15 of the Federal Rules of Civil Procedure states that permission to amend pleadings should be given freely. The purpose of the rule is to make it easy for parties to correct procedural oversights and bad drafting so the issues and evidence are accurately reflected in the pleadings. If amendments and supplements were not freely permitted, the parties would be hamstrung in their efforts to present the best possible case on clearly defined issues, and cases would be dismissed for procedural errors rather than tried on the real substance or merit. If, in the judgment of the court, the change to the pleading will significantly prejudice the other party, however, the motion to amend or supplement the pleading will be denied.

PROCEDURE

A party is permitted to amend a pleading without court permission any time before the responsive pleading is served. If no responsive pleading is required, and if the

INTERNET EXERCISE

Determine your state's rule of civil procedure for:
a. cross-claims
b. counterclaims
c. interpleaders
What are the differences between your state rules and the federal rules for these types of actions, if any?

action is not on the trial calendar, the pleading may be amended within 20 days after the pleading is served. Otherwise pleadings may be amended only with leave of the court—permission of the court—or with written consent (stipulation) of the opponent [Rule 15(a)].

It is necessary to respond to an amended pleading either within the remaining period to respond to the original pleading or within ten days of service of the amended pleading, whichever period is longer, unless otherwise ordered by the court [Rule 15(a)]. Response to a supplemental pleading is required only on order of the court [Rule 15(d)].

When leave of court is required to amend a pleading, the request is made by motion. Because of the policy to freely allow amendments to conform to the evidence, such motions can be brought any time, even after judgment [Rule 15(b)]. An amended pleading dates from the filing of the original pleading when *relation back* is permitted by the applicable state or federal statute of limitations law and as long as the claim or defense asserted in the amended pleading arose out of the conduct, transaction, or occurrence set forth in the original pleading [Rule 15(c)]. This avoids statute of limitations problems, especially for a party that filed the original pleading just before the deadline. If a party tries to amend the pleading with an entirely new claim based on a different fact situation, however, this new pleading will not date from the original.

In addition, a pleading may be amended to change the name of the party against whom the claim is brought. What happens if the statute of limitations runs out between the time the complaint is filed and the amendment is made? Federal Rule 15(c)(1) permits the amendment to date back to the filing of the original complaint if several conditions exist. The amendment must stem from the occurrence set out in the original complaint, and the new party must have notice of the action in time to defend against it and within the original time limit to serve the summons and complaint—the statute of limitations. Check state rules for variations.

The amended pleading should combine the amended language plus what remains of the original pleading. Pleading one complete, amended document is easier for the court and the parties than referring to both the original document and the amended one. The amended pleading should be captioned "Amended" or "Supplemented" for clarity. For example, an amended complaint would be entitled "First Amended Complaint" or an amended answer would be entitled "First Amended Answer and Counterclaim."

Amended and supplemental pleadings are served on the adverse party's attorney by mailing or delivering a copy of the pleading to the attorney or as otherwise directed in Rule 5. These pleadings should be filed with the clerk of court. Most state jurisdictions freely permit the filing of amended pleadings; local rules, however, should be consulted.

MOTION FOR JUDGMENT ON THE PLEADINGS

A motion for judgment on the pleadings may be the course of action if the supervising attorney believes the opponent's claim or defense is by law inadequate. The pleadings are normally closed after the filing of the complaint, answer, and reply to the counterclaim. Once the pleadings are closed, Rule 12(c) and parallel state rules permit the filing of a motion for judgment on the pleadings.

PURPOSE

A motion for judgment on the pleadings is a vehicle to end the litigation. In effect the motion says, "Even if what the opponent says is true, no claim is stated on which relief can be granted," or conversely, "No adequate defense is stated, and therefore I should win." For example, even if Mrs. Forrester's allegations in her complaint are considered to be true, if Richard Hart and Mercury Parcel could show that the statute of limitations had run prior to the action being filed, the defendants' motion would be granted.

On the other hand, if Richard Hart and Mercury Parcel's only defense is not recognized in the state, then the court is within its authority to grant the motion for the plaintiff. Their motion is to be considered without the assistance of the affidavits and matter outside the pleadings. If outside matter is presented with the court's permission, Rule 12(d) requires the motion to be considered a motion for summary judgment (discussed in the next section). A motion on the pleadings often results in an amendment to the pleadings rather than dismissal.

The motion is drafted, filed, and served in the same manner as other motions discussed in this chapter.

MOTION FOR SUMMARY JUDGMENT

A motion for summary judgment is another type of motion that, if granted, will end the litigation. With this motion, evidence can be presented that substantiates the moving party's claims against the opposing party.

TECHNOLOGY UPDATE: MOBILE FILE SHARING

Sharing case information among lawyers and support staff is commonplace. The question is what is the best way to share information in a case and also protect its confidentiality. Most of us use e-mail to share information, such as letters and documents. But how do we share larger amounts of information securely and confidentially? One method of sharing information in today's world is mobile file sharing. Generally, file sharing allows for individuals, such as those in a law firm, to share and access digital data and information on a case through electronic means, such as desktop computers, the Web, or mobile devices. This data sharing can be public or private and often has different levels of security access or sharing privileges.

Mobile Apps or Web-based sites like Dropbox or GoogleDocs provide for file sharing through the Internet. By uploading files to the sites, information can be shared so that you will have access to client cases for all business-related purposes, wherever you are, whenever you need it. When choosing mobile Apps, be mindful of the security issues and risks involved, as lawyers and paralegals have to consider confidentiality issues when using any mobile file sharing service or App. Security safeguards should be examined. What happens if your mobile device is lost or stolen? Does the system chosen provide for password and information wiping? Can the system or App permit editing? Some mobile file sharing Apps document receipt of letters, for example, and track when a document was reviewed, forwarded, and who viewed it. This can be an excellent evidentiary tool in litigation. The end result is that in the age of mobility, file sharing is inevitable. As a paralegal, you should be aware that you will be using mobile or Web-based file sharing and should know the best practices used to share and secure sensitive client information.

PURPOSE

A successful motion for summary judgment wins the case without the necessity of a trial. The motion does more, however, than a motion to dismiss or a motion for judgment on the pleadings, because it asks the court to look behind the pleadings at additional evidence. This evidence can be affidavits, statements made under oath by parties and witnesses (called depositions and interrogatories), admissions of facts, and stipulations of facts. Only admissible evidence is considered. A motion for summary judgment and the supporting evidence must allege two things: that there is no genuine issue of material fact (no crucial questions of fact that must be answered by a jury at trial) and that, according to the law, the movant is entitled to judgment [Rule 56(a)]. If the opponent's evidence can show a genuine issue of fact, the motion is denied.

A summary judgment might be granted in the following situation. Ann Forrester files a complaint for negligence against Hart and Mercury Parcel. The defendants' answer admits all the allegations, but as a defense, states that Forrester signed a release freeing the defendants from all liability. Since defenses are deemed controverted, there appears to be a factual issue: was a release signed? If, after filing a motion for summary judgment, the defendant can prove that the release exists or present affidavits of witnesses who read the release and saw it signed, the court can grant summary judgment. There is no longer an issue of fact because the evidence proves the release was signed. As a matter of law, the release bars recovery. If the plaintiff could prove facts to the contrary or show that the release was only a partial release, then the motion would be denied, or at best granted in part. Whether the party opposing a motion for summary judgment must rebut the movant's evidence varies in state practice. If a party cannot rebut the motion because the evidence needed is not yet available, the court may not grant the motion and has the option of granting a reasonable continuance until the evidence is available [Rule 56(f)]. Keep in mind that, under Federal Rule 12(b) and parallel state rules, a motion to dismiss for failure to state a claim shall be treated as a motion for summary judgment if the court permits presentation of matters outside the pleadings.

A recent case, *Boston v. Athearn*, 329 Ga. App. 890, 764 S.E. 2d 582 (2014), dealt with a parent's responsibility for their child's posting of a Facebook page which allegedly disparaged another child. At what point is a parent responsible for their child's actions and who are the true parties in interest? The case illustrates how a child can sue and be sued, but more importantly, it is an example of a summary judgment proceeding.

CASE STUDY: UNDERSTANDING THE LAW

In *Boston v. Athearn*, Alexandra Boston, a minor, brought an action through her parents, against Dustin Athearn, a minor, and his parents. Because Alexandra was not an adult she had to sue Dustin through her parents. Dustin, 13 years old, and a friend Melissa, created a fake Facebook page of Alex on the family computer and used a photo which was altered with a "Fat Face" application. Then both Dustin and Melissa added misinformation about Alex's orientation and posted graphically sexual, racist, and other offensive

CASE STUDY: UNDERSTANDING THE LAW (continued)

comments and pictures. They also stated that Alex was on medication for a mental disorder and that she took illegal drugs. Alex figured out who posted the page, then told her parents who went to school to report Dustin and Melissa. Dustin and Melissa were suspended from school in May, 2011. Dustin was disciplined. However, the Facebook account remained accessible and active until April, 2012. The question was what did the parents do, if anything, to determine the contents of the Facebook page and the extent of its distribution? They apparently never told Dustin to delete the page and thus, it remained active for nearly one year until the lawsuit was filed.

The question before the court was whether there were any genuine issues of material fact entitling the Athearns to judgment as a matter of law for the actions of their child who posted negative comments about Alexandra and the results of those actions. The court reviewed two issues related to their motion for summary judgment. First, did the Athearns negligently supervise their son and second, did the Athearns have the power to take down the Facebook page. The court reviewed the law relating to the liability of parents for the actions of their child. Ordinarily, parents are not responsible for the actions of their minor child. However, in this case, the court held that because the Athearns knew

for almost a year about the posting and did not act or require their son to act to close the Facebook page, the Bostons alleged sufficient facts to overcome a motion for summary judgment. Here, the Athearns negligently failed to supervise their son which resulted in harm to another. The court reversed the lower court's decision to grant summary judgment on that issue finding that there were genuine issues of material fact and the Athearns were not entitled to judgment as a matter of law.

However, on the issue of whether the Athearns had the ability to take down the Facebook page with the defamatory content, the court found in favor of the Athearns, granting their motion for summary judgment on that issue. Because the Athearns contacted Facebook, who indicated that only the user with the password could take down the page, they could not control the libelous comments. Therefore, there were no genuine issues of material fact and the Athearns were entitled to judgment as a matter of law on that issue.

Questions for Review: Review and analyze the *Boston* case. Why did the court require Alexandra's parents to be part of the lawsuit? Who was the true party in interest in the case? What facts would have changed the result in favor of the Athearns on the issue of negligent supervision?

PROCEDURE

Rule 56 states that any party seeking to recover on a claim, counterclaim, or cross-claim may, after 30 days following the close of discovery or set by local law or the court, move for summary judgment or do so after service of a motion for summary judgment by the adverse party. Any party defending against a claim, counterclaim, or cross-claim may move for a summary judgment any time. State rules and time requirements may vary. Either party may move for a summary judgment against the other. This is called a *cross-motion*.

The motion must be served at least ten days (more than the five days normally required in motion practice) before the hearing on the motion, and the opponent must file responding affidavits at least one day prior to the hearing.

The documents required to file the motion are typical of those required for most motions: the motion itself, the notice of motion, attached affidavits plus exhibits, a memorandum of law in support of the motion, and an order for the court to sign. The motion is filed and a copy served on the opponent. The following is an example of the motion (Exhibit 6.20), and an affidavit in support of the motion for summary judgment (Exhibit 6.21).

EXHIBIT 6.20 Motion for Summary Judgment by Plaintiff

[FED. R. CIV. P. Rule 56(a)]
[Title of Court and Cause]

Plaintiff moves this Court pursuant to Rule 56 of the Federal Rules of Civil Procedure to enter summary judgment for the plaintiff on the ground that there is no genuine issue as to any material fact, and the plaintiff is entitled to judgment as a matter of law.

In support of this motion, plaintiff refers to the record herein including the amended complaint, the answer thereto, the defendants' amendment to the answer, plaintiff's sworn affidavit, responses to admissions, deposition testimony, and [any other evidence that is relevant to the motion].

[Note: It is helpful to lay out for the Court the facts and cite the law in either the motion or independent memorandum of law.]

_____

Attorney for Plaintiff
Address: _____
Additional Required Information for
the Signature Block

Adapted from West's Federal Forms, § 4723, v. 4, with permission of West Group.

APPLY YOUR KNOWLEDGE

Prepare a corresponding chart for Exhibit 6.23, but use your state rules and cite the applicable time limits and rule number for your future use and reference.

EXHIBIT 6.21 Affidavit in Support of Motion for Summary Judgment—General Form

[FED. R. CIV. P. Rule 56(e)]

State of _____

    ss.

County of _____

_____, being first duly sworn, deposes and says:

1. I am _____, and have personal knowledge of the facts herein set forth. I am over the age of 18 and know the purposes for which this affidavit is being made. I have never been convicted of a felony or a crime involving moral turpitude.

2. This affidavit is submitted in support of the plaintiff's [or defendant's] motion for summary judgment herein, for the purpose of showing that there is in this action no genuine issue as to any material fact, and that the plaintiff [or defendant] is entitled to judgment as a matter of law.

3. *[State all the evidentiary facts within affiant's personal knowledge in support of motion, such as promissory note, if a debt; the fact the note has not been paid; that amounts still are owed in the amount of _____. Attach accounting of amounts paid, if any, and dates.]*

[Jurat]

Adapted from West's Federal Forms, § 4726, v. 4, with permission of West Group.

EXHIBIT 6.22 File Pleading Log

Title of Case _____ Client _____

_____ File No. _____

Our Pleading	Date Filed	Date Served	Opponent Acknowl. of Service	Opponent Response Due	Opponent Pleading	Date of Service	Our Response Due
Summons and complaint Reply to counter-claim					Answer and counterclaim		

KEEPING A PLEADING RECORD

Pleadings require good record keeping. A quick glance in the file should tell the reader exactly what pleadings have been filed, served, and replied to, and the applicable dates. A pleadings log in each file can provide this information. Exhibit 6.22 is an example of a pleadings log that can be regularly updated as each pleading is exchanged.

PLEADINGS, MOTIONS, AND TIME LIMITS

Exhibit 6.23 displays the most common pleadings in approximate chronological order, their purpose, any applicable time limit, and the pertinent federal rule. It continues through discovery, pretrial, and post trial tasks, time limits, and rules, so make a note to return to this chart as you learn about those phases of litigation.

EXHIBIT 6.23 Pleadings, Motions, and Time Limits

Pleading/Act	Purpose If Not Clear	Due	Federal Rule	State Rule/ Due
PLEADINGS/PARTIES				
Complaint				
Service of summons and complaint	For personal jurisdiction	120 days after filing complaint	4, 4(m), 5	

(continued)

CHAPTER 6

EXHIBIT 6.23 Pleadings, Motions, and Time Limits (*continued*)

Pleading/Act	Purpose If Not Clear	Due	Federal Rule	State Rule/ Due
Request for Entry of Default and Judgment of Default	To prevent defendant's response after time limit for answer, to get judgment concluding case and awarding remedy	Entry may be sought on first day after expiration of time limit for answer. Judgment sought as soon after as possible. Notice of hearing on application for default—three days prior to hearing when required.	55, 54(c)	
Motion to Set Aside Default Judgment		In reasonable time and not more than one year after judgment	55(c), 60(b)	
Motions Attacking Complaint or Action (in general)	To dismiss action for lack of subject matter jurisdiction, personal jurisdiction, improper venue, insufficiency of service, failure to state a claim, and failure to join a party, or to make complaint more definite or to strike language, or for *forum non conveniens*	Within time permitted to answer complaint, which depends on method used for service of process. Could be 21, 60, or 90 days. 20 days generally; motion to dismiss for lack of subject matter jurisdiction can be made any time, including on appeal.	12(a), (b), (e), (f), 28 U.S.C. § 1406(a), 28 U.S.C. § 1404	
Notice of Motion plus Affidavit		Served at least 14 days before hearing unless *ex parte*	6(c)	
Responsive Motion plus Affidavit		Served not later than seven days before hearing on motion, generally, or pursuant to local court rule	6(c) (2)	
Amendment to Pleadings (generally)	To correct errors, vagueness, or other inadequacies	Prior to service of a responsive pleading or within 21 days after service if no responsive pleading is permitted. If in response to order to make more definite, 14 days after notice of order.	15(a), 12(e)	

EXHIBIT 6.23 Pleadings, Motions, and Time Limits (*continued*)

Pleading/Act	Purpose If Not Clear	Due	Federal Rule	State Rule/ Due
Answer	To admit, deny, or state defenses to plaintiff's allegation; may include counterclaim and motions attacking complaint	Within 21, 60, or 90 days, depending on method used for service of process (U.S. has 60 days) or in 14 days after decision on motion attacking complaint	12(a) 12(a)(4)	
Answer in Response to Amended Complaint		In remaining time to respond to original or within 14 days, whichever is greater	15(a)	
Counterclaim	To state a claim defendant has against plaintiff, usually arising out of same transaction alleged by plaintiff	At same time answer is served or as permitted by court	13	
Cross-Claim	To state a claim against a party on the same side of the action and may allege that the party is the one fully or partially liable for claim alleged in complaint or counterclaim	With answer, reply to counterclaim, or other appropriate pleading	13	
Reply to Counterclaim or Cross-Claim	To admit, deny, or state defenses to allegations in counterclaim or cross-claim. May include motions attacking these pleadings	Twenty-one days after service of answer or 20 days after service of notice of order to reply to counterclaim or as otherwise directed (U.S. has 60 days)	12(a)(1) (B)	
Third-Party Complaint	To bring in third party who may be liable to one of the original parties for the claim or counterclaim brought against the original party	Fourteen days after service of original answer (counterclaim) or by leave of court	14(a)	
Third-Party Answer	To attack, or to admit, deny, or state defenses to the third-party complaint (may include counter and cross-claims)	Twenty-one days after service of answer	14(a)(2), 12(a)	

(*continued*)

EXHIBIT 6.23 Pleadings, Motions, and Time Limits (*continued*)

Pleading/Act	Purpose If Not Clear	Due	Federal Rule	State Rule/ Due
Motion to Dismiss: Not Real Party in Interest	To attack jurisdiction of court and to avoid harassment of defendant by parties having no right to claim	Within time permitted for regular response to complaint	17(a), 12(a), (b)	
Motion to Join a Party	To add either plaintiffs or defendants for the purpose of adjudicating all claims of all parties arising from same or series of transactions	In reasonable time after action begins	18, 19, 20	
Motion to Add Interpleader	To add a party to resolve all possible claims against a third party	In reasonable time after action begins	22	
Motions Regarding Class Actions	To certify a group of plaintiffs as a class or to dismiss or compromise	As soon as practical after start of action	23, 23(c)(1)	
Motion to Intervene	To permit party to enter lawsuit so can protect interest or where statute permits intervention	In reasonable time after start of action	24, 5	
Motion for Substitution of a Party	To permit continuation of action by substituting a party in the case of death, incompetency, transfer of interest, or resignation of office	Ninety days after death, etc., made part of record	25	
Motion for Enlargement of Time	To gain extension from original date pleading is due	In time within which pleading is originally due or after if due to excusable neglect	6(b)	
Motion for Judgment on the Pleadings	To get final judgment in case based solely on the pleadings	After pleadings closed but not so late as to delay trial	12(c)	
Motion of Application for Seizure of Property (Writ of Attachment)	To secure property so that if suit is successful, judgment can be paid. Also final remedy to collect judgment	After filing of lawsuit (generally) or after judgment	64 (incorporating state law)	

EXHIBIT 6.23 Pleadings, Motions, and Time Limits (*continued*)

Pleading/Act	Purpose If Not Clear	Due	Federal Rule	State Rule/ Due
Motion or Application for Injunctions including Temporary Restraining Order, Preliminary Injunction, and Permanent Injunctions	To prevent irreparable damage to persons or property involved in the original action, to require another party to do some act or to refrain from some act	After filing of lawsuit (temporary restraining order good for up to ten days unless extended by court for good cause); after ten days must secure preliminary injunction	65	
Motion for Summary Judgment	Seeks final judgment based on pleadings and supporting affidavits (may come after discovery). Alleges no genuine issue in case	Plaintiff: 20 days after filing complaint or after being served with such motions by adverse party. Defendant: Any time after action filed. Notice: Served ten days prior to hearing on motion	56	
DISCOVERY				
Parties' Planning Meeting	To decide on a plan for disclosure and discovery	As soon as practical and at least 21 days prior to 16(b) scheduling conference	26(f)	
Planning Meeting Report		Within 14 days after parties' planning meeting	26(f)(2)	
Initial Disclosure		Within 14 days of 26(f) meeting unless otherwise stipulated or ordered. At least 90 days before trial if expert witness information.	26(a)(1)(c) and (2)(D)	
Pretrial Disclosure	Witnesses, documents, exhibits, and other information for trial	At least 30 days prior to trial. Objection to admissibility within 14 days after disclosure.	26(a)(3)(B)	
Petition for Deposition Before Action or Pending Appeal	To preserve testimony or other evidence before action or appeal started	Notice to each party due 20 days before hearing on petition	27(a)(1–2)	
Notice to Take Deposition (notice to all other parties)	To gather evidence from the oral or written statements of others	After parties' 26(f) meeting	26(d), 30(a), 30(b)(1)	
Motion to Enlarge or Shorten Time for Taking Deposition			30(d)	

(continued)

EXHIBIT 6.23 Pleadings, Motions, and Time Limits (*continued*)

Pleading/Act	Purpose If Not Clear	Due	Federal Rule	State Rule/ Due
Notice to Take Deposition on Written Questions	Requested when oral deposition impractical	After parties' 26(f) meeting; cross questions within 14 days of service of original questions; redirect and recross questions within seven days of service of follow-up questions	31(a)	
Objections to Form of Written Deposition Questions		In time permitted for response as stated above and in five days after service of the last question	32(d)(3)(C)	
Interrogatories	To discover evidence through written questions to any party	After parties' 26(f) meeting; limited to 25 interrogatories	33(a)	
Answers or Objections to Interrogatories		Within 30 days after service of questions; must be written	33(b)(3)	
Request for Production of Documents and Things and Entry to Land	To inspect documents (writings, photos, data collections, etc.) and land to gather evidence	After parties' 26(f) meeting	34(a)(b)	
Response to Request for Production, Etc.		Within 30 days after service of request. Objection waived if no written responses served.	34(b)	
Motion for Order to Submit to Physical or Mental Exam	To require a party to submit to exam when condition in question (injury, emotional illness, other) relates to cause of action or damages	After parties' 26(f) meeting	35(a)	
Request for Admission(s)	To get opponent to admit to certain facts so they do not have to be proven at trial by separate evidence	After parties' 26(f) meeting	36(a)	
Answer or Objection to Request for Admission		Within 30 days after service of request	36(a)(4)	
Duty to Supplement Discovery Responses	To keep discovery current	Seasonably	26(c)	

EXHIBIT 6.23 Pleadings, Motions, and Time Limits (*continued*)

Pleading/Act	Purpose If Not Clear	Due	Federal Rule	State Rule/ Due
Motion to Compel Discovery	To get court to order party to provide discovery	On reasonable notice to all parties and all persons affected and after attempt to resolve	37(a)	
Motion for Protective Order	To get order permitting party to not respond to certain aspects of discovery or to prevent abuse of discovery by opponent	In reasonable period of time and after attempt to resolve	26(c)	
Motion to Enforce Subpoena	To require person to appear and/or produce documents for examination	Any time after objection to subpoena is made and upon notice to person commanded to produce	45	
Objection to Subpoena for Production and Inspection	To change or stop the enforcement of subpoena	Before time for compliance with subpoena or within 14 days after service of subpoena	45(d)(3)	
PRETRIAL				
Demand for Jury Trial		To all parties any time after action starts but no later than ten days after the last pleading directed to such issue. Check local rules.	38(b)	
Motion for Involuntary Dismissal	To dismiss action for failure of plaintiff to prosecute	120 days after filing of action absent service of summons and complaint	41(b), 4(m)	
Consolidation of Actions or Separation for Trial	To combine actions for the sake of judicial economy or to provide separate trials where combined trial would cause prejudice or inconvenience	In reasonable time before trial	42(a)(b)	
Motion for Voluntary Dismissal	So plaintiff or parties can agree to action dismissal	By notice of dismissal at any time before service by adverse party of an answer or motion for summary judgment, whichever occurs first, or by filing stipulation signed by all parties appearing in action	41(a)(1)	

(continued)

EXHIBIT 6.23 Pleadings, Motions, and Time Limits (*continued*)

Pleading/Act	Purpose If Not Clear	Due	Federal Rule	State Rule/ Due
Motion to Use Deposition at Trial	To use deposition as testimony at trial	Reasonable time before trial and on reasonable notice	32	
Motion in Limine	For protective order against prejudicial questions or statements by adverse party	Pursuant to scheduling order and usually a reasonable time before trial or reasonable time after selection of jury	16 generally (no specific deadlines for motion, except by court order)	
Motion to Exclude Evidence	To exclude evidence for a variety of reasons	Pursuant to scheduling order and usually a reasonable time before trial or as matter arises at trial	16(c)	
Offer of Judgment	To settle case by defendant offering to accept judgment for a specified amount	Any time more than 10 days before trial. Ten days to accept offer.	68	
TRIAL				
Motion for Judgment as a Matter of Law (Directed Verdict)	To have court enter judgment for moving party for failure of opponent to prove prima facie case	Any time before submission of case to jury	50(b)(3) 50 (1) and (2)	
Renewal of Motion for Judgment as a Matter of Law (JNOV)	To have court enter judgment contrary to that returned by jury on basis jury verdict goes against weight of evidence (may be joined with motion for new trial)	Within 28 days after entry of judgment	50(b)	
POST-TRIAL				
Motion for New Trial or to Alter or Amend Judgment	To have judgment set aside and new trial ordered because of error or other injustice at first trial	Within 28 days after entry of judgment	59, 52(b)	
Response to Motion for New Trial/ Affidavits	To oppose motion for new trial	Within 14 days after service of motion or 20 more days with leave of court	59(c)	
Motion to Correct Clerical Errors in Judgment		Any time	60(a)	

EXHIBIT 6.23 Pleadings, Motions, and Time Limits (*continued*)

Pleading/Act	Purpose If Not Clear	Due	Federal Rule	State Rule/Due
Motion for Stay of Execution of Judgment Pending Post-Trial Motions		Within 14 days after entry of judgment or with motion for post-trial relief	62(b)	
APPEAL				
Notice of Appeal	To notify all parties of appeal	Within 30 days after judgment or order; 60 days if U.S. or officer or agency	Rule 4(a) of Appellate Procedure	
Stay on Appeal	To prevent execution of judgment until appeal decided	At filing notice of appeal or soon after	62(d) and 62(e)	

SUMMARY

Chapter 5 emphasizes the role of formulating and filing a case for the plaintiff; Chapter 6 emphasizes the defense, how to attack the weaknesses in the complaint or action, how to remove a case to federal court, and how to respond in the form of an answer to the complaint.

The defendant has 20 days or more to respond to the complaint, depending on jurisdiction and method of service. The first likely response includes a host of motions to have the complaint dismissed or modified. These motions are your first introduction to what today has become an extensive motion practice. Motions drafted by the parties to the action request the court for an order directing the other side to comply, backed up with contempt of court or other sanctions for failure to do so. Because they can result in specific court action against one or more of the parties, motions are critical to sound representation.

The first motions to be filed in a case seek orders dismissing or modifying the complaint [Rule 12(b)]. These motions can attack jurisdiction, service, or venue; or they may attack a complaint for stating an incomplete, inaccurate, or misconceived premise. Your tasks are to review the complaint and spot its weaknesses, and to research and draft the motion and supporting documents, including memoranda of law and affidavits. If the motion is successful, the complaint may be dismissed or simply amended. If the latter, then the defendant must file the answer.

If the case is filed in state court but could be heard in federal court, the defendant may choose to have the case removed to federal court, which is accomplished through the drafting and filing of a Notice of Removal.

The defendant must answer the complaint regardless of removal. The answer is the formal pleading that states the defendant's specific admission, denial, or other responses to each of the plaintiff's assertions in the complaint. What determines the needed detail in the response is whether the jurisdiction is a notice pleading or a code (fact) pleading jurisdiction.

The answer must include affirmative defenses, such as the expiration of the statute of limitations, if the defense plans to assert these defenses at trial. In addition, counterclaims that the defendant has against the plaintiff should be asserted with the answer. Cross-claims against co-parties can be included in the answer after the counterclaim or may be filed as separate documents. To litigate all the claims arising from a single set of circumstances, the parties may bring in nonparties as third-party defendants. These are persons who may be liable to the defendant for part or all of the plaintiff's claim, or may be liable to the plaintiff for part or all of the defendant's counterclaim.

The filing of each of the pleadings and motions mentioned in this chapter follows strict time deadlines that, if not met, may result in default, the loss of the right to assert or claim a defense, or the loss of the case. One of your important roles is knowing each of the time limits and then seeing to it that they are met. It also involves noting when the other parties fail to meet their deadlines.

Pleadings may be liberally amended or supplemented under Rule 15 as long as the time limits for doing so are followed. When the pleadings are closed after the filing of the complaint, answer, and reply to counterclaim, either party may file a motion for judgment on the pleadings. A judgment on the pleadings essentially asserts that even if what the adversary says is true, there is no claim or there is no defense. A motion for summary judgment is similar, but goes further by asking the court to look behind the pleadings to consider additional evidence. Because of the importance of each of these pleadings and motions and their respective time deadlines as set out in state and federal rules, it is helpful for you to keep an accurate and timely pleading record.

KEY TERMS

affiant	counterclaim	motion
affidavit	cross-claim	order
answer	demurrer	third-party practice (impleader)
argumentative denials	memorandum of law (memorandum of points and authorities)	
bill of particulars		
brief		

QUESTIONS FOR STUDY AND REVIEW

1. What is a motion? State the purposes of motions in general.

2. What are the requirements for a motion under federal and your state rules? Identify the particular rules that apply.

3. What is the purpose of a supporting affidavit in motion practice? A supporting memorandum of law? What is the difference between the two?

4. Describe the detailed procedure for filing and serving motions. What federal and state rules apply?

5. What is a motion to dismiss? What purpose does it serve?

6. What is a demurrer? What purpose does it serve?

7. What method should you use to determine the weaknesses in a complaint subject to a motion to dismiss the complaint? Explain how the method works.

8. Explain the procedure, applicable rules, and time deadlines for filing and serving a motion to dismiss in both federal and your state courts.

9. What are the other Rule 12(b) motions? Must they be made separately?

10. What are the other motions attacking the complaint? State their purposes.

11. When may an action be removed to federal district court? What is the correct procedure and what form is needed to remove an action to federal court?

12. What is the purpose of the answer? When must it be filed? What rule is applicable?

13. Be able to list style and content considerations for drafting an answer, including those that apply to denials.

14. What are the components of an answer? Be able to define each of them. What is the procedure for locating the possible defenses to a claim?

15. What is the purpose of the following: third-party practice, amending and supplementing the pleadings, a motion for judgment on the pleadings, and a motion for summary judgment?

SYSTEMS FOLDER ASSIGNMENTS

1. Locate in your state rules the requirements, procedures, and time limits that apply to motions. Write a checklist for drafting, filing, and serving motions for both state and federal court, and place it in your systems folder. Verify the time limits pertaining to motions in the Pleadings, Motions, and Time Limits table at the end of the chapter. Add state deadlines.

2. Enter a reference to or copy of the notice of removal to federal court in your systems folder. Develop your own brief checklist for the required procedural stages and place that in your systems folder.

3. Note the rules for calculating time for both the federal and your state jurisdiction [see Rule 6(a) and (e)] in your systems folder. Include the formula and the example on how to calculate the due date.

4. From the steps for preparing and filing a third-party complaint, create a checklist for third-party practice and place it in your systems folder. Note any variations in local practice.

5. Enter state time limits parallel to Rule 56 (summary judgment) in the Pleadings, Motions, and Time Limits exhibit at the end of the chapter. Fill in the state rule and deadline section up to the discovery section and add the table or page reference to your systems folder.

APPLICATION ASSIGNMENTS

1. You are directed to look over a complaint for negligence. The body of the complaint reads as follows:

   a. On March 22, _____, Defendant owned and operated the Bay View Motel.

   b. On that date Plaintiff was descending a stairway at the motel, and as a result of Defendant's conduct, tripped and fell down the stairway.

   c. As a result of Defendant's conduct, Plaintiff suffered a broken wrist, a brain concussion, and numerous bruises over much of his body.

  d. Because of the above injuries, Plaintiff had extensive medical bills and lost six weeks of work, to the sum of $25,000.

Using the method suggested in the Determining What to Attack section, determine if the body of this complaint is defective, and if so, why. Explain how the syllogism method of finding defects applies to this case. Be prepared to defend your conclusion.

2. Draft the Notice of Removal to have the case against Allen Howard removed to federal court, as Mr. McDuff requested.

3. Review the basic facts set out in Chapter 1 for Case IV, *Briar Patch Dolls, Inc. v. Teeny Tiny Clothing Manufacturing Co.*, a contract case. Using the method described in the Affirmative Defenses section of the text, make an initial determination of what affirmative defenses under the topic "discharge" might be available to the defendants. Make a list of these defenses and suggest some facts that might be necessary to support the defense. Because there are numerous defenses in contract law, confine yourself in this assignment to those defenses within the concept of "discharge."

4. Prepare the Request to Amend Pleadings in Case IV, based on the defendant's answer and affirmative defenses presented in assignment 3 above.

5. Exhibit 6.15 is a copy of the code (fact) complaint in Case II, the *Ameche/Maple Meadows Campground* case. Assume that your firm is defending the owner of the campground. Review the complaint and draft an Answer and Counterclaim for a code-pleading state. Then draft one for a notice-pleading jurisdiction.

CASE ASSIGNMENTS

1. Using the complaint that was prepared in the *Forrester* case in Chapter 4, prepare the answer and affirmative defenses for Richard Hart and Mercury Parcel Service, Inc.

2. Assume that Mercury Parcel Service can sue the manufacturer of the brakes and van. Prepare the Interpleader action of Mercury against International Brake Distributors Company and General Car Company, the manufacturer of the van. Both entities are located in the State of Columbia, Capitol County. Be creative. (You are only restricted by your imagination.)

DISCOVERY AND ELECTRONIC DISCOVERY: OVERVIEW AND INTERROGATORIES

OUTLINE

OBJECTIVES

AFTER READING THIS CHAPTER, YOU WILL BE ABLE TO:

- Delineate the purpose of discovery
- Identify the scope of discovery and its limitations
- Understand the requirements and obligations of electronic discovery
- Prepare a set of interrogatories
- Assist in answering interrogatories from an opposing party

OVERVIEW OF DISCOVERY

INTRODUCTION

discovery

The process in a lawsuit involving the exchange of information, exhibits, and documents between parties according to specific rules of procedure.

Discovery is the process in a lawsuit involving the exchange of information, exhibits, and documents between parties according to specific rules of procedure. That information helps form the evidentiary basis for both sides of the lawsuit. The exchange involves the following procedures or devices listed in Federal Rule of Civil Procedure 26:

1. **Disclosure:** giving to the opponent a broad spectrum of relevant information about the case without a specific request or use of other discovery devices

2. **Interrogatories:** written questions submitted to a party

3. **Deposition:** sworn oral testimony of a witness or litigant taken prior to trial

4. Production of documents, tangible items, or entry to property for inspection

5. **Expert's report and opinion:** the name, subject matter, and substance of the report of scientists and other experts to be used at trial

6. **Medical examinations:** requirement upon motion that a party submit to a physical or mental examination by a doctor chosen by the opposing party

7. **Request for admission:** asking the opponent to admit certain facts in writing, which then do not have to be proven at trial

Employ these devices more or less in proportion to the complexity of the case and the amount in dispute. Small cases use discovery sparingly, large cases extensively. These chapters emphasize the full use of discovery, including the discovery of electronically stored information. Read the discovery section of Exhibit 6.23 for a helpful overview of the discovery devices and the rules and time limits that pertain to each. Discovery is an essential area of paralegal practice. Learn it well. Exhibit 7.1 is a summary of the different types of discovery methods.

PURPOSE OF DISCOVERY: LEARNING ABOUT THE CASE

Justice is served when a case is tried on its merits (the evidence) rather than on some tactic of surprise or deception. "Trial by ambush" is no longer accepted. The rules of discovery attempt to achieve this result by making it possible for both sides in a lawsuit to be informed about the evidence and witnesses that will be presented by the opponent. More information should result in better preparation by both sides, which in turn provides the trier of fact with better information for ascertaining the truth. Despite these laudatory goals, discovery is expensive, comprising a high percentage of the cost of litigation.

Discovery Reveals Strength of the Case. More practical purposes exist as well. Discovery helps reveal whether there is a basis for the lawsuit or its defense. Therefore, discovery may lead to summary judgment or voluntary dismissal, ending the lawsuit and saving the time, expense, and anguish of a trial. The early access to information provided by discovery is more likely to lead to an early settlement based on a more

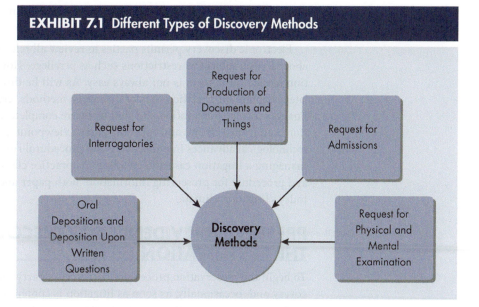

EXHIBIT 7.1 Different Types of Discovery Methods

accurate assessment of the case. Discovery also serves to identify undisputed facts, leaving for trial only those issues clearly in conflict. Fewer issues may result in a shorter, less expensive trial.

Discovery Gathers Information. Another purpose of discovery is to gather information from the opponent that can strengthen one's own case or allow one to be better prepared to refute the accuracy of the evidence presented by the other side. For example, if a witness says one thing at a deposition and another at trial, the earlier statements can be used to weaken the inconsistent trial testimony.

Discovery Preserves Evidence. Discovery also helps preserve evidence. If a witness gives testimony at a deposition and is later unavailable for trial, the court might permit the prior testimony to be entered at trial. **Electronically stored information**, commonly known as "ESI," which might be destroyed in the normal course of business, must be preserved for discovery. As will be discussed, ESI is becoming the focal point of discovery and has developed into an expertise, especially for paralegals.

ELECTRONIC DISCOVERY: A NEW AGE IN LITIGATION

The importance and impact of electronic discovery cannot be overstated. It is here to stay. With its advantages come extreme pitfalls for those who are not adequately schooled and prepared to deal with the intricacies and complications that invariably comprise electronic discovery. **Electronic discovery or e-discovery** is that process in civil litigation that deals with electronic formats and information. Contained in e-discovery is the information it envelops—electronically stored information, "ESI." ESI encompasses many forms and includes what we typically use in our daily life, such as e-mail, texts, instant messaging, Web sites, blogs, photographs, and virtually anything stored in electronic form. ESI also is information that we normally do not think about such as **metadata**, embedded data, backup information,

---

electronically stored information (ESI)
Information stored within any electronic device.

electronic discovery or e-discovery
Process in civil litigation that deals with electronic formats and information.

metadata
Data that explains other data.

GPS tracking information, or any information that can be electronically retrieved into a useable form.

Electronic discovery permits parties to review all relevant electronic information about a case, subject to restrictions such as privilege. However, producing information in electronic form is not always easy. As will be discussed in this chapter and later chapters on specific types of discovery methods, electronic discovery and its nuances involve preparation and skill to assure complete access to relevant information both from a client's and opposing party's viewpoint. Keeping abreast of the latest technological advances in e-discovery and procedural rule amendments is critical in managing a litigation case and avoiding malpractice claims. Thus, having a process and procedure for preserving information, both paper and electronic, is essential in today's litigation climate.

PRESERVING EVIDENCE FOR DISCOVERY: THE PRESERVATION LETTER

preservation letter
A letter sent to the opposing party requesting preservation of evidence.

To begin the preservation process for discovery, a party may need to act prior to discovery and, occasionally, as soon as litigation is contemplated to see that the opponent preserves potentially important evidence, particularly where the discovery of electronically stored information is contemplated. Early action is important not only because e-stored information is easily altered or lost, but also because the prospective opponent may not anticipate the need to preserve the evidence nor know what needs to be preserved and where it is located. The **preservation letter** accomplishes this end. It also alerts the opposing party to possible sanctions for carelessly or willfully losing evidence. Read the sample preservation letter for electronically stored information in Exhibit 7.2 to understand the focus and necessary detail of the letter.

EXHIBIT 7.2 Sample Preservation Letter

[LAW FIRM LETTERHEAD]

[date/address]

Re: Notice to Preserve Electronic Evidence
[Legal Matter]

Dear _____:

Our law firm represents [name] in the above legal matter in which you [your business] are [is] [will be] named as a defendant. This letter requests your immediate action to preserve electronically stored information that may contain evidence important to the above legal matter. Briefly, the matter involves [short statement of facts in case].

This notice applies to your [company's] on- and off-site computer systems and removable electronic media plus all computer systems, services, and devices (including all remote access and wireless devices) used for your [company's] overall operation. This includes, but is not limited to, e-mail and other electronic communications; electronically stored documents, records, images, graphics, recordings, spreadsheets, databases; and calendars, system usage logs, contact manager information, telephone logs, Internet usage files, deleted files, cache files, user information, and other data. Further, this notice applies to archives, backup and disaster recovery tapes, discs, drives, cartridges, voicemail, and other data.

EXHIBIT 7.2 Sample Preservation Letter (*continued*)

All operating systems, software, applications, hardware, operating manuals, codes, keys and other support information needed to fully search, use, and access the electronically stored information must also be preserved.

The importance of immediate action cannot be overstated. Electronically stored information is easily corrupted, altered, and deleted in normal daily operations. Even booting a drive, running an application, or reviewing a document can permanently alter evidence. An important method for preserving data in its original state is to have a forensic image (mirror image or clone image) made of pertinent hard drives of both office and home computers used for business and of network servers. This image captures all current data, including the background or metadata about each document. Simply copying data to a CD-ROM or other common backup medium is not adequate. For each captured image file, record and identify the person creating the image and the date of creation. Secure the file to prevent subsequent alteration or corruption and create a chain of custody log. Once the forensic data image file is created, the pertinent computer or other device can be placed back into operation.

[If known, identify any key persons', officers', supervisors', and employees' computers to which special attention for forensic imaging must be directed.]

This preservation notice covers the above items and information between the following dates: [state dates]. Follow the above procedures to preserve electronic information created after this notice.

Current law and rules of civil procedure clearly apply to the discovery of electronically stored information just as they apply to other evidence, and confirm the duty to preserve such information for discovery. You [company] and your officers, employees, agents, and affiliated organizations must take all reasonable steps to preserve this information until this legal matter is finally resolved. Failure to take the necessary steps to preserve the information addressed in this letter or other pertinent information in your possession or control may result in serious sanctions or penalties.

Further, to properly fulfill your preservation obligation, stop all scheduled data destruction, electronic shredding, rotation of backup tapes, and the sale, gift, or destruction of hardware. Notify all individuals and affiliated organizations of the need and duty to take the necessary affirmatives steps to comply with the duty to preserve evidence.

Sincerely,

[attorney's name]

---

disclosure

The procedure automatically triggered early in a case requiring a party to give to the opponent a broad spectrum of information relevant to the case.

A good preservation letter should be as specific to the case and narrowly drawn as your knowledge of the opponent's e-storage system permits and reasonableness dictates. Consult with your office's information technology person or a consultant to provide you with the necessary technology guidance before sending your first preservation letter. Discuss the letter with your supervising attorney and plan how the legal team can effectively respond to the opponent's questions about the technology addressed in the letter. Send the letter by certified mail, return receipt requested.

MANDATORY DISCLOSURE: WHAT IS REQUIRED UNDER THE RULES?

Introduction

Mandatory **disclosure** is the procedure automatically triggered early in a case requiring a party to give (disclose) to the opponent a broad spectrum of information pertinent to the case. It is designed to focus the attention of opposing lawyers on the details of the case at an early stage in the litigation to facilitate fairness and efficiency in the handling and resolution of the dispute.

Initial Disclosure

Within 90 days after the defendant has made an appearance in the case and within 120 days after the complaint has been served on the defendant, the court holds a scheduling conference with the attorneys to establish a time frame for the case and to issue a scheduling order. At least 21 days prior to the scheduling conference or the date that a scheduling order is due from the court, sooner if practicable, the attorneys must hold a meeting to discuss and establish a plan for disclosure and discovery in the case. Within 14 days after the attorneys' planning meeting, unless otherwise stipulated or directed by the court, the *initial disclosure* of information must occur. This disclosure is automatic; it eliminates the need to start the process with a motion or request for discovery submitted to the court. Initial disclosure is defined by Federal Rule of Civil Procedure 26(a)(1). It requires the parties to disclose the following information to the other parties:

(a) The name, address, and phone number of persons likely to have discoverable information that the disclosing party may use to support its claims or defenses, unless solely for impeachment, identifying the subjects of the information

(b) The production or description of relevant documents, electronically stored information, and tangible things in the possession, custody, or control of the disclosing party that may be used to support its claims or defenses, unless solely for impeachment

(c) A computation of damages, with the source of information on the nature and extent of the injuries made available to the other party for inspection and copying

(d) Any insurance agreement likely to cover the damages, made available for inspection and copying

This initial disclosure is designed to eliminate the need for an initial set of interrogatories or other early discovery devices. Occasionally, the new disclosure process occurs later in the case than some discovery opportunities under the former rules or current state rules. This delay may cause some information to be lost or a witness's memory to fade. A good paralegal is alert to such possibilities early in the case, and notifies the attorney that disclosure on that particular information needs to occur ahead of the normal schedule.

Note that the first item (a) encompasses persons with discoverable information as well as persons likely to have discoverable information. Also, the duty to disclose no longer includes information favorable to the opponent. Instead, the duty to disclose is confined to what a "party may use to *support* its claims or defenses" [emphasis added]. The phrase "claims or defenses" strictly narrows disclosure from the former language ("relevant to disputed facts") to that which the disclosing party intends to use. "Use," as defined in the advisory committee's notes, includes any use at a pretrial conference, to support a motion, or at trial.

Mandatory disclosure is not required in eight types of cases including administrative appeals, *habeas corpus* petitions, and actions by the United States to recover student loans. Also, the parties may stipulate to forgo mandatory disclosure, or a party's objection to mandatory disclosure may prevent disclosure until the court rules on the objection. Mandatory disclosure is also required of newly added parties. To move the process along, initial disclosure "must" be made based on what is reasonably available at the time. An incomplete investigation or the failure of the other party to properly disclose does not excuse a party from the obligation to disclose under this rule.

Disclosure of Information on Expert Testimony

Rule 26(a)(2) requires the disclosure of information on expert testimony in the case. This rule provides for disclosure of the following information:

(a) The identity of any expert (Federal Rules of Evidence 702, 703, or 705) who may be used at trial

(b) A written report prepared and signed by the expert witness, which includes a complete statement of all of the opinions to be expressed, the reasons for the opinions, the data or information relied on, the expert's qualifications and publications in the last ten years, the expert's compensation, and other cases the witness has testified at or been deposed for in the last four years

The disclosure of expert-related information must occur as directed by the court or by stipulation between the parties. In the absence of such direction, this disclosure must occur at least 90 days before trial unless it pertains to a rebuttal expert. If the latter, disclosure must be made within 30 days after disclosure of the other party. Complying with disclosure requirements regarding expert witnesses continues to be a problematic area in practice, especially regarding what attorney work product, if any, must be revealed to comply with Rule 26(a)(2)(b). Special cooperation and frequent communication between opposing sides is crucial to having this part of disclosure work effectively.

Pretrial Disclosures versus Initial Disclosures: The Differences

Pretrial disclosures, as distinguished from initial disclosures, must be made at least 30 days prior to trial. Pretrial disclosures include the following information regarding evidence for trial, unless it will be used strictly for impeachment purposes:

(a) The names, addresses, and phone numbers of each witness designated as "expected" to be or "may" be called at trial

(b) The designation of witnesses who will testify by deposition with a transcript of the pertinent testimony unless stenographically recorded

(c) The identification of each document or exhibit, including summaries of other evidence, labeled as "expected" to be used or "may" be used at trial

Within 14 days after the receipt of pretrial disclosures, a party must serve and file a list disclosing objections to the use under Rule 32(a) of any deposition proposed in (b) and any objection and grounds for the objection to the admissibility of materials stated in (c). Objections not disclosed are waived, unless the failure to disclose is excused for good cause or the objection is pursuant to Rule of Evidence 402 (relevance) or 403 (undue prejudice).

Disclosure Procedure, Certification

All disclosures under these provisions must be in writing, signed by the attorney, and served on the other party. Include the attorney's address. Note that the filing of disclosure and discovery documents in court is prohibited until the material is used in the proceeding or the court orders filing [Rule 5(d)]. Further, Rule 26(g) adds Rule 11–type requirements and certification. The attorney's signature certifies that the disclosure is complete and correct to the best of the signer's knowledge. When applied to discovery, the signature certifies that any discovery request, response, or objection is consistent with the rules and warranted by existing law or a good faith argument for the extension, modification, or reversal of existing law; is not interposed for an improper purpose such as to harass, unnecessarily delay, or needlessly increase the cost of litigation; and is not unduly burdensome or expensive regarding the needs of the case, previous discovery, the amount in controversy, and the importance of the issues at stake.

Any discovery request, response, or objection shall be stricken if it is not signed or promptly corrected on notice of the defect. An attorney or the party represented may be sanctioned by the court for making a certification in violation of the rules.

SCOPE OF DISCOVERY AND ITS LIMITATIONS

Introduction

The courts liberally apply the rules of discovery, including those on disclosure, to carry out the rules' laudatory purposes. Some important limitations apply to what may be discovered, however. The limitations are defined in Rule 26(b) and parallel state rules.

Relevance [26(b)(1)]

Any matter that is relevant to a claim or defense of any party of the lawsuit and is not protected by one of the limitations discussed here must be disclosed and is discoverable. Recall that information is relevant, and thus admissible for trial, if it is of consequence to the determination of the action and tends to prove or refute a fact of consequence to the lawsuit. The broad purpose of discovery, however, reaches beyond relevant information that is admissible for trial purposes to include information that "appears reasonably calculated to lead to the discovery of admissible evidence." The Advisory Committee Notes state that the emphasis on discovering admissible evidence takes allowable discovery beyond a strict limitation of relevance to a claim or defense to encompass, for example, evidence to be used to impeach a witness. Although such impeachment evidence, strictly speaking, may not be relevant to the claim or defense, it is admissible and, therefore, discoverable.

Rule 26(b)(1) creates two different areas of discovery. In the first, the attorneys are charged with and limited to carrying out discovery consisting of matters relevant to the claim or a defense to the claim. In the second, the court manages any discovery that goes beyond the claim or defense and can, on a showing of good cause, order discovery that is "relevant to the subject matter" of the action. This subsection emphasizes the court's authority to prevent unnecessarily broad and sometimes voluminous discovery requests. As a matter of practice, the legal teams for each party need to determine when the court should be brought into the process and concerning what material.

Privilege [26(b)(1)]

The rule of privilege, discussed in Chapter 3, that protects some information from being admissible for trial (attorney-client privilege and others) also protects that same information from discovery [Rule 26(b)(1)]. Therefore, privileged information may be withheld from disclosure and any other discovery. A party withholding privileged information, however, must provide a list (or privilege log) to the other party. The list must identify the document or other information along with a description of its nature so the other party can "assess the applicability of the privilege or protection."

When a discovery issue arises regarding whether a particular communication is privileged, Rule 501 of the Federal Rules of Evidence indicates that where a case in federal court relies on state law for its determination, such as in diversity cases, the state rule defining privilege controls [*Jewell v. Holzer*, 899 F.2d 1507, 1513 (6th Cir. 1990)]. If, however, the case involves both federal and state claims, then privilege is normally defined by the federal case law interpreting Rule 501 [e.g., *Hancock v. Hobbs*, 967 F.2d 462, 466–467 (11th Cir. 1992)].

Trial Preparation Materials [26(b)(3)]

The other major limitation on the scope of discovery is the attorney's work product or trial preparation materials exception. It bears repeating that documents and tangible things prepared in anticipation of litigation or trial may be discovered only if the party wanting discovery can show a substantial need for the materials in preparation for trial, and that obtaining the information any other way would cause undue hardship. This rule protects the work of the attorney as well as the work of the attorney's agents. This rule especially protects from disclosure the mental impressions, conclusions, opinions, and legal theories of the attorney. As in the case of privileged information, the party withholding the trial preparation material must provide a 26(b)(5)(a) list to the other party. Failure to do so can result in the loss of any work product protection for the item not listed. Although Rule 26 leaves the federal judge some discretion, the protection afforded trial preparation materials is absolute in some states. Rule 26(b)(3) also provides that a party may obtain a copy of any statement made by that party or by a nonparty without any special showing of need. Should discovery disputes arise, federal law defines trial preparation materials in all cases in federal court [*Toledo Edison Co. v. G. A. Technologies, Inc.*, 847 F.2d 335, 338–341 (6th Cir. 1998)].

Time and considerable experience are required for a paralegal to learn the delicate boundaries of what is protected and what is not. Sanctions for failure to comply with these rules, as well as court orders and procedures to protect material requested under these rules, are discussed in Chapter 9.

Procedure When Produced Information Contains Privileged or Trial Preparation Material [26(b)(5)(b)]

The 2006 Federal Rule amendments that address electronic discovery issues recognize how difficult and costly it is in the electronic information age to prevent completely the production of protected information. Rule 26(b)(5) was amended with a new subsection (5)(b) to provide remedial procedure in such circumstances. The producing party may notify any recipient party of what produced information is later claimed to be privileged or protected trial preparation material and the basis for that assertion. The longer the time between the production and the notice, however, the more likely it is the court may find that any privilege or protection claimed has been waived. The recipient party must "promptly return, sequester, or destroy" the specified information and may not use or disclose it. The recipient party may challenge the claim of protection by presenting the pertinent information to the court under seal for determination of the issue. If the recipient disclosed the information prior to notification of the claim, the recipient must "take reasonable steps" to recover it. The information for which the protection is claimed must be preserved by the producing party until the question is resolved. It remains for the court to determine whether the inadvertent or other production of the information waives the privilege or protection.

Clawback and Quick Peek Agreements: A Smart Investment

The American Bar Association has established ethical guidelines that recognize the likelihood that confidential information will be inadvertently sent to opposing parties at one time or another. When it happens, the attorney or paralegal receiving the information should avoid reading the information or sharing it with anyone else [Formal Opinion 92-368 (1992)]. If part of the confidential information is read, any unexamined part should not be read. The attorney receiving the confidential information should contact the attorney who inadvertently sent it and determine the best way to return it. This is a matter between attorneys, and a client need not be notified before the item is returned. The opinion strongly implies that inadvertently revealed confidential information should not be used by the receiving party. The Federal Rules of Civil Procedure reflect an approach consistent with the ABA's.

clawback agreement
Sets forth the procedures the parties will follow when inadvertent privileged or work product information is disclosed in response to a discovery request.

non-waiver agreement
Another term for clawback agreement.

One way to address this potential situation is to have a **clawback agreement** or **non-waiver agreement** executed between the parties in a case. A clawback agreement sets forth the procedures the parties will follow when inadvertent privileged or work product information is disclosed in response to a discovery request. This agreement protects the parties from any waiver of privileges due to the mistaken disclosure of information. How this occurs in discovery is as follows: A request for documents or information in any form is sent by one of the parties. Often enormous amounts of electronic information are produced. The producing party checks for documents that are privileged. As is often the case, privileged documents are inadvertently produced to the opposing party.

Producing the document could waive any privilege, but with a clawback agreement, the privilege is not waived and the opposing counsel is under an obligation to return the privileged information and cannot use that information in the case. The basis of the clawback agreement is that the disclosure is not voluntary and any error, which is usually human, should not be held against the client. In preparing a clawback agreement, consider the following:

- Any mistaken or inadvertent disclosure does not waive any privileges.
- When requested by the producing party, opposing counsel must return or destroy the information disclosed. The information disclosed cannot be used in any form in the case.
- If the opposing counsel realizes that privileged information was disclosed, counsel must notify the opponent. Setting a time period is appropriate, such as within 24 hours of the discovery, immediately, or in a timely manner.
- Opposing counsel must identify each person who had access to the privileged information, and if disseminated to any third party, secure the return of the information. The agreement should have language that places an obligation on the opposing counsel or party to safeguard the use of the information in any manner.

Having a clawback agreement is simply good practice and acts as an insurance policy for inadvertent disclosures.

quick peek agreements
An agreement between parties where one party is given access to all, or substantially all, of an opposing party's ESI with the understanding that any disclosure of privileged information is not a waiver of privilege.

Quick Peek agreements are another form of protection for privileged documents. In a Quick Peek agreement, a party is given access to all, or substantially all, of an opposing party's ESI with the understanding that any disclosure of privileged information is not a waiver of that privilege. After review of the documents, the receiving party identifies the documents that they wish to have formally produced. If in that production there are privileged documents that were inadvertently produced to the opposing party, that party must return and destroy any improperly produced documents.

Recognizing some of the issues encountered with electronic discovery, Congress passed Rule 502 of the Federal Rules of Evidence. This rule addresses inadvertent discloses and waiver of privilege. Under Rule 502, the party claiming the inadvertent disclosure must show that the disclosure was accidental and that reasonable precautions were taken to protect the information that was disclosed. The party claiming the privilege also must make attempts to correct the inadvertent disclosure in compliance with Rule 26 of the Rules of Civil Procedure. Essentially, Rule 502 attempts to tackle the practical problems that are encountered when voluminous amounts of ESI are disclosed and bridge the gap between the harsh effects of inadvertent waiver and fairness. A recent interpretation of Rule 502 was in *Clarke v. J.P. Morgan Chase & Co.*, 2009 WL 970940, 2009 U.S. Dist. LEXIS 30719 (S.D. N.Y., April 10, 2009) where the district court found that J.P. Morgan's inadvertent disclosure of an e-mail containing some legal advice was not privileged and even if privileged, Morgan did not take adequate steps to prevent the disclosure of the information and did not act in a timely manner to notify opposing counsel of the inadvertent disclosure. Rule 502 requires that reasonable steps were taken to prevent the disclosure and subsequent steps were taken to rectify the error of the disclosure. None of this occurred in the *Clarke* case. Therefore, although courts will examine how the disclosure occurred and the time lapse after the disclosure was identified, courts will not rubber-stamp carelessness in the disclosure process. Diligence is critical when discovering inadvertent disclosures to protect the client's interest and the privileges that attach to those disclosures.

ETHICAL CONSIDERATIONS: COMPETENCY AND E-DISCOVERY

ABA Model Rule of Professional Conduct 1.1 requires competent representation consisting of the "legal knowledge, skill, thoroughness and preparation reasonably necessary for the representation." Although most lawyers and paralegals are comfortable with their competency in conducting discovery in the traditional context, many are far less comfortable with, and even fearful of, taking cases involving e-discovery. Comment 2 to Model Rule 1.1 sensibly states that Rule 1.1 allows attorneys to take cases where new areas of expertise will be required, if the attorney and legal team are diligent and thorough about acquiring the reasonably necessary skill and knowledge. Practically speaking, some preparation prior to accepting a case involving e-discovery is necessary to make a realistic assessment of the level of expertise needed and the time and cost involved in the case and in acquiring the requisite level of competency to handle it. The lack of competence regarding the process of determining how and where electronic information is stored, and the ethical duties related to its preservation and discovery, can result in severe and costly sanctions. Both the supervising attorney and the paralegal must be prepared to have a frank discussion about this issue with the client, who otherwise might blindly assume that the firm has the requisite knowledge and skill to adequately conduct and respond to e-discovery requests. More importantly, the paralegal should not be burdened with the responsibility to compensate for the attorney's lack of expertise and knowledge in the area. Therefore, paralegals should be honest and forthcoming in their competency in the area. Neither party wants to be surprised during a case and be subject to the ire of the opposing counsel or sanctions by the court.

APPLY YOUR KNOWLEDGE

Determine whether your jurisdiction has passed legislation or amended its procedural rules to address the issue of inadvertent disclosures in e-discovery. If so, identify the statute or rule and detail the requirements an attorney must take to protect any attorney-client or work product privilege.

Trial Preparation: Experts [26(b)(4)]

An opposing party may depose an expert who will testify at trial only after the expert's 26(a)(2)(b) report has been disclosed to the opponent. The party requesting the deposition must pay the expert a reasonable fee for the deposition or the expert's response to any other discovery device. An expert employed by the opponent but not expected to testify at trial may be deposed or requested to answer interrogatories. If so, the party requesting discovery must pay a fair portion of the expert's fee and expenses.

Court Discretion and Other Limits [26(b)(2)(A–C)]

The federal court may change the number of interrogatories or depositions or other discovery devices sought if the following conditions are present:

- The discovery sought is unreasonably burdensome, cumulative, or duplicative, or is obtainable from a more convenient and less expensive source.
- The party seeking discovery has had ample opportunity to obtain the information sought.
- The discovery is unduly burdensome or expensive, taking into account the needs of the case, the amount in controversy, limitations of the parties' resources, and the importance of the issues at stake in the litigation [Rule 26(b)(2)(c)].

New language was added to Rule 26(b)(2) addressing the difficulty of producing some kinds of electronically stored information. Rule 26(b)(2)(b) permits a responding party not to produce requested electronically stored information when it is "not reasonably accessible because of undue burden or cost." That party, however, must "identify" for the requesting party those specific sources of information. Some examples of e-information that may not be reasonably accessible include backup tapes not indexed or easily searched, residual but fragmented data from previous deletions, and other data that can only be searched by very expensive and time-consuming forensic processes. The party asserting that the requested information is not reasonably accessible must convince the court of that fact. Despite that showing, the court may, for good cause shown by the opponent, still order production. In making that decision, the court must consider the three conditions in 26(b)(2)(c) stated above. Check your state rules for similar limits on discovery.

INTERNET EXERCISE

Identify your state's discovery rules. What are the practice and procedures for your state's discovery process? Are there any local rules or local court practices that apply to the discovery process? Has your state addressed e-discovery issues through their rules of procedure or case law? Review both your state and federal court procedures.

PARTIES' PLANNING MEETING AND RESULTING DISCOVERY PLAN

Discovery may not start until the parties hold a planning meeting. The planning meeting is governed by Rule 26(f). The parties shall meet as soon as practicable and at least 21 days before a scheduling conference is held or a scheduling order is due under Rule 16(b). The meeting should cover:

- the nature and basis for the claims and defenses asserted
- the possibility of a prompt resolution of the case through a settlement or other resolution
- disclosure or arrangement for disclosure as required in Rule 26(a)(1)

APPLY YOUR KNOWLEDGE

Determine whether your state rules require a planning meeting between the parties and if so, what that meeting entails. Check your state and federal court Web sites to determine whether any of the judges have specific forms to follow for the discovery plan which resulted from the planning meeting between the parties.

- any issues concerning the preservation of discoverable information, including electronically stored information
- the plan for discovery, including interrogatories, depositions, and other devices
- the parties' plans (discovery plan) concerning:
  1. disclosures and changes to be made in the timing, form, or requirements for disclosure under 26(a) or a local rule
  2. subjects in which discovery is needed, a date for completion of discovery, whether discovery should be conducted in phases or limited to particular issues
  3. disclosure or discovery issues regarding e-stored information, including in what form(s) it should be produced
  4. issues about claims of privilege or protection of trial-preparation material, including whether the parties agree on how to assert such claims after production and on asking the court to include any agreement in an order (the Committee Note to this item encourages the parties to consider an agreement on what post-production protocol, if followed, will avoid the waiver of the pertinent privilege or protection)
  5. what limitations on discovery imposed by the Rules or local rules should be changed and what other limitations should be adopted
  6. any other orders to be entered by the court regarding protective orders or matters under the Rule 16 pretrial and management conference.

The attorney for each party and any unrepresented party must meet and attempt in good faith to agree on a plan. The plan must be submitted in writing to the court within 14 days of the meeting. The times for holding the parties' planning meeting and for submitting the report may be altered by the court if needed to comply with an expedited schedule for Rule 16(b) conferences. The form for the Report of Parties' Planning Meeting, Federal Form 35, is in Exhibit 7.3. Some judges have developed their own report forms to ensure a thorough meeting and reporting of that meeting by the parties.

A Word on the Internal Discovery Plan: Your Work Product

Under the Federal Rules of Civil Procedure as discussed in the chapter, a discovery plan is required to be developed by the parties. This plan includes those items required under the rules, such as dates of disclosures, completion of discovery, e-disclosure and format, non-waiver of privilege, and limitations on the process. Another type of discovery plan is one that is developed internally between the paralegal and supervising attorney. This plan is considered privileged and is attorney work product. Used in conjunction with your evidence and investigative plans, in this plan, the paralegal should focus on the discovery phase of the case. After identifying the issues, the paralegal should consider including such areas as

- what documents support the claims or defenses alleged in the case
- who may possess the documents and where they are located
- where e-documents are located and the format
- whether expert assistance is needed in evaluating e-documents and their format

- how to retrieve e-documents
- who can best identify documents and testify to the contents
- what forms of discovery are best for a particular issue or situation, e.g., deposition, interrogatories, admissions.

Important to the plan is the deadlines which were ordered by the court and the scope of the discovery. Attach a copy of the court's order or amended order to the discovery plan. The document should not be a static document. As the case progresses, things will change and the discovery plan should be changed accordingly. Any discovery plan prepared for a case should be placed in the systems folder.

EXHIBIT 7.3 Form 35. Report of Parties' Planning Meeting

[Caption and Names of Parties]

1. Pursuant to Fed.R.Civ.P. 26(f), a meeting was held on (date) at (place) and was attended by:
   (name) for plaintiff(s)
   (name) for defendant(s) (party name)
   (name) for defendant(s) (party name)

2. **Pre-discovery Disclosures.** The parties [have exchanged] [will exchange by (date)] the information required by [Fed.R.Civ.P. 26(a)(1)] [local rule _____].

3. **Discovery Plan.** The parties jointly propose to the court the following discovery plan: [Use separate paragraphs or subparagraphs as necessary if parties disagree.]

Discovery will be needed on the following subjects: (brief description of subjects on which discovery will be needed), Disclosure or discovery of electronically stored information should be handled as follows: (brief description of parties' proposals).

The parties have agreed to an order regarding claims of privilege or of protection as trial-preparation material asserted after production as follows: (brief description of provisions of proposed order).

All discovery commenced in time to be completed by (date). [Discovery on (issue for early discovery) to be completed by (date).]

Maximum of _____ interrogatories by each party to any other party. [Responses due _____ days after service.]

Maximum of _____ requests for admission by each party to any other party. [Responses due _____ days after service.]

Maximum of _____ depositions by plaintiff(s) and _____ by defendant(s). Each deposition [other than of _____] limited to maximum of hours unless extended by agreement of parties.

Reports from retained experts under Rule 26(a)(2) due:
   from plaintiff(s) by (date)
   from defendant(s) by (date)

Supplementations under Rule 26(e) due [time(s) or interval(s)].

4. **Other Items.** [Use separate paragraphs or subparagraphs as necessary if parties disagree.] The parties [request] [do not request] a conference with the court before entry of the scheduling order.

The parties request a pretrial conference in (month and year).

Plaintiff(s) should be allowed until (date) to join additional parties and until (date) to amend the pleadings.

Defendant(s) should be allowed until (date) to join additional parties and until (date) to amend the pleadings. All potentially dispositive motions should be filed by (date). Settlement [is likely] [is unlikely] [cannot be evaluated prior to (date)] [may be enhanced by use of the following alternative dispute resolution procedure:

_____].

EXHIBIT 7.3 Form 35. Report of Parties' Planning Meeting (*continued*)

Final lists of witnesses and exhibits under Rule 26(a)(3) should be due
    from plaintiff(s) by (date)
    from defendant(s) by (date)
Parties should have _____ days after service of final lists of witnesses and exhibits to list objections under Rule 26(a)(3).
The case should be ready for trial by (date) [and at this time is expected to take approximately (length of time)]. [Other matters.]
Date: _____

Source: Federal Rules of Civil Procedure.

UNIQUE ISSUES IN ELECTRONIC DISCOVERY: THE UPS AND DOWNS

Electronics have made the world accessible in a way many of us never contemplated. With the Internet, receiving news, contacting friends and family, and shopping can occur with just a click. Gone are the days when mail was transmitted solely through the post office and faxing a document was the fasting way to communicate with a colleague. Now, we have an electronic device to do everything. Smartphones, tablets, iPads, and laptops are just a few of the ways we communicate. With those communications, we are transmitting information in electronic form and electronic form only. No paper documents result. This technology revolution has created some headaches for attorneys and paralegals in developing a case. No longer are boxes of papers delivered in response to discovery, but now information is delivered on CDs, DVDs, flash or zip drives, or other forms which comply with discovery demands. Electronic discovery produces an avalanche of information, which is considered a good advancement. We can discover someone's e-mails, Facebook or Twitter accounts, and texts or instant messaging. These forms of information usually do not have a hard or paper copy associated with them. The means to review this data is electronic.

When retrieving data, be sure the data received is in a compatible form to the firm's computer system. Often the form of data is determined by the parties during the initial pretrial conference, but when that does not occur, identify the form the firm requires the data to be transmitted in. Forms such as TIFF (or TIF) (Tagged Image File Format) and PDF (Portable Document Form) are the common forms. Coupled with these formats may be the need to use computer assisted analytic software, such as C.A.R., computer assisted review, or T.A.R., technology assisted review. These tools help the attorney's review of the documents produced by narrowing the number of documents required for review and prioritizing those documents identified as relevant.

Some computer systems automatically and routinely delete information, such as e-mails. Include a warning not to delete any information automatically in the "hold letter," and be sure the IT people assisting in the case can determine whether information was deleted and when. There are programs that determine this information. Most information, deleted or not, is retrievable. This is important as most individuals believe that once they have deleted information from a phone or other electronic device, it is gone forever. Not so. Therefore, clients should be advised that anything they transmit

TECHNOLOGY UPDATE: E-FORENSICS AND CIVIL LITIGATION

Gone are the days when forensics was limited to the criminal context. With the advent of e-discovery and its requirements, a new area of the law and expertise has evolved known as e-forensics, cyber-forensics, digital forensics, or computer forensics. Whatever we call it, e-forensics developed in response to the myriad of issues from e-discovery. E-forensics is a process that collects, analyzes, and preserves evidence from a particular electronic device. Used in electronic discovery, this process verifies how and where electronically stored information is located and can assist in restoring information that was seemingly lost. The general goal of e-forensics is the preservation of all electronic data in its original form, which will assist in reconstructing past events that may be relevant in a civil litigation matter. This is not an easy process. Challenges arise when searching for data and preserving it in suitable form acceptable to the legal principles

required in our jurisprudence. Critical to this search is the ability to maintain a link in the chain of evidence or chain of custody, similar to the process used in a criminal case. To overcome legal challenges, a forensic computer expert must be able to show how information was acquired, who authored the information, and in some instances, who received it. It is a delicate technical balance that must be bridged for electronic evidence to be admissible in a court of law. (Recall the Chapter 3 discussion on evidence and evidence preservation.) E-forensics is particularly important in examining and searching hidden folders where deleted or encrypted information may be present. Similarly, retrieving damaged electronic files through e-forensics can be useful in the discovery process. This is a science and legal expertise that is developing as the electronic age unfolds and e-discovery procedures gain more sophistication.

electronically may be retrieved regardless as to when the information was transmitted or whether it was deleted. Think about the texts we send, the Apps we download, and the videos we record. Even when deleted, this information is retrievable and discoverable in a case. Think about when you shop online and view an item. Then when you are on a completely unrelated site, such as a news site, a pop-up appears showing the item of clothing that was just viewed on another Web site. Eerie. But, through hidden data engines, such as cookies, information we search for and seek is being monitored. Now, translate that into all the sites, both social and personal, we visit and now we see how information stays with us forever and thus, with today's technology, is discoverable.

SUPPLEMENTING DISCLOSURE AND DISCOVERY: THE CONTINUING OBLIGATION

The parties are under a continuing obligation to supplement or correct any disclosure or discovery information if they learn the information given is incomplete or incorrect in some material respect. This duty encompasses information previously provided by experts in depositions. Supplementation is to be made at "appropriate intervals" for disclosure and "seasonably" for discovery and must be made no later than 30 days before trial.

Because paralegals work so closely with discovery information, they are frequently the ones in the law firm who know when responses need updating. A good paralegal notices outdated or inaccurate information and calendars regular reminders to seek supplementation of discovery from the opponent and to reciprocate. Such an obligation cannot be overemphasized. Plaintiffs in *Shapiro v. Plante & Moran, LLP* (*In re Connolly N.Am., LLC*) 376 B.R. 161 (S.D. Mich. 2007), a complex bankruptcy matter, learned this the hard way.

CASE STUDY: UNDERSTANDING THE LAW

Misleading the court and failure to supplement discovery can have a chilling effect. The underlying case in *Shapiro v. Plante & Moran, LLP (In re Connolly N.Am., LLC)* was filed by Mark Shapiro, the Chapter 7 **trustee** for the estate of Connolly North America, LLC, the debtor, against Connolly's accountant, Plante & Moran. The case centered around the trustee's claims for damages of $4.8 million for malpractice in a 2001 audit of Connolly's financial statements. During discovery, Plante & Moran made numerous document requests. Not until nine days into the trial on the malpractice claims did information come to light that the trustee failed to produce 36 boxes of relevant documents that had been requested 2 1/2 years earlier. Incredibly the trustee testified that the boxes had been discarded "to save storage expense."

This trial (or adversary proceeding) stemmed from the trustee filing a malpractice claim against Plante & Moran claiming that malpractice in the financial audits and resulting statements caused Connolly to file for bankruptcy. Discovery requests from both parties ensued with detailed document requests from Plante & Moran. The trustee's consistent response to document and interrogatory requests was that the documents did not exist. A deposition of the trustee occurred where he testified that the requested records had been destroyed. He also testified that 38 bankers' boxes that were discovered only contained information on the accounts receivable and not operating records and other related corporate information that was relevant to the claims of malpractice against Plante & Moran. Even though Plante's attorneys attempted to review the 38 bankers' boxes, they were told that the information contained inside the boxes were irrelevant. The trustee did not properly or adequately review the bankers' boxes initially. However, in 2003, the trustee did discover that his information about the relevancy of the boxes was erroneous, but failed to communicate this to Plante and their attorneys and never supplemented his

discovery responses. Instead, the trustee continued the charade with defense counsel and the court, maintaining that the records sought were destroyed even though in truth they were not. Not until days into the trial were the existence of the boxes and their contents discovered.

Because of the trustee's repeated erroneous information (and lies), Plante filed a motion to dismiss the case as a sanction for the trustee's continued discovery failures. The issue for the court was whether the trustee's misconduct was so egregious as to warrant dismissal of the case. Focusing on the required duty to supplement discovery requests, the court stated that this duty is a "continuing duty." Examining whether dismissal was the appropriate sanction, the court noted that dismissal is a harsh sanction which should only be used with caution. Only when the conduct is willful and in bad faith should a court impose the sanction of dismissal. Focusing on a Sixth Circuit case, the court examined a four-prong test which includes (1) whether the conduct of the party was willful, (2) whether the adverse party has been prejudiced, (3) whether the offending party was warned that the sanction of dismissal could be imposed, and (4) whether less drastic measures were considered before ordering dismissal. *Id.* at 182. Evaluating each standard, the court found that dismissal was the appropriate remedy because of the trustee's conduct and those for whom he had control. The court did not grant attorney's fees, stating that adding that penalty would be too harsh.

Questions for Review: Locate a copy of *Shapiro v. Plante & Moran.* Outline the chain of events that led to the discovery of the existence of the documents requested in discovery. Did the court find the trustee's conduct willful in its discussion of the law? Support your response with the court's reasoning. Was the court's order reasonable and justified? Why or why not?

trustee

Person appointed by the court to represent the debtor's estate in a bankruptcy case.

ETHICAL CONSIDERATIONS FOR DISCOVERY AND DISCLOSURE

Preserving the benefits of discovery (including disclosure) demands vigilance, honesty, and cooperation. The paralegal and attorney who fail to adhere to the relevant ethical standards do a disservice not only to their profession, but also to the fairness that is the goal of discovery. The relative newness and complexities of electronic discovery only intensify the need to understand and conform to applicable ethical standards.

Numerous ethical provisions apply directly or indirectly to discovery. Several are worth noting. Model Rule 3.4, previously discussed in Chapter 3, addresses fairness to the opposing party and counsel. It lists serious unethical actions that prevent an open and fair fact-finding process, including unlawfully altering, destroying, or obstructing access to evidence, inducing others (including paralegals) to do so, and other equally injurious acts. Some of these acts are crimes. Disobeying an obligation imposed by the rules for strictly obstructionist reasons is unethical. Rule 3.4(d) adds that a lawyer shall not "make a frivolous discovery request or fail to make a reasonably diligent effort to comply with [an opponent's] legally proper discovery request." The ethical standards set in Model Rule 3.4 are further buttressed by the anti-obstructionist certification by signature in Civil Procedure Rule 26(g)(1)(3), previously discussed. Most state ethics codes have provisions similar to those in Rule 3.4.

Model Rule 1.4 regarding communication with a client is by inference important to discovery in general and to electronic discovery in particular. Under 1.4, an attorney must take reasonable steps to consult with and inform the client about the means to accomplish the client's objectives and the status of the matter to the "extent reasonably necessary" for the client to make informed decisions [Model Rule 1.4(a) and (b)]. In the discovery context, this means the legal team must not only understand the ramifications of the lawsuit and the necessary scope of discovery and disclosure (competence), but also take the required steps to alert the client to the significance of each step of the discovery process and what information and action is required from and by the client to comply. This obligation of communication is invoked early in the process, even in anticipation of litigation, and is necessary to prevent destruction of evidence (spoliation).

Other areas of ethical concern are the attorney work product (trial preparation materials) and attorney-client privilege. As discussed earlier, careless review and screening of materials and electronically stored information by a paralegal or an attorney may result in the improper revelation of a client's confidences or secrets in direct violation of the code of ethics [Model Rule 1.6(a)]. This rule covers information gained before and after the representation and does not require the client to indicate what is to be held secret; nor does it ask the lawyer to speculate what is embarrassing or detrimental. The rule does permit a lawyer to make disclosures when authorization is implied. The example given in the commentary to Rule 1.6 applies directly to the discovery process and states that a lawyer may disclose information by admitting facts that cannot properly be denied.

You must strive to identify any confidential or protected information and consult with the attorney prior to disclosing that information to anyone outside the firm. This is critical. Practical suggestions on how you can help your attorney meet ethically mandated discovery obligations are discussed in the section on document production in Chapter 9.

And finally, as previously discussed, competency issues arise when attorneys accept cases with electronic information implications, but do not possess the skill and expertise to conduct e-discovery properly and adequately. Here, the attorney places him or herself in a compromising situation where the client's case suffers, the attorney is exposed to potential violations of the rules of discovery and sanctions.

Sanctions for Failure to Preserve Electronic Evidence and Spoliation

sanctions

court imposed remedy that can include dismissal of the lawsuit, imposition of attorney's fees and expenses, contempt orders, and adverse jury instructions.

Failing to comply and follow the discovery rules can result in **sanctions** for the offending party. Sanctions are a court-imposed remedy that can include dismissal of the lawsuit, imposition of attorney's fees and expenses, contempt orders, and adverse jury instructions to name a few. Sanctions can be awarded against the attorney directly, the law firm, and even the client. Willful failure to comply with discovery or a court's order can affect the lawsuit and outcome, even if the lawsuit has merit. Sanctions can be awarded due to spoliation. Spoliation was defined in *Zubulake v. UBS Warburg LLC*, 229 F.R.D. 422, 430 (S.D.N.Y. 2004), as the "destruction or significant alteration of evidence, or the failure to preserve property for another's use as evidence in pending or reasonably foreseeable litigation." One of the leading cases on sanctions relating to spoliation is *Zubulake*. In that case sanctions, including an adverse jury instruction on willful destruction of evidence, led to a $29 million jury award. A closer look at the *Zubulake* case and its history is warranted.

CASE STUDY: UNDERSTANDING THE LAW

Zubulake stems from a discrimination and retaliation lawsuit by filed by Laura Zubulake against her employer UBS Warburg LLC. Five opinions were written because of the various discovery violations by UBS. These opinions by Judge Scheindlin have become the barometer for evaluating discovery violations in the civil context. Essentially the facts are straightforward. Zubulake was an equities trader at UBS. Zubulake claims that she was discriminated against, was not promoted, and was thus retaliated against by UBS because of her legal actions. After filing her case under federal, state and city law, she filed a production of documents requesting certain documents important to proving her case against UBS. Specifically, Zubulake requested certain e-mails from UBS employees which were stored on the UBS computer systems. The initial request by Zubulake was in 2002. *Zubulake I* established "the legal standard for determining the cost allocation for producing e-mails contained in backup tapes"—*Zubulake v. UBS Warburg LLC*, 216 F.R.D. 280 (S.D.N.Y. 2003). *Zubulake II* focused on Zubulake's reporting obligations—*Zubulake v. UBS Warburg LLC*, No. 2 Civ. 1243, 2003 WL 21087136 (S.D.N.Y. May 13, 2003). *Zubulake III* discussed how costs associated with backup tape restoration would be allocated between the parties—*Zubulake v. UBS Warburg LLC*, 216 F.R.D. 280 (S.D.N.Y. 2003). *Zubulake IV* reinforced the employer's duty to preserve backup tapes

and why the costs of deposing certain witnesses would be borne by UBS—*Zubulake v. UBS Warburg LLC*, 220 F.R.D. 212 (S.D.N.Y. 2003). Finally, *Zubulake V* resulted in sanctions for UBS's failure to comply with the prior orders and permitted adverse inferences in the jury instructions—*Zubulake v. UBS Warburg LLC*, 229 F.R.D. 422 (S.D.N.Y. 2004). The precedential importance of *Zubulake* cannot be overstated as it established important guidelines in the discovery process. One of the most important concepts reinforced in *Zubulake* is the duty to preserve electronic information and when that duty arises. Under *Zubulake* that duty arises when a party reasonably anticipates litigation and with that duty any policies regarding routine document destruction/retention are on hold to preserve potential relevant documents. In the *Zubulake* decisions, the court analyzed the duty to preserve documents and the scope of that preservation. That duty encompasses relevant documents related to the claims in the lawsuit. As part of the duty, destruction/retention policies are supposed to be suspended and, thus, any backup tapes are required to be preserved as well. Somehow UBS employees destroyed relevant information, such as e-mails, by not preserving the backup tapes, even after instructed otherwise. Initially this conduct was considered negligent and culpable; however, Zubulake had not proven that the backup tapes would have produced relevant information. However, because

(continued)

---

of the lost information, prior depositions had to be re-taken and the court ordered UBS to pay those costs. The saga does not end there. In the final *Zubulake* case, UBS was sanctioned for its willful destruction of relevant e-mails after continually being told not to and its failure to timely produce certain relevant e-mails. That sanction included not only monetary costs, but an adverse inference jury instruction relating to the e-mails that were not produced. In *Zubulake V*, after re-deposing certain witnesses occurred as ordered in *Zubulake IV*, it was learned that more e-mails had been deleted and others never produced that were still available. After four lengthy admonishments, the court had enough and discussed in detail UBS's failings in discovery. Finding the actions of UBS willful in the final *Zubulake* opinion, the court ordered UBS to restore and produce relevant documents from backup tapes,

pay re-deposition costs, attorney fees, expenses and perhaps the most harmful, an adverse jury instruction stating that the jury could find that the actions of UBS in withholding information contained evidence that would have been unfavorable to UBS suggesting that UBS was deliberating trying to hide information and its conduct. Ultimately, as stated in the text, a $29 million verdict was entered against UBS.

Questions for Review: Locate copies of the *Zubulake* decisions and closely examine them. What are the facts surrounding Laura Zubulake's complaint against UBS? What discovery standards and guidelines are drawn from the *Zubulake* cases? Identify what process and pro-cedures should be followed by attorneys when potential litigation becomes apparent.

Other cases have examined the discovery sanction issues. Following the lead in the *Zubulake* cases, *Pillay v. Millard Refrigerated Servs.*, No.9 C 5725, 2013 WL 2251727 (N.D. Ill. May 22, 2013) held that a jury could find an adverse inference if it deter-mined that the company's automatic deletion of computer information/data was in bad faith or intentional. In *Metropolitan Opera Assoc., Inc. v. Local 100, Hotel Employ-ees and Restaurant Employees International Union*, 212 F.R.D. 178 (2003), the court granted Metropolitan Opera's motion for judgment due to opposing counsel's willful and bad-faith failure to comply with discovery. The number of e-discovery sanction cases grows. However, the offending party is not always the target of the court.

In *Stephen Slesinger Inc. v. The Walt Disney Co.*, 2004 WL612818, Calif. Super. Ct., Slesinger's case looked strong, partly because the court found that Disney had destroyed records and made false and evasive discovery responses. Unsatisfied, Slesinger's pri-vate investigator trespassed onto Disney property and found numerous privileged and protected documents in Disney's dumpsters. The documents were distributed among Slesinger's attorneys. The court found Slesinger's conduct so egregious that it dismissed Slesinger's once-promising suit. For a summary of the *Zubulake* cases see Exhibit 7.4.

DISCLOSURE TIME FRAME SUMMARY (FEDERAL)

1. Parties' planning meeting: as soon as practical, but at least 21 days before court scheduling conference.

2. Court scheduling conference/date for scheduling order: as soon as practical, but within 90 days of first appearance of defendant and within 120 days since complaint served on defendant.

3. Written report to court of parties' planning meeting: within 14 days after parties' planning meeting.

EXHIBIT 7.4 Summary of the Zebulake Cases

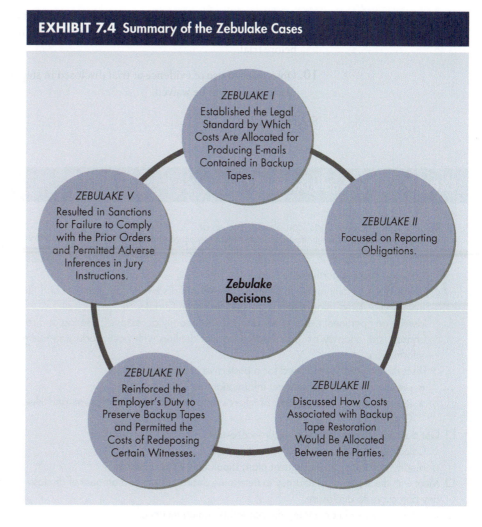

ZEBULAKE I
Established the Legal Standard by Which Costs Are Allocated for Producing E-mails Contained in Backup Tapes.

ZEBULAKE II
Focused on Reporting Obligations.

ZEBULAKE III
Discussed How Costs Associated with Backup Tape Restoration Would Be Allocated Between the Parties.

ZEBULAKE IV
Reinforced the Employer's Duty to Preserve Backup Tapes and Permitted the Costs of Redeposing Certain Witnesses.

ZEBULAKE V
Resulted in Sanctions for Failure to Comply with the Prior Orders and Permitted Adverse Inferences in Jury Instructions.

Zebulake Decisions

APPLY YOUR KNOWLEDGE

Using your state and federal courts as a guide, determine whether any of the state or federal court judges have local rules to follow when addressing discovery and e-discovery issues. Find any forms, if available, that the judges require relating to discovery. Familiarize yourself with the local practice of the judges in your jurisdiction.

4. Objections to disclosure: at parties' planning meeting and set out in planning report.

5. Disclosure (of persons likely to have supporting discoverable information; copy or description of supporting documents, data, and tangible things; calculation of damages and supporting materials; and applicable insurance agreements): unless otherwise stipulated, ordered, or properly objected to, within 14 days after parties' planning meeting.

6. Disclosure from party served or joined after parties' planning meeting: unless otherwise stipulated or ordered, within 30 days after served or joined.

7. Disclosure of expert testimony: unless otherwise stipulated or ordered, at least 90 days prior to trial or date set to be ready for trial. If solely to rebut previously disclosed evidence: within 30 days after opponent's disclosure.

8. Response to notification from party that information produced is subject to claim of privilege or protection: "promptly."

9. Pretrial disclosure (of witnesses, expected trial testimony of witness by deposition, and documents or exhibits): unless otherwise directed, at least 30 days before trial.

10. Objections to use of evidence at trial disclosed in step 9: within 14 days after disclosure or will be waived.

See Exhibit 7.5.

EXHIBIT 7.5 Paralegal's Disclosure Checklist

- ☐ Review case file, pleadings, complexity, and so on.
- ☐ Give special attention to e-disclosure and discovery needs [26(b)].
  - ○ Unless previously done, consult with attorney and meet with client regarding assessment of client's e-information storage system, if pertinent to case.
  - ○ Unless done, communicate to client disclosure and discovery requirements and the need to preserve evidence, including e-stored information (discussed further in Chapter 9).
  - ○ Identify any pertinent e-stored information "not readily accessible"; use log and record basis for conclusion.
  - ○ Consult with attorney on preferred method of dealing with post-production claims of privileged or protected information.
  - ○ Discuss with attorney the need for a protective order to:
    - ▪ preserve opponent's pertinent information or
    - ▪ legitimately protect aspects of client's information from disclosure and discovery (discussed further in Chapter 9).
- ☐ Get date for court scheduling conference/order.
  - ○ Calculate other deadlines based on this date.
  - ○ Modify according to subsequent plan, stipulation, or court order.
- ☐ Meet with the supervising attorney to determine desired depth and amount of disclosure and discovery needed and any objections to disclosure.
- ☐ Assist the attorney in arranging the parties' planning meeting.
  - ○ Assist at meeting.
  - ○ Draft agreed plan (Exhibit 7.2), stipulations, and objections as directed.
  - ○ Submit the parties' planning report to court if so directed.
- ☐ Using the investigation plan (Chapter 3) or similar approach, identify, gather, and organize the supporting evidence to be disclosed as set out in Rule 26(a). Remember to include any pertinent e-stored information.
- ☐ Review each item to be disclosed to raise any concerns about client confidentiality and/or attorney work product. Do this throughout the disclosure and discovery process.
- ☐ Format materials to be disclosed as directed. They must be written, unless court orders "otherwise" [26(a)(4)].
  - ○ Include signature line and attorney's address.
- ☐ Give formatted materials to supervising attorney for final review and signature.
- ☐ Serve disclosure materials on all parties.
- ☐ Upon receipt of disclosure materials from the other parties, review these materials carefully to see that all disclosure requirements have been met.
- ☐ Prepare disclosure of any expert witness, accompanying report, and other materials as set out in Rule 26(a)(2). Review parallel materials from other parties.
- ☐ Using the pertinent steps outlined above, serve and promptly file with the court all pretrial discovery, including witnesses to be called, exhibits, and other evidence described in Rule 26(a)(3). Do at least 30 days before trial.

EXHIBIT 7.5 Paralegal's Disclosure Checklist (*continued*)

☐ In consultation with the supervising attorney, prepare any objections to pretrial material disclosed by the other party within 14 days of its receipt.

☐ Check calendar dates periodically to see whether supplementation of previously submitted disclosure is needed. Supplement as required [Rule 26(e)].

☐ Use a tracking log for all disclosure and discovery.

INTERNATIONAL DISCOVERY

Under 28 U.S.C. § 1782(a), a person located in the district of a U.S. district court may be ordered to provide testimony or produce information, including documents, for use in a proceeding in a foreign or international tribunal. The order may be made pursuant to the request of the foreign tribunal or upon the application of any interested party. The U.S. Supreme Court has given this statute a broad interpretation that facilitates discovery and cooperation in international legal matters [*Intel Corp. v. Advanced Micro Devices Inc.*, 1261 S.Ct. 2466 (2004)].

AMENDMENTS TO THE RULES OF CIVIL PROCEDURE: CONSTANTLY MOVING THE BAR

The rules of civil procedure are constantly changing. This means that being current on amendments is essential to your job and performance as a paralegal. In 2006 and 2007, significant changes to the rules of civil procedure were proposed and passed. More changes were proposed in 2014 and will likely be passed in some form in 2015. Many of the proposed changes involve the discovery rules. What is important for you as a paralegal is always to check the rules for civil procedure, or any rule for matter, for

---

TRADE SECRETS: CERTIFICATION IN ELECTRONIC DISCOVERY

As a paralegal, you may be called upon to assist in evaluating a client's ESI and participate in the discovery process. You may be asked to ensure compliance with federal discovery rules and draft policies to ensure compliance with those rules. Because of the importance of e-discovery, understanding the e-discovery process is essential to your job and marketability as a paralegal. The field of e-discovery relating to the needs of law firms is a growing area, and paralegals can reap the benefits. Many programs offer certification in e-discovery. Becoming certified will demonstrate an expertise that is increasingly invaluable. Learning how to preserve, collect, and review the data produced in a client's case will only increase the paralegal's value to the litigation team. Often attorneys rely on their IT specialist to guide them through the e-discovery process. You can be one of those professionals as well. Knowing the different types of ESI and their characteristics along with understanding the processes involved in their retrieval serves as a basis to a successful and productive career. Similarly, certification and training will allow the paralegal to assist the attorney in evaluating e-evidence for admissibility, and determining the best methods to assure authentication of the e-evidence and reduce challenges in court from opposing counsel.

their current status. Do not assume that the rules will stay static. Pay attention to your and your attorney's professional journals for updates on changes that are proposed or final enactments on the rules of civil procedure and other related court rules.

INTERROGATORIES

TASK

Mr. White wants you to draft a set of interrogatories in the next three days to be answered by a yet-unidentified officer at Mercury Parcel Service, Inc.

PURPOSE OF INTERROGATORIES

interrogatories
A discovery device consisting of written questions submitted to another party and answered by that party in writing and under oath.

Interrogatories are a discovery device consisting of written questions submitted to another party and answered by that party in writing and under oath. They are authorized in Federal Rule 33 and parallel state rules. The person submitting (propounding) interrogatories, or other matters, for consideration by another party or the court is the "proponent." The replying party is the "respondent." Interrogatories provide a relatively inexpensive way to gather information from the opposing party. Useful information on the parties, witnesses, documents and records, evidence, and leads thereto can be obtained through questions such as the following:

- State the name and address of each person who has knowledge concerning . . .
- Identify and give the location of each document or record in your possession regarding . . .

The answers to the questions can aid in drafting other interrogatories or in preparing for depositions, and can provide the supporting information for summary judgment.

Interrogatories have some outstanding advantages. They are relatively inexpensive and the answering party cannot say "I do not know" or "I have forgotten." The rules impose a duty on the answering party to seek out the answer if the information is in the possession or control of that party. Interrogatories are especially helpful in "piercing the corporate veil" to gain information about internal structure, policies, and records of a corporation or agency.

PROCEDURE

Interrogatories must be carefully planned and drafted. They may be served by any party on any other party following the parties' discovery planning meeting [Rule 26(d)]. State rules may permit service with or following the service of the summons and complaint. Rule 33(a) permits a party without leave of court or written stipulation to serve no more than 25 interrogatories (counting each question and discrete subpart separately) on any other party. Leave to serve more interrogatories may be granted by the court if dictated by the needs of the case and the other principles stated in Rule 26(b)(2) [Rule 33(a)]. The number of interrogatories allowed by state courts varies. Check your local rules. Each question of the interrogatory must be answered separately and completely, or objections noted in lieu of the answer. The answers to the interrogatories must be returned within 30 days of service of the interrogatories unless otherwise agreed to by the parties or ordered by the court. State time limits may vary.

Answers to the interrogatories must be verified by the party, or by a designated official or agent in the case of a corporation or other entity. The answers, however, are actually drafted by the attorney and the paralegal.

In some cases it is not fair to place the time-consuming and difficult burden solely on the responding party to search through documents and locate the exact information. Rule 33(d) (Option to Produce Business Records) is designed to reduce or transfer that responsibility when the burden of locating the answer is about the same for the proponent as it is for the respondent. It permits the responding party to identify the specific business documents and records, including e-stored information, as well as where the information is likely to be found. It also gives the requesting party the opportunity to review the documents and locate the specifically requested information. The danger for the responding attorney in allowing the opponent to access and examine a block of the client's business information, including computerized information, is the unintended revelation of privileged or protected material. In such circumstances, the responding party may choose to carefully screen the block of information first or not invoke the 33(d) option. Relying on Rule 33(d) has positives and negatives. Your supervising attorney will have to evaluate the best course of action when ESI is involved, especially in more complex cases.

If a party objects to a question or refuses to answer, the requesting party can seek the assistance and sanctions provided by Rule 37(a)(4). The scope of the interrogatories is the same as that for any discovery device as set out in Rule 26(b)(1) and the Rules of Evidence. Although interrogatory practice is similar in most jurisdictions, become familiar with your local practice.

PLANNING INTERROGATORIES

Introduction

Interrogatories can be extremely useful as a discovery tool if they are planned carefully. If they are not planned carefully, the opponent may pose valid objections that preclude or delay discovery or produce information so general that it is useless.

Interrogatories are generally used to obtain the following information:

(a) Identities of persons who provided statements

(b) Identities of persons interviewed

(c) Facts elicited from a person interviewed who is now unavailable

(d) Identity of documents, witness statements, e-stored information, and physical evidence, including the nature, condition, location, and custody

(e) Information on all correspondence written by, read by, or mentioning a specific party, witness, or other person involved in the case

(f) Summary explanations of technical matter, data, and documents

(g) Transactions relating to the parties prior or subsequent to the events of the case

(h) Similar incidents related to the case involving the parties or others

(i) Information on the business or corporation including its organization, principal place of business, and other relevant data

(j) Information on the finances, related records, and status of the business or party

(k) Licenses relevant to party's business or conduct

(l) Identities of experts who will testify at trial and their opinions and bases for each opinion

(m) Insurance coverage, if permitted by state rule

(n) Data on time, speed, distance, and other relevant measurements, tests, or estimates

(o) Information on property and other assets for purposes of pre- or post-judgment collections

(p) Jurisdictional facts

(q) Protected work product where sufficient cause exists

The applicable discovery rules determine, in part, how the interrogatories can and should be used. For example, if the applicable rules include a substantial mandatory disclosure provision, as does federal Rule 26(a)(1), interrogatories serve more as a follow-up than as an initial discovery device, their focus depending on information obtained through disclosure. This narrowed use corresponds to the Rule 33 limit of 25 interrogatories, which gives the court, up front, control to prevent the deliberate drowning of an opponent in a sea of interrogatories.

Interrogatories are normally done in several sets. One set, for example, may be submitted early in the litigation to obtain leads for further investigation and discovery, and another set may be submitted later to obtain detailed information on a particular subject. Be aware of any limitations on the total number of questions that may be submitted. If the limit seems unworkable due to the complexity of the case, the supervising attorney may choose to move the court to expand the limit. [Rule 33(a)].

Determining Objectives of Interrogatories

A significant step in the planning of interrogatories is determining what information suitable for interrogatories is needed from the opponent. Ultimately the attorney will decide this issue, but you will often have responsibility for initiating the work. The following steps provide a guideline for this task:

(a) Keep the task clearly in mind, noting any special directions. In this case the task is to draft interrogatories to be submitted to Mercury Parcel Service.

(b) Review the case file including the pleadings and any other documents exchanged, as well as information obtained through informal investigation. Note areas that need clarification or more information. Review the complaint, answer, and counterclaim found in Chapters 4 and 6. Also review the information obtained in the informal investigation stages found in Chapter 3.

(c) Review or determine the elements of the cause of action according to the method outlined in Chapter 3. Also, know the elements of any alleged defense and counterclaim.

(d) Review the broad goals to be accomplished against the defendant at trial. In this case, one goal is to show that Mercury Parcel is Richard Hart's superior and is, therefore, liable for the negligent actions of Mr. Hart, its agent. Interrogatories would be needed, depending on what information was produced in any previous mandatory disclosure, to establish agency and to establish the following facts:

> That Mercury is a business
> That Hart was in the employ of Mercury on the date of the accident
> That Mercury owned the vehicle driven by Hart
> That Hart was working within the scope of his employment
> That Mercury had insurance to cover Hart and the vehicle

A further goal is to establish that Mercury was liable as a matter of its own fault. By applying imagination, one might produce the following possibilities for Mercury's negligence:

> That the van was defective
> That regular maintenance was ignored
> That complaints of defects were ignored
> That a pattern of poor maintenance procedures existed
> That maintenance reports were falsified to cover up poor or hurried maintenance procedures
> That drivers were asked to work unusually long shifts
> That Hart was asked to work an unusually long shift
> That hiring procedures disregarded or did not adequately screen for poor driving records
> That training of drivers was inadequate or non-existent regarding special circumstances, such as dangerous weather and road conditions

(e) Determine what information, including electronically stored information, is needed to reveal evidence or lead to evidence that supports such theories. The specific elements of the cause of action should be used as focal points for ideas on what information, witnesses, records, procedures, and so on might reveal evidence supportive of the proffered theories. Under each element, the following may prove helpful:

Duty of Care

- Laws or regulations imposing standards of care, such as a mandatory program for maintenance and vehicle and driver safety
- Records that must be kept to prove compliance with legal requirements
- The names of those responsible for recording and storing these records
- The existence of a company policy on maintenance or a regular maintenance program and records verifying such

- The existence of drivers' schedules, in-out reports, mileage, and so on
- The existence, quality, and use of a safety program and safety library
- The existence of any internal or external memos, letters, e-mails, and other communications indicating awareness of problems, failure to act, and other errors and omissions

Breach of Duty

Specifically on the van operated by Hart on the day of the accident:

- Maintenance records since the vehicle was purchased
- Source of purchase (new or used vehicle), name and address of previous owner(s)
- Records containing drivers' complaints or notes on performance
- Names and addresses of mechanics or others who worked on the vehicle
- Records relating to the history of maintenance and repair
- Maintenance and repair records for all vehicles covering the eighteen months prior to the accident
- Names and addresses of all persons responsible for implementing and supervising vehicle maintenance and repair
- Names and addresses of all drivers who operated the van
- Record of Richard Hart's driving schedule one month prior to the accident
- Dispatch logs for one month prior to the accident through the date of the accident
- Records of road hours put in by all drivers eighteen months prior to accident
- Names and addresses of all drivers employed within the last eighteen months prior to accident
- The existence of any internal or external communications pertinent to the previous items

Breach Was Substantial Cause of Injury

- Possible expert witness to testify at trial denying that any defect caused or contributed to the accident (depending on applicable disclosure rule)
- Possible expert witness to testify at trial that no defect existed at the time of the accident (depending on applicable disclosure rule)

The previous lists are by no means exhaustive, but illustrate the type of brainstorming process helpful in developing goal-related questions.

(f) Consult form or "canned" interrogatories as a reference. Although determining your own specific objectives will lead to better-focused and more useful interrogatories, the form interrogatories can act as reminders of goals or specific objectives that you may have missed. Form interrogatories are often available in the firm's form files or in the case folder of a similar case. The advantage to the latter is that the answers to the questions are available and can tell the drafter if the questions were too easily avoided or otherwise unproductive.

Form interrogatories may also be found in the law library, on the Internet, in books written specifically on interrogatories and arranged by topic, or in various litigation practice manuals and form books, which are in electronic form as well. Remember, however, that form interrogatories are good sources for ideas but not so good for the final product. Form interrogatories that will meet the drafter's specific needs are rare.

(g) Once you have set out the goals and specific related objectives, organize them by topic. One approach is to use the elements of the action and defenses as topics. Another is to follow the paragraphs in the pleading. No one method is best. Each law firm or each case may require a different approach. The following list contains frequently used topics in particular types of actions:

Contract
- Identification of parties, addresses, background
- Events leading up to breach of contract
- Details of the breach
- Events following the breach
- Communications between parties
- Documents relating to breach, location, and other evidence
- Defenses raised
- Damages
- Basis for calculation of damages
- Witnesses/statements
- Elements, information, documents, and so on related to counterclaim

Personal Injury Case
- Identification of parties, addresses, background
- Jurisdictional matters (for example, determination of diversity of citizenship)
- Duty of care
- Breach of duty
- Damages/basis for calculation
- Breach as substantial cause of damages
- Defenses
- Documents and related information
- Witnesses/statements
- Elements, information, documents, and so on related to counterclaim

Products Liability
- Parties, addresses, place of business, and so on
- Product's purchase and use
- Advertising, warranties, representations, operator's manual, posted cautions, and so on
- Events leading to injury
- History of product/similar incidents and claims
- Product testing and related reports

- Details of injuries or damages (emotional, mental, and physical)
- Basis for calculations of damages
- Witnesses/statements
- Documents
- Defenses

Based on these three types of cases, one might construct a list of common categories:

- Parties, addresses, background, and so on
- Events leading up to injury or incident
- Injury
- Damages
- Basis for damages
- Witnesses/statements
- Related documents
- Defenses
- Elements, information, documents, and so on related to counterclaim

Regardless of the topics suggested here, usually other topics or subtopics are unique to the case and require special attention.

(h) For e-interrogatories and ESI, determine what information you need on the opponent party's computer system. This is necessary for locating the relevant stored ESI and exchanging it in a form that you and your attorney can use. Here are some ideas on what to request:

- Kind of network used and its configuration
- Operating system used
- Details on machines (hardware) used
- Applications (software) used, including any that are custom-made
- Backup system used
- When backup media is overwritten
- System's administrator (other key technicians)
- Whether home computers are used for business
- Whether laptops, notebooks, cellphones, pagers, or other digital devices are used for business
- Whether any digital copier is connected to network
- Any remote access
- E-mail application used
- Firewall application used
- Any e-mail server
- Internet network provider
- Where e-mail is stored
- Any user and administrator manuals not commercially available
- Any archive of obsolete or returned e-files
- Key personnel, managers, executives, supervisors using computers

Along the personnel issue, when drafting interrogatories addressing ESI, consider including in your requests, either in a direct interrogatory or through the definition section, information seeking the ownership of electronic devices, such as smartphones,

COPE—company owned personally enabled devices
Electronic device issued by employer and used exclusively for work purposes only.

BYOD—bring-your-own-device
Personal electronic device used for work purposes.

laptop computers, and tablets. Who owns electronic devices and how they are used has become a critical issue in the discovery process. Some companies or firms issue electronic devices, known as **COPE—company owned personally enabled devices**—while others permit employees to use their own personal devices, known as **BYOD—bring-your-own-device**. Both can be discoverable and should be on your radar screen.

BYOD permits employees to bring their own devices for use in the workplace. Usually these devices are programmed by the IT departments to segregate work information from personal information in a secure manner. This allows employees to receive e-mails, texts, and other work-related information in the secure area. COPE devices are issued by the employer and are the sole property of the employer. Personal use is usually not permitted with these devices. What is important from the discovery standpoint is that electronic devices, whether personal or company issued, may be subject to discovery requests if it can be shown that company work was performed on the device and such information may be relevant and discoverable.

Interrogatories may be a valuable discovery device, but they are not without pitfalls. Interrogatories should not be used to cover an area exhaustively; their primary function is to get background information, determine the existence and location of evidence, and elicit leads to other evidence. Determining the detailed content of the evidence is best left to other discovery devices such as depositions and document production. Using interrogatories exhaustively will likely elicit valid objections for length, scope, and harassment, and achieve unsatisfactory results. The practice will also engage the parties in a costly and inefficient paper war.

DRAFTING INTERROGATORIES

Review Rules and Examples

Although most jurisdictions have similar rules on the style and format for interrogatories, consult the local rules and acquire examples of interrogatories used in that particular jurisdiction. They will serve as important guides to drafting. Also consult state and federal annotated versions of the rules of procedure, such as the United States Code Annotated®, to obtain judicial rulings on the form, limits, scope, and successful objections to interrogatories and other discovery devices.

Introductory Paragraphs

After the case caption, an introductory paragraph should be drafted. Formats vary, but generally state to whom the interrogatories are directed, that an answer is required within a specified period of time, and the appropriate state or federal rule. For example, see Exhibit 7.6.

INTERNET EXERCISE

Search the Internet for your state's rules regarding interrogatories. Determine the (1) rule number, (2) limitations on number permitted by each party, (3) time period to respond to interrogatories, and (4) format required.

EXHIBIT 7.6 Introductory Paragraph

Plaintiff hereby requests defendants to answer under oath, pursuant to Rule 33 of the Federal Rules of Civil Procedure, the following interrogatories within thirty days of the date service is made upon you.

The introductory paragraph addressed to a corporation or other company might appear as in Exhibit 7.7.

EXHIBIT 7.7 Introductory Paragraph for a Corporation

To _____, Defendant:

The Plaintiff, pursuant to Rule 33 of the Federal Rules of Civil Procedure, requests that the following interrogatories be answered under oath by any of your officers competent to testify in your behalf who know the facts about which inquiry is made, and that the answers be served on plaintiff within thirty days from the time these interrogatories are served on you.

Adapted from West's Federal Form, § 3512, v. 3A, with permission of West Group.

Definitions and Abbreviations

The interrogatories should be preceded by a section on definitions and abbreviations to provide clarity and make it unnecessary to define terms repeatedly throughout the questions. Definitions also reduce the number of questions and subquestions needed. For example, if "identity" has been defined in the case of a document to include type, date, author, recipients, and other matters, specific questions addressing each of those points are avoided. An example of such a section appears in Exhibit 7.8.

EXHIBIT 7.8 Definitions

I. Definitions

1. As used herein, the words "document" or "documents" include any written, printed, typed [electronically stored], or graphic matter of any kind or nature however produced or reproduced, now in the possession, custody, or control of a defendant, or in the possession, custody, or control of the present or former officers, agents, representatives, employees of a defendant or any and all persons acting in its or his/her behalf, including documents at any time in the possession, custody, or control of such individuals or entities, or known by the defendants to exist.

2. As used herein, the words "identify," "identity," or "identification" when used in reference to a natural person mean to state his or her full name and present or last known address, and his or her present or last known position and business affiliation; when used in reference to a document mean to state its date, its author, the type of document (e.g., letter, memorandum, telegram, chart, photograph, sound reproduction, etc.), or, if the above information is not available, some other means of identifying it, and its present location and the name of each of its present custodians. If any such document was but is no longer in your possession or subject to your control, or in existence, state whether it (a) is missing or lost, (b) has been destroyed, (c) has been transferred voluntarily or involuntarily to others, or (d) is otherwise disposed of, and in each instance, explain the circumstance surrounding and authorization for such disposition thereof and state the date or approximate date thereof.

EXHIBIT 7.8 Definitions (*continued*)

3. The words "you" and "your" mean the defendants, their present or former members, officers, agents, employees, and all other persons acting or purporting to act on their behalf, including all present or former members, officers, agents, employees, and all other persons exercising or purporting to exercise discretion, making policy, and making decisions.

(Include any abbreviations or acronyms [ABA for example] if appropriate.)

Adapted from West's Federal Form, § 3513.10, with permission of West Group.

DEFINING ESI-RELATED TERMS

With the number of interrogatories limited, and possibly even more limited with future amendments to the rules of civil procedure, utilizing the definition section to streamline or lessen the number of questions is a smart approach. Include in your definition section the term "computer." This definition should encompass virtually any type of electronic device so that the response will provide the information that is necessary to understand the opponent's computer system, and provide information for follow-up discovery in the form of depositions or document productions or any other relevant information which will assist in leading to relevant and discoverable electronically stored information, ESI. An example of the definition of computer may be "smartphones, laptops, any mobile device, iPads, desktop PCs, tablets, any digital recording device, and any electronic device that may be part of a network either at home or business." This definition is not all-inclusive but provides guidance as to what could be considered in the definition.

Similarly, defining ESI will assist in identifying the type and extent of information that needs to be produced. Definitions vary and include a myriad of information. Review law firm form interrogatories for potential definitions, Internet examples, or forms—either electronic or book—to locate the best definitions of ESI for your situation.

As part of the process, be sure your interrogatories—either in the definition section or through the interrogatory itself—include that hidden data known as metadata. Metadata is data that describes the inner data within the computer. It is the data on the data. For example, metadata may contain information on when a document was created and edited, who created the document, and what people accessed the document, when, and how often. Metadata also can be retrieved from e-mail systems. Virtually anything that could be known about the origin of an e-mail can be discovered through its metadata. Defining the electronic-related terms in your definition is critical in gaining the type of information desired in discovery.

Instructions

The inclusion of a section of instructions has become increasingly common, especially in more complex cases and when local rules do not proscribe the desired

APPLY YOUR KNOWLEDGE

Using the Internet or, if access is available, a law firm's form banks or court cases, locate five examples of a definition section for Request for Interrogatories. Compare the definition sections and note the differences and similarities from the examples.

EXHIBIT 7.9 Instructions

II. Instructions

1. To the extent that information sought by any Interrogatory can be furnished by reference to the Answer furnished to another Interrogatory, appropriate reference will be acceptable to the plaintiff. However, a separate answer should be accorded to each Interrogatory, and Interrogatories should not be joined together and accorded a common answer.
2. Each Answer should be preceded by identification and verbatim quote of the Interrogatory to which the Answer regards.
3. If any Interrogatory is objected to by you as inquiring into privileged matter, set forth fully in the objection the facts which form the basis for your objection.
4. If any document, report, study, memorandum, or other written material is withheld or not identified under claim of privilege, furnish a list identifying each such document for which the privilege is claimed, together with the following information: date, author, sender, recipient persons to whom copies were furnished, together with their job titles, subject matter of the document, the basis on which the asserted privilege is claimed, and the paragraph or paragraphs of these Interrogatories to which the document responds.
5. (Add others as needed.)

Adapted from West's Federal Form, § 3513.10, with permission of West Group.

procedure. These instructions provide the opposition with some guidance and allow the questioner to shape the form of the answers. An example is shown in Exhibit 7.9.

Another typical instruction reads: Divulge in your Answer all pertinent information in your possession, or in possession of the corporation, or your attorney's agents, investigators, employees, or other representatives.

If you are requesting production of electronically stored information, an instruction on the form in which you want the information produced is important. For example, you might encourage that e-stored information be produced on CD or DVD. If so, include a detailed instruction requiring that each CD or DVD contain an index that identifies each document or item and its assigned identification (Bates stamp) number; describes its content; references the specific interrogatory to which it responds; states the format it is in; lists a detailed physical or electronic location of the original document; states, if not the exact original, what subsequent generation it is; requires that it should be in its metadata format; identifies the pertinent application and version of creation; and, if created in proprietary metadata format, requires that a copy of the software and user manual be included. Included in this request should be the file format of the document. Common formats are PDF (Portable Document Format) and TIFF (Tagged Image File Format). Depending on the system used, the proponent of the interrogatories may request that any electronically produced documents be in a certain format. This is an area that should be discussed with the IT department to determine the file format for production of any electronic documents.

Questions: The Body of the Interrogatories

GENERAL BACKGROUND. One or more questions on the general background of the person or corporation being questioned frequently follow the introductory paragraph. For example:

What is your:	What is:
full name	the full name of the corporation
age	the date and place of incorporation
current address	the corporation's principal place of business
marital status	the type of corporation
employment address	
employment position	
education	

When the number of interrogatories is limited, it may be best to define the term "background" or "identity" to include all of the details set out in the preceding lists. Then only one question needs to be asked. "What is your background?" or "Identify your corporation."

PLEADINGS. Good interrogatories elicit information based, in part, on the most recent pleading of the opponent. Since the pleading states factual allegations to show that the elements of the cause of action exist or are denied or state a defense, the opponent has the right to discover the underlying basis of the alleged facts: the who, what, when, where, why, and how (the five Ws and an H) of the factual allegations. Therefore, the pleading in question should be reviewed carefully and interrogatories should be drafted to acquire information on each allegation. For example, assume the complaint alleges the following in paragraph 3:

> Defendant operated vehicle in a negligent manner by failing to keep a proper lookout and by operating said vehicle at an excessive rate of speed.

The defendant should draw upon the five Ws and an H to formulate questions to elicit information that is clear and complete. For example:

> Regarding paragraph 3 of Plaintiff's Complaint, describe and explain all the specific facts on which you rely to support your contention that the defendant failed to keep a proper lookout.
> Regarding paragraph 3 of Plaintiff's Complaint, describe and explain all the specific facts on which you rely to support your contention that the defendant "operated vehicle at an excessive rate of speed."

On the other hand, the plaintiff should draft questions to elicit information that forms the basis for the defendant's answer. For example, assume defendant's answer to paragraph 3 was "Denied," an appropriate interrogatory would be:

> Regarding paragraph 3 of Defendant's Answer, describe and explain all the specific facts on which you rely to support your denial of the allegation that defendant failed to keep a proper lookout.

In another paragraph of the complaint, assume that the following allegation is made:

> As a consequence of Defendant's negligence, Plaintiff has incurred numerous expenses for doctor bills, hospital bills, nursing care, and medications to the sum of $17,000.

In a section on damages in the interrogatories, the defendant might request the following information:

> In regard to paragraph 8 of Plaintiff's Complaint, identify each doctor, hospital, source of nursing care, and medication and all records related thereto to support the allegation that Plaintiff incurred expenses "to the sum of $17,000."

BASIC AREAS OF THE CASE. The next section of the interrogatories goes beyond the pleadings and focuses on areas not yet addressed by the questions on the pleadings. Use the ideas generated in the brainstorming process to mold questions for this section. Recall the ideas and areas for inquiry implicating Mercury Parcel in the negligence apart from the negligence of Mr. Hart. The ideas generated in the planning stage might take the following form in the drafting stage. Some of the ideas generated under duty of care were: laws or regulations imposing standards of care such as a mandatory program for maintenance and vehicle and driver safety, records that must be kept to prove compliance with legal requirements, the names of those responsible for recording and storing these records, and the existence of a company policy on maintenance or a regular maintenance program/records indicating such.

Interrogatories based on these points should then be drafted:

1. Identify any corporate or department policies or mandatory programs regarding:
    a. Regular maintenance of your delivery vehicles
    b. Repair of your delivery vehicles
    c. Driver safety (including training, required breaks, limits to operating hours, vehicle safety checks, precautions on ice, speed, etc.)
    d. The maintaining of records on a.–c.
2. Identify all types of records kept by your company on a.–c. in interrogatory no. 1.
3. Identify all records and communications (both oral and written) on a.–c. in interrogatory no. 1 specifically pertaining to Mr. Hart and the van operated by Mr. Hart that was involved in the accident of February 26, _____.

Because "identify" has previously been defined, it is not necessary to repeat all the requests associated with the term "identify." Following this method, you should be able to continue drafting pertinent questions to cover all the necessary points for each element of the cause of action.

It is also appropriate in many jurisdictions to ask questions about insurance coverage (company, coverage, limits), the existence of physical things (evidence), persons with knowledge of the facts, witnesses and exhibits to be relied on or "may" be relied on, and the identity of persons who helped prepare the interrogatories or acted as consultants. Keep in mind that the information needed depends on whether initial disclosure is required.

OPINIONS AND LEGAL AND FACTUAL CONTENTIONS. Rule 33(c) and parallel state rules permit questions calling for "an opinion or contention that relates to fact or the application of law to fact." The information gained in the answer to such a question reveals the opponent's position on a key point of possible contention and calls for the opponent to reveal the facts and other evidence relied on to support the contention. If the answer to an interrogatory reveals the matter is not contended, or the opponent is without evidence to support the contention, the area could be a productive one for the party seeking the answer. An example of such a question appears as follows:

> Do you contend that Defendant Hart was not operating the van at an excessive rate of speed at the time of the accident? If so, what are the facts and the evidentiary basis relied on to support the contention?

This type of question is often reserved until the end of the discovery period to gain maximum information and avoid responses like "not sure yet," or "investigation still continuing," or "not available at this time." This type of question can be more effective than a request for admission because it calls for the basis of the contention.

ELECTRONICALLY STORED INFORMATION. As previously stated, to ignore e-discovery today is likely to be serious malpractice and invoke costly sanctions. Involving an information technology expert is helpful, if not essential, to avoid oversights and the loss of data. See Exhibit 7.10 for an example of interrogatories needed for e-discovery.

EXHIBIT 7.10 Sample Interrogatories for Electronic Discovery

UNITED STATES DISTRICT COURT
DISTRICT OF [Jurisdiction]

Court File No.:

_____,

Plaintiff,

INTERROGATORIES TO [Party Name]

v.

_____,

Defendant.

I. Definition. The definitions below will apply to the interrogatories requested in this document.

   A. *Application* An application is a collection of one or more related software programs that enable a user to enter, store, view, modify, or extract information from files or databases. The term is commonly used in place of "program," or "software." Applications may include word processors, Internet browsing tools, and spreadsheets.

   B. *Backup* To create a copy of data as a precaution against the loss or damage of the original data. Most users back up some of their files, and many computer networks utilize automatic backup software to make regular copies of some or all of the data on the network. Some backup systems use digital audio tape (DAT) as a storage medium. Backup Data is information that is not presently in use by an organization and is routinely stored separately upon portable media, to free up space and permit data recovery in the event of disaster.

   C. *Deleted Data* Deleted data is data that, in the past, existed on the computer as live data and which has been deleted by the computer system or end-user activity. Deleted data remains on storage media in whole or in part until it is overwritten by ongoing usage or "wiped" with a software program specifically designed to remove deleted data. Even after the data itself has been wiped, directory entries, pointers, or other metadata relating to the deleted data may remain on the computer.

   D. *Document* Fed.R.Civ.P. 34(a) defines a document as "including writings, drawings, graphs, charts, photographs, phonorecords, and other data compilations." In the electronic discovery world, a document also refers to a collection of pages representing an electronic file. E-mails, attachments, databases, word documents, spreadsheets, and graphic files are all examples of electronic documents.

(continued)

EXHIBIT 7.10 Sample Interrogatories for Electronic Discovery (*continued*)

E. *Hard Drive* The primary storage unit on PCs, consisting of one or more magnetic or solid-state media platters on which digital data can be written and erased.

F. *Mirror Image* Used in computer forensic investigations and some electronic discovery investigations, a mirror image is a bit-by-bit copy of a computer hard drive that ensures the operating system is not altered during the forensic examination.

G. *Network* A group of computers or devices that is connected together for the exchange of data and sharing of resources.

H. *Operating System (OS)* The software that the rest of the software depends on to make the computer functional. On most PCs this is Windows or the Macintosh OS. Unix and Linux are other operating systems often found in scientific and technical environments.

I. *Spoliation* Spoliation is the destruction of records which may be relevant to ongoing or anticipated litigation, government investigations, or audits. Courts differ in their interpretation of the level of intent required before sanctions may be warranted.

J. *Software* Coded instructions (programs) that make a computer do useful work.

II. Documents and Data.

A. *Individuals/Organizations Responsible* Identify and attach copies of all company organizational and policy information including:

1. Organizational charts;
2. A list of the names, titles, contact information, and job description/duties for all individuals (or organizations) responsible for maintaining electronic process systems, networks, servers, and data security measures; and
3. A list of the names, titles, contact information, and job description/duties for all individuals employed in the following departments (or their equivalents) for [Plaintiffs/Defendants/Third Party]:

   (a) Information Technology;
   (b) Information Services;
   (c) Incident Response Teams;
   (d) Data Recovery Units; and
   (e) Computer Forensic or Audit/Investigation Teams.

B. *Relevant Products/Services* Identify and attach copies of all documents related to (including marketing, selling, leasing, sharing, or giving to another party) the computer system, programs, software, hardware, materials, tools or information that [Plaintiffs/Defendants/Third Party] uses or has used in relation to the sale or use of [Product/Service]. This includes all electronic data and necessary instructions for accessing such data relating to:

1. The pricing of [Product/Service] in the United States and internationally;
2. Customer invoices for [Product/Service], including the customer names/addresses, purchase volume, prices, discounts, transportation changes, and production information;
3. E-mail sent or received by [Plaintiffs/Defendants/Third Party] to customers relating to [Product/Service];
4. Accounting records relating to [Product/Service], including work-in-progress reports, billing records, vendor invoices, time and material records, and cost completion reports for each of [Plaintiffs/Defendants/Third Party] customers;
5. Construction and development information relating to Web pages offering sale of [Product/Service] to the public;
6. Internal reports, sales reports, customer backlog reports, supplier backlog reports, and operation reports related to [Product/Service];
7. Financial reporting information on a monthly and annual basis including profit and loss statements, branch costs, contribution margins, and corporate overhead relating to [Product/Service];
8. Budgeting, projection, and forecasting information relating to [Product/Service]; and

EXHIBIT 7.10 Sample Interrogatories for Electronic Discovery (*continued*)

    9. Sales booked, gross profit dollars and percentage for the sales booked, net sales shipped, and gross and net profit dollars and percentages for [Product/Service].

C. *Networks* As to each computer network, identify the following:

    1. Brand and version number of the network operating system currently or previously in use (include dates of all upgrades);

    2. Quantity and configuration of all network servers and workstations;

    3. Person(s) (past and present, including dates) responsible for the ongoing operations, maintenance, expansion, archiving, and upkeep of the network; and

    4. Brand name and version number of all applications and other software residing on each network in use, including but not limited to electronic mail and applications.

D. *Hardware* Identify and describe each computer that has been, or is currently, in use by [Plaintiffs/Defendants/Third Party] (including desktop computers, PDAs, portable, laptop and notebook computers, cell phones, etc.), including but not limited to the following:

    1. Computer type, brand, and model number;

    2. Computers that have been re-formatted, had the operating system reinstalled or been overwritten, and identify the date of each event;

    3. The current location of each computer identified in your response to this interrogatory;

    4. The brand and version of all software, including operating system, private and custom-developed applications, commercial applications, and shareware for each computer identified;

    5. The communications and connectivity for each computer, including but not limited to terminal-to-mainframe emulation, data download and/or upload capability to mainframe, and computer-to-computer connections via network, modem, and/or direct connection; and

    6. All computers that have been used to store, receive, or generate data related to the subject matter of this litigation.

E. *Software* Identify and describe all software programs that have been, or are currently, in use by [Plaintiffs/Defendants/Third Party] including, but not limited to, the following:

    1. Titles;

    2. Version Names and Numbers;

    3. Manufacturers;

    4. Authors and contact information; and

    5. Operating systems that the programs were installed on.

F. *Operating Systems* Identify and describe all operating systems that have been, or are currently, in use by [Plaintiffs/Defendants/Third Party] including, but not limited to, operating systems installed during [time period] for the following individuals:

    1. [Name & Job Title]

G. *E-mail* Identify all e-mail systems in use, including but not limited to the following:

    1. All e-mail software and versions presently and previously used by you and the dates of use;

    2. All hardware that has been used or is currently in use as a server for the e-mail system including its name;

    3. The specific type of hardware that was used as terminals into the e-mail system (including home PCs, laptops, desktops, cell phones, personal digital assistants, etc.) and its current location;

    4. The number of users there has been on each e-mail system (delineate between past and current users);

    5. Whether the e-mail is encrypted in any way and list passwords for all users;

    6. All users known to you who have generated e-mail related to the subject matter of this litigation; and

(continued)

EXHIBIT 7.10 Sample Interrogatories for Electronic Discovery (*continued*)

7. All e-mail known to you (including creation date, recipient(s), and sender(s)) that relate to, reference, or are relevant to the subject matter of this litigation.

H. *Internet Use* Identify any Internet policies and procedures in use, including but not limited to the following:

1. Any Internet Service Providers (ISPs) that [Plaintiffs/Defendants/Third Party] has provided its employees and the method used to access the Internet;
2. The names and titles for all individuals who had Internet access;
3. Any Internet hardware or software documentation that is used to provide Internet access to the above individuals during [time period];
4. Internet use/access manuals, policies and procedures, including limitations on Internet access and use; and
5. All Internet-related data on the electronic processing systems used by [Plaintiffs/Defendants/Third Party] including but not limited to saved Web pages, lists of Web sites, URL addresses, Web browser software and settings, bookmarks, favorites, history lists, caches, and cookies.

I. *Other Electronic Data* Identify any other electronic data in use, including but not limited to the following:

1. Activity log files contained on [Plaintiffs/Defendants/Third Party] network and any equipment needed to access the log files;
2. Manual and automatic records of hardware and equipment use and maintenance;
3. The names of Internet newsgroups or chat groups that [Plaintiffs/Defendants/Third Party] subscribe(s) to; include the name and title of the individuals subscribing to each group as well as any information necessary to access the groups, including passwords; and
4. Any portable devices that are not connected to [Plaintiffs/Defendants/Third Party] network and that are not backed up or archived.

J. *Data Transmission* Describe in detail all inter-connectivity between the computer system at [opposing party] in [office location] and the computer system at [opposing party #2] in [office location #2] including a description of the following:

1. All possible ways in which electronic data is shared between locations;
2. The method of transmission;
3. The type(s) of data transferred;
4. The names and contact information of all individuals possessing the capability for such transfer, including list and names of authorized outside users of [opposing party's] electronic mail system; and
5. The name and contact information of the individual responsible for supervising inter-connectivity.

K. *Data Security Measures* List all user identification numbers and passwords necessary for accessing the electronic processing systems or software applications requested in this document. During the course of this litigation, you must supplement all security measures with updated information, if applicable. Include:

1. Computer security policies;
2. The name(s) and contact information of the individual(s) responsible for supervising security; and
3. Information about each application's security settings, noting specifically who has administrative rights.

L. *Supporting Information* All codebooks, keys, data dictionaries, diagrams, handbooks, manuals, or other documents used to interpret or read the information on any of the electronic media listed above.

III. Backup Protocols.

A. *Current Procedures* As to data backups performed on all computer systems currently or previously in use, identify and describe the following:

1. All procedures and devices used to back up the software and the data including, but not limited to, name(s) of backup software used, the frequency of the backup process, and type of tape backup drives, including name

EXHIBIT 7.10 Sample Interrogatories for Electronic Discovery (*continued*)

and version number, type of media (i.e. DLT, 4mm, 8mm, AIT). State the capacity (bytes) and total amount of information (gigabytes) stored on each tape;

2. The tape or backup rotation, explaining how backup data is maintained, and stating whether the backups are full or incremental (attach a copy of all rotation schedules);

3. Whether backup storage media is kept off-site or on-site. Include the location of such backup and a description of the process for archiving and retrieving on-site media;

4. The name(s) and contact information for the individual(s) who conduct(s) the backup and the individual who supervises this process;

5. A detailed list of all backup sets, regardless of the magnetic media on which they reside, showing current location, custodian, date of backup, a description of backup content, and a full inventory of all archives;

6. All extra-routine backups applicable for any servers identified in response to these Interrogatories, such as quarterly archival backup, yearly backup, etc., and the current location of any such backups; and

7. Any users who had backup systems in their PCs, and the nature of the backup.

B. *Backup Tapes* Identify and describe all backup tapes in your possession including:

1. Types and number of tapes in your possession (such as DLT, AIT, Mammoth, 4mm, 8mm);

2. Capacity (bytes) and total amount of information (gigabytes) stored on each tape; and

3. All tapes that have been re-initialized or overwritten since commencement of this litigation, and the date of said occurrence.

IV. Spoliation of Electronic Evidence.

A. *Document Retention and Destruction Policies* Identify and attach any and all versions of document/data retention or destruction policies used by [opposing party] and identify documents or classes of documents that were subject to scheduled destruction.

1. Attach copies of document destruction inventories/logs/schedules containing documents relevant to this action.

2. Attach a copy of any disaster recovery plan.

3. Also state:

(a) The date the policy was implemented;

(b) The date, if any, of the suspension of this policy in toto or any aspect of said policy in response to this litigation;

(c) A description by topic, creation date, user, or bytes of any and all data that has been deleted or in any way destroyed after the commencement of this litigation. State whether the deletion or destruction of any data pursuant to said data retention policy occurred through automation or by user action; and

(d) Whether any company-wide instruction regarding the suspension of the data retention/destruction policy occurred after or related to the commencement of this litigation. If so, identify the individual responsible for enforcing the suspension.

B. *Document Destruction* Identify any data that has been deleted, physically destroyed, discarded, damaged (physically or logically), or overwritten, whether pursuant to a document retention or destruction policy or otherwise, since the commencement of this litigation. Specifically identify those documents that relate to or reference the subject matter of the above referenced litigation.

C. *Organizations or Individuals Responsible for Maintaining the Document Retention and Destruction Policies* List the job title, description, business address, telephone number, and e-mail address of any individuals or organizations that are/were responsible for creating, implementing, or retaining any and all versions of your document retention or destruction policies.

D. *Meetings or Documents Discussing Document/Data Destruction* Identify with specificity any meetings or conversations referencing document spoliation in relation to this action:

1. Identify and attach any and all related meeting minutes/notes from [time period here];

(continued)

EXHIBIT 7.10 Sample Interrogatories for Electronic Discovery (*continued*)

    2. List the job title, description, business address, telephone number, and e-mail address of any individuals or organizations that are/were responsible for retaining the meeting minutes/notes.

E. *Data Wiping* For any server, workstation, laptop, or home operating system that has been "wiped clean," defragmented, or reformatted such that you claim that the information on the hard drive is permanently destroyed, identify the following:

    1. The date on which each drive was wiped, reformatted, or defragmented;

    2. The method or program used (i.e., WipeDisk, WipeFile, BurnIt, Data Eraser, etc.).

F. *Data Recycling* Identify the person(s) responsible for maintaining any schedule of redeployment or circulation of existing equipment and describe the system or process for redeployment.

Source: Reprinted with permission of Kroll Ontrack, Inc., http://www.krollontrack.com.

CONCLUDING OR SUMMARY INTERROGATORIES. Consider adding one or more general interrogatories to cover any oversights and prevent the opponent from later using evidence at trial that should have been elicited in the interrogatories. For example:

> Do you have any additional information relevant to the subject of this lawsuit not set out in your previous answers? If so, please state that information.

Be mindful of the fact that this summary style interrogatory may prompt objection as overly broad or even vague. As the number of permitted interrogatories diminishes, including this type of question may give way to other questions that elicit more substantive information.

DRAFTING TECHNIQUES

The following list provides some specific pointers for drafting well-written interrogatories:

- Test the appropriateness of the question by asking whether the information requested will lead to evidence that is admissible. There is no restriction that the information requested be admissible, only that it be reasonably calculated to lead to admissible evidence.

- Draft the question as concisely and precisely as possible. Keep it simple and easy to understand. If you do, the answer will be more to the point.

- Avoid an excessive number of questions.

- Number the questions sequentially with extra sets starting where the last set left off.

- Use the following techniques when the number of interrogatories is severely limited:

    1. Avoid numbering or lettering sublistings.

    2. Do not make your subtopics conspicuous; avoid "and," "or," "the," semi-colons, and colons. For example, do not write, "Please state the names, addresses, and phone numbers of the defendant's employers for each job

held by the defendant during 1980, 1981, 1982, 1983, 1984, and to the present." Write, "Please identify all the defendant's employers beginning with 1980."

3. Reduce lengthy phrases to a single word or class. For example, instead of asking the defendant to "list all repairs to the wheels, brakes, engine, exterior, hood, etc.," ask the defendant to "list all repairs to the car."

4. Ask singular questions that require multiple answers rather than the other way around. For example, instead of saying, "State the name of the corporate president, vice president, and associate vice president," say, "Identify each corporate officer by name and office held."

5. Use multiple-choice questions if appropriate, unless you do not want to suggest the answer: "State whether the bonds in question are Series E bonds, Series F bonds, or Series Y bonds."

- Draft interrogatories in the correct verb tense. "Who had custody of the documents?" is a different question and may elicit quite a different answer than "Who has custody of the documents?" The careful drafter must be sure the correct question is being asked. If it is not, lost time and a permanently lost answer may be the consequence.

- Phrase questions to determine whether an answer is based on firsthand knowledge and whether impediments to accuracy exist. Since secondhand knowledge is less reliable and likely to be excluded as hearsay, for evidentiary reasons, the questions should be phrased to determine whether knowledge is first or secondhand. "Did you personally observe ice on the road?"

- Questions should also be devised to determine the ability of the party to observe the facts. "Was there anything obstructing or limiting your view of the pedestrian? If so, explain the nature of the obstruction or limiting factor, and how it affected your view of the pedestrian. Are you required to wear glasses with corrective lenses when you drive? Were you wearing your glasses at the time of the accident?"

- Keep in mind, however, that the deposition may be a better time to ask some of these questions because the answers will be more spontaneous. If answered in the interrogatories, the answer will be carefully planned and probably more self-serving than a deposition answer. The most appropriate discovery device for each type of question needs to be weighed carefully.

- Avoid questions that allow a yes or no answer unless you include a follow-up. Questions that permit the answering party to respond yes or no rarely provide much useful information. Normally such a question should be followed by others that require more detail or an explanation of the answer.

- Evaluate and proofread the questions. The purpose of an interrogatory is to force the opponent to relinquish information that you need. It should be drafted to restrict the answering party's ability to provide an uninformative though truthful answer. Evaluate each question drafted to see if it is sufficiently restricted by trying to see how the question could be evaded. If it leaves room for evasion, it requires redrafting. It is essential to go through this evaluation process prior to giving the interrogatories to the attorney for review. Further, proofread the interrogatories carefully to eliminate typos, misspellings, grammatical mistakes, and so on. Such mistakes, if left uncorrected, create a negative impression of your abilities and may result in confusion, unresponsive answers, and the time-consuming and embarrassing process of asking the opponent to stipulate to a correction.

Exhibit 7.11 contains sample interrogatories for an auto accident case. These interrogatories are drafted in the context of mandatory disclosure.

EXHIBIT 7.11 Sample Interrogatories to Defendant (Auto Accident)

State of _____

County of _____

Civil Court Branch

Dennis Diamond

        Plaintiff,

    v.   CIVIL ACTION NO._____

Janet McDonald

        Defendant,

INTERROGATORIES TO _____

Pursuant to section _____, _____ hereby submits the following interrogatories to _____ These interrogatories are to be answered by _____ under oath and served on the attorney for _____ within _____ days.

INSTRUCTIONS AND DEFINITIONS

A. Supplement your answers to these interrogatories as information is acquired by you, your agents, attorneys, or representatives.

B. Precede each answer with a verbatim restatement of the pertinent interrogatory.

C. Answer each question completely with all information possessed by you or your attorneys, investigators, agents, employees, and representatives.

D. The term "accident" as used here, means the incident that is the basis of this lawsuit, unless otherwise specified.

E. The term "identify" when applied to an individual ... [add other instructions and definitions as needed.]

F. [Consider adding request for opponent party to sign and return an attached HIPAA-compliant authorization form for release of protected information when applicable to case or counter-claim.]

INTERROGATORIES

1. State your full name, address, date of birth, marital status, and all former names or aliases.
2. Identify each person you consulted to provide information for your answers to these interrogatories.
3. State your occupation, wages, and dates of employment in reverse chronological order for the last ten years, identifying each respective employer beginning with the present.
4. State whether you were driving for your business, employer, or personal reasons at the time of the accident.
5. State in detail the purpose of your trip on the day of the accident, your complete itinerary with dates, times, locations, mileage covered between locations, passengers, purpose of stops, whom you saw, and what you did at each location.

EXHIBIT 7.11 Sample Interrogatories to Defendant (Auto Accident) (*continued*)

6. Identify all persons known to you or your attorneys possessing personal knowledge of the facts and circumstances of and surrounding the accident including any eyewitnesses, medical witnesses, and others, and describe the pertinent knowledge and likely testimony of each party.

7. Identify all persons or organizations, other than your attorneys, who investigated the cause and circumstances of this accident for you and/or your employer, and state whether a written report of such was submitted, and, if so, identify the current custodian of any such report.

8. Identify the make, model, year, registration number, license number, fleet number (if applicable), and owner of the vehicle you were operating at the time of the accident, and, if the owner is a person or entity other than you, state whether you had permission to operate the vehicle.

9. State whether you have made any oral or written statements regarding the accident, and identify the date of each statement, its substance, the person to whom the statement was given, and, if written or recorded, the current custodian of each statement.

10. State whether you, your attorneys, employer, insurance carrier, or anyone acting on your or their behalf obtained written or recorded statements from any person regarding the accident, and, if so, identify each person giving a statement, the date of each statement, its substance, the person to whom the statement was given, and the current custodian of the statement.

11. State whether you, your attorney, employer, insurance carrier, or anyone acting on your or their behalf have or know of any photographs, videos, motion pictures, maps, drawings, diagrams, measurements, surveys, or other depictions regarding the accident, the scene of the accident, and the persons and vehicles involved, and, if so, state what each item purports to depict and identify the person who created the item and the current custodian of the item.

12. State the facts of the accident specifying speed, position, directions, condition, and location of each vehicle and any pertinent light, traffic, weather, road, visibility, mechanical defects, or other conditions.

13. Describe in detail all evasive steps taken by you to avoid the accident.

14. State whether you contend that plaintiff's or any other person's actions or omissions caused or contributed to the accident, and state the facts that support each contention.

15. State whether you consumed any alcoholic beverages, drugs, or medications within the twenty-four hours preceding the accident, the nature of the substance, where obtained, when consumed, and in what amount, and identify any person having knowledge as to the consumption of each item.

16. Identify any physician whose care you were under at the time of the accident, the pertinent illness or condition, the nature of treatment, and prescribed medications.

17. State whether you had any physical, mental, emotional, or other disability, disease, impairment, limitation, or restriction at the time of the accident, and identify any pertinent physician or health care professional who diagnosed each such condition.

18. State whether you had a valid driver's license, including any specialized driver's license, permit, or certifications, at the time of the accident, and list the issuing state, expiration date, license or permit number, and any restrictions on the license or permit and the nature of the restrictions.

19. State whether your driver's license has ever been revoked or suspended, and, if so, provide full details.

20. Identify all insurance policies covering the vehicle you were operating at the time of the accident, the insurance company, policy owner, policy number, coverage type, amount of coverage (including upper and lower limits), and the effective dates of coverage.

21. List all prior motor vehicle accidents in which you were involved, whether persons and/or property were involved, the name of the other driver or property owner, the accident's location, date, time, and outcome of the matter.

22. List violations of all motor vehicle or traffic laws or ordinances with which you have been charged in the State of _____ or in any other jurisdiction.

(continued)

EXHIBIT 7.11 Sample Interrogatories to Defendant (Auto Accident) (*continued*)

23. State whether you have been convicted of any crime other than a traffic offense, and state the nature of the offense, the date, county, and state or federal court, and any sentence received.
24. State whether the plaintiff had any conversation with you after the accident, and, if so, state the substance of the conversation and identify any persons present during that conversation.
25. State whether at the time of the accident you had any eye condition that impaired your vision or required corrective lenses and, if so, state the nature of the impairment, your visual rating, the date and results of your last eye exam, whether you were wearing corrective lenses at the time of the accident, and identify your eye doctor or other person who prescribed treatment or the corrective lenses.

CONCLUDING MATERIAL, FINAL PREPARATION, AND SERVICE OF INTERROGATORIES

The opponent should be advised of the continuing obligation to supplement the answers to the interrogatories. This notice can be given in the instructions or as a reminder at the end of the interrogatories. Here is an example:

> Please note that you have a continuing obligation to supplement your answers to these interrogatories as information is acquired by you, your agents, attorneys, or representatives.

After the attorney has reviewed the interrogatories, make all final corrections. Make sure that copies are prepared for each defendant, the court (if needed), and the client's file.

The interrogatories should end with a signature line for the attorney and the address of the firm or office. Prior to service, obtain the attorney's signature. Some firms enter interrogatories onto CD-ROM, using software compatible with that used by the opponent. The opponent receives the disk, copies the interrogatories, enters answers, and returns a completed CD, saving time and paper. E-mail and e-mail with attachments are the most efficient ways to deliver such information. Check local court rules and consult your supervising attorney, however, before using electronic delivery of discovery devices.

Effect service pursuant to Rule 5 of the Federal Rules and parallel state rules that permit service by mail or in person to the opponent's attorney. Execute the certificate of service, sometimes called proof of service or certificate of mailing. Although many courts require the filing of interrogatories or other discovery documents, the federal courts prohibit it. If filing is not required, place the original interrogatories and the certificate of service in the file. This is important to preserve the record should a discovery dispute arise later. If filing is required, file the original interrogatories and the certificate of service with the clerk. Check to see if e-filing is permitted in any applicable state court. An example of the certificate of service appears in Exhibit 7.12.

Exhibit 7.13 is a checklist for planning and drafting interrogatories.

EXHIBIT 7.12 Certificate of Service

CERTIFICATE OF SERVICE

A copy of Plaintiff's First Set of Interrogatories was served on Defendant Mercury Parcel Service, Incorporated's attorney, Lynn Ott, located at 518 S. Maple Street, Cincinnati, Ohio, by U.S. Mail this 21st day of November, _____.

_____

Arthur White
Attorney for Plaintiff
(address)

EXHIBIT 7.13 Checklist for Planning and Drafting Interrogatories

☐ Planning the Interrogatories
   o Have the attorney's directions for the task firmly in mind.
   o Review the file, especially the pleadings, and all related information discovered to date.
   o Review the elements of the claim, defense, counterclaim, and so on.
   o Determine the goals to be accomplished.
     ■ Review the pleadings for areas needing more detail or explanation.
     ■ Brainstorm on each element of the claim, defense, counterclaim, and so on, to develop useful theories of liability and areas of inquiry.
     ■ Determine what must be discovered (witnesses, documents, physical evidence, etc.) and the likely leads to it.
     ■ Assess the initial need for and scope of interrogatories on the opponent's electronic information storage system.
   o Acquire and read form interrogatories for suggested areas of inquiry, format, and questions.
   o Organize areas of inquiry by logical topics.
   o Avoid pitfalls.
     ■ Do not try to cover entire areas exhaustively if other methods of discovery are available and better lend themselves to the specific objective.
     ■ Keep brief to avoid setting off a paper war.
     ■ Avoid forcing the other side to prepare their case.
☐ Drafting the Interrogatories
   o Acquire the civil practice rules for interrogatories and locate samples of interrogatories in the jurisdiction for the particular case.
   o Draft an introductory paragraph stating to whom the interrogatories are directed, applicable rules, and time required for a reply.
   o Provide a definition and abbreviation section.
   o Provide an instruction section so the answer and any objections will be placed in a format most useful to the questioner.
   o Draft questions that focus on finding out more about the basis for the allegations in the opponent's pleadings.
   o Draft questions that cover the theories of liability and defenses thereto as they relate to the elements of the offense.
   o Draft questions calling for opinion and legal and factual contentions [Rule 33(b)].
   o Draft questions covering the e-storage system and the information stored.
   o Draft concluding or summary interrogatories.
   o Include notice of continuing obligation to update answers.
   o Provide for attorney's signature and certificate of service.

(continued)

EXHIBIT 7.13 Checklist for Planning and Drafting Interrogatories (*continued*)

☐ Specific Drafting Techniques
  ○ Ask whether the question elicits information that is likely to lead to admissible evidence.
  ○ Keep questions concise, precise, and easy to understand.
  ○ Avoid excessive questions.
  ○ Number questions and sets of questions sequentially.
  ○ If the number of interrogatories is limited:
    ■ Do not number or letter subdivisions.
    ■ Avoid making subtopics conspicuous: avoid "and," "or," "the," semicolons, and colons.
    ■ Reduce lists to a single word or class.
    ■ Ask singular questions that require multiple answers.
    ■ Use multiple-choice questions where appropriate.
  ○ Use correct verb tense.
  ○ Phrase questions to determine if answers are based on firsthand knowledge and if impediments to accuracy exist.
  ○ Avoid questions that permit yes or no answers unless more detail is requested.
  ○ Phrase questions to restrict evasiveness in the answer.
  ○ Proofread carefully prior to submitting to attorney for review.

☐ Final Preparation and Service of Interrogatories
  ○ Make all final corrections.
  ○ Get attorney's signature.
  ○ Prepare copies for each opponent and the court, if the court requires filing.
  ○ Serve copies on the opposing attorney by mail or in person.
  ○ Execute the certificate of service and file it and the original interrogatories with the court clerk.

ANSWERING INTERROGATORIES

NOTE DEADLINE, REVIEW CASE FILE

Ms. White comes to you and says, "Here are the interrogatories in the Forrester case. Please begin preparing answers to these questions. We have 30 days to respond. Let me know if you need any help." First calendar the deadline. Rule 33(b) (3) requires answers to be served in 30 days unless otherwise ordered by the court or agreed to by the parties. State rules vary. Failure to answer on time waives any objections to the questions, except questions that are grossly improper or call for privileged information or an expert's opinion [*Bohlin v. Brass Rail, Inc.*, 20 F.R.D. 224 (S.D.N.Y. 1957)]. An enlargement of the time limit for responding may be needed. If so, consult Rule 6(b) or parallel state rules. In some jurisdictions a stipulation between parties to enlarge the time is adequate. In other jurisdictions, a court order is required.

Become thoroughly familiar with the facts and all the evidence and sources of evidence that might be called on in answering the interrogatories. This will make answering easier and give you confidence that the facts and evidence support the answers.

REVIEW POSSIBLE OBJECTIONS

Before reading the interrogatories, have firmly in mind what kinds of objections can be raised to any particular question. Then read through the interrogatories and note

APPLY YOUR KNOWLEDGE

Research your states rules for requesting additional time to respond to interrogatories. What are the steps that must be taken to extend the time to respond to the interrogatories in your jurisdiction? Based on your research, prepare the document following your state's court rules to request additional time to respond to a set of interrogatories.

questions believed to be objectionable. These common types of objections are based on the definition of what is discoverable found in Rule 26(b)(1) and limitations stated in 26(b)(2):

Irrelevant: A question is objectionable if its ultimate aim is to elicit evidence information that is not relevant to the issues in the case.

Privileged: A question that calls for information protected by the attorney-client, husband-wife, and like privileges is objectionable.

Work product (trial preparation materials): If a question calls for the mental impressions, conclusions, legal theories, and like matters related to the attorney's preparation for trial, it need not be answered. Objectionable questions typically ask for the names of witnesses that will be called at trial and for the names and opinions of experts who are hired as consultants and not as trial witnesses. The work product objection, however, is often invoked too broadly and abused.

Vague, ambiguous, and unintelligible: Occasionally a question is so unspecific or worded so unclearly that it requires the answering party to guess at the meaning of the question. Such a question is objectionable. This objection may also apply to the instructions.

Too broad: A question can be so inclusive that its limits are excessive. For example, a question calling for the names of all the documents gathered over the last 20 years pertaining to the incident in question is so sweeping in its coverage that it is overly burdensome, while also calling for irrelevant material. Questions requesting information covering an unduly lengthy time span are objectionable. The scope of the question must be reasonable.

Unduly burdensome: Paragraph (c) of Rule 26 allows a party to seek a protective order from unduly burdensome or expensive discovery requests. It is a valid objection to a particular interrogatory or an entire set of interrogatories. If a question or set of questions requires a response that is excessively detailed, costly, time-consuming, or embarrassing relative to the opponent's need for the requested information, then the question or set of questions is objectionable.

Questions can also be too numerous, call for previously disclosed information (unreasonably cumulative or duplicative), be premature or too late, call for a scientific opinion from a lay person, call for purely legal conclusions, or for information that is just as easily obtainable by the other side. The last point is especially true if the information is not in the answering party's custody or is in the public domain. Requesting the attachment of documents or other evidence is objectionable if a request for production of documents and things (Rule 34) has not been submitted; therefore, interrogatories are often submitted with a Rule 34 production request.

Some common objections that are *not valid* are that the information is already known by the opponent; the question calls for inadmissible evidence (it may); the question seeks an admission (it may); the information is better obtained at deposition (so what!); the question seeks factual opinions, conclusions, and legal contentions (it may); and it is not the business of the questioning party.

There are some strategic concerns to have in mind. Although the decision to object is the realm of the attorney, keep in mind that it is sometimes better to answer an objectionable question than to have to request the court for a protective order, especially

EXHIBIT 7.14 Summary of Common Objections

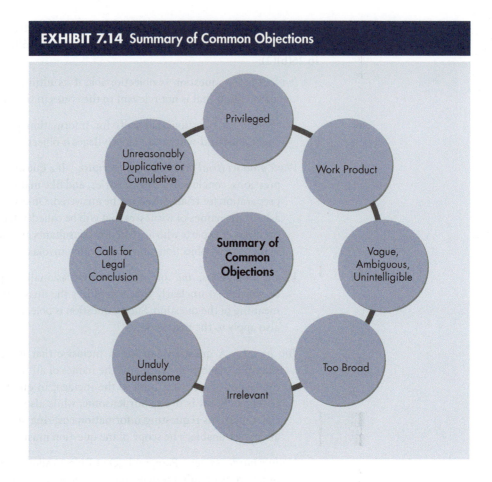

if the information to be revealed does not hurt the answering party or might improve their case in the eyes of the opponent. See Exhibit 7.14.

REVIEW QUESTIONS

Copy the interrogatories so your working notes can be written or electronically entered on the copy. Read each definition, instruction, and question thoroughly, noting any observations. These observations might include questions, ideas on where to gather information, possible objections, or a note that an objectionable question might be answered without harm to the case. Make sure the instructions are consistent with the applicable rules of discovery and do not ask for more than the opponent is entitled to know.

Before attempting to answer the questions, confer with the attorney to discuss the questions and your notes. As each question is approached, note any comments, suggestions, or possible sources of information from the attorney.

GATHER AND RECORD INFORMATION

Interrogatories are directed to a party (the client), and that party has the duty to respond. The client and the client's agents, representatives, investigators, information technology staff, and attorney will provide much of the information needed to answer the interrogatories. It is well-accepted practice for the attorney to take this information and, with your help, mold it into the answers for the client. The client should become involved as early as possible in the interrogatory process. Before contacting the client, however, review the file and note what information you already have. That way you will not ask the client to do unnecessary work. Copy each question as a separate page and send the questions to the client with a cover letter and instructions. Some firms will ask the client to answer the questions and return them to the firm, as requested in the letter in Exhibit 7.15. Other offices prefer to have the client come in to go over each question and possible answer. Check with your supervising attorney to see which procedure is preferred. Make sure your client understands the process, and do what you can to reduce the client's anxiety over what may be unfamiliar ground.

Prepare a working copy of each question and its comments on a separate page. Organize the pages so that all information gathered can be kept in order with the appropriate question. This method prevents loss and simplifies the task of drafting answers to the questions.

The primary source of information must be the party requested to answer the interrogatories. In the case of a corporation or agency, it must be those officers or employees, either individually or collectively, who have the knowledge to answer the questions. Generally, a party (including a corporation) is not responsible for investigating information or records beyond that party's possession or control. In theory, such information is equally obtainable for the opponent and is, therefore, not the responding party's duty to provide.

If you have become familiar with the case, it should not be difficult to determine where the information will come from. Some of the techniques discussed in Chapter 3 on investigation might be drawn on to answer interrogatories properly. Do not overlook your client's electronically stored information.

When gathering information, keep in mind that the answer should be based on thorough investigation; it does not, however, require the searching of every possible nook and cranny. Also, the questions require a reasonable interpretation, not an irrational or hypertechnical one.

REVIEW TECHNIQUES FOR ANSWERING INTERROGATORIES

- Answer each interrogatory separately and fully in writing under oath.
- Precede each answer with a restatement of the applicable question. This technique is called *engrossing* the question.
- State the reason for any objection and answer any part of the question that is not objectionable.
- Write the answer clearly and concisely. Avoid confusing answers that lead the opponent to the answers of several previous questions or to answers in other documents (depositions) incorporated by reference.
- Draft objections by stating with particularity the nature of the objection and its basis, which may be done in the interrogatory or separately.

EXHIBIT 7.15 Letter to Client on Answering Interrogatories

WHITE, WILSON & McDUFF
ATTORNEYS AT LAW
FEDERAL PLAZA BUILDING, SUITE 700
THIRD AND MARKET STREETS
LEGALVILLE, COLUMBIA 00000
(111) 555-0000

November 1, _____

Mrs. Ann Forrester
1533 Capitol Drive
Legalville, Columbia 00000

Dear Mrs. Forrester:

I have enclosed a set of questions called "interrogatories" submitted by the attorney for Mercury Parcel Service. The rules of the court require your full cooperation in answering each of the questions. We are permitted to assist you. Our office has the information to answer questions 1, 2, 8, 9, and 10. We need information from you to draft answers to 3, 4, 5, 6, 7, and 11.

We must have the information and your answers no later than November 15. Failure to return the answers when they are due may be harmful to your case. On receipt of this information and your answers, we will integrate them into our draft and return the answers for your review and verification before a notary public. Should it be necessary to have you come to the office to discuss your answers, we will inform you.

Please begin gathering all the documents and other information needed to answer the questions identified above. When writing answers to the questions, keep the following in mind:

1. Answer all questions completely but concisely.
2. Always be truthful.
3. Do not try to withhold information or be evasive. For example, if asked about witnesses (and you know of three), name all three; or, if you are asked about prior injuries, lawsuits, or criminal convictions, state them with identifying dates, times, location, etc. Any evasiveness is a serious matter and can definitely affect the outcome of the case.
4. Look up all dates, amounts, times, and other information requested.
5. You are not required to make an unreasonable search or incur unreasonable expense. If you do not have access to the information, you are not required to provide it. State any reasons for not answering a question.

After answering the questions, return them in the enclosed envelope.

Thank you for your assistance. If you have questions, please let me know.

Sincerely,

Terry Salyer
Paralegal
White, Wilson & McDuff

Here is an example of how an objection would appear in the answer to an interrogatory:

> Defendant objects to this interrogatory because it requests information that is irrelevant and cannot reasonably lead to evidence that is admissible on any issue in this action.

- Answer ethically with accurate and complete information; do not be evasive or deceptive. If an interrogatory asks for the name and location of a person, it would not be adequate to state only his first name and "I do not remember where he lives."

- Disclose as little harmful information as possible, but not by deliberate concealment or unreasonable interpretation of the question.

- Place the client in the best possible light without distorting or misrepresenting the facts.

- Consider using the alternative option to produce business records found in Rule 33(d), which places the burden on the opposing party to search or audit your client's records. In such cases one need only identify the documents available, which should not be done, however, if other information sensitive or harmful to the client will be revealed.

- Review your office's or your own interrogatory answer bank for previous answers to parallel questions, especially for routine interrogatories. Regularly expanding and consulting such a bank of boilerplate responses can save time if used prudently. Computerizing the answer bank permits rapid copying and pasting.

- Use the following techniques for answers you are unable to complete or are unsure of:

  Indicate that supplements will follow.
  State "on information or belief" or "based on secondhand information."
  State according to person Y or records in office X.
  Indicate that you do not know the answer but received information that

  _____.

- Consider attaching as an exhibit a document or business record inquired about if to do so will be helpful and if it is subject to document production under Rule 34 or parallel state rule. (See Chapter 9 for guidelines on producing documents and electronic information.)

DRAFT ANSWERS AND HAVE THEM REVIEWED, SIGNED, AND SERVED

Draft the answers, incorporating the information gathered for each question. The attorney should then review the answers. Once prepared in final form, the person answering the interrogatories (usually the client, or in the case of a corporation, a representative of the corporation) must carefully review each answer for accuracy and sign the document under oath, usually in the presence of a **notary public**. If objections have been made, the attorney must sign as well. Attach any necessary exhibits. Prepare a certificate of service and effect service according to Rule 5, or as dictated by state rules.

UPDATE ANSWERS

In most jurisdictions, the answering party has a continuing obligation to supplement or amend responses to questions as additional information or inaccuracies in the answers previously submitted are discovered. A good way to do this is to simply

notary public
Individual who is authorized to administer oaths and attest or certify signatures for their authenticity.

replace the out-of-date page of the former answer with a revised one. The new page should restate the question accompanied by the complete new answer.

Exhibit 7.16 is an example of a defendant's answer to a plaintiff's first set of interrogatories submitted under Rule 33.

EXHIBIT 7.16 Answer to Interrogatories

[Case Caption]
DEFENDANT UNITY DELIVERY SERVICES, INC.'S ANSWERS TO PLAINTIFF'S
FIRST SET OF INTERROGATORIES
INTRODUCTION

A. The enclosed responses are intended for and restricted to use in this case only.
B. No enclosed answer should be taken as an admission to the existence of any facts for purposes of trial.
C. *[Others]*

ANSWERS

INTERROGATORY NO. 1
Identify the physician(s) who conducted the company's annually required physical exams of Donald Jordan (defendant driver) and the dates of the last two exams.

ANSWER
Walter P. Hayes, M.D., 1644 W. Endover Ave., South Town, Columbia 11000, phone: (500) 000-0000. Exams were held on June 15, _____ and April 28, _____.

INTERROGATORY NO. 2
State Rodney Robert's (your disclosure material, page 3) qualifications at the time he worked on the van in question, and the dates, hours, and nature of the work performed, and identify any records and documents not previously disclosed that record what was done on the van, including any of Mr. Robert's comments and assessments concerning repairs made or that should be made.

ANSWER
Mr. Roberts worked on the van in question on September 2, _____, for 2.2 hours. He was an apprentice mechanic at that time, having been employed at that job for seven months. He had previous vocational training at Warton County Tech. On September 2, Mr. Roberts gave the van a forty-point safety inspection, changed the oil, and replaced the air filter. A parts department form 3510 reflects any parts ordered by a mechanic for a vehicle. The daily work order form was disclosed previously.

INTERROGATORY NO. 3
What company correspondence exists for the three-year period immediately preceding the accident regarding your policies or proposed notices on driver health and safety?

ANSWER (OBJECTION)
Defendant corporation objects to interrogatory 3 because it is too broad in scope, the burden or expense of the proposed discovery outweighs its likely benefits, and it covers material that is protected by defendant corporation's attorney-client privilege.

INTERROGATORY NO. 4
State defendant driver Donald Jordan's traffic record for the last five years.

EXHIBIT 7.16 Answer to Interrogatories (*continued*)

ANSWER/OBJECTION

To defendant corporation's knowledge, Mr. Jordan has no violations in the last five years, but objects to interrogatory no. 4 insofar as it requests information that is in the custody of the Columbia Division of Motor Vehicles and is as easily obtainable by plaintiff as it is by defendant.

INTERROGATORY NO. 5

State the number of vans of the same make and model as the van in question purchased by your company in the last three years.

ANSWER (OBJECTION)

Defendant corporation objects to interrogatory no. 5 because the information requested is irrelevant to issues in this action and is not likely to lead to the discovery of admissible evidence.

INTERROGATORY NO. 6

State each fact on which you rely to support your allegation in paragraphs 3 and 4 of your counterclaim that plaintiff assumed the risk of injury and caused the accident in question.

ANSWER

1) Plaintiff was intoxicated at the time of the accident and 2) plaintiff entered the road and thumbed her nose not only at defendant driver, but also at the driver of a vehicle that passed seconds earlier.

Date _____   _____

                          Barbara J. Lane, CEO
                          Unity Delivery Service, Inc.

Date _____   _____

                          Lincoln Case, Attorney
                          789 Courthouse Square
                          Legalville, Columbia 00000
                          Phone: (111) 111-1111

ANALYZING THE ANSWER AND COMPELLING A RESPONSE

When the opponent's answers to interrogatories are received, promptly read each answer, carefully noting the opponent's objections and any deficits in completeness, responsiveness, or clarity. Prompt review of e-discovery information is particularly important in the event the information cannot be accessed or searched as contemplated. Inform the attorney of each objection and defect. If the attorney believes some clarification or other action is needed, the following options are available:

1. The attorney will handle the matter at this point.

2. You will be directed to contact the opponent's attorney or paralegal and request more information, possibly offering an extension of time. This action should

be followed by a confirming letter identifying the incomplete answer, acknowledging the extension of time granted, and stating that the time for a Motion to Compel Further Answers will be assumed tolled until the opponent files a corrected response or does not make a correction within the allotted time.

3. You will draft a motion to compel [Rule 37] and have it filed and served. Certification that a good faith effort was made to resolve the matter with the other party is required in federal and many state courts.

MOTIONS TO COMPEL

The federal discovery rules and those in most states are designed to encourage cooperation in the mutual discovery process with a minimum of court involvement. Despite the emphasis on cooperation, the court must sometimes become involved. When one of the parties refuses to respond or cooperate in disclosure or a request for discovery, the other party can invoke the power of the court to compel that party to produce the information or give valid reasons for not doing so.

A party may seek the aid of the court when the other party does not provide the required disclosure or answer questions in interrogatories or a deposition (discussed in Chapter 9), when a corporation or other entity fails to designate the person who will provide the required interrogatory or deposition answers, when a party does not permit the inspection of documents (discussed in Chapter 9), or when a party provides an evasive or incomplete answer [Rule 37(a)(2) and (3)].

Motions to compel discovery are common vehicles used by litigants when responses to discovery, such as interrogatories, appear to be insufficient, evasive or nonresponsive. These motions will be discussed in more detail in Chapter 9. However, the issue of motions to compel relating to interrogatories was front and center in *McNearney v. Washington Department of Corrections*, 2012 U.S. Dist. LEXIS 108386 (W.D. Wash. August 2, 1012). In that case a prisoner sued prison officials for failure to provide proper medical care for an orthopedic problem presumably suffered by the inmate.

CASE STUDY: UNDERSTANDING THE LAW

Jill McNearney was incarcerated. She claimed in a civil rights action that she had orthopedic issues but the Washington Department of Corrections refused to provide her with medical care. After she filed suit, McNearney filed interrogatories. The interrogatories at issue involved requests for documentation and information on McNearney's medical and mental health issues, and an interrogatory involving ESI and the steps the Corrections Department took to respond to a document request and its steps in locating ESI. The Department objected to the interrogatories stating that they were overbroad,

burdensome, irrelevant, and noted other general objections as well.

The court reviewed McNearney's request and the Department's responses. As stated in the court opinion, McNearney's counsel attempted on numerous occasions to gain compliance by the Department. They promised information and promised to supplement, but never adequately responded to the interrogatories. McNearney's counsel even warned defense counsel of their intention to file the motion to compel. In its discussion of the law, the court agreed with McNearney that the Department failed to act in good faith in their response to the

CASE STUDY: UNDERSTANDING THE LAW (*continued*)

interrogatories and produce the requested information as required by the rules of civil procedure. The Department failed to produce e-mails and other electronic information related to the interrogatory requests after repeated attempts to garner the Department's compliance. The Department did not dispute its conduct. Finding that the Department did not adequately respond to the interrogatories in dispute, the court ordered the Department to pay attorney's fees as a sanction. Therefore, the court granted the motion to compel.

Questions for Review: Read the *McNearney* case. What actions by the Department caused the court to find noncompliance with the request for interrogatories? What defenses did the Department raise to the motion to compel? Why did the court find the Department's responses inadequate? Was the court's conclusion justified? Support your response.

SUMMARY

Your work often focuses on the stage of litigation called discovery—the formal process of investigation that invokes the cooperation of all parties in producing and exchanging information so that facts can be determined, evidence revealed, and issues narrowed before the matter goes to trial.

The discovery process continues to evolve in federal and state courts. Federal Rule 26(a) makes mandatory an initial disclosure process for all parties. Mandatory disclosure, and similar state provisions, requires each party to disclose information about parties, witnesses, records, experts, and other information early in the lawsuit and without court order.

The scope of discovery encompasses any matter, not privileged, that is relevant to the claim or defense of any party, including any information appearing to be reasonably calculated to lead to admissible evidence [FED. R. EVID. 26(b), as amended]. Information relevant to the subject matter of the action, a broader category of discovery, is discoverable by court order only. Pay special attention to any differences in the scope of discovery in your state rules.

Only those discovery requests that are unreasonable, unduly burdensome, unnecessary, or seek privileged information or protected work product information may be excluded. Cooperation and honesty in discovery are important ethical requirements.

The tools employed for discovery vary depending on the magnitude of the case and the financial strength of the client. The available tools include interrogatories; depositions; requests to produce and inspect documents, land, and other things; requests for physical and mental examination; request for admission; and use of the Freedom of Information Act. You must be adept at employing and responding to each of these tools to gain the maximum benefit for your client within the scope, limits, and ethical standards applied to discovery. Discovery is an area quite suitable for the talents of the paralegal. When exercised knowledgeably, these discovery talents are extremely valuable to the law firm, the client, and you.

One of the areas that paralegals are particularly valuable is in the e-discovery process. E-discovery permits review of the electronically stored data, known as ESI, in a case. Virtually anything in electronic form may be requested in the discovery process. Preservation of electronic data is important when litigation is anticipated or has commenced. Litigation preservation letters are a common form used to alert clients regarding the duty to preserve electronic information that may be discoverable in a case. Failure to preserve electronic data may result in sanctions by a court. The Federal Rules of Civil Procedure set forth the process and procedures for discovery and as a paralegal familiarity with those rules is critical.

KEY TERMS

bring-your-own-device (BYOD)

clawback agreement

company owned personally enabled device (COPE)

disclosure

discovery

electronically stored information (ESI)

electronic discovery or e-discovery

interrogatories

metadata

non-waiver agreement

notary public

preservation letter

Quick Peek agreement

sanctions

trustee

QUESTIONS FOR STUDY AND REVIEW

1. Define the term *discovery* and describe its purposes in the context of litigation practice.

2. List and define the seven discovery devices set out in the Federal Rules of Civil Procedure.

3. What is the function of a preservation letter? What are its benefits? What makes a good preservation letter?

4. In general, what kinds of information must be provided under the federal disclosure rule and under your state rule? How does your state rule differ from the federal rule?

5. When must mandatory disclosure occur? What must occur before an opposing party can depose an expert under this rule?

6. What must be disclosed under initial disclosure? "Pretrial" disclosure? When must objections to the disclosure of any item occur?

7. What is the scope of discovery as defined by Federal Rule 26(b) and parallel state rules? Has your state adopted the Federal Rules of discovery? If so, cite the statute or rule numbers.

8. What reason is permitted for not producing some requested electronically sorted information under Fed. R. Civ. P. 26(b)(2)(b)?

9. What are the important ethical rules that apply to discovery? What is their significance?

10. What are interrogatories, and their purpose and advantages? What federal and state rules govern interrogatories? What is the limit on the number of interrogatories for federal and your state practice?

11. What are the basic procedures that must be followed when utilizing interrogatories? What are the specific steps in planning a set of interrogatories?

12. What kinds of information lend themselves to exploration through interrogatories?

13. What are the typical divisions of and types of questions that make up a set of interrogatories? Explain their usefulness.

14. What are the basic reasons discovery requests are objectionable under Rule 26(b)(1)? Explain each objection.

15. What are the steps to be followed in preparing answers to interrogatories?

SYSTEMS FOLDER ASSIGNMENTS

1. In both the ethics and discovery sections of your systems folder, place your own restatement of the ethical principles covered in this chapter, and cite the pertinent ethical rules.

2. Place page references or copies of the following items in their respective sections of your systems folder. Add any suggestions from your instructor. Enter citations to the pertinent federal rules and your state rules on disclosure.

   • Preservation Letter

   • Form for Reporting Parties' Planning Meeting

   • Paralegal's Disclosure Checklist

   • Sample Interrogatories in E-Discovery Cases

   • Sample Interrogatories to Defendant (Auto Accident)

3. Verify the deadlines for interrogatory practice by checking the Pleadings, Motions, and Time Limits table in Chapter 6 or in your systems folder. Add the time limits from your state rules. Place citations to the pertinent federal and state rules in your systems folder, including the number of interrogatories permitted by both federal and your state rules.

4. Create a form letter to the client from the letter in Exhibit 7.15 and place it in your systems folder.

5. Drawing from the interrogatory section of the chapter and any information added in class, draft a checklist for answering interrogatories and place it in your systems folder. The checklist should cover the basic steps and techniques for preparing, drafting, serving, and updating interrogatories.

APPLICATION ASSIGNMENTS

1. Drawing from the discussion on the scope and limitation of disclosure and discovery plus the pertinent rules of evidence discussed in Chapter 3, indicate whether the following would be discoverable in the *Ann Forrester* case. If an item would be discoverable only on a showing of undue hardship, indicate that as well. The first item is completed for you as an example. D = discoverable, ND = not discoverable, R = reason not discoverable, E = exceptional circumstances, H = undue hardship.

   ANSWER:

ITEM	D	ND	R	E	H
1. Photo of accident scene taken by plaintiff's attorney		☑	work product		
2. Defendant Hart's driving schedule for day of accident and previous week					
3. Mercury Parcel's maintenance schedules on van					
4. Hart's statement to his attorney					
5. Forrester's medical bills					
6. Identification and opinion of plaintiff's trial expert on auto defects					

7. Statement Hart made to Mr. Forrester in plaintiff's possession

8. Defense attorney's diagram of accident (not for trial exhibit)

9. Forrester's alleged confession to her priest that she felt responsible for accident

10. Plaintiff's request for a second copy of Hart's driving schedule

11. Statement of Forrester tape recorded by her attorney's paralegal

12. Letters between attorneys for defendants discussing strategy

2. Assume that a complaint was filed and served on the defendant in the *Forrester* case on Friday, March 29, or on another date supplied by your instructor. Using the Disclosure Time Frame Summary (Federal), determine the last possible date for the following:

   a. The court scheduling conference

   b. Parties' planning meeting

   c. Report to court on parties' planning meeting

   d. Disclosure from party joined on Tuesday, August 6

   e. Objections to disclosure

   f. Objections to any pretrial disclosure, assuming the trial date has been set for Monday, December 9

3. Assume that you are the paralegal whose firm is representing Carl Ameche in Case II, the campground fire case. Draft answers to several of the questions in the sample set of interrogatories (Exhibit 7.11). Also practice objections and how to respond when unsure of your information in your answers. Alternatively, answer your own interrogatories for practice and to evaluate the quality of your interrogatories. Use the requirements set out in the preceding paragraphs.

4. Go to the law library, Westlaw, LEXIS, or an Internet-based Web site and find at least five federal or state court decisions that found specific kinds of discovery requests not discoverable. List these and return to class ready to report the cases and the types of requests that were denied by the court.

5. Assume that you are a paralegal for a firm representing Make Tracks, Inc., Case III. In the discovery stage, your attorney asks you to draft as many questions as you can because she wants to "paper the plaintiff to death." She also directs you to answer the plaintiff's questions as narrowly as possible, and respond that requested safety test reports have been temporarily misplaced, even though you saw them in the file yesterday. What specific ethical concerns arise and what rules of professional conduct apply?

CASE ASSIGNMENTS

1. (A) Drawing from the material in this chapter on planning and drafting interrogatories (including the checklist in Exhibit 7.13) and using the form interrogatories as a guide, draft a set of carefully planned interrogatories on behalf of Mrs. Forrester to Mercury Parcel Service. For the purposes of this assignment, confine your drafting to the following:

    a. Caption and instructions

    b. Questions on:

        1. Background information, employment, and agency of Hart

        2. Inadequate maintenance of van and possible defects

        3. Time standards for operation of vehicles by drivers, and Hart and Mercury Parcel's compliance prior to accident

    c. Concluding questions and directions

    d. Signature and certificate of service

    (B) To gain additional practice and confidence, reverse the situation and draft a set of interrogatories from Mercury Parcel to Mrs. Forrester. Confine your drafting to:

    a. Caption and instructions

    b. Questions on:

        1. Her background information (current employment information only)

        2. Her statements to others about the accident

        3. Her own possible negligence

    c. Concluding questions and directions

    d. Signature and certificate of service

2. Exchange the interrogatories you drafted in Assignment 1 above with a classmate, then draft answers to the classmate's interrogatories, using the checklist you developed. For practice, object to at least one question and explain the basis of the objection. Also assume you do not trust the accuracy of the information you have for the answer to one other question. You may have to create some information to answer the questions adequately.

8

DISCOVERY: DEPOSITIONS

OBJECTIVES

AFTER READING THIS CHAPTER, YOU WILL BE ABLE TO:

- Identify the different types of depositions
- Prepare and serve the notice of deposition
- Draft proposed deposition questions for the case
- Assist in preparing the client or witness for testifying at a deposition
- Develop and identify the best techniques for digesting depositions

DEPOSITIONS

INTRODUCTION

deposition

A discovery device permitting a party's attorney to question a witness or party spontaneously and under oath before trial, and to record the testimony.

deponent

A witness or party giving testimony under oath and recorded before trial.

Chapter 8 continues the discussion of discovery devices and related paralegal tasks. Its focus is deposition practice, including the important art of summarizing depositions. A **deposition** is a significant discovery device permitting a party's attorney to question a witness spontaneously (including parties) before trial. The witness, called a **deponent**, is under oath and generally must respond orally to the questions, much as a witness responds to questions at trial. The advantage of the deposition is its spontaneity; the disadvantage is its relatively high cost.

The deposition is a commonly used discovery device with many purposes. Depositions are used to discover information or lead to information based on the deponent's testimony and any accompanying physical evidence. They are used to find out more information about the opponent's case, to further explore points raised in the interrogatories and pleadings, and to evaluate the witness and the opposing attorney. Because the answers offered at the deposition may be used later in court, depositions have purposes related to their potential use at trial. Federal Rule of Civil Procedure 32 and parallel state rules allow depositions to be used to impeach the trial testimony of the deponent. If the deponent testifies at trial that the van was going 25 miles per hour, but said at the deposition that it was going 55 miles per hour, the earlier answer may be used to throw doubt on the reliability of the trial testimony. Likewise, if a party takes the stand at trial, the party's answers at the deposition may be used as an admission of key facts or for impeachment of the party [Rule 32(a)(2)]. Further, if a witness is unavailable for trial (dead or out of the country, for example), that witness's deposition may be offered into evidence at the trial as if the witness were present [Rule 32(a)(3)].

The well-prepared legal team also may use the deposition less as the broad information-gathering tool that it has been in the past and more as a sharply focused device to support the team's theory of the case. Such an approach is more likely to lead to an earlier resolution of the case, while reducing the opponent's opportunities to exploit unfocused and unsupportive deposition testimony at trial.

SCOPE AND LIMITS OF THE DEPOSITION

One real advantage of the deposition over interrogatories is that persons besides the parties may be deposed: bystanders, experts, document custodians, character witnesses, and the like. Rule 30(c) requires that the deposition, examination, and cross-examination be conducted in accordance with the Federal Rules of Evidence. In all other respects the scope is the same as that for other discovery devices.

A deposition may be taken without leave of court but not until the parties' planning meeting, unless otherwise ordered or agreed to by the parties. Leave of court is needed to depose an imprisoned person or if (absent a written stipulation of the parties) the limit of ten depositions per party is exceeded, the deponent has already been deposed, or a party seeks to take a deposition before the parties' planning meeting. An exception to the last condition allows the deposing party to certify in the notice of the deposition that the deponent is expected to leave the country and needs to be

INTERNET EXERCISE

Determine your jurisdiction's rule for taking deposition testimony. What are the requirements, and are they different from the Federal Rules of Civil Procedure? If so, identify the differences in the rules.

examined before then. To reduce costs and inconvenience, a deposition is limited to a seven-hour day (including any needed examination of documents by the deponent) unless otherwise authorized by the court or stipulation. Many state rules limit the length of a deposition or give the court power to do so. Additional time may be granted by the court, especially if the deponent impedes or delays the examination. Such impediments can lead to court sanctions. If at any time during a deposition a deponent believes the examination is being conducted in bad faith or to annoy, embarrass, or oppress the deponent or a party, the court, upon motion, may suspend the deposition and invoke sanctions under Rule 37(a)(4).

TYPES OF DEPOSITIONS

Three types of depositions are set out in the federal and parallel state statutes. They are depositions on oral examination, depositions on written questions, and depositions before the action is filed. The most commonly used of the three is the deposition on oral examination (Rule 30), and for that reason will constitute the primary basis for discussion in the following section.

Depositions on written questions are an underused device providing for direct questions from one party and cross questions from the opposing party to be read to the deponent who orally answers the questions in the presence of a person authorized to administer oaths. This relatively low-cost procedure is governed by Rule 31 and is used primarily to gain information on noncontroversial matters or on documents from a person *other than a party*. Depositions on written questions have been used as a method to gain information by pro se plaintiffs, especially in the prison setting. *Eggleston v. Mitchell*, 2013 U.S. Dist. LEXIS 135455, 2013 WL 5351053 (M.D. Pa 2013) is a recent case where the court evaluated the use of deposition upon written questions.

CASE STUDY: UNDERSTANDING THE LAW

The plaintiff, Prince Eggleston, filed a lawsuit against the Department of Corrections where he was incarcerated. Numerous motions were filed, including one to depose a number of witnesses from the Department on written questions. Under Rule 31 of the Rules of Civil Procedure, certain formalities must be completed before deposition upon written questions can proceed. The court noted in its opinion that before a request for deposition on written questions will be granted, the plaintiff must show how he intends to pay for the deposition witness fees, retain an officer to administer the oath, and serve subpoenas on the witnesses. Simply because he is *pro se* and indigent does not excuse him from following the procedures under the rules and paying relating costs in his civil lawsuit. Additionally, in the opinion, the court recognized how depositions upon written questions are not always the inexpensive method of discovery that

some, including the plaintiff, may think. And, as the court pointed out in following and citing a California opinion, the process is not a simple and straightforward one. The rules are specific and their requirements rigorous. In the case, the court permitted Eggleston to take the depositions upon written questions, but he had to shoulder the burdens of the expense and comply with the procedural rules. He was unable to meet these burdens, and ultimately his request for depositions upon written questions was denied.

Questions for Review: Examine *Eggleston*, specifically the section on depositions upon written questions. What procedures did the court set out for depositions upon written questions? What are the pitfalls of depositions upon written questions? Under what circumstances will a court pay for the expenses of an indigent party?

The third type of device is the taking of a deposition before the action and is governed by Rule 27. The purpose of this device is to preserve testimony that may be unavailable later. Such a situation might arise when a witness or party is gravely ill and may not be available to testify at the trial, or when a witness will be out of the country for a long time. In circumstances such as these, a person may, with court permission, take the deposition of a person before an action is filed. Rather strict requirements set out in Rule 27 must be met before the court will grant permission. If you are asked to assist the attorney on depositions of written questions or depositions before trial, check Rules 31 and 27 and parallel local rules for any limitations or special procedures that must be followed. See Exhibit 8.1 for a summary of the different types of depositions.

PROCEDURE

court reporter

Individual who records and transcribes verbatim testimony or court proceedings, such as depositions, by stenography.

The party conducting the deposition must set a time and place and arrange for a person authorized to administer oaths and able to record the testimony. Notice of the deposition is then sent to each party. The witness is subpoenaed by the court and must be present at the designated time and place. The other parties may also attend and ask questions. At the deposition the officer or **court reporter** swears in the witness, and the attorney requesting the deposition asks the witness questions. The opponent may cross-examine. All questions and answers are recorded by the officer, a court reporter, or other recording device. The record may be reviewed by the witness and certified as accurate.

If the deposition is conducted by written questions, the requesting party must serve the questions on every other party along with the notice of the deposition. The notice must identify the deponent and the officer, usually a court reporter. Within 14 days after service of the questions, a party may serve cross questions on all other parties. Questions in response to cross questions (redirect questions) must be served on all parties within the next seven days, and recross questions in seven days thereafter.

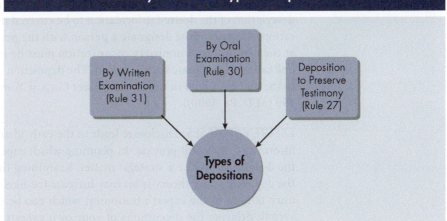

EXHIBIT 8.1 Summary of Different Types of Depositions

PRELIMINARY TASKS

Determine Whom to Depose

ORGANIZE INFORMATION TO IDENTIFY POTENTIAL DEPONENTS. The attorney decides who should be deposed, but a well-informed paralegal can be helpful in organizing the material needed to make that decision.

To identify potential deponents, extend the case analysis process discussed in Chapter 3 on investigation and in Chapter 7 on preparing for disclosure and interrogatories. Thoroughly review the facts of the case, the key elements, the pleadings, information gained through investigation, and especially the opponent's answer to any interrogatories.

After reviewing the information, organize it in a format favored by your supervising attorney. This could be a summary, outline, or chronology of the facts of the case. Important points to include are the parties and attorneys, the court, the issues in the case as indicated by the pleadings and any disclosure and discovery to this point, and the evidence and its source such as witnesses or documents pertinent to each issue. After the supervising attorney reviews this summary, it may help to have the attorney identify the theory of the case if not previously discussed.

Next, sift through the summary of the case for material that points to persons who can provide needed evidence as testimony or documents. From this information, prepare a list of potential deponents, describing each person's role in the case, what evidence they need to address, and what documents or other information pertains to the deponent or the deponent's testimony. Developing a list of potential deponents is a detailed process requiring thoroughness. Both the process and the result, however, can be interesting and exceptionally helpful.

Your understanding that the basis for deciding whom to depose is both practical and tactical is also helpful to the attorney who must decide if the expected information is worth the expense of the deposition. Little benefit is derived from deposing friendly witnesses or opposition witnesses who are very old or ill, or those who have previously provided a favorable statement.

DESIGNATED CORPORATE OR AGENCY DEPONENT. The difficulty of determining what person in a corporation or government agency is the best person to depose has been eliminated by Rule 30(b)(6) and parallel state rules. Upon proper notice to the corporation or agency, including a reasonably particularized description of the desired information to be covered in the deposition, the corporation or agency must designate a person with the pertinent knowledge to testify at the deposition. A nonparty organization must be informed by subpoena of its obligation to designate such a person. The deposition questions cannot be limited to the matters stated in the notice [*Cabot Corp. v. Yamulla Enterprises,* 194 F.R.D. 499 (M.D. Pa. 2000)].

EXPERT WITNESSES. Disclosure leads to the early identification of experts and the information they will provide. In planning which experts to depose, the timing of the deposition may be a strategic matter. Examining the opponent's experts before the opponent's case theory is set may increase the likelihood of inconsistencies and uncertainties in the expert's testimony, which can be exploited later at trial. Conversely, delaying the depositions of your own experts until your legal team's case theory is developed reduces the opposition's opportunities to exploit the deposition testimony at trial.

Conduct a Preliminary Interview

The list of persons to be deposed is narrowed by conducting preliminary interviews. Paralegals are frequently assigned this task. The purpose of the interview is to determine whether the person possesses information worth an expensive deposition. It might also reveal that the person is gravely ill or will soon be leaving the country, thus influencing the decision on whether to depose. The information gained can also help your attorney develop a case theory early in the process, which can better focus decisions regarding depositions and other discovery. Before conducting such an interview, obtain from the attorney a clear idea of what is needed from that particular witness. Then proceed in the manner described in Chapter 3 on investigation and interviewing, keeping in mind the ethical restrictions on making direct contact with a represented party. Occasionally a brief phone call may be all that is necessary to make the determination.

COORDINATE THE DEPOSITION: EASIER SAID THAN DONE

Arrange for Site and Necessary Components

TIME. Set up the time for the deposition after consulting the applicable rules and any Rule 16 scheduling order and getting your attorney's approval. Allow adequate time for any special preparation, as in the case of deposing an expert witness. Check with the attorney, the client (if attending), the parties, and possibly the person to be deposed to determine a mutually convenient date. Taking the time to coordinate the date may be time-consuming, but it will save rescheduling and paperwork in the future. Be sure to have the deposition calendared into the deadline system.

SITE. In most instances, the site for the deposition is a standard one often used by the firm: a conference room at the office, or if a more formal atmosphere is sought, a room at the courthouse. Occasionally a deposition must be taken in another jurisdiction. In such circumstances, a law firm in that area might permit use of a room, or a clerk of court in the foreign jurisdiction may be able to arrange for a room. If an overnight stay is required, a conference room at a hotel may be convenient. In determining the location for the deposition, remember that the plaintiff can be required to attend a deposition in the jurisdiction where the action was brought. Other persons must be deposed in the jurisdiction where they live and work or within 100 miles of where they live, work, or conduct business. Occasionally the deposition of a doctor is taken in the doctor's office. Regardless of the location, a suitable room should be reserved well in advance. Suitability may depend on atmosphere, adequate space, power outlets, and convenience to refreshments, meals, and rest rooms.

METHOD OF RECORDING. The party taking the deposition must arrange to have the deposition recorded and bears the cost of the recording. Depositions can be stenographically recorded (typed) or recorded by audio or videotape. The notice of the deposition must state the method to be used. At its own expense, another party can

TRADE SECRETS: PREPARING THE SITE AND FAULTY FURNITURE

Making sure that the venue where a deposition is to take place is safe seems like stating the obvious. But, a New Jersey law firm was sued by a male witness who fell off his chair while being deposed. Apparently, Thomas Hickey, the plaintiff, leaned back in the chair he was sitting in and fell on the floor. He claimed that the law firm was negligent in not checking the chair and its setting before the deposition. He claimed the chair was a safety hazard which the lawyer knew about. The trial court judge disagreed and granted a summary judgment in favor of the law firm; he appealed. The New Jersey appellate court agreed with the lower court and dismissed the appeal. According to the facts, the man had been sitting in the chair being questioned for approximately 90 minutes before falling off. The court stated in its opinion that having sat in the chair for that period of time was "sufficient time for him to learn the chair was designed to tilt and to appreciate its tension setting." *Hickey v. Wolff, Helies, Duggan, Spaeth &* *Lucas*, 2014 N.J. Super. Unpub. LEXIS 2656 (Appellate Div. N.J. November 5, 2014). Although this may seen amusing at first blush, it is a matter to be taken seriously. As a paralegal, make sure that the venue where a deposition is to be taken is clean and safe for all who will be present, including the legal professionals, court reporter, and witnesses. View and check the deposition site, especially if the site is away from the office. Broken furniture can be a hidden liability that could disrupt the deposition and produce unanticipated issues and problems. Of course, the paralegal or lawyers cannot guard against the unexpected, but, at least attempt to secure the venue and perform an inspection of the room where the deposition will be taken. Chairs may not be the only culprit to consider. Look for extension cords or any other obstructions in the room that may that may cause a dangerous condition. The objective is to focus on the subject of the deposition and not potential hazards at the venue.

employ an additional, alternative means of recording. Many law firms use stenographic recording for making objections, preparing deposition summaries, and for use at trial. Audio and videotape are more appealing to a jury when used at trial as compared to the dry reading of a typed deposition. Some vendors can synchronize the audio portion of a digital video recording with the typed deposition transcript. Then the use of split-screen technology allows a jury to see and hear the deponent while highlighted portions of the transcript appear simultaneously in the other window.

Videotaping a deposition provides the jury with the nearest thing to a real picture of a since-deceased individual, of a laboratory demonstration conducted by an expert witness, or testimony describing a thing or location inaccessible or inconvenient to the jury. Some disadvantages accompany the use of video, such as improper camera angles, bad or misleading lighting, and poor sound quality. Consequently, in arranging a video deposition or reviewing a stipulation for video recording, make sure that the camera is unobtrusive, the operator is well trained, the lighting and setting are fair, the audio is of high quality, and the camera angles are fair but sufficiently varied for interest. The camera operator should not totally exclude the examiner from view. Two cameras permit a split-screen image of the witness as the dominant view and the examiner as the smaller view. Some attorneys and paralegals use a computer-networked, stenographically recorded system. Such a system produces an immediate copy of the deposition on the attorney's or paralegal's computer screen and allows simultaneous highlighting and annotating. Several companies offer real-time Internet transcript services that permit, for example, a paralegal in New York to monitor a deposition in Seattle and provide immediate research and other assistance to the attorney conducting the deposition. There are limitations as to who can assist the deponent in a deposition and the extent of communications between the deponent and counsel. In *Wei Ngai v. Old Navy*, 2009 U.S. Dist. LEXIS 67117 (D. N.J. 2009), an attorney learned the hard way that texting to his client during a deposition is a recipe for sanctions from the court.

CASE STUDY: UNDERSTANDING THE LAW

Wei Ngai, a minor, suffered an eye injury from a clothing rack at an Old Navy store in New Jersey. The parties agreed to depose the General Liability Claims Manager for GAP through video conference. Counsel for the plaintiff and defendant were in Fort Lee, New Jersey. Another counsel for the defendant participated from Southfield, Michigan. The witness was in Sacramento, California. The plaintiffs claimed that during the deposition, the witness and defendant's counsel in Michigan were communicating surreptitiously by text. The plaintiffs alleged that during the deposition, the witness was only visible from the chest up and could not see her hands. Apparently, the Michigan attorney and the witness exchanged numerous texts before and five during the deposition. The Michigan attorney commented on the witness's performance by texting "you are doing fine." The plaintiff's attorney wanted the texts, but the Michigan attorney claimed attorney-client privilege. Soon thereafter, the Michigan counsel requested to withdraw from the case, which was granted, but his conduct at the deposition was still before the court. The trial court's decision focused on the issue of attorney-client privilege and when and under what circumstances that privilege attaches. Ordinarily communications between a client and attorney are privileged. The privilege attaches when the attorney is rendering legal advice. When communications are in the presence of third parties, such as in the context of a deposition with outside individuals present, the privilege is destroyed. The court evaluated when the communications took place. Those communications prior to the deposition were privileged, but once the deponent was sworn, those communications were not privileged. Comparing the communication to the trial setting, the court observed that the deponent and attorney cannot communicate as this would defeat the purpose of the deposition as the attorney would be influencing responses. This is prohibited under the rules. Additionally, the court stated that the communications between the attorney and witness violated Rule 30 of the Rules of Civil Procedure. The end result was that the conduct of the attorney and witness were wrongful and the plaintiff was permitted to view the texts messages and present a future motion to determine whether the information could be used at trial.

Questions for Review: Read the *Wei Ngai* case. Who had the burden of proving that the communications between attorney and client were privileged and why? Why was the conduct of the Michigan attorney a violation of Rule 30 of the Rules of Civil Procedure? Why did the court determine in this instance that private communications between attorney and client were not privileged?

Rule 30(b)(7) permits a deposition to be taken by telephone or other electronic device, such as Skype or other types of telecommunications application software, if the parties so stipulate or the court so orders. Some state rules do not accommodate such technology. Where permitted, these methods can result in considerable savings in cost and time. It would be difficult by phone, however, to evaluate such a deponent as a potential witness unless the deponent were simultaneously videotaped. Telephone depositions are not common. If the deposition is on written questions, it is still necessary to reserve a site and to have the answers recorded.

Consult with your attorney about the method for recording the deposition. Strategy may determine whether videotaping is more or less advantageous than traditional transcription.

OATH OFFICER. Regardless of the type of deposition or the method used to record the deposition, a person is needed to administer the oath and take testimony. Normally, this person is a certified court reporter authorized to administer oaths. Otherwise, the court can appoint a person to administer the oath. Some court reporters are also trained in audio and videotaping techniques and can perform these services. If not, you need to locate a person trained in the needed technology.

The clerk of court and the law firm are likely to have a list of court reporters and video operators available for recording depositions and administering oaths. Not all lists cover all situations, however, and since it normally falls to the paralegal to locate a court reporter and other technicians, you need some resources to do so. You can contact paralegals you know in the area where the deposition is to be held. They or their attorneys may be able to help. They may also offer a conference room for the deposition. The National Court Reporters Association provides lists of qualified court reporters and sells a directory. Some commercial companies locate out-of-town court reporters and legal videographers. It is wise to choose a court reporter certified either by the state in which they practice or by some reputable national organization.

DEPOSITION TRACKING LOGS. Two types of logs can help you prevent costly and embarrassing oversights in coordinating depositions. A Deposition Arrangements Checklist for each deposition lists all the arrangements to be made, those completed, and those pending; and the Log of Items Sent to Witness helps you track all materials sent to a witness, such as an expert witness, in preparation for a deposition.

Prepare and Serve Notice of the Deposition

After the arrangements are made, you must serve notice of the deposition on the deponent and each of the other parties as required by Rule 30(b)(1). If a party or a person designated to represent a party is to be deposed, service of the notice of deposition is all that is needed, and failure to attend is subject to sanctions under Rule 37(d). A nonparty deponent must be subpoenaed, as discussed later.

The notice must state the time and place, the name of the attorney conducting the examination, the name and address of each person to be deposed, and the method of recording the testimony. If the name of the person is not known, Rule 30(b)(1) permits a general description sufficient to identify the person or his or her class or group. If the deponent is a business, association, or agency, the notice should describe in some detail the matters that the examination will cover [Rule 30(b)(6)]. If documents, books, papers, or tangible things are requested to be brought to the deposition, they should be designated in the notice to take deposition. An example of a Notice of Taking Deposition appears in Exhibit 8.2.

The notice should be drafted and served on the deponent, all parties, and the court reporter. A certificate of service should be executed. If the deposition is rescheduled or other changes occur, draft a letter notifying the deponent, all parties, and the court reporter.

APPLY YOUR KNOWLEDGE

Verify the deadlines for deposition practice from your state and local federal district rules. Place citations to the pertinent state or federal rules, including those covering scope and other limitations on depositions, in your systems folder.

> **EXHIBIT 8.2** Notice of Taking Deposition of a Witness Including Reference to Materials Designated in Attached Subpoena
>
> [Fed. R. Civ P. Rule 30(b)(1)]
>
> [*Title of Court and Cause*]
>
> TO: [*Attorney for Plaintiff*] or Counsel of Record
>   [*Law firm*]
>   [*Address*]
>
>   PLEASE TAKE NOTICE that pursuant to Rule 30 of the Federal Rules of Civil Procedure, Plaintiff will take the oral deposition of _____ before a notary public or other authorized officer by stenographic means on [date], at _____ P.M. and there-after from day to day until completed or adjourned, at the offices of [*law firm name and address*].
>
>   PLEASE TAKE FURTHER NOTICE that the Defendant requests that deponent bring to the deposition all documents, materials, and tangible things described in the attached ADDENDUM to Civil Subpoena.
>
>   PLEASE TAKE FURTHER NOTICE that this deposition will be taken through instant visual display of testimony. Plaintiff reserved the right to record the deposition testimony by videotape for use at trial, pursuant to the Rules of [jurisdiction] Civil Procedure. [alternative paragraph]
>
>   _____
>   Attorney for Defendant
>   Address: _____
>
> Adapted from West's Federal Forms § 3429, v. 3A (5th ed.), Notice of Taking Deposition, with permission of West Group.

Subpoena the Deponent

subpoena

A document pursuant to a court order that commands a person to appear to testify.

OBTAIN THE SUBPOENA. A **subpoena** is a document issued by the clerk or officer of the court commanding a person (nonparty) to be present and, if indicated, bring physical items to a specified place at a designated time. Failure to comply with the subpoena may result in contempt of court and appropriate penalties. Subpoenas are the documents used to require attendance of witnesses at depositions and at trial. Rule 45 of the Federal Rules and parallel state rules set out the requirements for a subpoena and its service. Of the two types of subpoenas, the most common is a subpoena for a person to give testimony. The second type is a **subpoena duces tecum**, which requires a person to appear and produce books, documents, electronically stored information, or tangible things. Because parties to an action do not have to be subpoenaed, it is appropriate to serve a Rule 34 request for production of documents with the notice of the deposition. It serves the same function as the subpoena duces tecum for nonparties. If a Rule 34 production is requested, the other party must receive notice 30 days before the date of the deposition.

subpoena duces tecum

A document pursuant to a court order that commands a person to appear with certain books, documents, electronically stored information, or tangible things.

In the federal system a nonparty deponent must be deposed within 100 miles of where that person resides, works, or regularly transacts business in person. Although some court decisions say the 100-mile limit should be calculated by a straight line, the cautious practice is to figure it according to the actual driving mileage. If the deponent is located in the district where the case is pending, the subpoena is issued by that court. If not, the subpoena must be issued by the court in the district where the deponent is located. Federal subpoenas may be served anywhere in the district of the issuing court, or anywhere outside the district if it is within 100 miles of the place of the deposition or anywhere in the state where state statute or court rule permits service of a subpoena issued by a court of general jurisdiction sitting in the place of the deposition. Generally, a deponent in a state action may not be required to go beyond the county of residence, work, or personal transaction of business. Check your state rule.

To obtain a subpoena for a deponent, provide the appropriate clerk of court with a copy of the notice to take deposition and proof of service on the parties. In the federal system the subpoena must be issued by the clerk in the district where the deposition is to be taken or by the attorney. In some states it is issued where the action is pending. Consult local rules. The clerk will sign the subpoena *in blank* in most jurisdictions, which means that you will need to fill in the necessary information.

Following the dictates of Rule 45, be sure that the following information is on the subpoena: the name of the issuing court; the title and docket number of the action and the court in which it is pending; the name of the paralegal's attorney; the witness's name and address with directions for the witness to attend and give testimony; and the date, time, and place for the deposition. The caption of the subpoena must state the name of the issuing court. This is easy to overlook if the issuing court is different from the court where the action is pending. If done incorrectly, neither court has jurisdiction to enforce the subpoena. Indicate whether the production of documents is commanded. In addition, Rule 45(a)(1)(iv) requires that the text of sections (d) and (e) of Rule 45 be set out in the subpoena. These sections define the duty of an attorney not to abuse the subpoena process and on what basis and how one objects to a subpoena. Note that Rule 45 now requires a deposition subpoena to state the method for recording the deposition. Add the details just mentioned and designate the documents or physical evidence to be produced, inspected, copied, tested, or sampled. If the items are numerous or require a lengthy description, a rider may need to be attached to the subpoena. Rule 45 does not require the personal presence of a person subpoenaed to produce documents and things.

Revisions to Rule 45 address electronically stored information. A subpoena duces tecum may designate the form in which e-stored information should be produced. If it does not so designate, the responding person must produce the information in the form or forms in which it is normally maintained or in a reasonably usable form, Other provisions similar to those added to Rules 26 and 34 address how to deal with privileged information, the right to refuse production of e-stored information as not reasonably accessible because of undue burden or cost, and the right to object to or compel the requested production. An example of a subpoena duces tecum appears in Exhibit 8.3.

HIPAA AND SUBPOENAS. The HIPAA privacy regulations and parallel state laws impact deposition and subpoena practice. Keep in mind that you must comply with any stricter respective state requirements, as well as HIPAA. If you need to obtain medical information from a health care provider for discovery, the simplest procedure is to get the patient's signed authorization, as previously discussed. If a

EXHIBIT 8.3 Subpoena for Production of Documents (Duces Tecum)

AO 88B (Rev. 02/14) Subpoena to Produce Documents, Information, or Objects or to Permit Inspection of Premises in a Civil Action

UNITED STATES DISTRICT COURT
for the

_____ District of _____

_____ *Plaintiff* v. _____ *Defendant*	))))))

Civil Action No.

SUBPOENA TO PRODUCE DOCUMENTS, INFORMATION, OR OBJECTS
OR TO PERMIT INSPECTION OF PREMISES IN A CIVIL ACTION

To:

_____
(Name of person to whom this subpoena is directed)

❑ *Production:* **YOU ARE COMMANDED** to produce at the time, date, and place set forth below the following documents, electronically stored information, or objects, and to permit inspection, copying, testing, or sampling of the material:

Place:	Date and Time:

❑ *Inspection of Premises:* **YOU ARE COMMANDED** to permit entry onto the designated premises, land, or other property possessed or controlled by you at the time, date, and location set forth below, so that the requesting party may inspect, measure, survey, photograph, test, or sample the property or any designated object or operation on it.

Place:	Date and Time:

The following provisions of Fed. R. Civ. P. 45 are attached – Rule 45(c), relating to the place of compliance; Rule 45(d), relating to your protection as a person subject to a subpoena; and Rule 45(e) and (g), relating to your duty to respond to this subpoena and the potential consequences of not doing so.

Date: _____

CLERK OF COURT

OR

_____   _____
Signature of Clerk or Deputy Clerk   *Attorney's signature*

The name, address, e-mail address, and telephone number of the attorney representing *(name of party)* _____
_____ , who issues or requests this subpoena, are:

_____

Notice to the person who issues or requests this subpoena
If this subpoena commands the production of documents, electronically stored information, or tangible things or the inspection of premises before trial, a notice and a copy of the subpoena must be served on each party in this case before it is served on the person to whom it is directed. Fed. R. Civ. P. 45(a)(4).

(continued)

EXHIBIT 8.3 Subpoena for Production of Documents (Duces Tecum) (*continued*)

AO 88B (Rev. 02/14) Subpoena to Produce Documents, Information, or Objects or to Permit Inspection of Premises in a Civil Action (Page 2)

Civil Action No.

PROOF OF SERVICE
(This section should not be filed with the court unless required by Fed. R. Civ. P. 45.)

I received this subpoena for *(name of individual and title, if any)* _____

on *(date)* _____ .

☐ I served the subpoena by delivering a copy to the named person as follows: _____

_____ on *(date)* _____ ; or

☐ I returned the subpoena unexecuted because: _____ .

Unless the subpoena was issued on behalf of the United States, or one of its officers or agents, I have also tendered to the witness the fees for one day's attendance, and the mileage allowed by law, in the amount of

$ _____ .

My fees are $ _____ for travel and $ _____ for services, for a total of $ _____ .

I declare under penalty of perjury that this information is true.

Date: _____

_____
Server's signature

_____
Printed name and title

_____
Server's address

Additional information regarding attempted service, etc.:

| Print | Save As... | Add Attachment | | Reset |

EXHIBIT 8.3 Subpoena for Production of Documents (Duces Tecum) (*continued*)

AO 88B (Rev. 02/14) Subpoena to Produce Documents, Information, or Objects or to Permit Inspection of Premises in a Civil Action(Page 3)

Federal Rule of Civil Procedure 45 (c), (d), (e), and (g) (Effective 12/1/13)

(c) Place of Compliance.

(1) *For a Trial, Hearing, or Deposition.* A subpoena may command a person to attend a trial, hearing, or deposition only as follows:
   (A) within 100 miles of where the person resides, is employed, or regularly transacts business in person; or
   (B) within the state where the person resides, is employed, or regularly transacts business in person, if the person
      (i) is a party or a party's officer; or
      (ii) is commanded to attend a trial and would not incur substantial expense.

(2) *For Other Discovery.* A subpoena may command:
   (A) production of documents, electronically stored information, or tangible things at a place within 100 miles of where the person resides, is employed, or regularly transacts business in person; and
   (B) inspection of premises at the premises to be inspected.

(d) Protecting a Person Subject to a Subpoena; Enforcement.

(1) *Avoiding Undue Burden or Expense; Sanctions.* A party or attorney responsible for issuing and serving a subpoena must take reasonable steps to avoid imposing undue burden or expense on a person subject to the subpoena. The court for the district where compliance is required must enforce this duty and impose an appropriate sanction—which may include lost earnings and reasonable attorney's fees—on a party or attorney who fails to comply.

(2) *Command to Produce Materials or Permit Inspection.*
   (A) *Appearance Not Required.* A person commanded to produce documents, electronically stored information, or tangible things, or to permit the inspection of premises, need not appear in person at the place of production or inspection unless also commanded to appear for a deposition, hearing, or trial.
   (B) *Objections.* A person commanded to produce documents or tangible things or to permit inspection may serve on the party or attorney designated in the subpoena a written objection to inspecting, copying, testing, or sampling any or all of the materials or to inspecting the premises—or to producing electronically stored information in the form or forms requested. The objection must be served before the earlier of the time specified for compliance or 14 days after the subpoena is served. If an objection is made, the following rules apply:
      (i) At any time, on notice to the commanded person, the serving party may move the court for the district where compliance is required for an order compelling production or inspection.
      (ii) These acts may be required only as directed in the order, and the order must protect a person who is neither a party nor a party's officer from significant expense resulting from compliance.

(3) *Quashing or Modifying a Subpoena.*
   (A) *When Required.* On timely motion, the court for the district where compliance is required must quash or modify a subpoena that:
      (i) fails to allow a reasonable time to comply;
      (ii) requires a person to comply beyond the geographical limits specified in Rule 45(c);
      (iii) requires disclosure of privileged or other protected matter, if no exception or waiver applies; or
      (iv) subjects a person to undue burden.
   (B) *When Permitted.* To protect a person subject to or affected by a subpoena, the court for the district where compliance is required may, on motion, quash or modify the subpoena if it requires:
      (i) disclosing a trade secret or other confidential research, development, or commercial information; or

      (ii) disclosing an unretained expert's opinion or information that does not describe specific occurrences in dispute and results from the expert's study that was not requested by a party.
   (C) *Specifying Conditions as an Alternative.* In the circumstances described in Rule 45(d)(3)(B), the court may, instead of quashing or modifying a subpoena, order appearance or production under specified conditions if the serving party:
      (i) shows a substantial need for the testimony or material that cannot be otherwise met without undue hardship; and
      (ii) ensures that the subpoenaed person will be reasonably compensated.

(e) Duties in Responding to a Subpoena.

(1) *Producing Documents or Electronically Stored Information.* These procedures apply to producing documents or electronically stored information:
   (A) *Documents.* A person responding to a subpoena to produce documents must produce them as they are kept in the ordinary course of business or must organize and label them to correspond to the categories in the demand.
   (B) *Form for Producing Electronically Stored Information Not Specified.* If a subpoena does not specify a form for producing electronically stored information, the person responding must produce it in a form or forms in which it is ordinarily maintained or in a reasonably usable form or forms.
   (C) *Electronically Stored Information Produced in Only One Form.* The person responding need not produce the same electronically stored information in more than one form.
   (D) *Inaccessible Electronically Stored Information.* The person responding need not provide discovery of electronically stored information from sources that the person identifies as not reasonably accessible because of undue burden or cost. On motion to compel discovery or for a protective order, the person responding must show that the information is not reasonably accessible because of undue burden or cost. If that showing is made, the court may nonetheless order discovery from such sources if the requesting party shows good cause, considering the limitations of Rule 26(b)(2)(C). The court may specify conditions for the discovery.

(2) *Claiming Privilege or Protection.*
   (A) *Information Withheld.* A person withholding subpoenaed information under a claim that it is privileged or subject to protection as trial-preparation material must:
      (i) expressly make the claim; and
      (ii) describe the nature of the withheld documents, communications, or tangible things in a manner that, without revealing information itself privileged or protected, will enable the parties to assess the claim.
   (B) *Information Produced.* If information produced in response to a subpoena is subject to a claim of privilege or of protection as trial-preparation material, the person making the claim may notify any party that received the information of the claim and the basis for it. After being notified, a party must promptly return, sequester, or destroy the specified information and any copies it has; must not use or disclose the information until the claim is resolved; must take reasonable steps to retrieve the information if the party disclosed it before being notified; and may promptly present the information under seal to the court for the district where compliance is required for a determination of the claim. The person who produced the information must preserve the information until the claim is resolved.

(g) Contempt.
The court for the district where compliance is required—and also, after a motion is transferred, the issuing court—may hold in contempt a person who, having been served, fails without adequate excuse to obey the subpoena or an order related to it.

For access to subpoena materials, see Fed. R. Civ. P. 45(a) Committee Note (2013).

Source: U.S. Courts.

request for the authorization is refused, a subpoena is needed. A subpoena signed by a judge fulfills HIPAA requirements, because the subpoena is a court order. In jurisdictions where judges do not sign subpoenas, however, HIPAA and the health care provider require written assurance that the patient has been notified of the intent to subpoena the records, the medical professional, or both, and that the patient has been given sufficient time to object to the release of the protected information. In practice, this requires that a "notice letter" be sent to the party's attorney containing:

- reference to the governing HIPAA and state provisions;
- the intent to obtain the party's medical records by subpoena duces tecum;
- the health care provider(s) to be subpoenaed;
- copies of the subpoenas to be issued; and
- a date by which written objection must be communicated.

If an objection is raised, the attorneys must resolve the issue.

Once the date for objection has passed or any objection has been resolved, then the subpoena with a copy of the notice letter and a cover letter must be sent to the provider's record custodian. The cover letter along with a copy of the notice letter gives the provider the assurance that HIPAA requirements have been met. The Sample Cover Letter to the Records Custodian in Exhibit 8.4 sets out the necessary assurances.

Another HIPAA option for subpoenaing medical records is the qualified protective order. A qualified protective order specifies that the protected records will be used for

---

EXHIBIT 8.4 Sample Cover Letter to Records Custodian (Subpoena/HIPAA)

Dear Records Custodian:

Please find enclosed a subpoena duces tecum for you to provide us with a certified copy of the complete medical file on __(patient)__.

This letter is to assure you of our compliance with the privacy requirements of the Health Insurance Portability and Accountability Act [45 C.F.R. § 164.512(e)]:

1. a copy of the letter that provided notice of our intent to subpoena the patient's medical records;
2. sent with sufficient time (a specified deadline) to give the patient the opportunity to object to the subpoena; and
3. our assurance that no objection has been raised by the specified deadline, which has expired.*

Please send a certified copy of the requested records to the address specified on the subpoena and bill us to get prompt reimbursement of your cost in producing the records.

Thank you,

_____

Counsel

*Note: Some states may have additional requirements and/or may require that the custodian receive a Notice to Take Deposition with an option to produce the records without having to appear.

INTERNET EXERCISE

Determine what fees must be attached to a deposition conducted in your state courts. How are witnesses served with a deposition notice and subpoena in your state? Identify the statute or civil rule of procedure that applies for each.

a qualified purpose, such as litigation in the pertinent case, and will be returned to the provider or be destroyed at the end of the defined use. When the subpoena is sent to the provider, this option requires an accompanying cover letter, similar to Exhibit 8.4, that assures the records custodian that the parties in the pertinent legal action have agreed to a qualified protective order or the attorney seeking the records has requested the protective order from the court.

If a provider still refuses to release the medical records, the final option for the party seeking the records is to get a court order for their release. Similar procedures must be followed when a treating physician is to be deposed. A Notice to Take Deposition must be added to the process and all parties notified.

ATTACH FEES. Before serving the subpoena, determine if it is necessary to attach witness and mileage fees. The Federal Rules require that such fees be tendered at the time of service of the subpoena to have a valid subpoena. Determine the distance to be traveled by the deponent and calculate the round trip mileage. A call to the federal clerk of court or checking the court's Web site will give you the most recent witness fee and the mileage allowance. Prepare a check and attach it to the subpoena for service. The procedure is the same for most states. Some states require a witness fee only for witnesses from outside the county where the deposition is to be taken.

SERVE THE SUBPOENA. The subpoena and attached fee must be personally served on the deponent. Because a subpoena can be unnerving to its recipient, it may be a good idea, if your attorney approves, to warn the witness and explain why the subpoena is necessary. This explanation might keep a witness in your camp. In the federal system a subpoena may be served by a person not a party and not less than 18 years of age. Service in state cases is performed by a sheriff, special bailiff, or any person of legal age (check local rules). Paralegals are frequently asked to serve subpoenas. Professional servers are available in some areas. When delivering the subpoena or directing someone else to do so, make sure the server fully understands the correct way to serve a subpoena. Consult local rules, but in most instances, the subpoena must be personally handed to the deponent and the deponent told what the subpoena is, where the deponent is to go, and what is expected of the deponent. The server must then acknowledge service in writing on a copy of the subpoena or execute an affidavit of service.

When service is to be on an out-of-town deponent, it is best to call the local clerk of court for the correct procedures and, if necessary, call each day to ensure issuance of the subpoena and service on the witness. If a person objects to the commands of the subpoena, objections must be served on the deposing attorney within 14 days of service of the subpoena, or on or before the deposition if it is scheduled in less than 14 days from service.

In the case of a deposition, the objecting party must move the issuing court for an order to quash or modify the subpoena. A detailed list on subpoena practice is in Chapter 11 under Subpoena Witnesses.

A case where the subpoena power of a court was tested was *Toyota Motor Corp. v. Superior Court,* 197 Cal.App. 4th 1107, 130 Cal.Rptr. 3d 131 (2011), where the court attempted to subpoena Japanese residents for a deposition in California. A closer review sheds some light on the issue.

CASE STUDY: UNDERSTANDING THE LAW

A California state trial court issued subpoenas for five employees of Toyota Motor Corporation who resided in Japan. Initially, the plaintiffs in the case filed the request for subpoenas. The main case was a products liability case filed by the Stewart family against Toyota. The Stewarts owned a Toyota pickup truck which was involved in a fatal car crash in Idaho. The allegations focused on a defective steering rod that cracked causing the fatal crash. Toyota had issued a recall on the truck. When the plaintiffs in the case issued deposition subpoena requests, they argued that a California statute permitted the Japanese employees to be deposed in California and not in Japan. The statutes in question are sections 2025.250, 2025.260, and 1989 of the California Code of Civil Procedure. Section 1989 states, "A witness, including a witness specified in subdivision (b) of Section 1987, is not obliged to attend as a witness before any court, judge, justice or any other officer, unless the witness is a resident within the state at the time of service." Section 2025.250 limits the distance that a witness must travel for a deposition to 75 miles of the deponent's residence or if within the county of the pending action within 150 miles of the deponent's residence. Toyota refused to produce the five employees for depositions in California. In their challenge, Toyota claimed that the Superior Court exceeded its jurisdiction by issuing the subpoenas against Japanese residents. Toyota appealed the Superior Court order in the form of a writ of mandate. The Appeals Court agreed with Toyota and reversed the lower court order. In its opinion, the appeals court discussed the legislative history of California statutes and the extent of the jurisdictional limitations of a state court. There had been changes to section 1989 which limited the jurisdiction of the Superior Court of nonresidents. These changes were plain, clear, and unambiguous. Although the (original) plaintiffs relied on two cases to support their conclusions that the Superior Court had jurisdiction over the Japanese nonresidents, the Appeals Court declined to follow those decisions and stated that the cases had not been cited in any decision for over 22 years and did not apply. The end result was that the Superior Court exceeded its authority in issuing subpoenas for nonresidents to submit to depositions in California. The Appeals Court decided the issue on strict interpretation of the applicable statutes.

Questions for Review: Read the *Toyota* case. What was the legislative history that the court relied upon to reach its result? Why did the Court reject the plaintiffs' reliance on the *Glass* and *Twin Lock* decisions? What significant changes were made to section 1989 that persuaded the court to find for Toyota?

PREPARE FOR DEPOSITION

Draft Questions or an Examination Outline

Although the attorney will determine what questions will be asked the deponent, you can provide considerable assistance by drafting a proposed set of questions or a detailed outline for the examination, indicating each point to be addressed. The outline may be better because it is less time-consuming, often more complete, easily amended, and provides flexibility during the examination. Adequate preparation is important.

Carefully review all file information, paying particular attention to those areas for which the witness can provide proof, information, or leads, including any documents or physical items that can or need to be introduced through this witness or otherwise impact on the witness's testimony. Pay special attention to answers to interrogatories or admissions from this case or other cases made by the witness. If the witness is a party, these items just mentioned will permit you to eliminate some areas of questioning, especially if the other party has already admitted certain facts. Make notes.

Meet with the attorney, review the notes, and determine as specifically as possible what the attorney wants from this witness. For example, the attorney for Mrs. Forrester may wish to examine Mr. Hart to determine his version of the facts, lock him into that version, and establish any breaches in company policy or defects in the vehicle that may have contributed to the accident. The attorney may want to depose the head of Mercury Parcel's maintenance shop to produce his records of repairs on the van, explain the shop procedures and policies to see if they were followed in this case, or reveal any problems or defects in the van. Or the attorney for Mercury Parcel might want to depose Mrs. Forrester to lock her into her story, assess how high the jury sympathy factor will be, probe her attitude on any negligence on her part, or to hear her description of her injuries and pain. Or Mercury's attorney may want to depose Mrs. Forrester's surgeon and other doctors to get detailed assessments of injuries, possible causes, treatment, and prognosis. Since the witness has been previously identified, you will find that it is easier than you might think to determine what the witness needs to be asked and what can be eliminated. The discussion with the attorney ought to make clear the objectives and areas of examination.

Look at similar witness examinations from other office files or form depositions. Several publishing companies have published detailed deposition outlines to cover a variety of types of witnesses. An example of a deposition outline appears in Exhibit 8.5.

The outline in Exhibit 8.5 can be adapted to a particular witness and set of facts. If no sample is available, check the objectives carefully and brainstorm topics and subtopics that must be covered. In most circumstances, it is necessary to get detailed information on the witness's background (including possible areas for future impeachment), and then on the details of the event, documents, or other matters relevant to the case. Remember that in a deposition the attorneys have more latitude in the types of questions they may ask than they have at trial. The scope is confined to what is relevant to the case, is admissible evidence, or might reasonably lead to admissible evidence. Therefore, hearsay may be legitimate, as is the identification of other possible witnesses, documents, and physical evidence. In deposition preparation it is probably better to err on the side of going too far rather than being too cautious.

One of the best techniques for generating questions for an outline is to sit down with your notes, form depositions, and a recording device, and dictate every question you can possibly think of to elicit the desired information. You will be surprised once you get rolling how many useful questions you can generate. Or try preparing questions on your desktop, laptop, or tablet. Some of us compose better on one of those devices rather than a recording device. Having a working document typed that you can edit and add to as needed is helpful.

As you are going through materials and generating questions, be sure to list each document that needs to be gathered for your attorney to use or introduce at the deposition.

EXHIBIT 8.5 Deposition Outline/Checklist (Plaintiff—Automobile)

PRELIMINARY INFORMATION

Title of Case and Court Number _____

Deponent's Name _____

Place of Deposition _____

Date and Time _____

Lawyers in Attendance: _____

IDENTIFICATION OF DEPONENT

Name and general information _____

SPECIFIC INFORMATION

- Prior traffic convictions _____
- Has driver's license ever been revoked? _____
- Does deponent have restrictions on driver's license? _____
- Does the deponent carry liability insurance?
  Name of company _____
  Policy number with liability and medical limits
  _____
  Effective period _____
- Was any reimbursement received for medical expenses, loss of income, property damage, or Workmen's Compensation, or other? _____

EMPLOYMENT BACKGROUND

Name of employer and address _____

Job description and rate of pay _____

DETAILS OF DEPONENT'S VEHICLE

- Make, model, year, color _____
- Unusual accessories on car _____
- Owner's name and address _____
- Approximate mileage on car at time of accident
  _____
- Last repairs and where performed _____
- Condition of Vehicle (such as brakes, tires, headlights)
  _____
- Last safety check before the accident _____
- Previous accidents _____

Other Passengers

- Seatbelts _____
- Clear view of the accident? _____

- Passenger's conduct before impact _____
- Warnings to the driver of impending danger
  _____
- Passenger injuries _____

LOCATION OF ACCIDENT

- Road conditions and surface _____
- Type of area (e.g., residential, business, rural, etc.)
  _____
- Structures near scene (e.g., building at each corner) _____
- Obstructions of the driver's view _____
- Traffic controls and location of each _____
- Speed limit _____
- Familiarity with the scene _____

DETAILS SHORTLY BEFORE ACCIDENT

- Deponent destination at time and route _____
- Last stop made before the accident, other than for traffic _____
- Deponent talking on phone or texting _____
- Deponent talking to others _____
- Deponent smoking _____
- Deponent drinking _____
- Right before accident _____
  Deponent had anything of an alcoholic nature to drink _____
  Deponent under medication _____
  Deponent: _____
  – Sleepy _____
  – Emotionally upset _____
  – Ill _____
  – Other _____

Deponent Agent for Business

- List details of reason for trip _____
- Owner's permission to drive car _____

DETAILS OF OCCURRENCE

- Speed of vehicle _____
- Direction of vehicle prior to impact _____
- Actions to avoid impact _____
  – Sound the horn _____

EXHIBIT 8.5 Deposition Outline/Checklist (Plaintiff—Automobile) (continued)

– Use flashing lights _____

– Other _____

- Actions prior to impact _____
- Other car _____
- Warn the deponent _____

– Sounding the horn _____

– Flashing lights _____

– Other _____

- Speed of the other vehicle _____
- Damage to deponent's auto _____
- General details of impact and damage _____
- Contributory factors _____

Automobile failures _____

Human error _____

Distractions _____

Road surfaces _____

- General injuries _____
- Ambulance service or first aid _____
- Person treating at scene _____
- Nature of treatment _____

POLICE INVESTIGATION

- Name of police department and investigating officers _____
- Traffic citation issued or not _____

Charges _____

Outcome of charges _____

- Get copy of photographs _____
- Police report _____
- List of eyewitnesses _____

WITNESSES

- Identify witnesses (name and address) _____
- Witnesses knowledge/observations _____

At scene _____

In car(s) _____

INJURIES AND MEDICAL INFORMATION

- Description of injuries _____

- Name of treating physician and address/contact number _____
- Names and addresses/contact numbers of specialists _____
- Name of hospital(s) with address and contact number _____
- Medical treatment with dates and doctors giving treatment _____

PRIOR MEDICAL HISTORY

- Prior injuries _____

dates _____

- Prior Hospitalization _____

Dates _____

- Any physical or mental illnesses _____
- Any prior claims or lawsuits _____

DAMAGES TO DATE WITH AMOUNTS

- Hospital _____
- Ambulance service _____
- Private nurses _____
- Physicians _____
- Drugs & prescriptions _____
- X-rays _____
- Loss of income _____
- Property damage _____
- Total to date _____
- Additional details _____

ATTORNEY'S APPRAISAL OF DEPONENT

- Physical description, and general appearance

_____

- General impressions _____
- Negative observations or impairments _____
- Any past or present behaviors that would impact case _____
- General attitude _____
- and impressions _____

Source: Adapted from: Alan E. Morrill.

Submitted by: _____

Prepare a document that can be edited as needed similar to your general outline. A possible format for the outline appears in Exhibit 8.6.

The advantage of such an outline form is that it lists the questions or topics on one side and permits comments, notations, documents that need to be introduced, or evaluation of the answer on the other side. This format will help the attorney at the deposition. It also permits highlighting of questions that the attorney may choose to use out of chronological sequence to elicit a more spontaneous and less planned answer from the deponent.

Once the outline is in good draft form, it should be reviewed by the attorney. Amendments should be added, and a final outline prepared. Extra copies should be made for the form file if there are no other good examples.

Gather and Prepare Documents and Exhibits

Each of the documents or photographs the attorney plans to introduce for authentication or needs for reference should be gathered and placed in separate, clearly labeled manila folders. Sufficient copies of each document should also be in the folder, allowing the attorney to mark up one copy as needed or to give copies to

---

EXHIBIT 8.6 Sample Deposition Outline

CASE: Smith v. Jones
DEPONENT: Albert Smith-Plaintiff

DEPO DATE: 6 Jan 2015
LOCATION: 1421 6th Avenue, Sacramento

ATTYS: E. Gibson for Jones
N. Mason for Smith

Items to Cover	Testimony	Exhibit Desc. & No.
ID Name, Address, & Telephone	Albert Smith 2130 "I" Street Sacramento 777/333-2222	
SSN	238-45-9726	
Age, DOB	54, 9/14/60	
Education	Wilson HS, Sacramento, 1978 Stanford, BS Math, 1982 UCLA, MS Math, 1984	
Employment	Stanford, Asst. Prof, Math Dept; 1983-1984 State of CA Dept of Highways Statistician; 1984-present	

Docs reviewed prior to deposition	Accident report
	Statistics on accidents in location of
	  accident in this matter
	Report of raw data on which statistics
	  are based
		Acc. Report, Exh. 1
		Statistics, Exh. 2
		
		Raw data docs, Exh. 3

the other attorneys at the deposition. Other physical items requiring introduction should be gathered.

Some exhibits may need to be located, purchased, or prepared. Preparation of exhibits will be discussed later in the text on preparing for trial. Most attorneys agree that witnesses have an easier time and are more accurate if they refer to a diagram or some other visual exhibit. These should also be organized in the order they will be needed by the attorney.

Set Up Witness Files

A good witness file is particularly important to conducting a good deposition. You can begin to organize a witness file as it becomes clear that a particular witness will play a role at deposition and probably later at trial. The file should be organized prior to the scheduled deposition of the witness and should contain the following:

- A witness information sheet (see Chapter 3)
- The deposition outline or questions
- Documents by or concerning the witness arranged chronologically or as needed at the deposition
- An extra set of documents that you or the attorney may mark on during the deposition
- Discovery information gained through interrogatories, admissions, or other requests
- Allegations in the pleadings
- Notice of deposition, subpoenas, and certificate of service

The witness file should be arranged according to the specifications of the supervising attorney. A small three-ring binder with all pertinent documents placed loosely at the back in separate, clearly labeled folders seems to aid organization and quick access. A separate witness file should be maintained for each witness to be deposed or later examined at trial.

Assist in the Preparation of the Client or Witness for Testimony

Preparing clients or witnesses for deposition testimony is extremely important, because what they say, how effective they appear, and how certain they are of the facts may well determine whether the case is settled in the client's favor or heads for a full-blown expensive trial. Further, if the case does go to trial and the witnesses' answers are not well thought out, there is considerable likelihood that the opponent will use the deposition to show inconsistencies and inaccuracies that will harm the witnesses' credibility in the eyes of the jury.

You can play an important role in seeing to it that the witnesses do the best job they can. In many law offices the paralegal's role is primarily one of communication, keeping the witness informed on what to expect and when to expect it. This task involves timely correspondence, phone calls, and coordinating meetings with the attorney. In some offices the paralegal is used even more effectively by working directly with the witness. In this case the client or witness comes to the office where the paralegal assists the attorney by addressing the witness's anxiety, counseling on testifying techniques, and answering questions. Frequently the firm takes the witness through a mock examination. The paralegal can help by having questions ready that are likely to be asked by the opponent.

The experienced paralegal occasionally participates in questioning the witness during the mock examination.

There are numerous ways you can assist at a preparation conference: making suggestions to the witness, observing the witness in mock examination and noting weak or ineffective areas, doing the questioning while the attorney notes problems, and other possibilities. You may need to be assertive at this stage in suggesting ways to render assistance.

Exhibit 8.7 is a sample letter that serves two purposes: first, it shows the form of a letter that many paralegals are called on to draft and send to clients, and second, it covers the most significant tips that should be passed on to a client, whether by letter or in a conference at the office. Some attorneys would rather not send out detailed instruction letters to clients. Such letters may be used against the client or attorney, so they prefer to handle such things in an office visit. Check with your supervising attorney. The proposed letter can be used as a checklist on what to tell the client at such an appointment.

EXHIBIT 8.7 Letter to Client Regarding Deposition

WHITE, WILSON & MCDUFF
ATTORNEYS AT LAW
FEDERAL PLAZA BUILDING, SUITE 700
THIRD AND MARKET STREETS
LEGALVILLE, COLUMBIA 00000
(111) 555-0000

Mrs. Ann Forrester
1533 Capitol Drive
Legalville, Columbia 00000

November 1, _____

Dear Mrs. Forrester:

As we previously discussed, the time has come when you will need to testify about the accident and your injuries at a deposition. We will work with you to prepare for the deposition. Mr. White will be with you and is confident you will do just fine.

The deposition is scheduled for Wednesday, December 2, _____, at 10:00 am in room 202 in the Federal District Court Building at Third and Race Streets. Parking is available at the Municipal Parking facility behind the courthouse. Please be there by 9:30 am.

A deposition is an examination of a witness under oath by the opposition and in the presence of a court reporter. The examination is to determine the witness's version of the facts, the evidence in support of those facts, and the location of the evidence and names and addresses of persons having information about the evidence. It is an important stage in the lawsuit because the other side will be evaluating you as a witness, including your appearance, ability to recall facts, truthfulness, etc. Depositions produce evidence that might lead to a settlement of the case. They may also be used at trial to test the consistency and credibility of a witness. Therefore, good preparation on your part is important. It will give you confidence.

EXHIBIT 8.7 Letter to Client Regarding Deposition (*continued*)

In preparing for the deposition, please keep the following in mind:

1. Depositions are occasionally postponed, and if so, you will be informed.
2. Chronologically review the facts of the case up through your current medical status; anticipate questions on dates, times, directions, distances, speeds, weather, clothes, events, injuries, medical treatments, expenses, witnesses, statements, etc. If you do not know distances and the like for sure, reasonable approximations are acceptable. A return to the scene of the accident to check distances, obstructions, and other details before your deposition might be helpful.
3. Be sure you have informed your attorney of all matters about the incident and those that reflect on your own honesty and credibility. Do not allow your attorney to be surprised to your detriment.
4. Expect the opponent's attorney to do most or all of the questioning. Your attorney will object when it is necessary.
5. Dress neatly, be pleasant, and speak up.
6. Listen to each question carefully. If you do not understand the question, *do not guess at its meaning*, simply state you do not understand.
7. Think about your answer; do not blurt out answers. Be cautious of a series of questions in quick succession that intend to lead you to the answer your opponent desires. Answer thoughtfully at your own pace.
8. Above all, tell the truth. You will be under oath and should avoid giving in to the temptation to fill in gaps of information. Do not guess. Should you want to correct an earlier answer, simply indicate your desire to do so. The attorney will assist you.
9. If you are asked, "Did you speak with your attorney about testifying today?" answer "yes." There is nothing wrong with speaking with your attorney about testifying. If the question is, "Did your attorney tell you what to say?" the correct answer is, "He told me to tell the truth." Other than that, your attorney will not tell you what to say.
10. While testifying, it is preferable that you not seek guidance from your attorney. You must answer the question as best you can. If your attorney feels a question is improper, an objection will be stated. An objection is a signal to you to stop answering.
11. A common technique of adverse attorneys is to remain silent after your answer. They frequently do this in the hope that you will feel compelled to add more information. It can be damaging information. Therefore, resist the temptation to add information and to fill silences.
12. Avoid discussing your case and any aspect of your testimony with anyone other than your attorney. Casual conversation about your case can be damaging.
13. You may be asked at the deposition to sketch a diagram of the accident scene. If you try some practice sketches, you should not have any difficulty with this.
14. During the deposition you may be given documents, diagrams, photographs, or other items to identify. Be sure to examine such items carefully to see that they accurately reflect what they intend to reflect before you agree to their accuracy.
15. Be prepared to describe your injuries and medical treatment in detail. Do not exaggerate or understate.
16. Be prepared to discuss any injuries you suffered or claims you made before this accident.
17. Bring any documents that you have been requested to bring.
18. Be prepared to discuss changes such as loss of pay, property damage, and other out-of-pocket expenses.
19. It is not necessary to memorize possible answers and is probably better if you do not.

(continued)

EXHIBIT 8.7 Letter to Client Regarding Deposition (*continued*)

In summary, you will do the best job at your deposition if you are well prepared, thoughtful, deliberate, and truthful. I will be contacting you soon to set up a time when you and Mr. White can meet to discuss the deposition. Meanwhile, if you have any questions or concerns, please feel free to contact me or Mr. White.

Very truly yours,

Terry Salyer
Paralegal

A letter such as in Exhibit 8.7 should be followed by an appointment with the attorney, possibly including yourself. At that time any additional directions can be conveyed. If given responsibility for guiding the witness, keep in mind some matters of concern:

- It is unethical for an attorney or attorney's agent to tell a client what to say to answer questions, either at deposition or at trial. To do so greatly influences the witness, and may unintentionally lead to perjury or cause the witness to believe that you or the attorney condones such dishonesty. Even if you or the attorney knows a particular answer is true, specific answers should not be suggested. Any breach of this ethical standard is extremely serious and the slightest implication of impropriety can be damaging to the case and the reputation of the attorney. This admonition applies to the substantive part of an answer. It does not, however, apply to a nonsubstantive preface to an answer. For example, it is not uncommon for an attorney to ask a question that states facts not yet proven. Rather than have the deponent answer the question as if the facts were true, it would not be unethical to coach the client to say, "assuming your facts are correct," as a preface to a substantive answer.

- In going over questions that might be asked the witness, watch for questions that call for privileged information or the attorney's work product. Such matters should be called to the attention of the attorney so the client can be instructed accordingly and any necessary protective orders can be sought.

- When working with a witness as opposed to a client, many of the same suggestions apply. One additional suggestion is to stress to the witness the importance of impartiality. If the witness appears too sympathetic to the client or too eager to help, it may cause the jury to question the reliability of the witness and possibly discount the testimony.

- It is not a good idea to have witnesses, including clients, review documents and recorded statements prior to depositions or trial. The other side is entitled to a copy of a document that a witness has reviewed to refresh his or her memory of the events. Such a document can be damaging and especially useful to the opposition for impeaching the friendly witness. The best approach is to try to get the client to recall facts by asking questions and discussing information rather than having the client read the document.

- A set of form deposition questions can be used to simulate the deposition. An attempt to anticipate unusual questions that will likely be asked by the opponent is usually well worth the effort.

- How a witness or client presents themselves is important. Neat business attire is always appropriate for a deposition. Seeming too casual may present the wrong impression. Suggesting what to wear may seem forward, but remember for most witnesses, this is their first time at a deposition or giving formal testimony.

ATTEND AND REVIEW THE DEPOSITION

You may be asked to attend the deposition with the supervising attorney. This may depend on the complexity of the deposition and whether the cost of a paralegal's

ETHICAL CONSIDERATIONS: SHOWING RESPECT TO OPPOSING COUNSEL

Treating opposing counsel and other legal professionals with respect and courtesy seems like stating the obvious. We all recognize that attorneys should represent their clients zealously, but there are limits. In a U.S. District Court case in Florida, styled *Bedoya v. Adventura Limousine & Transportation Service, Inc.*, Case No. 11-24432-CIV-Altonaga (S.D. Fla. 2012), a law firm was disqualified from representing the plaintiffs in a case because of their offensive and reprehensible conduct toward opposing counsel. The case made headlines because of the abusive nature of the attorneys. The attorneys, Richard Celler and Stacey Shulman of Morgan & Morgan, attempted to intimidate the opposing counsel's client by degrading the competence of his attorney. Interestingly, these acts of intimidation occurred in a prior case but spilled over into a current case between the parties. In the court's 39-page opinion and order, the U.S. District Court judge, Cecilia Altonaga, outlined Celler's actions from previous cases and encounters with the defendants; the court also detailed a deposition incident where Celler chose Dunkin Donuts as the location of the deposition. Apparently, using this venue was a means of intimidating and distracting opposing counsel. The court further observed that during the deposition at Dunkin Donuts, Celler had been drawing crude pictures of male genitalia and relating those pictures to opposing counsel, Jason Coupal. Celler also bragged that he was playing the video game Angry Birds during the deposition and boasted beating someone in Minnesota. To make matters worse, Celler wore a T-shirt and shorts to the deposition to attempt to gain a "psychological advantage." Celler taunted Coupal about his trial successes and how he would lose this case. Such conduct although from a prior proceeding, as the court stated, impacted their current proceeding. Coupled with disparaging e-mails between the attorneys that violated ethical rules, the court disqualified Celler, Shulman, and their law firm from representing the plaintiffs in the current case. The court was very conscious of the extremeness of the remedy against Celler, Shulman, and their law firm, but because of their extreme and consistent pattern of disrespectful, unprofessional conduct, disqualification was warranted.

This case shows extreme behavior, but behavior that may be encountered. The lesson legal professionals should take from this case is that this type of conduct should not be tolerated on any level. If an attorney acts unprofessionally to you or others, immediately report it to your supervising attorney and document it in the file. Civility is the practice of most attorneys and legal professionals and should be the standard that you, as a paralegal, should practice and live by.

INTERNET EXERCISE

Research whether your state permits any form of electronic depositions and identify the requirements for this type of deposition.

attendance is justified. Some insurance companies will not pay for the paralegal to attend. Ideally, you should have the opportunity to attend one or more depositions prior to doing any deposition work. That experience provides a better understanding of the entire process and leads to a better job of assisting the attorney and the witness in all steps of deposition practice.

At the deposition your most important role is to listen carefully. If your attorney is doing the questioning, follow along on the outline of questions. The paralegals for both sides should take notes on significant information, contradictions, objections, and observations about the effectiveness of the witness and opposing counsel. Listening and observing carefully are important factors because the supervising attorney will occasionally be too distracted to be a good listener. You should be able to make suggestions, catch topics or questions that have been missed, and detect evasiveness, inconsistencies, or lies. You can also make sure information and documents are quickly retrieved when needed, that the law is researched on a point that arises in the deposition, or that an important phone call is made. Keep in mind that a paralegal may not question the deponent. To do so is the practice of law. It is generally acceptable for a paralegal to be the only person from the office to attend a deposition if the paralegal's only role is to observe, listen, and take notes.

It is also important for you to understand the rules governing procedure at the deposition. Federal Rule of Civil Procedure 30(b) (5) calls for the oath officer to start the deposition by entering into the record preliminary information about the oath officer, date, time and place of the deposition, deponent, administration of the oath, and the parties. The parties may agree to have one of the attorneys do this preliminary task.

Objections made to the qualifications of the oath officer, the manner of taking the deposition, the evidence presented, conduct of any party, or any other aspect of the proceeding shall be entered into the record by the officer. Objections shall be concise, nonargumentative, and shall not suggest an answer to the deponent. The deposition continues, however, subject to the objections. A deponent may be instructed not to answer only if to preserve a privilege, to enforce any court-imposed limits on the deposition, or to present a motion regarding conducting the deposition in bad faith or for unreasonably annoying, embarrassing, or oppressive questioning. The appropriate court may stop or limit the deposition if serious bad faith or similar violations occur, and may impose any necessary sanctions. Once stopped, a deposition cannot resume except by court order.

If a deponent or a party wants to review the transcript, that request must be made before the deposition is completed, and the request is entered into the record. Under the Federal Rules, unless this request is made, a party or deponent waives the right to review and list changes in the form or substance of the testimony.

At the end of the deposition, the oath officer shall record that the deposition is complete and place any important stipulations into the record, such as who will have custody of the transcript. Immediately following the deposition, compare notes with the attorney and draft a summary of the deposition based on those notes and other impressions. This summary allows discovery to progress and avoids having to wait for the typed transcript before other discovery decisions are made.

Following the deposition, the court reporter will prepare the transcript. If the deponent or a party requested to review the transcript, the oath officer notifies the

APPLY YOUR KNOWLEDGE

Review your state's rules for the process of a deponent's review of their deposition. Identify (1) the state rule; (2) the time period for review; (3) the process for making changes to the deposition; and (4) the verification process of the deposition.

deponent that the record is ready, then the deponent has 30 days in which to review the transcript or recording. If the deponent wants to submit changes in the form or substance of the deposition, that must be done in a signed, written statement detailing the changes and the reasons for the changes. The officer certifies that this review was requested and appends the changes to the transcript or recording. Your state procedure may vary.

Where state rules require it, check to see that the deponent signs the transcript. If the deponent refuses to sign it, the court reporter should sign it and state the reason why the witness would not sign. Verify that the court reporter has certified in writing that the witness was duly sworn by the officer and that the deposition is a true record of the testimony given by the witness. The deposition is then sealed and filed with the court or sent to the attorney who arranged for the transcript or recording. That attorney has the duty to protect the integrity of the transcript or recording. The officer is required to keep a copy so the other parties can request and receive copies as well. On request of a party, documents and things produced for inspection during the deposition should be marked as exhibits and attached to the deposition following the procedures outlined in Rule 30(f). Verifying that the requirements have been met assures the deposition's effective use at trial if needed.

On receipt of the deposition transcript, review it carefully. Any questions omitted by the attorney should be noted so they can be asked through interrogatories or at trial. Inconsistencies in a witness's testimony should also be noted. For example, in one part of the transcript the witness might say the van was traveling at 35 to 40 miles per hour and 20 pages later say it seemed like less than 30. Such inconsistency can be used to impeach the witness. The review may also reveal inaccuracies or omissions in the reporting.

TECHNOLOGY UPDATE: THE STATE OF ELECTRONIC DEPOSITIONS

We live in a mobile electronic world, and the law has tried to keep pace with the impact of new technology. Depositions have normally been conducted in a face-to-face physical setting. This has advantages, but often with high costs. Today, more and more attorneys are investigating and investing in technology that permits different kinds of electronic methods for taking depositions. As observed in the *Wei Ngai* case discussed earlier, there are drawbacks to the convenience of electronic communications—the inability to observe all interactions between the witness and attorney. Under Rule 30(b)(4), any means of remote access is permitted when conducting a deposition. Laptops, tablets, and other electronic devices can be used to view and conduct depositions. Even smartphones have the capability to stream a deposition.

Although electronics have cost advantages, especially if the witnesses are from long distances, such as the witnesses in the *Toyota* case discussed earlier, electronic depositions have their drawbacks. Sometimes the reception and voice quality is compromised. Use of technology such as Skype, Tango, Facetime on iPhones and iPads and Oovoo is economical and readily available, but can be victim to transmission interruptions which could delay or sever the deposition altogether. One issue that is being addressed through new technology is the completely paperless deposition, that is software which permits the electronic sharing of documents remotely through e-mail, for example, and stored in the cloud (discussed in Chapter 1). As technology becomes better, electronic depositions will become increasingly common among the legal community. Whether electronic deposition will completely replace the face-to-face deposition remains to be seen. The face-to-face deposition still provides important tools such as the physical observation of a witness's demeanor and presence. Sometimes a picture is not worth a thousand words.

DIGESTING DEPOSITIONS AND OTHER DOCUMENTS

INTRODUCTION AND DEFINITION

Whether you are confronted with medical records, depositions, trial transcripts, a party's written statement, commercial records, expert reports, or other documents, it is critical to reduce the volume of information to a format that affords the attorney a concise and accurate summary with a handy reference for locating the complete language in the original documents. To that end, this section focuses on digesting (summarizing) documents, using depositions as the primary example. The methods used to digest depositions are applicable to most other documents. Once each deposition or each significant document is summarized, the information on each point can be organized under topical headings. Such a format permits evidence from one or more witnesses to be compared, evaluated for evidentiary weight, and examined for inconsistencies and weaknesses.

Paralegals practice the art frequently and soon become good deposition digesters. Digesting depositions can become tedious at times, but the task's overall importance to the success of the client's case cannot be overstressed. The attorney with good digests in hand at trial will be more organized, knowledgeable, decisive, and effective.

PURPOSES FOR DIGESTING DEPOSITIONS

Deposition digests are used to do the following:

1. Condense large amounts of material
2. Index testimony and topics
3. Facilitate questioning and cross-examination of witness at trial
4. Lay foundation for production or admissions for discovery
5. Identify items for follow-up investigation or discovery
6. Verify key or disputed facts
7. Reveal inconsistencies in evidence or testimony
8. Review for trial or additional depositions
9. Support summary judgment and other motions
10. Include relevant facts or testimony in briefs
11. Cross-reference topics, witnesses, evidence
12. Bring new attorneys or paralegals up to speed on a case
13. Inform client
14. Prepare correspondence, settlement brochures, and material relevant to pretrial and other hearings

TECHNIQUES FOR DIGESTING DEPOSITIONS

Being a good digester takes language skills, time, and experience. Doing a good digest, however, even the first time, is not difficult. Here are some techniques for a good start in this area:

1. Study the file to grasp the claim, defenses, issues, and legal theories.

2. Ask the attorney to provide the outline of the questions used at the deposition that gives an overview and suggestions for topical headings, and guidance on the type of digest and indexes desired, location of examples of similar summaries, desired detail, paraphrased or ellipsis format (see number 13 below), time frame, cost, need of extra assistance, key issues, key individuals, and any other special requests.

3. Skim the entire deposition first; develop a feel for its scope, importance, issues addressed, and topics for digest headings.

4. Draft a topical outline or tentative table of contents for the digest, placing topics in the order raised in the deposition, for example:
   - Personal background
   - Education
   - Prior injuries
   - Other information (repeat headings where necessary)

5. Schedule blocks of time to do actual digesting so you will not lose sight of the continuity of the entire deposition and forget what topics have previously been addressed.

6. Compose in electronic form your summary. Some may still handwrite or dictate the summary, but the end result should be a document that is editable by those who rely on it. Most depositions today are in some electronic form. Copy the deposition and do your editing and summarizing on the computer or electronic device. If the depositions are not in electronic form, make a photocopy, then delete unnecessary language and take notes on the photocopy.

7. Be as concise as possible. Eliminate unnecessary words: article adjectives such as "the," "an," "a"; previous or proper nouns if the reference is clear; exchanges between attorneys; and false starts in questioning or answering by the attorneys or deponent. Note, though, that reduction quotas, such as one digest page for every ten pages of transcript, are not particularly helpful.

8. Use abbreviations and short forms as much as possible, but be sure they are clear: re = regarding; ex = exhibit; 12/3/15 = December 3, 2015; w/ = with; w/o = without; ∴ = therefore, ≅ = approximately, and so on.

9. Be accurate about what witnesses said. Use the witnesses' key words. Avoid distortion for the sake of obtaining a briefer phrase or having the digest coincide with your own understanding of the material. *Do not interpret!*

10. Use subheadings frequently and write in short paragraphs.

11. Use page and line number references in the margins and/or in a paragraph of summarized material, indicating where the full text of the summarized information can be found in the original transcript.

12. Utilize the "paraphrase" or the "ellipsis" method of summary. The paraphrase method is a concise restatement in paragraph form of what the witness said. The ellipsis method is a chronological listing of significant statements in sentence fragments preceded by ellipsis points (. . .). An example of each appears in Exhibit 8.9, a sample deposition digest form.

13. Include, in addition to the obvious, all dates exactly as mentioned, all exhibits by name and number with attached exhibit list referring to pages where the exhibit is identified, court reporter's notes on the witness's behavior, substantive objections, admissions, stipulations, document requests, and any notes by the attorney or yourself on the effectiveness of the witness.

TYPES OF DEPOSITION DIGESTS AND INDEXES

The prior techniques can be applied to create various types of deposition digests. Deposition digests (summaries) have a variety of names and formats (Exhibit 8.8). Eventually, you will need to choose the format that works best for you in a particular situation. Here are some formats for your consideration.

The *chronological* (sequential or page/line) summary condenses the deposition in the order that matters were raised. Each summarized fact or answer is referenced to its page and line in the transcript. Appearance of exhibits and the deponent's comments on them are also noted. The chronological digest should have a table of contents or topical index that states the topics as they arise in the deposition with appropriate page references. These can be made easily from the information on the sheets or the slips. Exhibit 8.9 is an example of the format for a chronological deposition digest beginning with a table of contents or topical index and ending with an exhibit index.

The *topical* (category, subject) digest is organized by topics and subtopics. Each of the deponent's answers that addresses a particular topic, regardless of where it appears in the transcript, is collected under that topical heading. These answers may then be organized as they appear in the transcript. The slip method of recording lends itself particularly well to this type of summary. An appropriate table of contents should be prepared. Sample pages from a topical deposition digest appear in Exhibit 8.10.

EXHIBIT 8.8 Deposition Summary Techniques

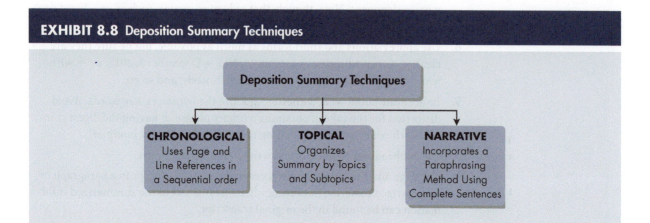

EXHIBIT 8.9 Deposition Digest (Chronological)

DEPOSITION DIGEST

CASE: Smith v. Jones Dixon Sup Crt #234 567
DEPONENT: Albert Hackston
DATE: 7/25/15

Page: Contents
Atty: G. Baker
L /A: N. LUONO

TABLE OF CONTENTS/TOPICAL INDEX

Topic	Page	Lines
1. Personal Data	1	6–12
2. Education		
High School	2	6–8
On-the-job Training	2	17–20
	10	3–5
3. Employment History		
Prior to Employment w/Plaintiff	5	
Employment w/Plaintiff	6	1–4
	11	17–20
	33	12–17

DEPOSITION DIGEST (CHRONOLOGICAL)

DEPONENT: Albert Hackston   Page 1

Pg.	Ln.	Topic	Summary	Exhib/Notes
1	6–12	Personal Data	Born 6/1/75, Detroit, MI, married, 2 children, lives at 1400 North Ave., Detroit	Speaks very softly
2	6–8	Education	Finished H.S. 92	
	17–20		OJT 1 year Army	Most recent training
3	10	Safety Training	(*Paraphrase method*) Hackston had read the instructions in detail and received 4 hours of OJT before operating the machine. In June 2013 he watched the disassembly and reassembly of the machine. It was frequently serviced and he specifically recalled preventive maintenance was performed on Sept. 8, '13.	
3	10	Safety Training	(*Ellipsis method*) . . . he had read the instructions in detail.	
	13		. . . he had 4 hours of OJT before using it.	
	18		. . . saw the apparatus disassembled and reassembled in June 2013 . . .	
4	6		. . . he was present when preventive maintenance was performed Sept. 8, '13	

(continued)

EXHIBIT 8.9 Deposition Digest (Chronological) (*continued*)

DEPOSITION DIGEST
DEPONENT: Albert Hackston   Page: Exhibit Index

EXHIBIT INDEX

EXHIBIT NUMBER	DESCRIPTION
1	Ch. 3, "Safety," ST 3 Trng. Man'l dated 5/10/12
2	St 3 Operating Instructions dated 9/20/12
3	OJT Training Certificate dated 2/19/12

An increasing number of court reporters prepare transcripts that condense several pages of deposition transcript into one. If this practice is the case in your jurisdiction, you may need to adapt the traditional page/line emphasis according to what your attorney prefers. In addition, many court reporters provide indexing services. With a list of topics (key words) provided by you, the reporter can compile an index showing on what page that topic is mentioned.

The *narrative* digest incorporates the paraphrase method of complete sentences and may be organized by topic, witness, or other categories depending on the attorney's needs. Narrative digests are particularly good to send to a client such as an insurance company so the client can get an understanding of the nature of the evidence in the case. An example of a page from a narrative digest arranged by topic is in Exhibit 8.11.

DIGEST AIDS FOR COMPLEX CASES

If there are numerous deponents, you may be asked to perform several tasks to assist the attorney in trial preparation as well as at the trial. First, a master topical digest can be developed to collect the comments of all deponents on a particular topic under the respective topical heading. This type of digest facilitates a quick review of all evidence, including exhibits, from all deponents on a particular key point. A master topical digest should also include references to page, line, and deponent. The preparation of more complex cases can also be assisted by the compilation of subindexes that list all deponents, all exhibits, or are organized by topic.

AUTOMATED DEPOSITION SUMMARIES

Most court reporters now provide depositions and other transcripts on disk. The transcript can then be downloaded to the law office computers, dramatically enhancing the paralegal's ability to summarize, annotate, index, locate, and otherwise manipulate the information. Software specifically for summarizing transcripts

EXHIBIT 8.10 Page Extracts from Topical (Subject) Deposition Summaries

TOPICAL DEPOSITION SUMMARY

Case: FORRESTER v. MERCURY PARCEL

Case File No. _____

Deponent: Ann Forrester

Date: 12/10/__

Page 1

Attorney: L. Ott

Paralegal: C. Sorenson

TOPIC: INJURIES

Page	Line	Summary	Exhibits/Notes
38	3	Date of accident 2/26/__ ... she felt sharp pain at point of impact.	
	6	... pain was extreme in hip, lower abdomen, and upper left leg.	
39	1	... she felt nauseated.	
53–54	28–1	Date: 3/10/__ ... after two weeks in hospital the leg felt numb and she could not move it. etc.	

TOPIC: EMPLOYMENT

Page	Line	Summary	Exhibits/Notes
62	7	... she said she rarely missed work before the accident.	
66	12	... believed she would have been promoted by now to master teacher.	
71	2	... does not see how she can return to teaching with her current disabilities. etc.	

and other information is readily available. Programs such as *Summation iBlaze®*, *Concordance*, and others make digesting more interesting and efficient, and are designed to utilize the summarizing formats already discussed, and others. This software enables the paralegal to monitor live depositions online, annotate and mark the deposition in real-time, access multiple depositions and other document depositories simultaneously, download documents, and, of course, summarize the deposition.

Exhibit 8.12 is an excerpt from the transcript (absent page and line numbers) of a deposition of Mr. Hart.

EXHIBIT 8.11 Deposition Digest (Narrative)

DEPOSITION DIGEST (NARRATIVE/TOPICAL)

CASE: Johns v. Brown No. Civ 880050   Page 1
DEPONENT: Catherine Johns

         Atty: H. Ray
DATE: 7/16/ _____   Plgl: C. Borden

Background

Catherine Johns is 34 years old, residing at 1437 Oak St., Legalville, Columbia, is divorced and has one child, Edward, 10. (pages 1–2)

She has a master's in business administration from Columbia State and her high school diploma from East Legalville H.S. (3)

Employment

She worked for two years after high school for Columbia Foods as a secretary from 2003-05. She has worked for Fairmont Computers as a market analyst from 2010 to the present, earning $60,000 per year. (4–5)

The Accident

On May 3, 2010, Johns was driving to work, proceeding north on Holiday Blvd. in Legalville at 7:40 A.M. She was wearing a seat belt. She drove a 2009 Chevrolet Camaro and was 200 feet from the intersection of Holiday and East Twenty-third St. when defendant, Harold Brown, suddenly backed out of his driveway at 3201 Holiday Blvd. in his 2010 Buick LaCrosse. (9, 32)

Johns "swung car to left" but the back of Brown's car hit hers in the Camaro's left front. (10–11)

Johns' car "lurched" into oncoming traffic lane, crossed lane avoiding car driven by Walter Forth, went up curb, and "smashed" into Roy's Hot Dog Stand and stopped. (11–12, 23)

Injuries

Johns hit her head on the steering wheel, breaking her nose and cheekbone. Ligaments in her left knee were severed, and she suffered muscle damage and internal injuries to the stomach lining causing internal bleeding. (14, 27)

Johns was rushed to Mount Sinai Hospital where she was admitted and operated on to correct fractures, stop internal bleeding, and repair ligaments in knee. Minor plastic surgery was performed on her nose by Dr. Kizar on 7/2/10. (15, 28)

One year after accident Johns still needs cane to walk. The fractures have healed satisfactorily but chewing is limited and painful, and one obvious scar remains on her nose. (16, 28–30)

Loss of Employment

(narrative continues)

EXHIBIT 8.12 Deposition of Richard Hart

UNITED STATES DISTRICT COURT FOR THE EASTERN DISTRICT OF COLUMBIA

ANN FORRESTER
   and
WILLIAM FORRESTER,
              Plaintiffs

     v.

RICHARD HART
   and
MERCURY PARCEL SERVICE, INC.,
              Defendants

Civil Action, File No._____

Cincinnati, Ohio, Wednesday, January 12, _____

    Pretrial examination of Richard Hart held in the offices of Ott, Ott & Knudsen, 444 Front St., Cincinnati, Ohio, at 10:00 A.M. on the above date before Bernadette Schaffer, Certified Court Reporter and Notary of Ohio.

    APPEARANCES:
    Arthur White
White, Wilson & McDuff
Attorneys for Plaintiffs

    Lynn Ott
Ott, Ott & Knudsen
Attorneys for Defendants

                                           (signature and certification omitted)

    Richard Hart, after having been duly sworn, was examined and testified as follows:

By Mr. White:
Q. Please state your full name.
A. Richard Hart
Q. Your residence?
A. 1223 Penny Lane, Cincinnati, Ohio.
Q. How long have you lived there?
A. Eight years.
Q. Where did you live prior to that?
A. 4313 East Wickland St., Columbus, Ohio.
Q. How long did you reside there?
A. Seven years.
Q. Are you married?
A. Yes.
Q. Your wife's full name?
A. Jessica Marie Hart.
Q. When were you married?
A. Seventeen years ago. June 19, _____.
Q. Do you have any children?

(continued)

EXHIBIT 8.12 Deposition of Richard Hart (*continued*)

A. Yes, two boys.

Q. What are their names and ages?

A. Brett is sixteen and Jerome is fourteen.

Q. When and where were you born?

A. August 13, 19 _____, I am forty-one.

Q. Where?

A. Oh, ah . . . Columbus, Ohio.

Q. How far did you go in school?

A. I graduated from high school.

Q. Where did you attend high school?

A. Taft High in Columbus.

Q. What, if any, schooling have you had since high school?

A. I was trained as an ambulance driver by the army and took a truck driving course about twelve years ago.

Q. When were you in the army?

A. Twenty years ago, 19 _____ to 19 _____, for two years.

Q. How extensive was your training?

A. A few weeks each year.

Q. Where was your training?

A. Fort Oglethorp, Georgia.

Q. Did you ever have any special training for driving on ice and snow?

A. No, but I have lived in Columbus most of my life and we get plenty of winter weather.

Q. Where was the truck driving course?

A. In Cincinnati.

Q. What was the name of the school?

A. The Cincinnati Vocational Institute.

Q. How long was the course?

A. Six weeks.

Q. Did you learn how to drive vans at this school?

A. No, it was for large rigs.

Q. Did they give you any special training for winter driving?

A. They were supposed to, but we never got to it.

Q. Have you ever received any formal training for driving in wintery weather?

A. No.

Q. Not even with Mercury Parcel?

A. No.

Q. What is your current occupation?

A. Route man.

Q. Would you explain what a route man is?

A. O.K. I drive a truck—or van—and deliver parcels and things to people and stores over a certain route.

Q. What route do you cover?

A. We cover several different ones—sometimes we fill in for a guy that's sick.

Q. Are you assigned to the Legalville, Columbia route very often?

A. Oh, sure.

Q. Have you ever made deliveries on Capitol Drive outside of Legalville before?

A. No . . . possibly . . . I'm not sure.

Q. Would any records of your deliveries indicate whether you had been out there before?

EXHIBIT 8.12 Deposition of Richard Hart (*continued*)

A. They might. It's probably been years ago.

Q. How long ago?

A. Maybe five or six years ago . . . I don't know.

Q. What records might show that?

A. We have to fill out a record of delivery form—it has addresses on it.

Q. Do they show every delivery?

A. Yes.

Q. Does this form have a number?

A. I think so. It . . . it's a Form 30.

Q. Who is your current employer?

A. Mercury.

Q. Do you mean the Mercury Parcel Service?

A. Yes.

Q. How long have you worked for them?

A. Let's see, two years in Columbus and eight years in Cincinnati. Ten years.

Q. Is this full-time employment?

A. Yes.

Q. Have you worked in any capacity other than route man for Mercury?

A. No.

Q. How much do you earn an hour?

A. $10.35 an hour.

Q. How many hours per week?

A. Usually 40 . . . unless we need to work overtime.

Q. How often do you work overtime?

A. Every so often when someone is sick or we have a lot to deliver . . . or if we volunteer to put in some extra time.

Q. Where did you work prior to working for Mercury?

A. I worked as an ambulance driver for the town of Jackson just outside Columbus. There was always trouble getting adequate funds to keep the service going, so I quit and went with Mercury.

Q. What is the address for that service?

A. If it's still there—it is Route 3, Highway 95, Jackson, Ohio.

Q. How long did you work for the ambulance service?

A. Six years.

Q. Have you had a good driving record?

A. Yes.

Q. Have you had any accidents either on or off the job?

A. Well, yes. I think most folks do.

Q. When did you have the accidents?

A. Well, I had one two years ago in Cincinnati, and . . .

Q. Were you driving for Mercury at the time of the accident?

A. Yes, I was.

Q. What happened?

A. I was trying to exit off I-75 and a guy was trying to enter I-75. They cross there. I thought he was by me and he slowed down. I ran into his left side. No one was hurt, thank goodness.

Q. Were any citations issued by the police?

(continued)

EXHIBIT 8.12 Deposition of Richard Hart (*continued*)

A. No.

Q. Have you had any other accidents?

A. Yes, I had one about five years ago in Columbus.

Q. What happened?

A. My family and I were heading for downtown Columbus to see a Fourth of July parade. I was in a line of stopped traffic. The line began to move. I turned to say something to my wife. The car in front of me stopped and I rammed into it. An elderly lady got hurt but my insurance company paid for her doctor bills.

Q. Were any citations issued?

A. Yes, I got a ticket for inattentive driving.

Q. Any other accidents?

A. Not that I recall.

Q. Have you received any other traffic citations?

A. Well, a few over the years.

L. Ott: Let the record reflect that I object to this question on the grounds that it is not relevant to the accident in question.

Mr. White: Counselor, if there is a pattern of reckless driving, then I believe it is relevant. Your objection is noted. May I proceed?

L. Ott: Yes.

By Mr. White:

Q. What were those citations for?

A. Mainly for speeding.

Q. How many in the last five years?

A. Oh, not too many.

Q. More than five?

A. I guess so.

Q. Six?

A. I think about six.

Q. Where have most of these violations occurred?

A. In the Cincinnati area.

Q. How many occurred on the job?

A. Oh, about half, I'd say.

Q. Mr. Hart, do you recall the accident you had on February 26, _____?

A. Yes, I do.

Q. Were you working for Mercury Parcel at the time of the accident?

A. Yes.

Q. When did you start work that day?

A. I was on the night shift and started at 11:00 P.M. on the twenty-fifth. I was supposed to be back in the barn by 7:00, but I was about two hours behind schedule because of the weather.

Q. So normally on night shift you work from 11:00 P.M. until 7:00 A.M.?

A. Yes.

Q. Were you driving the entire time the night of February 25 to 26?

A. Well, not constantly. We do stop and get out of the truck to deliver the packages or letters. However, because most of the deliveries were in Legalville, and due to the weather, I guess I was driving more than usual.

Q. Did you take any breaks?

A. Yes, the union says we're to get two breaks and a paid half-hour lunch break. That night, though, I only took a break at 3:00 A.M. By lunchtime and the second break I was too far behind to stop.

Q. Other than the weather, did anything else occur that was unusual that night?

EXHIBIT 8.12 Deposition of Richard Hart (*continued*)

A. Not that I recall.

Q. Were you having any mechanical trouble with the truck—like braking or steering problems?

A. Not really. Oh, the van pulls to the left a little when you brake hard, but I knew that and was able to allow for that when I stopped.

Q. How long had that problem existed?

A. Oh, about two weeks. I mentioned it to them about a week before the accident but told them it wasn't too serious.

Q. Who do you mean when you say "them"?

A. A couple of the mechanics at the barn—Mercury's shop.

Q. Can you name them?

A. Well, I think I told Arnie Hanson and I might have told Johnny Sloan . . . I'm not sure about Johnny.

Q. Is there a regular procedure for reporting problems with a vehicle?

A. No, not really . . . well, there is a form that we're supposed to fill out, but if it is not too serious, we just mention it to one of the mechanics.

Q. What does the mechanic do then?

A. If they can find the time, they'll look at it. If not they wait till their next regular servicing of the van.

Q. Had the problem of pulling to the left been worked on at the shop?

A. No, I don't think so.

Q. Do you always drive the same van?

A. Yes, almost always.

Q. Did you fill out a form on the braking problem?

A. No.

Q. Describe the weather conditions that night.

A. The roads were wet from melting snow at the beginning of the evening, but by mid-shift—say 3:30 a.m.—the roads began to freeze in spots. You had to be careful.

Q. Had you done any slipping that night?

A. Occasionally . . . but nothing serious.

Q. Was there a lot of ice on the roads?

A. Here and there.

Q. What was the road like just before the accident?

A. Well, it wasn't too bad. There were occasional patches of ice, but not too bad.

Q. Was there enough ice to slow you up some? In other words, did you reduce your speed?

A. Oh, maybe five or ten miles an hour . . . but not much. The road really wasn't too bad.

Q. How fast were you going just prior to the accident?

A. Well, I had just looked and I was going at about thirty-five miles per hour.

Q. What do you mean you "just looked"?

A. Well, I looked at the speedometer to check my speed.

Q. Why?

A. Well, I'm not sure . . . I think I was thinking about how late I was going to be getting back home.

Q. Were you anxious to get back to Cincinnati?

A. Yes, it had been a long night.

Q. Were you tired?

A. A little—because of the weather, I think.

Q. Couldn't you have stopped for a break?

A. I could have, but I didn't. I was late enough the way it was.

(continued)

EXHIBIT 8.12 Deposition of Richard Hart (*continued*)

Q. Had you had any other long shifts that week?

A. The last shift had been snowy, so I was about an hour late that night.

Q. How much sleep did you get the following day, the twenty-fifth?

A. About six hours, I think. My son had a basketball game that afternoon, so I didn't get to sleep quite as much as I usually do.

Q. Are there any company rules about how much sleep you are to have before your shift?

A. No.

Q. Are there any company rules about taking a break if you become tired?

A. Oh, they tell us to pull over if we are real tired, but I felt OK.

Q. How do they tell you to pull over? Is that a rule, or do they mention it at meetings? How is this done?

A. Well, anyone who drives knows that, but I think there are some safety rules posted in the shop.

Q. Do you read those rules?

A. Not really. They're nothing most drivers don't already know.

Q. Are there any limits on how many hours you are supposed to drive at any one time?

A. I think the rule is around seven hours of actual driving time.

Q. How many hours of actual driving time did you drive that night?

A. Oh, I'd say about eight, maybe nine.

Q. And had the accident not occurred, you would have had nearly two more hours of driving?

A. Yes.

Q. Is there any penalty for driving over the limit of hours?

A. Not that I know of.

Q. On bad weather nights, or if you're late for any other reason, do you get paid overtime?

A. Only if the extra hours are unavoidable, such as for bad weather.

Q. Would you please describe the road you were driving at the time of the accident?

A. The road was quite narrow, hilly, and curvy.

Q. What was the posted speed limit on that road?

A. I'm not sure.

Q. Would you characterize the road as tricky?

A. Oh, maybe a little . . . but I have driven a lot of roads worse than that.

Q. You mentioned before that you looked at your speedometer just before the accident. What happened next?

A. Well, I looked up and suddenly there was this lady stepping out onto the road.

Q. You looked at your speedometer just before the accident occurred?

A. Yes, I glanced at it—only for a split second.

Q. Had you seen the woman before you looked at the speedometer?

A. No.

Q. Why not?

A. Well, she was hidden by a rise in the road. See, there is a dip in the road where the lady was at. I was coming over the hill just before the dip. You can't see to the bottom of the dip. And that's where the lady was.

Q. What happened then?

A. I thought she would stop, but she just kept looking ahead and kept walking into the road.

Q. What do you mean she just kept looking ahead?

A. Well, when I came over the hill she was barely onto the road. I thought she would see or hear me and stop, but her head was tucked down into her coat and she just kept walking.

Q. Did you sound your horn?

A. No.

Q. What did you do?

EXHIBIT 8.12 Deposition of Richard Hart (*continued*)

A. I hit the brakes.

Q. Then what?

A. The truck began to pull to the left . . . it began to fishtail back and forth. I pumped the brakes to keep control. The lady looked up then, but hesitated and then went the wrong way. I couldn't avoid her. I was trying to get control of the van and then I heard the thump. I felt sick—I knew I'd hit her.

Q. What happened then?

A. The van was crossing the middle of the road. I saw the woman fall off from my side of the van. I tried to hold the van under control, but it went into the ditch and hit a tree.

Q. How hard did the van pull to the left when you applied the brakes?

A. It started that way almost immediately. I think it might have been the same problem I described before, or it might have been the ice. I don't know. (Assume that the examination went on to cover what happened after the accident, damages to the van, Mr. Hart's injuries, etc. The opposing counsel would have an opportunity to ask questions, and then the deposition would conclude.)

Mr. White: I have no other questions.
(Witness excused)
(Deposition concluded)

OTHER FOLLOW-UP TASKS

As discovery progresses you can enhance your value to the litigation team by keeping the file current. Important information from documents, interrogatories, digests, investigation, research, and other sources should be regularly integrated into a case summary that includes specific source location references. This process not only better preserves critical information about the case over a long period of time and facilitates a quick review of the case, it also helps identify specific areas of the case that need attention.

SUMMARY

Deposition practice is an indispensable area of paralegal knowledge. Understand what a deposition is, what it can be used for, and what the rules of civil procedure require when taking depositions. Tasks include setting up the deposition, locating a court reporter, sending out notices and subpoenas, assisting witnesses and the attorney in preparing for the deposition, attending the deposition, summarizing it, and performing other follow-up tasks.

Deposition digests come in several formats adaptable to the special needs of a case. Computer software specifically for summarizing depositions and other documents greatly enhances your ability to work efficiently and effectively.

Knowing the issues in a case and what testimony is necessary to prove or refute proof of these issues is the key to good digesting. Condensing large documents and transcripts of testimony down to concise summaries that are well indexed to the originals saves countless hours when planning strategy, negotiating, preparing for trial, and appealing a case.

KEY TERMS

court reporter

deponent

deposition

subpoena

subpoena duces tecum

QUESTIONS FOR STUDY AND REVIEW

1. What is a deposition? What is the purpose of a deposition? What are the advantages and disadvantages of a deposition?

2. How many kinds of depositions are there, and what are their unique functions?

3. What is the time limit on the length of a deposition in federal cases? Your state's cases?

4. What is your role in the deposition process?

5. How do you obtain a subpoena for a deponent? What should be included on the subpoena?

6. What are the HIPAA-imposed assurance procedures and pertinent documents that must be employed when using a subpoena to get protected medical information?

7. When are witness and mileage fees required under Rule 45?

8. What should you do to plan and draft an outline for taking a deposition? What should be included in a witness file for the attorney?

9. Why is it important to prepare friendly witnesses or clients for deposition testimony?

10. What are some of the most significant things a witness can be told in preparing for the deposition?

11. What are significant ethical and other considerations that you need to be aware of in working with witnesses?

12. Why should the deponent's signature on the certified copy of the deposition not be waived in most instances?

13. What do you look for when reviewing a deposition?

14. What is the purpose of digesting litigation documents? List the techniques for digesting depositions.

15. What are the important uses of a deposition summary?

SYSTEMS FOLDER ASSIGNMENTS

1. Write a brief outline on the definition, purpose, scope, and the procedure of depositions to place in your systems folder.

2. Draft a checklist on preparing and serving subpoenas and place it and references to the pertinent documents in your systems folder. Include citations to both state and federal rules. Note the time limits for objection to a subpoena in this section of your systems folder. Add a section to the checklist on the relationship between a subpoena duces tecum and HIPAA procedural requirements. Place a copy or the page reference to the HIPAA-compliant Sample Cover Letter to Records Custodian in your systems folder.

3. Draft a checklist for planning and preparing for deposition based on the steps and recommendations made in this chapter, and place it in your systems folder.

4. Prepare a checklist for attending and reviewing the deposition and place it in your systems folder.

5. Place copies of or page references to the deposition summary examples in this chapter in your systems folder. Add any other examples provided in class.

APPLICATION ASSIGNMENTS

1. Assume you represent Mr. Hart. Prepare a deposition outline for your attorney to use in examining Mrs. Forrester. For purposes of this assignment only, limit the scope of your outline to the time immediately before and during the accident. Do not get into injuries or other damages. Use the sample outline, your checklist, and Exhibits 8.5 and 8.6 as guides for your work.

2. Exhibit 8.12 contains excerpts from a deposition of Mr. Hart. Skim the deposition transcript first. Then read it and carefully draft the corresponding section of a chronological digest. Prepare a table of contents for the digest. Count lines from the top of each page of the deposition, since no lines are provided. Then do a topical summary.

3. What limits are imposed on what can be asked in a deposition? What federal and state rules apply?

4. What are some of the ways to take depositions, other than orally, and their governing rules? What are the advantages and disadvantages of such procedures?

ANSWER:

Method	Advantage	Disadvantage	Rule

5. Assume that you are working to prepare Mr. Hart for his deposition by Mrs. Forrester's attorney. Mr. Hart says that he is unsure about the road conditions at the time of the accident. You and the attorney know that it works against Hart to appear unsure about important facts.

   a. The attorney says to Hart, "It's best not to be unsure and, after all, the road was not very icy." Are there any ethical concerns?

   b. The attorney has left the room and you say, "Mr. Hart, do you recall that during our first interview you told me the road was not very icy?" Are there any ethical concerns?

CASE ASSIGNMENTS

1. Mrs. Forrester needs to have the deposition of the driver, Richard Hart. Prepare the oral deposition notice and the documents that should be produced by him. Use information from previous chapters to prepare the document. Similarly, Richard Hart's attorney wants to depose both Mr. and Mrs. Forrester. Draft the deposition notices for each and the corresponding document request, if needed. Be creative and imaginative.

2. Assume that Henry Herbert, III, is the executive officer for Mercury Parcel Service, Inc. Draft a subpoena duces tecum requiring Mr. Herbert to appear at a deposition and to bring the employment and safety records of Mr. Hart. Find information in the Forrester complaint in Chapter 4 and make up the remaining information, remembering the rules for deposing persons in another district.

9

DISCOVERY: DOCUMENT PRODUCTION AND CONTROL, MEDICAL EXAMS, ADMISSIONS, AND COMPELLING DISCOVERY

OUTLINE

OBJECTIVES

AFTER READING THIS CHAPTER, YOU WILL BE ABLE TO:

- Draft a request for production of documents, request for admissions, and request for medical examination

- Outline the procedures for preparing and responding to a request for production of documents

- Analyze the documents produced for responsiveness, relevancy, and compliance

- Identify the best use for request for admissions

- Prepare a motion compelling discovery and identify the range of sanctions that could be ordered by a court

INTRODUCTION

This chapter covers requests for production of documents and things and entry upon land for inspection and other purposes, the related process of document management, and request for physical and mental examination. The section on medical record analysis illustrates techniques a paralegal can use to analyze discovery or other information in a highly technical field. Following this section, we take a look at the request for admissions. In addition, you will find that you can use federal and state freedom of information requests and their benefits as a device that is independent of the formal discovery process. The Federal Rules covering the subject of discovery also contain provisions for compelling discovery, and courts may make use of applicable sanctions against uncooperative parties. The final section suggests how to organize the client's file with the information accumulated through investigation and discovery.

PRODUCTION OF DOCUMENTS AND THINGS AND ENTRY UPON LAND FOR INSPECTION AND OTHER PURPOSES

INTRODUCTION

Production of documents and things is a request made of one party by the other to physically produce and permit the requesting party to inspect, copy, test, or sample documents, electronically stored information, physical evidence, and land and buildings, and is governed by Federal Rule of Civil Procedure 34. Its purpose is to make evidence available to both sides to assess its value and to prevent surprise at trial. More specifically, the requesting party uses the device not only to discover what evidence the other side has, but also to locate evidence damaging to the other side that supports any theories propounded by the requesting party. The request for production and inspection is particularly valuable in business cases and for accessing any tests or information used to form the basis for the testimony of the adversary's expert witnesses. Information discovered in this manner can be valuable in preparing for depositions, settlement proposals, or trial. With the Rule 26(a) disclosure of documents provision or similar state rules, the request for documents and things is more a narrow, follow-up device than a sweeping discovery tool.

Documents may be produced in the context of interrogatories, depositions, and subpoenas. Rule 34 and parallel state rules, however, are the primary means to require production of documents from another party and, therefore, are the focus of this section.

SCOPE

Rule 34(a) defines the scope of the request and includes the following evidence:

(1) . . . writings, drawings, graphs, charts, photographs, phono recording, and other data compilations from which information can be obtained, translated, if necessary, by the respondent through detection devices into reasonably usable

form, as well as any tangible things which constitute or contain matter within the scope of Rule 26(b) and which are in the possession, custody, or control of the party upon whom the request is served; or (2) to permit entry upon designated land or other property in the possession or control of the party upon whom the request is served for the purpose of inspection and measuring, surveying, photographing, testing, or sampling the property or any designated object or operation thereon, within the scope of Rule 26(b).

The scope of the rule covers not only tangible (physical) information such as paper documents, but also any type of e-stored information. The request, however, cannot be unreasonably burdensome, oppressive, or unduly disruptive, such as when going to observe the internal workings of a business or manufacturing plant. Businesses are not expected to disclose commercially valuable trade secrets. Of course, privileged and work product materials and information that are irrelevant or cannot reasonably be expected to lead to admissible evidence are beyond the reach of the rule. Rule 34 contains no specific limits on the number of requests or documents that may be requested; it is, however, objectionable to be unreasonable in the number requested or the period of time (dates) covered by the request. Reasonableness is dictated by the type, value, and complexity of the case.

PROCEDURE

In many nondisclosure jurisdictions the request for production and inspection can be made with the service of the summons and complaint, or at any time after the action starts. Where Rule 26(a) or similar disclosure is in effect, production of documents and things cannot be requested until at or after the parties' discovery planning meeting, unless authorized by the court or otherwise stipulated. The request can be made to any other party. Third persons can be asked to produce documents and things or submit to an inspection through the subpoena duces tecum.

The request may be served directly on the other party without leave of the court and must state the items to be inspected either by individual item or by category with reasonable particularity. It also shall specify a reasonable time, place, and manner for conducting the inspection and any related activities, such as copying or testing. The form or forms in which e-stored information is to be produced may be specified as well.

The responding party must file a reply within 30 days of receipt of the request. A longer period may be in effect in nondisclosure jurisdictions. A shorter or longer period may be required by the court or agreed to by the parties in writing, subject to the restrictions in Rule 29. Rule 29 states that only the court can extend the time specified in Rules 33, 34, and 36 if the requested extension would alter the date for completion of discovery, hearing a motion, or starting a trial. The reply must be written and shall indicate, with respect to each item or category, compliance or any objection (including objection to the requested form for producing e-stored information), specifying the particular part or section of the request objected to and the reasons. If the form for producing e-stored information is not indicated in the request or is objected to, the responding party must state in which form it intends to produce the information. Any unobjectionable part of an item or category objected to must be produced or made available for inspection. One may not withhold a set of documents because one of the documents requested is objectionable.

The requesting party may move for a court order under Rule 37(a) if they think the refusal or objection is improper. Most states have either parallel or similar procedures, but it is always wise to check.

Unless otherwise agreed or ordered, documents shall be produced either as they are kept in the usual course of business or organized and labeled according to the categories in the request. Unless specified in the request or otherwise agreed or ordered, e-stored information must be produced in a form (or forms) in which it is ordinarily maintained or that is "reasonably usable." A party may not take usable information and produce it in a form "that removes or significantly degrades" that usability [Committee Note, Civil Rule Amendments 2006, Rule 34, Subdivision (b)]. To reduce the burden of production, the producing party need only produce any item of e-stored information in one form.

The cost of complying with a request to produce documents and things in the federal system is generally borne by the producing party [*Oppenheimer Fund Inc. v. Sanders*, 437 U.S. 340 (1978)]. Where costs are particularly burdensome, such as in large e-discovery cases, courts are increasingly inclined to shift some of the costs to the requesting party [*Rowe Entertainment Inc. v. The William Morris Agency Inc.*, 205 F.R.D. 421 (S.D.N.Y. 2002)]. Shifting any costs should be considered, however, only regarding data described as inaccessible, such as fragmented, "deleted," or damaged data or that on storage or archival back-up tapes [*Zubulake v. UBS Warburg LLC*, 217 Fed. R. D. 309 (S.D.N.Y. 2003)]. Inaccessible data is usually the most expensive to produce.

Practically speaking, attorneys informally work out cost issues according to local practice and the amount in controversy, the resources of the respective clients, and the degree of significance of the issues. It is common for the requesting party, once the information is produced, to pay for such things as copying the information, reproducing photos, and like procedures that facilitate the requestor's subsequent analysis and use of the material in preparing for trial.

INITIAL PREPARATION FOR PRODUCTION AND INSPECTION REQUEST

Decide what to request, keeping in mind the facts of the case and the legal theories gained through a review of the file. Give particular attention to the answers to interrogatories or deposition questions that identify pertinent documents. It might be useful to determine the types of documents or things often used in a particular industry or business. Clients may help here, or experts, or persons in similar businesses and trade and professional associations. The law office's or client's technology manager may be helpful in an e-discovery case. In a highly complex or technical matter, a consultant may be needed. If disclosure has occurred, focus on documents and things missed in or suggested by the initial disclosure. Review the Rule 26 discovery plan. Consider the opponent's cost and the likely benefit of each item requested. For electronically stored information, the cost hierarchy, from least expensive to most expensive, runs as follows:

active data

Active data is the information stored on the hard drive or network.

Active Data: **Active data** is the information stored on the hard drive or network. Think of active data as your regular day-to-day data—the current data and information that you access every day on your computer. Data such as documents, calendars, e-mail, and other information currently accessible on

metadata

data about data.

embedded data

another term for metadata.

backup data

Backup data is that data that duplicates information as a protective method.

residual data

Residual data is the fragmented data that is from deleted or corrupted files. Also known as latent or ambient data.

computers, networks, and the like are considered active data. This type of data is the least expensive and easiest to retrieve.

Metadata: **Metadata** is defined as data about data. It is the data that explains other data—the hidden data or information on author creation and alteration. It is also known as **embedded data**. With metadata, attorneys and paralegals can discern not only who prepared a document, but when and the number of drafts. By evaluating the metadata, determining when a document was printed is possible. Similarly, information on e-mails including recipient and blind copies, plus other information, can be identified as well from the metadata.

Backup Data: **Backup data** is that data that duplicates information as a protective method. It is data that is stored on backup tapes, optical storage, and hard disks. The trend, however, is to store data remotely through broadband services, as this provides for the most secure measures.

Residual Data: **Residual data**, also known as latent or ambient data, is the fragmented data such as that from deleted files and corrupted files. This data can be found on hard drives and is not readily accessible from normal use. Effectively, residual data is data that seemingly was deleted and lost forever but is still potentially retrievable. It is the most expensive data to produce in the discovery process.

Determine, as well, whether the office has adequate resources, both in technology and personnel, to handle and analyze the information to be requested. In particularly voluminous cases, the cost of hiring an outside vendor should be weighed. Consult with the attorney to arrive at a mutual list of specific items or categories of items that should be requested.

Frequently the production and inspection occurs in a room in the office of the attorney whose client has possession of the documents. In some cases it involves arranging to go to a particular building to inspect machinery, observe a production process or a test, or copy computerized data forensically. If so, a time and manner of inspection of copying should be agreed on that is reasonable and not disruptive, which may require setting a time outside normal business hours; otherwise, most requests are timed for normal business hours. Production and inspection may simply be a process of exchanging a CD, DVD, flash or zip drive, or sharing access to an online document bank.

DRAFTING THE REQUEST FOR PRODUCTION AND INSPECTION

A good sample of a request, preferably in a similar case, should be obtained for reference. Office copies or the standard form books and electronic sources should be consulted. Exhibit 9.1 is a general form for a Request for Production. Some practitioners include, at the beginning of the request, a definitions section similar to equivalent sections in interrogatories. In drafting a request, remember the following guidelines:

1. Describe the items or categories with sufficient specificity so that a person of average intelligence has enough information to know what must be produced. The standard is flexible and is determined by how much the requesting party can reasonably be expected to know and whether the respondent has sufficient

EXHIBIT 9.1 Request for Production, Inspection, and Copying of Documents, and Inspection and Photographing of Things and Real Property—General Form

[Fed. R. Civ. P. Rule 34]

[*Title of Court and Cause*]

Pursuant to the Federal Rules of Civil Procedure, Rule 34 [or your state rule] [plaintiff] or [defendant] _____ requests [plaintiff] or [defendant] within _____ [30 days or (state a number)] after service of this request, to respond to the following requests: [include a definition section here which will assist in assuring that the documents requested will be produced] [Such as:

Documents include writings, drawings, graphs, charts, photographs, and other data compilations from which information can be obtained, or translated in necessary, by the [party] through detection devices into reasonably usable form.]

1) That defendant produce and permit plaintiff to inspect and to copy each of the following documents:
[*List the documents either individually or by category and describe each of them to be inspected or copied. State the time, place, and manner of making the inspection and performance of any related acts.*]

2) That defendant produce and permit plaintiff to inspect and to copy, test, or sample each of the following objects:
[*List the objects either individually or by category and describe each of them. State the time, place, and manner of making the inspection and performance of any related acts.*]

3) That defendant permit plaintiff to enter [here describe property to be entered] and to inspect and to photograph, test, or sample [here describe the portion of the real property and the objects to be inspected].
[*State the time, place, and manner of making the inspection and performance of any related acts.*]

_____
Attorney for Plaintiff

Address: _____

Adapted from West's Federal Forms, § 3551, v. 3A, with permission of West Group.

knowledge to determine what is requested. Phrases such as "financial records" or "all correspondence between" have been found to be inadequate descriptions. More specificity in name, topic, and time is required.

2. Organize the request by the type of evidence requested (see Exhibit 9.1) and include a paragraph on the continuing obligation of the respondent to produce pertinent documents that come into the respondent's possession after the original production date.

3. Include an instruction that directs the producing party to designate clearly what documents and things produced respond to each respective item of the request, if your request is pursuant to a rule that does not specify how the information should be produced.

4. Regarding electronically stored information, apply the knowledge gained from your e-discovery interrogatories (Exhibit 7.10) and any subsequent deposition of the other party's technology manager; identify the form in which you want the data produced, such as in native format (which includes metadata), paper or electronic form, and other considerations; and confine the request to cover a reasonable period of time.

Assume Mercury Parcel has indicated in its answer to Mrs. Forrester's interrogatories that the following items do exist: rules and regulations of the Interstate Commerce Commission on the required maintenance of vehicles used in interstate commerce, copies of Form ICC-2010 needed to report compliance with those rules on a quarterly basis, Form ICC-2010A used to record regular maintenance information on a specified vehicle, and Form ICC-2015 for recording specific complaints and resulting repairs to a specific vehicle. Also assume that the answer revealed that the van was vehicle number 23 and that photographs had been taken of the van and the accident scene. Although more records might be available, these examples should be sufficient for purposes of illustration. Assume Mr. White has asked you to draft that request. After reviewing the file and forms and consulting with the attorney, you might draft a form that looks like Exhibit 9.2.

EXHIBIT 9.2 Example of a Production and Inspection Request Form

UNITED STATES DISTRICT COURT FOR THE EASTERN DISTRICT OF COLUMBIA

ANN FORRESTER,

                Plaintiff

   v.   Civil Case, File No. _____

MERCURY PARCEL SERVICE, INC.,

                Defendant

PLAINTIFF'S REQUEST FOR PRODUCTION AND INSPECTION OF DOCUMENTS, THINGS, AND REAL PROPERTY

According to Rule 34 of the Federal Rules of Civil Procedure, Plaintiff requests Defendant Mercury Parcel Service to respond within thirty days to the following requests:

1. That Defendant produce and permit Plaintiff to inspect and to copy each of the following documents:
   a. The specific rules and regulations of the Interstate Commerce Commission requiring regular safety checks, maintenance, and repair of vehicles used in interstate commerce.
   b. Defendant's file copies of all Form 2010s submitted to the ICC between Feb. _____ and Jan. _____.
   c. All Form ICC-2010As recording the regular maintenance and safety checks on van number 23 over the two-year period preceding the accident on February 26, _____.
   d. All Form ICC-2010As for all other Defendant's delivery vehicles over the two years preceding the accident.
   e. All Form ICC-2015s recording complaints and needed repairs and subsequent repairs made to van number 23 for the two years preceding the accident.
   f. All Form ICC-2015s on all other vehicles for the two years preceding the accident.
   g. All photographs or negatives thereof that Defendant had taken of the accident scene and the damage to the van. Plaintiff will inspect and copy these items at the office of Plaintiff's attorney on November 1, _____ at 9:00 A.M., or at any other reasonable time and place convenient to counsel in this action.

                                               Respectfully submitted,

                                               _____

                                               Arthur White
                                               Attorney for Plaintiff
                                                 (address)
                                                 (telephone number)

INTERNET
EXERCISE

Locate your state's rule
for production of doc-
uments and identify
(a) the rule number,
(b) the procedure,
(c) time to respond,
and (d) limitations,
if any.

The wording in Exhibit 9.2 can be customized to encompass electronic forms of the requested information, plus any memos or e-mails that address maintenance of van number 23 or other matters related to the ICC reports.

SERVICE OF THE REQUEST FOR PRODUCTION

The request should then be signed by the attorney, and you should serve the request by mail and execute the appropriate certificate of mailing. A copy should be kept for the file. Follow the filing dictates of Rule 5(d) as previously discussed or any applicable local rules, including those governing e-filing. The response date should be noted on your calendar and in the deadline calendar so that the failure of the other party to respond will not go unnoticed. The attorney should be informed if no reply is forthcoming so remedial measures can be taken.

PREPARING FOR PRODUCTION OF DOCUMENTS AND THINGS

INTRODUCTION

This section focuses on the significant procedure and techniques for preparing for the production of documents and things. We start, however, on what the law firm must do, even before there is a request for production, to protect the client from accusations of spoliation and potentially costly sanctions.

SPOLIATION AND THE DUTY TO PRESERVE EVIDENCE: PROTECTING THE CLIENT FROM SANCTIONS

spoliation

The destruction or loss
of evidence, including
the failure to preserve it.

As noted in Chapters 3 and 7, a party has the duty to preserve evidence, even if it is harmful. Correspondingly, **spoliation** is the destruction or loss of evidence, including the failure to preserve it. Spoliation can be intentional or careless, and can so negatively impact on the laudatory aims of discovery as to warrant serious judicial sanctions. Protecting the client and the law firm from accusations of spoliation, made even more difficult with e-information, is a paramount concern for the legal team.

A client's duty to preserve evidence is clear, but the exact time at which the duty arises is not. Case law and good practice suggest that the duty to preserve arises when the party becomes aware or should have become aware that there is a real potential for litigation. At that time, a client must prepare to produce documents and things in a manner consistent with the obligation to preserve evidence and avoid spoliation. Your awareness of the following guidelines, which are specific to the preservation of e-information, will enhance your value as a litigation paralegal:

1. Have the client—particularly businesses, organizations, and institutions—develop a comprehensive ongoing *document retention policy*. The policy should address active and archival e-storage systems; what types of information are necessary, practical, and reasonable to retain in the ordinary course of business; what can and should be routinely destroyed (e-shredding); proper use and storage of e-mail, instant messaging,

and voice mail; proper use of portable devices such as stick drives, handhelds, and laptops; proper business use of home computers; what applications and programs provide useful access and search functions; who will manage, monitor, and enforce the policy; security; and other considerations. Include a section on the special response required for litigation. Inform the client and the client's technology person or staff why it is important that the policy be developed with an eye toward litigation.

2. Fully inform the client of the duty to preserve evidence and the consequences of spoliation.

3. When the potential for litigation is real, the attorney should promptly notify the client. Include in the notice process a *litigation hold letter* that is similar in content to the model preservation letter in Chapter 7. The letter advises the client immediately to implement a *litigation hold order*. The order informs employees of the potential for litigation and directs them to take prompt steps to preserve and not destroy evidence. Some parties shut down their entire computer system so a mirror image copy can be made of all data. This, of course, is extremely costly, usually includes volumes of unneeded information, and is seriously disruptive to the client's operations. The better practice may be to continue with routine backup and destruction processes while a previously designated litigation response team quickly begins to narrow down what must be preserved. The response team should consist of the attorney, the paralegal overseeing discovery, and, at least, the client's technology manager. Your legal team must anticipate, as well as you can at this early stage, the cause of action and related legal issues. Promptly interview key employees to determine who created relevant information, who received it, and what computer applications and equipment were involved. The technology people then identify where it is electronically stored and how best to locate, isolate, and preserve the information in a usable form. Establish a chain of custody log and address security issues. Choose a method to review for privileged and protected information. This process should reasonably balance discovery requirements with fiscal responsibility. See Exhibit 9.3 for the steps that should be used to preserve a client's documentary information.

4. If the client is an individual, such as Mrs. Forrester in her personal injury case, the preservation of her e-stored information, which should not be ignored, is likely to be a far less complicated undertaking.

In addition to drafting document production and inspection requests and assisting in the earliest efforts to protect your client from spoliation sanctions, you must also know how to prepare documents either for initial disclosure or to respond to a production request. Mr. White has asked that you oversee the production of a sizable number of documents pursuant to a request for production submitted by the adverse party in one of our cases. The following material suggests a variety of techniques and steps for performing this task.

The purpose of production is to provide the opponent an opportunity to review documents pertinent to the case to determine if and how the documents support the facts to be alleged at trial. From the point of view of the person producing the documents, the more practical objectives are to locate and produce documents thoroughly, accurately, and efficiently. In order to do this effectively, the documents must be well organized and easy to retrieve. The entire process should interfere as little as possible with the daily business needs of the client or the client's employees.

EXHIBIT 9.3 Steps to Preserve a Client's Documentary Information

Develop a Document Retention Policy With the Client if One Does Not Exist

Notify Key Personnel of the Document Retention Requirements

Inform the Client of the Duty to Preserve Evidence

Inform the Client of the Consequnces of Spoliation of Evidence

Always Advise the Client of the Information and Document Hold Through a Litigation Hold Letter.

Advise Client to Continue Backup Process of Data

Begin Interviewing Key Personnel for Data Preservation

Establish a Chain of Custody Log

Address Security Issues

Begin Determining Privileged Documents and Protected Information

Assume that the legal team on a case has done everything according to the rules. Documents have been produced and the client has been queried numerous times regarding what documents are in their possession. The client communicates that all documents, both copies and originals, have been produced. Trial commences and during an exchange between the court and the attorneys regarding the production of an original document, the plaintiff's attorney states unequivocally that all originals have been produced and if they have not, they do not exist. Out of the blue, the client states, "Oh, I have the original document that you are talking about in my home." The attorney is stunned; so is the court and opposing counsel. Such was the case in *Bull v. United Parcel Service*, 665 F. 3d 68(3d Cir. 2012) where the Third Circuit Court of Appeals was faced with interpreting the definition of spoliation and whether the producing party spoliated evidence warranting the dismissal of the case.

CASE STUDY: UNDERSTANDING THE LAW

Laureen Bull worked for United Parcel Service ("UPS"). She injured her neck and shoulder on the job in 2005 and was restricted as to the physical duties she could perform. Bull was examined by two doctors who produced medical notes. UPS claims that they requested the two original notes from a Dr. Faber throughout the course of discovery as the copies that were produced were illegible. One note requested had been cut off at the bottom. UPS continued to request the original doctors' notes. Although better copies were turned over to UPS prior to trial, no originals were ever produced. At trial, the issue of producing the original doctors' notes was discussed between counsel and the court. All appeared to be satisfied that the original was non-existent and a copy of the note was going to be admitted, when the court asked Bull: "Well, before we do that: Where's the original of this note?" Bull answered: "The original note is in my home." Stunned, Bull's attorney quickly attempted to clarify his client's response to no avail. The trial court declared a mistrial. Bull produced the originals five days after the mistrial was declared, but the trial court ultimately dismissed the case with prejudice as a sanction for Bull's conduct.

Bull appealed the verdict. The issue that the Third Circuit then had to address was whether the production of copies instead of the original document is spoliation and whether Bull's acts were considered spoliated evidence warranting dismissal with prejudice. In its opinion the court first addressed whether nonproduction of original documents falls under the definition of spoliation. Spoliation normally refers to destroyed or altered evidence. In analyzing this definition, the court determined that failure

to produce documents can have the same effect as spoliation. However, although agreeing with the trial court that in some instances withholding original documents may prevent a party from discovering critical information, the court did not believe this was the case here. First the court reviewed UPS's demands for the originals. According to the Third Circuit opinion, UPS did not show that it (1) requested the originals during discovery and (2) made any demands directly to Bull though any means. UPS did not show it properly requested the originals and therefore, Bull did not intentionally fail to produce information. The second part of the opinion discusses what Bull knew and when she knew it. Her attorney stated that he repeatedly asked Bull for the originals. The evidence in the record shows the contrary. At a post-trial hearing, Bull and her attorney attempted to explain the situation, but the trial court refused to permit any further explanation and found spoliation of evidence. The Third Circuit found, however, that the District Court abused its discretion by ordering the sanction of dismissal with prejudice when it failed to develop the record of facts that Bull acted intentionally by withholding the original documents.

Questions for Review: Review *Bull v. UPS*. How does the court define spoliation and what factors are considered in a spoliation analysis? Why did the Third Circuit find the trial court abused its discretion in finding against Bull? What case did the court review in analyzing the factors to dismiss a case and how did the court apply those factors? What were the Third Circuit's conclusions regarding the dismissal and why?

APPLY YOUR KNOWLEDGE

Research how your state defines spolia-tion. Does your state permit sanctions or an adverse inference through a jury instruc-tion for an attorney or client's spoliation?

TASK AND PROCEDURE

Background

Certain steps should be performed prior to preparing a production of documents and things. These steps include reviewing the file and the opponent's production of documents. Be sure to consult with the client for thoroughness, which should include the IT experts. Once a thorough understanding of the needs of the case is determined, prepare a plan for the execution of the production of documents, taking into account the complexity of the case, the number of documents to be produced, and the time needed to accomplish the task. The following is a suggested approach in preparing for a production of documents.

Initial Steps Checklist for Preparing for Production of Documents and Things

(a) Review the case thoroughly.

- Completely review the file.
- Understand the cause of action, the elements that must be proved, defenses, and the corresponding evidence requirements.
- Draft a brief summary of these things and ask your supervising attorney to review it for accuracy and omissions.
- Develop a sense of what is at stake and the complexity of the case.

(b) Review the opponent's request for production.

- Note the items requested, possible objections, privilege concerns.

(c) Meet with the client and key personnel.

- If applicable to the type of case and if the information has not been gathered previously, determine:
  - how the client's business or organization is structured.
  - its chain of command.
  - the departments most relevant to the case.
- Go over the document request with the client's technology manager and any documents custodian to find out:
  - what kinds of documents (electronic or paper) are responsive to the request.
  - likely volume.
  - who created them.
  - where they are stored.
  - how they are accessed.
- This is a good time to have your attorney remind the custodians of the duty to preserve evidence and, possibly, the need to issue a more specific litigation hold order.

(d) Develop a document production plan.

- Using the information gathered above and working closely with your supervising attorney, a technology manager, perhaps an experienced paralegal, and a consultant (if needed), plan for the entire production process. Lack of a plan leads to confusion and spiraling costs.

- Address the complexity of the case:

  - the extent of both paper and e-information sought.
  - the expertise level needed to implement and manage the production.
  - the time required for the project.
  - the human and technology resources needed.
  - whose staff and equipment will be used to produce (the law office's, the client's, or outsourced).
  - the ability of both the law office and the client's staff to pull employees off what they normally do to work on the production.
  - where the information will be stored and secured.
  - access policies.
  - how attorney-client privilege and other protected information will be screened.
  - who will be on the production team.
  - what the chain of command will be.
  - what policies and procedures (such as those for coding and classifying relevant documents) will be implemented.
  - what logs must be kept.
  - in what form documents will be produced.
  - how the chain of custody will be maintained.
  - who will be the designated expert to testify should chain of custody, spoliation, or other production and technical issues arise.
  - who will serve as liaison to the other party to work out production issues.
  - what procedures will be the least disruptive to the client's operations.
  - what quality control will be needed to see that the established policies and procedures are followed.
  - after looking at comparative costs and production times, will the production be paper, electronic, or a combination of the two.
  - is production better done in-house or by an outside litigation production vendor.

- Estimate costs (in large e-information cases, this may require expert assistance):

  - Screen representative samples of documents for:

    - types of documents requiring screening.
    - page length and data space of documents.
    - time required to review, code, and log documents manually or electronically.

  - Once you know how many boxes of documents you have, time to do a project and employee needs can be estimated according to the following procedure. Note how many boxes of documents have been located to be produced plus an estimate of the number of boxes to be produced by other parties. Most standard storage boxes contain about 2,000 pages. You can check this by filling one of your empty storage boxes with reams of copying paper. Estimate the average document size, say seven pages. Divide the number of pages (2,000) by seven to get the number of documents per box (286). Assume you have fifty boxes of documents or the electronic equivalent, which equals 14,300 documents.

14,300 documents	×	5 minutes each	=	71,500 minutes
71,500 minutes	÷	60 minutes	=	1,192 hours
1,192 hours	÷	8 hours	=	149 days
149 days	÷	30 days/deadline	=	5 coders
14,300 documents	÷	30 days	=	477 documents/day
477 documents	÷	5 coders	=	95 documents per coder per day

- Also, consider the following:
    1. 2,000 pages (1 box) is about 650 megabytes (MB) of data.
    2. 1 GB (gigabyte) of data is approximately 45,000 to 50,000 pages (25–30 boxes).
    3. 1 CD-ROM holds 15,000 pages.
    4. 1 DVD holds 7 CD-ROMs of data.
    5. 1 double-sided, dual-layer DVD holds 15.9 GB.
    6. 1 typical case production takes six to twelve weeks.
    7. Zip or jump drives vary according to size.

As a general rule, the greater the number of documents and data to be produced, the more efficient and economical it is to create and use an all-electronic, searchable database. Also, the more complex the case is, the greater the need for experience and expert assistance.

Locate Documents

The difficulty in locating documents varies with the particular case. Locating the medical records on Mrs. Forrester's injuries and treatment and her employment records is relatively easy. Locating all the records pertaining to the manufacture, maintenance, and operation of the van driven by Mr. Hart could be more difficult. Much more difficult is locating all pertinent documents and the full gamut of electronically stored information generated by a large multinational corporation with numerous subsidiaries and branch offices.

For locating both paper and e-stored information, meet with the client and key personnel and follow section (c) of the Initial Steps Checklist. The document retention policy, if one exists, may tell you what is most likely to have been retained or destroyed. The likely flow of memos, e-mails, reports of problems, and comments and discussion of such reports or problems is important. Whether the information is active, metadata, archival data, or residual data provides insight into how difficult and costly it will be to recover. Prepare a detailed list of potentially relevant information, subject matter, type of data, and the specific location or likely location of the information. Develop an atmosphere of cooperation. Be sensitive to the need for keeping disruption of the office routine to a minimum, and express appreciation for any help extended to you and the production team.

Pull Files and Documents

PULLING PAPER MANUALLY. By this stage the document production team, if one is called for, should be in place and trained. In coordination with each of the client's designated document custodians and carefully following the guidelines set up by the attorney or the document production team leader, pull the files or individual documents likely to contain the responsive information. For each relevant file, do the following:

- Pull the file and fill out a file checkout card or leave a temporary replacement sheet or file cover indicating by whom the file has been pulled, for what case, its next location (office or room number), and the date. When in doubt whether to pull a file, the best practice is to pull it.

- Check with the custodian to see if the file is so critical to daily operations of the office that an immediate copy of the file or of certain documents needs to be made for the convenience of the office. If so, have the document or file photocopied. Tape a legend reading: "Copy: original in case file _____ v. _____" to the photocopy machine so it will appear on each copy. This provides notice that the new file is a copy and indicates where the original can be located.

- Label each file or document as it is pulled to indicate its place in the case file. For example, the first file pulled for the *Forrester* case could be labeled F-1 indicating that it is now in the first file folder of the *Forrester* case.

- On your laptop, prepare a log of each file pulled. The log should contain at a minimum the source of the file, a description of the file (exact title is best), the new working file number (F-1, F-2) assigned to it, and the custodian. The log might also contain other information as indicated in Exhibit 9.4, which shows an original source log.

- The original source log provides immediate information on the source of the document or file and is invaluable when the files or documents are returned.

- If any files cannot be found, this fact should be noted in the log, and a memo so indicating should be addressed to the case file and attached to the log. Such a memo protects you from accusations of sloppy work and the firm from possible sanctions from the court for failure to comply with a discovery order.

- Log books, journals, or other unique items should be specially noted to indicate their unique nature for easier identification in the future.

- Remove the pulled files and documents to a separate office or screening room with limited access to ensure control over the documents and enhance the efficiency of additional screening. When dealing with a large number of

EXHIBIT 9.4 Document Production Original Source Log

New File No.	Description	Source
F-1	Maint. form 20's _____	Merc. Parcel Rm 108 drawer 31 Ralph Johnson
F-2	Maint. form 20's _____	Merc. Parcel Rm 108 Dr. 31 R. Johnson
F-3	Driver Hour Logs _____	Merc. Parcel Rm 108 Dr. 81 Betty Robinson

documents, place the files into file boxes and label them—for example, Box 1 files F-1 to F-50, Box 2 files F-51 to F-100, and so forth.

- As a courtesy, inform the custodian what documents have been removed.

CONVERTING PAPER TO ELECTRONIC FILES (IMAGING). Some law offices strive to be paperless. All documents are created and stored electronically; all incoming paper documents (correspondence, contracts, memoranda, etc.) are scanned into the computer. This same process is invaluable to document production. Electronic conversion of paper documents prevents loss, eliminates filing cabinets or boxes, greatly enhances portability, quickens retrieval, speeds copying and organization into folders of related files for a particular purpose, and facilitates access by multiple parties at any time.

In this process, done in-house or by a vendor, the paper document is scanned and converted into a "read only" electronic document, meaning that the text cannot be edited. Many office photocopiers now double as digital scanners. When equipped with the right software, scanners can produce the document in PDF or TIFF format. A more dated process is to scan paper or a digital image with an optical character reader (OCR). Despite regular upgrades, these readers are relatively slow and prone to interpretation errors regarding character recognition and formatting. Once the documents are converted to digital files, they can be processed like any other electronically stored information.

"PULLING" ELECTRONICALLY STORED INFORMATION. The client's potentially responsive e-stored information must be "pulled" or captured with great care. Capturing data is often the costliest stage of e-discovery and requires intense scrutiny so that complete compliance with the request is accomplished along with preserving the integrity of the data. Close cooperation among the firm's technology manager, the client's technology manager, and any expert consultant is imperative. A big stakes case may require data to be captured by an expensive forensic expert. That is not necessary in most cases, however.

Here is a practical approach for a typical (assuming there is such) e-discovery case:

- Verify that any routine or other destruction of potentially relevant e-stored information has stopped.
- Capture mirror images of the data, including residual data, on each pertinent person's PC and portable devices. This can be done with commercially available applications. Expand the capture to other likely data sources, but only after the team has thoroughly weighed what is likely to be found, the hierarchy of usefulness, and the realities of difficulty and cost of capture.
- Keep a source log and expand the information to include the method of capture.
- Once the data is captured, secure it.

Screen Pulled Files and Documents

OBJECTIVES OF THE SCREENING PROCESS. This next stage lies at the heart of good document control and production. It requires the review of each piece of paper or electronic page for its relevancy to the request and for any privileged or sensitive material. Although laborious at times, the importance of the process cannot be overstated.

Some high-profile cases have completely turned on the hero paralegal's ability to find and recognize a key piece of evidence hidden among thousands of pages of a document review. The objectives and guidelines for this step of the document production process should be specific, and normally include the following:

- To identify documents that are responsive to each particular request for production.
- To number those documents, if so directed, for easy identification and retrieval.
- To identify documents that are privileged or sensitive to avoid disclosure of that information.
- To classify documents for rapid identification, retrieval, and return.
- To prepare documents for photocopying or other electronic recording.
- To have documents readied for review by the attorney.

SCREENING PAPER. The tasks for manual paper screening involve the following:

- Aim to pass through all documents once and to record all necessary information at that time. If several people are reviewing, logs should be maintained by each person to show who has reviewed what.
- Place the files and documents on their sides in boxes. As each relevant document is identified, the document should not be removed from the file but placed in an upright position so it protrudes from the file. See Exhibit 9.5.
- Number each document page in sequential order as the pages are turned up. Since these are the original documents and need to be preserved in their original state, a decision must be made by the attorney if numbering

EXHIBIT 9.5 Place Documents in an Upright Position

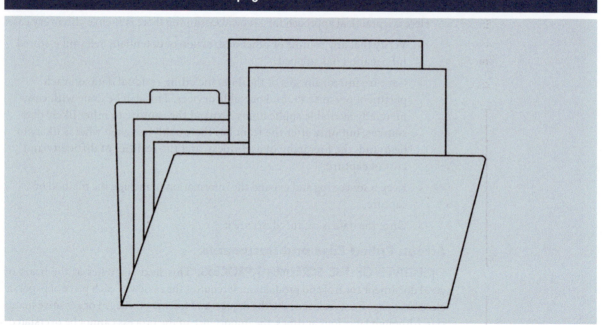

and other notations should be penciled on the document or a Post-it label used on which to record the necessary information. If the Post-it labels are the type that reliably stay on and can be removed without damaging the original document, this method is probably the best. Some firms number the documents directly; others do not. Some firms still use a manual Bates stamping device. Others use a computerized Bates numbering system, bar codes, and computer-generated labels. Numbering now saves much time later. In large-volume cases this entire process may be contracted to a private vendor.

- Indicate the number on each document, the set and paragraph of the production request to which it responds, the numbered source file in which it belongs (F-1, F-2), how many copies of the document are needed, and to which cross files the copies of the document should go. The files normally kept include three files of original documents: one as numbered, one of privileged and other undiscoverable documents, and one of unresponsive documents. Copies of all the files and documents are made to be returned to the original custodian. Additional copies of the numbered documents go into cross files: chronological files and files sorted by production request set and paragraph. Some firms also want copies of the documents sorted into files by issue and by person. Systems may become even more detailed than this. With all of the sorting, cross referencing, and photocopying, the benefits of converting paper to digital data quickly become apparent.

- Indicate whether the document is privileged or contains work product or other sensitive material. In such cases a colored cover sheet should be placed in front of the document so it can be readily identified and pulled when necessary.

- Index the documents. The number of indexes maintained will depend on what the supervising attorney has requested. A master index should record the number of the document, subject matter on the document, and its nature (memo, letter, tax return, phone log, etc.), the new file number, the date of the document, the author of the document, the recipient of the document, whether the document is privileged or otherwise undiscoverable, the set and item of the production request that it responds to, and eventually whether the document was produced to the adversary. If other files, such as personality files, are requested, information such as names of persons mentioned or receiving copies or drafts of the document might be included.

- This master index can then be used to create other indexes. Even if screening paper is done manually, indexes are best done electronically.

USE A STANDARDIZED NUMBERING SYSTEM. A standardized or uniform numbering system will prove most efficient and can be adapted to most cases in the office. Many attorneys set up a numbering system as it occurs to them in a particular case, resulting in confusion for others not privy to its logic. Further, such haphazard systems often prove inadequate as the case expands, or result in telltale gaps in the numbering system as privileged or attorney work product documents are removed. The method used by many law firms is the decimal system. The numbers become a shorthand description of the document, and the system can be used for all appropriate cases. Here is how the system works.

First, an estimate of the number of documents involved must be made. The number of documents equals the degree of digits needed for numbering. Ninety-nine (99) or fewer documents is a second-degree case, 100–999 documents equals a third-degree case, 100,000 documents equals a sixth-degree case, and so forth. The number of digits needed for numbering is based on the formula: degree + 3 = digits needed. Therefore, a third-degree case is simply calculated: degree = 3 + 3 = 6 digits. A sixth-degree case calculates: 6 + 3 = 9 digits (xxx,xxx,xxx).

The first digit refers to the first assigned category or grouping. In many firms this first grouping is the *role* the document will play in the proof process according to the elements of the case and related factors. A sample group one in a negligence case might appear as follows:

Group I, Role in Case

1. Jurisdiction (to establish or challenge)
2. Parties (to identify)
3. Existence of duty
4. Breach
5. Causal connection to damage/injury
6. Damages
7. Defenses
8. Others

If the first document to be numbered for production (or the first to be received in response to a request for production) pertains to the existence of a duty, the first digit will be numbered 3xx, xxx, xxx. In other words, anyone familiar with the categories will know at a glance the expected role the document will play in the case. The other digits, as you will see, provide similar information at a glance. This information will be based on categories carefully planned by the attorney. The categories will generally be the same for all negligence cases or all product liability cases. The attorney-paralegal team, however, can alter these categories as the unique nature of a case dictates.

A document might play several roles. In that case, number it for its major role, but also number a reference insert page according to the secondary role, which refers the searcher to the original numbered document. When the documents are sorted by categories, this additional numbering will prevent a document with dual purposes from being overlooked and may make an extra copy of a lengthy document unnecessary.

The second digit may be designated to show the *source* of the document. Group two, therefore, might appear as follows:

Group II, Source of Document

1. Mrs. Forrester
2. Dr. Harris
3. Mr. Hart
4. Mercury Parcel Service
5. Others

If the first document came from Mrs. Forrester, the numbered document would appear as 31x, xxx, xxx. Other groupings for remaining digits could include the *type* of document (correspondence, memo, others), *production mode* (how produced—with pleadings, pursuant to a request for production, subpoena duces tecum, etc.), *potential for evidentiary exclusion* (admissible, privilege, hearsay, etc.), and any other grouping predetermined by the attorney.

The order in which the document was pulled or received can be indicated by using the right-hand digits in the number. If your first document is numbered by all its categories and appears at 318,720,001, it would be recorded on the general index as the first document. The next document (whatever its categories would indicate) would end in xxx,xxx,xx2 and would be the second document entered into the general index. If there are numerous groupings, digits may have to be added to accommodate the sequential numbering. If the document is multipaged, pages are indicated simply by inserting a decimal and the page number. The ninth page of your first document would be numbered 318,720,001.9. This uniform decimal system is computer-compatible.

SCREENING THE CAPTURED ELECTRONICALLY STORED INFORMATION. The process of screening the captured e-information loosely parallels the process for screening paper documents. Whether done by a person or by automated software or a combination thereof, each document must be reviewed for relevance to the document production request and for privileged and protected information. The final production set must ultimately be numbered, coded, and indexed like the paper documents, but with the assistance of software designed for these document management tasks. This software offers far more fields, numbering options, indexing and cross-indexing options, and other benefits over the manual paper process. Whether in small or large volume, the documents are placed into a separate discovery data bank where they can be retrieved quickly and further organized into groups responsive to each item of the document request. The documents can be kept in their native format or converted to PDF, TIFF, or other form agreed on by the parties.

A document production company is often the best approach in large-volume cases. They can automatically filter data to eliminate all duplicate files, application and system files, unneeded file types, dated material that falls outside any specified date range, and other data not pertinent to the case. Additional filtering can be done by keywords and even concepts. This filtering process can narrow the original captured data and reduce the cost of production. The savings in temporary staff and hours of document review can be dramatic.

Once reduced, metadata and text can be extracted and the documents converted to a universally usable form. This much leaner database can be returned to the production team for final review, numbering, indexing, privilege checking, and so on. The final production data can then be provided to the requesting party in CD, DVD, or other form. Some attorneys agree to have the final production set of documents placed on an online repository. This permits both sides to access the production set securely from any place at any time. These services often facilitate searching and manipulating the documents into subsets by issues, names, witnesses, and other criteria. Any final production data set can be downloaded into document management and litigation support software for retrieval, organization into subsets, searching, further narrowing to a trial set of documents and exhibits, and other functions.

Have the Attorney Review the Documents

Once the production set (whether paper, electronic, or both) is ready, have your supervising attorney verify that the documents are responsive to the production requests, that all privileged and other protected documents have been identified, that the paper documents have been kept in original format (stapled, bound, paper-clipped), that the electronic documents have been kept in native form or in a form agreed on by the attorneys, and that any necessary paper copies will be prepared. Your supervising attorney also will appreciate anything you can do to red-tag or point out documents that stand out as particularly significant to the case.

Extract Privileged Documents

Each of the privileged or sensitive documents should be extracted from the original file and placed in a separate paper or electronic folder. If the document is paper, pull the colored privileged document sheet as well. A sheet of paper with the document's number on it should be substituted in the original file.

Recall that Federal Rule 34(b) requires a party to produce any unprotected and relevant information from the same document that contains privileged or otherwise protected information. Therefore, once the privileged information is identified, it must be removed from the original document that will be produced. The process of editing out irrelevant, privileged, or protected information from the text of a document is called **redaction**. A brief notation indicating that the document has been redacted and why should be entered on the document. Return the redacted version of the document to the production set. Maintain an original (unredacted) version of the document in a secured folder.

redaction
The process of editing out irrelevant or privileged information from the text of a document.

Keep in mind that Rule 26(b)(5)(a) requires the disclosing or producing party to inform the other party of any material otherwise discoverable that is withheld from discovery because it is privileged or is attorney's work product. Either the master index, referred to previously, or a privileged/work product index can be used to create a privileged/work product log for the other party. This entire extraction, redaction, and return process must be done in very thorough consultation with your supervising attorney. See Exhibit 9.6 for an example of a privilege log.

Have Documents Copied

Determine how many copies of each paper document are needed. Usually four or five are necessary: one to replace the originals in the files of origin, one to duplicate

---

EXHIBIT 9.6 Example of a Privilege Log

Bates No.	Document Date	Document Type	Document Description	Author(s) Document	Recipient	Basis of Privilege
Priv. 001	Feb. 28	Ltr	Ltr to Atty	Pres. Mercury Parcel	Mr. White	Atty/client

the original file, one for a chronological file, one for each item of the response request, and any other need such as a person or issue file. The person making copies substitutes a sheet in the original file indicating what documents are being copied and by whom. The copies should contain a legend indicating that they are a copy of the original and where the original can be found, as described previously. The copies should be in the same format, paper-clipped, stapled, and so on, as the original. Unless it is impractical, an entire document should be copied even if only one page of the document is responsive. All oversized, reduced, and otherwise nonreproducible or altered documents should be noted. Any bad copies should be destroyed. The copies should then be sorted into expandable file folders or boxes as initially indicated on the original. The originals should be placed in an original document file in numerical order as they were identified. A copy of the originals should be reinserted in the files of origin, and they may be returned to their custodians and refiled. A letter of return to the custodian should be drafted and the copy placed in the case file. The custodian should be directed to keep the files in their original state. It is wise to request a receipt. If a case is small, it may be adequate just to set up a three-ring binder and place the copied documents into the needed categories or according to the sets of the discovery requests with a simple table of contents at the front.

Prepare Documents for Examination

A copy of the documents should be arranged and noted according to the set and item of the request they pertain to or as they are kept in the normal course of your client's business. Some firms prefer to renumber the documents at this time. (This renumbering is not necessary with the decimal numbering system.) Others wait for the examination and number only those documents selected by the opponent. Either way, an index showing the original number of the document, the item to which it responds, that it was produced, and if it was selected by the adversary should be kept. Be sure to keep a copy of all documents produced to the opponent.

For electronic information, document management or litigation support software facilitates the ultimate arrangement of the production set, that is, either in subsets corresponding to each item of the opponent's production request or as the e-information is kept in the ordinary course of the client's business. *Make sure that you retain at least one exact duplicate of what is produced to the opponent.* This point cannot be overemphasized.

Retrieve the Documents

During the case it may become necessary to retrieve a particular document or several documents, which could be necessary to prepare for a deposition, to find documents for an expert to review, to prepare for the examination of a witness, or to make a critical rebuttal point at trial. Using the indexes that have been prepared, you can retrieve the pertinent documents efficiently with one or more of the following: the date of the document, the name of the author or recipient, the number of the document, the issue that it pertains to, key words, concepts, and so on. A checkout system for all paper documents should be carefully maintained.

It is in search and retrieval that document management and litigation support software saves enormous amounts of time and facilitates numerous trial preparation and presentation functions.

TECHNOLOGY UPDATE: PREDICTIVE CODING

Often considered technology-assisted document review, predictive coding is a technology that filters and selects information from documents to determine relevancy to e-discovery document requests with human guidance. Through the use of keyword searches and other sampling mechanisms, the paralegal or attorney can identify and reduce the number of potential irrelevant or nonresponsive documents in a document search. Through the use of computer programs, searches can be created to refine document production. Think of predictive coding as a prioritization and filtering system for documents. For example, software is used that will scan ESI and find the most relevant documents based upon the search initiated. From the search, documents are categorized and narrowed to match key search terms and concepts that are inputed by the legal professionals. They are

searching for broad language patterns. The result is that relevant documents are identified from the search, narrowing the pool of information that needs to be reviewed by the legal team. It is probably fair to conclude that predictive coding will be used more and more in cases, especially those cases involving large volumes of documents. The question to be asked is "how will predicative coding be interpreted and judged by the courts?" This remains to be seen. It is still a new area in discovery and case law on the subject is sparse. As a paralegal, if you use predictive coding when responding to a document production, be sure your tracking process is documented so you can detail how you did things and why. Transparency is key in defending your methodology in case opposing counsel challenges the process used for a document production response.

Return the Documents and Retain Indexes

At the close of the case, usually after all appeals have been exhausted, the original paper documents may be returned to their original locations. The return of each document or identifiable group of documents should be logged and receipted. Any of the client's original documents filed with the court or in the possession of the other parties should be retrieved and returned. All copies should then be shredded or burned. All the indexes, return letters, and receipts should be kept in the case file.

If your task is to review the documents sent by the opponent in response to a request for production submitted by your firm, a similar system of selecting and organizing can be used.

Quality Control

Every document production system requires regular checking either by the attorney or an experienced auditor or litigation manager. Checks should be made to see that uniform terminology, coding, and other systems are being followed and that test retrievals produce the anticipated results.

Security

Once the data is computerized, precautions should be taken to protect it. As mentioned earlier, original hard-copy documents should be placed in a room with limited access. Make a backup copy of the final production set, whether paper or electronic, in case something happens to the originals. The backup should be stored in a completely separate and well-protected location. Some law offices store backup sets in more than one secure off-site location. If the documents are in an online repository, the vendor provides security. All originally mirrored and collected data and duplicates should be placed in locked facilities or otherwise secured to prevent and detect any unauthorized access to and use of the information. Should any document be challenged, its chain of custody must be verifiable. Of course, extracted privileged, protected, and private information must be secured as well. As attorneys and paralegals work with the documents in preparation for trial, the usual protection of computer data should be in place, such as passwords, firewalls, virus protection, locked server rooms, wireless use prohibition, encryption, e-mail attachment metadata removers, and access shut-offs for those unexpectedly extended step-out-of-the-office moments.

Today law offices and their clients are seeking highly technical security advice to protect the integrity of their computer data.

PRODUCTION PROCEDURE

REPLYING TO A REQUEST FOR PRODUCTION AND INSPECTION

A party must respond to a request for production in writing and within 30 days of service of the request, unless ordered by the court or otherwise agreed to by the parties. Again, state rules may vary. Before drafting the response, review each item of the request once more. For each item of the request, outline:

- What documents or information responsive to that item, if any, were located in the search of information.

- Any objection and the reasons for the objection (failure to object may waive the objection).

- In what form or forms the opponent wants the information produced and in what form or forms it is best for your client to produce the item.

- What differences or concerns need to be worked out with the other party prior to seeking a protective order.

- What process is best for the client and the opponent for delivering the information or conducting any inspection, copying, testing, or sampling of the information.

Prior to raising an objection in the response, it is good practice to research case law on what kind of information courts have protected from production. Only the specific part of the document that is objectionable may be excluded from production.

Go over your outline with your supervising attorney and identify who will do what in negotiating differences and arrangements with the other side. Cooperation with the opponent can greatly simplify the production and reduce the number of subsequent problems. The written response can be easier to draft following such negotiations.

Then draft the response to the request for production. A general form for the response is shown in Exhibit 9.7. The preferred practice is to respond specifically to each enumerated item in the request for production by restating the item requested, then adding your response or objection and the explanation for the objection.

EXHIBIT 9.7 Response to Request for Production—General Form

[FED. R. CIV. P. Rule 34]

[*Title of Court and Cause*]

_____

Attorney for Plaintiff

Address_____

In response to plaintiff's request to produce and for inspection in the above-entitled action, served upon plaintiff [*date*], _____, the inspection and related activities requested will be permitted at [*if a different place than requested*] with respect to each item and category as requested [add "with the exception of Items as follows, _____, to which inspection defendant objects, respectfully on the following grounds:" list each request objected to, the objection and the reasons_____] [or, the inspection and related activities requested are objected to on the ground that _____]. [Possible objections or response: (1) No such documents exist after a reasonable and diligent search; (2) The request is overly broad or unduly burdensome; (3) The request is vague, ambiguous or unintelligible; (4) The request is not reasonably calculated to lead to the discovery of relevant, admissible evidence; or (5) any other stated reason for the non-production.]

Respectfully submitted,

_____

Attorney for Defendant

Address: _____

Adapted West's Federal Forms, § 3557, v. 3A, with permission, West Group.

Here are a few examples of how to respond to a specific, enumerated request:

Request: All Form ICC-2012s referred to in defendant's answer to plaintiff's interrogatories.

Answer: Defendant will produce these documents, copies of which are included with this response.

Or,

Answer: Defendant will produce the documents requested for the two years prior to the accident, but objects in so far as the request is for documents from an unlimited time period, which is unduly burdensome [FRCP 26(b)].

Or,

Answer: Defendant will not produce these documents because the request was served after the court order staying discovery.

Have the attorney review and sign the response. Serve the response on the other parties and execute the return of service. Calendar any dates and times scheduled for the examination of the documents and other information.

ASSISTING AT THE PRODUCTION, EXAMINATION, OR INSPECTION

In many smaller cases, production is handled informally between the law offices. Requested documents are copied, logged as submitted to the other party, and exchanged. Some productions still occur in the traditional on-site manner, however. Paralegals frequently oversee the on-site production of documents or play an important role in examining the documents produced by the other party.

If your task is to oversee the examination of your client's documents, arrange for the location and remind those concerned of the time and place. Normally, production is held at the responding party's law office, the client's place of business, or a storage facility. See that the room is secure and has a phone and a copying machine. Check with your supervising attorney and the other party regarding any use of scanners at the production. Review the case, the request, and the written response so you know what is to be produced. Verify that the documents to be examined, whether paper or electronic, have been properly indexed as previously indicated, and that the nature of the documents, time periods, and other factors are responsive to, and do not exceed, the bounds of the request. Determine if there are any documents in a foreign language, and notify the examining party accordingly. Schedule any technical assistance for the examiner, such as when specialized proprietary software is needed for the review. Arrange the documents *according to how they are kept in the client's usual course of business or organized and labeled to correspond to the categories in the request.* Any attempt to obscure or bury key documents or produce them in a form that is less usable than the original form is unethical and subject to sanction. Take a note pad or laptop and a numbering or tabbing device, know where to reach your supervising attorney, and be ready to stay for the duration of the examination. If you use a commercial copying service, consider having the other party billed directly for its copies. During the examination, see that the documents are kept in order and that none are removed from the room. Keep a log of all documents chosen by the opponent and note if special attention is given to any particular document. Strictly avoid conversation about the case or judgments on the value of any of the documents. If issues come up, do not leave the room. Use the phone to call the attorney. When breaks are needed, ask all persons to leave the room and lock the door. In the alternative, phone out for someone else to fill in for you. Immediately after the examination, summarize anything noteworthy, and give the summary to your supervising attorney. Then proceed with any needed follow-up, such as photocopying selected documents, copying them to a CD, and getting them to the opponent.

If your role is examining the documents, prepare by reviewing the file and the specifics of the request for production and the response. Have the issues of the case and the examination objectives clearly in mind. Seek suggestions from your supervising attorney on what to look for and what the client's budget will allow for copying, scanning, photographing, testing, or whatever method best suits the particular examination. Make sure the method of copying is clear to both sides and that the necessary equipment and technical support will be available. Determine cost allocation and billing procedures. Inquire whether any of the documents are in a foreign language and the number, which may necessitate the hiring of a certified translator.

Take a laptop, tablet, or note pad, a tagging or numbering device in case none is provided by the opponent, and a small recording device such as can be found on most mobile or smart phones. The laptop or recording device facilitates efficient recording of observations and descriptions of documents, especially if they cannot be numbered or copied. A laptop, tablet, or smart phone may be just as expedious to record observations. No one methodology is better. As a paralegal, you will learn which method works best for you.

At the examination, methodically work through the documents, noting type, date, author, addressee, pages, and attachments. Pay special attention to any extraneous marks or handwriting. Such scribbles can provide valuable insights, or even evidence, against the opponent. See that all documents requested are produced and that the opponent provides a list of each document not produced under the claim of privilege or other objection. Note and index each document you want and have documents copied or see that arrangements are made to have them copied later and delivered to your office. If a vendor or others will be responsible for copying your selections:

- Consider bringing a hand-held scanner for those especially important documents to ensure against loss in the copying process.
- Be certain they know the specific date by which you need the documents.
- Send a follow-up verification letter.
- Calendar the return date.

For budgetary reasons, copy only useful documents. If in doubt as to whether to copy a particular document, it is best to copy it. You may not be able to review the document again. Always err on the side of caution and copy a document that may be questionable.

Immediately after the examination, summarize your notes and taped comments and share them with your supervising attorney. The summary also will help you recall what you were thinking at the time of the examination, which can be beneficial when you review the documents later.

In the rarer instance of being given direct access to the other party's computer system for purposes of examination, testing, or sampling, a qualified technician will be needed to make a complete examination of the e-system, deal with viruses, detect tampering or changes since the date of the preservation hold, extract meta- and residual data, and properly duplicate the selected information. In this process, it is essential that the technician know the agreed-on protocol involving the exposure of privileged or protected information.

ANALYZING DOCUMENTS PRODUCED BY THE OPPONENT

The documents produced by the opponent need to be analyzed immediately. Apply the same processes described earlier (preparing the client's documents for production) to number, code, digest, index, scan where needed, retrieve, and review the documents. Employ document management and good litigation support software to make full use of your opponent's information, including deposition transcripts, video, photos, and the like, not only for discovery, but also for trial preparation.

The documents should be reviewed for compliance with the original request. Are the time periods requested covered? Are all of the pertinent attachments referred to in the document properly attached? Are the objections appropriate? Are there gaps in the records or chronology? Have items been lost or destroyed? Is an additional request for production necessary; for example, do you need to request production in native format (including metadata) of a suspicious document that was initially produced in PDF or TIFF? Concerns raised by the analysis should be discussed with the attorney.

EXHIBIT 9.8 Sample Production Log

Document	Bates No.	Document Date	Author of Document	Date Produced	Produced by (party)	Privilege	Comments

An expert may be needed to help interpret highly technical material. If any points of concern cannot be resolved in discussion with the other party, a Rule 37 motion to compel discovery may be needed. Compelling discovery is covered later in this chapter.

Regardless whether you are retrieving or producing documents for a case, always keep a detailed production log. Organization is often a learned skilled and one that should be practiced in earnest. Firms often have a template for their production logs. However, Exhibit 9.8 is a sample of a typical production log and the type of information that it should contain.

REQUEST FOR PHYSICAL AND MENTAL EXAMINATION

PURPOSE AND SCOPE

guardian ad litem
An individual appointed by the court to protect a minor or incompetent person's interest.

Rule 35 and parallel state rules permit an adverse party, with good cause, to have the other party submit to a medical examination. The exam is requested to confirm the opponent's allegations of mental or physical injury and to prevent fraudulent claims. The exam may be to confirm a child's blood type in a paternity action, the permanency of a physical injury in an automobile accident, or the mental capabilities and awareness of a person who may be claiming incapacity in a contract challenge.

The request may reach parties and persons who are in the custody or legal control of a party. For example, a mother suing for paternity may need to bring the child for a blood test, or a **guardian ad litem**, an individual appointed by the court to protect a minor or incompetent person's interest, may be requested to produce an incompetent person to have injuries examined that the guardian alleges disabled that person in an automobile accident. Co-parties may also be reached under the rule.

According to Rule 35(a) an examination may be ordered if two tests are met: (1) the alleged condition is in controversy (i.e., the nature and extent of the condition is at issue) and (2) good cause exists to have the examination. In this context, good cause refers to a legitimate need to confirm the injury or to discover information likely to have a direct bearing on the case. Because of the potential for abuse, and the obvious and sometimes painful intrusion into the privacy of the person subject to examination, the courts tend to interpret "good cause" rather strictly and deny motions for medical examinations if the information can be acquired through less intrusive

INTERNET EXERCISE

Research your jurisdiction's requirements for a request for physical and mental examination. Are your state rules different from the Federal Rules of Civil Procedure? If so, identify those differences.

means. Medical examinations are most routinely ordered in personal injury cases. Another area where requests for mental examinations have become common are in employment discrimination cases where the plaintiff alleges emotional distress. An example where a request for examination by a psychiatrist was challenged was *Montana v. County of Cape May Board of Freeholders*, 2013 U.S. Dist. LEXIS 151660 (D.N.J. 2013).

CASE STUDY: UNDERSTANDING THE LAW

Arthur Montana was a Juvenile and Family Crisis Counselor employed by the County of Cape May Board of Freeholders. Montana filed a lawsuit against the Board alleging First Amendment and hostile work environment and retaliation claims. As part of his damages, he alleged emotional distress. The defendants filed a request for mental examination which was reviewed and denied by the U.S. Magistrate judge. The defendants appealed that denial to the U.S. District Court judge. Because of certain reports produced by the plaintiff claiming that he was a victim of bullying in the workplace and his emotional state, the defendants claimed that the plaintiff's mental state was at issue. Therefore, the plaintiff should be required to submit to a psychological examination un Rule 35.

The District Court judge affirmed the Magistrate's decision and analyzed when a mental examination was appropriate. Basing its decision on a 1964 U.S. Supreme Court case, *Schlagenhauf v. Holder*, 379 U.S. 104, 117, 85 S. Ct. 234, 13 L.Ed. 2d 152 (1964), the District Court stated that the "in controversy" and "good cause" requirements of Rule 35 are more than just conclusory assertions. A person's mental health must "really and genuinely" be in controversy and good cause must exist for the examination. The showing for a mental examination is a higher requirement than simple relevancy. In quoting the U.S. Supreme Court, the District Court observed that "Rule 35 is meant to act as a shield against unnecessarily subjecting a plaintiff

to a mental examination on just general allegations of emotional distress, or using it as a means to harass the plaintiff" (*Id*. at 8). Then the court reviewed the request in the context of employment discrimination cases. Relying on *Bowen v. Parking Authority of Camden*, 214 F.R.D. 188 (D.N.J. 2003), the court observed that additional elements need to be met to comply with Rule 35. *Bowen* listed five elements to consider in determining whether a person's mental health was at issue. The elements are: "(1) a cause of action for intentional or negligent infliction of emotional distress; (2) an allegation of specific mental or psychiatric injury or disorder; (3) a claim of unusually severe emotional distress; (4) plaintiff's offer of expert testimony to support a claim of emotional distress; and/or (5) plaintiff's concession that his or her mental condition is 'in controversy' within the meaning of Rule 35(a). *Id*. at 10. Citing to the "garden variety" allegation of suffering emotional distress, the court stated that after reviewing the complaint, discovery and depositions, the plaintiff had not placed his mental state at issue and thus did not meet the requirements of Rule 35. Motion denied.

Questions for Review: Read the *Montana* case. What facts in discovery led the defendants to allege that the plaintiff's mental health was at issue? Under what circumstances is a mental health examination proper according to the *Montana* case? Why did the U.S. District Court judge affirm the decision of the Magistrate judge?

PROCEDURE

Attorneys for the parties are usually quite cooperative regarding such exams. Often a phone call and a confirming letter are all that is needed to secure the examination. However, a request to a party to undergo an exam does not require the party to undergo the exam. If an informal overture is rejected or ignored, a motion for a court order is required. A refusal to submit to the exam in violation of a court order may result in dismissal of the case. The party subject to the exam may object or seek a protective order.

Once the exam is completed, a physician's report is prepared for the party requesting the exam, who then is responsible to forward a copy of it to the examined party if requested.

SET UP THE EXAM

You may be asked to perform several tasks in conjunction with the Rule 35 examination. Contacting the other party's attorney to see if there are any objections to the exam and proceeding informally will be the initial task. Consult with the supervising attorney to see if a confirming letter or a more formal stipulation is appropriate, or if a motion is required.

Contact the physician to discuss the purpose of the exam and the method of payment. Schedule an appointment and convey this information to the party to be examined.

DRAFT THE DOCUMENTS

Draft the necessary documents. An example of a motion for compulsory physical examination appears in Exhibit 9.9.

The motion may require a notice of motion, an accompanying affidavit, and/or a proposed order for the judge. Check local practice. The motion should be reviewed by the attorney, signed, and served on the other party. After the exam, obtain

---

EXHIBIT 9.9 Motion for Compulsory Physical Examination

[Fed. R. Civ. P. Rule 35(a)]

[*Title of Court and Cause*]

Defendant, _____, moves the court for an order requiring the Plaintiff, _____, to submit to a physical examination for the purpose of determining the exact nature and extent of his [or her] injuries, if any, and disabilities and states the following:

1. There is a controversy between the Plaintiff and Defendant as to the physical injuries, if any, sustained by the plaintiff [or _____], and the disabilities, if any, resulting therefrom, and that the physical examination of the Plaintiff [or _____] is necessary in order that the Defendant, _____, may be in a position to defend as to the claimed injuries of the Plaintiff and to prepare his case for trial.

WHEREFORE, _____, Defendant, requests an order that the Plaintiff undergo an independent medical examination and for such other and further relief as the Defendant may be entitled.

[Date]

Respectfully submitted,

_____

Attorney for Defendant

Address: _____

Adapted from West's Federal Forms, § 3601, v. 3A, with permission of West Group.

a report from the doctor and consult with the supervising attorney. When the report is approved, send a copy to the opposing party if requested or as directed by your attorney. Pay the doctor and record the expense so it can be added to the client's bill.

INFORM THE CLIENT

If your party is subject to the exam, tell the client as soon as it is determined that the exam should be taken. Although the client may have been forewarned of a possible exam, the reality of it calls for further explanation, support, and instruction, which may be done by letter as in the Exhibit 9.10 example. In the alternative, the client might be instructed on these points at the office. In some circumstances you may be asked to accompany the client to the exam. In a Colorado case, a judge ruled that a paralegal could attend the Rule 35 physical exam of the paralegal's client. The court ruled that the exam was more adversarial than medical, giving rise to the need of the paralegal to protect the client from overreaching and unfair questioning.

EXHIBIT 9.10 Notice to Client of Physical Examination

WHITE, WILSON & MCDUFF
ATTORNEYS AT LAW
FEDERAL PLAZA BUILDING, SUITE 700
THIRD AND MARKET STREETS
LEGALVILLE, COLUMBIA 00000
(111) 555-0000

December 15, _____

Mrs. Ann Forrester
1533 Capitol Drive
Legalville, Columbia 00000

Dear Mrs. Forrester:

You may recall I mentioned in our initial interview the possibility that the other side in this case may request an examination by a doctor of their choosing to confirm the existence and extent of your injuries. Lynn Ott has contacted me to request such an exam.

The exam is scheduled for January 23, _____, at 1:30 in the afternoon. The examining physician is Dr. Melissa Ward, whose office is at 1644 Fountain Drive near exit 103 off I-275 in Legalville. Please make arrangements to be at Dr. Ward's office at the appointed time.

The exam will consist of a routine examination of your injuries, brief strength and movement tests, and a discussion with the doctor about your injuries and disabilities. The exam should last about an hour.

Before going to the examination, you may choose to make a list of your injuries, treatments, pain, disabilities, and current status. A review of your injury diary should help you.

You should cooperate fully in the exam and be sure neither to overstate nor understate the progress of your condition.

Mr. White believes the exam will be beneficial to your case. If you have any concerns, please let me know.

Very truly yours,

Terry Salyer
Paralegal

REQUEST THE REPORT

Following the exam, check with the supervising attorney on whether to request a copy of the report. Once the report is requested by the examined party, Rule 35(b)(2) says all privilege regarding other examinations of that party pertaining to the condition in question is waived. Normally this waiver of privilege would not be a problem, but in some unusual cases it may be. You may be asked to review and summarize the report noting any significant findings or comments for the attorney.

REVIEWING AND INTERPRETING MEDICAL RECORDS AND OTHER TECHNICAL DOCUMENTS AND REPORTS

INTRODUCTION

Most litigation paralegals review and summarize medical, commercial, industrial, scientific, and other technical records and reports that come into the case file as the result of a request for a medical examination, initial disclosure, document production, or other investigation. This can be exciting not only when you come upon information critical to your client's case, but also because you are learning entirely new areas of knowledge. Steps for dealing with such material are as follows:

1. Start the process of review as soon after receipt of the information as is practical.

2. Review the case file for the facts and issues.

3. Check each document against the list of requested documents to see if all are present. If not, note any absence and explanation for the attorney.

4. Read each document to categorize it and check its completeness, legibility, and accuracy. Missing words, letters left out of an abbreviation, misused words, and any other inaccuracies should be noted to avoid misreading or inaccurate conclusions. Certain documents providing critical information should be summarized.

5. Interpret each technical document by translating it into plain English.

6. Digest each document by summarizing the most significant information. Note inconsistencies or anything unusual. Highlight things that are particularly important to a determination of the issues.

The following section describes how this methodology is applied in the particular example of interpreting medical records.

MEDICAL RECORD INTERPRETATION

Resources

Assume that you have received the medical records for Ann Forrester. The hospital has sent each record that you requested. It is now your job to read that record, verify its accuracy, and understand it so that you can summarize it in lay terms for the benefit of the attorney. The stumbling block, however, is that you cannot interpret what you do not understand. Therefore, it becomes your task to educate yourself. In the case of medical records, as is true of many other technical documents, the major obstacle is the terminology and abbreviations. To overcome this obstacle, you need specialized dictionaries and other guides. A good medical dictionary is an essential for litigation paralegals working in personal injury cases. It is a good idea to create a concise, working glossary of obscure or technical terms raised in a particular case for quick reference for the duration of the case. An electronic version of the glossary is convenient for such a task and provides organizational flexibility and mobility.

Some reports use abbreviations or codes that may not be readily found in a dictionary. The people who work regularly with such documents have a code key or some other guide to abbreviations. For example, a tactful request to the medical records librarian of a hospital usually produces a list of abbreviations used by that hospital. Medical report abbreviations are somewhat standardized, but each hospital or each form may have its own peculiarities. Professional associations often have uniform abbreviations or code guides. Diagrams on human anatomy and physiology should be obtained. They are available in basic biology or nursing textbooks, as well as in appropriate sections of the medical or law library. Much of this information is also available online.

You should have a guide to pharmaceutical (drugs) and therapeutic terminology. The *Physician's Desk Reference* is an excellent reference for medicines, their purposes, and side effects. A current guide to medical tests and procedures is also helpful. Another good source is *Paralegal Medical Records Review* by Kristyn S. Appleby and Joanne Tarver. See the list of investigative resources in Chapter 3 for relevant online sites. Equipped with such resources, you should have little difficulty interpreting and summarizing hospital and physicians' records. Many other technical fields have similar references.

Preparing a Mini-Guide to Medical Terminology

Having acquired the necessary dictionaries and other resources, it may be worthwhile to create a mini-guide that can be used repeatedly as a quick reference when interpreting technical records. This type of tool is built over time and generally is personal in nature. It is the paralegal's personal "bible." The mini-guide method is adaptable to any technical field.

Once the record is translated, it can be summarized or digested in the same manner that depositions are digested. Be sure to have a section for observations and notations from your review, which includes areas such as inconsistencies or record omissions. These observations are important to identify and provide to your supervising attorney. Some medical or other specialized records can be provided in electronic form or can be converted. Commercial vendors and consultants are available to assist when working with such records.

Once medical records are received, preparing a medical timeline is helpful. This timeline assists both the attorney and paralegal in formulating positives and negatives in a case. It also serves as an organizational tool for the case. A medical timeline graph should be specific to a case, but Exhibit 9.11 offers a template to follow.

EXHIBIT 9.11 Timeline of Medical Treatment

Date of Treatment	Physician or Provider of Treatment	Type of Medical Treatment	Charges for Treatment	Diagnosis	Comments

REQUEST FOR ADMISSION

PURPOSE AND SCOPE

A request for admission is a document that sets out statements on specific facts, opinions, or the application of law to facts for the other party to admit or deny. Once admitted, the matter cannot be controverted. The purpose of admissions is to clarify which matters are no longer in dispute and, thus, unnecessary to prove at trial. This device is authorized by Rule 36 of the Federal Rules and parallel state rules. By narrowing the issues and related areas of proof, admissions can reduce the amount of time devoted to investigation and discovery, as well as the number of witnesses needed for trial. The need for the trial itself can be eliminated by clarifying the desirability of a settlement or possibility of a summary judgment. In short, it aims to achieve efficiency and frugality. The request for admission generally follows other discovery devices. It is not a request for information like a deposition or an interrogatory, but a confirmation of the truthfulness and accuracy of the previously discovered information. Requests for admission are a productive but often underused discovery device.

The scope of the request is defined by Rule 26(b) and for all practical purposes is the same as for the other discovery devices. The request may be directed to any other party in the lawsuit, and its use is limited solely to the particular lawsuit. In addition to facts, opinions, and application of law to facts, the request may seek admission on the genuineness of documents, photographs, exhibits, and physical evidence (things). When an admission should be forthcoming, failure or refusal to admit can lead to significant sanctions.

PROCEDURE

The steps in requesting admission include the following:

1. The request for admission with pertinent documents attached must be served on the responding party with copies to other parties.

2. The request may not be made prior to the Rule 26(f) discovery planning meeting unless ordered by the court or stipulated to by the parties. Check local rules.

3. The response must be made within 30 days or *matters are deemed admitted* unless extension of time is requested and granted.

4. The party responding may choose to seek a Rule 26(c) protective order on any particular matter. If so, other parties must be notified, the motion argued, and order entered.

5. The party responding may withdraw an answer and amend it with leave of the court. A timely withdrawal is granted if the original response is inaccurate and has not prejudiced the other party's case. If a party relied on the truthfulness of a response, and as a result did not pursue an expert opinion or evidence at that time available but now lost, the withdrawal can be denied.

6. The party requesting admission may accept the opponent's replies and objections or seek an order compelling either an answer or an expanded answer through a motion to determine the sufficiency of the response [Rule 36(a)].

7. Motions for court-imposed sanctions may be made if a denial is ruled improper or the challenge to an objection improper. The court may then require the other party to pay for costs of having to bring or argue a motion or for having to prove the matter at trial when it should have been admitted [Rules 36(a) and 37(c)(2)]. The court will not order sanctions if the request was held objectionable at the time of the 36(a) motion, or the admission sought was inconsequential, or there were reasonable grounds to believe the refusing party would prevail on the unadmitted issue at trial, or for other good reason not to admit.

PREPARING THE REQUEST FOR ADMISSION

Your role in working with requests for admissions can range from simply keeping track of what has been admitted and what has not, to a more intensive involvement, including the drafting of questions and answers for such requests. The following is a list of suggested steps in assisting the attorney with requests for admissions:

1. Review the pleadings, interrogatories, depositions, statements, and other relevant information if it is not fresh in your mind.

2. Prepare a list of admissions you need from the opponent. In the *Forrester* case it would be helpful if Mercury Parcel admitted that Mr. Hart was their employee and on duty at the time of the accident, or that Mr. Hart had exceeded the recommended number of shift hours just prior to the accident, if discovery had so revealed. Depending on the nature of the case, the list could become quite lengthy.

3. Seek suggestions and comments on the list from the attorney.

4. Draft a set of requests, keeping the following suggestions and techniques in mind:

    a. Check to see if court rules impose any limits on the number of admissions that may be requested. The Federal Rules have no such limitations.
    b. Locate a form for requests for admissions to learn format, types of questions, style, detail, and other matters that will help in visualizing the task.
    c. Set forth each point in a separate request or clearly delineated subsection. Combining points can be confusing and may lead to evasive or misleading answers.

d. Write brief and concise questions that elicit yes or no or otherwise brief answers. Eliminate unnecessary qualifiers from the questions.

e. Avoid use of incorporations by reference unless it is the only alternative.

f. Number questions sequentially and from the end of one set of requests to the beginning of another.

g. Research any request formats that raise questions of appropriateness.

h. Request admissions that relate to facts, statements or opinions of fact, or of the application of law to fact. Include admissions regarding the genuineness of documents or other physical evidence including diagrams and exhibits [Rule 36(a)].

An example of a request for admission of a fact:

> Please admit:
> That Mr. Hart was driving said vehicle on the date of said accident.

An example of a request eliciting an admission of an opinion:

> Please admit:
> That Defendant Hart was tired at the time of the accident.

An example of a request relating the application of law to fact:

> Please admit:
> That Defendant Hart was acting in the scope of his agency to Defendant Mercury Parcel at the time of the accident.

Agency and its scope are defined by law; therefore this question requires the application of legal principles on agency to the specific facts of the case.

An example of a request related to a document:

> Please admit:
> That Exhibit 5, a form MSA dated June 12, _____, signed by Mr. Hart:
> a. is an accurate copy of the original document,
> b. is kept in the ordinary course of Mercury Parcel Service's business,
> c. is a document used for drivers to report complaints about Mercury Parcel's vehicles.

This example demonstrates how a document should be identified and how a question on one item can be broken down to elicit admissions on each important sub-point. These points, if admitted, not only establish the copy of the document as a true copy, but also seek an admission that will lay the necessary foundation for the document to be admitted into evidence at trial. If admitted, these points will eliminate the need of a special witness to lay the foundation.

Usually a copy of the document is also included as an exhibit for review by the opponent; however, attaching the document is not necessary if the other party has the original document or a copy acquired through discovery. The description of the document must be sufficiently detailed to enable the other party to determine what document is addressed.

5. Have the request for admission reviewed, signed, and served on all parties.

Exhibit 9.12 is the form for a request for admissions based on Official Form 25 of the Federal Rules of Civil Procedure.

EXHIBIT 9.12 Federal Form 25: Request for Admission under Rule 36

[Caption]

Plaintiff A.B. requests Defendant C.D. within _____ days after service of this request to make the following admissions for the purpose of this action only and subject to all pertinent objections to admissibility which may be interposed at the trial:

1. That each of the following documents, exhibited with this request, is genuine. (Here list and describe each document.)

2. That each of the following statements is true. (Here list the statements.)

Signed: _____
Attorney for Plaintiff
Address: _____

Source: Federal Rules of Civil Procedure, with Forms.

RESPONDING TO A REQUEST FOR ADMISSION

1. Calendar the necessary response date figured on the basis of 30 days, otherwise deemed admitted.

2. Review the request thoroughly and the particular case file as needed.

3. Consult with the supervising attorney on how to respond to each request.

4. Draft the response keeping the following in mind:

   a. Answer each question unless told to do otherwise. Failure to answer means the item is admitted.

   b. Engross questions and then add the corresponding response for purposes of convenience and clarity.

   c. Answer with one of the following choices: admit, deny, qualify, object, move for extension of time, or move for a protective order.

   d. You must admit if you believe the matter is at least substantially true; however, if you have a reasonable doubt, such as when the veracity (truthfulness) of a witness is doubted, a denial is permissible.
   Misspellings and other minor inaccuracies are not sufficient grounds for denial unless they go directly to the substance of the dispute.

   e. If an item is denied, you must state "denied," not "refuse to admit" or "not accurate."

   f. You may admit in part and deny in part, but be clear.

   g. You may qualify a response and say, "Cannot admit or deny," as long as you give adequate reasons such as, "After reasonable inquiry, there is insufficient information to admit or deny."

   h. If an objection is made, the reason must be stated.

   i. You may object if a specific question does not fall within the usual scope of discovery. The most common objections are irrelevancy and privilege. Other acceptable objections may include vagueness, trade secrets, compound question, and others. Typical invalid objections include: request presents issue for trial, disputable matter, factual opinion, mixed question of law and

EXHIBIT 9.13 Response to Defendant's Requests for Admissions

(Caption)

The Plaintiff, _____, in answer to the Defendant's request for admissions served on the _____ day of _____, _____, in the above stated matter, states:

1. Denied. However, Plaintiff admits that [state basis for that part of request for admission that will be admitted; for example: apart from the fact that the premiums were waived by the terms of the policies on account of Plaintiff's then existing total and permanent disability, premiums would have become due as set out in that statement.]

2. Admitted.

3. Admitted in part and denied in part. [If admitting part of the admission and denying part of the admission, be specific in your response. For example: Plaintiff admits that the check referred to in Statement No. 2, when deposited by the Defendant, was not honored by the bank. Plaintiff denies that the check was not paid thereafter.]

4. Plaintiff objects to Request No. 4, which request is as follows: _____. The objection is: _____. [State as ground for objection that the requested admission is privileged, irrelevant or otherwise improper, unintelligible, vague, etc.]

5. Plaintiff can neither admit nor deny Request No. 5, which request is as follows: _____. [state your basis for the response.] or Plaintiff does not have the knowledge to admit or deny the request.

Respectfully submitted,

_____

Attorney for _____
(address)

Adapted from Forms § 3632 and § 3635, West's Federal Forms, v. 3A, with permission of West Group.

fact, other party already knows the answer, and requesting party has burden of proof.

5. Have the draft reviewed, typed, signed, and served on all parties.

Exhibit 9.13 is the form for the Response to Defendant's Requests for Admissions.

REVIEW OF AND REPLY TO RESPONSE

1. List all admissions, denials, objections, or improper responses.
2. Consult with the supervising attorney concerning the response and the list you made on it.
3. Draft motions to test the appropriateness of answers or objections as instructed.
4. Keep a record of all costs related to proving points denied by the other party for recovery if denial is shown to be improper.

AMENDING RESPONSES

If a response is discovered to be untrue because of inaccuracies or change in facts, you may be requested to draft a motion for a court order to withdraw the answer and to submit an amended response [Rule 36(b)]. Or, a response may be withdrawn due to inadvertence or mistake. Such was the case in *New Albertsons, Inc. v. Superior Court*, 168 Cal.App. 4th 1403, 86 Cal. Rptr. 3d 457 (2008).

APPLY YOUR KNOWLEDGE

Review your state's rule or statute on requests for admissions. Under what circumstances will your state court's permit a request for admissions to be either amended, withdrawn, or deemed admitted? Identify the case law that supports your conclusions.

CASE STUDY: UNDERSTANDING THE LAW

The *Albertsons* case centers on a personal injury case filed by a customer, John Shanahan, who fell and became unconscious while shopping at an Albertsons store in California. This case focuses on the Superior Court's denial of Albertsons' motion to withdraw an admission in response to a request for admission. In its response to the request, Albertsons admitted that a bag of ice was found near the plaintiff, John Shanahan. Albertsons claims that this admission was in error and would not cause Shanahan any prejudice if withdrawn. The Superior Court denied Albertsons' motion to withdraw the admission, and Albertsons filed a petition for writ of mandate effectively requesting that the Superior Court change its ruling. Albertsons claimed that the admission was a mistake—inadvertent or excusable neglect. The admission centers on whether Albertsons withheld or destroyed pictures showing either a wet floor or an ice bag near the area where Shanahan was injured. One of Albertsons personnel, Mr. Wells, admitted that there was a photograph showing a bag of ice. It was later shown that the clear plastic bag on the floor may not have been a bag of ice, suggesting his mistake. There was evidence that the bag may have been placed there by the paramedics and was not involved in the injury

suffered by Mr. Shanahan. This information led to the argument of mistake.

Since the Shanahans believed the photograph was their "smoking gun," they rigorous opposed the withdrawal of the admission. But the appeals court, in its opinion, stated that there is a policy of favoring trial on the merits especially when there is no proof that Albertsons' actions were deliberate or inexcusable. Thus, the appeals court found that the Superior Court abused its discretion by not permitting the withdrawal of the admission. The court did not reach this conclusion lightly, but because the applicable legal principles dictated a contrary result and the court transgressed those principles, the appeals court reversed the Superior Court's order and found abuse of discretion.

Questions for Review: Read the *Albertsons* case. What are the critical facts that led to the court's decision? What legal principles did the court rely upon to reverse the Superior Court's decision? Why did the court determine that the sanctions issued were not proper or authorized under the law?

However, the paralegal on the other side may have to draft a response to the motion demonstrating that the client would be prejudiced by the withdrawal. A party may be prejudiced, for example, if he or she had stopped discovery on an issue or failed to seek witnesses because of reliance on the admission.

OBJECTIONS, COMPELLING DISCOVERY, AND SANCTIONS

OBJECTING TO DISCOVERY: PROTECTIVE ORDERS

A discovery request may go too far. It may request privileged information or attorney work product, be unduly expensive, or be excessive in some other way. When this happens, it is necessary to object to the specific question or request. If after a good faith attempt to resolve the matter between the parties, the requesting party persists, the resisting party may by motion request a protective order from the court. This motion must be accompanied by a certificate stating that the party requesting the

TRADE SECRETS: DEALING WITH A MISSED DEADLINE

Requests for admissions are due within 30 days from receipt or they are deemed admitted. A nightmare scenario is when a request for admissions is served but goes unanswered. Your first reaction is to panic and even perhaps to cover up the mistake—make believe that you never received the document or that it was not your responsibility. Forget that response. Fess up immediately! The faster you acknowledge the error, the faster it can be addressed. Missing a critical deadline is possible in so many situations in litigation. Filing an answer to a complaint has a deadline; responding to a motion has a deadline; responding to discovery has a deadline. There is probably a case on virtually any litigation scenario where someone missed a deadline. Are all the results from the courts positive? Are all mistakes fixable? Truthfully, no. But, more often than not, coming clean to the court and admitting the mistake goes a longer way than making up excuses or blaming someone else for the error.

Humans make errors. We are not perfect. We strive for perfection, but hope for competence. As Denzel Washington's character in *The Equalizer* says to a co-worker trying to reach a weight goal to apply for a security job,: "Progress. Not perfection." Learn from your mistakes. Do not hide your mistakes from your attorneys thinking that the issue will go away. It will not. When you realize a deadline was missed or a mistake occurred and you cannot correct it, let your attorney know. Motions can be filed to address the problem. Is it embarrassing? Yes. Is it fatal? Hopefully, it is not. It is surprising how empathetic judges can be when presented with a case of human error. They were once practicing attorneys. Courts have discretion in many instances and can right seemingly fatal situations. Therefore, if for someone reason a deadline is missed, no matter the case or the form it takes, tell your attorney or someone in authority and let them make the decision on how to proceed. Do not sweep the mistake under the carpet, so to speak. It will only make the situation worse. Fess up; move on. It will not be the end of the world. Stuff happens.

protective order made a good faith attempt to resolve the issue with the other party. The court has the duty to protect a party or person from annoyance, embarrassment, oppression, or undue burden or expense. It is empowered to provide these remedies set out in Rule 26(c):

1. Deny the requested disclosure or discovery.

2. Grant discovery on specific terms and conditions, including time and place.

3. Grant discovery but by a different method than requested.

4. Grant discovery provided certain items are not inquired into, or if the scope of the inquiry is limited.

5. Grant discovery but only in the presence of certain individuals named by the court.

6. Grant discovery provided the deposition is sealed and opened only by court order.

7. Deny discovery of trade or commercial secrets, or grant discovery in a limited way.

8. Grant discovery only if parties simultaneously file specified information or documents in sealed envelopes to be opened as directed by the court.

The court has the power to deny the motion and order the resisting party to permit the discovery. If the motion is denied and justice requires, the court may order the resisting party to pay the costs and attorney fees incurred by the party seeking discovery [Rules 26(c) and 37(a)(4)]. The protective order may be sought in the district where the case is pending or in the district where the discovery is sought.

COMPELLING DISCOVERY MOTION, ORDER, AND SANCTIONS

When a party has failed to cooperate, the adverse party may file a motion requesting an order to compel disclosure or discovery. The court may then order the uncooperative party to pay the costs (reasonable expenses) and attorney fees incurred by the other side in bringing the motion, unless the failure was substantially justified or if the moving party did not make a good faith attempt to resolve the matter with the other party. Conversely, if a motion to compel is filed, denied, and found to be without substantial justification, the filing party may be ordered to pay costs, including attorney's fees [Rule 37(a)(4)].

If the motion is filed, and the court orders compliance but the party does not comply, the court may impose a number of severe sanctions. The court in the district where the deposition is taken may fine the uncooperative deponent for contempt of court if the person has refused an order to be sworn in or to answer a deposition question [Rule 37(b)(1)]. If a party or the designated person for an entity fails to obey an order to permit discovery, the court may impose certain sanctions:

a. Order that the matter or evidence sought be considered proved for the benefit of the party requesting the order;

b. Order the uncooperative party not to oppose certain claims or defenses or not to introduce designated matter into evidence;

c. Order the pleadings or parts thereof be stricken;

d. Stay (stop) further proceedings until the order is obeyed;

e. Dismiss the action, or any part thereof;

f. Render a default judgment against the disobedient party;

g. Find the party in contempt of court;

h. Order sanctions a, b, and c, when there is a refusal to submit to a medical exam, unless the party can show that the person to be examined cannot be produced [Rule 37(b)(2)(a–e)].

In lieu of or in addition to these sanctions, the court may impose the payment of costs, including attorney's fees, unless such failure to respond is substantially justified [Rule 37(b)(2)]. Also, when a party breaches the duty to preserve potentially discoverable information, an *adverse jury instruction* can be given the jurors. This instruction permits the jury to infer that the lost information was damaging to that party.

In addition, Rule 37(c)(1) sanctions for failing to disclose information required by Rule 26(a) or 26(e)(1) or failure to comply with the continuing duty to disclose, unless there is substantial justification or the failure to disclose is harmless, include not

APPLY YOUR KNOWLEDGE

Determine the sanctions that are available to a party in your jurisdiction when a party fails to comply with discovery requests. Identify the case law and civil rule of procedure that supports your position.

being able to use the undisclosed evidence or witness at trial or other hearing; having to pay reasonable expenses caused by the failure, including attorney's fees; and the other sanctions set out in (a) through (f) in the preceding list. These sanctions do not require a motion.

As mentioned in the section on requests for admission, if a party receives a request for admission and fails to admit the genuineness of any document (or e-stored information) or the truth of any matter as requested under Rule 36, and the other party proves the genuineness or truth of the matter, the court on motion may order the refusing party to pay the other party's expenses in proving the matter [Rule 37(c)(2)].

If a party or an officer, director, or managing agent of a party or a designate for a corporation or other entity fails to appear at the deposition after receiving proper notice, or fails to serve answers or objections to interrogatories after proper service, or to serve a written response to a properly served request for inspection, the court may on motion impose the sanctions previously mentioned in (a) to (f), including payment of costs [Rule 37(d)].

If pursuant to Rule 26(f) a party requests a discovery conference to set up a discovery plan and the other party fails to participate in good faith in the framing of a discovery plan, the court may impose the payment of costs incurred by the other party, including attorney's fees, due to the failure to cooperate [Rule 37(g)].

Rule 37(f) recognizes that the standard operation of e-information systems can lead to the non-culpable loss of discoverable information. Under subsection (f), a party is protected from court sanctions if the information is "lost as a result of the routine, good faith [non-culpable] operation of an electronic information system."

ETHICAL CONSIDERATIONS: SOCIAL MEDIA, DISCOVERY, AND PRIVACY

Before the Internet and social media, privilege and the privacy rights of a client were more easily defined and, in turn, more easy to protect. Enter Facebook, Twitter, YouTube, and other social media outlets and the lines of privilege and privacy become quite blurry. Discovery disputes invariably arise during the course of litigation. But now privilege, sometimes even involving communications between attorneys and their clients, may be waived in what normally are private domains. Pictures, for example, are posted on Facebook, Instagram, or Twitter. Are these pictures fair game in discovery, even though considered private? The answer is most likely "no." What about a YouTube video post of your vacation, is that private? The answer, of course, is "it depends." If a user/client strictly adheres to privacy settings, there is the argument that the information is private. However, more and more courts are permitting the discovery of social media websites and their contents as public information,

especially if it can be shown that the information sought leads to discoverable information.

But, how far is too far? If a discovery request borders on fraud or misrepresentation, are ethical rules breached? Here is the scenario. Opposing counsel in a case knowingly sends a "friend" request on Facebook to the plaintiff knowing that is the only way to access to the information she wants. It is sneaky and most likely unethical. Many courts and bar associations are concluding that attorneys under these circumstances must reveal their professional capacity so as not to lure unsuspecting parties to permit access to private social media accounts. These ethical rules will apply to witnesses and other parties involved in the opposing party's case. Privacy may be dwindling, but attorneys' access to social media must meet ethical standards before information may be discovered or compelled. Future court cases will set the parameters for what is acceptable behavior in the spheres of privacy and social media. This area is developing and growing as social media becomes more and more prolific in our lives and the litigation process.

Routine overwriting and other loss of data in the normal operation of the system are acceptable. Conversely, once a party is aware of the duty to preserve discovery information in the context of particular litigation, routine loss of potentially relevant data is not acceptable.

Local rules may provide different procedures and sanctions and should be consulted.

PROCEDURE FOR COMPELLING DISCOVERY

When the opponent has not provided disclosure or responded to a request for discovery or has objected to a request for discovery, the supervising attorney should be informed. If, after the required good faith effort to resolve differences, the decision is made to compel disclosure or discovery and seek sanctions, draft the necessary documents to file the motion to compel discovery. The documents include the motion, certification of attempt to resolve, the notice of motion, usually a memorandum of law, the desired order, and the certificate of service. Before you draft the motion, however, the attorney must decide what court should receive the motion. A motion for an order to compel a party may be filed in the court where the action is pending; if to compel a nonparty, the motion should be made in the court in the district where the discovery is sought [Rule 37(a)(1)]. The caption should be drafted accordingly. An adaptable form for a motion to compel appears in Exhibit 9.14, the affidavit in support of the motion in Exhibit 9.15, and a proposed order to compel in Exhibit 9.16.

EXHIBIT 9.14 Motion to Compel Production, Inspection, and Copying of Documents in Case of Objection or Failure to Respond Plus Rule 26(c) Certification—General Form

---

[FED. R. CIV. P. Rules 34(b), 37(a)]

[*Title of Court and Cause Number*]

Defendant, _____, moves the court for an order compelling Plaintiff, _____, to produce and to permit Defendant to inspect and to copy or photograph the documents requested and states: each of the following documents [*here list the documents and describe each of them*].

1. This motion is made on the ground that the Defendant served a written request upon the Plaintiff for production, inspection, and copying or photographing the above-mentioned documents, a copy of which is attached hereto as Exhibit A.

2. The Plaintiff objected to the production by a response, a copy of which is attached hereto as Exhibit B [*or* and that Plaintiff has failed and refused to respond to Defendant's request as required by Rule 34, Federal Rules of Civil Procedure].

3. The documents requested by the Defendant contain relevant and material evidence in the above-entitled action and their production is necessary for the Defendant to prepare for trial.

4. The Defendant has attempted to resolve this matter as required by the Federal Rules of Procedure, but the Plaintiff continues to refuse to comply with the Defendant's request. See Exhibit C.

WHEREFORE, the Defendant requests an order compelling the Plaintiff to answer and produce documents as requested in the Defendant's Production of Documents and Things and for such other and further relief as the Defendant may be entitled.

Attorney for Defendant

Address: _____.

EXHIBIT 9.14 Motion to Compel Production, Inspection, and Copying of Documents in Case of Objection or Failure to Respond Plus Rule 26(c) Certification—General Form (*continued*)

Certification of Attempt to Resolve [Rule 26(c)]

I [*attorney's name*], attorney for [*Defendant, Plaintiff*], certify that prior to filing this motion to compel discovery I made a good faith attempt to resolve this discovery issue as follows:

1. [*Briefly state facts and dates of attempt and failure to resolve.*]

2. _____

Date _____

_____

Attorney for _____
Address:
Phone:

Source: Reprinted with permission of West Group.

EXHIBIT 9.15 Affidavit in Support of Motion to Compel

[FED. R. CIV. P. Rules 34, 37(a)]

[*Title of Court and Cause Number*]

[*Venue*]

_____, being first duly sworn, on his oath states:

1. That, _____,is one of the attorneys for the above named Defendant and makes this affidavit in support of the Motion for Production of Documents and Things for Inspection, Copying, and Photographing which is attached hereto.

2. The production of the documents, papers, statements and things requested is made in good faith pursuant to the Federal Rules of Civil Procedure.

3. The undersigned counsel has been informed and therefore believes that the matters and things so sought in the motion are relevant and permitted under the Federal Rules of Evidence by reason of the fact that the facts sought to be elicited are facts necessary to be shown and produced in this cause in securing all the facts necessary to prove the issues to be tried.

4. The motion herein made is made in good faith and the affiant as one of counsel for the Defendant desires to inspect the documents solely for the purpose of establishing facts to be used as evidence in the above entitled cause.

Dated this _____ day of _____, _____.

[*Jurat*]

Adapted from West's Federal Forms § 3560, v. 3A, with permission of West Group.

EXHIBIT 9.16 Proposed Order That Interrogatories Concerning Personal Jurisdiction Are Answered and That Personal Jurisdiction Is Established

[FED. R. CIV. P. Rule 37(b)(2)]

[*Title of Court and Cause Number*]

On [*date*], _____, an order was entered, requiring the Defendant to file answers to written interrogatories on or before [*date*], _____. No such filing has been made to the present day, and no motion has been made for an enlargement of time in which to comply with the order.

Sanctions under Rule 37(b) of the Federal Rules of Civil Procedure are therefore appropriate.

It appears to the court that the unresolved issues to which the interrogatories went are those designated in Exhibit C of the order on pretrial conference, filing _____, as:

"1. Personal jurisdiction on The _____ Company, a _____ corporation.

(a) Was The _____ Company, a _____ corporation doing business in _____?

(b) Was the involvement of The _____ Company substantial enough to give this court jurisdiction over this Defendant?"

Those questions will now stand as answered in the affirmative, and personal jurisdiction waived by that Defendant.

IT IS SO ORDERED:

1. That the motion to impose sanctions for failure to comply with the order of the court, filing is granted: That the Defendant The _____ Company, a _____ corporation, was doing business in _____ and its involvement was substantial enough to give this court jurisdiction over that Defendant; that personal jurisdiction over the Defendant The _____ Company, a _____ corporation, is deemed admitted and established and the issue of personal jurisdiction over the defendant is waived by that defendant;

2. That the Defendant The _____ Company shall pay within fifteen days of the date of this order to the Plaintiffs' counsel the amount of $ _____ as the expense of obtaining this order.

[*Date*]

_____
United States District Judge

Adapted from West's Federal Forms §3721.5, v. 3A, with permission of West Group.

A copy of the motion and supporting documents should be reviewed by the attorney and served on the attorney for the adverse party. All documents plus proof of service should be filed with the appropriate clerk of court. These procedures and the required documents may vary in state practice.

THE FREEDOM OF INFORMATION ACT

DEFINITION AND PURPOSE

In addition to the formal discovery devices covered in Chapters 7, 8, and 9 and the informal investigation devices covered in Chapter 3, paralegals can enhance the client's case by accessing government sources of information. In 1976, the Freedom of Information Act, 5 U.S.C. § 552 (FOIA) was passed to provide the general public access to the records of many government agencies. The public policy underlying the law is that a more informed public will enhance the accountability and performance of government agencies and officials. Such openness is deemed desirable and consistent with our democratic form of government. Several states have passed similar laws.

The FOIA might be helpful in a suit against a particular government agency or in a suit against a private party. The Consumer Products Safety Commission, for example, might be able to provide information on the safety record of the make of van involved in Mrs. Forrester's accident, on the type of extension cord used by the campground in Case II, or on the all-terrain vehicle that led to the death of Sean Coleman in Case III.

Use of the FOIA offers some advantages over most other discovery devices:

1. It is not necessary to file an action or order to gain access to the information. In the examples just given, a request for information about faulty products could be submitted well before the filing of the action, and could be useful in determining whether the manufacturer of the product in question should be joined as one of the defendants in the case.

2. Because the law is not oriented toward litigation, the Rule 26(b) prerequisite of relevancy does not apply. Consequently, one can go on "fishing expeditions" regardless of relevancy in the hope of turning up something useful.

3. Access is available to anyone with a bona fide request.

4. The request is not restricted to information from a party as is true of some discovery devices; therefore, the range of information that can be obtained is greater.

PROCEDURE AND LIMITS

The requesting party invokes the FOIA by submitting a request to the pertinent agency through that agency's designated information officer. The request must demonstrate that the information requested is in the records of an agency covered by the act. Specific exemptions to the disclosure requirement are listed in section 552(b) of the act:

- Properly classified national defense or foreign policy documents.
- Internal personnel rules and practices.
- Material specifically exempted from disclosure by statute.
- Trade secrets and commercial or financial information obtained from a person which are of a privileged or confidential nature.
- Inter- and intra-agency communication (letters and memos) otherwise not available through discovery in actions against an agency.
- Personnel, medical, and similar files of a private nature.
- Law enforcement records and information if disclosure would impede investigation, violate personal privacy, or permit circumvention of the law.
- Reports related to the regulation or supervision of financial institutions.
- Geological and geophysical information on oil and natural gas wells.

Once the request is submitted, the agency must indicate within 20 days whether it will comply or deny the request [§ 552(a)(6)(a)(i)]. That decision may be appealed, and if so, a determination must be made within 20 days [§ 552(a)(6)(a)(ii)]. If the agency

INTERNET EXERCISE

Using www.justice .gov/oip/foiacontacts. htm, locate the contact person for a FOIA request from the following agencies: 1) Office of Inspector General; (2) Centers for Medicare & Medicaid Services; (3) Department of Veteran Affairs; (4) Central Intelligence Agency.

upholds the decision to withhold the information, the administrative remedies are exhausted and relief must be sought in federal district court.

A reasonable fee for producing the information will be charged. The agency may waive the fee, however, if release of the information is likely to contribute significantly to public understanding of the operation or activities of government and is not primarily in the commercial interest of the requester [5 U.S.C. § 552(a)(4)(a)(iii)].

THE ROLE OF THE PARALEGAL

Your task as paralegal regarding a request for information under the FOIA will be to draft the request. Exhibit 9.17 is a form that can be used as a guide when drafting the document. FOIA forms can usually be found at the website of the applicable agency.

You may also be called on to research the likely availability of particular information and whether it is accessible under the act. Agency websites now post information of public value that is likely to be requested, so you may find what you need with a simple search. Excellent resources on making FOIA requests are a Bureau of National Affairs pamphlet entitled, "The Freedom of Information Act: Business Uses" and the extensive Department of Justice information at http://www.usdoj.gov/04foia.

EXHIBIT 9.17 Freedom of Information Act (FOIA) Sample Request Letter

Agency Head [*or Freedom of Information Act Officer*]
Name of Agency
Address of Agency
City, State, Zip Code

Re: Freedom of Information Act Request

Dear _____.

This is a request under the Freedom of Information Act [*or state applicable state freedom of information statute or opens records act*].

I request that a copy of the following documents [*or documents containing the following information*] be provided to me: [*identify the documents or information as specifically as possible*].

In order to help to determine my status to assess fees, you should know that I am [*insert a suitable description of the requester and the purpose of the request*].

[*Sample requester descriptions:*

(A) a representative of the news media affiliated with the _____ newspaper (magazine, television station, etc.), and this request is made as part of news gathering and not for a commercial use.

(B) affiliated with an educational or noncommercial scientific institution, and this request is made for a scholarly or scientific purpose and not for a commercial use.

(C) an individual seeking information for personal use and not for a commercial use.

(D) affiliated with a private corporation and am seeking information for use in the company's business.]

[*Optional*] I am willing to pay fees for this request up to a maximum of $ _____. If you estimate that the fees will exceed this limit, please inform me first.

[*Optional*] I request a waiver of all fees for this request. Disclosure of the requested information to me is in the public interest because it is likely to contribute significantly to public understanding of the operations or activities of the government and is not primarily in my commercial interest. [*Include a specific explanation.*]

EXHIBIT 9.17 Freedom of Information Act (FOIA) Sample Request Letter (*continued*)

[*Optional*] I request that the information sought be provided in electronic format, such as a computer disk or CD-ROM.

[If the information needs to be expedited, state the basis for the request.]

If you need any additional information or further clarification about this request, please contact me at [state a telephone number] or [e-mail address].

Thank you for your consideration of this request.

Sincerely, _____

_____

Name
[Address
City, State, Zip Code
Telephone number (Optional)]*

* (Note: If this information is included in the letterhead, it is not necessary in the closing salutation.)
Adapted from West's Legal Forms § 19.2, v. 28 (3d ed., 1997), with permission of West Group.

ORGANIZING FILES

INTRODUCTION

You see yourself sitting next to your supervising attorney at counsel's table at a dramatic point in the trial. The attorney turns to you and whispers, "I need the follow-up medical report from Dr. Grimes!" Your eyes shift to a dog-eared folder swollen beyond its capacity with corners of various pages slipping toward chaotic freedom. You begin to perspire as you feverishly page through the documents. Your attorney helps by loudly whispering, "Hurry up! Hurry up!"

As you fly through the folder, it creeps toward the edge of the table, and suddenly papers come flushing out like water through a broken dam as the file and its contents spread over the floor.

Then you wake up from the nightmare and swear that you will never let that happen to you.

The documents gathered and analyzed in discovery and investigation, plus the pleadings and other materials, must be organized in the case file. This document management is essential for efficient use of the information and to reduce the risk of loss or misplacement. A variety of methods can be used for organizing a client's file. More than likely you will use the method preferred by your supervising attorney. The following systems are only two methods of organization. Should you be asked to set up a system for organizing client files, law office management books will provide a variety of other methods from which to choose. The Association of Records Managers and Administrators, Inc. (http://www.arma.org) provides numerous aids. Case management software that allows an entire case file to be stored and updated electronically, Internet access, and laptop computers and mobile printers for in-court access and printing may soon make the hard-copy case file an endangered species. Even electronic files, however, need some organizational structure.

EXHIBIT 9.18 Small Case File Folder

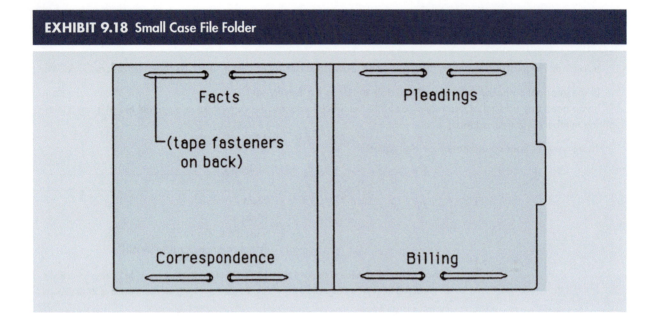

SMALL CASE FILE

The documents needed in most small case files can be neatly organized into one manila folder. By attaching some of the documents at the top and some at the bottom of each of the two flaps of the folder, four general categories of file documents can be maintained. Four common file categories include pleadings, correspondence, factual items, and billing documents. The folder would appear as indicated in Exhibit 9.18.

The fact section should include such things as client background sheet (see Exhibit 2.1), client interview or summary, accident reports, contracts, pertinent business records, medical reports and authorizations, witness statements, medical bills, damage estimates, and so on. The client data sheet can contain a checkoff section indicating what was done last in the case and what should be done next. This section can be a separate form (see Exhibit 11.2) that can be standardized and computerized for ease of updating and determining the status of a case at a glance. The subcategories of the fact section may be organized into subgroups and placed in chronological or reverse chronological order and tabbed with gummed labels.

The pleadings section should contain the complaint, answer, motions, affidavits, memoranda of law, proofs and acknowledgments of service, requests for admissions, and other documents filed in the case. These documents are normally filed in chronological order and may also be tabbed and color-coded for plaintiff's and defendant's pleadings.

The correspondence section consists of all letters, memos, and other correspondence, which may be divided and tabbed in subgroups and filed in reverse chronological order. Some firms use special colored carbons to allow quick identification of correspondence originating from their offices.

The billing section should include all items that will go into the client's bill: records of travel, phone calls, conferences, witness fees, filing fees, service of process expenses, time slips, and others. Having these items organized in such a manner facilitates figuring the bill and provides the basis for status reports requested by the client.

A current index of each section of the folder should be kept at the top of one leaf of the folder for quick reference.

This type of file provides some organization, allows the file to be updated in an organized way, and should reduce the amount of time needed when the supervising attorney says, "Hurry up!"

LARGE CASE FILE

When the case involves lots of documents or outgrows the small case file, a more involved system is called for. The following method is one of several ways that it can be done.

The first step is to gather all of the documents and file folders that pertain to the case, and separate these materials into six broad divisions:

- Correspondence, bills, and miscellaneous
- Pleadings
- Transcripts
- Photographs
- Documents and exhibits
- Medical records (or other relevant category).

The second step is to take the "correspondence, bills, and miscellaneous" material and make file folders assigning the following file numbers and titles:

Correspondence, Bills, and Miscellaneous: Numbers 10–99

- 10 Correspondence
- 20 Bills
- 30 Research
- 40 Investigations
- 50 Miscellaneous memos and notes
- 60 Deposition summary and notes
- 70 Answers to interrogatories summaries
- 80 Witnesses (background, memos, statements, etc.)
- 90 Miscellaneous (as needed).

Each of the subcategories can be further broken down as needed:

10 Correspondence

- 10.1 Client (to or from)
- 10.2 Insured (to or from)
- 10.3 Plaintiff's counsel (to or from)
- 10.4 Co-defendant's counsel (to or from)
- 10.5 Court (to or from)
- 10.6 Miscellaneous.

If folders need to be broken down further, then use 10.1(a), (b), (c), and so on. The other categories in the division should then be broken down into logical and relevant subdivisions.

The "pleadings" division should be assigned the number 100 and subdivided accordingly. Pleadings are placed in chronological order in their subdivision and numbered in red. For example, the complaint would have a 1 in its lower right corner, the answer a 2, and so forth.

Pleadings: Numbers 100–199

110 Complaints, answers, motions, and other related pleadings

120 Discovery pleadings to plaintiff and plaintiff's responses

121 Interrogatories to plaintiff

122 Plaintiff's response to interrogatories

123 Requests for admissions to plaintiff

124 Plaintiff's responses to admissions request

125 Requests for production and so on

130 Discovery pleadings to defendant and defendant's responses

131 Interrogatories to defendant

132 Defendant's responses to interrogatories and so on

140 Notice of depositions and related pleadings

150 Open (to be used as specific case dictates)

160 Open

170 Pretrial/trial pleadings

180 Miscellaneous pleadings by plaintiff

190 Miscellaneous pleadings by defendant.

The remaining divisions should be numbered and subdivided in like fashion. As the file folders are being created for each subdivision, a detailed index should be made of each division and the contents of each category and each subcategory. The master index should show the divisions and subdivisions with their assigned numbers. The subsequent sheets of the index should be assigned to each subfile, and as new items are placed in the subfile, a description of the item should be entered on the appropriate subfile index sheet. Exhibit 9.19 is an example of how the master index sheet might appear and Exhibit 9.20 shows the subfile index sheet.

The index can be kept and regularly updated as the first file in the case or as a three-ring binder to facilitate the rapid retrieval of needed documents. All the subfiles of the case can then be expandable case files in numerical order.

These index sheets kept at the top or front of a case file provide a quick overview of where everything is filed, and a more detailed log of the current holdings in each

---

EXHIBIT 9.19 Master File Index Sheet

Case: *Forrester v. Mercury Parcel Service* Case File No. _____

File No.	Categories
10–99	Correspondence, bills, miscellaneous
10	Correspondence
20	Bills
30	Research
100–199	Pleadings
110	Complaints, answers, motions, and other related pleadings
120	Discovery pleadings to plaintiff
200–299	Transcripts
210	Depositions of plaintiff's witnesses
220	Depositions of defendant's witnesses
230	Trial transcripts
300–399	Photographs

EXHIBIT 9.20 Subfile Index Sheet

Case: *Forrester v. Mercury Parcel Service* Case File No._____

File No.	Subtitled Components
10.1	Client (to or from)
(a)	6/26/___ letter from seeking our representation
(b)	7/11/___ letter to setting up interview
(c)	7/13/___ letter to describing items to bring
(d)	7/20/___ letter to accepting case
10.2	Insured (to or from)
(a)	9/01/___ letter to requesting payment of damages
(b)	9/20/___ letter from stating not responsible for damages

file. When kept current, such an index is a great organizer and time saver. If the case is going to be particularly voluminous, there are advantages to using the uniform decimal numbering system discussed earlier in the chapter.

SUMMARY

This chapter concludes the three-chapter discussion on disclosure and discovery. You have now been introduced to one of the most significant areas of litigation practice and paralegal responsibility.

Interrogatory and deposition practice were covered in the previous chapters. The focus of Chapter 9 is the production of documents and electronically stored information in disclosure and by request for production of documents and things, request for medical exam, and request for admission. Each of these procedures requires paralegals to know the applicable rules of procedure and the forms and techniques for seeking and providing the necessary information. The awareness of when and how to compel disclosure and discovery and to protect the client against improper discovery provides the weapons and armor needed to ensure that the system works for you and the firm's clients.

Further, techniques for organizing and analyzing large amounts of information, including the application of the latest computer technology to the tasks, can make an otherwise overwhelming discovery process manageable. When exercised knowledgeably and ethically, these discovery skills are extremely valuable to the client, the firm, and our system of civil justice. This knowledge plus experience will help make you an indispensable member of the litigation team.

KEY TERMS

active data	guardian ad litem	residual data
backup data	metadata	spoliation
embedded data	redaction	

QUESTIONS FOR STUDY AND REVIEW

1. What is the definition, purpose, and scope of the request for production of documents and things?

2. What are the procedural steps and time requirements involved in the production of documents?

3. In what form should e-stored information be produced? What are the concerns regarding the format of such material? How do you determine what documents and things should be requested for a production of documents and things?

4. What are some of the initial steps in preparing a production of documents and things and who can be helpful in assisting in this preparation?

5. What steps need to be followed in pulling document files, both electronic and paper? Describe the objectives and each step in screening the pulled files or documents, both electronic and paper.

6. What steps should be followed and indexes kept at the examination stage? What steps are important when returning documents that have been produced to the original custodian?

7. What security techniques should be taken to protect computerized data?

8. What is the procedure for replying to a request for production and inspection? What rules apply?

9. What is the purpose of a Rule 35 mental or physical exam? What nonparties may be reached through this rule, and what showing is needed for such a request to be granted?

10. What are the procedures and tasks you perform in working with requests for compulsory medical examination?

11. What is the definition, purpose, and scope of Rule 36 requests for admissions? What are the steps in the procedure for requesting admissions and responding to them?

12. What sanctions can be imposed on a party by the court for failure to cooperate and adequately comply with a disclosure or discovery request, or for failure to comply with a court order compelling discovery? What is the procedure for compelling discovery and the role of the paralegal?

13. What is the Freedom of Information Act? Why is it potentially useful to you as a litigation paralegal?

14. What must be demonstrated to be granted a FOIA request, and what procedure must be followed to have such a request approved?

15. How do you organize a small case file, and what kinds of documents go in each subsection? How do you organize a large case file?

SYSTEMS FOLDER ASSIGNMENTS

1. Insert the following in separate subsections of your systems folder for production of documents and things and entry upon land for inspection and other things; request for physical and mental examination; request for admissions; and objections, compelling discovery, and sanctions:

   Outline on definition, purpose, scope, applicable rules, and procedures; text page references, a copy or your own draft of pertinent checklists, techniques, and tips; copies of relevant sample forms for each device.

2. Note parallel state rules and time limits for each of the above discovery devices in the Pleadings, Motions, and Time Limits Chart (Exhibit 6.23) and in each respective subsection of your systems folder.

3. To better understand and retain an overall picture of the document production process, draft a chronological list of the procedural steps in the federal production process. (See the Procedure subsection at the beginning of the chapter.)

4. Draft a procedural checklist for making a request pursuant to the Freedom of Information Act, both federal and state, and place it in your systems folder. Include a copy of or page reference to the sample FOIA request in the chapter. (Note: Your state may have a specific statute for requesting public documents. It should be consulted in responding to this assignment.)

5. In a subsection in your systems folder on organizing files, insert text page references to or your drafted checklists for organizing small and large case files, copies of the master and subfile indexes, any alternative methods for organizing case files, and your organized case file to date for the *Forrester* case. (See relevant Application Assignment 5 below.)

APPLICATION ASSIGNMENTS

1. Draft a response to Mrs. Forrester's request for production of documents and things found in this chapter.

2. Using the procedures described in this chapter, the form in Exhibit 9.8, and examples of the types and forms of questions to ask, draft a five-item set of requests for admissions from Mrs. Forrester to Mercury Parcel that covers:

    - Caption
    - Admissions on employment and agency of Hart
    - Admissions on forms that reflect irregular maintenance—as well as inaction on complaint about wheels locking when braking

    Draft requests for admissions regarding both documents and statements. Assume that you have previously discovered certain facts needed to justify the requests.

3. Assume that you are a paralegal for Mercury Parcel and have received the following requests for admissions from Mrs. Forrester's attorney:

    a. Defendant Hart was an employee of Mercury Parcel Service, Inc. on Tuesday, February 23, _____.

    b. Plaintiff Forrester's conduct did not negligently contribute to the accident on February 26, _____.

    c. No follow-up maintenance was performed on vehicle 23 regarding locking wheels between the time of the filing of the complaint and the accident on February 26, _____ as confirmed by the unchecked follow-up item on form ICC-2015, No. 37.

    d. Defendant Hart's supervisor John Roosevelt, was advised to tell Defendant Hart not to fill out a company accident report after the accident.

    Reflect on each item and draft what you think would be the proper response to each item. Your responses should vary. Use the format that follows:

    REQUEST NO. 1: Defendant Hart. . .

    RESPONSE: (Admit, Deny, Other)

4. In Case V from Chapter 1, assume that Carlos Montez has refused Ms. Rakowski's request to produce reports of previous incidents of harassment. He has objected on the grounds that this is irrelevant. Briefly stating that this may lead to relevant evidence, draft a motion to compel the answer.

5. Using the small case filing method described in the text, under which of the four general categories and, if pertinent, in what order would you place the following:

    a. a letter to Mrs. Forrester dated December 2 of this year

    b. the complaint

    c. a motion to dismiss the complaint

    d. a time slip carbon for 3 hours of legal research

e. the client's background sheet

f. a memorandum on the admissibility of inflammatory photographs

g. the client's medical bills

h. a letter to Mrs. Forrester dated May of this year

i. a note on fee paid to witness for deposition

j. a memo from you to Isadora Pearlman

k. a written statement by Ms. Schnabel

CASE ASSIGNMENTS

1. Prepare the Request for Production of Documents and Request for Admissions to Mrs. Forrester from (1) Mercury Parcel Service, Inc. and (2) Richard Hart. (Prepare each document separately. Use the examples from the Application Assignments to expand your discovery documents.)

2. Draft the Request for Physical and Mental Examination from Mercury Parcel Service, Inc. to Mrs. Forrester. Be sure you comply with your state rules.

10

SETTLEMENT AND OTHER ALTERNATIVE DISPUTE RESOLUTIONS

OBJECTIVES

AFTER READING THIS CHAPTER, YOU WILL BE ABLE TO:

- Understand the paralegal's role in the settlement process
- Prepare a settlement précis or letter for your supervising attorney
- Assist your supervising attorney in preparing for a pretrial conference
- Draft settlement agreements and release documents
- Identify the different methods of alternative dispute resolution

INTRODUCTION

The purpose of litigation is to resolve disputes. Going to trial is one method of resolving the differences between parties. Most cases, however, never go to trial. They may be negotiated and settled, or the parties may seek some alternative form of resolution as required by contract or court process, or by choice. This chapter focuses on settlement as the primary method of resolving a case, but it also addresses other resolution procedures including arbitration, mediation, summary trials, and related processes that are growing in importance. As in trial preparation, the paralegal organizes information and prepares it for presentation in alternative dispute resolution. Paralegals with appropriate training also can have a more direct role in alternative dispute resolution by working as mediators and arbitrators.

SETTLEMENT

INTRODUCTION

Definition and Purpose

settlement

The process whereby both sides review strengths and weaknesses of a case and reach a mutual agreement on how to dispose of the case.

Settlement is the process whereby both sides review strengths and weaknesses of a case and reach a mutual agreement on how to dispose of the case. Approximately 98 percent of all federal civil cases are settled or resolved without a trial. A case may be settled at nearly any stage of the litigation process, with some cases being disposed of before a complaint is filed, most before trial, some at trial, and a few during appeal.

Cases are settled for a variety of reasons, the most obvious being to save time, trouble, and expense. Settlement is encouraged in our system. If cases were not settled at the rate they are, our courts would be overloaded (even more so), and the endless litigation that lasts over several generations as portrayed in Dickens's *Bleak House* would be a reality. Settlement removes the uncertainty of the outcome of a trial, eliminates or reduces adverse publicity, and ends the fear of the ordeal of trial.

Settlement is based on a combination of factors: amount of damages, ability of the defendant to pay, insurance coverage, ease with which liability and damages can be proven, nature of the injury (permanency, horror factor, disability), sympathy for the plaintiff, whether the plaintiff needs to be paid right away or can hold out through trial, amount of verdicts in similar cases in the same area, respective ability of attorneys, attitude of the judge, desire of either party for vindication, and others. Though most of these matters are assessed by the attorney, an alert paralegal often spots things otherwise overlooked that might make a difference.

Role of the Paralegal

The primary role of the paralegal is to gather, organize, and draft materials to help the attorney evaluate the case and present it in negotiation to the other side. If a settlement is reached, it generally falls to the paralegal to draft the necessary settlement documents.

ETHICAL CONSIDERATIONS: THE POWER TO ACCEPT A SETTLEMENT OFFER

Both attorneys and paralegals must remember that the decision to accept a settlement is up to the client. ABA Model Rule 1.2 states, "A lawyer shall abide by a client's decision whether to accept an offer of settlement of a matter." This language incorporates the spirit of the old code, which is still the ethical standard in some states.

Regardless of confidence in the facts or fairness of a case, a paralegal *may not make settlement offers, accept offers, or counsel the client on the advisability of accepting a settlement*. Take caution in discussing such matters with the client and in conveying advice of the attorney. It must be crystal clear that the paralegal is not giving the advice, and the information conveyed must be accurate.

Take care when discussing matters with an adverse (or opposing) attorney, paralegal, or others, since a client's opportunity for settlement may be adversely affected if information is unwittingly revealed. Settlement précis and brochures (to be discussed in this chapter) or other items prepared for review by the opponent or an insurance adjuster must not reveal harmful information. Confidential information must be protected, and should be revealed only with the client's permission and approval of the attorney.

Throughout the process, you may be expected to keep the client readily informed of the progress in negotiation and any proposals. Professional ethics require the attorney to keep the client informed (Model Rule 1.4a and b).

PREPARING FOR SETTLEMENT

Introduction

The importance of the preparation needed to conduct and ultimately reach a negotiated settlement is generally underestimated. Attorneys and paralegals alike tend to focus on the trial and frequently establish all preparation timetables accordingly. Since so many cases are settled, however, timetables and preparation need to be geared to the settlement process as well. An important by-product of preparation for settlement, if done correctly, is that it becomes a significant part of the preparation for trial.

The paralegal contributes to two significant stages in settlement: the attorney's evaluation of the case and the presentation of the case for settlement. If the opponent's side is presenting the case for settlement, the paralegal's work will help prepare the attorney to evaluate the opposition's proposal.

Evaluation of the case involves a thorough look at all the elements that make up a case, such as liability, damages, ability to pay, and others. Presentation of the settlement involves organizing information in an economical, informative, and persuasive format to convince the opponent that the claim is a good one and worth settling.

Early Investigation and Collection of Information

A thorough early investigation is important because settlement can come early in the litigation process. To assist in the attorney's preparation, you need to collect and summarize the following information from the beginning of the action:

PARTY'S SOCIAL OR BUSINESS BACKGROUND. Note age, race, sex, personality, family, education, character, occupation, income, benefits, advancement potential, lifestyle, activities, and interests both before and after the accident or claim. Determine whether your plaintiff is receiving or about to receive Medicaid or Medicare assistance.

If so, the federal and state governments may have claims against any monetary settlement or judgment received by your client. The courtroom effectiveness of witnesses should also be evaluated. For a commercial plaintiff, note reputation, age, income, and status before and after the alleged injury. Comparative wealth of parties in both commercial and personal injury cases is also important.

PARTY'S MEDICAL CONDITION. Note prior injuries and their possible implications for injuries caused by the accident (may reduce or, in rare cases, increase the amount of damages); details of injuries from accident; diagnosis; post-accident impediments such as shock, unconsciousness, embarrassment (these often explain statements or actions inconsistent with allegations of injuries); unwillingness to admit disability; causal relationship between alleged wrong and injury; treatment required (emergency, surgery, tests, hospital care, home care, checkups, other medical consultations); progressive stages of healing; hideous nature of injury or effects; temporary injuries and disability; permanent injuries and disability; disfigurement; psychological and emotional injury; effect on personality and happiness; prognosis; need for future medical care (nursing care, prosthetic devices); pain and suffering (at time of injury, during medical treatment, permanent); change in life expectancy because of injuries; occupational implications of injuries; effect on hobbies, interests, and home life; all out-of-pocket expenses for medical bills, travel for treatment, and prosthetic devices; and projection of future medical care and related out-of-pocket expenses. Collect all the items (bills, medical reports, witness statements, etc.) necessary to prove or disprove these factors. Consider if the injured party has the three strikes: has not seen a doctor, has not lost work, has not used home remedies.

PARTY'S COMMERCIAL CONDITION. Note the value of land and other property involved; replacement value of property; value of property after injury; income before injury and after; loss of markets; loss of customers; loss of opportunity; loss of profits; past, present, and future losses; loss of rents; loss of business reputation; loss of the entire business; cost of any delay caused by injury; cost of finding alternatives for lost services or property; attempts to mitigate damages; and relationship of the alleged wrong to the injuries. Collect all evidence to prove these factors.

SPECIAL AREAS OF INVESTIGATION. You can assist by investigating other items as well. Research can be conducted on the recent verdicts rendered by juries or judges in the jurisdiction where the case will be tried. If this research is done very early in the case, it may help determine the best venue for the client. For example, rural juries are likely to produce lower awards than urban juries. Recent verdict information can be obtained from the clerk of court or from other attorneys in the vicinity. Some good sources on jury awards and amounts of damages include: the American Trial Lawyers Association's *ATLA Law Reporter,* the damages section of *West's Digests,* and sections on jury verdicts, damages, and settlements in *American Law Reports.* Such information is also available through Westlaw, Lexis, and other electronic services. This information will help the attorney determine a fair settlement range in a particular jurisdiction.

Expert witnesses (including doctors) to be relied on should be researched on their reputation, background, intelligence, and courtroom abilities. Their friends, colleagues, and attorneys who have dealt with them can be helpful here.

The trial judge's attitude and previous decisions in similar cases should be researched. Other attorneys and paralegals can provide insights.

The opponent's lawyer needs to be assessed as well. If the adverse attorney is a good trial lawyer, tough minded on negotiations, and takes lowest offer to mean lowest offer, then settlement requests may differ from those of an experienced lawyer who starts high but caves in fast, and never goes to trial. Attorneys, clerks of court and assistants, and, in some cases, paralegals may be helpful in giving such information.

The track record of the insurance company in settling cases for the defendant and for how much may also be valuable.

Life expectancy statistics, vocational opportunities for the client, estimated inflation trends that may affect the cost of a child's college education, future medical care, estimated lost income and benefits, and basic cost of living (vocation experts and economists may need to be consulted) are areas that may need to be researched. Most of this kind of information can be obtained through the help of a reference librarian in most libraries or through pertinent online services.

Costs of litigation, trial, and attorney's fees should also be researched and collected if the attorney does not have a basis for this.

Communicating with Client and Insurance Adjuster

Continue to send to the client copies of letters and documents that will keep the client informed of the status of the case as well as items needing attention. In personal injury cases, track the client's medical treatment schedule so you can request resulting records and follow up with the client if medical appointments are missed. Gaps in treatment can appear to show an improvement in the client's condition and, therefore, can affect the level of damages.

Especially if settlement is being negotiated before a complaint is filed, initiate a positive and professional relationship with the defendant's insurance adjuster. Provide the plaintiff's identification information and regular updates on your client's condition, treatment, and current subtotal of medical bills, enclosing authenticated copies of the bills and medical progress reports. Respond promptly to the adjuster's requests for other information or documentation. If the insurer's investigators have taken written or recorded witness statements, request copies from the adjuster.

If the statute of limitations deadline is near and a complaint must be filed, the insurance adjuster may turn the case over to an attorney for litigation, possibly narrowing the chances for settlement, so time is important in completing settlement tasks.

Calculating Damages

The most important settlement objective in most cases is a dollar amount the plaintiff claims to deserve from the defendant. You can be of considerable assistance by recording and calculating the dollar amount of the damages. For a review of the types of damages (general, special, and exemplary), see the remedies section of Chapter 4. All bills, expenses, receipts, and so on should be collected and categorized. Damages should be itemized to ensure they are clear, accurate, reviewable, and believable. Exhibit 10.1 is an example of a form that can be used to list and calculate damages in personal injury and other cases. Read the form carefully and note each category of damages so you will know what to look for in this and future cases.

It may be useful to note that in some state courts and in some federal actions for personal injury, survival, and wrongful death, the "loss of enjoyment of life" (LOELs, hedonic damages) is separated from "pain and suffering," and in other jurisdictions

EXHIBIT 10.1 Damage Summary and Worksheet

Plaintiff _____ Date of Accident _____

Case _____ v. _____ Case No. _____

Attorney _____ Prepared by _____

Date _____

I. Damage Totals

Special Damages _____

General Damages _____

Other Special and Exemplary Damages _____

_____

Total Damages _____

ITEMIZATION

II. Special Damages

  A. Special Damages (Medical)

1. Ambulance Service: Name _____ Date _____

                                       Amount _____

2. Hospital: Name _____ Address _____

                Date _____ Service, Test, or Treatment _____

                                    Amount _____

                Name _____ Address _____

                Date _____ Service, Test, or Treatment _____

                                    Amount _____

  (add as needed)

3. Doctor: Name _____ Address _____ Date _____

           Purpose or Treatment _____ Tests _____

                              Amount _____

  (add as needed)

4. Pharmaceutical:

           Pharmacy _____ Address _____ Date _____

           Medication or Prosthetic Device _____ Purpose _____

                              Amount _____

           Pharmacy _____ Address _____ Date _____

(continued)

EXHIBIT 10.1 Damage Summary and Worksheet (*continued*)

Medication or Prosthetic Device _____ Purpose _____

Amount _____

(add as needed)

5. Travel for Medical Purposes:

Purpose _____ Date _____

Mileage _____ × _____ ¢/mile = $ _____ Lodging $ _____

Meals $ _____ Airfare, cabs, etc. $ _____

Amount _____

(repeat as needed)

6. Home Care (Nurse or Attendant):

Purpose _____ Date(s) _____

Amount per day _____ × no. of days _____

Amount _____

(add as needed)

7. Psychologists and Physical Therapists:

Name _____ Address _____

Purpose _____ Date _____

Amount _____

(add as needed)

TOTALS $ _____

TOTAL PAST MEDICAL COSTS $ _____

8. Future Medical Expenses:

a. Special

☐ Hospitalization: no. of days _____ × cost _____ Amount _____

☐ Doctor: Purpose _____ $ _____

☐ Surgery: Type _____ $ _____

☐ Therapy: Type _____ $ _____

☐ Travel: Purpose _____ miles _____ × _____ ¢/mi. $ _____

Airfare, etc. _____ $ _____

☐ Pharmacology: Nature _____ $ _____

☐ Nurse: Cost/wk. _____ × no. of wks. _____ $ _____

☐ Other: _____ $ _____

b. Daily: Itemize current daily needs: nurse, equipment, medications, etc.

Item: _____ Purpose: _____ Daily Cost $ _____

Item: _____ Purpose: _____ Daily Cost $ _____

Total _____

EXHIBIT 10.1 Damage Summary and Worksheet (*continued*)

(add as needed)

Total daily cost _____ × _____ days/yr. × _____ years + special costs + that figure × _____ % for growth in medical costs = gross expenses × _____ % for present cash value* = $ _____

TOTAL FUTURE MEDICAL EXPENSES $_____

*Present cash value (present value discount) reduces the future gross expense to a current lump sum, which if invested will provide for the total gross expenses when needed. The percentage of reduction is usually based on projected annuity tables or average yields for savings accounts or U.S. bonds over a reasonable historical period.

B. Special Damages (Economic Loss)

1. Current wage _____ Date returned to work _____

2. Units (hours, days, months, etc.) or percentage of annual income lost _____

Total wages lost to date _____

3. Lost fringe benefits, bonuses, perquisites _____

_____

(list if needed)   Total benefits lost to date _____

Total lost wages and benefits to date _____

4. Lost household services to date:

(Market value of household chores: bookkeeper, parent [care giver, tutor, chauffeur], maid, cook, decorator, gardener, etc.) $ _____/wk. × no. of wks. _____ = $ _____

5. Lost other considerations: _____

_____ $ _____

Total lost wages, benefits, household services to date _____

6. If the person's income is reduced by any disability, for example a need to change to a job with less pay, then that loss should also be added. $ _____

7. Future economic loss

a. Future wages (if complete disability or death):

Most recent normal year's wages $ _____ × years of work expectancy** _____ (including any remaining portion of current year) + that figure × compounded annual growth rate*** of _____% = gross wage loss $ _____

Gross wage loss $ _____ less _____% reduction to present cash value = $ _____

☐ If the person has partial disability, gross wage loss can be computed by applying the same formula to the percentage of current yearly wage lost because of disability. If death, reduce gross wage loss by the percentage of annual wage actually consumed by that person. See family expenses over a period of several years.

**Years to age of retirement or Department of Labor Statistics for work life in specific occupations or may be set by state law.

***Based on average % raise over same number of past years as work expectancy years for that person or industry standard. Consult Department of Labor statistics but usually between 4–8%. Adjust figure upward if raises show marked increase in recent years. Note: Provide alternative set of figures if promotion, career change, or other variable is likely.

(continued)

EXHIBIT 10.1 Damage Summary and Worksheet (*continued*)

b. Future fringe benefits:

Annual fringe benefit $_____ $\times$ ____ years of work expectancy + that figure $\times$ compounded annual growth rate for benefits of _____% = gross benefits loss

$ _____

Gross benefits loss $ _____ less _____% reduction to present cash value =

$ _____

☐ Annual growth rate for benefits is usually higher than wages. See Department of Labor statistics for occupation. Adjust if recent rise in %.

c. Future investments (if applicable)

Amount of annual income placed in savings or other investments $_____ $\times$ compounded annual growth rate _____% (based on average return over past years)

Total lost future investment income $ _____

(reduced to present cash value if necessary)

d. Future household services

Annual lost market value for each service (bookkeeper, cook, maid, painter, gardener, child-care giver, etc.) _____ Annual cost $\times$ ____ yrs. life expectancy = $_____ + that figure $\times$ _____% annual growth rate in cost of household services‡ =

Total future household services $ _____

Life expectancy: based on readily accessible projections (consult reference librarian or insurance sources).

‡Annual growth rate for household services is often tied to projections based on history of consumer price index adjusted for any recent increases. The percentage usually ranges from 3–5%.

e. Adjustments for income taxes: consult with attorney

f. Adjustments for inflation:

(Being allowed more frequently. See published reports from trustees of Federal Old Age and Survivors Insurance and Disability Insurance Trust Funds for inflation projections and what that means in real wage increases.)

Total future income loss $ _____

C. Special Damages (Property)

1. Personal property:

Item _____

Destroyed: Market value $_____ less salvage $_____ = $ _____

Damaged: Cost of restoration $_____ or if cannot be restored, value before damage $_____ less value after damage $_____ plus costs to attempt to preserve or restore $_____ = $_____

Other Property:

List: Portraits, heirlooms, pets, etc., with appraiser's valuation or some other reasonable standard

$_____

Appliances, furniture, clothing, worth at time of loss $_____

EXHIBIT 10.1 Damage Summary and Worksheet (*continued*)

2. Real Property (land, buildings):

Item _____

If permanent: value before damage $_____ less value after $ _____ plus interest to date =

$ _____

If temporary: reduction to rental or other profit value $ _____ plus injury to crops, buildings, improvements $ _____ plus restoration costs $ _____ plus any applicable interest =

$ _____

(consult local law)

Total Property Damages $ _____

Total Special Damages $ _____

III. General Damages

Pain and Suffering: fear, humiliation, inconvenience, anxiety, horror of injury, pain, discomfort; loss of companionship, status stimulation of job, enjoyment of life's experiences; and other subjective factors caused by injury. Briefly summarize: _____

_____

_____

_____

Standard: as estimated by party or reasonable person as fair.

Value per day $_____ × no. of days/yr. _____ × yrs. of life expectancy _____ × _____% inflation factor if allowed = $_____

Consortium: value per day $_____ × no. of days/yr. _____ × yrs. of life expectancy × _____% inflation factor if allowed = $_____

Note: Review current jury verdicts for reasonable estimates. Check local statutes for any limits on awards. Most states do not require a reduction to present cash value for pain and suffering.

Total pain and suffering and general damages $ _____

IV. Other Special and Exemplary Damages

1. Funeral expenses $ _____

2. Exemplary:

   Punitive $ _____

   Attorney's fees $ _____

3. Miscellaneous damages $ _____

Total of other special and exemplary damages $ _____

TOTAL DAMAGES $ _____

APPLY YOUR KNOWLEDGE

Determine whether your state permits hedonic damages either by statute or case law. Identify the case or statute which provides support for your state's position.

it is still an element of pain and suffering. The decision in *Kansas City Southern Railway Co. v. Adams*, 2001WL107864 (Miss. 2001, *unpublished opinion*) drew a clear line between LOEL, limitations on "ability to enjoy the pleasures and amenities of life," and pain and suffering, the "physical and mental discomfort caused by injury, such as anguish, distress, fear, humiliation, grief, shame, and worry." It also affirmed that expert testimony on LOEL meets evidentiary standards; some other jurisdictions reject such testimony. Most states bar hedonic damages in wrongful death suits and when the injured person is comatose on the theory that the person cannot feel anything, so enjoyment of life is irrelevant. Loss of companionship is recoverable for the family, however. Some states and federal civil rights suits under 42 U.S.C. 1983 allow hedonic damages in wrongful death suits. Plaintiffs try to separate the LOELs; defendants fight that separation.

A damages summary and worksheet similar to Exhibit 10.1 can be devised for a commercial case stressing actual and anticipated damages. Pulling a file from a previous case where such damages applied can help in devising the worksheet.

Spreadsheet programs or damage calculation software can be used to enter and calculate damages and update them regularly. They also can be used to explore variables and make the calculation of annuities, interest, and other settlement figures much easier. A damage calculation Internet search will give you names of consulting and accounting services offering damage calculations in several fields.

When asked to review the damage claims of the other side, employ a similar process to test the thoroughness and accuracy of the opponent's proposal. In either case, all arithmetic should be double checked, and all the supporting documents should be reviewed for accuracy and applicability. Forward the damage sheet to the attorney for review and amendment.

Verify that the following items also are gathered and readied to support or contradict a settlement claim: all doctors' summaries, discovery summaries, photographs, videos, charts, diagrams, legal memoranda, witness statements, accident reports, and any other material needed to help convince the other party.

PRESENTING THE SETTLEMENT REQUEST

Introduction

The gathered and summarized information can now be evaluated by the attorney to determine the strength of the case and a fair settlement. The settlement request usually comes from the plaintiff and is presented to convince the defense that this settlement is fair and reasonable and in their client's best interests. The actual form in which the case is presented depends to a large degree on the amount of damages. It makes little sense to prepare a settlement brochure costing $500 in a $1,200 lawsuit. There would be nothing left for the client after attorney fees and other expenses. In this kind of case, a small narrative summary sheet or letter outlining the key information may suffice. A large case may justify a more detailed version of the summary, called a **settlement précis**. In the big cases involving many thousands of dollars, a thorough settlement brochure may be prepared.

A settlement letter, précis, or brochure needs to be as convincing as possible. In marshaling the facts of the case, it must stress the obviousness of the opponent's liability; the serious and sympathetic nature of the injuries; the amount of damages

settlement précis
A brief presentation of the client's case designed to persuade the opposing party to settle the case on terms satisfactory to the client.

that have been and will be incurred; but most of all, the presentation must stress how the accident has torn up the life of the injured person as a productive or potentially productive individual. If liability is likely to be proven, it is the human factor that will impress the jury and affect the amount of their award. A settlement presentation, therefore, can use the leverage of a potentially sympathetic jury to move the defendant to settle.

Settlement Précis or Letter

The précis or demand letter must be brief and should cover the following: the identification of the plaintiff; the facts of the case that reflect the liability of the defendant; the theory of liability; the injury and past, current, and future medical consequences; all expenses; a summary of the evaluation; and a proposed figure for settlement. Exhibit 10.2 is an example of a settlement précis.

The précis can be reduced to an even more concise statement, if appropriate.

EXHIBIT 10.2 Settlement Précis—Illustration

Social history—Sharon Williams was born July 10, 2004, the fourth of four children born to John and Virginia Williams. The family lives at 2305 Grand Vista, Columbus, Missouri. Mr. Williams is employed as a machinist at Eagle Air Craft Co. A position he has held for six years.

Sharon is a student in the second grade of Middleton Grade School. She is a member of Girl Scout Troop 378 and is a member of the YMCA girls' swimming team.

Medical History—Sharon had a normal prenatal history and a normal birth. She has been attended by Dr. Grant Fry, a pediatrician, from birth. She has suffered from the childhood diseases of chicken pox and measles. She has never suffered any disability to her lower limbs and has never sustained any injuries to her legs, back, or spine. Dr. Fry's medical report is attached.

Facts of Accident—On April 5, 2012, Sharon was en route from her home to school. The attached police report confirms that the day was clear and warm and the streets were dry. Sharon was by herself and crossing Grand Avenue at its intersection with Washington Street moving westwardly from the southeast to the southwest corner, approximately six feet south of the south curb line and within the designated crosswalk. Grand Avenue is forty feet wide with two lanes of traffic moving in each direction. It is straight and level and surfaced with asphalt. There were no cars parked within sixty feet of the intersection. A sign located one hundred feet south of the intersection on Grand has the legend "Caution Children." Police report confirming the description of the scene of the accident is attached.

Sharon was struck by the northbound automobile of defendant at a point five feet from the center line. The attached photographs show the following:

Photo 1: skid marks ten feet long, blood on street
Photo 2: damage to left head light

Sharon states that when she left the southeast corner of the intersection the light was in her favor. She never looked at the light again. She walked at a normal pace until she was hit. She was looking forward and never saw or heard the defendant's automobile. The accident occurred at 8:35 A.M. The school is two blocks away and convenes at 8:45 A.M.

A statement taken from the defendant, a copy of which is attached, acknowledges that he didn't see the plaintiff until she was fifteen feet from him and that his automobile came to a stop twenty feet after impact.

(continued)

EXHIBIT 10.2 Settlement Précis—Illustration (*continued*)

Theories of Recovery

The plaintiff has three theories of recovery:

1. That defendant violated a red light.

2. That defendant failed to keep a lookout.

3. That defendant failed to exercise the highest degree of care to bring his automobile to a stop or slacken after plaintiff came into a position of immediate danger.

The proof of the first theory is supported by plaintiff's testimony that when she left the curb the light was green for westbound traffic. By reason of the plaintiff's age the court may not permit her to testify. In that event, the defendant's failure to keep a lookout could be submitted as an alternate theory of recovery. Defendant has acknowledged that he didn't see plaintiff until he was fifteen feet away from her and she was already in his path. This would place Sharon at least twelve feet from the curb. The court will judicially notice that the pace of walk is approximately two or three miles an hour or 2.9 to 4.4 feet per second. *Wofford v. St. Louis Public Service Co.*, Mo., 252 S.W.2d 529. Sharon was in the street and visible to defendant for almost three seconds before the accident. At defendant's acknowledged speed of twenty-five miles per hour he was traveling at approximately thirty-six feet per second or was approximately one hundred feet away when he should have seen Sharon. He was further alerted by the warning sign as he approached the intersection.

By reason of her age, it is questionable whether Sharon would be held responsible for her own actions. *Malott v. Harvey*, 199 Mo. App. 615, 204 S.W. 940; *Quirk v. Metropolitan St. Ry. Co.*, 200 Mo. App. 585, 210 S.W. 103.

In the event Sharon could be held accountable for not maintaining a proper lookout, a third theory of recovery is available: defendant's failure to stop or slacken after plaintiff came into a position of immediate danger. By defendant's admission he came to a stop twenty feet after the impact and he did not attempt evasive action until he was fifteen feet from Sharon, therefore his overall stopping distance was thirty-five feet. A jury could find that by reason of Sharon's obliviousness that she was in immediate danger as she approached the path of the vehicle and when defendant's automobile was more than the thirty-five feet that was available to bring his vehicle to a stop.

The skid marks indicate that no slackening took place until the defendant's vehicle was within ten feet of the impact. The damage to the automobile indicates it was the left front headlight which struck Sharon. Sharon was within two feet of safety beyond the path of the car when she was struck. Moving at 4.4 feet per second, in one-half second she would have escaped injury. From this the jury could assume that a failure to slacken at an earlier time was the proximate cause of the injury.

Medical

The police report states that Sharon was "bleeding about the face and mouth" and complaining of "pain in the left hip." She was taken by police cruiser to Welfare Hospital where it was discovered that she had suffered the loss of a front upper left tooth which was permanent, a laceration of the lip necessitating six stitches, and a bruise of the right hip. Portions of the hospital record are attached. She was examined by her pediatrician Dr. Fry who referred her to Dr. William Jones, a dentist, for examination. He confirms the loss of the permanent tooth and outlines the dental prostheses which will be needed throughout her growth stage and into adulthood. His report is attached. The stitches were removed after six days by Dr. Fry leaving a hair line scar one-fourth inch long near the upper lip.

Expenses

Emergency room Welfare Hospital	$550
Dr. Grant Fry	$150
Dr. William Jones	
Examination	$175
Anticipated Treatment	$4,000

EXHIBIT 10.2 Settlement Précis—Illustration (*continued*)

Analysis of Evaluation

Actual out-of-pocket expenses total $875 with anticipated costs for dental prosthetic devices throughout Sharon's growth period adding $4,000 for a total of $4,875. The loss of the tooth is permanent and will necessitate special prophylactic care to maintain the prosthetic devices which must be employed. The scar above the lip is discernible and will be permanent.

It is anticipated that a jury verdict could fall within the $60,000 to $70,000 range. If the case could be settled without further legal procedure I would recommend a settlement of $45,000.

Adapted from Jeans, Trial Advocacy 398-403, 1975, with permission of West Group.

Settlement Brochure (Demand Package)

The settlement brochure is the product of a serious commitment of time and money. Brochures are unlikely to be used unless injuries are serious and the liability of the defendant is sufficiently clear. It does little good to "sell" the pain and suffering of a client if the opponent has a good shot at disproving liability at trial. Many firms cut costs by using their own computer desktop publishing to print brochures or produce them on DVD. The decision to commit resources to a brochure rests with the attorney, but you should be prepared to give impressions and evaluations of the case if asked.

The brochure is an orderly, dramatic, and persuasive presentation of the facts, statements, reports, and exhibits in the case. When done well and prepared early in the case, it tells the other side that this is a case to be taken seriously, that the plaintiff is thorough, organized, and likely to win. In addition, the preparation of the brochure forces the attorney to evaluate the case early in the process, identify its strengths and weaknesses, and see where more investigation or evidence is needed. It also facilitates the preparation of the trial brief (see next chapter) for the pretrial conference or trial. The fact that the plaintiff has set everything out in the case can be used as evidence of the plaintiff's desire to deal openly and in good faith from the start. A juror may decide to vote for higher damages if it appears that the defendant could have avoided the time-consuming trial by settling weeks or months before.

Paralegals with good communication skills can increase their value to the law firm by being able to organize and draft an effective settlement brochure. It not only can be of tremendous assistance to the attorney, but also may be the tool that wraps up the case.

The brochure should be organized to include the following areas:

(a) The facts of the case as supported by the evidence
This section includes summaries of the cause of action; details of the accident, witnesses, and reports; photos of the accident scene, vehicle, and injured party; dramatic newspaper clippings; and other evidence to support the claim.

(b) The personal history of the plaintiff
This section introduces the client and makes a statement as to who this person is, what kind of life he or she has had, what the person has enjoyed, what joy the

client has brought to others, what services he or she has provided others, employment, earnings, service and professional organizations, stature in the community, religious affiliation, education, awards, recognition, services to family, letters of citation, evidence of advancement, future prior to accident, and other "get-to-know-this-person" facts and evidence. One or several carefully selected before-the-accident photos can be effective here.

(c) The prior medical history of the plaintiff

This section is a concise summary of the plaintiff's medical history prior to the accident. Any previous injuries or medical conditions, even if they tend to reduce the damages, should be candidly presented. This promotes credibility and makes the brochure more effective. Previous medical reports should be included if relevant and if they clearly define the extent and limits of previous problems.

(d) Injury and its present and long-term effects

This section should graphically depict the fear, pain, and anguish of experiencing the accident. The injuries should be described in detail and be supported by physicians' reports, hospital summary sheets, records of surgery, tests, treatment, therapy, photos, and reference to videos of healing progress.

The current and future status of the client should also be described, supported by physician reports on the prognosis of the injured party. This section should evoke sympathy and meaningfully portray the pathetic physical and social existence faced by the plaintiff. One or two letters written by a friend, family member, or co-worker in their own words can provide an effective personal account of the impact of the injury on the life of the plaintiff.

(e) The economic and related psychological impact of the injury

The brochure describes how the injury affects future employment and that impact on the plaintiff and the plaintiff's family. The economics of disability, reduced status, lowered self-esteem, continual problems, and the like should be thoroughly covered.

(f) Damages

The special, general, and exemplary damages are summarized and explained where necessary. Copies of all bills, checks, receipts, and so on are included to substantiate the claims.

(g) Evaluation of claim

The brochure ends with a summary reiterating the most significant aspects of the claim and statement of a proposed settlement figure.

Some attorneys believe that any pertinent legal memoranda and such questions as the legal issues in the case, evidentiary matters, and itemized damages should be included. Others believe the brochure is not the place for such arguments. Some attorneys also like to include copies of the pleadings, enclosing at least the complaint, summons, and answer, or go so far as to include the pertinent jury instructions. It can be effective to show that pertinent law clearly and persuasively supports your position, but be sure to discuss these items with the attorney before you draft a brochure.

The brochure should be honest and professional. It should not be overblown, simplistic, or unduly sentimental. How much it should reveal is sometimes a difficult question. A brochure should be forthright, but it can be a disadvantage if it only succeeds in better preparing the opposition to rebut creative and imaginative arguments. Supporting medical reports and witness statements should at least appear to be objective. If they show a strong bias for the plaintiff, they may simply alert the opponent to the fact that the attending physician has lost objectivity and is vulnerable to attack. These questions are addressed by the supervising attorney, but, again, an alert paralegal can point out areas that may have been overlooked and can contribute to an improved brochure.

Exhibit 10.3 is an example of a settlement brochure. Although it does not strictly follow the category arrangement previously proposed, most of these elements are contained in this sample.

It is a common practice to include a cover letter that sets a date after which the offer will be withdrawn and a date for return of the brochure. A statement is included that the brochure is the property of plaintiff's counsel and that there are restrictions on its use. A request for the acknowledgment of receipt of the brochure and an agreement to abide by the restrictions is accompanied by a proposal to meet and reach a mutually agreed-upon settlement.

Video: "Day in the Life"

An increasingly persuasive settlement and trial aid is a digital video of the injured party that tastefully and graphically demonstrates the injuries, treatment, progress, and likely future of the victim. These videos have been named "Day in the Life" videos because they focus primarily on one day in the life of the injured party. Recently, for example, a law office assigned a paralegal to videotape the progressive stages in the medical treatment of an accident victim. This videotaped record provided credible, otherwise unobtainable documentation of the pain and suffering of the client and strikingly illustrated that the healing process was going to take a long time with recovery clearly doubtful. The recordings were edited into a concise and powerful presentation by the paralegal. The cost was minimal. The "Day in the Life" video or DVD can include much of the settlement brochure including photographs, television commentary, and newspaper clippings.

Some firms video family and friends as well. Their out-of-court comments on what impact the serious injuries have had on the plaintiff's life and on their own can be moving.

Calendaring

It is important to calendar dates the attorney has designated to initiate settlement or follow up on a demand letter or a brochure. Continue to inform the client of the progress in settlement negotiations.

ROLE OF THE DEFENDANT'S OR INSURANCE COMPANY'S PARALEGAL

The process of preparing for settlement on behalf of the defendant or an insurance company is, in many respects, the same as preparing for settlement for the plaintiff. Although the defense rarely, if ever, prepares a settlement précis or brochure, you may be asked to draft a letter proposing settlement and summarizing significant elements of the case from the defendant's perspective. Further, you will often be responsible for organizing and summarizing the information that arrives for the case. If the plaintiff submits summarized medical reports and witness statements rather than copies of

EXHIBIT 10.3 Settlement Brochure

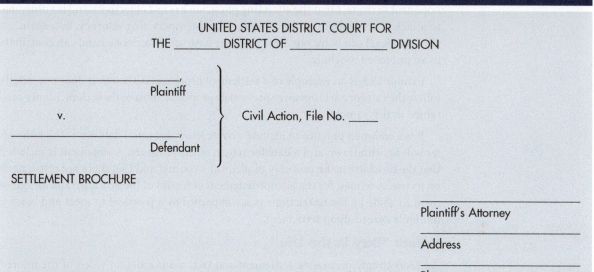

UNITED STATES DISTRICT COURT FOR

THE _____ DISTRICT OF _____ _____ DIVISION

_____,
                    Plaintiff

        v.   Civil Action, File No. _____

_____,
                    Defendant

SETTLEMENT BROCHURE

                                                            _____
                                                            Plaintiff's Attorney

                                                            _____
                                                            Address

                                                            _____
                                                            Phone

Note: (Optional)

The exhibit, statements, and reports incorporated in this brochure are submitted for settlement purposes only. They are not to be copied or reproduced in any fashion. In the event this case is tried, none of the contents of this report, neither facts, representations, nor opinions are to be used without plaintiff's permission. (Some offices place a legend on each page of the brochure so it cannot be used by the other party.)

Index (or Table of Contents)

I. Description of Accident
   Photos of Accident
   Newspaper Reports
   Police Reports
   Witness Statements (or Summary)
   Photos: Injuries, Plaintiff Today, Others

II. Memorandum on Admissibility of Photos (Optional)

III. Personal History of Plaintiff
   Photos of Catherine Brown: Family, Teaching, Recreation

IV. Medical History of Plaintiff—Summary

V. Medical History and Physical Report by Initial Attending Physician

VI. Operative Record of Initial Attending Physician

VII. Consultation Report by Doctor Johnson, Orthopedic Surgeon

VIII. Operative Record of Doctor Smith, Oral Surgeon

IX. X-Ray Interpretation

X. Discharge Summary

XI. Medical Report of Doctor Anderson, Orthopedic Surgeon

XII. Medical Report of Doctor Holt, Plastic Surgeon

XIII. Medical Expenses

XIV. Effects of Injuries

XV. Evaluation of Claims

EXHIBIT 10.3 Settlement Brochure (*continued*)

Settlement Brochure

page 1

I. Description of Accident

Photo of Accident

News Clipping

News Clipping

News Clipping

(continued)

EXHIBIT 10.3 Settlement Brochure (*continued*)

Settlement Brochure

   Police Report   page 2

                                    (Own summary could be substituted)

Settlement Brochure

   Witness Statements or Summary   page 3

Settlement Brochure

   Photo of Injuries   page 4

Settlement Brochure

   Photos of Plaintiff Today   page 5

                            (Showing scars, limitations, wheelchair, etc.)

Settlement Brochure

                                                                                        page 6

   II. Memorandum on Admissibility of Photographic Evidence

EXHIBIT 10.3 Settlement Brochure (*continued*)

III. Personal History of Plaintiff

Catherine Brown was born June 8, 1984, and at the time of the accident was twenty-six years of age. She was reared in Texas where she completed four years of high school at Lockhart, Texas, and four years of college at Southwest Texas State College. On March 13, 2006, she was married to Fred Brown and his change of employment necessitated a move before her last semester of college could be completed.

On January 29, 2007, Catherine gave birth to her only child, Carl Robert.

Upon arrival in the Kansas City area Catherine enrolled in the Music Conservatory of the University of Missouri—Kansas City and graduated with a B.M.E. in music in 2008. She served as a substitute music teacher in the public schools of Kansas City in the Spring of 2009 and in the fall of that year was hired as Music Director of the R-7 School District in Center City, Missouri, at a salary of $24,800 for the school year.

Catherine's responsibility included the directorship of three bands and two choirs. In addition she served as a sponsor for the Pep Club and Cheerleaders. Her outside activities included membership in the Mu Phi Epsilon Music Sorority and the Center City Music Club.

IV. Medical History of Plaintiff—Summary

Prior to the date of the accident, June 16, 2010, Catherine Brown was in excellent health. She had never suffered any physical disability and her only hospitalization was for the birth of her son.

The accident was unusually violent. The loaded gravel truck struck the vehicle in which plaintiff was a passenger with such force that the automobile was carried seventy-six feet and seven inches beyond the point of impact. The side on which plaintiff was sitting was literally "run over." (See attached photo from police report.)

The injuries, detailed in the hospital record and medical reports which follow, consisted primarily of the following:

disfiguring lacerations of face;

multiple fractures of the jaws;

fracture of clavicle with loss of bone;

multiple fractures of the pelvis;

fracture of radius and ulna right arm;

fracture of left forearm;

severe cerebral contusion.

V. Medical History and Physical Report by Initial Attending Physician

[*Date*]

BROWN, Catherine.

CHIEF COMPLAINT: Auto accident.

PRESENT ILLNESS: The patient is a 26-year-old Gravida I, Para I, Aborta O, white female who was involved in an auto-truck accident. The patient was brought immediately to the Emergency Room of General Hospital at which time the patient was admitted through the Emergency Room by Dr. Smith. The patient was then seen by this doctor in the Intensive Care Unit at which time the patient presented with a blood pressure systolic between 80 and 90. The patient had a very rapid pulse of 120. The patient was cool and appeared to be in shock.

PHYSICAL EXAMINATION:

NEUROLOGICAL: The patient was confused as to time and place with episodes of incoherence. The pupils were dilated and extremely sluggish but were reactive. Fundoscopic examination revealed the discs to be sharp. There was no evidence of papilledema. Cranial nerves appeared to be intact. There was no evidence of motor or sensory loss of the extremities. The patient had obvious multiple fractures.

(*continued*)

EXHIBIT 10.3 Settlement Brochure (*continued*)

HEENT: Tympanic membranes were intact. There was no evidence of fluid or blood in the auditory canals. Posterior pharynx was clear. Oral cavity: The patient had palpable fractures of the mandible bilaterally.

NECK: Supple with no palpable masses or tenderness. No bruits. Thyroid was not palpable.

CHEST: Lungs were clear on auscultation and percussion. The patient had palpable fractures over the right chest.

ABDOMEN: No palpable masses or tenderness. Bowel sounds hypoactive. No CVA tenderness. Patient had a mild suprapubic tenderness.

EXTREMITIES: Symmetrical. The patient had marked deformity of the right forearm and wrist area with marked swelling. The patient also had deformity of the left forearm with some swelling. Pressure applied to the pelvic cage caused excruciating pain. Peripheral pulses in all extremities were grade III and equal bilaterally.

SKIN: The patient had multiple large facial lacerations that covered the entire right face, forehead and parietal area. The patient also had a laceration of the right submandibular area, and left face at the outer canthus of the mouth. The patient had multiple abrasions over the upper extremities and a large laceration over the dorsum of the left hand with no evidence of tendon involvement.

IMPRESSION: Shock syndrome secondary to blood loss and multiple fractures; fracture of the right radius and ulna; right thoracic fractures; pelvic fractures; severe cerebral contusion; multiple lacerations.

DISPOSITION: Patient will be treated for shock syndrome with intravenous fluids, plasma expanders, antibiotics, and patient will then have splinting of the extremities and lacerations closed.

DIAGNOSIS: Compound fracture right and left body of the mandible. The patient sustained the injuries in an auto accident.

RECOMMENDATIONS: Closed reduction by the application of maxillary and mandibular arch bars.

Thank you for this consultation.

[*Signed*]

_____

C. A. Jones, M.D.

VI. Operative Record of Initial Attending Physician

_____

[*Date*]

BROWN, Catherine.

PRE-OP DIAGNOSIS: Auto accident with shock syndrome, multiple facial lacerations, laceration of the left lower lip, laceration of left hand, open fracture of the clavicle, fracture of radius and pelvic fractures, cerebral concussion, moderate, severe.

SURGEON: C. A. Jones

OPERATIVE PROCEDURE: The patient was placed in the supine position. Utilizing 1% Xylocaine diluted to 1/2% the patient had local infiltration and field blocks for closure of lacerations. The patient had multiple lacerations around the right eye, eyebrow, and scalp. The patient also had a through and through laceration of the left lower lip and mouth. The patient had multiple small lacerations on the left arm and dorsum of the left hand. All the lacerations were infiltrated and thoroughly scrubbed with Betadine and Betadine solution. The patient then had excision of the margins of the lacerations. The patient had a moderate amount of skin loss on the right temporal area which required undermining of the scalp flap for primary closure. This was repaired with interrupted 4–0 chromic suture and 5–0 nylon suture. Through and through laceration of the left lower lip was repaired with closing the subcutaneous tissue beneath the submucosa of the oral cavity with interrupted 3–0 chromic. The wound was thoroughly irrigated with saline. The subcutaneous tissue and muscle tissue was then approximated with interrupted 4–0 chromic. The skin was closed with interrupted 5–0 nylon. The subcutaneous tissue and muscle tissue was then approximated with interrupted 4–0 chromic. The skin was closed with interrupted 5–0 nylon suture. The lacerations on the hand and arm were handled in a likewise manner. The patient also had an open comminuted fracture of the right clavicle with a portion of the bone sticking up

EXHIBIT 10.3 Settlement Brochure (continued)

through the skin and remaining attached by a piece of periosteum. The bone had apparently been ground into the dirt. It was therefore thought advisable and with consultation by Dr. Peterson that this portion of the clavicle should be excised and removed. The wound was opened and thoroughly irrigated with approximately two liters of saline solution. The wound was then closed with interrupted 3–0 chromic and interrupted 4–0 nylon suture. All the wounds were then bandaged with Garamycin and 4 × 4 dressings. The patient also had an obvious fracture of the forearm. The forearm was thus splinted due to severe edema at that time; it was felt that casting was not indicated. The arm was splinted with a posterior splint and Ace bandage.

The patient was then returned to surgical ICU for further followup. Post-operative condition was guarded.

[Signed]

_____

C. A. Jones, M.D., Surgeon

VII. Consultation Report by Doctor Johnson, Orhopedic Surgeon

[Date]

BROWN, Catherine.

This 26-year-old woman was seen in consultation with Dr. Jones. The initial care had been provided when the patient came into the hospital by Dr. Jones for a compound fracture of the right clavicle and thoracic fractures. The patient also had fractures of the pubis which were also treated by Dr. Jones. I saw the patient at Dr. Jones' request for treatment of a fracture of the right distal radius, and this was treated with a closed reduction 6/18/10, and immobilized in a long arm cast.

Review of x-rays of the right clavicle revealed satisfactory position of the fracture of the clavicle and also fractures of the right pubis were in satisfactory position. The patient was treated with bed rest for the fractures of the pubis. The patient responded quite nicely to this.

Because of persistent pain in the forearm, left, x-rays were taken several weeks following the accident and these revealed a cracked fracture of the distal ulna. Although it was a good position it was felt that immobilization in a short arm cast was indicated and this was applied. At the time of discharge the patient was instructed to return to my office to be followed as an outpatient as treatment for fractures of the right radius and ulna and the left ulna.

[Signed]

_____

A. B. Johnson, M.D.,
Consultant

VIII. Operative Record of Doctor Smith, Oral Surgeon

[Date]

BROWN, Catherine.

OPERATIONS: Closed reduction and application of maxillary and mandibular arch bar with manual reduction.

PRE-OP DIAGNOSIS: Compound fracture of the right and left body of the mandible.

SURGEON: A. B. Smith.

OPERATIVE PROCEDURE: The patient was brought to the operating room in satisfactory physical condition. General anesthesia was induced. The patient was intubated through the right nares and draped in the usual manner for an intra-oral procedure. Mouth and throat were thoroughly cleansed. Deep throat pack was placed. Following this a maxillary arch bar was ligated to the remaining maxillary teeth. After this had been accomplished manual reduction of the fracture sites was accomplished, circumferential wires were placed around the teeth on either side of the fracture site. After this had been accomplished a mandibular arch bar was ligated to the mandibular teeth thus holding the

(continued)

EXHIBIT 10.3 Settlement Brochure (*continued*)

fracture sites in good alignment. Deep throat pack was removed. Elastids will be placed this evening or in the morning. Dr. Johnson then continued with his part of the procedure, reduction of the right arm.

[*Signed*]

_____

A. B. Smith, D.D.S.

IX. X-ray Interpretation

_____

[*Date*]

BROWN, Catherine.

RIGHT FOREARM EXAM including the ELBOW AND WRIST REGION with multiple views with a metal splint in place reveals recent fracture of the distal one-third of the shaft of the radius approximately 2 inches from the wrist joint. There is minimal comminution. The fragments are not widely displaced or separated. There is very slight anterior angulation. There is also a fracture of the ulna slightly more than one cm from the distal end with minimal displacement of these fragments. There is no dislocation.

RIGHT SHOULDER REEXAM WITH AP VIEW shows the lateral fracture fragments of the clavicle to be displaced completely inferiorly in relation to the medial fragment. The major fragments are separated approximately one-half cm. The fracture fragments of the right 2nd rib are separated almost one-half cm. There is little callus formation in the fracture region but the fragments are not stabilized by bony union. There are also fractures of the right 5th and 6th ribs posteriorly in good position.

LEFT FOREARM EXAM reveals a fracture in the ulna about 7 cm above the wrist joint. The fragments are in close opposition with less than 1/2 cm displacement and no significant degree of angulation.

PELVIS EXAM WITH FILMS MADE AT THE BEDSIDE reveals recent fractures of the superior and inferior pelvic rami and the symphysis pubis on the right side. The fragments show only minimal displacement. There is no dislocation. There is also irregularity in the right side of the sacrum due to fracture in this region with minimal impaction of the fragments. The sacroiliac joints are not disrupted.

RIGHT FOREARM AND ELBOW reading including with reading of the films of night before examination of the Rt Arm.

EXAMINATION OF THE SKULL AND MANDIBLE WITH MULTIPLE VIEWS reveals recent fracture of the body of the mandible on the left side. The anterior fragment is displaced medially one cm. No other definite fracture of the mandible is seen at this time. There is no apparent fracture of the skull or depression. The sella turcia is regular.

RIGHT CLAVICLE AND CHEST EXAM reveal the markedly comminuted fracture near the mid portion of the right clavicle. The major fragments are separated almost one-half inch. There is complete inferior displacement of the lateral major fragment. There is no definite rib fracture or lung injury.

RIGHT FOREARM EXAM with AP AND LATERAL VIEWS with films made at the bedside shows fracture of the radius 2 inches from the distal end with minimal comminution, and approximately 10 degrees anterior angulation of the fragments. The fragments are not widely displaced. There is also a fracture of the ulna approximately one cm from the distal end with minimal comminution and slight impaction of these fragments. There is no dislocation.

[*Signed*]

_____

Radiologist

X. Discharge Summary

_____

[*Date*]

BROWN, Catherine.

PRESENT ILLNESS: The patient is a 26-year-old white female who was involved in an auto-truck accident. The patient was apparently struck broadside by the truck and carried out through a field. The patient was brought to the Emergency

EXHIBIT 10.3 Settlement Brochure (*continued*)

Room for treatment. The patient was admitted through the Emergency Room by Dr. Smith, who initiated treatment. The patient was then seen in ICU with a blood pressure of 60 to 90 systolic. The patient was confused as to time and place. Neurological examination revealed both pupils to be extremely dilated and sluggish. Discs were sharp. The patient was able to move all extremities. The patient also had multiple facial lacerations and fractures of the extremities. PERTINENT PHYSICAL FINDINGS: Revealed multiple facial lacerations involving the right face and right temple area. There was no palpable skull fracture. The patient had bilateral fractures of the mandible, fractures of both forearms, and pelvic fracture. The patient was also seen in consultation by Dr. Peterson, Dr. Johnson, and Dr. Smith. Patient initially had closure of the facial lacerations, repair of lacerations of the lower lip and left hand. The patient had an open fracture of the right clavicle which was debrided. A small portion of bone was removed. The wound was thoroughly irrigated and closed. The patient had splinting of both forearms. The patient was treated vigorously for shock with intravenous fluids, vasopressors, and blood. The patient was also started on massive doses of antibiotics. The patient became more responsive 36 hours after admission at which time the patient then had maxillary fractures and fractures of the radius and ulna bilateral corrected. The patient was then treated with bed rest for four weeks due to large pelvic fracture. The patient's hospital course following the first four days of admission was unremarkable except for slow progression of activity. The patient was ambulated on the 3rd week post-admission. At the time of the discharge the patient was ambulatory without assistance, however, the patient had a wide base gait due to instability of the pelvis. The patient's forearms were in plaster splints. The patient's maxillas were still wired. The patient was on a full liquid diet. The facial lacerations had healed well with minimal amount of scar defect. The patient was given a one week return office appointment for followup examination. The patient was discharged from the hospital on Keflex 250 mgms q.i.d.

FINAL DIAGNOSIS:
- (1) Shock syndrome, secondary to multiple fractures and blood loss
- (2) Fracture of right radius and ulna
- (3) Fractures of left ulna
- (4) Fracture of right clavicle and right second rib, anteriorly
- (5) Multiple pelvic fractures
- (6) Severe cerebral contusion
- (7) Multiple facial and extremity lacerations

[*Signed*]

_____

C. A. Jones, M.D.

XI. Medical Report of Doctor Anderson, Orthopedic Surgeon

_____

[*Date*]

Re: Catherine Brown

(including history, previous injuries, physical exam, summary and prognosis)

XII. Medical Report of Doctor Holt, Plastic Surgeon

_____

James P. Holt, M.D.

Plastic and Reconstructive Surgery Maxillo-facial Surgery

[*Date*]

Mr. James W. Jeans, Attorney
U.M.K.C. Law Building
5100 Rockhill Road
Kansas City, Missouri 64110

(continued)

EXHIBIT 10.3 Settlement Brochure (*continued*)

Dear Mr. Jeans:

The following is a medical report on Catherine Brown, a 26-year-old music director, who was seen in my office on December 9, 2010, for evaluation of scars resulting from injuries in an automobile accident on June 16, 2010.

The patient states that she was hospitalized for over a month in Joplin, Missouri, with fractures of the pelvis, jaw, right forearm, left forearm, right clavicle and ribs.

She has multiple atrophic scars running from the eyebrow and temple to above the ear (4–5 inches in total length), a scar at a right angle to the mandible and lower part of the ear (3–4 inches) which is also atrophic, a transverse atrophic scar of the lower lip (2 inches) with a ridge inside the labial mucosa, a scar of the dorsum of the right hand (3 inches), two scars of the radial aspect of the wrist (1 inch) and a scar of the right lower neck (1 1/2 inches).

There is sensitivity around the right temple and clavicle and over the right wrist due to the injuries and scarring. She has some limitation of supination at the wrist and difficulty in abduction of the right fifth finger. These limitations interfere with playing the piano which is her professional activity.

My recommendation in this case would be a revision of the scars mentioned above which would require hospitalization and general anesthesia. The surgical fee for the procedures over the entire areas could be estimated at $5,000–$7,000 not to include the cost of hospitalization, anesthesia, surgical suite, laboratory fees, etc. After the initial revision, it is possible that a dermabrasion procedure might further minimize the scarring after a period of 4–6 months.

In any event, regardless of the improvement that could be obtained from the surgery, the patient would still undoubtedly have permanent, visible scarring and some cosmetic disfigurement in the areas enumerated.

[*Signed*]

_____

James P. Holt, M.D.

XIII. Medical Expenses

The cost of the medical services necessitated by the injuries incurred in the accident are itemized as follows:

General Hospital	$25,846.27
Dr. Smith	2,000.00
Dr. Chess	600.00
Dr. Johnson	1,200.00
Dr. Jones	4,500.00
Misc.	525.00
Dr. Murphy	560.00
Dr. James Holt	150.00
Total	$35,381.27

In addition Dr. Holt, the plastic surgeon, estimates $5,000–$7,500 for surgical fees for remedial surgery plus a like amount for hospitalization, anesthesiologist, etc. It appears fair to state that total medical will approximate fifty thousand dollars.

XIV. Effects of Injuries

The effects of the injuries upon Catherine Brown and her family have been pronounced. She has lost weight, has been moody and depressed and has been unable to resume her activities in music. Although rehired in 2011 at $26,000 (as evidenced by the employment contract) because of her physical and emotional effects of her injury she was unable to satisfactorily perform her duties and was not rehired. In addition her private music lessons (which accounted for approximately $150 per month) had to be discontinued.

EXHIBIT 10.3 Settlement Brochure (*continued*)

Fred Brown, at the time of the accident, was working toward a master's degree in Counselor Education at U.M.K.C. His wife's need for constant attention and encouragement has delayed the completion of his education and has worked a real hardship on the family. Even though Catherine is no longer employed in the Bronaugh area, they continue to live there because they secure their present housing by Fred doing farm chores for the owner. He must commute over 100 miles to Kansas City for his schooling and work forty to sixty hours on the farm for house rent and living money.

XV. Evaluation of Claims

The injuries speak for themselves and anyone so victimized would be entitled to a substantial sum for the resulting pain and disability. For Catherine Brown the effects were particularly disabling. The loss of strength, flexibility, and dexterity of her right hand has seriously impaired her capacity as a musician and thus has affected her earning potential. The effects of the disfiguring facial scars on this 26-year-old woman have been aggravated by the fact that her employment brings her before the public as well as numerous students. Although future plastic surgery may ameliorate some of the disfigurement of the skin, some will remain. The contour of the jaw and teeth have been permanently altered. The loss of bone in the clavicle has resulted in a permanent postural change.

We evaluate the damages for Catherine Brown as follows:

Medical expenses to date	$35,381.27
Medical expenses projected	15,000.00
Loss of earnings school year 2011	26,000.00
Loss of earnings private lessons to date at $150 per month	2,250.00
	$78,631.27

Future loss of wages depends on the hireability of a physically impaired candidate suffering from permanent head injuries manifested by "nervousness, irritability, anger, fatigue, memory changes, forgetfulness, headaches, concentration difficulties." The impairment of Catherine's earning capacity is a fact—only the amount is uncertain. A strong argument could be advanced that a fair estimate could be figured at $5,000 a year or a total of $190,000 until her work expectancy of sixty-five.

If permanent disability and future pain and suffering were to be evaluated on the same basis of $5,000 for each year of expectancy, one could argue an additional $280,000 for the expected life span. A total of these sums is $548,631.27.

This computation is advanced as an example of jury argument that could be legitimately advanced with, in my opinion, a good chance of acceptance. I appreciate that for settlement purposes the sum of $548,631.27 is not a valid figure—but it does represent the degree to which each of the parties is exposed as individual or joint tort-feasor. Add to this the loss of consortium claim of the husband and the injury to the son and that exposure, again in my judgment, exceeds $750,000.

The plaintiff is assured of recovery against someone. The nature of the accident, the extensiveness of the injury, and the "jury appeal" of the plaintiff lead one to conclude that a jury would be generous in evaluating the case. Our settlement demand for all claims is $525,000.

Adapted from Jeans, Trial Advocacy 444-462, 1975, with permission of West Group.

the original, it may mean that there are some weaknesses in those reports. The originals should always be obtained, using discovery if more informal means have not been productive. The same process of researching jury verdicts, assessing pain and suffering, and submitting final summaries for attorney review are employed.

You should inform the attorney if there appears to be a need for an independent medical exam or special surveillance of the adverse party.

Calendar the date indicated by your supervising attorney to respond or initiate the settlement process. Note in your calendar when tasks must be done in preparation for that date.

PREPARING FOR THE PRETRIAL CONFERENCE

Federal Rule of Civil Procedure 16, individual state rules, local practice, and the preference of a particular judge determine what happens at the pretrial conference. In some jurisdictions the conference is mandatory, and the judge is active in trying to settle the case. In other jurisdictions the conference must be requested, and the judge may refrain from any involvement in settlement discussions.

A pretrial conference is normally conducted in the judge's chambers and is attended by the attorneys for the parties and the judge. Clients may be required to attend. Traditionally the conference is a discussion by the attorneys of the facts in the case, the evidence to prove those facts, the issues remaining in the case, when and how long trial will be, and, if possible, whether settlement is in the offing. Federal Rule 16 now requires a more extensive pretrial conference process involving more than one meeting in many cases. In this context the pretrial conference takes on the important role of facilitating the overall planning and management of the progress of the case beginning at a much earlier point in the litigation (within 90 days of the defendant's first appearance or within 120 days of serving the complaint on the defendant, whichever is shorter). Rule 16 describes the pretrial process (Exhibit 10.4).

EXHIBIT 10.4 Rule 16. Pretrial Conferences; Scheduling; Management

(a) Pretrial Conferences; Objectives. In any action, the court may in its discretion direct the attorneys for the parties and any unrepresented parties to appear before it for a conference or conferences before trial for such purposes as

(1) expediting the disposition of the action;

(2) establishing early and continuing control so that the case will not be protracted because of lack of management;

(3) discouraging wasteful pretrial activities;

(4) improving the quality of the trial through more thorough preparation, and;

(5) facilitating the settlement of the case.

(b) Scheduling and Planning. Except in categories of actions exempted by district court rule as inappropriate, the district judge, or a magistrate judge when authorized by district court rule, shall, after receiving the report from the parties under Rule 26(f) or after consulting with the attorneys for the parties and any unrepresented parties by a scheduling conference, telephone, mail, or other suitable means, enter a scheduling order that limits the time

(1) to join other parties and to amend the pleadings;

(2) to file motions; and

(3) to complete discovery.

EXHIBIT 10.4 Rule 16. Pretrial Conferences; Scheduling; Management (*continued*)

The scheduling order may also include

(4) modifications of the times for disclosures under Rules 26(a) and 26(e)(1) and of the extent of discovery to be permitted;

(5) provisions for disclosure or discovery of electronically stored information;

(6) any agreements the parties reach for asserting claims of privilege or of protection as trial-preparation material after production;

(7) the date or dates for conferences before trial, a final pretrial conference, and trial; and

(8) any other matters appropriate in the circumstances of the case.

The order shall issue as soon as practicable but in any event within 90 days after the appearance of a defendant and within 120 days after the complaint has been served on a defendant. A schedule shall not be modified except upon a showing of good cause and by leave of the district judge or, when authorized by local rule, by a magistrate judge.

(c) Subjects for Consideration at Pretrial Conferences. At any conference under this rule consideration may be given, and the court may take appropriate action, with respect to

(1) the formulation and simplification of the issues, including the elimination of frivolous claims or defenses;

(2) the necessity or desirability of amendments to the pleadings;

(3) the possibility of obtaining admissions of fact and of documents which will avoid unnecessary proof, stipulations regarding the authenticity of documents, and advance rulings from the court on the admissibility of evidence;

(4) the avoidance of unnecessary proof and of cumulative evidence, and limitations or restrictions on the use of testimony under Rule 702 of the Federal Rules of Evidence;

(5) the appropriateness and timing of summary adjudication under Rule 56;

(6) the control and scheduling of discovery, including orders affecting disclosures and discovery pursuant to Rule 26 and Rules 29 through 37;

(7) the identification of witnesses and documents, the need and schedule for filing and exchanging pretrial briefs, and the date or dates for further conferences and for trial;

(8) the advisability of referring matters to a magistrate judge or master;

(9) settlement and the use of special procedures to assist in resolving the dispute when authorized by statute or local rule;

(10) the form and substance of the pretrial order;

(11) the disposition of pending motions;

(12) the need for adopting special procedures for managing potentially difficult or protracted actions that may involve complex issues, multiple parties, difficult legal questions, or unusual proof problems;

(13) an order for a separate trial pursuant to Rule 42(b) with respect to a claim, counterclaim, cross-claim, or third-party claim, or with respect to any particular issue in the case;

(14) an order directing a party or parties to present evidence early in the trial with respect to a manageable issue that could, on the evidence, be the basis for a judgment as a matter of law under Rule 50(a) or a judgment on partial findings under Rule 52(c);

(15) an order establishing a reasonable limit on the time allowed for presenting evidence; and

(16) such other matters as may facilitate the just, speedy, and inexpensive disposition of the action.

(continued)

EXHIBIT 10.4 Rule 16. Pretrial Conferences; Scheduling; Management (*continued*)

At least one of the attorneys for each party participating in any conference before trial shall have authority to enter into stipulations and to make admissions regarding all matters that the participants may reasonably anticipate may be discussed. If appropriate, the court may require that a party or its representatives be present or reasonably available by telephone in order to consider possible settlement of the dispute.

(d) Final Pretrial Conference. Any final pretrial conference shall be held as close to the time of trial as reasonable under the circumstances. The participants at any such conference shall formulate a plan for trial, including a program for facilitating the admission of evidence. The conference shall be attended by at least one of the attorneys who will conduct the trial for each of the parties and by any unrepresented parties.

(e) Pretrial Orders. After any conference held pursuant to this rule, an order shall be entered reciting the action taken. This order shall control the subsequent course of the action unless modified by a subsequent order. The order following a final pretrial conference shall be modified only to prevent manifest injustice.

(f) Sanctions. If a party or party's attorney fails to obey a scheduling or pretrial order, or if no appearance is made on behalf of a party at a scheduling or pretrial conference, or if a party or party's attorney is substantially unprepared to participate in the conference, or if a party or party's attorney fails to participate in good faith, the judge, upon motion or the judge's own initiative, may make such orders with regard thereto as are just, and among others any of the orders provided in Rule 37(b)(2)(B), (C), (D). In lieu of or in addition to any other sanction, the judge shall require the party or the attorney representing the party or both to pay the reasonable expenses incurred because of any noncompliance with this rule, including attorney's fees, unless the judge finds that the noncompliance was substantially justified or that other circumstances make an award of expenses unjust.

Source: Federal Rules of Civil Procedure.

Paralegal tasks in preparation for pretrial conference are to make available to the attorney all needed information and supporting documents, and to place the conference time in the docket control and reminder systems.

A pretrial preparation checklist should contain the following:

Pretrial Conference Preparation Checklist

1. Docket conference date and reminder dates for yourself and the attorney.

2. Enter reminder dates to inform the client of upcoming conferences, their significance, and whether the client should plan to be present. Check with the attorney.

3. Determine rules of pertinent jurisdiction and expectations of the assigned judge. Most courts publish their local rules; call the judge's deputy clerk for clarification. Summarize for the attorney.

4. See that the client has signed all needed documents authorizing the attorney to enter into stipulations and to settle the case (see example following this checklist).

5. Have available for the attorney summaries of the following:
   - The facts, acts, and omissions that form the basis of the claim.
   - Any specific statutes or ordinances that have been violated.

- Documents, photos, diagrams, and other tangible evidence that will be entered into evidence at trial.
- All witnesses (names, addresses, and area of testimony), including expert witnesses.
- All injuries, damages, and monetary amounts.
- All points of factual and legal contention.

6. Gather and organize all documents and other evidence needed by the attorney to submit to the other side for stipulations.

7. Gather all needed records, bills, and other documents, and evidence to support claim.

8. Gather and organize all motions to be made or that are pending in the case.

9. Gather and organize any briefs, memoranda to the court, or other summaries of the law, or any points of contention.

10. Confer with the attorney to see that all that is needed is prepared.

In order for the attorney to negotiate in good conscience and to be in a position to make an offer to settle and to agree to settle at the most opportune time, the client must sign a written authorization for the attorney to negotiate and settle the lawsuit. Some firms incorporate an authorization in the fee agreement. Prior to signing, the client should be fully informed as to the likelihood of settlement negotiations, a realistic settlement figure, and what is given up when settlement is elected. If the authorization has not been obtained earlier, it should be obtained by the time of the pretrial conference. Exhibit 10.5 is an example of a general authorization.

Some attorneys and courts require the preparation of a pretrial statement following the pretrial conference. It includes an overall summary of the items mentioned in the previous checklist. If you have summarized the damages as previously indicated and prepared a settlement précis or brochure, the preparation of a pretrial statement should be relatively easy. The only new wrinkle is to determine the exact format preferred by the attorney or the court requiring the statement.

Some courts require the pretrial statement (memorandum) to be prepared jointly, furthering the opportunity for settlement. This may be followed by a pretrial order drafted by the judge or one or more of the parties. Because the required format varies with the jurisdiction, it is best to locate a local example of these documents. Exhibit 10.6

APPLY YOUR KNOWLEDGE

Identify the state court rule in your jurisdiction for pretrial memorandum/ conference. What are the requirements? Compare your state rule with the federal rules and note the differences.

EXHIBIT 10.5 Power to Settle Personal Injury Claims

I, [name] authorize [attorney or person] to represent me in any negotiations with _____, or his/her attorney, with reference to his/her claim for damages against me on account of personal injuries received in a collision with my automobile on or about the ____ day of _____, hereby authorizing my attorney either to compromise the claim for such amount as he may deem best, or to defend an action in the courts, if he deems that necessary to protect my interests.

Adapted from West's Legal Forms § 28.223, v. 30, with permission of West Group.

EXHIBIT 10.6 Pretrial Memorandum

[Caption]
PRETRIAL MEMORANDUM

Pretrial Conference
   Attorneys, date, location, etc.
Statement of Uncontested Facts
   Agreed times, events, damage, etc.
Contested Issues of Fact
   Disputed facts: Speed of vehicle, signature on document, intent of contract, etc.
Contested Issues of Law
   Disputed application of rules of law, defenses, and other matters for the judge to decide.
Witnesses
   A list of witnesses with their position, title, and relationship to case to be called by each party.
Exhibits
   A list and brief description of each exhibit to be presented at trial. In some jurisdictions this is added as an appendix; in others it is placed in the body of the memorandum with a column for any objections to the exhibits, i.e.,

               <u>Exhibit</u>   <u>Objections</u>

Other Categories
   Other categories that may be included, depending on the jurisdiction and nature of the case, such as a statement of agreed damages or special damages, attached jury instructions and any objections to them, and a statement of any agreed findings of fact and conclusions of law.

   Respectfully Submitted this _____ day of _____
   By:

                                                    _____
                                                    Attorney for Plaintiff

                                                    _____
                                                    Attorney for Defendant

---

is an outline of one format. The pretrial order generally follows the same format as the pretrial memorandum.

SETTLEMENT CONFERENCE

settlement conference

A meeting between the parties to discuss settlement of the case.

A **settlement conference** is a meeting between the parties to discuss settlement of the case. Its purpose is, therefore, more narrow than the pretrial conference. A settlement conference may be part of the extended pretrial conference procedures under Rule 16 and parallel state rules, or it may come after a pretrial conference or occur as the parties or the court deem necessary. A party may request a settlement conference, or the court may order it. A magistrate judge or other judge particularly skilled in settlement may conduct the settlement conference. Procedures, settlement conference statements, and local rules vary. Failure to attend or act in good faith in participating in the settlement conference may result in sanctions by a court. Examine *Pitman v. Brinker International, Inc.* 216 F.R.D. 481 (D. Az. 2003)

CASE STUDY: UNDERSTANDING THE LAW

Carl Pitman, a former employee of Brinker International, filed an age discrimination case. During the course of the litigation, the court ordered a settlement conference with specific requirements. One of those requirements was to bring a representative with complete authority to discuss and settle the case. The plaintiff and his attorney attended the settlement conference. However, the defendant attended the conference with a representative who did not have real settlement authority. After the court questioned the defendant's representative, it became clear that the defendant had violated the court's order by not bringing someone who could participate in meaningful discussions about settlement with the plaintiff. The defendant's representative had settlement authority of only $1,075.00, when the plaintiff's demand was over $400,000.

The court then set the matter for sanctions. Citing to the court's inherent authority to issue sanctions for failure to comply with the court's order, the court evaluated the circumstances surrounding the order and the defendant's compliance. The court then evaluated whether disobedience of the court was intentional. Finding that the defendant's counsel was experienced and knew what to expect from the settlement conference, his actions in failing to comply with the court's order and acting in good faith warranted the imposition of sanctions. Those sanctions included the plaintiff's counsel's preparation time and were imposed on both the defendant's attorney and the defendant, joint and severally.

Questions for Review: Review *Pitman v. Brinker International*. What facts led to the plaintiff filing the discrimination lawsuit? What are the standards the court must follow before imposing sanctions on a party? What facts supported the court's imposition of sanctions and why?

Your role in preparing for a settlement conference incorporates many of the tasks previously discussed in this chapter. The objective is to see that your supervising attorney has all needed material organized for quick, logical access. Settlement conference material includes identification of all remaining issues and supporting authority; highlighted parts of crucial reports, records, medical bills, and transcripts; key statements of experts and other witnesses; and important photographs, diagrams, and exhibits. As in the case of a pretrial conference, preparation is the key.

SETTLEMENT FORMS

release

A document executed by the plaintiff or claimant that frees the defendant from any further obligations or liability stemming from the incident causing the damages in return for consideration (money).

RELEASES AND SETTLEMENT AGREEMENTS

Once the parties have agreed to settle, there are several forms that you may be asked to draft or review for accuracy. One such form is the **release**. A release is a document executed by the plaintiff or claimant that frees the defendant from any further obligations or liability stemming from the incident causing the damages in return for consideration (money). The document ends litigation on the matter between the two parties. Two common types of releases are set out in Exhibit 10.7, an easily adapted example of a release for personal injury, and Exhibit 10.8, a mutual release used when both sides in a lawsuit have claims against the other.

EXHIBIT 10.7 Release and Settlement of Suit for Personal Injuries

Received from _____ the sum of _____ dollars ($ _____), lawful money, to me in hand paid, the receipt of which is hereby acknowledged, the same being in full payment, satisfaction and discharge of any and all claims, demands or causes of action, of whatsoever nature which I or my heirs, executors, administrators, personal representatives, successors or assigns, may now or hereafter have against the _____, its officers, agents or servants, its successors and assigns, for damages for or by all reason of all personal injuries, all pain and suffering, damage to property, all losses and expenses, of whatsoever character, sustained as a result of an accident which occurred to me on or about the _____ day of _____, at or near _____ Avenue, on which date and at which time and place I was injured when attempting to board a bus, and especially from the cause or causes of action set forth in a petition filed by me in the Court of _____, _____ County, _____, in an action entitled "_____ vs. _____ Case No. _____ on the docket of said Court, in which entry may be made "Settled and dismissed at defendant's costs."

I hereby certify that this release is fully understood by me and is entirely satisfactory.

In Witness Whereof,

Adapted from West's Legal Forms § 330.66, v. 30, with permission of West Group.

EXHIBIT 10.8 Mutual Release of All Claims and Demands

_____, of _____ and _____, of _____, each hereby releases the other from all sums of money, accounts, actions, suits, proceedings, claims, and demands whatsoever which either of them at any time had or has up to this date against the other for or by reason of or in respect of any act, cause, matter, or thing whatsoever dated _____ in [identify the place and incident, if necessary].

Signed and sealed on _____ at _____.

_____ [Seal]

_____ [Seal]

Adapted from West's Legal Forms, § 12.34, v. 10, with permission of West Group.

settlement agreement

A contract between the parties setting all the terms, conditions, and obligations of the parties, including how the action will be dismissed.

Releases may be general in nature or specific, tied to a particular claim or injury. It is a good idea to consult local law on what must be included in a valid release. Some states, for instance, do not require consideration. In some circumstances a covenant not to sue is executed, which is not a release of past wrongs but simply an agreement not to sue on a claim in return for consideration. Exhibit 10.9 is an example of a covenant not to sue. This type of release is also called an indemnification agreement or hold harmless agreement.

Settlement agreements are often used in more complex cases and provide a more detailed description of the settlement than a typical release from liability. The **settlement agreement** is a contract between the parties setting all the terms, conditions, and obligations of the parties, including how the action will be dismissed.

EXHIBIT 10.9 Covenant Not to Sue (with Reservation of Rights as to Others)

COVENANT NOT TO SUE

In consideration of _____ dollars ($ _____) paid to me by _____, of _____, individually of _____, receipt of which I acknowledge, I hereby covenant not to sue _____individually and refrain forever from instituting, pressing, collecting or in any way acting or proceeding upon any and all claims, judgments, debts, causes of action, suits and proceedings of any kind at law or in equity which I ever had, now have or may have against any of the aforementioned covenantee(s) or their legal representative(s), successor(s) or assign(s), arising out of the following matters: _____

_____

   I have received the consideration of $ _____ in full payment for this covenant not to sue, notwithstanding any injuries or damages sustained, whether known or unknown.

   This instrument is not intended as a release or discharge nor as an accord or satisfaction with any person whomsoever, but only as a covenant not to sue upon any and all claims and matters whatsoever which have been or may be made against covenantee by me. I acknowledge that covenantee, in making payment of the consideration for this covenant, does not thereby admit any liability on account of any of the above-described matters but expressly denies all of such liability whatsoever.

   Signed and sealed on _____.

_____ [*Seal*]

Witness:

_____

Adapted from West's Legal Forms, § 12.54 v. 10, with permission of West Group.

If requested to draft such an agreement, review local examples of the document and ask the attorney for specific guidelines. Exhibit 10.10 is an example of a settlement agreement.

An issue generating increased debate is whether settlement agreements should be permitted by the courts to be secret (or sealed) and whether such agreements should be permitted to contain restrictions on parties, particularly plaintiffs, from providing information to government investigative bodies. On one hand, secrecy encourages settlements, while opening secret settlement provisions to public scrutiny may discourage them. On the other hand, anti-secrecy proponents argue that there is strong public policy in support of revealing settlement information that might prevent additional harm to the public or facilitate health and safety investigations of public agencies. It is likely that courts will increasingly scrutinize what settlement information can be sealed or subjected to revelation prohibitions.

SPECIAL PROVISIONS TO CONSIDER IN SETTLEMENT AGREEMENTS

As discussed above, confidentiality and nondisclosure provisions are important provisions to consider when preparing a settlement agreement. These provisions restrict

EXHIBIT 10.10 Settlement Agreement

SETTLEMENT AGREEMENT

[*Name of first party*] of [*address*], hereafter referred to as _____ and [*Name of second party*] of [*address*], here-after referred to as _____ in order to settle the controversy between them designated as _____ v. _____ civil case file number _____ filed in the [name of court] by the dated signatures below, HEREBY AGREE AND INTEND TO BE LEGALLY BOUND BY THE FOLLOWING TERMS:

1. (Here state in detail each term, condition, and covenant agreed to by both parties: amount, time, and terms of payment; nature and extent of releases that will be executed and delivered; when and how the action will be dismissed; how court costs and legal fees will be handled; whether goods or documents will be exchanged or discharged; what collateral, if any, will be used to insure the agreement; and any other items suggested by the attorney.)

(Seal)

Attest _____

(First Party)

by _____

Party (or duly authorized officer)

_____

Address

Date _____

(Seal)

Attest _____

(Second Party)

by _____

Party (or duly authorized officer)

_____

Address

Date _____

what can be discussed regarding the settlement between the parties. Some examples of confidentiality and nondisclosure provisions are:

(1) The terms and conditions of the Agreement are absolutely confidential between the parties and shall not be disclosed to any person or entity, except as shall be necessary to effectuate its terms. Any disclosure in violation of this section shall be deemed a material breach of the Agreement. The breaching party may institute the appropriate legal action.

(2) The parties agree that they shall treat the fact of this settlement and its contents between the parties as confidential. Neither party shall disclose any information regarding this settlement to any other person or entity, unless legally compelled to do so, and then, only upon timely notice to the [opposing party] giving it sufficient time to contest such disclosure. Confidentiality is a material part of this Agreement and is intended to apply to and be upon all parties, including its employees, agents and other representatives. The parties shall take

TRADE SECRETS: CONFIDENTIALITY PROVISIONS AND THEIR ENFORCEMENT

Often parties to a settlement want the terms of the settlement secret or confidential. Recall the highly publicized case of Mel Gibson and his former girlfriend Oksana Grigorieva, with whom he had a child. The facts of the case were a bit salacious, enough so that Gibson appeared to be willing to pay for Grigorieva's silence. In exchange for Grigorieva's silence she received a large cash amount, a house, and generous child support. All she had to do was not discuss the details of her relationship with Gibson. However, it appears she wanted to extend her 15 minutes of fame and agreed to be interviewed on the Howard Stern Show. Gibson claimed foul and sued Grigorieva for breach of their agreement. She still had $375,000 to receive on her settlement. A judge agreed with Gibson and Grigorieva did not receive the final payment. The confidentiality/nondisclosure provision was alive and well.

Therefore, it is prudent to include a confidentiality or nondisclosure provision in a settlement agreement, especially when sensitive terms or circumstances should not be disclosed to the public. This provision should include language that nullifies the settlement if the confidentiality provision is breached as happened in the Gibson/Grigorieva case. This provision is not exclusively for the rich and famous but should be considered for any settlement that contains sensitive facts. What also is important when including a confidentiality/nondisclosure provision is monitoring it. Pay attention to social media posts or other media communications when determining whether provisions of a settlement agreement have been followed. As we often find out, oversharing can have dire consequences. To ensure clear understanding of these provisions, have the parties initial those provisions or have the language stand out through underlining or bold print. That will ensure full knowledge of the provision and more evidence of assent.

APPLYING
THE LAW

Determine whether your jurisdiction permits settlement agreements to be sealed. What is the law in your jurisdiction for allowing confidentiality clauses in a settlement agreement? Do settlement agreements resulting from litigation require filing and approval of a court? Set forth your jurisdiction's policy and law on the issue.

all necessary steps to assure that this provision is communicated to and followed by those intended to be bound.

Another type of special provision to consider is a general media provision. This provision restricts any discussion about the case and often provides the response that must be communicated when disclosure of a settlement is broached. A common provision is:

Neither party shall issue a press release or otherwise, directly or indirectly, disclose the terms of this Agreement to any third person, entity or media except as necessary to effectuate its terms, secure its enforcement, as compelled by a court order, or to his attorneys. In conjunction with any communication regarding this lawsuit, the parties shall reply only with the following statement and nothing more: "All matters between the parties have been resolved."

Enforcement of these types of provisions are not uncommon with parties filing court actions for enforcement of the terms and conditions of the mutually agreed to settlement. This was the case of a Florida man who told his daughter about a settlement with his former employer; she then posted the information on Facebook. A motion to compel enforcement of the agreement was filed in *Gulliver Schools, Inc. v. Snay*, (App. Fla. 2014)

CASE STUDY: UNDERSTANDING THE LAW

Gulliver v. Snay stems from a dispute between Gulliver Schools and Patrick Snay, its former headmaster. Snay claimed discrimination and retaliation when his contract was not renewed and filed claims under the Florida Civil Rights Act. The parties ultimately reached a settlement and executed an agreement with a full release. At issue was the confidentiality provision, which stated that the terms of the agreement would be strictly confidential and that if he or his wife disclosed any terms of the agreement, $80,000 would be forfeited from that settlement. The specific provision stated:

> *The plaintiff shall not, either directly or indirectly, disclose, discuss or communicate to any entity or person, except his attorneys or other professional advisors or spouse any information whatsoever regarding the existence or terms of this agreement…. A breach … will result in the disgorgement of the plaintiff's portion of the settlement payments.*

Less than four days after signing, Snay's daughter posted on Facebook the following:

> *Mama and Papa Snay won the case against Gulliver. Gulliver is now officially paying for my vacation to Europe this summer. SUCK IT.*

Gulliver sent a letter to Snay's counsel citing the breach. Snay filed a motion to enforce the settlement in the trial court which conducted hearings to determine whether a breach had occurred. The trial court deemed that the settlement agreement had not been breached and Gulliver appealed. Focusing on black letter contract law that the agreement was unambiguous, the appeals court found that the mere disclosure that the case had been settled to his daughter was a breach of a material provision of the agreement. The court continued that the Snays did exactly what the agreement had prevented—disclosure to another party, even his daughter, who then broadcast the settlement over social media. The appeals court reversed the trial court and found that the settlement agreement had been breached.

Questions for Review: Locate a copy of *Gulliver v. Snay* and read it. Why did the Snays breach the settlement terms? What was the legal basis for the appeals court enforcement of the settlement agreement? Were the actions of the appeals court justified? Why or why not?

---

without prejudice
In the dismissal of a case, the understanding that the action may be brought again.

with prejudice
In the dismissal of a case, the understanding that the action may not be brought again.

adjudication on the merits
A judgment by the court deciding the issues of an action, precluding that action from being brought again.

STIPULATION AND ORDER FOR DISMISSAL

Once an action has been filed and settlement agreed upon, the parties generally have two options for finalizing the settlement. The first is a stipulation and order for dismissal; the second is a consent decree and order.

A stipulation and order for dismissal notifies the judge that the case has been settled and the parties want an order dismissing the action. Under Federal Rule 41(a)(1) and parallel state statutes, the plaintiff without order of the court may file a notice of dismissal at any time before the opponent has filed an answer or a motion for summary judgment, whichever occurs first. If later than this, the parties may file a stipulation for dismissal signed by all the parties that have appeared in the action. Such a dismissal is normally **without prejudice**, meaning the action may be brought again. A signed release is important in this case, since it serves as a defense to the action being brought again. If requested, however, the court may dismiss the action **with prejudice**, meaning it may not be brought again. The case is treated as an **adjudication on the merits**, as if the court had considered and decided all remaining issues. One advantage to this process is that the parties do not have to make public the terms of the settlement. If one of the parties breaches the agreement, the court may impose sanctions. Exhibit 10.11 is an example of a stipulation and order for dismissal. Local rules and examples should always be consulted.

EXHIBIT 10.11 Stipulation and Order for Dismissal

IN THE UNITED STATES DISTRICT COURT FOR
THE _____ DISTRICT OF _____

_____

           Plaintiff

    v.   Civil Action, File No. _____

_____

           Defendant

STIPULATION AND ORDER FOR DISMISSAL

On this _____ day of _____, it is stipulated between counsel for Plaintiff and counsel for Defendant that this action be dismissed *[with or without prejudice]* regarding all claims and counterclaims of the parties and without costs to the parties, and that an order consistent with this stipulation be entered without further notice to the parties.

_____
Attorney for Plaintiff

_____
Address

_____
Attorney for Defendant

_____
Address

So Ordered

_____, Judge United States District Court of the _____ District of _____

Date _____

INTERNET EXERCISE

If a minor is a party to a settlement agreement, what are your state's requirements for its approval? Identify the statute, rule, or case that supports your research.

CONSENT DECREE AND ORDER

The parties may instead choose a consent decree and order. This method differs from the stipulation for dismissal by including the details of the settlement and by asking the judge to review and approve the terms of the settlement. A number of states require any settlement on behalf of a minor to be approved by the court. Judgment is entered according to the terms as approved. Exhibit 10.12 is an example of a stipulation and consent decree and order.

SETTLEMENT DISTRIBUTION STATEMENT

The attorney or firm should give the client a settlement distribution statement that clearly itemizes the amount of the settlement and how it will be distributed. The drafting of such a statement is not difficult and can be instrumental in avoiding unnecessary conflicts and misunderstanding with the client both now and in the future. Also, to avoid misunderstandings and the appearance of impropriety, settlement checks cannot be deposited in the law firm's bank account before distribution to the client. Note that a firm's share of any settlement is usually documented in the fee agreement between the attorney and client. Exhibit 10.13 is an example of a settlement distribution statement.

EXHIBIT 10.12 Stipulation and Consent Decree and Order

(Caption omitted)

STIPULATION AND CONSENT DECREE

The parties to this action, having agreed to settle this case, hereby consent to the entry of the following order. This order and stipulation shall not be interpreted as an admission of wrongdoing by either party.

THE PARTIES, BY THEIR ATTORNEYS, STIPULATE THAT THIS CASE SHALL BE SETTLED BY CONSENT DECREE AS FOLLOWS:

1. The Defendant, _____, shall pay to the Plaintiff, _____, the agreed upon sum of $_____ for all injuries, pain and suffering, and damages, past, present, and future sustained from [*state accident or other source of claim*] on [*date*] .

2. The Defendant, _____, shall pay the sum in the following manner: _____.

3. The Plaintiff, _____, shall pay to the Defendant, _____, the sum of $_____, for all damages, past, present, and future, incurred by the Defendant as a consequence of [*restate accident as source of claim*] as alleged in Defendant's counterclaim against Plaintiff.

4. The Defendant shall pay the costs of this action in the sum of $_____.

5. The parties will pay their own attorney's fees.

6. At the time of compliance with all terms of the stipulation and decree, the above captioned action shall be dismissed with prejudice.

For Plaintiff,   For Defendant,

_____   _____
Attorney for Plaintiff   Attorney for Defendant

_____   _____
Address   Address
Date _____

(Caption omitted)

ORDER

Having reviewed the above entitled case and the Stipulated Consent Decree freely entered into by both parties to this action as evidenced by the signature of their respective counsel, the Court ORDERS, ADJUDGES, and DECREES that the Stipulation is approved, as set forth and attached hereto, so ordered this _____ day of _____.

_____
Judge, United States District
Court for the _____
District of _____

FAILURE TO SETTLE AND THE RULES OF EVIDENCE

Settlement discussions are confidential and cannot be disclosed or used against a party if they fail. Under the Federal Rules of Evidence, Rule 408, use of information disclosed during settlement discussions to prove disputed facts or claims or to impeach are prohibited and inadmissible in a trial. The basis for the rule is to encourage settlement and honest and candid conversations about the case which could assist in reaching a settlement. If attorneys or the parties believe that information during settlement discussions could be used against them in a future proceedings, cases would rarely settle. Consequently, when participating in settlement discussions, remember Rule 408.

EXHIBIT 10.13 Settlement Distribution Statement

WHITE, WILSON & MCDUFF
ATTORNEYS AT LAW
FEDERAL PLAZA BUILDING, SUITE 700
THIRD AND MARKET STREETS
LEGALVILLE, COLUMBIA 00000
(111) 555-0000

SETTLEMENT DISTRIBUTION STATEMENT

CASE: _____ vs. _____   CLIENT: _____

   Civil Case No. _____

   Court _____

Total Gross Settlement (received from _____) $_____

   Less Attorney's Expenses (Itemized)

      Travel $_____

      Printing $_____

      Doctors' Report Fees $_____

      Medical Records Fees $_____

      Phone Calls $_____

      Court Costs and Filing Fees $_____

      Photocopies $_____

      Others $_____

               Subtotal $_____ $_____

Less Attorney's Fee (figured by percentage of gross in contingency fee
case or by itemized billing entries)

                                    $_____

             Total Net Settlement Due Client $_____

OTHER ALTERNATIVE DISPUTE RESOLUTIONS: ARBITRATION, MEDIATION, AND SUMMARY TRIALS

INTRODUCTION

alternative dispute resolution (ADR)
Any means of settling disputes outside of a courtroom or without litigation.

Paralegals are becoming increasingly involved in assisting attorneys and clients in preparing for **alternative dispute resolution** (ADR) processes. Alternative dispute resolution is any means of settling disputes outside of a courtroom or without litigation. These processes include various forms of arbitration, mediation, summary trials, and others. The remaining portion of this chapter focuses on these procedures and the role of the paralegal in assisting in these processes.

The interest in and use of alternative dispute resolution continues to grow dramatically. Three primary reasons explain the increasing use of these systems. First, alternative dispute resolution keeps many cases out of an already overcrowded court docket, which not only relieves pressure on our courts, but also allows thousands of ADR cases to be resolved more quickly than if they had been adjudicated in the courts. Complex trials can go on for months or over a year. ADR hearings usually are completed in several hours, a day, or, in complex cases, a series of one- or two-day sessions over several months.

Second, because ADR takes less time and is less formal with relaxed standards of evidence, procedure, and location than a court procedure, it also saves parties a considerable amount of money. Costs may be waived for indigency in some cases. A greater fee in large commercial cases is still a bargain.

Third, ADR processes are less adversarial and confrontational than a trial and substantially reduce the emotional trauma and bitterness associated with trials. Cases involving family law, business associates, employers and employees, landlords and tenants, and a host of other kinds of disputes are better served by a process that stresses reconciliation, common ground, and the mutual desire to get the matter over with as congenially as possible.

At one time ADR was reserved for small cases. Today, however, cases involving millions of dollars and complex technical issues have been resolved through alternative dispute resolution. An increasing number of courts require ADR in at least some types of cases. Some states require ADR in all civil cases. All federal courts have been required to have mandatory ADR programs since 1998. In 1991, the Administrative Dispute Resolution Act amended the Administrative Procedure Act of 1946 specifically to authorize and encourage the use of ADR processes in federal agencies. In 1996, President Clinton signed an executive order requiring all U.S. government lawyers to use alternative dispute resolution when warranted. (Incidentally, this same order called for a greater use of nonlawyer representatives in federal administrative agency practice.) Although satisfaction with ADR generally runs high, concerns exist, particularly in regard to arbitration.

ARBITRATION

arbitration

An alternative dispute resolution process consisting of the submission of a dispute to a neutral decision maker.

Arbitration is an alternative dispute resolution process consisting of the submission of a dispute to a neutral decision maker. It is, generally speaking, a private contractual process that is encouraged by state and federal law. Most states have adopted a version of the Uniform Arbitration Act. The Federal Arbitration Act (9 U.S.C. § 10) applies to arbitrations when they are part of contracts involving interstate commerce.

Although the parties surrender decision-making power to the arbitrator, they have considerably more control over the process than they do in litigation. They can determine whether the award will be binding or advisory, and they can select the time, place, the arbitrator (who may or may not be an attorney), the conditions that invoke arbitration, the procedures, and even the standards for the arbitrator's decision. The terms of the arbitration are set out in a formal agreement and signed by each party. Parties are bound by the agreement as they would be by a contract. The parties pay the arbitrator's fee, a filing fee, and expenses. The losing party frequently covers the prevailing party's filing fee. Arbitrators and guidelines for arbitration are available through various arbitration associations, including the American Arbitration Association and the Society of Professionals in Dispute Resolution.

The procedure in voluntary arbitration is initiated by a "demand for arbitration," a "statement of claim," or some similar document. This document sets out the dispute, a remedy, and the amount of the award sought. It serves the same purpose as a complaint, but is generally more informal in nature. The "demand" is usually accompanied by a "submission agreement" signed by both parties agreeing to the arbitration. Alternatively, the claim may be filed with the arbitration association, which serves the claim on the opposing party. A reply may be required.

A list of arbitrators may be sent to the parties who, generally, can cross out the names of a specified number of arbitrators. The arbitrator is then selected from the remaining names.

A form of discovery is also available: Documents, information, and depositions are exchanged when deemed necessary by the arbitrator. Generally, 30 days are permitted for the response to such requests. A hearing date is set, and notice is given allowing approximately 45 days for preparation.

The hearing is similar to a trial but more informal. Opening arguments are given, witnesses are heard, some cross-examination is allowed, and evidence is presented. The rules of procedure and burdens of proof are more relaxed; for example, hearsay evidence is generally not objectionable. The complaining party may be given the choice on whether to go first or last in closing arguments.

Sometimes summary briefs are requested after the hearing. The decision is usually rendered within 30 days. An appeal to the courts is available, but generally the court's latitude in overturning a decision is limited to the grounds stated in the Federal Arbitration Act (9 U.S.C. § 10) and similar statutes. Generally they are as follows:

1. The award was obtained by fraud or corruption.

2. The arbitrator was obviously partial or corrupted.

3. The arbitrator was guilty of misconduct or some obvious abuse of fairness or discretion, or otherwise exceeding delegated powers.

The standard of proof in arbitration varies depending on the type of case. It can be as indefinite as "the party whose evidence is most persuasive viewed as a whole."

Despite the success of arbitration or because of it, concerns have developed. One such concern stems from the expanded use of mandatory arbitration clauses in a variety of commercial and employment contracts. For individuals, if you want the job, merchandise, credit card, mortgage, service, or other contracted benefit, you must agree to arbitration, rather than litigation, as the means to resolve any claim against the employer or the merchant. These clauses are criticized for being a product of unequal bargaining power where there is no practical alternative for the weaker party and where the clauses contain additional obstacles that make it difficult or often too costly to pursue a claim or seek judicial relief. Despite these concerns, courts have largely upheld mandatory arbitration clauses, even extending enforcement of the Federal Arbitration Act to employment contracts [*Circuit City Stores, Inc. v. Adams*, 121 S.Ct. 1302 (2001)].

TECHNOLOGY UPDATE: ARBITRATION AND THE FUTURE

Not surprising is the trend toward Internet-based arbitration. Known as Online Dispute Resolution, ("ODR"), this area of ADR is changing the face of how parties resolve disputes, especially in the e-commerce arena. ODR has been generally defined as the relationship between ADR and Information and Communication Technology ("ICT"). Primarily conducted online, this type of arbitration uses technology almost exclusively from the initial filing of the dispute to oral presentations and the resulting arbitration award. Sometimes ODR is referred to by other names, such as Internet Dispute Resolution ("iDR"), Electronic ADR ("eADR") to name a few. But the implication is the same—online technology based methods to resolve disputes. The issue with ODR is its regulation, due process and enforceability. Arbitration is normally contractual. Assume that a consumer agreement contains an online dispute resolution clause. If the consumer believes that the process does not protect or afford due process, the ODR could be challenged and nullified. This area of arbitration is developing, with the key consideration focused on providing the same protections that face-to-face arbitration provides. For example, the parties must be able to properly question witnesses, with both direct and cross examination. This requires online services that provide audio and visual connections, such as Skype or similar technologies. As a developing alternative in dispute resolution, be mindful of its existence and the issues that it raises. ODR is probably the future of ADR as it presents a more efficient and economical method of resolving disputes in both the e-commerce and standard dispute resolution scenarios. However, be sure that if ODR is the chosen methodology, you take care in protecting due process rights to minimize any possible legal challenges that could arise.

INTERNET EXERCISE

Locate a copy of *Artificial Intelligence: Robots, Avatars and the Demise of the Human Mediator,* by David Allen Larson, *Ohio State Journal on Dispute Resolution,* Vol. 25, No. 1 February 26, 2010. What is the premise of the article? Does this present the future of arbitration and mediation? Why or why not? How does the author define "artificial intelligence" and its applications?

Other concerns include the lack of hard data on whether arbitration, especially in complex commercial cases, actually saves money and time; whether individuals have adequate information on which to base their choice of an arbitrator; whether arbitration agreements can prohibit class actions; and whether dissatisfaction with aspects of arbitration, especially mandatory arbitration, is leading to increased and more frequently successful court challenges.

Another form of arbitration is court-annexed arbitration. It is controlled by the court in which the action is filed and, if the arbitration is not successful, the case may still be tried by that court. Procedurally, a complaint is filed in court as it would be in any lawsuit. The defendant answers the complaint. Court personnel screen the filings and assign certain cases to the arbitration process. The assignment may be challenged by a party not wanting to go to arbitration or, if a case is not assigned to arbitration, a party or the parties may request that it be so assigned.

The arbitrator or panel of arbitrators are generally selected by the court or by the parties from a court list. Arbitrators are usually attorneys and normally paid by the court. In some jurisdictions they are expected to work hard to facilitate a settlement prior to the hearing. The hearings may be quite trial-like and formal, or informal where each side simply states its case and no witnesses testify. A decision is rendered in as little as a week in some programs. The award is entered as the court's judgment.

If a party is unsatisfied with the decision, that party may request that the case be tried in a *trial de novo* (a trial as in any other case and as if no previous hearing had been held). Usually, however, such a request is discouraged by disincentives such as the requirement of a party to pay the other party's court costs and attorney's fees if it does not do significantly better at trial than it did under the arbitration award.

This requirement helps prevent abuse of arbitration as just another pretrial discovery tool, and upholds its purpose in freeing court dockets. Appeals are limited when arbitration is used, and the scope of the court's review is limited as well. Decisions can be challenged on very narrow grounds, such as fraud, bias, disregarding the law, or against public policy. *Eastern Associated Coal Corp. v. Mine Workers,* 531 U.S. 57 (2000) was a case where an arbitration award was challenged.

CASE STUDY: UNDERSTANDING THE LAW

Eastern Associated Coal Corporation, the employer, filed a challenge to an arbitration award in favor of a unionized employee. The facts are straightforward. James Smith worked for Eastern as a truck driver where he drove heavy truck-like vehicles on the highways. Under Department of Transportation regulations, Smith was subject to random drug testing. Smith tested positive for marijuana use twice over a period of time. His collective bargaining agreement required that dismissal be based on "just cause." In his defense, the union had argued alternative measures rather than suspension. On two occasions, an arbitrator found in favor of the employee and ordered Smith's reinstatement with strict conditions. From the second infraction, the arbitrator order a lengthy suspension, participation in a substance abuse program, reimburse to Eastern for the costs of the arbitration, continued random drug testing, and finally, a signed undated letter of resignation if Smith tested positive within five years of the arbitrator's decision.

Eastern challenged the arbitrator's decision, stating that it was against public policy for those in public safety positions to have continued employment. Both the district court and court of appeals affirmed the arbitrator's award stating that the conditions of reinstatement did not violate public policy. The U.S. Supreme Court accepted the petition for certiorari and affirmed the arbitrator's

award. The Supreme Court focused on the terms of the collective bargaining agreement and the interpretation of "just cause." The issue before the court was "does a contractual agreement to reinstate Smith with specified conditions run contrary to an explicit, well-defined, and dominant public policy, as ascertained by reference to positive law and not from general considerations of supposed public interests?" *Id.* at 63. Eastern argued that failure to pass a drug test in a position such as Smith's violates public policy without regard to any rehabilitation considerations. However, the Union/Smith argued that rehabilitation is not contrary to the spirit of the law or the bargaining agreement. The award takes into account the severity of the infraction and ordered specific consequences if another failed drug test occurred by Smith. In evaluating the award in context of the law, the agreement, and regulations, the Supreme Court did not find the arbitrator's award against public policy.

Questions for Review: Read the *Eastern Associated Coal* case. What attorney argued for the petitioner? Why did the Supreme Court accept the petition for writ of certiorari? Outline Eastern's arguments for dismissal rather than reinstatement for Smith. Why did the court find in favor of Smith?

Arbitration is also important to the global market. Since the vast majority of international business agreements now contain an arbitration clause, paralegals practicing in international business law need to consult the International Arbitration Rules of the American Arbitration Association, the Rules of Arbitration of the International Chamber of Commerce, or the Arbitration Rules of the United Nations Commission on International Trade Law, depending on the system being used. The collection and presentation of evidence in international arbitration hearings is not usually covered by these rule systems, however. In 1999, the International Bar Association approved its updated *IBA Rules on the Taking of Evidence in International Commercial Arbitration,* balancing the requirements of differing legal cultures and clarifying the limits of discovery and use of witnesses.

MEDIATION

mediation

An alternative dispute resolution process incorporating a neutral person (the mediator) who facilitates a mutual resolution of the dispute.

Mediation is an alternative dispute resolution process incorporating a neutral person (the mediator) who facilitates a mutual resolution of the dispute. The parties reach their own decision as to how to resolve the matter. Arbitration focuses on a somewhat adversarial fault-finding process of presenting evidence to decide a case and render an award; mediation focuses on common ground, how the parties can conduct themselves in the future (not how they conducted themselves in the past), and conciliatory compromise to resolve the dispute. In a 1999 survey, lawyers stated their overwhelming preference for nonbinding mediation over binding arbitration, because of savings in both time and money.

Generally, the two types of mediation are voluntary and mandatory. In voluntary mediation the parties realize that they are unable to resolve a dispute on their own or, at least, realize that they need assistance. They seek assistance through mediation programs or mediation associations. Mandatory mediation is generally imposed in specific types of cases by statute or by court order. Its purpose is to require the parties to mediate their differences before exercising their right to a trial or to other procedures, such as a strike in labor disputes. In either case the agreement is strictly voluntary with few if any sanctions for going ahead with other dispute resolution processes, including litigation if mediation fails. Voluntary mediation provides more party control over the process—selection of mediator, objectives, written agreement—than does mandatory mediation.

Procedurally, the processes used in the two types of mediation are similar. First, the parties select a mediator or are assigned one by the court or under a procedure established by the controlling statute. The parties meet with the mediator to gain an understanding of the goals of the process and how it works, and to establish some rules within which the mediation will be conducted. Where arbitration may have more formal and sometimes set rules of procedure, mediation is far more flexible with rules often created according to what will best serve the parties. For example, arbitration normally sets some standard or burden of persuasion. There is no such burden in mediation. Once the rules are formulated, then the parties or their representatives meet together or individually with the mediator in private to set out some facts and to propose solutions. Generally, these discussions are considered confidential and cannot be used as evidence in court.

When these discussions are completed, the effort focuses on the drafting of a mutually agreed plan to resolve the dispute. This agreement is to be the agreement of the parties' own work and ideas and not an agreement imposed on the parties by the mediator. Indications are that parties stick more readily to the terms of a mediated settlement because the terms are their own. Sometimes the parties will be able to agree on all issues, other times only on some—but even then progress has been made. When the parties cannot agree, the process returns to more formal remedies such as litigation. Many agreements provide for further mediation if disputes on clarifying terminology or some other matter arise later. An attempt at mediation is not a step in litigation and does not interrupt the tolling of the statute of limitations, however, so timing is important [*Gallagher v. Cook*, 775 So. 2d 79 (La. App. 2000)].

Mediation programs are growing, keeping numerous cases out of court, and preserving congeniality and civility in what might otherwise be far more seriously estranged relationships. While mediation lends itself well to family, neighborhood, and consumer disputes, it is now being more widely used in complex labor, environmental, and intellectual property cases. The American Bar Association joined forces with the American Arbitration Association and the Association for Conflict Resolution to develop the Model Standards of Conduct for Mediators (2005), uniform ethical guidelines.

A hybrid form of dispute resolution is med-arb. **Med-arb** is a combination of mediation and arbitration methods in which the matter is first mediated, then any unresolved issue is decided by the same or a different person who serves as an arbitrator. This approach incorporates the best features of a nonconfrontational process while still providing a decision to better ensure finality of the matter.

Before leaving arbitration and mediation, brief mention of some related concepts may be helpful. One is *collaborative law*, a process where attorneys for disputing parties agree in writing to work diligently for a negotiated settlement to the dispute. If no settlement is reached, the attorneys will refer their client to another attorney for litigation of the matter. The aim is to increase the likelihood of settlement by committing the parties and their agents to the sole purpose of settlement.

Another is the *high-low agreement*, where the parties agree to no more than a maximum (high) award and a set minimum (low) award, regardless of the jury's verdict or the arbitrator's decision. The high-low agreement removes some of the uncertainties of the final result. For example, if a plaintiff sees the potential that a jury may find the plaintiff partly responsible for an accident or more responsible than the defendant, the low part of the agreement assures the plaintiff that the very least awarded will be enough to cover hospital bills, attorney fees, and other expenses. If the verdict is more than the agreed low but less than the agreed high, the plaintiff will get the amount of the verdict. For the defendant, if the verdict goes beyond the agreed high, the plaintiff gets the agreed high and no more.

Finally, Federal Rule of Civil Procedure 68 and equivalent state rules are relevant to both the discussion of settlement and arbitration. Under Rule 68, more than 10 days prior to trial, the defendant may serve the plaintiff with an *offer of judgment*—an offer to allow entry of judgment against the defendant for a specified amount. If the plaintiff refuses the offer, and the result after trial is not more favorable to the plaintiff than the offer of judgment, the plaintiff must pay the defendant's costs incurred after the offer. The rationale for the rule is to encourage another thoughtful analysis of the case and possible settlement before accruing the added costs of trial. The Rule 68 approach of shifting the costs of trial to an unreasonable party is not just limited to civil court actions, but also applies to arbitrations in some states.

Exhibit 10.14 identifies some of the differences between arbitration and mediation.

EARLY CASE ASSESSMENT

Most federal courts have implemented early case assessment or early neutral evaluation programs. These programs attempt to head off the substantial expense of discovery by having a neutral court employee, an appointed attorney with pertinent expertise, or a different judge facilitate the exchange of only the information that

Med-arb

A combination of mediation and arbitration; the matter is first mediated, then any unresolved issue is decided by the same or a different person who serves as an arbitrator.

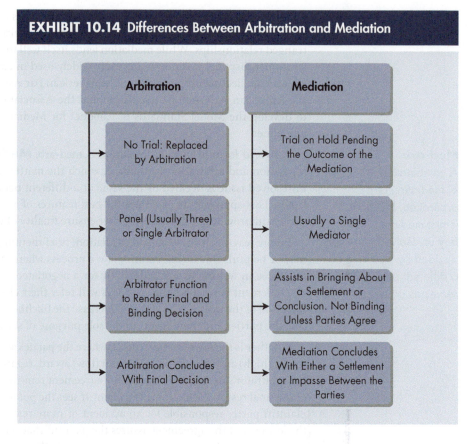

EXHIBIT 10.14 Differences Between Arbitration and Mediation

Arbitration	Mediation
No Trial: Replaced by Arbitration	Trial on Hold Pending the Outcome of the Mediation
Panel (Usually Three) or Single Arbitrator	Usually a Single Mediator
Arbitrator Function to Render Final and Binding Decision	Assists in Bringing About a Settlement or Conclusion. Not Binding Unless Parties Agree
Arbitration Concludes With Final Decision	Mediation Concludes With Either a Settlement or Impasse Between the Parties

summary trial

A nonbinding, abbreviated trial before a summary jury to see whether either side's case merits a real trial; encourages settlement of especially large cases.

INTERNET EXERCISE

Research your jurisdiction's rules on summary trials. Identify the civil rule of procedure or statute that permits summary trials. Outline the process for summary trials in your jurisdiction. Place your outline in your systems folder for future reference.

is key to resolving the dispute. After this minimal exchange, the parties may enter mediation for a resolution of the case. These programs have been quite successful in settling cases before expensive discovery occurs.

SUMMARY JURY TRIAL

Courts also utilize the **summary trial**. Used most often in expensive, complex trials, its purpose is to let both sides try the key points of their respective cases before a small jury in an abbreviated format. The purpose of a summary trial is to get at the results quickly, and then encourage the parties to settle the case on the basis of the additional information. Summary trials have a way of pointing out theories and evidence that will not work in fact, despite their appeal on paper. When this happens, settlement often occurs and much time and money are saved. The summary trial verdict, however, is not binding, and the case may still go to a full trial.

ROLE OF THE PARALEGAL IN ALTERNATIVE DISPUTE RESOLUTION

You may find that a case you are working on goes to arbitration, mediation, or some other ADR procedure. Or an attorney in the office becomes the arbitrator or mediator in a case and requires your assistance. In such circumstances your role will be similar to the role you normally play in preparing for settlement—that is, gathering facts, cooperating with the other side on a form of discovery, and drafting and filing necessary documents to start an action and present it at a hearing. You may work with witnesses in some cases, research the client's best choice of arbitrators or mediators, and research and draft summaries of evidence that can be similar to settlement packets or briefs. Most of your tasks in ADR are similar in technique to what you do in trial or settlement preparation, only abbreviated for alternative dispute resolution.

In some instances experienced paralegals may serve as layperson mediators. Should you become involved in assisting in a mediation or arbitration process, keep in mind that forms and procedures and names of arbitrators and mediators can be obtained from sponsoring associations such as the American Arbitration Association, Neighborhood Justice Forums, the Federal Mediation and Conciliation Service, National Academy of Arbitrators, local and federal courts, chambers of commerce, landlord/tenant associations, and others. The entire area of alternative dispute resolution, including efforts to negotiate a settlement, can be an exciting endeavor, especially when you realize that your work has resulted in the resolution of a conflict without the cost in time, money, and emotional trauma often associated with a court trial.

SUMMARY

Chapter 10 focuses on the resolution of civil cases without trial. Under the umbrella of alternative dispute resolution (ADR), this chapter addresses settlement, procedures that encourage settlement such as pretrial and settlement conferences, the summary trial, early case assessment, and the alternatives to litigation offered by arbitration and mediation. You serve the client in each procedure by gathering and organizing pertinent information and by drafting persuasive and other necessary documents.

Settlement is the traditional method of ending a case through the negotiation and agreement of the parties. It is facilitated by summarizing the collected facts and carefully totaling the damages. You may be asked to prepare a presentation of this summary in the form of a settlement request. The request can be brief in small cases or involve the preparation of a detailed settlement brochure in more complex cases. The request, regardless of size, normally includes a summary of the facts and the evidence to support those facts, background of the injured party, description of injuries or damage, impact or consequences, a summary of the actual cost in dollars of the damages, and a proposed settlement amount. It becomes the task of the defense paralegal to examine such proposals with a fine-toothed comb and to note weaknesses, inaccuracies, and inconsistencies in the settlement request.

The pretrial conference is a meeting of the opposing lawyers in the case and the judge. Its purpose is to decide what issues remain to be tried and whether the parties can reach a settlement. Again by utilizing a system and checklist approach, you can assist the attorney in preparing for the conference. The process for a settlement conference is similar. If a settlement agreement is reached, the necessary releases, covenants, settlement agreement, and other documents must be drafted and filed. Some courts—in complex cases in which settlement has not been reached—use abbreviated summary trials to identify additional motivation for settlement.

Disputes are being resolved at an increasing rate through arbitration and mediation to keep costs down, reduce the time for ending a dispute, minimize adversarial confrontation, and keep large numbers of cases off the court trial dockets. In arbitration the parties ask a neutral third party to decide the dispute; in mediation the parties utilize a third party to help them work together to come up with a solution to their dispute. Med-arb combines the best features of both arbitration and mediation to bring a dispute to a conclusion. Collaborative law, high-low agreements, and Rule 68 offers of judgment also enhance the dispute resolution effectiveness.

KEY TERMS

adjudication on the merits	mediation	settlement précis
alternative dispute resolution (ADR)	release	summary trial
arbitration	settlement	with prejudice
med-arb	settlement agreement	without prejudice
	settlement conference	

QUESTIONS FOR STUDY AND REVIEW

1. What is a settlement?

2. What is your role in the settlement process?

3. What are the ethical considerations applicable to the settlement process? Why are they important?

4. What must be investigated and summarized in preparing for settlement? Why is this information necessary?

5. What kinds of information needed in preparing for settlement and in evaluating a case can be obtained from a reference librarian or online service?

6. During the settlement process, what are the goals of communication with clients? With insurance adjusters?

7. What formulas and processes are utilized to calculate various kinds of damages?

8. How do hedonic damages differ from pain and suffering?

9. What is included in a settlement brochure and a settlement letter or précis? What is the difference between the two and the primary reason for the difference?

10. What is the definition and purpose of a pretrial conference? What Federal Rule applies? What state rule applies?

11. What things should you do to assist the attorney in preparing for the pretrial conference?

12. What is an authorization to negotiate (compromise), and why is its execution by the client important?

13. What are the contents and what is the purpose of a release? A settlement agreement?

14. What is ADR and its advantages and disadvantages?

15. In general, explain the paralegal role in ADR processes.

SYSTEMS FOLDER ASSIGNMENTS

1. In the ethics section of your systems folder, add page references to ethical considerations for the settlement process, the cited sections of the Model Rules of Professional Conduct, and the rules or ethical standards in your state.

2. Draft a checklist of or enter text page references to the items that need to be researched and summarized in preparation for settlement. Indicate the sources for such information. Place the checklist in the settlement section of your systems folder.

3. Place a page reference or copies of the Pretrial Conference Preparation Checklist and the attorney's authorization from the client to settle in your systems folder.

4. Locate three examples of settlement agreements. Review the provisions and identify the common provisions in each for future reference.

5. Your attorney has asked you to find examples of mediation and arbitration provisions that may potentially be used in a settlement agreement. Locate five sample provisions for her review and place them in your systems folder.

APPLICATION ASSIGNMENTS

1. What factors either favoring or discouraging settlement do you see present in the *Forrester* case? Discuss.

2. Draft an outline of the contents of a settlement brochure for the *Forrester* case indicating what should appear and in what order. Compare your list of components and discuss the advantages of each in small groups with class members. Make a list of the typical components of a settlement brochure and place it in your systems folder.

3. By researching your state statutes and local federal rules, determine whether your state has a provision for arbitration or mediation. If so, determine what types of cases and dispute amounts are considered for the program. If your state has no such system, write a proposal to your local or state bar association on why you believe there should or shouldn't be such a system. Discuss and defend your proposals in class.

4. Assume that the Congletons, the campground owners in Case II, are told by you that their attorney, your supervisor, advises them to agree to settle their case by paying Mr. Ameche $60,000. The Congletons say no and want to go to trial. Your attorney believes that the jury will hold the Congletons liable for $150,000.

   a. Considering that lawyers are supposed to exercise their independent judgment, may the attorney ethically accept the offer since it is such a good one?

   b. Are there any other ethical concerns raised in this scenario?

5. What are the primary reasons for the use of alternative dispute resolution? Now, applying your reasoning, assume that Teeny Tiny Manufacturing and Briar Patch Dolls from case scenario IV agree to arbitrate or mediate their dispute. To whom might they turn for assistance? How can this assistance be located?

CASE ASSIGNMENTS

1. Using your imagination and creativity, prepare the settlement précis or letter from Mrs. Forrester to Mercury Parcel Services, Inc. and Richard Hart. Prepare a joint letter to Mercury Parcel and Mr. Hart and then prepare individual letters to both defendants.

2. (a) Assume that Mr. Hart has agreed to the terms of your settlement. Draft the settlement documents between Mrs. Forrester and Mr. Hart.

   (b) For purposes of this case assignment, assume that Mercury Parcel and their insurance company has agreed to settle with Mrs. Forrester. Mercury has agreed to pay the maximum limits under its insurance policy and will admit that Mrs. Forrester was not negligent, but also will not admit their liability. Prepare the final settlement documents between Mercury and Mrs. Forrester. Be creative in preparing your document. Review other settlement agreements to determine the types of provisions that should be included in the document.

TRIAL PREPARATION AND TRIAL

OUTLINE

OBJECTIVES

AFTER READING THIS CHAPTER, YOU WILL BE ABLE TO:

- Determine the preliminary tasks in preparation for trial
- Prepare witness subpoenas
- Identify different sources to locate information on prospective jurors
- Outline the necessary components of a trial notebook
- Understand the role of a paralegal during the trial process

TRIAL PREPARATION

INTRODUCTION AND TRIAL PREPARATION CHECKLIST

Late yesterday afternoon Mr. White said that despite all our efforts, it did not appear that the *Forrester* case was going to settle, and that we should begin our final preparation for trial. The trial date, set at the pretrial conference, is two months from yesterday. It will be your job to perform much of the preparation and to assist Mr. White at trial. Good trial work is based on thorough preparation; much of that responsibility rests in your hands.

Use the trial preparation checklist (Exhibit 11.1), adapting it to the unique features of each case. The remaining materials will help explain what must be done at each step on the checklist. Study the checklist, carefully noting each task.

EXHIBIT 11.1 Trial Preparation Checklist

At Least Three Months Prior to Trial

☐ If a trial has not yet been set, check with the attorney and file any request or praecipe needed to have trial date set.
☐ Calendar the trial date, unless done previously, and check for any scheduling conflicts.
☐ Check case status sheet and calendar more frequent updatings right up to trial.
☐ Check to see that all required disclosure to date has been completed, including exchange of expert witness names and written report (federal rules).
☐ Check time deadline chart and confirm that key dates are calendared and that litigation team members are reminded.
☐ Meet with team to assess need for special exhibits and technology at trial.

At Least Six Weeks Prior to Trial

☐ Meet with litigation team to review case status and establish countdown work schedule.
☐ Review the case status sheet and keep it updated in the file. Inform the attorney of any depositions, discovery, or other steps needing completion or updating.
☐ Review the facts of the case to determine if there is a need to amend the pleadings.
    ☐ Keep the client fully informed. Meet as needed.
    ☐ Prepare witnesses' statements or witness sheets.
    ☐ Highlight important facts both for and adverse to client.
☐ Review pretrial order to determine if the issues have been narrowed.
    ☐ List documents, exhibits, and witnesses needed on each point, including refutation of the opponent's key points and evidence.
☐ See that legal memoranda have been completed on all questions of law including any likely questions relating to the admissibility of evidence or any motions likely to be made at trial.

At Least Three Weeks Prior to Trial

☐ Prepare a list of all witnesses needed; confirm with the attorney and have subpoenas prepared and served.
☐ Conduct the jury investigation.
☐ Conduct an investigation of the judge, the opposing attorney, and the community if not previously done.

EXHIBIT 11.1 Trial Preparation Checklist (continued)

☐ Prepare any exhibits, diagrams, audiovisual aids.
☐ Visit courtroom to determine general set-up and electronic capabilities, such as electrical outlets and accessibility.
☐ Check with clerk or appropriate court personnel to determine process for electronics and any other needs, such as monitors, graphs, white boards and audio capabilities.
☐ Acquire necessary tools and electronics based upon courtroom set-up.

At Least One Week Prior to Trial

☐ Verify the court date.
☐ Complete the trial notebook.
☐ Verify service of all subpoenas.
☐ Prepare client and witnesses for testimony.
☐ Make final arrangements for the following:
    ☐ Lodging of the client, witnesses, and staff as needed.
    ☐ Payment of lost wages for witnesses if committed by the attorney.
    ☐ Transportation of all files, documents, audiovisual equipment, computer terminal, and other items needed at trial.
    ☐ Petty cash needed for parking, meals, phone calls, and so on.
☐ Verify courtroom readiness for trial needs.

One Day Before Trial
Check and verify one last time for courtroom readiness for trial needs.

☐ Meet one last time with the trial team.
☐ Meet with the client.

PRELIMINARY TRIAL PREPARATION TASKS

You should confirm the exact trial date and time if available. Some judges, however, do not set specific times. They follow a docket list for a one- or two-month period, and as cases set for trial are either settled or tried, the client's case moves up on the docket. Where such a system is used, the attorney can normally guess the approximate day of the trial, but you need to keep the attorney and all witnesses informed as the court docket progresses. Court dockets are often accessible online. The date and time must be calendared with related reminder dates for the completion of various tasks prior to the trial.

Well before trial, verify that all disclosure to date, as set out in the applicable rules or in the court's scheduling order, is complete. About 90 days before trial is a good time for the litigation team to meet to review the status of the case and to assess the need for the preparation of trial exhibits and other courtroom presentations, especially if the presentation will be high tech.

Although trial preparation time frames vary with the complexity of the case, at least six weeks prior to trial check the case status sheet to verify that all necessary investigation and discovery are complete. Exhibit 11.2 is an example of a case status sheet.

The case status sheet, or its computerized equivalent, should be set up early in the case and reviewed monthly, and possibly weekly within the last six weeks before trial. The attorney should be informed on any matters that are outstanding, so the necessary action can be taken.

EXHIBIT 11.2 Case Status Sheet

Trial date: Case name and no.:
Client: (plaintiff, defendant)   Defendant:
Attorney: Court:
Paralegal: Date filed:
Date client interviewed: Judge:

PLEADINGS AND MOTIONS ON PLEADINGS

Description	Date filed and served	Response date	Check if met	Hearing date
Complaint				
Motion to dismiss				
Answer and counterclaim				
Motions				
Reply				
Amended pleadings (list)/dates filed/response date				

Default: Date: Judgment for default: Date

Jury trial demanded   ☐ yes   ☐ no

INVESTIGATION

Signify investigations to be conducted and witnesses to interview

☐ Done/date:
☐ Done/date:
☐ Done/date:

DISCOVERY

Interrogatories

	Date served	Due date	Response date served	Motion to object or compel
Plaintiff's				
Defendant's				

Depositions (by plaintiff)

Deponent/date	Notice/fee	Subpoena/fee	Location	Court reporter	Done
					☐
					☐
					☐

Depositions (by defendant)

					☐
					☐
					☐

Request for Production of Documents and Things (Plaintiff's)

Describe	Served	Due	Answer/served	Objections/motions	Conducted	Copies delivered
					☐	☐

(Defendant's)

					☐	☐

EXHIBIT 11.2 Case Status Sheet (*continued*)

Request for Mandatory Physical Examination   ☐ yes   ☐ no

Person examined: Date: Physician:

Request for Admissions (Plaintiff's)

Served	Due	Answer/served	Objections/motion to compel	
				☐
				☐
				☐

(Defendant's)

				☐
				☐
				☐

MOTIONS

Describe	Notice	Served	Response	Argued	Result

CASE EVALUATED

Plaintiff's damages: Total:

Other notes:

PRETRIAL CONFERENCE

Date: Judge:

Preparation (describe):   Done

                                                      ☐

                                                      ☐

Notes on result:

SETTLEMENT

Settlement précis or brochure   ☐

Date: Terms:

Releases/settlement agreement   ☐

Stipulation, consent decree, order for dismissal   ☐

Settlement distribution statement   ☐

FINAL PRETRIAL

Witness	Address	Subpoenaed	Fees
Jury Investigation			☐
Preparation of Exhibits and Diagrams			
			☐
			☐

(continued)

EXHIBIT 11.2 Case Status Sheet (*continued*)

Preparation of Trial Notebook (Proof chart, voir dire questions, witness sheets, legal research, motions, jury instructions, etc.)   ☐

Preparation of Witnesses, Including Experts   ☐

Final Arrangements (Lodging, meals, parking, petty cash, transportation of trial materials)   ☐

Trial Date: Verdict/Date: Judgment/Date:

Motions: Served   Reply due   Reply

☐

☐

APPEAL

Notice filed: ☐

Order transcript and preparation of record   ☐

File brief: Plaintiff/date   Defendant/date

Oral argument: Date:

Court Decision

Motion for reconsideration: ☐

Bill of costs   ☐

Review the file, the case evaluation sheets, summaries and digests of information, witness sheets, and so on to see that all is in order and the issues are clearly in mind. Case management and litigation support software, as previously noted, enhance this preparation process. A discussion with the attorney and other litigation team members at this point to verify the issues (possibly narrowed by the pretrial conference), and to review the evidence, exhibits, and documents needed for each issue would be helpful in better completing the tasks to follow.

The attorney should pinpoint the need for any further research on legal questions as well, in preparation for motions either before or during trial and to deal with objections or arguments that might arise at trial. These items should be researched and any memoranda or rough drafts should be completed. The writing of some of these may be assigned to you depending on the personal preference of the attorney. Memorandum preparation is good work for paralegals well versed in research skills. Offering to do this kind of work is one way to enhance your value to the law firm.

SUBPOENA WITNESSES: DON'T ASSUME YOUR WITNESS WILL SHOW UP!

The client and friendly witnesses should be informed as soon as possible about the trial date and when they will be expected to testify. Client and witness preparation sessions should be calendared at this time so the client or witness can be notified of the trial and preparation session dates. The availability for trial of each witness should be determined.

The attorney should be consulted to finalize the list of witnesses to be called on behalf of the client. Some attorneys prefer to subpoena only the witnesses who are not considered friendly; however, the best practice is to subpoena all the witnesses needed for your case. Do so unless instructed otherwise. Some witnesses prefer to be subpoenaed so that it can be made clear that they have been ordered to testify, especially if the witness has a business or friendly relationship with both parties of the lawsuit and wants to remain, or at least appear, neutral. A subpoena also gives the witness something to show an employer for the absence from work. It is a good idea to explain to each witness the necessity of serving them with a subpoena.

Subpoenas for trial are obtained and served in the same way they are obtained and served for depositions. The following are important points to remember:

1. Service of subpoenas is covered in Rule 45 and parallel state and local rules.

2. Local rules and procedures for the issuing and service of trial subpoenas should be reviewed.

3. The clerk of the court issues the subpoena signed and sealed but otherwise blank in most state courts. Attorneys can issue subpoenas in federal court [Rule 45(a)(3)].

4. In most jurisdictions any person over 18 years of age can serve subpoenas. Professional process servers may be used.

5. It is best to read the subpoena to the person being served.

6. The subpoena is not valid until it is personally served on the witness, the required witness and mileage fees are tendered, and the return of service is completed and filed with the court (28 U.S.C. § 1821). Normally only the first day's fee plus round trip mileage is tendered.

7. Check with the clerk for amount of fee and mileage.

8. If a subpoena is issued on behalf of the United States or its officer or agency, fee and mileage need not be tendered.

9. Subpoenas reach to the boundaries of the state for both state and federal court trials. Hardship exceptions may be made in some circumstances. Subpoenas are valid outside the federal district to within 100 miles of the place of trial or as specifically authorized by the pertinent federal statute.

10. A witness in a foreign country is subpoenaed pursuant to 28 U.S.C. § 1783.

11. A subpoena duces tecum must describe documents with reasonable certainty— that is, so they can be identified without an extensive search. Wording such as "every" or "all" is suspect.

12. If a subpoena is directed to a corporation, it is best to name the corporate official in charge of the specific documents.

INTERNET EXERCISE

Determine the procedure for obtaining a trial subpoena under your state's rules of civil procedure. Note the differences between your state and federal rules.

13. Subpoenas are generally valid for the date or dates entered on them and for the remainder of the trial unless the person subpoenaed is dismissed by the court or the party that subpoenaed the person.

14. Subpoenas remain in effect for continuances and postponements.

15. Subpoenas need to be reissued if there is a change of venue.

16. A subpoena can be challenged as insufficient, oppressive, or unreasonable through a motion to quash, vacate, or modify. Exhibit 11.3 is an example of a subpoena form for a witness in federal court.

At least one week prior to trial, verify that all subpoenas have been served. Occasionally a subpoena will have to be obtained at the last minute of the last working day before trial. In such a situation, the relationship that you have nurtured with court personnel will pay off. Keep a record to show that all subpoenas have been obtained, served with amounts of fees paid, and returns have been filed with the clerk, if required.

JURY INVESTIGATION

Introduction

Regardless of the size of the case, if a jury has been requested, some investigation of the jury will be needed. The extent of that investigation depends on the nature and size of the case. The degree that you will be involved varies, but this area is another in which you can assume responsibility.

The purpose of the jury investigation is to gather the best possible information on each prospective juror and that juror's likely response to the issues in the case. The information will guide the attorney during **voir dire** (which means to speak the truth), when the jurors are selected at trial. The overall purpose is to rid the jury of those persons biased against or not likely to be sympathetic with your client, and to shield or protect the selection of those individuals who are likely to favor your client.

Exhibit 11.4 is a juror data sheet. It can serve as a summary sheet for the attorney before and at trial, as well as your checklist in determining what information should be gathered. Check with the attorney to see if special concerns or information are needed in addition to that requested on the form.

voir dire

The questioning of potential jurors by the judge (and attorneys in state court) to reveal disqualifying information in the process of selecting an impartial jury.

Sources for Juror Information

The amount of information a paralegal is asked to gather and the money that can be spent gathering it is proportional to the size and significance of the case. The following sources are listed in approximate order from the least expensive to most expensive. Choose appropriate methods in consultation with the attorney.

a. *Jury Panel List.* A list of the names of all jurors for the upcoming term can be obtained from the clerk of court's office. This list may not be available in some jurisdictions.

b. *Juror Information Sheets.* These forms are filled out by each juror providing a minimum of information on background, marital status, education, occupation, previous jury service, and litigation. They may be copied or reviewed in the

EXHIBIT 11.3 Subpoena Form

AO 88 (Rev. 02/14) Subpoena to Appear and Testify at a Hearing or Trial in a Civil Action

UNITED STATES DISTRICT COURT
for the

_____ District of _____

_____ *Plaintiff* v. _____ *Defendant*	))) Civil Action No. _____))

SUBPOENA TO APPEAR AND TESTIFY
AT A HEARING OR TRIAL IN A CIVIL ACTION

To: _____

(Name of person to whom this subpoena is directed)

YOU ARE COMMANDED to appear in the United States district court at the time, date, and place set forth below to testify at a hearing or trial in this civil action. When you arrive, you must remain at the court until the judge or a court officer allows you to leave.

Place:	Courtroom No.:
	Date and Time:

You must also bring with you the following documents, electronically stored information, or objects *(leave blank if not applicable)*:

The following provisions of Fed. R. Civ. P. 45 are attached – Rule 45(c), relating to the place of compliance; Rule 45(d), relating to your protection as a person subject to a subpoena; and Rule 45(e) and (g), relating to your duty to respond to this subpoena and the potential consequences of not doing so.

Date: _____

CLERK OF COURT

OR

_____   _____
  Signature of Clerk or Deputy Clerk   *Attorney's signature*

The name, address, e-mail address, and telephone number of the attorney representing *(name of party)* _____
_____ , who issues or requests this subpoena, are:

Notice to the person who issues or requests this subpoena
If this subpoena commands the production of documents, electronically stored information, or tangible things before trial, a notice and a copy of the subpoena must be served on each party in this case before it is served on the person to whom it is directed. Fed. R. Civ. P. 45(a)(4).

(continued)

EXHIBIT 11.3 Subpoena Form (*continued*)

AO 88 (Rev. 02/14) Subpoena to Appear and Testify at a Hearing or Trial in a Civil Action (page 2)

Civil Action No.

PROOF OF SERVICE
(This section should not be filed with the court unless required by Fed. R. Civ. P. 45.)

I received this subpoena for *(name of individual and title, if any)* _____

on *(date)* _____ .

☐ I served the subpoena by delivering a copy to the named person as follows: _____

_____

_____ on *(date)* _____ ; or

☐ I returned the subpoena unexecuted because: _____

_____ .

Unless the subpoena was issued on behalf of the United States, or one of its officers or agents, I have also
tendered to the witness the fees for one day's attendance, and the mileage allowed by law, in the amount of

$ _____ .

My fees are $ _____ for travel and $ _____ for services, for a total of $ _____ .

I declare under penalty of perjury that this information is true.

Date: _____   _____
                                                                   Server's signature

                                                               _____
                                                                   Printed name and title

                                                               _____
                                                                   Server's address

Additional information regarding attempted service, etc.:

| Print | Save As... | Add Attachment | | Reset |

EXHIBIT 11.3 Subpoena Form (*continued*)

AO 88 (Rev. 02/14) Subpoena to Appear and Testify at a Hearing or Trial in a Civil Action (page 3)

Federal Rule of Civil Procedure 45 (c), (d), (e), and (g) (Effective 12/1/13)

(c) Place of Compliance.

(1) *For a Trial, Hearing, or Deposition.* A subpoena may command a person to attend a trial, hearing, or deposition only as follows:
(A) within 100 miles of where the person resides, is employed, or regularly transacts business in person; or
(B) within the state where the person resides, is employed, or regularly transacts business in person, if the person
(i) is a party or a party's officer; or
(ii) is commanded to attend a trial and would not incur substantial expense.

(2) *For Other Discovery.* A subpoena may command:
(A) production of documents, electronically stored information, or tangible things at a place within 100 miles of where the person resides, is employed, or regularly transacts business in person; and
(B) inspection of premises at the premises to be inspected.

(d) Protecting a Person Subject to a Subpoena; Enforcement.

(1) *Avoiding Undue Burden or Expense; Sanctions.* A party or attorney responsible for issuing and serving a subpoena must take reasonable steps to avoid imposing undue burden or expense on a person subject to the subpoena. The court for the district where compliance is required must enforce this duty and impose an appropriate sanction—which may include lost earnings and reasonable attorney's fees—on a party or attorney who fails to comply.

(2) *Command to Produce Materials or Permit Inspection.*
(A) *Appearance Not Required.* A person commanded to produce documents, electronically stored information, or tangible things, or to permit the inspection of premises, need not appear in person at the place of production or inspection unless also commanded to appear for a deposition, hearing, or trial.
(B) *Objections.* A person commanded to produce documents or tangible things or to permit inspection may serve on the party or attorney designated in the subpoena a written objection to inspecting, copying, testing, or sampling any or all of the materials or to inspecting the premises—or to producing electronically stored information in the form or forms requested. The objection must be served before the earlier of the time specified for compliance or 14 days after the subpoena is served. If an objection is made, the following rules apply:
(i) At any time, on notice to the commanded person, the serving party may move the court for the district where compliance is required for an order compelling production or inspection.
(ii) These acts may be required only as directed in the order, and the order must protect a person who is neither a party nor a party's officer from significant expense resulting from compliance.

(3) *Quashing or Modifying a Subpoena.*
(A) *When Required.* On timely motion, the court for the district where compliance is required must quash or modify a subpoena that:
(i) fails to allow a reasonable time to comply;
(ii) requires a person to comply beyond the geographical limits specified in Rule 45(c);
(iii) requires disclosure of privileged or other protected matter, if no exception or waiver applies; or
(iv) subjects a person to undue burden.
(B) *When Permitted.* To protect a person subject to or affected by a subpoena, the court for the district where compliance is required may, on motion, quash or modify the subpoena if it requires:
(i) disclosing a trade secret or other confidential research, development, or commercial information; or

(ii) disclosing an unretained expert's opinion or information that does not describe specific occurrences in dispute and results from the expert's study that was not requested by a party.
(C) *Specifying Conditions as an Alternative.* In the circumstances described in Rule 45(d)(3)(B), the court may, instead of quashing or modifying a subpoena, order appearance or production under specified conditions if the serving party:
(i) shows a substantial need for the testimony or material that cannot be otherwise met without undue hardship; and
(ii) ensures that the subpoenaed person will be reasonably compensated.

(e) Duties in Responding to a Subpoena.

(1) *Producing Documents or Electronically Stored Information.* These procedures apply to producing documents or electronically stored information:
(A) *Documents.* A person responding to a subpoena to produce documents must produce them as they are kept in the ordinary course of business or must organize and label them to correspond to the categories in the demand.
(B) *Form for Producing Electronically Stored Information Not Specified.* If a subpoena does not specify a form for producing electronically stored information, the person responding must produce it in a form or forms in which it is ordinarily maintained or in a reasonably usable form or forms.
(C) *Electronically Stored Information Produced in Only One Form.* The person responding need not produce the same electronically stored information in more than one form.
(D) *Inaccessible Electronically Stored Information.* The person responding need not provide discovery of electronically stored information from sources that the person identifies as not reasonably accessible because of undue burden or cost. On motion to compel discovery or for a protective order, the person responding must show that the information is not reasonably accessible because of undue burden or cost. If that showing is made, the court may nonetheless order discovery from such sources if the requesting party shows good cause, considering the limitations of Rule 26(b)(2)(C). The court may specify conditions for the discovery.

(2) *Claiming Privilege or Protection.*
(A) *Information Withheld.* A person withholding subpoenaed information under a claim that it is privileged or subject to protection as trial-preparation material must:
(i) expressly make the claim; and
(ii) describe the nature of the withheld documents, communications, or tangible things in a manner that, without revealing information itself privileged or protected, will enable the parties to assess the claim.
(B) *Information Produced.* If information produced in response to a subpoena is subject to a claim of privilege or of protection as trial-preparation material, the person making the claim may notify any party that received the information of the claim and the basis for it. After being notified, a party must promptly return, sequester, or destroy the specified information and any copies it has; must not use or disclose the information until the claim is resolved; must take reasonable steps to retrieve the information if the party disclosed it before being notified; and may promptly present the information under seal to the court for the district where compliance is required for a determination of the claim. The person who produced the information must preserve the information until the claim is resolved.

(g) Contempt.
The court for the district where compliance is required—and also, after a motion is transferred, the issuing court—may hold in contempt a person who, having been served, fails without adequate excuse to obey the subpoena or an order related to it.

For access to subpoena materials, see Fed. R. Civ. P. 45(a) Committee Note (2013).

Source: U.S. Courts.

EXHIBIT 11.4 Juror Data Sheet

Case: File no: Court: Date:

Attorney: Paralegal:
_____

Juror no. _____ Name: Aliases:

Overall Evaluation: Good _____ Bad _____ ? _____

Place and date of birth: Race: Ethnic group:

Address:

Previous addresses (list most recent first):

Grew up at:

Home phone: Work phone:

Employment (list most recent first):

Occupation: Employer: Address: Phone: Dates:

Present annual income:

Highest level of education completed: Date:

Health:

Marital status: single: married: divorced: widowed: remarried:

Immediate family

    Parents: Age: Occupation/education:

    Where lived most of life: Current address

    Spouse: Age: Occupation/education:

    Children: Age: Occupation/education:

    Grandchildren: Age: Occupation/education:

Juror's political affiliation: Rep ( )   Dem ( )   Ind ( )

                                 Liberal ( )   Middle of road ( )   Conservative ( )

Juror's professional and service associations:

    Veteran:

    Religious affiliation: Active: Inactive:

Hobbies and activities:

Friends and relatives:

Financial concerns in case:

Relationship to parties:

EXHIBIT 11.4 Juror Data Sheet (*continued*)

Prior jury service: Where: When:

   Type of case: Verdict: Foreperson:

Previous or current litigation: Plaintiff: Defendant:

   Where: When: Type: Outcome:

Close family or friend involved in litigation: Plaintiff: Defendant:

   Where: When: Type: Outcome

Prior experiences related to trial and issues: (for example, ever injured in an accident, ever at fault in

accident)

Assessment of opinion on: Issues:

   Source of information: Survey: Fellow workers: Other:

Assessment of jury leadership potential and strength of personality:

   Source of information:

      Record of juror on current panel:

      Overall evaluation: Good: Bad: ?:

      Explanation:

      Additional comments:

clerk's office and are a good source of information with minimal copying cost and inconvenience. The American Bar Association recommends that judges permit lawyers to expand the jury information sheet with jury questions, especially in complex cases (ABA Civil Trial Practice Standards, Standard 1, 1998). Such questions go beyond the typical limited background information to solicit views and experiences that could impact a case or trial strategy. Useful in the *Forrester* case, for example, would be questions about the juror's opinion of proper training for truck drivers, whether the juror had ever had to care for a seriously ill or injured person, whether the juror ever worked for an insurance company or conducted claims evaluations, and on the importance of partial but lesser fault to assigning liability in an unrelated accident scenario. Juror information sheets or questionnaires can be customized for any type of litigation. The key is determining what, out of a list of possibilities, are the most critical things to learn.

c. *Internet Research.* With a juror's name and background, including affiliations, search that person's name, website, and sites of relevant organizations for valuable, inexpensive information.

d. *Voter Registration Lists.* Available in the county clerk's offices, these lists provide information on political party affiliation where such information is required by law.

e. *Co-workers, Friends, Others.* Sometimes your co-workers, attorneys, paralegals, relatives, friends, and others may be able to recognize the names of people on the jury list and provide valuable information. It is not uncommon in a small town for a few people to know practically everyone. Sometimes a friend of a friend can tap into that information. If attorneys or paralegals in another firm have recently had experience with this jury panel, they might also be willing to provide some insights. The client might be able to help, or have friends or relatives that can help.

f. *Clerk of Court Personnel.* If you are on particularly good terms with one or more of the local clerk's staff, that person might prove helpful.

g. *Jury Files Kept by Law Firms.* Some law firms keep extensive records on jurors. Information on particular jurors may often be purchased from these firms.

h. *Professional Jury Services.* Usually in big cities, these services compile extensive background information on prospective jurors and conduct a thorough investigation of specific jurors on request. These services can be valuable, but are expensive.

i. *Jury Surveys.* These extensive phone surveys are more or less scientifically based. If the law firm does not have the internal expertise, a consultant on surveying techniques should be employed to guarantee an accurate random sampling of the prospective community and to assure that questions are worded to elicit accurate and meaningful responses. Such a survey reaches only qualified jurors; their religion, occupation, and other background is recorded. The responses can then be evaluated by types or categories of persons, providing some information on how that type of person would vote as a member of the jury. Depending on how it is done and who does it, a survey like this can be quite expensive to conduct and to analyze, but can be useful for general guidance. If you are asked to conduct such a survey, a good source to consult is *Jurywork: Systematic Techniques*, 2nd, 2014–2015 ed. prepared by the NJP Litigation Consulting (formerly National Jury Project) in cooperation with the National Lawyers' Guild and National Conference of Black Lawyers.

j. *Employment of Psychologists and Other Experts.* Some firms may choose to send a synopsis of the case to a psychologist, social scientist, or other jury selection consultants to evaluate and give advice on what type of person should be chosen and what type should be avoided. This process can be helpful but expensive. Nationally recognized resources include NJP Litigation Consulting (formerly National Jury Project), The Jury Research Institute, and Decision Quest.

k. *Mock Juries.* Some firms employ mock juries or focus groups. A scaled-down version of the trial is held or a summary of the key issues is presented to persons who represent the expected composition of the jury. After their decision, the jurors are questioned at length about why they decided as they did and what impressed them the most and the least. This simulation helps the firm make decisions on what jurors to select, what theory of the case works best, and how to improve their presentation.

l. *Social Media, Blogs, and other Internet sites.* Social media sites, such as Facebook, Twitter, LinkedIn, and others are a means to acquire information about prospective jurors, but there are limitations. A juror's general Internet presence is fair inquiry, but any communications with a prospective juror must be done pursuant to current ethical standards. This issue is addressed in the ethical considerations for this chapter. Blogs are generally readily accessible and may not create the ethical concerns as social media sites which have

APPLY YOUR KNOWLEDGE

Locate a copy of ABA Opinion 466 and outline the issues it raises. Determine whether your state or local bar associations have issued ethics opinions on what is considered an *ex parte* communication with a prospective juror through the use of social media or the Internet. Place the ethical opinions in your systems folder.

ETHICAL CONSIDERATIONS: SOCIAL MEDIA AND JUROR INFORMATION

Social media and one's Internet presence is a boon for information, but for attorneys and legal professionals examining prospective jurors' backgrounds can blur the lines between ethical and unethical behavior. The issue as to how far attorneys and legal professionals can delve into a prospective juror's postings raises many concerns. Can an attorney or hired professional "friend" a prospective juror to learn more about that person? How far can legal professionals investigate a prospective juror before crossing ethical boundaries? The answers to these questions has been recently answered by the American Bar Association (ABA) Formal (ethics) Opinion 466 stating that such acts as friending a prospective juror amounts to an *ex parte* contact and violates the rules of ethics. Under the ABA Model Rule 3.5, *ex parte* communication with a prospective juror is prohibited either directly or through another person or entity. What this means is that a legal professional cannot send an access request to a prospective juror. If a prospective juror has privacy settings and a legal professional attempts to contact that juror, this is a potential violation of the rules of ethics.

What the opinion also addressed was the discovery of jury misconduct through the attorney or legal professional's Internet search. The opinion cited Model Rule 3.3, which requires disclosure to the court or tribunal of the discovered misconduct. Additionally, courts have addressed this issue through standing orders, jury instructions, and other judicial means to curb potential violations of ethical rules by either legal professionals or prospective jurors. Since technology changes so rapidly, attorneys and paralegals should be mindful of the rapid transformation of the Internet and its sites. With these changes, ethical questions arise. As a paralegal you should keep abreast of the social media and Internet issues that persist in the ethics area for legal professionals.

privacy restrictions. Keep checking your state's ethical opinions and other professional sites for guidance on using Internet-related sites as sources for juror information.

When investigating jurors, remember that it is unethical to have any direct contact with a juror. Take every precaution to avoid having jurors become aware that they are being investigated. This awareness not only might disturb some jurors, but also can cause reactions potentially damaging to the firm and the client.

All the information on a particular juror should be recorded and summarized for quick reference by the attorney. Be prepared to add your own evaluation of the juror to such a summary sheet, if requested. Summary sheets will be used at trial. A case where a motion for new trial was granted due to a prospective juror's failure to disclose critical information when a direct question was asked is *Johnson v. McCullough*, 306 S.W. 3d 551 (Mo. 2010).

CASE STUDY: UNDERSTANDING THE LAW

In *Johnson v. McCullough*, plaintiff Phil Johnson filed a medical malpractice case against defendants, Edward McCullough and Mid-America Gastro-Intestinal Consultants. Johnson claimed permanent throat damage due to a surgery that was performed. During *voir dire*, jurors were asked about their prior involvement in

(continued)

litigation. The question was direct, requiring jurors to be forthcoming in their response. Many jurors responded in the affirmative, except that **venire member** Mims did not respond, indicating that there was no prior involvement in any litigation. Mims was chosen for the jury. After a six-day trial, the jury found against the plaintiff. For some reason, Johnson's counsel investigated Mims and found numerous court cases, through a case record service, where she had been a defendant in numerous debt collection cases and a personal injury case. A number of the lawsuits were recent. Johnson then filed a motion for new trial and presented evidence of the prior lawsuits.

A hearing was held by the court where the motion for new trial was granted based upon the juror's intentional failure to disclose and concealment of critical information during the *voir dire* process. The defendants, Edward McCullough and Mid-America Gastro-Intestinal Consultants, appealed. In reviewing the lower court decision, the Missouri Supreme Court stated that a venire member had a duty to be truthful and disclose information when asked a clear and unambiguous question. Other venire members disclosed participation in lawsuits; Mims did not. Since the question was clear, Mims had a duty to disclose and the trial court correctly evaluated the facts.

The next inquiry for the court was whether the trial court abused its discretion in determining whether the lack of disclosure was intentional or unintentional. The distinction is important because it is from that, that the court will determine if prejudice occurred. No new trial is warranted unless prejudice can be shown. Intentional withholding of information during *voir dire* is considered prejudice as a matter of law. Although Johnson did not provide an affidavit or other evidence, which would have been the better practice, the court found that the litigation records from the website *case.net* were sufficient.

The final issue that the court addressed was the timeliness of the challenge. Although the court found that the challenge was timely, it noted that with the advances in technology, litigants should bring this information to the court's attention at the earliest possible stage. The granting of the new trial was affirmed.

Questions for Review: Read *Johnson v. McCullough*. What are the facts surrounding the appeal? What arguments were advanced by the defendants to support their position against the granting of the motion for new trial? Under what circumstances would the Missouri Supreme Court have found for the defendants?

venire member
Pool of people that can be called to be on a jury.

Ancillary Investigation

The judge, opposing counsel, and the community should be researched if not already done in preparation for settlement. It is important to know the judge's practice on jury information sheets, extent of voir dire, preferred jury instructions relevant to the respective type of case, and other trial practices. It is also important to determine if the judge permits jurors to take notes at trial, have mid-trial discussions about the case, ask questions of the witnesses, take evidence and instructions into the deliberation room, and other modern jury practices. In this regard, it is useful to review the ABA's *Principles for Juries and Jury Trials*, American Jury Project (2005).

PREPARING DEMONSTRATIVE EVIDENCE

Introduction

Imagine for a moment a hushed courtroom at a dramatic moment in a trial where a jury will decide whether the tobacco industry is liable to a class of plaintiffs for making cigarettes more addictive. Then the plaintiffs' paralegal presses a button and in mid-air, before the jurors, appears a stunning 3D holographic image of a human brain. In real time, the hologram shows how quickly nicotine invades the brain and causes addiction. Jurors return a $600 million verdict for the plaintiffs. This has already occurred in a state courtroom.

Jurors learn more and retain more when they can read something, hear about it, and see it. Generations X (born 1966–1981) and Y (born 1982 and later), raised with e-technology and expect its use. Work conducted at the William and Mary School of Law, called the Courtroom 21 Project and established in 1993, analyzes the use of demonstrative technology and how it contributes to juror understanding and efficient trials. The project and its research offers a great source of information especially on how legal technology is used by legal professionals in the courtroom.

Further, today's courtrooms are more and more high-tech driven. Therefore, the legal team of the 21st century, including the paralegal, not only must understand the importance of demonstrative evidence in general, but also must apply it competently to effectively represent a client. Like the competent use of e-discovery, the competent use of e-technology in the courtroom may be required for the ethical practice of law. Of course the maxim applies that the bigger and more important the case, the larger and more justified is the expense.

In addition to use at trial, demonstrative devices can play an important role in interviewing, depositions, settlement negotiations, mock trials, and focus groups.

Evidentiary Concerns

Some evidentiary foundation is essential to the use and admission of demonstrative evidence (see Chapter 3). Diagrams for purely illustrative purposes need only be a fair representation of what is depicted. On the other hand, if a diagram or scale model is presented as evidence to be taken to the jury room, it must be accurate: drawn to scale and based on accurate measurement and timely observation. Local rules may vary on what is admissible as demonstrative evidence and what is not, and should be thoroughly researched according to the type of item to be prepared (photo, video, diagram, document, computer animation, etc.).

Technology

As the use of the holographic image in the tobacco case indicates, technology is dramatically changing trial presentations. Computer software enables the creation of colorful charts, graphs, and diagrams, and the recording of photos, audio material, and videos. Software like PowerPoint and similar programs colorfully highlight key presentation points in the form of sequential "slides." Anything computer-generated or recorded can be vividly projected, using a laptop computer, a television, or a liquid-crystal large-screen projector. High-powered software programs facilitate the integration of audio, video, animation, and PowerPoint-type slides into an efficient and precise trial presentation. Documents and transcripts can be displayed on a split screen with carefully edited clips of a witness's deposition or other video. With a properly wired court, some witnesses who might otherwise be unavailable to testify can do so by two-way conference technology. Similar technology can be used to access foreign language interpreters, especially for rare or less common languages.

Physical evidence including documents can be viewed on a large screen by the use of color video document cameras, which can zoom in on an important detail such as

APPLY YOUR KNOWLEDGE

Visit your local federal and state trial courts and determine what technology is available in the courtroom. Determine who your future contacts should be for your technology issues and questions and prepare a list to include in your systems folder. Be sure to periodically update your list for changes to the courtroom technology or personnel.

a particular paragraph in a document or the serial number on a key piece of evidence. Microscopic video cameras can expose minute detail, revealing otherwise hidden defects. The paralegal who understands presentation technology and, better yet, learns how to operate it can be instrumental to the success of the litigation team.

The minimum courtroom presentation equipment list includes an LCD large-screen projector, a regular movie screen or multifunction white board or TV monitors, document camera (Elmo, Dean, others), DVD player, laptop with corresponding trial presentation software, an all-in-one printer-scanner-photocopier, cables, cords, power strips, and a bar code reader (wand). With a list of trial exhibits and the corresponding paste-on bar code tags, the lawyer or paralegal simply scans the bar code of the needed item on the list, and the exhibit is instantly projected. Some courtrooms are equipped with all or most of these items, some are not. In the latter situation, it is necessary to provide your own equipment, rent equipment, or hire a presentation technology vendor.

A variety of audiovisual aids can be used at trial to help the jury understand your client's viewpoint in the case.

- *Diagrams.* Diagrams are probably the most often-used audiovisual aid. They can depict almost anything and, if kept simple, can be inexpensively created. The diagram of the site of an accident, for example, is frequently used in automobile injury cases. Witnesses can use the diagram to identify streets and the location of witnesses, traffic signals, obstructions, and vehicles before, at the time of, and after the accident.

  The preparation of diagrams does not require any special artistic ability. To make an effective diagram, keep it simple; strive for reasonable accuracy; make it concise and readable by using short titles and descriptions, horizontal wording, letters easily seen from the required distance, and clear lines. Keep in mind how the jury will see it.

  If you choose not to use computer software to make the diagram, the art department of a bookstore or school supply store can provide the necessary materials. If you tell the clerks what you are trying to do, they may have suggestions for techniques and products that can simplify your job. Some universities have an instructional media department with personnel who specialize in preparing audiovisual aids. They can provide sound, free advice on a variety of techniques, and equipment. Professional services are available that provide diagram preparation or preprinted diagrams. Several companies specialize, for example, in medical diagrams of every part of the human body.

- *Charts and Graphs.* Charts and graphs also lend themselves to simple construction by the paralegal. Follow the guidelines mentioned for diagrams to make graphs and charts that convey complex and hard-to-picture data in an easily understood manner. For example, a vertical bar graph may better dramatize the decreasing ability of an intoxicated person to react to emergencies than a simple reference to a percentage.

- *Google Maps, Map Quest, and other Internet Demonstrative Products.* Using Google Maps or Map Quest to identify locations is becoming commonplace. With an extensive database, both sites provide information on most street locations. Google Maps provides details on an area's terrain and other important details that could assist in a case as well. However, be sure that your trial team will be prepared to authenticate the documents used. Sometimes there will be legal challenges to presenting documents from these sites.

- *Timelines.* A timeline is a form of diagram or chart that graphically portrays a single sequence of events or shows the relationship between two or more independent lines of conduct or occurrences. Although timelines have always been important to help jurors visualize a chain of events, timeline software has greatly simplified their creation and enhanced presentation quality.

- *Animation.* Digital animation can provide a moving recreation of events such as those leading up to, during, and immediately after a traffic accident or a work injury. Animation can show various viewpoints and is particularly effective when demonstrating obscured and unsafe viewpoints. Professional vendors are available but are expensive and need a lot of lead time.

- *Models.* Models are often used to display parts of the body, buildings, equipment, and a variety of other items. Construction of scaled, admissible-quality models usually requires professional skill. Companies that construct, sell, and rent models advertise in trade journals. Costs are usually quite high for such services. Computerized models create the illusion of three dimensions and can be manipulated to show various perspectives. Such models are expensive but effective. Holographic imaging is the cutting-edge technology for model presentations.

- *Photographs.* Photographs of injuries, damages, individuals, equipment, settings, and other items can be extremely helpful. The paralegal with minimal training can be the photographer, or professionals can be employed. Blown-up photographs can be particularly dramatic if allowed by the court. Digitized photos can be projected onto a large screen, and key features zoomed for emphasis.

- *Slides.* Simply another form of photograph, slides have largely been replaced by the use of digital photography and scanners. Film is still used where the highest professional quality is needed. It is expensive.

- *Video.* Video is relatively inexpensive and does not always require a professional technician. Some firms use professional video services if the case justifies it. Large screen projectors greatly enhance video presentations, making a "day-in-the-life" video or a video clip a powerful piece of evidence. When the defense in a medical malpractice trial claimed that the victim was in a persistent vegetative state and could not feel pain, and therefore did not deserve compensation for pain and suffering, a "day-in-the-life" video showed otherwise, resulting in a record verdict for the victim and also for her husband for loss of consortium.

Be an opportunist and make yourself even more valuable to the law office by seeking training in the effective operation of trial presentation technology. The American Bar Association's *The Lawyers' Guide to Creating Persuasive Computer Presentations*, 2nd edition, is a useful resource. As trial approaches, visit the trial courtroom well in advance to determine the most advantageous placement of displays, the adequacy of lighting and electrical hookups, and the availability of teleconferencing

TECHNOLOGY UPDATE: WHAT TECHNOLOGY IS BEING USED IN THE COURTROOM

More and more judges use the latest technology in their courtrooms. Quickly fading are the traditional practices of the past; they are being replaced by the electronics of the present and future. What the future holds is the paperless case and paperless courtroom. That means that as a paralegal, you should familiarize yourself with the courtrooms in your jurisdiction or where a case will be tried. Probably the first question you should ask is whether the courtroom is wired for use of computers and general audiovisual systems which assist the parties, the court, and the participants in the case. Many courtrooms have installed multi-screen displays—large television-like screens—that permit multiple types of displays during a hearing or trial. If the courtroom is not technologically advanced, then it is incumbent upon the legal team to determine what technology is permitted by the judge and what parameters the judge has set in using that technology. Oftentimes, judges will issue orders, and post them on their court websites, which specify the procedures for use of technology in their courtrooms. One of the main uses for technology is the display of exhibits, video, video depositions, PowerPoints, and any other visual means that will assist the judge and jury in the case. You often use a laptop computer or visual presenter to display this information.

Whatever your choice for displaying the digital information, be sure the equipment works and have a back-up plan for electronic failures. One important issue about using technology in the courtroom is who controls the presentation of the evidence, especially when objections are made. Normally a member of the legal team controls the presentation of the electronic evidence. When an objection is made to that evidence, the image is projected on the screens within the courtroom. This can allow the jurors and witnesses to scrutinize an exhibit which ultimately may be objectionable. In most technology-wired courtrooms, the judge is provided with a mechanism to turn off or disconnect the challenged evidence. Known as a **kill switch**, this device permits the judge to shut down monitors or displays with the click of the switch. A kill switch is used when admissibility of evidence is questioned or when a judge is asked to determine whether certain images should be shown to a jury, such as a graphic image of an injured party.

These are just some of the technology issues that face the legal team in today's courtrooms. As technology advances and courtroom accessibility to that technology increases, stay abreast of the latest technological additions not only in your jurisdiction but also in courtrooms around the country.

kill switch

Device that permits a judge to shut down monitors or displays with the click of the switch; used when admissibility of evidence is questioned.

and court-supplied electronic and audio-visual equipment. Be ready for technical problems. Have an extra projector lamp, a backup laptop containing a duplicate of the presentation, a set of video tapes should you not be able to run the digital video clips, and hard copy backups of each exhibit. Learn the judge's rules and preferences on the use of technology and what electronic exhibits, if any, will be allowed in jury deliberations. Review the relevant ABA standards.

ABA Standards: Guidelines for Trial Practice

The American Bar Association's Civil Trial Practice Standards address the use of technology for trials. This is a fluid document that is periodically updated by the ABA. Guided by the use of Standards, this practice guide offers judges and attorneys an overview of general evidentiary and procedural rules. For example, Standard 11 urges judges to have adversaries view all demonstrative evidence before trial to facilitate objections and save time at trial. Judges are encouraged to rule on admissibility of demonstrative evidence well ahead of trial to avoid significant expenditures on ultimately unusable presentations. As with all the Standards, they are a suggested approach and are a guide only. Always refer to your court rules, case law, and internal operating procedures for the specifics on your jurisdiction.

TRIAL NOTEBOOK

Introduction

A trial notebook (often notebooks) consists of everything an attorney needs at the trial organized for easy and quick retrieval. The information it contains ranges from names of everyone involved in the case to a court opinion in support of admission of evidence. In some respects it is an outline of each step that must be taken to try the case, complete with indexes and cross-indexes. Trial notebooks are critical to successful courtroom litigation. If well prepared, they can make the difference between winning and losing and, regardless of the outcome, assist the attorney and the paralegal in being organized, effective, and confident.

Mr. White has asked that a trial notebook be assembled for the *Forrester* case. It is your job to put it together. The following material will help guide you in that process.

Begin organizing the sections of a trial notebook from the beginning of the case. This provides several advantages: (1) organization of case materials with indexes for quick retrieval of original documents, (2) paralegal control over the case materials with a checkout system for materials that have to be removed from the notebook, (3) easy reduction and editing of materials as issues narrow, and (4) quick preparation for settlement, pretrial conferences, meetings with the client or witnesses, and other procedures.

If prepared in hard copy, the trial book should consist of one or more loose-leaf three-ring binders, preferably of different colors, for standard 8 1/2-by-11-inch paper. If some 14-inch pages must be used, they can be reduced in the copying process to the standard size. Plenty of tabbed dividers will be needed to place between major sections and their subsections. In today's technology-driven world, most paralegals prepare trial notebooks electronically for review by their supervising attorney. This is done using standard word processing software or software designed specifically for that purpose. Electronic trial notebooks are easily customized, edited, and updated. They provide organizational structure, effortless duplication, quick retrieval, and are conveniently loaded into the trial laptop.

The actual contents and order of a trial notebook vary according to the type of case and the preference of the attorney. A lot of time can be saved by asking the attorney for a detailed outline of what is wanted in the notebook, or by preparing an outline of the notebook and asking the attorney to express preferences on the outline.

Read Exhibit 11.5 for a detailed outline of the basic structure of a trial notebook. The sections are arranged chronologically as they would come up at trial. Such an arrangement allows the attorney and the paralegal assisting at trial to work methodically through each section as needed. Each attorney has an organizational preference, however, so consult your supervisor. You can provide assistance by preparing the overall structure of the trial notebook and many of its components.

Legal Research

You can do much of the trial brief section of the trial notebook. Initial background research on evidence, elements of a cause of action, the appropriateness of a jury instruction, and the composition of concise memoranda and lists of legal authorities for the attorney's perusal are tasks a paralegal can handle competently. These may have to be edited, expanded, or changed in other ways, but your winnowing will form a sound base for further work.

EXHIBIT 11.5 Outline of Trial Notebook

Page or tab number	Divisions

Section One: Reference

1. Table of contents (complete last)
2. Persons and parties at trial
   a. Court, courtroom, judge, clerks, bailiff: name, phone, office e-mail
   b. Own staff at trial: attorneys, paralegals, others: names, phone numbers, e-mail, motel, etc.
      (1) Firm's office numbers for assistance
      (2) Client
      (3) Witnesses   Names, addresses, phone numbers, affiliations
      (4) Expert witnesses
      (5) Others
   c. Opponent's staff at trial and witnesses, experts, phone, affiliation, etc.
3. Case summary: factual and legal issues
4. Proof chart: elements and proof in case

EXAMPLE OF PROOF CHART

Plaintiff's elements and facts to prove	Source of proof
Negligence:	
Excessive speed	Wit: Schnabel "between 45–50 mph" Statement
	Client: "over 45" deposition p. 26 (Tab___)
	Photo: skidmarks, test. of Officer Timms
Inattentiveness	Hart's test.: "looking at speedometer" deposition p. 35 (Tab___)

Same for defendant's proof

Section Two: Pleadings and Pretrial

1. Major pleadings as amended: complaint, answer, defenses (all tabbed and color coded to separate plaintiff's from defendant's with key sections highlighted)
2. Alternative method: (Simply summarize pleadings stating allegations, admissions, and denials. Highlight remaining issues.)
3. Any pretrial order could go here

Section Three: Last-Minute Motions

1. Any remaining pretrial motions with supporting authorities
2. Authority to oppose any expected last-minute motions by the opposition

Section Four: Voir Dire (Jury Selection)

1. Jury challenge chart: (usually 18 to 20 boxes on standard sheet of paper to enter no. and name of each juror, plus attorney's and paralegal's notes on suitability)

EXHIBIT 11.5 Outline of Trial Notebook (*continued*)

2. Profiles of jurors most and least wanted (predetermined by jury investigation)

3. Outline of voir dire questions: (if the attorney is permitted to conduct voir dire—if not, proposed questions for the judge to ask jurors with copies for the judge and opponent. Questions are usually drafted by the attorney or an experienced paralegal with attorney review. There are numerous sources on conducting voir dire.)

4. List grounds and authority for challenges for cause (a challenge for cause is a request to remove a juror for lawful reasons such as inability to be impartial)

5. List of authorities on any anticipated jury issues (including legality of any voir dire questions)

6. Jury panel chart (usually 12 boxes to place names and comments about jurors finally selected to hear the case)

7. Blank loose-leaf sheets to write notes on voir dire or to record any objections

Section Five: Opening Statement

1. Complete text

2. Alternative: outline (both drafted by attorney. Use large orator's type.)

Section Six: Outline of Order of Proof and of Opponent's Proof

Section Seven: Witness Examination

1. Own witnesses: direct examination (tabbed subsections for each witness in the order they will be called by the attorney). Each witness subsection should include:

    a. A synopsis of witness information, whether subpoenaed and interviewed

    b. An outline or chronological list of the questions that will be asked on direct examination on each critical issue. Use wide margins so notes can be added

    c. Notations of what exhibits will be introduced by the witness with inserted copies of the exhibits

    d. Notations inserted on any references to diagrams or other audiovisual aids

    e. Conflicting testimony of witness (references to prior statements, depositions, interrogatories, admissions)

    f. Questions to rehabilitate witness, especially if harmful cross-examination by opponent is expected

    g. Summaries of any statement, letters, memos, or depositions with key quotations highlighted. Cross-indexed to section containing copy of full statement, deposition transcript, memos, etc.

    h. Copies of subpoena with proof of service

2. Opponent's witnesses: cross-examination (Some attorneys prefer an entirely separate, different colored notebook for dramatic effect.)

    a. Similar structure to item 1 above with emphasis on conflicting and inconsistent statements, testimony, or other impeachment material

    b. Inserted copies of necessary exhibits, criminal records, etc.

(continued)

EXHIBIT 11.5 Outline of Trial Notebook (*continued*)

Section Eight: Exhibits (sometimes kept as separate book)

    1. Exhibit log

EXAMPLE OF EXHIBIT LOG

Ex. no. (as premarked or as assigned at trial)	Descript. or title of exhibit	Whether introduced, accepted or rejected. Notes.		
<u>Own ex.</u> (in order of introduction)	Title	Introduced ( )	Accepted ( )	Rejected ( )
		Notes:		
P-1 (Plaintiff)				
<u>Opponent's ex.</u>	Title	Introduced ( )	Accepted ( )	Rejected ( )
		Notes:		

    2. Each exhibit in expected order of introduction (may be separated by identifying tabs, including exhibit no. if premarked by clerk

    3. Each exhibit section should include:

       a. Exhibit summary sheet paper-clipped to exhibit (includes brief description of exhibit and significance, case file location or code no., witness needed for introduction, foundation, brief statement of authorities on admissibility

       b. Exhibit

         (1) Marked copy for judge, opponent, one for each juror if desired, one for witness section, one for exhibit section

         (2) If oversized, specially indexed to separate container or if cannot be hole punched, place in three-hole plastic envelopes

       c. Place exhibits in box if there are too many for notebook.

    4. List of all audiovisual props and accessories indexed to specially numbered containers if necessary.

Section Nine: Trial Motions and Authorities

(Any motions such as for dismissal or for directed verdict. Reminders to make motions should be placed at chronologically appropriate places and cross-indexed to this section. Consult with the attorney for what and where.)

Section Ten: Jury Instructions (Charge to Jury)

    1. Attorney's copy of all instructions proposed to be read to the jury. (Should contain complete language of instruction, one instruction per page, plus any legal authorities supporting its use. Each should contain a checkoff for given, modified, or refused. Have enough copies for all parties and the judge.)

    2. Opponent's proposed instructions with checkoff

    3. Final copy of instructions read by the judge

    4. If no jury, copy of request for findings of fact and conclusions of law for the judge

Section Eleven: Proposed Verdict Form (General, Special, General with Interrogatories)

(Optional section depending on detail of verdict desired by attorney. Necessary copies for judge and opponent. Section for supporting authorities.)

EXHIBIT 11.5 Outline of Trial Notebook (*continued*)

Section Twelve: Closing Statement

1. Text or outline of closing statement (orator's size print)
2. Props or list of props
3. Notepad for recording items to add as trial progresses

Section Thirteen: Law Section

1. Trial memo or brief covering the law on all significant questions of law concerning the issues, evidence, motions, and other anticipated objections or conflicts
2. Geared to the judge's bench book (legal authority book)
3. Should include points and responses to law likely to be argued by opponent
4. May include concisely typed copy of the Rules of Evidence and pertinent Rules of Procedure with authorities
5. Cross-indexed to relevant sections in notebook

Section Fourteen: To Do, Notes, and Reminders

1. List of items to do before trial in completing notebook, serving subpoenas, gathering exhibits, etc.
2. Reminders of motions to make, whether to poll jury, and others
3. Notepad for items that come up at trial that should be commented on, argued, noted for appeal, etc.

Motions

The attorney will have a good idea of what standard motions are likely to be needed just before and during trial. Many of these motions, such as a motion to dismiss or a motion for a directed verdict (called a motion for judgment as a matter of law in the federal system), require grounds that can be stated generally. The attorney will be able to fill in needed details as more specific reasons develop at trial. Authorities that generally state the legal standards necessary to grant or deny the motion can be cited. Therefore, you can prepare a skeletal or general version of the motion, along with an accompanying order. See Chapter 6 on motion drafting. Exhibit 11.6 and Exhibit 11.7 contain examples of several common trial motions to include in the trial notebook.

motion in limine
A motion filed for protection against prejudicial questions and statements at trial.

You might be assigned the task to draft a **motion in limine**. This motion asks the court for protection against prejudicial questions and statements. It is usually made when the attorney realizes that the opponent is likely to ask questions of a witness or refer to matters that will prejudice the jurors, making a fair trial difficult to achieve. An example of a motion in limine appears in Exhibit 11.8.

Voir Dire Questions

You can research possible voir dire questions. A trial attorney generally has these in mind, but each case has its own peculiarities. Furthermore, new ideas and approaches are always being developed along with a current body of literature that you can review and digest into a list of questions with supporting legal authority for the attorney's consideration.

EXHIBIT 11.6 Motion for Mistrial

(*Caption*)

MOTION FOR MISTRIAL

_____ (Plaintiff/Defendant) respectfully moves this court for an order declaring a mistrial in this action and discharging the jury from further consideration of this case.

As grounds for the motion, _____ (Plaintiff/Defendant) states that [*state grounds*]. Consequently, it is impossible for _____ to receive a fair trial by the jury.

This motion is made on the basis of all records, files, and proceedings in this case.

Date _____

Attorney for _____

Address _____

_____

EXHIBIT 11.7 Motion for Directed Verdict

At Close of All Evidence
(*Caption*)

MOTION FOR DIRECTED VERDICT

_____ (Plaintiff/Defendant) respectfully moves this court, at the close of all the evidence in this case, to instruct the jury to return a verdict in favor of _____.

As grounds for the motion, it is asserted that [*state grounds*].

Date _____

Attorney for _____

Address _____

_____

EXHIBIT 11.8 Motion in Limine

For Order Prohibiting Reference During Trial to Insurance Payments Received by Plaintiff
(*Caption*)

MOTION IN LIMINE

The Plaintiff respectfully moves this Court to order counsel for the Defendant to avoid any reference during the course of trial to any compensation received or likely to be received by the Plaintiff from the Plaintiff's insurance carrier for his/her hospital and medical expenses.

Grounds for this motion are that reference to such insurance payments would be improper and prejudicial, and that such prejudice could not be corrected by any court ruling or admonition of the jury.

Date _____

Attorney for plaintiff _____

Address _____

_____

APPLY YOUR
KNOWLEDGE

Research the source
of the standard jury
instructions in your
jurisdiction. Determine
whether particular
judges in your state
have rules for prepar-
ing and submitting
jury instructions to
the court. Place these
guidelines in your
systems folder.

Jury Instructions

Not unlike voir dire questions, jury instructions can be researched, revealing new ideas and cases where jury instructions favorable to the client's position have been given and upheld as proper. Jury instructions or charges are read to jurors by the judge and cover a review of the evidence, burden of proof, the pertinent law, and application of the law to the facts in this case. If your client's case will be tried by a judge who permits jurors to take printed jury instructions into the jury room for deliberations, this phase of preparation becomes even more important.

Most states have a standard jury instruction sources in both electronic and book form used by judges in the state. Many of the federal courts use standardized instructions as well. Extensive, annotated collections of jury instructions are now available in many electronic forms. The instructions are organized by topic, so it is not difficult to find those covering each area of the case. Research into other case files, periodical literature, recent books on the topic, and recent case law may reveal instructions better suited to the client than the standard instructions. From these, you can draft a set of instructions to be reviewed by the attorney and altered or expanded where necessary. These special instructions, when supported by good legal authority, can give the attorney that needed edge. Exhibit 11.9 is an example of how jury instructions can be

---

EXHIBIT 11.9 Jury Instructions

JURY INSTRUCTION

Instruction no. _____

Crossing between intersections, not in marked crosswalk, last clear chance

1. Although the Plaintiff had the duty to yield the right of way to vehicles on the highway, the Defendant had the duty to exercise ordinary care for pedestrians and others, including the duty of keeping a proper lookout. If you are satisfied from the evidence that immediately prior to the accident it was no longer possible for the Plaintiff, by exercise of ordinary care for his/her safety, to avoid the Defendant's vehicle, while the Defendant still had time, by the exercise of ordinary care, to discover the Plaintiff's danger and avoid the accident, you will find for the Plaintiff; otherwise you will find for the Defendant.
2. (Definition of ordinary care from other standard instructions.)
3. (Damages from other standard instructions.)

Authorities (List relevant statutes and cases.)

ALTERNATIVE JURY INSTRUCTION

1. It was the Defendant's duty while operating his/her vehicle to exercise ordinary care for others, including:
   a. keeping a lookout for others close enough to pose a danger
   b. keeping vehicle under reasonable control
   c. driving at a reasonable and prudent speed as dictated by speed limits and conditions of the road

If you are satisfied from the evidence that the Defendant failed to comply with one or more of these duties, and that such failure was a substantial factor in causing the accident, you will find for the Plaintiff; otherwise you will find for the Defendant.

2. If you are satisfied from the evidence that the Defendant complied with all of these duties and that the Plaintiff moved into the path of the Defendant's vehicle so suddenly that the Defendant could not avoid the accident, you will find for the Defendant.
3. (Add definition of ordinary care from other standard instructions.)
4. (Add standard instruction on damages.)

Authorities

worded to approach the same facts, but from slightly different viewpoints. Which instruction do you believe is preferable for Mrs. Forrester?

Witness Questions

You may be asked by your attorney to draft proposed questions for witnesses at trial, or to draft an outline of topics to be covered in direct or cross-examination. Apply the pertinent techniques discussed in Chapter 8 on preparing for a deposition. If this task is not assigned, you can propose to do it.

Juror Notebooks

Some judges have permitted parties to give notebooks to jurors for use at trial, especially in complex cases (ABA Civil Trial Practice Standard 2). This notebook consists of exhibits, photos, expert witness resumes, glossaries, and other useful information. If asked to prepare a juror notebook, consult your attorney about content and how polished it should look.

Noting Special Details

While working on a case, you will undoubtedly become very familiar with its facts and evidence. Use that familiarity to identify those special details and pieces of reality that will help sway a jury. Note these for the lawyer. If you are able to attend the trial, hearing reference to something you contributed will be very satisfying.

PREPARING THE CLIENT AND WITNESS FOR TESTIFYING AT TRIAL

Task

Your role in assisting the attorney to prepare a witness for testifying can go beyond that of preparing a witness for a deposition. Trial means some new challenges for the witness, and you can be an instrumental part of the legal team preparing the witness for trial.

Most obvious is the task of communicating more frequently with the client or witness as the trial date approaches. Inform the client of the trial date, appointments at the office, and those things that the witness will need at trial. The client or witness may need to be reminded to review their deposition several weeks before the trial and again just before a final preparation session with the attorney.

You can take witnesses to the courtroom to familiarize them with the surroundings and procedures: where they should report the day of the trial, what they should and should not wear, what to do when called to the stand, where the witness box is, what it is like to sit in the witness box, how important it is to address the jury and speak up, how to refer to diagrams and other props and still communicate with the jury, how to look at the attorney asking the question and turn to the jury to answer it, what it feels like to be in the jury box, and how important it is for the jury to see and hear. The need for any special accommodations for the witness should be reviewed. A brief dry-run direct examination can be conducted here. Learn how to set the stage. Such efforts will give the witness confidence and reduce a lot of unnecessary anxiety. Witnesses will greatly appreciate it.

Most attorneys try to prepare the client and most important witnesses, even in the simplest of cases. The preparation can range from a rather brief, informal discussion about the case and things to keep in mind, to a complete courtroom-like direct and cross-examination with a critique of the witness's performance. In such circumstances, most attorneys prefer to do the fine tuning with the witness, but you can still play an important role by observing, noting behavior or idiosyncrasies, listening for inconsistencies, and relating any impressions to the attorney. The facilities also have to be readied and witnesses made comfortable just as in preparing for the first client interview.

Critiquing witnesses must be done tactfully because of the anxious state most witnesses are in. You can help here by saying a few words of encouragement and letting them know that they will do fine.

Videotaping the witness during mock testimony can be helpful. You can do the taping and review it with the witness. Witnesses frequently note and comment on their obvious mistakes and distracting mannerisms that need to be worked on. On the other hand, most people will be pleasantly surprised that they were more effective and confident than they thought. Videotaped presentations on how to be an effective witness can also be prepared for viewing by each witness. This could prove to be a great time-saver when used repeatedly.

With the proper guidelines and authorizations from the attorney, you can help locate and enlist the expert witness. All the necessary data on the expert's qualifications should be gathered and placed in a summary format for the attorney. The expert might suggest publications, evidence, props, testing devices, and audiovisual material that need to be gathered and organized for trial or mock testimony. Summaries of the facts, theories in the case, and other relevant information may also have to be gathered and prepared for the expert. Caution regarding confidentiality is in order here, however, because no attorney-client privilege exists between the attorney and the expert. The expert can benefit from a trip to the courtroom as well. Experts need to be told not to get defensive during cross-examination, that they are there to give an opinion based on their best work and what they consider the best principles and theories of their area of expertise, despite contrary opinions of other experts and authors. Experts must also be guided tactfully to avoid appearing condescending or pompous, and cautioned against using jargon. Mock sessions with an expert can be helpful, and their time on the "stage" should be well orchestrated down to the finest detail.

The attorney may give you permission to inform some witnesses that, for their convenience, they will be called to court only at the time they will be needed, even if that is not the time listed on the subpoena. Witnesses should be fully informed of their place in the trial and how other witnesses are likely to testify. The client should be well informed as to the theory of the case.

You may be asked to produce a list of suggestions for testifying. In addition, knowing the primary tips for a trial witness will help in setting-the-stage visits to the courtroom and in critiquing witnesses. Exhibit 11.10 is a list of common suggestions provided to a witness. Such a list should not be given a witness without the direction of the attorney and should be reviewed thoroughly by the attorney for any additions or deletions.

EXHIBIT 11.10 Guidelines for a Witness's Trial Testimony

- ☐ Dress neatly in clothing that helps you feel secure.
- ☐ Arrive at court one half hour before the designated time.
- ☐ Do not discuss your testimony or the case with or in the presence of others.
- ☐ Look at the attorney asking the question, then look at the jury when answering.
- ☐ Speak up.
- ☐ Try to be as relaxed as possible. Remind yourself that you are not there to match wits or to outsmart someone, but you are there simply to tell the truth as best you can. Let the chips fall where they may.
- ☐ Do not try to memorize your testimony. If you have reviewed the facts in your own mind, and anticipated likely questions, your answers will be informed but spontaneous.
- ☐ Listen to the opening statements of the attorneys to better understand the opposing theories and where your testimony will fit. Be prepared, however, if you are not a party, that you may be sequestered (set off in a separate room) so your testimony will not be influenced by the testimony of others.
- ☐ Listen to each question very carefully. Do not try to answer if you do not understand the question or a term in the question. Ask for clarification.
- ☐ Do not guess at an answer. If you do not know, say so, and do not be led into guessing or agreeing with the cross-examiner when you really do not know.
- ☐ Do not look at the attorney for help, guidance, or approval. Once on the stand, all responses should be your own.
- ☐ Pause if a question seems inappropriate; give your attorney a chance to object.
- ☐ Do not continue to answer a question if your attorney objects.
- ☐ Do not get trapped by the opposing attorney into a yes or no answer even if the attorney says "Just yes or no." State what needs to be said. You have the right to answer a question fully.
- ☐ Avoid qualifying your answer with "maybe," "I think," "to tell you the truth," or "honestly."
- ☐ Your attorney will give you a chance to explain your side fully, but if the opponent gives you an opening, take it.
- ☐ Do not over explain. State your point clearly and briefly and let it be.
- ☐ If you are a party, be prepared to be called by the opposition for cross-examination during their presentation of the case.
- ☐ If you are asked by the opposing attorney whether you remember saying something, agree only if you do remember it. If you do not, or are not sure, ask to see the statement. If refused, make it clear that you will have to guess.
- ☐ If asked, "Is that everything that occurred?" give yourself an out by saying, "That is all I recall at this time."
- ☐ Visit the scene prior to testimony, review photos, videotape, and diagrams; note any current changes or differences from the original scene.
- ☐ Review the statements or testimony of other likely witnesses.
- ☐ Have an understanding of the case, the theories of both sides, and the order of presentation.
- ☐ Bring all records and documents requested.
- ☐ Do not fabricate or mislead.
- ☐ If you have spoken with the attorney before testimony and the opponent asks, "Have you spoken with attorney so-and-so prior to testifying?" state "Yes." There is nothing improper about this as long as you have been instructed to tell the truth.
- ☐ If you have been reimbursed for lost wages or travel to testify or have been paid as an expert witness, acknowledge this when asked. Witnesses are frequently reimbursed and experts are paid for their time and experience. They are not paid to mislead or state something other than their well-founded, expert opinion.
- ☐ If an expert witness, do not readily accept other authorities as sole authority in the field.
- ☐ Avoid jargon and technical language.
- ☐ Do not get defensive if challenged by the opposition; relax and avoid a battle of egos or wits.
- ☐ If an expert, testimony should be extremely well prepared and planned.
- ☐ Be ready to show how measurements and calculations were made.

An Ethics Reminder

Remember that any attempt to have a witness conceal evidence, give misleading testimony, or lie is a serious ethical violation. It is best, therefore, to avoid even the appearance of impropriety. If any questions do arise, consult the attorney immediately. Also, keep in mind that just because an attorney tells you to do something, especially if you know it is improper, you are not relieved from exercising independent judgment based on a sound knowledge of professional ethics.

ADDITIONAL PREPARATION

The paralegal is often charged with supervising the following arrangements:

- All hotel reservations for the trial team
- All transportation to the trial site
- Parking and payment for parking, including change when necessary for parking meters
- A prearranged system for meals and payment
- A system for collecting receipts for all expenses
- Arrangements and cash for emergency copying, phone calls, etc.
- Delivery of all trial materials, diagrams, files, equipment, etc., to court

STAGES IN THE TRIAL PROCESS

Before we discuss the role of the paralegal at trial, understanding the key stages in trial procedure is essential. Each stage of the trial builds on the other until a result is reached.

Jury Selection (Voir Dire): The initial selection and questioning of prospective jurors by the judge and often the attorneys to choose an impartial jury is known as **jury selection**. To begin jury selection, names are drawn from the jury pool to form the potential jury panel. The judge in federal court and the judge and attorneys for each side in state court question the potential jurors during voir dire to reveal bias or personal interest in the case. When voir dire reveals information that disqualifies a juror, the attorney makes a **challenge for cause** to strike that person from the panel. The challenge must be based on grounds, and is decided by the court. Each side also may make a certain number of **peremptory challenges** to strike jurors without justification by the attorneys. Attorneys exercise challenges for cause and a predetermined number of peremptory strikes to eliminate unwanted jurors. These challenges reduce the panel to the required number of jurors.

Opening Statements: The **opening statement** is introductory remarks by the opposing attorneys on the case and what they will be proving during the trial. The defendant's attorney may reserve the opening statement for later. This is the first time the trier of fact, a judge or a jury, has to hear the details of a case. Opening statements should not be too long. They should be a general roadmap as to what each side intends to present during the course of the trial. It is each party's theory of the case. Opening statements are not evidence and should not be considered in the trier of fact rendering a verdict or judgment. Attorneys should take care to avoid presenting an opening statement that is argumentative. Remember it is the first impression of the case, especially if being tried before a jury.

jury selection
process of questioning prospective jurors by a judge, or sometimes the attorneys, to choose an impartial jury.

challenge for cause
The attorney's request to remove a potential juror on the grounds of bias or other reason.

peremptory challenges
The authority of an attorney to strike the name of a potential juror without having to express any reason for the strike; limited in number.

opening statement
Introductory remarks by the opposing attorneys on the case and what they will be proving during the trial.

direct examination
The initial questioning of the plaintiff's or party who called that particular witness.

Plaintiff's Case in Chief: The plaintiff's attorney presents their case first. This is known as the case in chief. The attorney presents the plaintiff's case through **direct examination**. Direct examination is the initial questioning of the plaintiff's or party who called that particular witness. Questions cannot be leading, which means that the answer cannot be suggested in the question. Most direct examination questions are more open-ended, such as "when did the accident occur?" "What injuries did you sustain?" Were you treated by a doctor?" Physical evidence also is presented through the appropriate witnesses that assist in building the plaintiff's case in chief.

When the plaintiff has completed the direct examination of a witness, the defendant's attorney may cross-examine each of the plaintiff's witnesses. Cross-examination generally uses leading questions to elicit information. Often times, cross-examination is used to discredit a witness, such as showing that memory has faded or sight of vision was impaired. It normally calls for a yes or no answer. For example, a defendant may ask, "Isn't it true that you failed to wear your glasses on the day of the accident?" Or, "Isn't it a fact that there was a large tree blocking your line of vision so that you could not see when the van hit the car?" This allows the defense attorney more control of the witness, who is usually not friendly to the opposing attorney. Normally, the plaintiff's attorney is given the opportunity for redirect examination, with the defense counsel being permitted to have another bite at cross-examination known as recross. But, both parties are limited to the information and evidence elicited and normally cannot exceed the scope of the initial direct and cross-examinations, respectively. Once all the witnesses have been questioned and evidence admitted, the plaintiff will rest. This gives the opposing counsel the opportunity to present motions arguing that the plaintiff has not proven the case.

Defendant's Motion for Dismissal, Motion for Judgment as a Matter of Law, or Directed Verdict: After the close of the plaintiff's case in chief, the defendant may move for dismissal of the action, motion for judgment as a matter of law, or a directed verdict requesting the judge to dismiss the case on the grounds the plaintiff has failed to prove the allegations sufficiently. If the plaintiff, in the judge's opinion, has met the requisite burden of proof, it is a **prima facie case** (sufficient to prove a claim prior to any rebuttal), and the case will continue. If the evidence is inadequate, the judge will dismiss the case.

prima facie case
The minimum evidence sufficient to prove a case, prior to any rebuttal by the defense.

Defendant's Case in Chief: Assuming that the plaintiff has met the burden of proof, the case will continue with the presentation of evidence through the defendant's witnesses. The defendant will now present evidence and testimony to support their theory of the case, which will include any defenses to the plaintiff's allegations that show why the plaintiff should not recover from the defendant. With the presentation of the defendant's case in chief, the defense now will question witnesses through direct examination with the plaintiff cross-examining those witnesses. Now, the defense will ask more general questions and cannot ask leading questions. This will be permitted for the plaintiff in their cross-examination of the defense witnesses. Redirect and recross-examination will be permitted with the defense resting when they have completed their presentation of the their witnesses and evidence.

plaintiff's rebuttal
Last chance for plaintiff to discredit the evidence admitted during the defense's case.

Plaintiff's Rebuttal: After the completion of the defense's case, the plaintiff is permitted to present witnesses or evidence to rebut any new items raised in the defendant's case in chief. Know as **plaintiff's rebuttal**, the plaintiff presents evidence to discredit the evidence elicited and admitted during the defense's case. The rebuttal is not an opportunity for the plaintiff to bring in new issues or evidence, but rather is limited to the case already presented—the cases-in-chief.

defendant's rebuttal (rejoinder)
last opportunity for defendant to challenge the fact that plaintiff has not proven the case.

Defendant's Rebuttal or Rejoinder: When the plaintiff has completed the rebuttal, the defendant has the opportunity to present witnesses or evidence to rebut evidence offered in the plaintiff's rebuttal. Known as the **defendant's rebuttal**, and by such other names as rejoinder or surrebuttal, the result is that the defendant is given one last chance to show why the plaintiff has not proven its case. Rebuttal is not a free-for-all and is limited to the plaintiff's presentation on rebuttal.

Motion for Directed Verdict or a Motion for Judgment as a Matter of Law: Depending on the court, this type of motion by either side states that the other side has failed to prove or sufficiently rebut the evidence such that, as a matter of law, the verdict is clear. If the motion was presented by the defense at the end of the plaintiff's case, the motion would be a "renewed" motion. The renewed motion would build on the arguments presented by the defense at the close of the plaintiff's case in chief. If granted for either party, the judge enters the verdict and the case ends.

Conference to Determine Jury Instructions: Determining the jury instructions is the domain of the judge. It is the judge's responsibility to advise the jurors on the law, the required burdens of proof, how to weigh evidence, and how to reach its final result—the verdict. Attorneys do offer *suggested* jury instructions and can object to a judge's jury instructions prior to delivering them to the jury. Objections are important as they will preserve any legal issues if an appeal is necessary, which will be discussed more fully in Chapter 12. Ultimately, it is the judge that will control the delivery and final instructions to the jury. The jury instructions are presented to the jury *after* the closing arguments.

closing arguments
summation given by the parties at the end of a trial.

Closing Arguments: In **closing arguments**, the parties sum up the case. This is when the attorneys review the evidence, summarize the case, and request the jurors to enter a verdict in favor of their client. Unlike opening arguments which are general in nature, the closing arguments are persuasive. This is the final chance the attorneys have to argue the positives and negatives of the case and show the jurors, based on their theory of the case, why their client should win. In most civil cases the plaintiff closes first, then the defendant, and then the plaintiff's rebuttal if needed. Some jurisdictions vary on the order of presentation, but the purpose of the closing argument is the same— to persuade jurors why a party should win or lose. Although rare in the civil context, sometimes attorneys make improper statements during closing arguments. Opposing counsel may object to the statements, but sometimes attorneys miss the opportunity. Ordinarily issues for an appeal must be preserved at the trial court unless the appellate court determines that the statement was so egregious as to warrant error in the trial court. Such was the issue in *Murphy v. International Robotic Systems, Inc.*, 766 So. 2d 1010 (Fla, 2000), where the Florida Supreme Court was asked to address whether unobjected comments at closing so affected the rights of a party that a new trial was required.

CASE STUDY: UNDERSTANDING THE LAW

The facts of *Murphy v. International Robotic Systems, Inc.* involve the development of an unmanned remote-controlled marine vehicle known as the OWL. The inventors of this vehicle were attempting to sell and market this concept to the U.S. Navy. The main developers Robert Murphy and Howard Hornsby set up

(continued)

International Robotic Systems, Inc. to market the OWL. As with so many business transactions, Murphy and Hornsby had a falling out resulting in this lawsuit. With allegations of misrepresentation, breach of fiduciary duties among others, the jury found for the defendants except for one count. During the defendant's closing, no objections by plaintiffs were made. However, when the plaintiff filed a motion for new trial, they raised the issue of improper comments by the defendant during closing arguments, although conceded that no objections were made by them.

Since there was conflict among the various appeals districts in Florida on this issue, the Florida Supreme Court agreed to hear the issue to settle the legal conflicts. The court acknowledged previous precedents that had permitted relief under a narrow exception to unobjected-to improper comments in the criminal context. However, different appeals courts questioned whether a civil exception should exist and what the standard of review should be under those sets of circumstances. Discussing the requirement that contemporaneous objections must be made during a closing argument of improper comments, reinforces a basic tenet of trial practice. Following that tenet, the court then reviewed four of its decisions that dealt with the issue. The decisions varied in their results, but the message of those cases was that if comments made by opposing counsel were so egregious as to result in an unfair trial, even though unobjected to by counsel, the court had a duty to protect the integrity of the process and not sanction jury prejudice. The court then reviewed cases from other jurisdictions, both state and federal, many of which do not recognize an exception in the civil context. After analyzing all the cases from other jurisdictions, the Florida Supreme Court clarified its previous position and found that "a civil litigant may not seek relief in an appellate court based on improper, but unobjected to, closing argument, unless the litigant has at least challenged such argument in the trial court by way of a motion for new trial even if no objection was voiced during trial." *Id.* at 1027.

The next issue that the court addressed was the standard of review that should apply when this issue is raised. The court found that when a new trial is requested based upon unobjected-to comments in a closing argument, the moving party must show that the argument challenged was "improper, harmful, incurable, and so damaged the fairness of the trial that the public's interest in our system of justice requires a new trial." *Id.* at 1031. The standard of review to be applied in this instance is abuse of discretion. Ultimately, the court found that the comments made by the defense did not comport with the new standard and affirmed the decision of the trial court to deny the new trial.

Questions for Review: Review *Murphy v. International Robotic Systems, Inc.* What Florida cases were at the center of the court's opinion and what were their holdings? What persuaded the Florida Supreme Court to change its position on unobjected-to comments during closing arguments? Why did the Florida Supreme Court affirm that trial court's decision?

Instructions or Charge to Jury: The judge reads instructions to the jury on their duties and the law governing their decision. This also is known as the charge to the jury. The jury instructions are the roadway or guidelines that a jury must follow in deciding a case. It is their legal bible. In the jury instructions, the judge explains not only the law and burdens of proof, but how certain terms are legally defined. The judge will advise jurors that their interpretation of the evidence and the credibility of witnesses is what counts within the parameters set forth by the judge in the instruction. Ultimately, it is the jury that interprets the facts and evidence and applies it to the standards set by the judge in the instruction. The jury is the fact finder and reaches a verdict—the

verdict

The final decision of the jury regarding the questions of fact submitted to it by the judge.

general verdict

Pronounces the result, whether finding for the plaintiff or the defendant, with any damages associated with that result.

general verdict with interrogatories

Requires jurors to answer questions relating to the verdict.

special verdict

Requests jurors to respond to specific questions relating to the case.

final result—based upon the evidence and testimony presented using the jury instructions as its guideline.

Jury Decides Case: After the judge's instructions, the jury adjourns to the jury room, deliberates, and reports its **verdict** to the judge. A verdict is the jury decision. Verdicts can be general, general with interrogatories, or special. Like its name, the **general verdict** pronounces the result, whether finding for the plaintiff or the defendant, with any damages associated with that result. A **general verdict with interrogatories** requires jurors to answer questions relating to the verdict. The jury enters a general verdict based on its required answers to one or more prerequisite questions of fact. Whether the answers to the interrogatories are consistent with the general verdict determines whether the court enters a judgment consistent with the general verdict, enters a judgment as a matter of law, sends the jury back to reconsider the inconsistencies, or orders a new trial. This process reveals inconsistencies in the decision-making process. The final category is the **special verdict**. A special verdict requests jurors to respond to specific questions relating to the case. It is factually based. From those responses, the judge then applies the law to determine which party prevails in the case. Additionally, usually the jurors choose a foreperson who acts as the spokesperson for the jury. Think of the foreperson as the chairperson of the board—the person who ushers the other jurors through the deliberation process, such as the general discussion of the evidence and its application to the law, and facilitates votes in reaching a verdict. Once a verdict is reached, the jury foreperson notifies the bailiff, and in turn, notifies the judge that a verdict has been reached. Sometimes the jury foreperson reads the verdict of the jury; other times it is the judge. When a verdict is reached, that decision is read in open court.

Polling the Jury: Normally the losing party asks that the jury be polled on their result. Each juror is asked if he or she is in agreement with the verdict. It is a way to verify the validity of the verdict to assure the parties that the verdict announced is correct and the actual verdict of the jury. Once a verdict is announced and the jury polled, the jury is discharged of their duties and dismissed. This simply means that their jury service is concluded and the case is finished.

Motion for Judgment Notwithstanding the Verdict (JNOV) or Renewal of the Motion for Judgment as a Matter of Law: Either party may move the judge to enter a judgment contrary to the jury's verdict on grounds the verdict is against the great weight of the evidence. This motion essentially states that despite the jury's verdict, the evidence does not legally support their decision, and should be changed. Thus, the losing party should win.

Motion for New Trial: Another type of motion after a verdict is rendered is a motion for new trial. Either party may move for a new trial based on serious errors occurring at trial. These types of motions are time sensitive, and may even be required to perfect a party's appeal rights. If granted, the case will have to be retried.

Entry of Judgment: Simply announcing a verdict does not formally dispose of the case. The court must enter a judgment consistent with the jury verdict, motion for judgment as a matter of law, or JNOV. The judgment is the document which is filed publicly showing the results of the trial. From this judgment, the unsatisfied party may appeal. Exhibit 11.11 is a chart that summarizes the trial progression of a civil trial.

EXHIBIT 11.11 Civil Trial Process

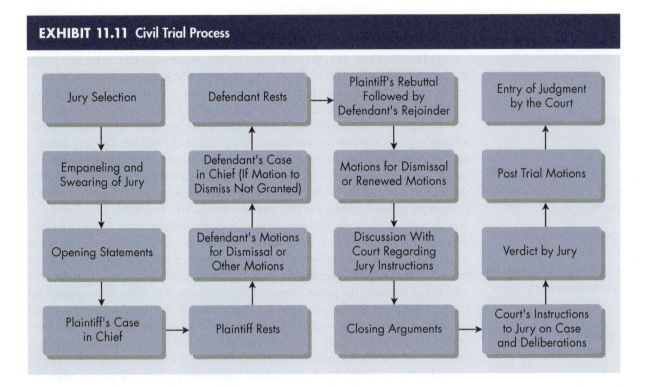

ASSISTANCE AT TRIAL

INTRODUCTION

Some law firms have a paralegal do much of the background preparation for the case and then make the mistake of failing to utilize the knowledge and skills of that paralegal at trial. The firms that utilize paralegals at trial realize the tremendous benefits that can be derived from such assistance.

RESEARCH YOUR JUDGE

One of the most important jobs for the legal team, and one with which a paralegal can assist, is knowing as much as possible about the judge before whom you will be appearing prior to beginning a trial. Research a particular judge's decision making through LEXIS and WESTLAW or consult others who have appeared before them. Know the rules of their court. Many judges have local rules of court that can be found on the court's websites. Study them and make them part of your trial notebook and trial preparation. Learn about a judge's idiosyncrasies—what he or she likes or dislikes. The more you learn and understand about the judge where your case will be tried, the less room for surprises that could have a negative impact on the case and the proceeding. Research, research, research!

DECORUM AT TRIAL

Discuss courtroom decorum with your supervising attorney so you know what is expected of you. Additionally, here are a few reminders. Dress for your role as

---

TRADE SECRETS: YOUR TRIAL SURVIVAL KIT

Think of the trial and the courtroom as your home (office) away from home—your mobile office. You want all your creature comforts and conveniences at your fingertips. To achieve this, litigation paralegals preparing for trial have what most call a trial box. It is your trial survival kit, which contains a hodgepodge of necessities and supplies. What you choose to use as your trial box is a matter of preference. The supervising attorney in the case may have a trial box to use or you could use a tool box, child's school box, or find your own. No matter what you use, your trial box should contain items such as post-it notes, pens, pencils, highlighters, markers, paper clips, rubber bands, stapler, extra staples, staple remover, scissors, extra notepads, extra manila folders, exhibit stickers, and scotch tape. You also should consider the needs of the litigation team and items they may want or need. Consider including in your trial box mints, antacids, granola bars or protein bars, or any other energy-boosting products that will assist team members. Also consider additional extension cords, telephone and tablet cords, external batteries for electronics, or any other electronic-related items. Each trial team is different and items should be added or subtracted as the situation dictates. Communicate with your supervising attorney and litigation team as to their needs and suggestions for what should be included in the trial box. There is no right or wrong way to prepare your trial box. By anticipating the needs of the trial team, you make yourself an invaluable asset of that team.

---

the professional representative of both your client and the law firm. Dress conservatively, yet comfortably. Assume that you will be observed by client, judge, jury, court personnel, and others in the court. Reflect confidence in and support for your client, witnesses, and colleagues. Place your cell phone on standby or vibrate, or as directed by the judge. Be aware of whether any personal electronic devices are likely to interfere with other courtroom technology. Use such devices only during court recesses, unless absolutely unavoidable. Avoid any personal interaction with jurors, because such contact could lead to accusations of improperly trying to influence the jury.

JURY SELECTION

Paralegals can be invaluable as part of the jury selection process that was discussed earlier in the chapter. While your attorney is listening to the questions being posed, you should be noting each person's name that is called as a potential juror. You can quickly note on the jury selection charts (or electronic equivalent) the juror's name and previous assessment of that person as good, bad, or intermediate for the case. Transfer key, relevant facts about the person to the chart for the attorney. At this point, all the jury investigation performed earlier pays off. As the juror answers voir dire questions, enter significant responses on the chart.

Paralegals are frequently asked to note their observations of both verbal and nonverbal actions of the potential juror during voir dire. Much popular literature, including quasi-scientific articles, has been written about body language and ways to tell if a person is being truthful. Some attorneys place stock in these articles and train paralegals in such techniques. The truth is, however, that most such techniques should be applied with great caution. Only the most obvious clues, requiring simply an observant eye, prove useful. A good paralegal is cautious and conservative in the use of even the obvious. The human mind is extremely complex and often does not reveal the experience or belief system behind the behavior. Common sense should serve as a guide. For example, if the attorney asks a juror a question and the juror turns away from the attorney and starts fidgeting, there is a high probability that the juror does not care much for the attorney. Or, if on questions regarding racial or ethnic prejudices a juror keeps referring to a certain group as "those people," it is probable that the person chooses to be distanced from the subject and is likely to be prejudiced. Even the most noticeable clues, however, are not foolproof; do not rule out manipulation by the knowledgeable juror.

During the questioning, keep track of the voir dire questions on a copy of the voir dire outline from the trial notebook so questions overlooked can be pointed out to the attorney. The attorney can use information recorded on the jury selection chart to make challenges for cause and to strike jurors. You may be consulted. Once the final panel is selected, fill in a chart showing these jurors.

Occasionally, paralegals are asked to observe potential jurors unobtrusively where they gather and take breaks. Every so often a paralegal overhears a juror say something that provides insight as to their suitability for the case. For example, if in the rest room a prospective juror was heard to say that she had a reliable cousin who felt Mrs. Forrester was akin to the wrong end of a horse, it would certainly affect the attorney's decision to strike that juror. Stranger things have happened.

Speaking of strange things, a recent case in the U.S. Virgin Islands, *Rivera-Moreno v. Government of the Virgin Islands,* 61 V.I. 279, 2014 V.I. Supreme Court LEXIS 46 (V.I. 2014) showed the importance of keeping track of which jurors have been excused for cause and the perils of losing track of dismissed jurors. Although a criminal case, the principles and lessons learned from this case can be applied equally in the civil setting.

CASE STUDY: UNDERSTANDING THE LAW

The facts are straightforward in this case. Ruben Rivera-Moreno had been charged with first degree murder and other offenses. At his trial in 1991 in the U.S. District Court, prospective juror 173, when questioned by the trial court judge, stated that he believed that Moreno was guilty of the crimes committed. He was excused for cause. All dismissed jurors were asked to leave the courtroom, but juror No. 173 remained. When jury selection concluded, somehow, juror No. 173 had been placed on the jury despite being previously excused for cause. Juror No. 173 sat for the entire trial with the other 11 members. A verdict was reached convicting Moreno of all charges including the first degree murder. He was sentenced to life in prison. Moreno appealed his sentenced to the Third Circuit Court of Appeals on a variety of issues. None involved the juror issue. The Third Circuit affirmed the District Court decision.

Nearly 15 years later, Moreno filed a petition under the habeas corpus statute. The petition languished for a number of years and finally in 2014, the Superior Court denied the petition for habeas corpus stating that there was no proof that juror No. 173 sat on the jury. Moreno appealed. The Virgin Islands Supreme Court reversed Moreno's conviction and ordered a new trial. Focusing on the constitutional and statutory guarantees, the court found that the merits of the case warranted further investigation. It was clear that excused juror No. 173 sat on Moreno's case, and under the Sixth Amendment to the Constitution, a defendant is entitled to an impartial jury. Somehow through inadvertence, juror No. 173 was empaneled. His participation, knowingly or not, tainted the process and violated his constitutional rights. Because of the court's, the attorneys', and court personnel's failure to keep track of which jurors had been excused and which had not, a conviction for murder was reversed.

Questions for Review: Review the *Rivera-Moreno* decision. What lessons can be applied from this case in the civil context? Was the result fair and appropriate? What steps should have been taken to avoid the issue occurring and what steps as a paralegal would you take to assure that this situation does not occur in any of your cases?

SHADOW JURY: ANOTHER TOOL FOR INFORMATION

A group of citizens who reflect the cross-section of the community represented in the jury and who are hired to sit in the public area of the courtroom and to give their impressions of the trial is called a shadow jury. These people listen to evidence the jury hears, leave the courtroom whenever the actual jury is excused, and receive no outside information about the case, just like the empaneled jury. The shadow jury renders no verdict, however, but reports to a consultant at the end of each day. This information gives the attorney an idea of what the jury is thinking, what points need to be clarified, what weaknesses need to be shored up.

Jury consultants charge substantial fees for managing shadow juries, but paralegals can do the work for much less cost to the client. In either case, shadow juries are a good investment when a large amount of money is at stake.

Setting up a shadow jury includes the following steps:

1. Decide the number of jurors needed (three to six is recommended) and costs (fees can be based on an hourly wage for temporary work or a flat payment per day), with guidance from your supervising attorney and client.

2. Choose individuals who reflect the jury pool in age, gender, race, educational background, and other factors important in your community. Observe the jury selection process in another case to learn typical jury characteristics.

3. Have the shadow jurors sign an agreement to avoid news and information about the case, and not to discuss the case with anyone but the paralegal or consultant in charge. It should be clear that this includes spouses, significant others, family members, friends and use of social media sites. This stipulation maintains their effectiveness as a reflection of the true jury. (Social media contacts from a juror could result in their dismissal from the jury. Shadow jury members should refrain from any use of social media during their time on the shadow jury.) The agreement should include a pledge not to speak to any regular jury member or court personnel. Tell the shadow jurors what will be expected of them, and give

them instructions as to how they are to respond if questioned by the judge or opposing counsel. Confidentiality is important as well.

4. Set up a location for the debriefing of the shadow jury each day. This site should be neutral if you do not want to reveal which side has employed them. This is important as you want to have the most honest and candid views from the shadow jury. If they know which side you represent that may affect their opinions in the case. Absolute candor is critical if the shadow jury is to be used as a barometer of the real jury in the case.

5. Set up a process for payment of fees and for communication in case of illness or other emergency.

6. Determine who will debrief the shadow jurors. Some attorneys prefer to do this themselves. Debriefing the jury individually allows comparison of opinions. Debriefing the group together may show the effects of group dynamics on the jury's decision. Which approach to use should be decided before the trial.

7. Prepare questions that elicit general impressions, irritations, or distractions; opinions about the case in general, attorneys, witnesses, experts, and testimony that are confusing or unbelievable; and questions about evidence or case theories. Try and create the same atmosphere as the trial, including only revealing facts presented at the actual trial.

8. Present the information to the attorney, noting significant areas to be considered, for example, in the closing argument. This will assist the attorney is focusing his or her presentation before a decision is rendered. In some cases, the information acquired by the shadow jury may impact how the attorney presents the remainder of the case.

WITNESS CONTROL

You can help during trial by keeping track of witnesses, notifying them when to appear, meeting them, and reducing their anxiety. Sometimes it is necessary to arrange for the witness's payment, lodging, and transportation. Occasionally a witness will have to be found and subpoenaed during trial.

DOCUMENTS AND EXHIBITS

You can also serve as custodian of exhibits, equipment, and other trial materials. In such cases you must see that everything is ready that will be needed that day at trial, and that each item is stored in a secure place at the end of the day. If others are to serve as custodians, you should have a list of who has what and where the items are stored.

EXHIBIT AND WITNESS LOGS

During testimony you should keep track of each exhibit that is presented by both sides. This record serves as a guide to what has been presented, objected to, and accepted. It also tells you when the attorney needs a reminder to present an exhibit. Refer to Section 8 of the Trial Notebook (Exhibit 11.5).

Witness logs should also be maintained to show what witnesses have been called and whether they have deviated significantly in their testimony from previous statements, or as otherwise anticipated. Outlines of questions for each witness can be followed as a check to make sure the attorney has not forgotten important questions. It is not unusual during the course of trial for the attorney to ask the paralegal, "Have I forgotten anything?" See Section 7 of the Trial Notebook.

TRIAL NOTES

Take notes at the trial. The attorney is frequently too busy to note or even observe some significant comment or action. These notes should be particularly detailed when your supervising attorney is cross-examining the opponent's witnesses. A good technique is to use a fresh spiral notebook with lined paper. Each page should be numbered ahead of time. A summary-outline of the proceedings can be recorded on the left page, with detailed notes on a particular witness's answer or other important notes on the right page. This provides a systematic means to take notes. Key entries at vital stages in the proceedings will be easier to locate when reviewing the notes. Notes should be kept on what the attorney specifies before trial; most commonly that includes the name of the case, judge, court reporters, and staff; all parties, attorneys, experts, and others. Indicate what witnesses have been called, by whom, and the essence of their testimony. Note exact quotations if particularly significant. Record the exhibits entered through each witness. Note all objections and judge's rulings, and the times of all recesses, conferences before the bench, conferences in chambers, and times trial resumed. Much of this process can be done on an in-court laptop computer. Many courts are now equipped with instant or real-time transcript reporting technology, providing attorneys and paralegals with an immediate on-screen copy of the typed testimony. Key portions can be highlighted and reviewed in conjunction with your notes.

TRIAL DAY REVIEW MEETINGS

Frequently the entire trial team gathers each evening to discuss the day's events and next day's strategies. Your notes of the day can be compared to the attorney's notes and recollections. Items can be noted for follow-up or emphasis in the closing arguments. You can offer suggestions when appropriate and receive instructions on what to do for the following day, which might involve last-minute subpoenas, arranging for transportation, or doing some last-minute legal research on a point expected to be argued the following day. Motions may need to be put into final form, or at least readied for the attorney's submission.

WHEN THE PARALEGAL MUST TESTIFY

Sometimes it becomes necessary for the paralegal to testify at trial. Such testimony is commonly used to prove that something was mailed on a specified date, that a photo is authentic, or that a chain of custody has been maintained to preserve certain evidence. The better practice is to refrain from involving the paralegal, but sometimes it is unavoidable.

When asked to testify, you should review the suggestions given to any witness. The attorney can prepare you through questions, since a review of actual documents to refresh recollection will make the documents accessible to the opposing attorney for cross-examination and can result in the revelation of attorney-client privilege.

Your testimony should be kept to a minimum, advocacy should be left aside, and the testimony should be professional and truthful. Any commitment to the client or the attorney cannot and does not supersede the commitment and responsibility to the truth.

VERDICT

As previously discussed in the chapter, the verdict is the final decision of the jury regarding the questions of fact submitted to it by the judge.

Prior to the judge's submission of the verdict document to the jury, each party has the opportunity to request what type of verdict it wants submitted to the jury. The paralegal can play a role in researching what form of verdict would be best and what legal authority supports the submission of that form, and drafting the necessary documents. The documents and supporting authority are placed in Section Eleven of the Trial Notebook.

findings of fact and conclusions of law
The document that contains the court's judgment summarizing the key evidence on the elements of the cause of action and the judge's conclusions that form the basis of the judgment.

FINDINGS OF FACT AND CONCLUSIONS OF LAW

In some states, in cases with no jury, the prevailing party has the duty of drafting the court's **findings of fact and conclusions of law**. This document summarizes the key evidence on the necessary elements of the cause of action and the judge's conclusion that form the basis of the judgment. The paralegal is often asked to draft this document for the attorney's review. You should consult several pertinent examples of findings of fact and conclusions of law before drafting the document. It is submitted to the court, signed by the judge, and distributed to the parties. Exhibit 11.12 is a skeleton form for drafting findings of fact and conclusions of law.

EXHIBIT 11.12 Findings of Fact and Conclusions of Law

(Caption)

FINDINGS OF FACT AND CONCLUSIONS OF LAW

The above entitled action, having been tried before this court without a jury on [date], with _____ appearing as the attorney for _____, and _____ appearing as the attorney for _____, and having heard the evidence in this case and the arguments of counsel, this court, being fully advised herein, makes the following findings of fact and conclusions of law:

Findings of Fact

(In separately numbered paragraphs state each finding of fact.)
From the foregoing facts, the court concludes

Conclusions of Law

(In separately numbered paragraphs state each conclusion of law.)

By the Court

_____

Judge

Dated _____

SUMMARY

Preparedness through organization continues to be a common thread that defines much of your responsibility as a paralegal. Preparing the litigation team for trial is not only crucial to success at trial, but also involves some of the most interesting and creative tasks that you may be asked to perform. You have learned to develop and utilize a checklist such as the Trial Preparation Checklist. You have learned the importance of and techniques for serving subpoenas, conducting jury investigations, creating demonstrative evidence, drafting motions in limine and motions to be used at trial, and preparing witnesses to testify. You have become familiar with the components and organization of an effective trial notebook.

Paralegals, as we have seen, also play an important role at trial by knowing each stage of the trial and anticipating how they can be of best use at each stage, by observing and recording information at jury selection, by coordinating witnesses and maintaining control over documents and exhibits, by taking careful notes for daily trial review, and other tasks. Although these tasks require energy and diligence, your hard work will be rewarded at the moment of victory.

KEY TERMS

challenge for cause	general verdict with interrogatories	plaintiff's rebuttal
closing arguments		prima facie case
defendant's rebuttal (rejoinder)	jury selection	special verdict
direct examination	kill switch	venire member
findings of fact and conclusions of law	motion in limine	verdict
general verdict	opening statement	voir dire
	peremptory challenge	

QUESTIONS FOR STUDY AND REVIEW

1. What are the trial preparation tasks to be performed by the paralegal well before trial? In the last six weeks before trial?

2. What is the importance of a case status sheet?

3. What steps must be followed in subpoenaing witnesses?

4. How can you help in conducting a jury investigation? What information should be gathered and from what sources?

5. What purpose does the juror data sheet serve?

6. What benefits are derived from diagrams and other audiovisual aids? Whom might you consult when preparing your own diagrams and charts?

7. List and describe current technology and some typical audiovisual aids used in the courtroom.

8. What are the rules in your jurisdiction on the admissibility of and proper foundation for demonstrative evidence, including diagrams?

9. What is a trial notebook? List and define its key components.

10. What aspects of the trial notebook can you draft?

11. What is a juror notebook?

12. What are jury instructions? What should you do to prepare a draft set of instructions for the attorney?

13. How can you assist the attorney in preparing the client or a witness for trial testimony?

What ethical considerations must be kept in mind?

14. How can you assist the attorney at voir dire and other stages of the trial?

15. Define three types of verdicts.

SYSTEMS FOLDER ASSIGNMENTS

1. Place a list of or page reference to the steps in obtaining and serving subpoenas in your systems folder. Having the list in both the deposition and trial preparations sections will prove useful.

2. Locate the applicable local, state, and federal rules of evidence on demonstrative evidence. Place these in your systems folder.

3. Add copies of or references to the trial and in limine motions to both the trial

and motions sections of your systems folder.

4. Draft a checklist for preparing clients and other witnesses for testifying at trial. Include a special section on preparing expert witnesses. Place the checklist in your systems folder.

5. Locate state examples of the three types of verdict forms and place them in an appropriate subsection of your systems folder.

APPLICATION ASSIGNMENTS

1. What special information might you want to know about jurors for Case II, the *Ameche* case?

Case II, *Ameche* Case

Pro Ameche

Pro Congden

Prepare a list of potential questions for your attorney.

2. What audiovisual aids would be useful in the *Forrester* case for the plaintiff? For the defendant? Using the information that you have gathered on the scene of the accident in the *Forrester* case, prepare a courtroom diagram of the accident scene.

3. Prepare a list of paralegal tasks to assist the attorney at trial and describe research and writing tasks that a paralegal can do in preparing the trial notebook.

4. Draft a brief checklist of the minimum courtroom presentation equipment and backup for courtroom technology problems. Place a copy of your list in your systems folder. Add a copy of or a page reference to the audio visual aids listed in the technology subsection of the chapter. If not provided otherwise, seek an opportunity to use some presentation technology.

5. In familiarizing yourself with courtroom decorum, trial preparation, and witness trial testimony, identify how a paralegal should conduct herself or himself regarding the following: (a) clothing, (2) demeanor, and (3) techniques and ethics for answering questions. What miscellaneous tasks can a paralegal do to help things go smoothly for the legal team outside the courtroom during trial?

CASE ASSIGNMENTS

1. Your attorney has requested that you assist in preparing a list of questions for prospective jurors in the *Forrester* case. What special information might you want to know about jurors for that case? Draft a list of questions for your attorney's review.

   Juror Information Case I, *Forrester* Case

   Pro Forrester

   Pro Mercury Parcel and Hart

2. Research form books, the Internet, case law or electronic forms for jury instructions in your jurisdiction. Place a list of the major sources in your systems folder. Prepare a list of instructions that you believe will be needed in the *Forrester* case for your attorney's review.

12

POST-TRIAL PRACTICE FROM MOTIONS TO APPEAL

OBJECTIVES

AFTER READING THIS CHAPTER, YOU WILL BE ABLE TO:

- Draft the different types of post-trial motions
- Assist in enforcing a judgment entered by a court
- Prepare a plan to locate a judgment debtor's assets
- Outline the steps to preparing and filing a foreign judgment
- Identify the components of an appellate brief

INTRODUCTION

This chapter covers the procedures employed after the verdict is rendered. Here you will learn the function, procedure, and forms for four post-trial processes: post-trial motions for judgment notwithstanding the verdict and a motion for a new trial, the proper filing of the judgment and bill of costs, enforcing a judgment, and appealing the case.

With experience, a good paralegal should be able to perform each of these tasks. Keep in mind, however, that not all law offices will readily delegate all of these tasks to the paralegal. It falls to you to earn the confidence of the law firm and, in many situations, to *make* the opportunity and reach out for enhanced responsibility.

POST-TRIAL MOTIONS

remittitur

A post-trial motion in which the defendant requests the court to reduce a jury award because of an error in determining the award or because the award is unreasonably excessive.

additur

A post-trial motion in which the plaintiff requests the court to increase a jury award.

INTERNET EXERCISE

Locate a copy of your jurisdiction's rules for motions for judgment as a matter of law and motions for new trial. What are the requirements for filing each motion? Are the time deadlines the same in your state courts as in the federal courts? Identify the similarities and differences. Place this information in your systems folder.

Even if the court has entered judgment in the case, the party against whom the judgment has been entered may move to have the judgment set aside.

Under Rule 50 of the Federal Rules of Civil Procedure and like state rules, a party who has moved for a motion for judgment as a matter of law (a motion notwithstanding the verdict) at the close of all the evidence may file a renewed motion for judgment as a matter of law. The motion must be filed within 28 days after judgment has been entered. The motion asks either that the judgment be set aside, combined with a motion for a new trial, or that judgment be entered in accordance with the previous motion for judgment as a matter of law. A motion for a new trial may also be filed separately. Generally speaking, a motion for judgment as a matter of law is granted if the weight of the evidence is contrary to the jury's verdict; in other words, if there is only one reasonable conclusion as to the verdict.

A motion for new trial must be filed within 28 days of the entry of judgment (Rules 50 and 59). Typically, this motion alleges procedural errors (improperly admitted or excluded evidence, improper argument by opposing counsel, prejudicial jury instructions, etc.), a verdict contrary to law, excessive or inadequate damages, and other grounds. The motion must be supported by affidavit. The opposing party has 14 days in which to file responsive affidavits.

Post-trial motions also include motions for remittitur and additur. **Remittitur** is a post-trial motion in which the defendant requests the court to reduce a jury award because of an error in determining the award or because the award is unreasonably excessive. If the plaintiff agrees to the remittitur, there is no new trial. Remittitur is used in both state and federal post-trial practice. **Additur** is a post-trial motion in which the plaintiff requests the court to increase a jury award. Although additur is used in a number of states, it is not used in the federal system since the Supreme Court declared it a violation of the Seventh Amendment in *Dimick v. Schiedt*, 293 U.S. 474 (1935).

Your role in post-trial motion practice can be significant. Immediately after trial, review with the attorney the copious notes you took at trial. From these notes the attorney develops theories on which the motion can be based.

Research the applicable local rules of procedure and the legal standards and authority for the motion in the pertinent jurisdiction. After a review of the authorities with the attorney, draft the motion and any supporting affidavit, brief, or memorandum required by local rules. Filing dates should be entered in the deadline control system. Once in final form, the motion and supporting documents are served on the opponent and filed in court. Exhibit 12.1 is a sample motion for judgment as a matter of law, and Exhibits 12.2 and 12.3 are examples of motions for new trial.

JUDGMENT AND BILL OF COSTS

Another task performed by the litigation paralegal is the preparation and filing of the bill of costs. Federal Rule 54(d) and parallel state rules provide that costs shall be awarded to the prevailing party unless otherwise directed by the court. The prevailing party files a bill of costs with the clerk of court. A copy is sent to the opposing attorney. The opposing attorney may object to all or part of the bill. If either party is dissatisfied with the clerk's determination, a motion for court review may be served within five days of the clerk's taxation of costs.

EXHIBIT 12.1 Renewal of Motion for Judgment as a Matter of Law (State: Motion for Judgment Notwithstanding the Verdict)

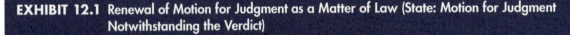

UNITED STATES DISTRICT COURT

THE _____ DISTRICT OF _____

_____ DIVISION

ABC

    Plaintiff

    v.   Civil Action File No._____

XYZ

    Defendant

RENEWAL OF MOTION FOR JUDGMENT AS MATTER OF LAW

[Plaintiff or Defendant] having, at the close of all the evidence, moved this court for judgment as a matter of law, which motion was denied, and subsequently a verdict was entered for [plaintiff or defendant], [plaintiff or defendant] now renews his/her motion for judgment as a matter of law pursuant to Rule 50(b), Federal Rule of Civil Procedure and as grounds would show:

1. [*state specific grounds for each point*].

2. [*reference the trial record where possible*]

WHEREFORE, the [Plaintiff or Defendant] moves this Court to consider the Renewed Motion for Judgment as a Matter of Law and for such other and further relief as [Plaintiff or Defendant] may be justly entitled.

Dated _____

Respectfully submitted,

_____

Attorney
Address:
Phone

[*Notice*]

Adapted from West's Legal Forms § 16.68. v. 25, with permission of West Group.

EXHIBIT 12.2 Motion for New Trial in a Nonjury Case

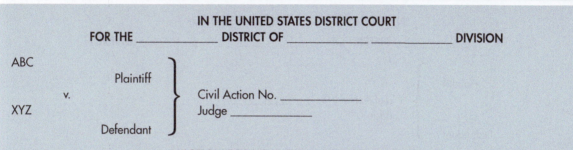

IN THE UNITED STATES DISTRICT COURT

FOR THE _____ DISTRICT OF _____ _____ DIVISION

ABC

Plaintiff

v.   Civil Action No. _____

XYZ   Judge _____

Defendant

MOTION FOR NEW TRIAL IN NON-JURY CASE

Plaintiff ABC moves the Court to set aside the Findings of Fact, Conclusions of Law and Judgment pursuant to Rule 52(b), Federal Rules of Civil Procedure, and to grant Plaintiff a new trial pursuant to Rule 59(a), Federal Rules of Civil Procedure on the grounds that:

1. The Court erred in ruling that *** [state the specific ruling and the legal basis as to why there was error for each challenge]
2. The Court erred in admitting the following evidence offered by the Defendant over objection of Plaintiff ***
3. The Court erred in excluding evidence of Plaintiff ***
4. The Court erred in admitting the following exhibits over objection for the following reasons ***
5. The Court erred in excluding the following exhibits ***
6. The Judgment is contrary to law in that *** [cite any case law that would support your argument here]

WHEREFORE, the [Plaintiff or Defendant] moves this Court to grant the Motion for New Trial and for such other and further relief as [Plaintiff or Defendant] may be justly entitled.

Respectfully submitted,

_____

J. Doe, Attorney for Plaintiff

[*Add Proof of Service*]

Adapted from West's Legal Forms § 16.778. v. 25, with permission of West Group.

APPLY YOUR KNOWLEDGE

Determine whether your jurisdiction permits remittitur and additur. Under what statutory or legal authority are they permitted? Locate cases in your jurisdiction that have addressed remittitur and identify the standards for its allowance.

Taxable costs allowed by 28 U.S.C. § 1920 include such things as filing fees, printing fees, pleadings, witness fees, and other items. A standard fee is usually established by the clerk of court, who can provide the necessary information. Generally, attorney's fees are not recoverable. There are exceptions, however, mainly in the form of statutes, including the Americans with Disabilities Act, the Privacy Act, and various civil rights acts. The recovery of attorney's fees under these acts is sought by a separate motion. Check local rules. In every respect, however, costs must be reasonable under the circumstances. What to include in the bill and what is necessary to support the charge is set out in Federal Form AO133. Some state courts provide similar forms. A supporting brief or memorandum may be required. Exhibit 12.4 is the federal form for a bill of costs.

It is advantageous from the start of the action to dedicate a section of the case file in which to note bills and costs and collect receipts and other pertinent records.

EXHIBIT 12.3 Motion for New Trial in a Jury Case

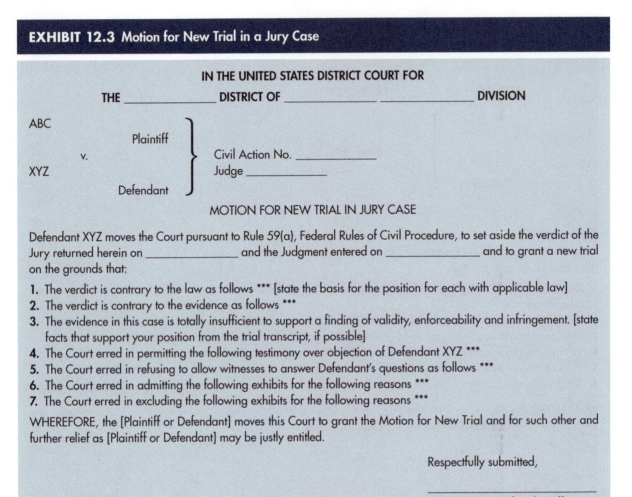

IN THE UNITED STATES DISTRICT COURT FOR

THE _____ DISTRICT OF _____ _____ DIVISION

ABC

        Plaintiff

    v.   Civil Action No. _____

XYZ   Judge _____

        Defendant

MOTION FOR NEW TRIAL IN JURY CASE

Defendant XYZ moves the Court pursuant to Rule 59(a), Federal Rules of Civil Procedure, to set aside the verdict of the Jury returned herein on _____ and the Judgment entered on _____ and to grant a new trial on the grounds that:

1. The verdict is contrary to the law as follows *** [state the basis for the position for each with applicable law]
2. The verdict is contrary to the evidence as follows ***
3. The evidence in this case is totally insufficient to support a finding of validity, enforceability and infringement. [state facts that support your position from the trial transcript, if possible]
4. The Court erred in permitting the following testimony over objection of Defendant XYZ ***
5. The Court erred in refusing to allow witnesses to answer Defendant's questions as follows ***
6. The Court erred in admitting the following exhibits for the following reasons ***
7. The Court erred in excluding the following exhibits for the following reasons ***

WHEREFORE, the [Plaintiff or Defendant] moves this Court to grant the Motion for New Trial and for such other and further relief as [Plaintiff or Defendant] may be justly entitled.

Respectfully submitted,

_____

J. Doe, Attorney for Plaintiff

[*Add Proof of Service*]

Adapted from West's Legal Forms § 16.78 v. 25, with permission of West Group.

judgment creditor
The winner in civil cases in which money has been awarded.

This will prevent loss and oversight of such items and ease the task of preparing and filing the bill of costs at this stage. You may be asked, as well, to review and determine the accuracy of a bill of costs submitted by the opposing party.

ENFORCEMENT OF THE JUDGMENT

INTRODUCTION

judgment debtor
The loser in civil cases in which money has been awarded.

One of the perplexing quirks in civil procedure is that the winner of a judgment, the **judgment creditor**, often must go back into court to force the **judgment debtor** to comply with the judgment. Although not a difficult process, it is time-consuming and adds additional expense to the lawsuit.

EXHIBIT 12.4 Bill of Costs

AO 133   (Rev. 12/09) Bill of Costs

UNITED STATES DISTRICT COURT

for the

_____ District of _____

)
)
v.   )   Case No.: _____
)
)

BILL OF COSTS

Judgment having been entered in the above entitled action on _____ against _____ ,
the Clerk is requested to tax the following as costs:

Fees of the Clerk . . . . $ _____

Fees for service of summons and subpoena . . . .   _____

Fees for printed or electronically recorded transcripts necessarily obtained for use in the case . . . . . .   _____

Fees and disbursements for printing . . . .   _____

Fees for witnesses *(itemize on page two)* . . . .   _____

Fees for exemplification and the costs of making copies of any materials where the copies are
necessarily obtained for use in the case. . . . .   _____

Docket fees under 28 U.S.C. 1923 . . . .   _____

Costs as shown on Mandate of Court of Appeals . . . .   _____

Compensation of court-appointed experts . . . .   _____

Compensation of interpreters and costs of special interpretation services under 28 U.S.C. 1828 . . . . .   _____

Other costs *(please itemize)* . . . .   _____

                                                                      TOTAL $ _____

SPECIAL NOTE: Attach to your bill an itemization and documentation for requested costs in all categories.

Declaration

I declare under penalty of perjury that the foregoing costs are correct and were necessarily incurred in this action and that the services for which fees have been charged were actually and necessarily performed. A copy of this bill has been served on all parties in the following manner:

❑   Electronic service   ❑   First class mail, postage prepaid

❑   Other: _____

s/ Attorney: _____

Name of Attorney: _____

For: _____   Date: _____
Name of Claiming Party

Taxation of Costs

Costs are taxed in the amount of _____ and included in the judgment.

_____   By: _____   _____
Clerk of Court   *Deputy Clerk*   *Date*

                                                                      (continued)

EXHIBIT 12.4 Bill of Costs (*continued*)

AO 133 (Rev. 12/09) Bill of Costs

UNITED STATES DISTRICT COURT

	ATTENDANCE		SUBSISTENCE		MILEAGE		Total Cost Each Witness
NAME , CITY AND STATE OF RESIDENCE	Days	Total Cost	Days	Total Cost	Miles	Total Cost	
						TOTAL	

Witness Fees (computation, cf. 28 U.S.C. 1821 for statutory fees)

NOTICE

Section 1924, Title 28, U.S. Code (effective September 1, 1948) provides:
"Sec. 1924. Verification of bill of costs."
　"Before any bill of costs is taxed, the party claiming any item of cost or disbursement shall attach thereto an affidavit, made by himself or by his duly authorized attorney or agent having knowledge of the facts, that such item is correct and has been necessarily incurred in the case and that the services for which fees have been charged were actually and necessarily performed."

See also Section 1920 of Title 28, which reads in part as follows:
　"A bill of costs shall be filed in the case and, upon allowance, included in the judgment or decree."

The Federal Rules of Civil Procedure contain the following provisions:
RULE 54(d)(1)

Costs Other than Attorneys' Fees.
　Unless a federal statute, these rules, or a court order provides otherwise, costs — other than attorney's fees — should be allowed to the prevailing party. But costs against the United States, its officers, and its agencies may be imposed only to the extent allowed by law. The clerk may tax costs on 14 day's notice. On motion served within the next 7 days, the court may review the clerk's action.

RULE 6

(d) Additional Time After Certain Kinds of Service.

　When a party may or must act within a specified time after service and service is made under Rule5(b)(2)(C), (D), (E), or (F), 3 days are added after the period would otherwise expire under Rule 6(a).

RULE 58(e)

Cost or Fee Awards:

　Ordinarily, the entry of judgment may not be delayed, nor the time for appeal extended, in order to tax costs or award fees. But if a timely motion for attorney's fees is made under Rule 54(d)(2), the court may act before a notice of appeal has been filed and become effective to order that the motion have the same effect under Federal Rule of Appellate Procedure 4(a)(4) as a timely motion under Rule 59.

Print	Save As...		Reset

Source: U.S. Courts.

More than likely, the judgment debtor will cooperate and make arrangements to pay. It may be a lump-sum payment in cash, a structured payment involving investments and annuities, installments secured by promissory notes and collateral, or some other method.

If, at the beginning of a lawsuit, the plaintiff fears that the defendant will try to hide or even transfer assets to avoid loss through judgment, the judgment creditor can seek court action to seize the property to satisfy a favorable judgment. Federal Rule 64 permits such procedure in accordance with the remedies and procedures available in the state in which the federal district court sits. Some typical prejudgment remedies include *attachment, garnishment, replevin,* and others. Some of these same remedies are available after judgment and will be discussed later in this section. Prejudgment remedies are less popular today than a few years ago, and courts are unlikely to grant them unless there is a good reason. If the action involves the title to specific property, a notice of **lis pendens** may be filed by the plaintiff. It places all other buyers of that property on notice that the plaintiff has claimed a right to that property depending on the outcome of the case. Exhibit 12.5 is an example of a notice of lis pendens.

The focus of this chapter, however, and the more common concern of the paralegal, is locating and obtaining assets after the judgment has been entered and the debtor refuses to cooperate.

lis pendens

Record to notify potential buyers that the plaintiff has asserted a claim against property in a lawsuit.

LOCATING THE ASSETS OF THE JUDGMENT DEBTOR

Prior to taking any action, the judgment creditor must determine whether the debtor has any assets. Most likely, this was determined to some extent in the early stages of the case. Few attorneys are willing to put forth the effort to win a case,

---

EXHIBIT 12.5 Notice of Lis Pendens

STATE OF _____   CIRCUIT COURT   COUNTY _____

_____
                    Plaintiff
    v.   Civil Case File No. _____
_____,
                    Defendant

NOTICE OF LIS PENDENS

NOTICE IS HEREBY GIVEN that an action has been filed in the above entitled court by _____, Plaintiff against _____, Defendant for an action [*state type of action such as "to quiet title"*].

This action affects title to real property in _____ County as described below:

(Provide legal description of property.)

Date _____   Attorney for Plaintiff _____
                       Address _____
                       Phone _____

judgment proof

Description of a party who has no assets with which to pay a judgment.

only to find at the end that the defendant has no assets and is, for all practical purposes, **judgment proof**. Whether at the beginning or end of the case, you need to gather this information.

A Guide to Locating Assets

Your objective is to compile a list of every asset that the judgment debtor has. As you search for assets, you will want to obtain the following basic information for each asset:

- A description of the asset. Be specific as to quantity, color, size or other measurements, function, component parts, or any other data relevant to the kind of asset in question.

- Location. Where is the asset? Give the exact addresses and names of people who have possession of the asset, including, of course, the judgment debtor.

- How did the judgment debtor obtain his/her interest in the asset? If by purchase, how much was paid, when acquired, etc.?

- What is the current fair market value of the asset? If the asset were sold on the open market, how much would it probably bring?

- When tracking assets in an attempt to obtain the above information, it is useful to think of the various categories of assets that are possible:

  1. Personal property—Real property
  2. Property solely owned by the judgment debtor—Property in which others also have an interest
  3. Tangible property—Intangible property
  4. Property in the possession of the judgment debtor—Property in the possession of a third person
  5. Property in the state where the judgment was rendered (forum state)—Property in another state (foreign state)
  6. Property the judgment debtor currently has—Property that will be received in the future
  7. Property the judgment debtor currently has—Property that the judgment debtor disposed of since the litigation began or just before it began
  8. Property that is exempt from creditor collection—Property not protected by exemption

Any single asset may fall into a variety of categories.

Personal/Real Property.   Personal property would include cash, bonds, securities, uncashed checks, cars, trucks, boats, jewelry, clothing, business inventory, equipment, pension rights, insurance policies, debts owed the judgment debtor (e.g., accounts receivable), and so on. Real property includes current residence, vacation home, fixtures on the land, buildings (business or personal use), and so on.

Solely Owned/Others with Interest.   The judgment debtor may own many assets in his/her own name without anyone else having a property interest in the asset.

On the other hand, there will usually be assets in which others will also have a property interest. For example,

- a spouse may jointly own a bank account or a home
- a spouse may have a dower or community property interest in assets acquired during the marriage
- an associate may have an equal partnership interest in a business
- a tenant will have a property right to remain on land owned by the judgment debtor as landlord
- the government may have a tax lien on property because of nonpayment of taxes
- a bank or some other creditor may have a security interest in property, e.g., the property was used as collateral in order to obtain a mortgage or borrow money in some other way
- a neighbor has an easement over the judgment debtor's land allowing the neighbor to use the land for a limited purpose

The following are some basic property terms with which you should be familiar. They all involve assets in which more than one person has a property interest:

Joint tenancy: individuals (called joint tenants) own the entire property together. They do not own parts of it; each individual owns all of the property. When one joint tenant dies, the property does not pass through the decedent's estate. The property passes immediately to the surviving joint tenants. This principle is known as the right of survivorship. (A joint tenant is not a tenant who rents an apartment; these are totally separate concepts of tenance.)

Tenancy by the entirety: a joint tenancy in which the joint tenants are husband and wife.

Tenancy in common: individuals (called tenants in common) who own a portion or a share of the whole property. There is no right of survivorship. When one tenant in common dies, his/her interest in the property passes through his/her estate and does not go to the surviving tenants in common.

Lien: a claim against property usually created to secure payment of a debt. The holder of the lien can force the sale of the property when the debt is not paid. The proceeds from the forced sale are used to satisfy the debt.

Mortgage: in some states, a mortgage is simply a lien of property used to secure the mortgage debt.

Tangible/Intangible Property. Tangible property has a physical form, which can be seen or touched, such as land, car, equipment. Intangible property is a "right" rather than a physical object; for example, the right to receive money from an employer, the right to the exclusive use of an invention, the right to have money repaid with interest. These rights may be described in documents that are tangible, for example, a stock certificate, a promissory note, a patent, but the rights represented by these documents are intangible.

Possession of Judgment Debtor/Possession of Others. Very often the judgment debtor will have assets in the possession of other persons or institutions. Banks and employers, for example, often hold money that belongs to the judgment debtor, which will be turned over upon request or when a set date arrives. Insurance companies, unions, and government agencies also hold ("possess") assets (often called benefits), which will be given to the judgment debtor at a certain time or upon the happening of a designated condition, such as retirement.

A bailment exists when someone else's goods are being held for use, repair or storage. Examples of bailment situations are furniture in storage, a borrowed or rented car, a car in a repair shop. The person holding the property (called the bailee) may or may not be receiving a profit for holding the goods of the other (called the bailor).

Garnishment is the process of trying to reach the assets of the debtor (here the judgment debtor), which are in the possession of a third party, in order to satisfy the debt.

Property in Forum State/Property in Foreign State.   The forum state is the state that rendered the judgment for the judgment creditor against the judgment debtor. A foreign state is any other state in the United States or any other country in the world. The judgment debtor may own land or other assets in a foreign state as well as in the forum state.

Current Property/Future Property.   Many of the judgment debtor's assets will already be in his/her possession. Other assets, however, may be on their way to the judgment debtor through the mail or other means of shipment. Some assets will not be received until the occurrence of a designated event or condition, such as a request for the asset is made by the judgment debtor, a certain age is reached, retirement, death, a designated date has arrived.

Assets the judgment debtor has a right to receive in the future can usually be *assigned* to someone else so that the latter will be entitled to receive the asset. An assignment is simply a transfer of rights from one person to another.

Current Property/Property Recently Disposed Of.   The great fear of a judgment creditor is that the judgment debtor will voluntarily render him/herself judgment proof by giving away, destroying, or otherwise disposing of the assets before the trial is over. The judgment creditor may or may not have obtained protection against this by the kind of pretrial attachment referred to above. Even if no such protection was obtained, the judgment creditor may be able to invalidate any transfers of assets made by the judgment debtor just before and during the trial on the ground that they were sham transfers, or were made with the intent to defraud the judgment winner.

Exempt Property/Nonexempt Property.   All the assets owned by the judgment debtor are not fair game to the judgment creditor. By law, certain property is exempt. This may include a designated percentage of the judgment debtor's salary, clothes, the tools of one's trade or profession, some furniture. Such property cannot be reached by the judgment creditor to satisfy the judgment debt. Consider researching the state rules for exempt and nonexempt property. Each state is different. States such as Texas and Florida have generous provisions for exempt property. What is permitted in one state to satisfy a judgment may be improper in another. Review, verify, and research a state's statutory laws before commencing the collection process. *Hickey v. Couchman,* 797 S.W. 2d 102 (Tex.App. Corpus Christi, 1990) places a responsibility on the entity executing on property to act diligently or be held liable for their actions.

CASE STUDY: UNDERSTANDING THE LAW

Hickey v. Couchman involves the judgment creditor and the sheriff's office who attempted to execute on a judgment. Texas has a statute that holds an officer liable for failure to levy or sell property subject to execution. In *Hickey v. Couchman*, Sheriff Hickey received a writ of execution from Carolyn Couchman. Couchman was awarded a judgment against her ex-husband in their divorce action. The judgment was for $2,000 in damages and $1,000 in attorney's fees. A writ of execution was prepared and sent to Sheriff Hickey's office. Along with Couchman's law firm's paralegal, a deputy sheriff went to Couchman's ex-husband Steve's condo and located a number of exempt pieces of property. No execution occurred. The two returned when Steve was present. He stated that he had filed bankruptcy. The paralegal checked and could not find a bankruptcy. The paralegal contacted the sheriff's office and told them that Steve was now selling his property. The property was sold even though no bankruptcy had yet to be filed. The sheriff's office told Carolyn that nothing could be done because Steve was going to file bankruptcy.

Carolyn's attorney filed an action against the sheriff's office alleging violation of Texas law in failing to execute on the property, because Steve's bankruptcy was filed nearly 90 days after the sheriff's initial encounter at the condo. The trial court found for Carolyn and the sheriff's office appealed. Following the long-standing history of the statute permitting judgment against a sheriff who fails to execute on property, the court analyzed the facts in the Couchman matter. Citing defenses that the sheriff's office could raise, the court focused on whether the judgment creditor—Carolyn—had been injured by the sheriff's failure to execute on the judgment. The court found that when the sheriff's office determined that no bankruptcy was filed and the assets were still in the debtor's possession, they had an obligation to execute on those assets immediately. Here, the debtor had assets to cover the judgment and were assets subject to execution. The court found that the sheriff's office violated the Texas statute and awarded Carolyn judgment and attorney's fees against the sheriff's office.

Questions for Review: Locate a copy of *Hickey v. Couchman* and read it. Who has the burden of proof to establish the value of the assets that are subject to execution? What defenses did the sheriff's office raise and were they successful? Explain your response. Is the trial court required to make findings of fact and conclusions of law and how did the appellate court interpret that requirement?

INTERNET EXERCISE

Research your jurisdiction's categories of exempt and nonexempt property. Identify the statutory authority for your state's rules. Compare your state's rules to a neighboring jurisdiction and identify the differences and similarities.

How then does the judgment creditor go about locating the assets of the uncooperative judgment debtor that fall into one or more of the eight categories of assets? There are some formal procedures that can be of assistance in discovering assets. Before discussing these, some thoughts will be presented on *informal* investigative techniques.

The judgment creditor has just been through a trial and perhaps an appeal with the judgment debtor. A good deal is already known about him/her. This data must be organized and evaluated at two levels. First, the data contains specific information on the possible assets and liabilities of the judgment debtor. Second, the data tells you a lot about the lifestyle of the judgment debtor. One's lifestyle is an excellent clue to assets and liabilities. You are interested in liabilities or other debts because the kind and extent of liabilities one assumes is often an indication of one's assets. The assumption is that someone with a lot of liabilities probably has a lot of assets to cover those liabilities. Someone who rarely gets into debt probably has very little to risk. Of course, you also want to know if the judgment debtor is over his/her head in liabilities since there may be little or nothing left for the judgment creditor to reach.

Source: Cengage Learning/Delmar, Statsky/*Torts: Personal Injury Litigation*, 1982.

postjudgment interrogatory

A method to discover the assets of the judgment debtor through written questions to be answered under oath.

SEARCHING FOR ASSETS: FORMAL METHODS

The power of the court can also be called upon to aid in locating assets of the judgment debtor. These more formal methods utilize devices designed for pretrial discovery to gather information important to the post-trial resolution of the case.

The least expensive method is the **postjudgment interrogatory**. The paralegal draws in part on the process of informally locating assets to design a set of questions for the judgment debtor to answer. The number of postjudgment interrogatories may be limited by local rules. Exhibit 12.6 is an example of interrogatories for the purpose of discovering assets.

EXHIBIT 12.6 Interrogatories in Aid of Judgment

[Caption]

INTERROGATORIES IN AID OF JUDGMENT

Because you have failed to pay the full amount of the judgment against you entered in favor of [*creditor*], [*creditor*] has the right to attempt to enforce that judgment by a judicial sale [*sheriff's sale*] of your assets. [*Creditor*] also may inquire concerning the existence and location of those assets.

Pursuant to the applicable [*state*] Rules of Civil Procedure you are required to make full and complete answers to the questions set forth on the following pages. These answers must be made in writing, under oath, within thirty (30) days after service upon you and sent to counsel for [*creditor*]; [*attorney's name and address*]. Please attach additional sheets if necessary to completely answer questions.

Should you fail to answer, the court may enter an order imposing sanctions against you.

If you do not understand your duty to answer these questions, you should consult a lawyer. If you do not have or know a lawyer, then you should go to or telephone the office set forth below to find out where you can get legal help.

[*Lawyer Referral Service address and telephone number*]

1. State the name of the person or persons with address, telephone number, and e-mail address who responded or assisted in responding to these interrogatories.
ANSWER:

2. State whether you are currently employed. If so, state whether you are paid weekly, semi-monthly, bi-weekly, monthly, or in some other fashion. If you are self-employed, state the name of your business, address, nature of your business and annual income.
ANSWER:

3. *ACCOUNTS:* State whether or not you maintain any checking or savings accounts. If so, state the name and location of the banks or savings and loan associations or building and loan associations or credit unions and the branch or branches thereof, the identification (account) number of each account, and the amount or amounts you have in each account. If you maintain any of these jointly with another person, give their name and address. Also provide the above information with respect to any such bank accounts which were maintained and which were closed within the past twelve (12) months.
ANSWER:

4. *REAL ESTATE:* Do you have an ownership or interest in any real estate anywhere in the United States? If so, set forth a brief description thereof, including the lot size and type of construction; the location, including the state, county,

(continued)

EXHIBIT 12.6 Interrogatories in Aid of Judgment (*continued*)

and municipality; the volume and page number of the official record; and state further whether you own it solely or together with any other person or persons and give their full names and addresses. If any of the above properties are mortgaged, supply the names and addresses of the lender[s], the date and amount of the mortgage, where it is recorded, the monthly payments and the balance now due.

ANSWER:

5. *DEBTS, NOTES, & JUDGMENTS:* State the names and addresses of any and all persons whom you believe owe you money and set forth in detail the amount of money owed, the terms of payment and whether or not you have written evidence of this indebtedness, and if so, the location of such writing. Also state if the matter is in litigation, and if so, give full details. If you hold a judgment or judgments as security for any of these debts, state where and when the judgment was recorded; and the county, number, and term where the judgment is recorded. If you hold this judgment jointly with any other person or persons, give their name and address.

ANSWER:

6. *INSURANCE:* State whether or not you are the owner of any life insurance contracts. If so, state the serial or policy number or numbers of said contract, the face amount, the exact name and address of the insurance company, the named beneficiary or beneficiaries, and their present address. If you own this insurance jointly with any other person or persons, give their name and address.

ANSWER:

7. *MORTGAGES:* State whether you own any mortgages against real estate owned by any other person in the United States. If so, state whether or not you own this mortgage with any other person or persons and, if so, supply their full names and addresses. State further the names and addresses of all borrowers and the state and county where said mortgage is recorded together with the number of the volume and the page number.

ANSWER:

8. *STOCKS, SHARES, OR INTERESTS:* State whether or not you own any stocks, shares, or interests in any corporation, or unincorporated association or partnership, limited or general and state the location thereof. Include the names and addresses of the organizations and include the serial numbers of the shares or stock. If you own any of the stock, shares, or interests jointly with any other person or persons, give their names and addresses.

ANSWER:

9. *GOVERNMENT, MUNICIPAL, OR CORPORATE BONDS:* State whether or not you own individually or jointly any corporate or governmental bonds including U.S. Savings Bonds. If so, include the face amount, serial numbers, and maturity date and state the present location thereof. If you own any of these bonds jointly with any other person or persons, give their names and addresses.

ANSWER:

10. *SAFETY DEPOSIT BOXES:* State whether or not you maintain any safety deposit box or boxes. If so, include the names of the bank or banks, branch or branches, and the identification number or other designation of the box or boxes. Include a full description of the contents and also the amount of cash among those contents. If you maintain any of these jointly with another person, give their full name and address.

ANSWER:

11. *TRANSFERRED ASSETS AND GIFTS:* If, since the date this debt to [*creditor*] was first incurred, you have transferred any assets (real property, personal property, chose in action) to any person and/or, if you have given any gift of any assets, including money, to any person, set forth, in detail, a description of the property, the type of transaction, and the name and address of the transferee or recipient.

ANSWER:

EXHIBIT 12.6 Interrogatories in Aid of Judgment (*continued*)

12. *INHERITANCE:* State whether or not, to your knowledge, you are now or will be a beneficiary of or will inherit any money from any decedent in the United States, and state the place and date of death, the legal representative of the estate, and the location of the court where the said estate is administered or to be administered.
ANSWER:

13. *ANNUITIES:* State whether you are a beneficiary of any trust fund, and if so, state the names and addresses of the trustees and the amount of the payment and when the payment is received.
ANSWER:

14. *PERSONAL PROPERTY:* Set forth a full description of all furnishings and any other items of personal property (including jewelry) with full description, value, and present location. State also whether or not there are any encumbrances against that property and if so, the name and address of the encumbrance holder, the date of the encumbrance, the original amount of that encumbrance, the present balance of that encumbrance, and the transaction which gave rise to the existence of the encumbrance. If you own any personal property jointly with any other person or persons, give their names and addresses.
ANSWER:

15. *RENTAL INCOME:* State whether you are the recipient, directly or indirectly, of any income for the rental of any real or personal property; and if so, state specifically the source of payment, the person from whom such payments are received, and the amount and date when those payments are received.
ANSWER:

16. *MOTOR VEHICLES:* State whether or not you own any motor vehicles. Include a full description of such motor vehicles including color, model, title number, serial number, and registration plate number. Also show the exact name or names in which the motor vehicles are registered, the present value of those motor vehicles, and their present location and place of regular storage or parking. State also whether or not there are any liens or encumbrances against those motor vehicles and if so, the name and address of the encumbrance, the present balance of the encumbrance, and the transaction which gave rise to the existence of the encumbrance.
ANSWER:

17. *PENSION:* State whether you are a participant in or the recipient of any pension or annuity fund, and if so, state specifically the source of payment, the person to whom such payments are made, the amount of the payments, and the date when those payments are received.
ANSWER:

18. *OTHER ASSETS:* If you have any asset or assets which are not disclosed in the preceding seventeen interrogatories, please set forth all details concerning those assets.
ANSWER:

19. *OTHER OBLIGATIONS:* State whether you currently owe any monies to any person, business, or entity other than the Plaintiff/Creditor herein. If so, provide the name and address of the creditor and the amount owed.

20. *EXEMPTIONS:* State whether you are claiming any exemptions, real property or personal property, tangible or intangible, from any claims of creditors. If so, state the item of property from which an exemption is claimed.

Respectfully submitted,

_____
Attorney for Plaintiff

Adapted from West's Legal Forms § 24.20, v. 11, with permission of West Group.

Postjudgment interrogatories, however, have disadvantages. The debtor can draft answers carefully to provide as little information as possible. If the debtor refuses to answer, the court must be asked to compel an answer, causing further delay.

post-trial request for production of documents
Method to obtain documents that will help in locating the assets of the judgment debtor.

As is true in discovery, the interrogatories could be joined with a **post-trial request for production of documents**, or the request could be submitted independently. The request can obtain a variety of documents including copies of tax returns, financial records and reports, bank statements, insurance policies, certificates of title, deeds, loan applications, mortgages, and others.

A more expensive and time-consuming process is the use of the **post-trial deposition**. This procedure is known as a *creditor's examination*. It can be used to bring the judgment debtor or other individuals knowledgeable of the debtor's finances into a setting where they can be questioned under oath about the location of the debtor's assets. Being able to question the debtor and others directly provides the opportunity for flexibility and immediate pursuit of newly raised areas of inquiry. Draft a list of those to be deposed and have them subpoenaed as approved by the attorney. Assist in preparing post-trial depositions in the same way you prepare for the discovery deposition. These procedures are referred to as **supplementary proceedings** and may be used before any action is filed to enforce a judgment or as part of separate actions to collect on the judgment. Sanctions can be imposed for failing to comply with these devices, including the contempt powers of the court. State rules and statutes should be carefully consulted before using any of these devices.

post-trial deposition
Device used to discover the assets of the judgment debtor through oral examination under oath.

supplementary proceedings
The methods used to acquire information about the judgment debtor to enforce a judgment; for example, the post-trial deposition.

COLLECTING A JUDGMENT: OBTAINING THE ASSETS OF THE JUDGMENT DEBTOR

Introduction

With a detailed list of the debtor's assets and consultation with the attorney, all that remains is the selection of an appropriate procedure and the drafting of the relevant documents. The easiest and least expensive collection method is to write a letter to the debtor. Keep in mind that the Federal Fair Trade Debt Collections Practices Act (15 U.S.C. § 1692) applies to attorneys. If the letter is to collect the judgment for a personal or consumer debt (as opposed to a business debt), consult the federal statute and locate form letters specific to collecting that type of debt. Exhibit 12.7 is an example. Exhibit 12.8 is an example of a follow-up letter.

supersedeas bond
Bond filed by the judgment debtor to secure the amount of the judgment while the execution of that judgment is stayed pending post-trial motions.

If the letters fail, procedures used to enforce a judgment include execution, garnishment, and domestication of a judgment. None of these actions may be taken, however, as long as any stay has been granted by the court on the execution of the judgment. Under Federal Rule 62 and parallel state rules, an automatic stay is imposed for the first ten days after judgment, and the court may grant longer stays in its discretion, including a stay pending the outcome of an appeal. The judgment debtor may have to post a **supersedeas bond** to secure the amount of the judgment during the stay. Absent a stay, enforcement actions may be taken.

Execution

execution
The process of carrying out or enforcing a judgment.

Execution is the process of carrying out or enforcing a judgment. Some judgments are self-executing. For example, a divorce decree or a quiet title action requires no further action. Some judgments require the transferring of title or a deed. When the party obligated to execute the transfer refuses to do so, the court may, on application,

---

EXHIBIT 12.7 First Letter to Judgment Debtor

JONES & SMITH
ATTORNEYS AT LAW
100 MAIN STREET
ANYWHERE, U.S.A. 00000
(000) 000-0000

By Certified Mail, Return Receipt Requested: [add in certified mail number here]

Mr. Henry I. Judgment-Debtor   [date] _____
110 North Sycamore Street
Anywhere, U.S.A. 00000

Dear Mr. Judgment-Debtor:

A judgment was entered against you in the _____ Court of _____ on [date], _____ in favor of our client _____, in the amount of $ _____. This amount is still owing to our client on account of the judgment.

Please contact this office to make arrangements for payment of this amount. By making such arrangements now, you will avoid the inconvenience and expense of further legal action against you to collect the judgment.

If we do not hear from you within 30 days of receipt of this letter, my client has instructed us to pursue all available legal options.

We trust you will give this matter your immediate attention.

                                                            Very truly yours,
                                                            JONES & SMITH
                                                            By _____
                                                            Attorneys for _____

cc: [Client]
    Clerk, _____ Court

Adapted from West's Legal Forms, 21.2, v. 11, with permission of West Group.

---

levy

To seize and sell property of the judgment debtor as specified by the court to satisfy the judgment.

APPLY YOUR KNOWLEDGE

Identify the process for a writ of execution in your jurisdiction. Create a checklist based upon your statutes and case law.

appoint a trustee to execute the necessary documents. In other states the court has the power to order done that which the judgment says should have been done. The court order has the effect of the deed when properly recorded.

A writ of execution is a device used to enforce a judgment for money. Both federal courts and the individual state courts rely on the procedure set out in the rules and statutes of that state. Check the local practice for the correct procedure. Most states have a local source book on the forms and procedures for collections.

Typically, the judgment creditor has a list of the property of the defendant needed to satisfy the judgment. A writ of execution is obtained from the court specifying the property to seize and sell (**levy**). A public officer, usually the sheriff, locates the property and physically or constructively seizes it. Only the property needed to satisfy the judgment may be seized. A procedure carefully outlined in state law is followed by which the property is sold. Some delay in the sale is common to give the debtor a chance to receive notice of the levy. The property is sold at auction or other sale, and proceeds are used to pay off the costs of execution, the judgment, and any interest accrued on the principal of the judgment since entry of the judgment. Any remaining

EXHIBIT 12.8 Follow-Up Letter to Judgment Debtor

JONES & SMITH
ATTORNEYS AT LAW
100 MAIN STREET
ANYWHERE, U.S.A. 00000
(000) 000-0000

Mr. Henry I. Judgment-Debtor   [date]_____
110 North Sycamore Street
Anywhere, U.S.A. 00000

Dear Mr. Judgment-Debtor:

Enclosed is a certified copy of the judgment which was entered against you in the _____ Court of _____ on [date], _____ in the amount of $ _____. We have not yet received any response to our letter to you dated, asking you to make arrangements for payment of this amount. Therefore, our client _____ has instructed us that, unless we hear from you by [date], we are to take further legal action against you. Such legal action may include but is not limited to seizure and sale at public auction of your nonexempt personal property, including your automobile, garnishment of a portion of your wages from your employer, and any other action provided under the laws of [state].

Please make arrangements to pay to our office not less than $ _____ by [date]. Otherwise, we will have no choice but to take further legal action against you.

Very truly yours,
JONES & SMITH
By_____
Attorneys for _____

cc: [Client]

Adapted from West's Legal Forms, 21.3, v. 11, with permission of West Group.

receivership
Placement of the assets of a business or an individual under the control of a court-appointed receiver who will protect those assets to pay a debt.

Garnishment
The process of trying to reach the assets of a judgment debtor that are in the possession of a third party in order to satisfy the judgment.

proceeds are returned to the judgment debtor. Exhibit 12.9 is an example of a writ of execution from the state of Maryland. Most states have available in preprinted form writs of execution from the court.

In some cases, such as where the judgment debtor owns business property, placing the property into **receivership** may be preferable to selling it. In this procedure, the court appoints a receiver who sees to it that the judgment is paid out of the regular income of the business until the debt is satisfied. It allows the debtor to maintain the business beyond payment of the debt unless the court orders the sale of the property.

GARNISHMENT

Garnishment is used to obtain property of the debtor held by or owed to the debtor by a third person. Property typically garnished includes money in bank accounts or wages regularly owed the debtor. The judgment creditor generally applies for a writ of garnishment. The writ is served with a summons by the sheriff

EXHIBIT 12.9 Writ of Execution

IN THE UNITED STATES BANKRUPTCY COURT
FOR THE DISTRICT OF MARYLAND
at <u>Greenbelt</u>   ▼

	*
	* Amount of Judgment $ _____
Plaintiff(s)	*
	*
vs.	* Case No. _____
	*
	* Chapter _____
	*
Defendant(s)	*
	*

WRIT OF EXECUTION OF PROPERTY

TO THE SHERIFF/CONSTABLE OF _____ **County** ▼:

You are to levy the property listed below, in accordance with MD Rule 3-642 (see attached):

The Judgment Debtor's last known address is _____.
The property to be levied is located at _____.

After levy you are to carry out the instructions of the Plaintiff as to the property, provided that, if bond is required for the payment of expenses that may be incurred by you in complying with this Writ, it had been posted in the amount and with the security approved by you. The Plaintiff instructs you to: ☐ leave the property where found. ☐ exclude others from access to/use of it. ☐ remove it from the premises. Please see the attached Writ of Execution Notice for additional instructions.

TO THE JUDGMENT DEBTOR:

The Court has ordered that your goods or land should be levied upon sold, and the proceeds used to pay the amount of the judgment shown above. In addition to those listed on the Writ of Execution Notice attached, FEDERAL AND STATE EXEMPTIONS MAY BE AVAILABLE to you. You may move to release some or all of the property from levy. You may avail yourself of these exemptions only by FILING A MOTION WITHIN 30 DAYS setting forth the items you select for exemption in the Office of the Clerk of this Court, U.S. Courthouse, <u>6500 Cherrywood Lane, Suite 300, Greenbelt, MD 2077</u> ▼. A copy of that motion must be mailed to the plaintiff or his attorney, and the original must be filed with the Court.

If any third person has any interest, lie, or claim in the goods or lands listed for levy, it is recommended that you notify such person immediately. By this levy, the goods and lands are subjected to a judicial lien and your right to sell or dispose of them is suspended. Since no complete statement of your rights and liabilities can be given here, you may wish to consult a lawyer.

_____   _____
Date Issued   Clerk/Judge

EXHIBIT 12.9 Writ of Execution (*continued*)

WRIT OF EXECUTION NOTICE

TO SHERIFF:

MD Rule 3-641(c)

Transmittal to sheriff; bond.- Upon issuing a writ of execution or receiving one from the clerk of another county, the clerk shall deliver the writ and instructions to the sheriff. The sheriff shall endorse on the writ the exact hour and date of its receipt and shall maintain a record of actions taken pursuant to it. If the instructions direct the sheriff to remove the property from the premises where found or to exclude others from access to or use of the property, the sheriff may require the judgment creditor to file with the sheriff a bond with security approved by the sheriff for the payment of any expenses that may be incurred by the sheriff in complying with the writ.

MD Rule 3-642

(a) *Levy Upon Real Property* – Except as otherwise provided by law, the sheriff shall levy upon a judgment debtor's interest in real property pursuant to a Writ of Execution by entering a description of the property upon a Schedule and by posting a copy of the Writ and the Schedule in a prominent place on the property.

(b) *Levy Upon Personal Property* – Except as otherwise provided by law, the sheriff shall levy upon a judgment debtor's interest in personal property pursuant to a Writ of Execution by obtaining actual view of the property, entering a description of the Schedule, and (1) removing the property from the premises, or (2) affixing a copy of the Writ and Schedule to the property, or (3) posting a copy of the Writ and Schedule in a prominent place in the immediate vicinity of the property and affixing to each item of property a label denoting that the property has been levied upon by the sheriff, or (4) posting a copy of the Writ and Schedule in a prominent place in the immediate vicinity of the property without affixing a label to each item of property, if affixing a label to each item of property is possible but not practical.

(c) *Possession of Personal Property By Third Person* – When the sheriff has been instructed to remove the property from the premises or exclude others from access or use and finds the property in the possession of a person, other than the judgment debtor, who asserts entitlement to possession and objects to the sheriff's removal of it or exclusion of that person from access or use, the sheriff shall notify the person retaining possession of the property of the legal effect of the levy.

(d) *Notice of Levy* – The sheriff shall furnish a copy of the Writ of Execution and Schedule to any person found by the sheriff to be in possession of the property. If that person is not the judgment debtor, the sheriff shall also mail a copy of the Writ and Schedule to the judgment debtor's last known address.

(e) *Return* – Following a levy, the sheriff shall promptly file a return together with the Schedule. If the Writ of Execution was received from another county under Rule 3-641(b), a copy of the Return and Schedule shall also be field in the county where the judgment was entered.

TO JUDGEMENT DEBTOR:

You have the right under Courts and Judicial Proceedings Article § 11-504 of the Annotated Code of Maryland to claim an exemption of certain kinds of personal property such as: wearing apparel, books, tools, instruments, or appliances in an amount not to exceed $5,000 in value necessary for the practice of any trade or profession except those kept for sale, lease, or barter; money payable in the event of sickness, accident, injury, or death of any person including compensation for loss of future earnings (however, disability income benefits are not exempt if the judgment is for necessities contracted for after the disability is incurred); professionally prescribed health aids for the debtor or dependent of the debtor; debtor's interest not to exceed $1,000 in value in household furnishings, household goods, wearing apparel, appliances, books, animals kept as pets, and other items that are held for the personal, family, or household use of the debtor or any dependent of the debtor. IN ADDITION, WITHIN 30 DAYS AFTER THE DATE OF SERVICE OF THE WRIT OF GARNISHMENT ON THE BANK OR OTHER PERSON HOLDING YOUR MONEY OR PROPERTY, YOU MAY ELECT TO EXEMPT A TOTAL OF $6,000. (This exemption does not apply to an attachment before judgment.) YOU MAY ALSO BE ENTITLED TO PROTECT OTHER MONEY OR PROPERTY NOT MENTIONED ABOVE. TO PROTECT YOUR RIGHTS FULLY, IT IS IMPORTANT THAT YOU ACT PROMPTLY. IF YOU HAVE ANY QUESTIONS, YOU SHOULD CONSULT A LAWYER.

Source: Maryland State Courts.

garnishee

The third party who is directed to surrender property owed to the judgment debtor to satisfy the judgment.

APPLY YOUR KNOWLEDGE

What is the process for domesticating a judgment in your state? Outline that procedure and place in your systems folder. What is your state's statute of limitations for collecting on a foreign judgment? Choose a neighboring state and identify what process you would have to follow to file a judgment from your state in that jurisdiction.

or some other public official on the third person (**garnishee**), and directs that person to disclose the amount of money being held by the garnishee. The garnishee usually has 20 days to respond to the summons. Once the amount is determined, an order for garnishment is requested and a writ issued for seizure of the property or for a lien on the property preventing its transfer to the debtor. When wages are involved, federal law exempts 75 percent of the employee's disposable earnings. Disposable earnings are all earnings less withholding taxes, Social Security, and other lawful deductions. Exhibit 12.10 is an example of a writ of garnishment from the state of Michigan. Many jurisdictions have forms for writs of garnishment. If tasked with preparing an application for a writ of garnishment, check state and local court websites for forms and other information.

Domesticating a Judgment

When a judgment is entered and recorded, it is good for a period of ten years in most jurisdictions. The recording of the judgment notifies all other creditors and potential buyers that a lien exists on the debtor's property. Most property will not be sold until all such liens are cleared. For a nominal fee, most judgments can be renewed. This procedure becomes particularly useful when a debtor is currently unable to pay the judgment but comes into money or property at a later date.

When the debtor has property in another jurisdiction, particularly another state, creditors can levy on that property by *domesticating the judgment*. In other words, the judgment from one state may be entered into a court in another state, and all rights will attach to that judgment as if it had been initially obtained in the foreign jurisdiction. This area is another in which a paralegal's investigation of assets can be valuable. The procedure involves locating the court that has jurisdiction over the debtor's

---

TECHNOLOGY UPDATE: USING THE INTERNET TO LOCATE ASSETS

It is no surprise that the Internet will enhance a creditor's ability to locate the assets of a debtor. Some common places to search are skip tracing websites as well as people locator sites. Skip trace sites assist in locating the whereabouts of a person. These sites accumulate public records and create databases on people. They can be helpful in locating a debtor. The Internet also has numerous sites which provide general people searches. On these sites information such as telephone numbers, addresses, dates of birth, and other general information is found. Common sites such as anywho.com, whitepages.com, and switchboard.com assist with this type of information. Companies can be hired who have access to extensive data bases that can locate individuals. And the ever-present social websites can provide information on people, such as whereabouts and general assets. Pictures speak a thousand words!

Be careful that ethical rules and statutory laws are followed when searching for a debtors' assets. There are restrictions as to how far you can go. Additionally, many court websites offer information on how to collect a debt. California, for example, offers detailed information on its website on how to get information about a debtor's assets. They have a mechanism called "debtor's examination" which allows a creditor to query a debtor about existing assets. The forms and procedure are listed as well. New York's court website also offers methods for locating assets and collecting a judgment. The possibilities are endless and a click away. But before you become the master investigator, *always, always, always* check state and federal laws and guidelines for collecting a debt. All your efforts can be thwarted if they are not done in accordance with state and federal law.

EXHIBIT 12.10 Writ of Garnishment

Approved, SCAO

Original - Garnishee (Part 1)
1st copy - Court (Part 2)
2nd copy - Defendant (Part 2)
3rd copy - Return (proof of service) (Part 2)
4th copy - Plaintiff/Attorney (proof) (Part 2)

• STATE OF MICHIGAN
_____ **JUDICIAL DISTRICT**
_____ **JUDICIAL CIRCUIT**

REQUEST AND WRIT FOR GARNISHMENT (PERIODIC)

• CASE NO.

Court address

• Zip code

Court telephone no.

Plaintiff's name and address (judgment creditor)

v

Defendant's name and address (judgment debtor)

Plaintiff's attorney, bar no., and address

Social security no.

Employee ID or account no.

Garnishee name and address

Telephone no.

| REQUEST | See instructions for item 2 on other side. |

1. Plaintiff received judgment against defendant for $_____ on _____ .
2. The total amount of judgment interest accrued to date is $_____ . The total amount of postjudgment costs accrued to date is $_____ . The total amount of postjudgment payments made and credits to date is $_____ . **The amount of the unsatisfied judgment now due (including interest and costs) is • $_____ .**
3. Plaintiff knows or with good reason believes the garnishee is indebted to or possesses or controls property belonging to defendant.
4. **Plaintiff requests** a writ of periodic garnishment.

I declare that the statements above are true to the best of my information, knowledge, and belief.

_____
Date

_____
Plaintiff/Agent/Attorney signature

| WRIT OF GARNISHMENT | To be completed by the court. See other side for additional information and instructions. |

TO THE PLAINTIFF: You must provide all copies of the disclosure form (MC 14), two copies of this writ, and a $6.00 disclosure fee for serving on the garnishee. You are responsible for having these documents served on the garnishee within 182 days. **NOTE:** The social security number field is blacked out for security reasons on all parts except the garnishee copy.

TO THE DEFENDANT:
1. You have **14 days** after this writ is mailed or delivered to you to file objections with the court. If you do not take this action within this time, without further notice, periodic payments owed to you may be withheld and paid directly to the plaintiff until this writ expires.

TO THE GARNISHEE:
1. Within **7 days** after you are served with this writ, you must deliver a copy of this writ to the defendant in person or mail a copy to his or her last-known address by first-class mail.
2. Within **14 days** after you are served with this writ, you must deliver or mail copies of your verified disclosure (form MC 14) to the court, plaintiff/attorney, and defendant. A default may be entered against you for failure to comply with this order.
3. Do not pay any obligations to the defendant unless allowed by statute or court rule.
4. If indebted, withholding must begin according to court rule (see instructions on the Garnishee Disclosure form). Unless notified that an objection has been filed, **28 days** after you are served with this writ you must begin forwarding withheld payments.
   You are ordered to make all payments withheld under this writ payable to:
   ☐ **the plaintiff**   ☐ **the plaintiff's attorney**   ☐ **the court**
   and mail them to: ☐ **the plaintiff.**   ☐ **the plaintiff's attorney.**   ☐ **the court.**
5. This periodic garnishment is effective until: a) the amount withheld equals or exceeds the amount of the unpaid judgment as stated in item 2 of the request, or b) the expiration date of this writ, whichever occurs first.
6. Within **14 days** after this writ expires, you must file a final statement of the total amount paid on this writ.

_____
Date of issue

_____
Expiration date

_____
Clerk of the court/Deputy

MC 12 (4/14) **REQUEST AND WRIT FOR GARNISHMENT (PERIODIC) (Part 1)**

MCL 600.4011 et seq., MCR 3.101

(continued)

EXHIBIT 12.10 Writ of Garnishment (*continued*)

Approved, SCAO

Original - Garnishee (Part 1)
1st copy - Court (Part 2)
2nd copy - Defendant (Part 2)
3rd copy - Return (proof of service) (Part 2)
4th copy - Plaintiff/Attorney (proof) (Part 2)

• STATE OF MICHIGAN _____ JUDICIAL DISTRICT _____ JUDICIAL CIRCUIT	REQUEST AND WRIT FOR GARNISHMENT (PERIODIC)	• CASE NO.

Court address   • Zip code   Court telephone no.

Plaintiff's name and address (judgment creditor)

Plaintiff's attorney, bar no., and address

Telephone no.

v

Defendant's name and address (judgment debtor)

Employee ID or account no.

Garnishee name and address

REQUEST | See instructions for item 2 on other side.

1. Plaintiff received judgment against defendant for $_____ on _____ .
2. The total amount of judgment interest accrued to date is $_____ . The total amount of postjudgment costs accrued to date is $_____ . The total amount of postjudgment payments made and credits to date is $_____ . **The amount of the unsatisfied judgment now due (including interest and costs) is** • $_____ .
3. Plaintiff knows or with good reason believes the garnishee is indebted to or possesses or controls property belonging to defendant.
4. **Plaintiff requests** a writ of periodic garnishment.

I declare that the statements above are true to the best of my information, knowledge, and belief.

_____   _____
Date   Plaintiff/Agent/Attorney signature

WRIT OF GARNISHMENT | **To be completed by the court. See other side for additional information and instructions.**

TO THE PLAINTIFF: You must provide all copies of the disclosure form (MC 14), two copies of this writ, and a $6.00 disclosure fee for serving on the garnishee. You are responsible for having these documents served on the garnishee within 182 days. **NOTE:** The social security number field is blacked out for security reasons on all parts except the garnishee copy.

TO THE DEFENDANT:

1. You have **14 days** after this writ is mailed or delivered to you to file objections with the court. If you do not take this action within this time, without further notice, periodic payments owed to you may be withheld and paid directly to the plaintiff until this writ expires.

TO THE GARNISHEE:

1. Within **7 days** after you are served with this writ, you must deliver a copy of this writ to the defendant in person or mail a copy to his or her last-known address by first-class mail.
2. Within **14 days** after you are served with this writ, you must deliver or mail copies of your verified disclosure (form MC 14) to the court, plaintiff/attorney, and defendant. A default may be entered against you for failure to comply with this order.
3. Do not pay any obligations to the defendant unless allowed by statute or court rule.
4. If indebted, withholding must begin according to court rule (see instructions on the Garnishee Disclosure form). Unless notified that an objection has been filed, **28 days** after you are served with this writ you must begin forwarding withheld payments.

    You are ordered to make all payments withheld under this writ payable to:
              ☐ the plaintiff   ☐ the plaintiff's attorney   ☐ the court
    and mail them to: ☐ the plaintiff.   ☐ the plaintiff's attorney.   ☐ the court.

5. This periodic garnishment is effective until: a) the amount withheld equals or exceeds the amount of the unpaid judgment as stated in item 2 of the request, or b) the expiration date of this writ, whichever occurs first.
6. Within **14 days** after this writ expires, you must file a final statement of the total amount paid on this writ.

_____   _____   _____
Date of issue   Expiration date   Clerk of the court/Deputy

MC 12 (4/14) **REQUEST AND WRIT FOR GARNISHMENT (PERIODIC) (Part 2)**   MCL 600.4011 *et seq.,* MCR 3.101

EXHIBIT 12.10 Writ of Garnishment (*continued*)

PERIODIC GARNISHMENTS

Definitions

Periodic Garnishment - garnishment of periodic payments which include, but are not limited to, wages, salary, commissions, bonuses, and other income paid to the defendant during the period of the writ; land contract payments; rent; and other periodic debt or contract payments.

Additional Instructions for the Plaintiff:

You must provide information that will permit the garnishee to identify the defendant such as the defendant's address, social security number, employee identification number, etc.

Instructions for Item 2:

If a civil judgment does not include judgment interest in the "total judgment" field, the interest amount reported in item 2 should be accrued from the date the complaint was filed.

If a civil judgment includes judgment interest in the "total judgment" field (as in the forms in use before the 5/07 revisions), the interest amount reported in item 2 should not include any postfiling interest already included in the judgment.

Additional Instructions for the Defendant:

1. This writ has been issued because there is a judgment against you that you have not paid. In order to collect on this judgment, income due to you may be garnished.

2. You may object to this garnishment if:
   a. your income is exempt from garnishment by law,
   b. you have a pending bankruptcy proceeding,
   c. the maximum withheld exceeds the amount allowed by law,
   d. you have an installment payment order,
   e. you have paid the judgment in full,
   f. the garnishment was not properly issued or is otherwise invalid.

3. Certain income is exempt from garnishment and the law gives you the right to claim this income as exempt to prevent it from being used to collect on this judgment. The following are examples of some types of income that are exempt from garnishment and the citations where each type may be found in the law. This is not intended as a complete list. You may want to contact your lawyer or legal aid agency for further assistance.

EXAMPLES OF INCOME EXEMPT FROM GARNISHMENT

The following are examples of **some** types of income that are exempt from garnishment and the citations where each type may be found in the law. **Please note that this is not intended as a complete list. You may want to contact your lawyer or legal aid agency for further assistance.**

- Individual Retirement Account (IRA) - [MCL 600.6023(1)(k)]
- Social Security Benefits - [42 USC, Section 407]
- Supplemental Security Income Benefits (SSI) - [42 USC, Section 1383(d)]
- Aid to Families with Dependent Children (AFDC) - [MCL 400.63]
- General Assistance Benefits (GA) - [MCL 400.63]
- Unemployment Compensation Benefits - [MCL 421.30]
- Veterans Assistance Benefits - [38 USC, Section 3101]
- Workers' Compensation Benefits - [MCL 418.821]
- The first $500.00 on deposit in a savings and loan savings account - [MCL 491.628]
- Cash value or proceeds of life insurance or annuity, payable to the spouse or children of the insured - [MCL 500.2207(1)]
- Income benefits under the Michigan Civil Service Act - [MCL 38.40]
- Income benefits under the Michigan Retirement Act - [MCL 421.30]
- U.S. Civil Service Retirement Benefits - [5 USC, Section 8346]

(continued)

EXHIBIT 12.10 Writ of Garnishment (*continued*)

| PROOF OF SERVICE | REQUEST AND WRIT FOR GARNISHMENT (PERIODIC) Case No. |

TO PROCESS SERVER: You must serve the garnishee with two copies of the request and writ of garnishment, a disclosure form, and the applicable fee, and file proof of service with the court clerk as directed by the plaintiff. If you are unable to complete service, you must return this original and all copies to the court clerk.

CERTIFICATE / AFFIDAVIT OF SERVICE / NONSERVICE

☐ **OFFICER CERTIFICATE**
I certify that I am a sheriff, deputy sheriff, bailiff, appointed court officer, or attorney for a party [MCR 2.104(A)(2)], and that: (notarization not required)

OR

☐ **AFFIDAVIT OF PROCESS SERVER**
Being first duly sworn, I state that I am a legally competent adult who is not a party or an officer of a corporate party, and that: (notarization required)

☐ I served two copies of the request and writ of garnishment, a disclosure form, and the applicable fee by:
  ☐ personal service   ☐ registered or certified mail (copy of return receipt attached) on:

Garnishee name	Complete address of service	Day, date, time

☐ I have personally attempted to serve the writ of garnishment, a disclosure form, and the applicable fee on the garnishee and have been unable to complete service.

Garnishee name	Complete address of service	Day, date, time

I declare that the statements above are true to the best of my information, knowledge, and belief.

Service fee $	Miles traveled Fee $		Signature
Incorrect address fee $	Miles traveled Fee $	TOTAL FEE $	Name (type or print)
			Title

Subscribed and sworn to before me on _____ , _____ County, Michigan.
                                        Date

My commission expires: _____   Signature: _____
                        Date   Deputy court clerk/Notary public

Notary public, State of Michigan, County of _____

ACKNOWLEDGMENT OF SERVICE

I acknowledge that I have received two copies of the request and writ of garnishment, a disclosure form, and the applicable fee on

_____ .
Day, date, time

_____   on behalf of _____
Signature

Source: Michigan State Courts.

exemplified

Authenticated as a true copy, as an official transcript to be used as evidence.

property and filing an application in the foreign court. The application includes statements that enforcement of the judgment is not barred by the statute of limitations in either state, that no stay of execution on the judgment is in effect, that the judgment remains unsatisfied, that no other action based on the judgment is pending, and that no judgment based on the original judgment has been previously entered in the foreign state. In addition the name and address of the debtor and the judgment creditor are included. An authenticated, **exemplified**, or otherwise certified copy of the original judgment should be attached.

Under Article 4, §1 of the U.S. Constitution, the foreign state must give "full faith and credit" to the judgment of a sister state. Once domesticated, the judgment can be entered with the foreign state in the same fashion as the original state.

The judgment debtor may challenge the judgment on the basis that the original court lacked jurisdiction or that the judgment has been paid. The burden of proof, however, rests with the judgment debtor. There is no retrial of the original issues. Judgment may be ordered in a similar manner in foreign countries, but in such cases the procedures may vary somewhat. *Bianchi v. Bank of America*, N.A. 124 Nev. 472, 186 P.3d 890 (2008) presented an interesting issue for the Supreme Court of Nevada regarding a foreign judgment from California and filed in Nevada.

CASE STUDY: UNDERSTANDING THE LAW

Maurice Bianchi, a judgment debtor of Bank of America, requested that a Nevada court vacate a domesticated judgment from California because the statute of limitations for enforcement of the judgment had expired in Nevada. The facts are straightforward. Bank of America acquired a judgment against Bianchi when he defaulted on a loan. The bank filed the judgment in Nevada under the Uniform Enforcement of Judgments Act. The bank did nothing to enforce the judgment in Nevada. Nevada had a statute of limitations of six years for the enforcement of judgments. California, however, had a ten-year statute of limitations. Before the judgment expired in California, the bank renewed the judgment and domesticated the judgment in Nevada.

Bianchi challenged the validity of the judgment arguing that the Nevada statute of limitations had run and thus, the judgment should be vacated. The District Court in Nevada denied Bianchi's motion. Bianchi appealed to the Nevada Supreme Court. The court reviewed two issues: (1) whether the renewed foreign judgment is valid under California law and (2) whether Nevada should give that judgment full faith and credit

since the Nevada statute of limitations for enforcement had run. The court determined that the bank had properly renewed its judgment under California law, which meant that the judgment was still a valid one. But, the court had to determine what effect its statute of limitations had on the renewed foreign judgment. Following the reasoning of an Oklahoma appeals court, the Nevada Supreme Court determined that when a foreign judgment remains valid and enforceable in the issuing state, that judgment will be enforceable in the foreign jurisdiction. Here, the judgment creditor must comply with all applicable laws and the judgment debtor is no worse off. Therefore, the Nevada statute of limitations did not preclude the bank from renewing its judgment from California.

Questions for Review: Read the *Bianchi* case. What facts gave rise to the initial lawsuit and judgment in California? Why did Nevada recognize the California judgment even though it would not have been otherwise enforceable in Nevada? Under what facts or circumstances would the Nevada Supreme Court have found the California judgment invalid and unenforceable?

Transferring federal court judgments for enforcement is quite simple. Title 28 U.S.C. at § 1963 permits the registering of a judgment from a federal court in any other federal court. Once registered, the judgment is treated as a local judgment.

Keeping Track of Collections of Judgment

Each case file should have a sheet kept at the front or top of the file that indicates the case, court, judgment, attorney, and the progress in collecting the judgment. If the judgment was not paid soon after its entry, a file record sheet should indicate all types of enforcement action taken and what has been collected on each action to date. You may decide to computerize the file record sheet.

You may also choose to keep a master list of all cases in which judgments have not been satisfied. Calendar all judgment expiration dates so that renewals of those judgments can be sought if the judgment remains unsatisfied. Review the unsatisfied judgment list with the attorney on a periodic basis to see if additional action needs to be taken.

APPEAL

INTRODUCTION

The purpose of an appeal is to ask a higher court to review the decisions of the trial judge that the person appealing believes are erroneous. The appellate court will review questions of law only, not questions of fact decided by the trial court judge or jury. A **question of law** is a point requiring the application and interpretation of statutes and case law. For example, was the statute in question constitutional? Did the lower judge erroneously instruct the jury on the burden of proof? On the other hand, a **question of fact** is a point decided on evidence. For example, was the traffic light red, or was the contract signed? In some issues, such as whether the verdict goes against the weight of the evidence, the appellate judge must review the evidence, but the question remains a question of law—whether the verdict was so erroneous that, as a matter of law, it must be reversed. Appeal also has become an effective tool against large jury awards.

Most parties choose not to appeal because appeals are expensive, and the majority of appellants are unsuccessful. The appeal, however, is an important part of our checks and balances system that guarantees a person the right to have a lower court's decision reviewed if there is a reasonable basis for the appeal. If the party did not raise an issue by objection or motion at the trial, the issue may be waived for purposes of appeal.

The person bringing the appeal is called the **appellant**; the person defending against the appeal is called the **appellee** or respondent. Appellate procedure generally involves the following stages. The appellant must file a notice of appeal that is conveyed to all the other parties. The appellant is responsible to see that a transcript of the pertinent aspects of the trial is ordered, prepared, and sent to the appellate court. Briefs are filed by both parties, stating the facts, the issues to be addressed, and the arguments and authorities on the issues. Oral arguments are presented by all parties during which the judges may ask questions. The judges meet to discuss the case,

---

question of law
A point requiring the application or interpretation of statutes and case law, to be decided by a judge; for example, whether a statute is constitutional.

question of fact
A point decided on evidence; for example, whether the traffic light was red.

appellant
The person bringing an appeal.

appellee
The person defending against an appeal.

and an opinion is written. The appellate court may affirm, modify, or reverse the judgment of the trial court. Even if the appellate judges rule that the trial judge was in error, the appellate court will not alter the judgment unless the error substantially affected the verdict in the case.

standard of review
Focuses on the deference an appellate court gives to a lower court decision or jury verdict.

Appellate courts must follow the **standard of review**, which is dictated by the issues raised on appeal, the lower court record, and case law. The standard of review focuses on the deference an appellate court gives to a lower court decision or jury verdict. There are a number of standards of review that a court may apply in a case depending on the issues raised by the parties. These standards are critical in determining outcomes in appeals and may be one of the most important components of your research for the appellate brief. Some common standards of review in civil cases are abuse of discretion, plenary, de novo, clearly erroneous, plain error, and harmless error. Each is discussed.

Abuse of discretion: Abuse of discretion is the most deferential standard of review. This standard leans toward accepting a trial judge's interpretation of the facts and law, unless that interpretation is egregious. When applied, the appellate courts will examine the record and application of the law and normally will reverse a trial court's decision only if the decision was unreasonable in its application of the law or facts of the case. Typical cases where an abuse of discretion standard applies is in the review of the admission of evidence, review of the granting or denial of a motion, and discovery issues.

De novo review: De novo standards of review usually include strictly legal issues. When a party challenges the constitutionality of a statute, the standard is de novo. As the words *de novo* suggest, the appellate court reviews the decision of the trial court "anew" which means that the review is independent—as though the trial court rendered no decision. Unlike the standard of abuse of discretion, there is no deference accorded the trial court's decision.

Clearly erroneous: When fact issues are raised by a party, the standard of review is clearly erroneous. Similar to abuse of discretion, this standard is extremely deferential to the trial court's decision and is difficult to overcome on appeal. For example, when a trial is before a judge (without a jury), the judge's findings will be reviewed under the clearly erroneous standard.

Plenary review: Under a plenary review standard, the court reviews the entire record completely and fully. The reviewing court does an exhaustive review of the lower court record, which includes all orders, hearings and the trial transcript presented in the record on appeal. Less deference is given to the trial court judge when a plenary standard of review is applied.

harmless error
An error found to have occurred at the trial court by the appellate court, but insufficient to substantially affect the verdict of the case, and therefore, insufficient to overturn the verdict.

Plain error review: Plain error review involves error that was not objected to or noted at trial, but would be prejudicial to the party if not corrected. Often, plain error involves constitutional rights. With this standard, error is not preserved in the court below. When further review of the lower court record occurs, a party raises the error for the first time on appeal. This standard is difficult to overcome since it was not raised in the original trial or proceeding. The key to success for plain error review is showing prejudice to the party raising the issue. Normally plain error is asserted in the criminal context.

Harmless error: With the **harmless error** standard, the court acknowledges that error occurred, but that the error did not affect the outcome of the case.

The error is insignificant. Taking the trial in its entirety, the error was not so harmful to prejudice the party and will not change the outcome. Think of harmless error as the "so what" of appeals. The error occurred, but it was harmless to the case as a whole.

Appeals may have different standards of review depending upon the issues raised by the parties. With four issues raised, there often are four standards of review. Every issue raised should be independently reviewed for the applicable standard of review.

The study of appeals in all their complexity is beyond the scope of this text, so the following discussion is simply an overview of the fundamentals in the process.

APPELLATE PROCEDURE CHECKLIST

Appellate procedure is fairly standardized in the federal courts, but it varies among states. Research the applicable state rules and adhere to them. Following is a list of the significant procedural steps and deadlines for the Federal Rules of Appellate Procedure (FRAP). These rules are amplified further by the local rules (LRs) and internal operating procedures (IOPs) of each respective circuit of the U.S. Court of Appeals.

- ☐ Consult with the attorney for go-ahead on the appeal.
- ☐ Develop a case appeal log for recording compliance with all requirements of the appellate process.
- ☐ File a petition for leave to appeal from *interlocutory order* pursuant to 28 U.S.C. § 1292(b).
- ☐ For post-trial appeals, verify that a judgment or order has been entered.
- ☐ Draft a notice of appeal (see following form).
- ☐ File the notice of appeal within 30 days of entry of judgment or order, or within 60 days if the United States or an officer or agency thereof is a party. Pay fees.
- ☐ File a bond for the cost of the appeal or a supersedeas bond if the execution of judgment is stayed. Seek stay or injunction pending appeal.
- ☐ File with the court of appeals a statement naming each party represented on appeal by the attorney within 14 days after filing the notice of appeal.
- ☐ Order a transcript of the trial proceedings (pertinent parts or pertinent videotape if so recorded) from the court reporter within 14 days after filing the notice of appeal or entry of an order disposing of the last motion such as a motion for a new trial, whichever is later. File a copy of the order with the clerk of district court. Unless the entire transcript is ordered, file a statement of issues on appeal. Notify all other parties of the issues on appeal and the parts of the transcript ordered so appellee can designate other parts of the record needed for appeal within 14 days of service of the order and statement of the issues. Appellant must order the added parts within the next ten days. Parties may stipulate to omit certain parts of the record.
- ☐ See to it that the reporter files a transcript with the clerk of district court within 30 days of the date ordered by the appellant. See that the record is complete (pleadings, exhibits filed in district court, transcript or parts

thereof, and certified copies of docket entries), prepared by the clerk, and submitted by the clerk of court to the court of appeals. Check to see if the record is sent by the clerk. The clerk of the court of appeals will docket the case upon receipt of the notice of appeal and the docket entries.

☐ Send to the appellee a designation of the parts of the record to be included in the appendix within 14 days of the filing of the record, unless there is an agreement on the contents (FRAP 30) or the alternative method of filing the appendix is chosen.

☐ File all papers with the clerk of the court of appeals by mail addressed to the clerk. Some courts of appeal permit electronic filing. All papers must arrive within the required time limit. Briefs are considered timely if mailed before expiration of the time limit. Proof of service should be filed with the papers. Rule 25(2)(d) now authorizes the adoption of local appellate rules to require electronic filing. Heed rules regarding redactions for privacy and security concerns.

☐ Service on the party or the party's counsel may be personal, by mail, by commercial carrier, or by electronic means.

☐ File a motion for extension of time if good cause can be shown. Check local appellate rules as many courts permit a one-time oral extension of time for filing briefs. The time for filing a notice of appeal may not be extended.

☐ Draft the brief and appendix according to the strict specifications in FRAP 28, 29, 30, 32, and 32.1 (unpublished opinions).

☐ File and serve the appellant's brief and appendix within 40 days after the date on which the record is filed. If the brief is not filed on time, the appellee may move for dismissal of the appeal. FRAP 31 calls for filing 25 copies of the brief, but check the respective local rule because the required copies often vary.

☐ File for an extension of time, if necessary.

☐ Note the date that the appellee's brief is due. (The appellee has 30 days after receipt of the appellant's brief to file and serve brief.)

☐ Check the opponent's brief for accurate statements of fact, case holdings and citations, and accurate recitation of the record.

☐ File and serve the appellant's reply brief within 14 days after service of the appellee's brief. (Double-check all case citations and citations of the record before filing.)

☐ Be sure all time limits are on the docket deadline control calendar.

☐ Record notice from the clerk of court whether oral argument is to be heard, and if so, the time, place, and duration of each side's oral argument. Notify the attorney and see that all deadlines are calendared.

☐ Assist in the preparation of oral argument as requested by the attorney. Prepare an oral argument notebook.

☐ Arrange delivery of any exhibits to the court, setup prior to oral argument, and removal immediately after argument.

☐ Attend oral argument to assist the attorney if requested.

EXHIBIT 12.11 Notice of Appeal

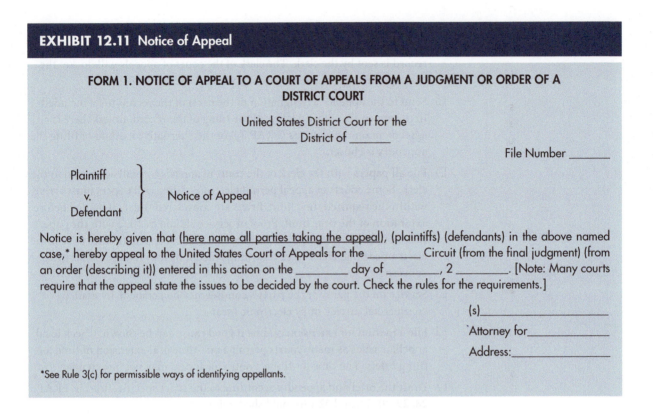

FORM 1. NOTICE OF APPEAL TO A COURT OF APPEALS FROM A JUDGMENT OR ORDER OF A DISTRICT COURT

United States District Court for the
_____ District of _____

File Number _____

Plaintiff
v.   Notice of Appeal
Defendant

Notice is hereby given that (<u>here name all parties taking the appeal</u>), (plaintiffs) (defendants) in the above named case,* hereby appeal to the United States Court of Appeals for the _____ Circuit (from the final judgment) (from an order (describing it)) entered in this action on the _____ day of _____, 2 _____. [Note: Many courts require that the appeal state the issues to be decided by the court. Check the rules for the requirements.]

(s)_____
`Attorney for_____
Address:_____

*See Rule 3(c) for permissible ways of identifying appellants.

☐ Note the receipt of opinion and judgment and convey it to the attorney.

☐ Submit an itemized and certified bill of costs to the clerk with proof of service within 14 days after entry of the judgment. Objection to the bill of costs must be filed within ten days of service of the bill.

☐ Draft and file a petition for rehearing if so directed by the attorney. The petition must be filed within 14 days after entry of the judgment, 45 days if the United States or its agency or officer is a party. The petition should follow the form prescribed by Rule 32(a) and served according to Rule 31(b).

☐ Consider with the attorney the filing of a motion to stay the mandate (direction of the Court of Appeals based on the judgment) pending an application to the U.S. Supreme Court for a writ of certiorari. The motion must be filed within 21 days of the entry of judgment. Note that Appellate Rule 27(d)(1) (e) requires that the typeface and type style requirements for motions must comply with Rules 32(a)(5) and (6), respectively.

Exhibit 12.11 is a notice of appeal, Exhibit 12.12 is a designation of record on appeal, and Exhibit 12.13 is a motion for enlargement of time.

ASSISTING IN THE APPEAL

Introduction

The checklist spells out the tasks you can and should perform. This section will focus on a few tasks that require some amplification.

EXHIBIT 12.12 Designation of Record on Appeal

IN THE UNITED STATES DISTRICT COURT FOR
THE _____ DISTRICT OF _____ DIVISION

ABC _____
                    Plaintiff

            v.   Civil Action No._____
XYZ _____   Judge_____
                    Defendant

DESIGNATION OF RECORD ON APPEAL

Plaintiff, _____, hereby designates the following documents, _____, to constitute the record on appeal.

> [*Here insert a list which includes docket numbers, date, and an identification of each docket entry which is being designated. Many courts have certain required documents for the record and the order in which they must appear in the Joint Appendix. Review the appellate rules for the court in which an appeal is filed.*]

Respectfully submitted,

_____

J. Doe, Attorney for Plaintiff

[*Add Proof of Service*]

Adapted from West's Legal Forms § 17.19, v. 25, with permission of West Group.

EXHIBIT 12.13 Motion for Enlargement of Time—Court of Appeals

IN THE UNITED STATES COURT OF APPEALS FOR THE _____ CIRCUIT

ABC _____,
            Plaintiff–Appellant
            }
            v.   Appeal No. _____
XYZ _____,   [lower court docket number]
            Defendant–Appellee

MOTION FOR ENLARGEMENT OF TIME

Appellant ABC respectfully moves for an order extending the time for filing its Brief by an additional _____ days, pursuant to Fed.R.App.P._____ or [state appellate rules] and would show as follows:

1. The basis for this request is that Appellant's attorney has been unable to complete the Brief within the requisite time period because of the length of the record and because of the loss of "working days" due to legal holidays [*insert any additional reasons, such as medical*].

2. Pursuant to Rule _____, this notice is filed five days before the due date of the brief, which is _____. [Note: Many courts require that a motion for enlargement of time be filed by a certain time before the due date. Check the rules.]

3. This motion is not filed for purposes of delay but so that justice may be done.

(continued)

EXHIBIT 12.13 Motion for Enlargement of Time—Court of Appeals (*continued*)

WHEREFORE, the Appellant prays that this motion for enlargement of time be granted and for such other relief as the Appellant be justly entitled.

Respectfully submitted,

_____

J. Doe, Attorney for Plaintiff

[*Add Proof of Service*]

Adapted from West's Legal Forms, § 17.23, v. 25, with permission of West Group.

Deadline Control and Appeal Management

The experienced paralegal can assume the role of appeals manager. To prepare for this role, study the appellate rules meticulously and record all deadlines, formats, and procedures. If you have questions, ask the appropriate clerk of court. An appeal program sheet should be kept for each case. Overall management can be achieved by using a master sheet with all pending appellate cases and points of progress for each case. Regular calendared reviews by all involved paralegals and attorneys can result in thorough and effective appellate management. With a little experience, the task will be easier and your benefit to the firm enhanced. Knowing and understanding appellate deadlines and timeframes cannot be overstated. A missed deadline can be catastrophic resulting in the dismissal of an appeal which can expose the attorney to malpractice claims. Understanding the intricacies of the appeals process is a learned skill. Read and review the Rules of Appellate Procedure and corresponding local rules to ensure proper handling of the case. As an attorney in *Enos v. Pacific Transfer & Warehouse*, 80 Haw. 345, 910 P. 2d 166 (1996) learned the hard way, misreading or not understanding the rules can lead to disastrous results.

CASE STUDY: UNDERSTANDING THE LAW

The Enoses filed a personal injury case against Pacific Transfer. A verdict was entered in favor of the Enoses. Judgment was filed on April 8. Notice of entry of judgment was filed on May 4. Pacific filed a motion to extend the time to file the appeal and other post-trial motions. The trial court granted Pacific's motion to extend the time to file the appeal, but denied their post-trial motions. Pacific filed their appeal on June 3. The Enoses filed opposing documents stating that the post-trial motions were untimely as well as the notice of appeal. They appealed the trial court's decision.

The Hawaii Supreme Court focused on a number of important issues. First, they applied a strict interpretation of their rules of procedure and then analyzed what constitutes excusable neglect and good cause in allowing a missed appeal deadline to be extended. Key to the court's analysis was appellate Rule 4, which stated that a notice of appeal had to be filed within 30 days after the date of entry of the judgment which was defined as "when it is filed in the office of the clerk...." *Id.* at 349. This rule is important as it is jurisdictional and cannot be waived. Here, as

CASE STUDY: UNDERSTANDING THE LAW (continued)

the court indicated in its opinion, Pacific's attorney became aware of the filing of the judgment through various means on April 14, but maintained that he believed the filing deadline was when the judgment was "entered." The court was not convinced of Pacific's argument and observed that the language of the statute was unambiguous. Pacific became aware of the filing of the judgment throughout the month of April, but did not file its appeal until June 3—56 days after the judgment was filed. However, the court opined on the meaning of excusable neglect and good cause found in its appellate rules, HRAP 4(a)(5). The Hawaii rule was patterned after the Federal Rules of Appellate Procedure. The court followed a First Circuit opinion observing that good cause was something that was out of the party's control. A five-day delay because of the postal service was held as good cause in one instance. The circumstances giving rise to the extension of time determine whether an extension is proper and not the timing of the filing of the motion for the extension of time. Determining excusable neglect requires a review of the record and the facts surrounding the failure to timely file the notice of appeal. In this case, Pacific's counsel's mistaken belief as to when the judgment was effective was the cause for the delay—a circumstance within their control. Therefore, the approach to the issue is not good cause, but whether the facts constituted excusable neglect. The court found it did not and reversed the trial court's decision and dismissed the appeal.

Questions for Review: Review the *Enos* decision. What standard of review did the court apply to the trial court's decision and why? What facts would have changed the court's decision? Distinguish between the standards for excusable neglect and good cause and how each standard is applied.

Research

The paralegal is frequently assigned to research potential theories for the appeal, locate authority in support of the theory, and verify the accuracy of all citations used by all parties in their briefs and oral arguments. You can frequently turn up misuse of authority by checking whether the authority cited actually stands for the principle of law being asserted, and whether the facts are as presented. Eliminating erroneous citations from one's own brief can only strengthen it, while being able to call the court's attention to misuse of authority by the opponent can be effective in challenging the overall credibility of their argument. Note that unpublished opinions issued after January 1, 2007, may be cited in federal appeals; earlier unpublished opinions may not be cited unless previously authorized by local court rule. Check state appellate rules on citing unpublished opinions.

Verifying the Record

Before the record is sent to the appellate court, review it to verify that the reporter has accurately portrayed what happened at the trial. If a partial transcript has been requested, verification of the accuracy of the key parts is particularly important. Further, determine whether everything needed in the record is ready to be sent by the clerk.

Assisting with the Appellate Brief

The appellate brief is a formal document drafted to specific standards that sets out the pertinent facts, legal questions, the legal argument addressing those questions, and legal authorities in support of that argument. The brief is usually accompanied by an appendix of exhibits, relevant transcript sections, and other materials. Knowing some basics about the court and judges in which a appeal is filed is a good start for any paralegal. Navigating through the rules and some of the minefields is critical to any appeal.

Each law office has a different approach to what the paralegal does here. Some firms do not use paralegals in brief preparation; others utilize experienced paralegals to prepare a full rough-draft brief that is reviewed by the attorney and then honed to a sharp edge.

If asked to research the brief, verify and update authorities on each key issue. Double-check each citation stated in the record and each citation to the record. Extract from the transcript those key lines that lie at the heart of the appeal. In addition, you may be asked to organize and write initial drafts of arguments based on the authorities. Good writing and organizational skills are needed at this stage. Observe the format and style of one or two appellate briefs previously filed in the particular court in question. If a brief of the exact same point can be found, it will substantially reduce the work (and also illustrate the value of keeping a brief bank on various topics). In reviewing these materials you will learn rules of drafting, such as "state your strongest argument first" and "use clear subheadings that state arguments." Relevance, fairness, and accuracy should characterize the statement of the facts, and crystal clarity and conciseness, the argument. Appellate handbooks and materials on brief writing provide more techniques and should be reviewed prior to writing the rough draft.

You should assume responsibility for organizing and indexing the brief. Old briefs are of great value here, but since court rules and specifications change, the latest edition of the appellate rules and specifications for briefs should be obtained. The Federal Rules of Appellate Procedure 28, 30, and 32 set the following specifications for briefs:

Rule 28 states that the appellant's brief shall contain a corporate disclosure statement, a table of contents, a table of authorities (cases listed in alphabetical order and statutes and other authorities cited to page of brief), a statement of jurisdiction, a statement of the issues on appeal, and a statement of the case including its nature, previous proceedings, and disposition. In addition, the brief shall have a statement of the relevant facts (with appropriate references to the record), a concise summary of the argument, an argument based on legal authority, a short conclusion stating the precise relief sought, and a certificate of word or line number compliance, if required by Rule 32(a)(7) (b) and (c).

Parties shall be referred to as "plaintiff" and "defendant" or by name rather than as "appellant" or "appellee." References in the briefs to the record shall be to the pages of the brief's appendix at which those parts appear. Relevant statutes, rules, regulations, and so on, or parts thereof, shall be reproduced in the brief, in an addendum, or supplied to the court in pamphlet form [Rule 28(d)–(f)].

The appellee's brief shall be the same, except that statements of jurisdiction, the issues, the case, and the standard of review need not be made unless the appellee is dissatisfied with the statement of the appellant [Rule 28(b)]. In some jurisdictions, the appellee may adopt the statement of facts presented by the appellant. Ordinarily, this is not a good idea. As the appellee, the facts should be drafted from that perspective. An appellant's statement of facts will be drafted in language that favors their point of view. The appellate court should read the statement of facts from the appellee's perspective; thus, adopting the appellant's statement of facts should only be done on a limited basis.

Appellant's and appellee's briefs generally shall not exceed 30 pages or 14,000 words, and the reply briefs 15 pages [unless they comply with Rule 32(a)(7) (b) or (c)], excluding the table of contents, tables of citations, and any addendum. However, check for the current limits on the number of words permitted. A certificate of

TRADE SECRETS: SOME PRACTICAL POINTS IN PREPARING AN APPEAL

Each appellate court has its own rules to follow regardless of whether they follow the Federal Rules of Appellate Procedure or state appellate procedures. Most appellate courts have local rules which modify the general rules of appellate procedure. Check both the general and local rules of procedure in the jurisdiction where an appeal is filed. For example, the Federal Third Circuit Court of Appeals allows for a one-time oral extension of time for the filing of a brief. That means that the attorney simply calls the case manager of the case and requests an extension. It is verbally granted over the telephone and documented in the court's electronic filing system. Many courts have page limits for briefs; others have word limits. Reviewing the rules and the court's requirements is essential to compliance with the filing requirements.

Similarly, many courts have font size requirements. Some courts require a 12-point font; others require a 14-point font. Not following the appellate requirements can cause a brief to be rejected by the court, which undoubtedly is not something anyone wants to have happen. Be sure all the required end affirmations are included. They are different in the appeals process. Usually at the end of the appellate brief along with the certificate of service, there must be a certificate of good standing of the attorney with the court in which the brief is being filed; there also is usually acknowledgment of the number of words used in the brief and a virus check. Some attorneys try and use footnotes as a means to circumvent page or word requirements. This ploy does not go unnoticed by the experienced appellate attorney—another means for a court rejecting the brief or the opponent filing a motion to strike or dismiss the appeal. This situation occurred in a recent appeal in a case filed in the Federal Court of Appeals. In a three-page nonprecedential opinion by the court, *Pi-Net International, Inc. v. JP Morgan Chase*, No. 14-1495 (Fed.Cir. April 20, 2015), the appellant's attorneys attempted to circumvent the word limitations by omitting spacing in citations and other tricks. This meant that a citation that would normally be 14 words would be one word. The attorneys did this throughout the brief, thus making the true word count over 14,000. The court did not appreciate this and dismissed the appeal altogether—a warning to all.

There are motions that can be filed if a brief exceeds court limitations. Slyness is not the answer. Additionally, cooperation in the preparation of the Joint Appendix will be an important function for the paralegal. Know the issues presented on appeal in a case. It is difficult to know what to include in a Joint Appendix if the issues are not identified. This is even more important if the party represented is the appellee. When exchanging information on the Joint Appendix, have the parties create the table of contents. Sometimes attorneys try and slip in items that were not included in the court below. This is generally improper and should not be before the appellate court. Have your attorney warn the opposing counsel of this and if there is a failure to comply, a motion to strike the appendix or that irrelevant portion may be appropriate when it is received.

And one final point relating to an attorney's credibility with the court, in the statement of facts every sentence should have a record reference from the Joint Appendix—"(J.A. 222)," for example. When this is done, this shows the court that the record contains the facts to support your client's version of the facts. Many attorneys fail to consistently cite to the record when presenting their statement of facts. By failing to do this, credibility is lost with the reviewing court. Not only cite to the record in the statement of facts, but also when arguing facts within the argument section of the brief. Again, showing the court where the facts were established in the record, brings a heightened sense of credibility to the case. Do not make the court fish for facts in the record. Your party's viewpoint is the one you want adopted by the court. The more you cite to the record, the higher likelihood the court will support your client's arguments and position. The end result for preparing for an appeal is knowing and understanding the rules of the court in which the appeal is filed, which will contribute to the success in prosecuting or defending the appeal.

EXHIBIT 12.14 Certificate of Compliance Pursuant to Rule 32(a)

1. This brief complies with the type-volume limitation of Fed.R.App.P. 32(a)(7)(b) because:

   - this brief contains [state the number of] words, excluding the parts of the brief exempted by Fed.R.App.P. 32(a)(7)(B)iii, or

   - this brief uses a monospaced typeface and contains [state the number of]lines of text, excluding the parts of the brief exempted by Fed.R.App.P. 32(a)(7)(b)iii,

2. This brief complies with the typeface requirements of Fed.R.App.P. 32(a)(5) and the type style requirements of Fed.R.App.P. 32(a)(6) because:

   - this brief has been prepared in a proportionally spaced typeface using [state name and version of word processing program] in [state font size and name of type style] or

   - this brief has been prepared in a monospaced typeface using [state name and version of word processing program] with [state number of characters per inch and name of type style].

/s/ _____

Attorney for _____

Dated:_____

compliance with Rule 32(a) is required under the appellate rules. This certificate is inserted at the end of the brief. See Exhibit 12.14.

Rule 30 requires the appellant to prepare and file the appendix to the brief containing the relevant docket entries in the proceeding; relevant portions of the pleadings, charge, findings, or opinion; the judgment, order, or decision in question; and any other parts of the record for the court.

Unless filing is to be deferred, the appellant shall serve and file the appendix with the brief. Ten copies of the appendix shall be filed with the clerk, and one copy shall be served on each party.

The parties are encouraged to agree as to the contents of the appendix [Rule 30(b)]. If they cannot, the appellant shall, not later than 14 days after filing the record, serve on the appellee a designation of the parts of the record that the appellant intends to include in the appendix and a statement of the issues for appeal. The appellee may, within 14 days after receipt of the designation, serve upon the appellant a designation of additional parts to be included by the appellant.

The cost of producing the appendix shall initially be paid by the appellant unless otherwise agreed. If parts of the record designated by the appellee for inclusion seem unnecessary to the appellant, the appellee shall pay for including those parts. The cost of producing the appendix shall be taxed as costs in the case. If either party shall cause matters to be included in the appendix unnecessarily, the court may impose the cost of producing such parts on the party [Rule 30(b)].

The court may permit the appendix to be filed after the brief in specific cases. In such cases the appendix may be filed 21 days after service of the brief of the appellee [Rule 30(c)].

The appendix shall include a table of its contents with page references. When transcripts are included in the appendix, the transcript page shall be indicated in brackets immediately before the matter that is set out. Omissions must be indicated by asterisks. Captions, subscriptions, acknowledgments, and so forth shall be omitted. The appellate rules have an order for the appendix. Review appellate rules for the court in which an appendix is filed for the order of the record. If documents are not presented in accordance with the rules, an appendix may be subject to rejection by the court.

Exhibits shall be included in a separate volume. Four copies shall be filed with the appendix and one copy served on each party [Rule 30(e)].

A court of appeals may by rule or in specific cases dispense with the appendix and permit appeals to be heard on the original record with such copies of the record [Rule 30(f)].

Rule 32 sets out the form of the brief. Briefs and appendices must be clearly reproduced on opaque, unglazed, white paper. Photos, illustrations, and other matter need only be a good copy of the original. Pages shall be 8 1/2 by 11 inches, double-spaced, with one-inch margins on all sides. The cover of the appellant's brief should be *blue,* the appellee's *red,* an intervenor's *green,* any reply brief *gray,* and the cover of the appendix, if separately printed, *white.* The front covers, if separately printed, shall contain the name of the court; the case number; the title of the case; the nature of the proceeding; the lower court, agency, or board; the title of the document; and the names, addresses, and phone numbers of counsel. Complete requirements can be found in Rule 32 and parallel state statutes.

Exhibit 12.15 is a skeletal example of the proper order and format of an appellate brief to be filed in the U.S. Court of Appeals. Exhibit 12.16 is a chart that shows the general process to follow in an appeal.

EXHIBIT 12.15 Sample Appellate Brief

IN THE UNITED STATES COURT OF APPEALS
FOR THE _____ JUDICIAL CIRCUIT
Case No. _____

_____
_____,
    Appellant

v.

_____
_____,
    Appellee

On Appeal from the United States District Court for the _____ District of _____

BRIEF AND ARGUMENT OF APPELLANT

(Attorney) _____
(Address) _____
Attorney for _____

(continued)

EXHIBIT 12.15 Sample Appellate Brief (*continued*)

(Table of Contents Page)
TABLE OF CONTENTS

(Authorities Page)
TABLE OF AUTHORITIES CITED

STATEMENT OF JURISDICTION

The basis for subject matter jurisdiction at the district court for the _____ district of _____ is _____. Appellate jurisdiction for . . .

STATEMENT OF THE ISSUES

The Honorable Walter F. DAVIS, Judge of the Northern District of Columbia, it is asserted made three errors at or following the trial in this case. The errors alleged are stated below:

1. _____

2. _____

3. _____

STATEMENT OF THE CASE*

   *(FED. R. APP. P. 28(a)(6) "a statement of the case briefly indicating the nature of the case, the course of proceedings, and its disposition in the court below.")

   This case is on appeal from the district court's ruling . . .

EXHIBIT 12.15 Sample Appellate Brief (*continued*)

STATEMENT OF THE FACTS*

*(7) a statement of the facts relevant to the issues submitted for review with appropriate references to the record [Rule 28(a)(7).

In February of _____, Ann Forrester, a brilliant and creative teacher and mother of two, was . . .

SUMMARY OF ARGUMENT*

*[FED. R. APP. P. 28(a)(8)]

ARGUMENT*

*[FED. R. APP. P. 28(a)(A)(B)].

I. BECAUSE THE JURY VERDICT WAS CONTRARY TO THE GREAT WEIGHT OF THE EVIDENCE, THE TRIAL COURT ERRED IN DENYING PLAINTIFF'S MOTION FOR JUDGMENT AS A MATTER OF LAW.

The law on when a motion for judgment as a matter of law is to be granted was reiterated in the recent Supreme Court case of *Abrams v. Pure Manufacturing, Inc.,* 500 U.S. 312, 33 L. Ed. 2d 419 (1995). The court stated the rule to be:

When the evidence in a case demonstrates . . .

CONCLUSION*

*(10) a short conclusion stating the precise relief sought [FED. R. APP. P. 28(a)(10)]. Under the rule of law stated in *Abrams v. Pure Manufacturing, Inc.,* the plaintiff must prove . . .

CERTIFICATE OF COMPLIANCE*

"(11) the certificate of compliance, if required by Rule 32(a)(7)."

JOINT APPENDIX

Page of Transcript		Page of Appendix
T–1	Amended Complaint	1
T–3	Answer	4
T–110	Motion for Judgment as a Matter of Law	8
T–19–21	Relevant Testimony of Ms. Forrester	9–11

INTERNET EXERCISE

Determine if your state or federal appellate courts stream oral argument. Watch recent arguments to learn about the process. This also will assist in learning about the court and judges' style in oral argument.

Oral Argument

The paralegal assists with oral argument by preparing an oral argument notebook in close consultation with the attorney. The notebook is organized to contain major arguments with references to supporting legal authority, applicable public policy, indexes to the most significant references in the record, major case authorities, copies of important statutes, jury instructions, and other key materials for quick reference.

You should attend the oral argument if possible. Your familiarity with the case, gained through months and years of work, can assist the attorney at significant points in the argument, especially in responding to unanticipated points made by the opposition or questions from the court.

EXHIBIT 12.16 Process to Follow in an Appeal

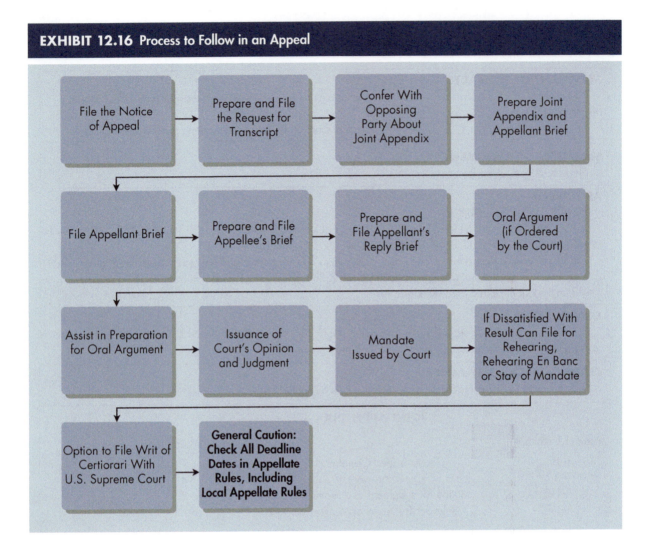

File the Notice of Appeal → Prepare and File the Request for Transcript → Confer With Opposing Party About Joint Appendix → Prepare Joint Appendix and Appellant Brief

File Appellant Brief → Prepare and File Appellee's Brief → Prepare and File Appellant's Reply Brief → Oral Argument (if Ordered by the Court)

Assist in Preparation for Oral Argument → Issuance of Court's Opinion and Judgment → Mandate Issued by Court → If Dissatisfied With Result Can File for Rehearing, Rehearing En Banc or Stay of Mandate

Option to File Writ of Certiorari With U.S. Supreme Court → **General Caution: Check All Deadline Dates in Appellate Rules, Including Local Appellate Rules**

ETHICAL CONSIDERATIONS: THE DO'S AND DON'TS IN APPELLATE PRACTICE

Professionalism before an appellate court is a given. That means being prepared for the questions that will be posed by the appellate panel. Although as a paralegal you will not be arguing before an appellate panel, assisting your attorney may well be one of your functions. From the time an appellate brief is filed to the time of oral argument, the law may change with new precedents being handed down that may directly affect your case.

Research whether any new cases affect your case. The appellate court surely will have any precedent-changing cases at their fingertips. Don't have your legal team be embarrassed, appear incompetent or unprepared.

Along those lines, if a case directly affects your case and was not cited or was not known at the time of the filing of the brief, bring it to your attorney's attention so that it can be addressed with the court. Sometimes one of the most difficult things to do is conceding a point or acknowledging a flaw in an argument. But the court will respect the candor and honesty—not to mention

ETHICAL CONSIDERATIONS: THE DO'S AND DON'TS IN APPELLATE PRACTICE (*CONTINUED*)

that it is required by the rules of ethics. However, admitting incompetency in representing a client is not the best approach for the successful conclusion of a case. Recently, a Kansas attorney dressed up like Thomas Jefferson to argue his case before the Kansas Supreme Court. He acknowledged his incompetency both at the trial level and appellate level—and he was disbarred. (Check YouTube for a video of the oral argument.)

There are lessons to be learned from the Kansas Supreme Court argument. The first take-away from oral argument is dress professionally before the court. That seems like stating the obvious, but some attorneys dress inappropriately when appearing before the appellate courts. Unprofessional attire does not go unnoticed, resulting in admonitions by the court or, worse yet, disallowing oral argument before the court. (Some courts require long sleeved clothing only when appearing before them.) The second take-away from the Kansas Supreme Court oral argument is

know the law. Know the current case law and be sure your attorney has the pertinent case law or statutes available. Having them in a binder is helpful as well. This goes to the competency of the arguing attorney. A final take-away from the Kansas argument is know your record. Know where important passages are cited within the record and note them for your attorney so he or she can reference them to the court. Prepare an outline of the record with references to the facts and evidentiary points within the record. And yes, that means page-by-page references. One guarantee in any appellate oral argument is that the court will be prepared—well prepared. The judges will not only have a command of the law, but will know the case's record inside and out. They often cite to pages from the joint appendix when questioning an attorney at oral argument. Do not underestimate the court's preparation as it could contribute to under-preparing or over-confidence—which will quickly be erased when the oral argument commences. Be sure your attorney has all the tools needed for a successful oral argument. Competency equals preparation, which equal success. As a paralegal, you can be instrumental in that success.

SUMMARY

In this chapter you have learned the function, procedure, and forms for post-trial practice. Paralegals often research and draft two post-trial motions. A motion for judgment as a matter of law, if granted, overturns the verdict as going against the weight of the evidence. A motion for a new trial because of procedural or other errors may be combined with the motion for judgment as a matter of law. A bill of costs is calculated and drafted by the prevailing party.

The paralegal for the prevailing party may assist the attorney in gaining the enforcement of the judgment. This process may be started in the initial stages of the case to guarantee that the property or funds will be available to cover any judgment. Notice of an expected judgment against the property is filed as a lis pendens. Enforcement procedures are more commonly employed after judgments, and involve investigating the location and amount of the debtor's assets through a variety of techniques. Interrogatories, post-trial depositions, writ of execution, garnishment, and domestication of the judgment may be used.

Appeal is a complex process allowing the losing party to seek appellate review of the trial judge's decision. Your role in this step includes developing a thorough appellate checklist, drafting and filing the necessary notice and other documents, maintaining a deadline control system, researching and drafting an appellate brief, and assisting at oral argument. See Exhibit 12.17.

EXHIBIT 12.17 Letter of Recommendation/Commendation

White, Wilson & McDuff
ATTORNEYS AT LAW
FEDERAL PLAZA BUILDING, SUITE 700
THIRD AND MARKET STREETS
LEGALVILLE, COLUMBIA 00000
(111) 555-0000

MEMO TO: Terry Salyer

FROM: Isadora Pearlman

Your preliminary work in post-trial procedure has been successful; you are now ready to assist Mr. White in the appeal of Ms. Forrester's case.

Better than that, you have come to the end of your training period. Now you have the skills to assist our attorneys in the variety of litigation cases that will be assigned to you. You know how to research what you need on your own. Always remember to ask questions and strive to improve your knowledge.

You are ready to be a highly professional litigation paralegal. Congratulations and good luck!

KEY TERMS

additur	judgment debtor	question of law
appellant	judgment proof	receivership
appellee	levy	remittitur
execution	lis pendens	supersedeas bond
exemplified	postjudgment interrogatory	standard of review
garnishee	post-trial deposition	supplementary proceedings
garnishment	post-trial request for	
harmless error	production of documents	
judgment creditor	question of fact	

QUESTIONS FOR STUDY AND REVIEW

1. What are the two most common motions to have the judgment set aside? What are they called in your state practice? Define each of these motions.

2. Rule 59 requires that a motion for a new trial must be filed within how many days of the entry of judgment? What is the rule in your state?

3. What is the bill of costs? What should you include when preparing a bill of costs? What form is used for a bill of costs?

4. To what law does a judgment creditor in federal court look to enforce a federal judgment? A state judgment in state court?

5. What is a prejudgment remedy?

6. What is a lis pendens?

7. What are the various types of property subject to execution? What is exempt in your state?

8. What are the formal methods that can be used by a judgment creditor to determine the assets of the judgment debtor?

9. Identify and describe the common procedures for enforcing a judgment.

10. What is the step-by-step process for executing on property in your state?

11. What procedure is followed to have a judgment rendered in one federal jurisdiction honored in another federal jurisdiction?

12. List the various ways you can assist in the appeals process.

13. Describe the key steps and time limits in the federal appellate process and in your state's appellate process.

14. What are the key components of an appellate brief?

15. What are the key components of an oral argument notebook?

SYSTEMS FOLDER ASSIGNMENTS

1. Research the rules of procedure and law in your jurisdiction on the availability of formal supplementary proceedings for locating a judgment debtor's assets. Check the U.S. Code as well for any such procedures. Then list the procedures and applicable rules and statutes in your systems folder. Place a copy of or a page reference to the notice of lis pendens and the Interrogatories in Aid of Judgment in your systems folder.

2. Research your state law to determine what assets of a judgment debtor are exempt from execution on the judgment. List these in your systems folder.

3. Make an outline of the procedure for domesticating a judgment in another state and in federal court. Place the outline in your systems folder.

4. Draft a step-by-step checklist for enforcing a judgment in your state. Place the checklist and any pertinent forms in your systems folder.

5. Place a page reference or copy of the Checklist for Federal Appellate Procedure (Appellant) in your systems folder. Research appellate procedure for your state and make a separate state appellate checklist for your systems folder. Verify appellate time requirements in the Motions, Pleadings, and Time Limits exhibit and add state time limits. Additionally, place page references or a copy of the skeletal appellate brief in your systems folder. Enter applicable rule references. Research the format of an appellate brief for your state. Include a copy in your systems folder plus references to rules on the required format.

APPLICATION ASSIGNMENTS

1. Assume that your client has a judgment for $250,000 against X, who lives in your state. You know that X has $100,000 in liability insurance, a $100,000 home and land, a small cottage worth $60,000 (but only $15,000 paid for), two vehicles each worth $10,000 (both paid for), a boat worth $7,000, and an online coffee business that generates $30,000 in gross annual income. Under your state statutes, what of X's assets are not exempt from execution on the judgment?

2. Assume that you represent a judgment debtor who has recently paid off a judgment. Under your state law, what procedure must one follow to record a release of judgment?

3. When must a notice of appeal be filed under your state's rule of appellate procedure? Can this time be extended by the court?

4. If a defendant has moved for a judgment as a matter of law (directed verdict) based on the weight of the evidence and the motion was denied, what motion may the defendant file after the trial if the defendant believes the jury's verdict is against the weight of the evidence? What motion should be filed if the defendant believes a serious procedural error was committed by the judge? What state rules govern these motions?

5. Compare and contrast your federal circuit court of appeals brief requirements with your state's appellate rules for briefs. Prepare a list of the differences and similarities for your systems folder. Note that some courts may have local rules that supplement these rules. Be sure to include any local rule requirements in your analysis.

CASE ASSIGNMENTS

1. Assume for purposes of this assignment that, contrary to the weight of the evidence, the jury returned a verdict against Mrs. Forrester. The areas that you believe the jury ignored are a) that Hart was looking at the van radio just prior to the accident; b) that several of Mercury Parcel's documents showed the van had faulty brakes; and c) that defendants offered no evidence whatsoever that Mrs. Forrester was careless or contributed in any way to the accident. Using your state form, draft a motion (no supporting affidavit or memorandum) for judgment notwithstanding the verdict or judgment as a matter of law.

2. Mercury Parcel has had a judgment entered against it for negligence against Mrs. Forrester.

   (a) Identify and prepare the motion(s) that Mercury Parcel can assert prior to filing a notice of appeal.

   (b) Assume that Mercury's motion(s) have been denied by the trial court judge, and prepare the notice of appeal in accordance with the rules in your jurisdiction.

   (c) Outline the components and requirements of an appellant's brief following your jurisdiction's rules of appellate procedure. Include in your outline such information as page limits, font size, margins, and any other requirements for filing a brief.

APPENDIX A

SYSTEMS FOLDER CONTENTS

The list of systems folder contents follows the text and the systems folder assignments in the workbook. It is a suggested list only. The systems folder is a student-created portfolio and can be created by using the following outline. A good systems folder has a table of contents, for which this list can be used, or a tab system for the quick location of any part of the system. Expand the system as you choose to accommodate local practice forms or alternative methods of practice.

QUICK REFERENCE INFORMATION

I. Preliminary and frequently used information

    A. Office structure and procedure

        1. Office structure chart

        2. Timekeeping forms and procedure

        3. Deadline control forms and procedure

    B. General information

        1. Court structure, names, addresses, and phone numbers for clerks of court and other persons frequently contacted

        2. Time deadline chart/rules and formula for computing time

        3. Statutes of limitations

        4. Case roadmap

        5. Ethics

        6. Professional organization information

INTERVIEW

I. Client interview

    A. Task and purpose

    B. Interview plan

        1. Interview plan checklist

        2. Steps in interview plan

            a. Interview forms and checklists

            b. List of information for client to bring to interview

            c. Appointment confirmation letter

            d. List of ethical considerations

    e.   List of interview techniques

    f.   Checklist of information to be given client at initial interview

    g.   Fee arrangement

    h.   Release of information forms (HIPAA)

    i.   Checklist for preparing interview site

    j.   Sample interview summary

INVESTIGATION

I.   Investigation

    A.   **Purposes of investigation**

    B.   **Quick guide to evidence**

    C.   **Investigative sources, including Internet sources**

    D.   **Sample investigation plan**

    E.   **Ethical Applications to Investigation**

    F.   **Medical information**

        1.   List of available medical records

        2.   Standardized request letter

        3.   Authorization to disclose protected health information (HIPAA)

        4.   Letter to doctor requesting medical summary/follow-up letter

    G.   **Accident scene checklist**

    H.   **Suggestions for locating witnesses and experts**

    I.   **Interviewing a witness**

        1.   Witness information cover sheet

        2.   Checklist for witness interview

        3.   Description of how to create interview questions

        4.   Checklist of considerations for conducting a witness interview

        5.   Tips for taking and drafting an effective statement (illustrative statement)

    J.   **Preserving evidence**

        1.   Accident diagram and other forms

        2.   Checklist

PLEADINGS AND SERVICE

I.   Drafting the complaint

    A.   **State and federal captions/pertinent rules including captions for multiple parties and privacy redaction**

    B.   **Common causes of action and remedies**

        C.   **Checklist for drafting a complaint**

        D.   **Sample notice and fact complaints**

        E.   **Other sample complaints**

II.   **Injunctions/sample forms**

III.   **Filing the lawsuit and service of process**

        A.   **Outline of tasks and purposes**

        B.   **Fee schedule for federal and state courts**

        C.   **Forms**

            1.   Federal and state summons

            2.   Federal civil cover sheet

            3.   Notice of lawsuit and request for waiver of service of summons

            4.   Waiver of service of summons

            5.   Form USM-285: process receipt and return and equivalent state form

            6.   Motion for special appointment to serve process

            7.   Affidavit of return of service

            8.   Consent to jurisdiction by magistrate judge

        D.   **Reference guide and checklists for methods of filing, e-filing, and service (add state)**

        E.   **Checklist for locating defendants**

        F.   **Checklist for service of process: federal and state**

        G.   **Checklist for filing and service of documents subsequent to the complaint: federal and state**

IV.   **Obtaining default judgment**

        A.   **Task and purpose**

        B.   **Checklist for default judgment: federal and state**

        C.   **Forms**

            1.   Affidavit and request for default judgments

            2.   Clerk's certificate of entry of default

            3.   Request to clerk for entry of default judgment and affidavit

            4.   Request to court for entry of default judgment and affidavit

            5.   Affidavit of nonmilitary service

            6.   Judgment of default

            7.   Notice of application for default judgment

            8.   Notice of motion for default judgment by court to defendant who has appeared in action

        D.   **Setting aside a default judgment/motion to set aside**

V.   Motions

    A.   Checklists for drafting, filing, and serving motions: federal and state

    B.   Motion to dismiss complaint

    C.   Notice of motion

    D.   Demurrer

    E.   Memorandum of law in support of motion to dismiss

    F.   Order for dismissal of complaint

    G.   Joint application for extension of time

    H.   Other motions to dismiss/Form 19 Federal Rules/Rule 12(b) motions

        1.   Federal Rule 12(b) motions to dismiss: Form 19 Federal Rules

        2.   Motion to make more definite and certain: Federal Rule 12(e)

        3.   Motion to strike: Federal Rule 12(f)

        4.   Motion for judgment on the pleadings

        5.   Motion for summary judgment/notice/affidavit

    I.   Other motions (add as they come up in text)

VI.   Removal of state action to federal court

    A.   Checklist for removal of action to federal court

    B.   Notice of removal

VII.   Answer, counterclaim, and cross-claim

    A.   Task and purpose: answer

    B.   List of style and content suggestions for answer

    C.   List of suggestions for drafting successful denials in the answer

    D.   Chart of forms of denial in pleadings

    E.   Steps in locating affirmative defenses

    F.   Sample answer, counterclaim, and cross-claim

VIII.   Third-party practice pleadings

    A.   Checklist for third-party complaint

    B.   Third-party summons

    C.   Third-party complaint

    D.   Third-party motion to implead

IX.   Amended pleadings

    A.   Checklist of procedures and time limits for amended pleadings

    B.   Amended complaint

    C.   Motion to amend the pleadings

X.   Motions for judgment on the pleadings and summary judgment: see motions

XI.   File pleading log

XII. Pleadings, motions, and time limit exhibit (or place in quick reference section at beginning)

DISCOVERY

I.   Discovery in general/motions to compel and for protective orders

    A.   Outline of definition and purpose, applicable state and federal rules on scope, limits, and sanctions

    B.   Preservation letter

    C.   Checklist of disclosure procedure

    D.   Report of parties' planning meeting

    E.   Ethical considerations and authority

II.   Interrogatories

    A.   Outline of definitions, purpose, scope, applicable rules, and procedure for interrogatories, including time limits

    B.   Checklist for planning and drafting interrogatories

    C.   Sample interrogatories in e-discovery cases

    D.   Form interrogatories for auto accident case

    E.   Copies of any other interrogatories or types of questions

    F.   List of objections to interrogatories

    G.   Form letter to client to gather information for answering interrogatories

    H.   Checklist for answering interrogatories

III. Depositions

    A.   Outline on definition, purpose, scope, applicable rules, and procedure, including time limits

B. Checklist on preparing and serving subpoenas, including subpoena duces tecum, HIPAA procedural requirements, and sample cover letter to records custodian

C. Notice to take deposition

D. Subpoena and subpoena duces tecum

E. Deposition checklist, plaintiff, auto

F. Deposition outline

G. Format for deposition outline

H. Checklist for planning and preparing an outline for taking a deposition

I. Checklist for preparing witness files

J. Letter to client on preparing for deposition

K. List on preparing witnesses for testifying

L. Checklist for attending and reviewing the deposition

M. Digesting depositions
   1. List of techniques for digesting a deposition
   2. Sample digests of deposition

IV. Production of documents and things and entry upon land for inspection and other purposes

A. Outline on definition, purpose, scope, applicable rules, and procedure for requests for production, including time limits

B. Checklist for production of documents and electronic information— request, response, examination

C. Sample request for production and inspection of documents, things, and real property

D. Response to request for production

V. Request for physical and mental examination

A. Outline on the definition, purpose, scope, applicable rules, and procedure for a request for physical and mental examination

B. Motion for compulsory physical examination

C. Letter to client regarding compulsory physical examination

D. Checklist on the paralegal's role in drafting and working with requests for compulsory physical examinations

E. Guide for reviewing and interpreting documents: creating the mini-guide on any technical topic

F. Sample mini-guide for interpreting medical records

VI.   Requests for admissions

   A.   Outline on definition, purpose, scope, applicable rules, and procedures related to a request for admissions

   B.   Form for request for admissions: Federal Form 25

   C.   Form for response to a request for admissions

VII. Objections, compelling discovery

   A.   Outline of definition, purpose, applicable rules, and procedures related to objections, protective orders, and compelling discovery

   B.   Checklist on compelling disclosure and discovery

   C.   Motion to compel

   D.   Affidavit in support of motion to compel

   E.   Order compelling discovery

VIII. Discovery through Freedom of Information Act

   A.   Checklist for making a request pursuant to the Freedom of Information Act (both state and federal)

   B.   Form for request pursuant to Freedom of Information Act

IX.   Organizing files

   A.   Checklist for organizing the small case file

   B.   Checklist for organizing the large case file
       1.   Master index sheet
       2.   Subfile index sheet

   C.   Alternative methods for organizing case files

   D.   Case file to date

SETTLEMENT

I.   Settlement

   A.   Definition and factors bearing on settlement

   B.   Outline of ethical considerations

   C.   Checklist of items to be researched and summarized in preparation for settlement

   D.   Damage summary and worksheet

   E.   Damage calculation formulas

   F.   Sample settlement précis or letter

G.   List of components of settlement brochure

H.   Related forms

1.   General authorization for settlement (power to settle)
2.   Release for personal injury
3.   Mutual release
4.   Covenant not to sue
5.   Settlement agreement
6.   Stipulation and order for dismissal
7.   Stipulation consent decree and order
8.   Settlement distribution statement

II.   Alternative dispute resolution

A.   State statutes on ADR

B.   State forms for mandatory or voluntary ADR

PRETRIAL CONFERENCE

I.   Pretrial conference

A.   Preparation checklist

B.   Applicable federal and state rules

C.   Outline for pretrial memorandum

TRIAL PREPARATION AND TRIAL

II.   Trial preparation

A.   Trial preparation checklist

B.   Case status sheet

C.   Steps in obtaining and serving subpoenas (cross-reference to section on deposition subpoenas)

D.   Juror data sheet

E.   Sources and methods for conducting jury investigations

F.   Applicable state and federal rules of evidence on demonstrative evidence

G.   List of commercial sources of demonstrative evidence

H.   List of ABA Civil Trial Practice Standards on technology and pretrial preparation

I.   Structure of a trial notebook

     J.   Sample trial motions (also add to motion section)

     K.   Sample motion in limine (also add to motion section)

     L.   Jury instruction sources

     M.   Sample jury instructions

III.   **Preparing the client and witness for trial**

     A.   Checklist for preparing clients, witnesses, and expert witnesses for trial

     B.   Guidelines for witness's trial testimony

IV.   **Trial**

     A.   List of tasks at trial

     B.   Form for drafting findings of fact and conclusions of law

     C.   Verdict forms (3 types)

POST-TRIAL PRACTICE

I.   **Post-trial motions and pertinent rules/deadlines**

     A.   Renewal of motion for judgment as a matter of law (JNOV for state)

     B.   Motion for new trial (place extra copies in motion section)

II.   **Bill of costs: state and federal**

III.   **Enforcement of judgment**

     A.   Pertinent rules of procedure and statutes

     B.   Notice of lis pendens

     C.   Interrogatories in aid of judgment

     D.   List of exempt assets under state law

     E.   Checklist for enforcing judgments under state law

         1.   Letter to judgment debtor
         2.   Follow-up letter
         3.   Writ of execution
         4.   Application and affidavit for a writ of garnishment
         5.   Writ of garnishment
         6.   State garnishment forms
         7.   Outline of procedure for domesticating a judgment in another state and in federal court

APPEAL

I. Checklist for federal appellate procedure, including rules and time limits

  A. Notice of appeal

  B. Designation of record on appeal

  C. Motion for enlargement of time

  D. Notice of filing of brief

II. Checklist for state appellate procedure/forms

III. Outline of federal and state appellate briefs plus rules on required format, sample appellate brief format

APPENDIX B

THE SUBSTANTIVE LAW OF TORTS

INTRODUCTION

The importance of learning the substantive law of torts,* or for that matter any other area of law, is that you will know the unique terminology of that area, its various causes of actions or defenses to which your client may be entitled, and its evidentiary requirements—all of which helps you to distinguish the relevant facts and information from the nonrelevant. In addition, your general knowledge of an area of law helps you to recognize issues and gives you the framework from which you can construct effective research and inquiry into issues or elements identified as relevant. The goal of this appendix is to provide you with the basic knowledge necessary to begin working effectively in the area of torts, and specifically tort litigation.

A tort is a civil as opposed to a criminal wrong for which the injured party can sue the wrongdoer for compensation. It is distinct from breach of contract and addresses harms to persons, property, rights, and economic and other relationships. Generally, torts have four common elements: (1) a legal duty of one person to another, (2) an act or omission that breaches that duty, (3) a harm, and (4) a finding that the harm was a direct result of the act or omission. Typical torts are driving recklessly and causing an automobile accident, manufacturing a product that is defective and causes injury, maliciously telling lies about a person that damages the person's reputation, and causing toxic industrial wastes to seep into the groundwater. Some torts, such as striking a person or wrongfully taking property, may also be crimes. When torts and crimes coincide, two distinct bodies of law are invoked, resulting in a government action for violation of a criminal statute and a private (or civil) action for violation of tort law.

The basic public policies underlying tort law are *fairness* (those who cause harm should bear its costs), *compensation* (an injured party ought to have access to a remedy

---

*See "A Brief Guide to Causes of Action and Remedies" in Chapter 4 for a concise statement of the elements that must be proved in several of the torts mentioned in this appendix.

for an injury inflicted by another), and *prevention* (holding people responsible for their wrongs will cause them to take steps to avoid those harms). This appendix will address the various kinds of torts and applicable defenses, and who can be held responsible for a tort.

SOURCES OF TORT LAW

Although many other areas of law, including contracts, have been substantially codified—placed into statutory form—tort law is founded in and primarily exists today as common (court-made) law. Some state and federal statutes create duties and define torts, but most of tort law and the individual torts are defined by a series of judicial opinions incorporating, interpreting, and adding to the common law. Some works such as the *Restatement (Second) of Torts* and treatises such as Prosser's *The Law of Torts* provide a general sense of tort law applicable in all jurisdictions, and they should be consulted along with existing statutes.

UNINTENTIONAL TORTS: NEGLIGENCE

INTRODUCTION

Unlike criminal law that emphasizes the intentional commission of a crime, tort law addresses unintentional, careless, or accidental harms. This substantive area of tort law is referred to as negligence law. Negligence is defined as "failure to use reasonable care, resulting in damage or injury to another." All persons have a duty to conduct themselves in their activities so as not to create an *unreasonable* risk of harm to others. The basic elements of negligence are:

1. Duty

2. Breach of that duty

3. Injury

4. Proximate cause—the breach has caused the injury.

In order to recover damages, the plaintiff must prove the existence of each of these elements by a preponderance of the evidence.

DUTY

A *duty* is the obligation of care exercised by one person in respect to another person as dictated by the circumstances and as imposed by common law or statute. For example, when you operate a vehicle at high speeds, you have a duty to the person in the vehicle in front of you to keep a reasonable distance between your car and the other vehicle. That distance is necessary to avoid a collision should the other vehicle have to stop quickly. The harm likely to occur under the circumstances if care is not exercised defines the duty.

In addition, some duties are not invoked until some action is taken. A person seeing another person stranded on a ledge on a tall building has no duty to try to save the person, because doing so may get two people killed instead of one or none. If the bystander, however, elects to help the stranded person, the duty to do so in a non-negligent fashion is involved. On the other hand, a firefighter has a duty to try to rescue the stranded person, as a lifeguard has a duty to try to rescue a drowning person.

Normally the harm must be *foreseeable*—likely and predictable. Airline baggage loaders who frequently toss luggage and packages do not have the same duty of care to those around them as they would if they were told package X contained nitroglycerin or other explosives. Therefore, the duty is defined by the circumstances that include any predictable harm resulting from the absence of due care.

BREACH OF DUTY—STANDARD OF CARE

A *breach of an existing duty* is the failure to conform to the required standard of care. The required standard of care is that which is reasonable under the circumstances. In other words, *what would a reasonable and prudent person do under similar circumstances?* If a person's conduct conforms to that standard, there is no breach; if the person's conduct falls short, there is a breach. Driving the speed limit on a dry, sunny day may be reasonable, but doing the same thing on an ice-covered road may not be.

A physically handicapped person is held to a standard that is reasonable for a physically handicapped person. Mental illness or infirmity does not generally change the standard, however. A child is held to a standard of reasonability for children of similar age. Professionals such as physicians, engineers, lawyers, and others are held to a higher standard, that is, that which is acceptable for a member of the profession as defined by professional competence in the community. Normally these standards are proven by expert testimony.

Businesses and other landowners must make reasonable efforts to see that their property is safe for those likely to come onto or be attracted to the property.

INJURY/DAMAGES

The third element requires that an injury actually occurs to the victim. The types of injuries that are compensated (with money) are medical bills and services related to physical injuries and disabilities, pain and suffering (distress, discomfort, emotional trauma), lost wages (only if because of some physical injury), lost enjoyment of life, and damages for injury to or destruction of land or other property.

CAUSATION

The final element of negligence is causation, proof that the injury was caused substantially by the negligent act or omission that comprises the breach of duty. Cause is shown by evidence that X's negligence is the direct cause of the injury—the factual cause.

But factual cause is not enough. The act or omission must be the legal or proximate cause as well. *Proximate cause* requires the consideration of foreseeable consequences and intervening causes. The general rule on foreseeability is that if the result is not foreseeable, then there is no liability. Liability is limited only to the harm that gave rise to the duty in the first place. A famous case on foreseeability is *Palsgraf v. Long Island R.R.*, 248 N.Y. 339, 162 N.E. 99 (1928). Railroad employees negligently caused X to drop a package containing fireworks. It exploded and caused railroad scales to fall on Mrs. Palsgraf, resulting in injuries. The court held that liability was limited to the foreseeable, that is, that contents in the dropped package would be damaged, which defined the original duty of care. A minority of courts rule otherwise and extend liability through to the damage caused by the last falling domino.

Persons causing an accident or other damages are also liable for the harms caused by the rescuers who attempt to undo or mitigate the damage. Since the wrongdoer (*tort feasor*) has placed the person in a state of danger or injury, the wrongdoer is also responsible for the action of those who will foreseeably come and attempt to administer to the injuries or rescue the victim from the danger. Further, the tort feasor is also liable for the full extent of the injuries even if the victim was in an unpredictably weakened or vulnerable state beforehand; that is, the person who slips on a banana peel in a store and suffers a serious heart attack because of a previous condition can recover damages for that injury in addition to the predictable and more likely injuries.

Tortious conduct may not incur liability if the cause of the injury is an *intervening* cause. This cause can be a human act or a natural occurrence (act of God) such as a tornado or lightning. The key is whether the intervening cause is a *superseding* cause. A qualifying superseding cause cannot simply be the foreseeable act of another that makes the situation worse or is the catalyst that sets off the harm. For example, if A carelessly erects a large flagpole, his neighbor bumps the pole with his lawn mower, and the pole falls injuring the mail carrier, A is still liable. The lawnmower bump is not sufficient to relieve the original tort feasor from liability; the cause is not superseding. The cause would probably be superseding if the neighbor deliberately pushed the pole onto mail carrier, or if lightning struck the pole causing it to fall on the carrier. If the intervening event was a wind not sufficient to blow over a well-secured pole, then it would not be a superseding cause.

Normally the victim must prove each of these four elements in order to prevail in an action for negligence. In a situation where negligence is the likely explanation for the injury, a high duty of care is expected, and the defendant has exclusive control over the product or activity, the doctrine of *res ipsa loquitur* ("the thing speaks for itself") comes into play. This doctrine shifts the burden to the defendant to prove there was no negligence. In cases involving airplane accidents, the airline has an enormous duty of care implying that if almost *anything* goes wrong, it is obviously the airline's fault. Also, an injured passenger would normally not have access to evidence revealing negligence, so the burden falls to the airline to prove no negligence was involved.

WRONGFUL DEATH

Common law prevented civil actions based on negligence or willful conduct that resulted in the death of the victim. Consequently, laws have been passed called *wrongful death statutes* that permit suits by representatives of the deceased's estate for the benefit of the deceased's family and other beneficiaries. These statutes permit actions based on negligence as well as willful conduct.

DEFENSES TO NEGLIGENCE

The defenses to negligence include the following:

1. *Comparative negligence.* The doctrine of comparative negligence—which is the law in the majority of states and in Columbia (unless your instructor indicates otherwise)—permits a plaintiff who is contributorily negligent to recover, but the award is reduced proportionately by the percentage of the plaintiff's

negligence. For example, if Ann Forrester stepped onto the highway without looking, then slipped as she tried to retreat, a jury might find her 30 percent negligent. If Mr. Hart was driving too fast to stop, a jury might find him 70 percent negligent. If Ms. Forrester's damages came to $100,000, the award would be reduced by 30 percent to $70,000. In some states, Ms. Forrester would be barred from any recovery if her comparative negligence was found to exceed 50 percent. Some states still use the term *contributory negligence* for this doctrine, although it is a modified version of contributory negligence [see (3) of this list].

2. *Assumption of risk.* This defense states that plaintiffs may not recover for damages if they knowingly place themselves in danger. For example, if Ms. Forrester had decided to stay in the middle of the road and thumb her nose at any oncoming vehicle, she would be assuming the risk of injury, and Mr. Hart would have a defense to Ms. Forrester's action for negligence.

3. *Contributory negligence.* Although most states have abolished contributory negligence as a defense, its use should be understood. If the action of the plaintiff, the person suing for injuries, was a contributing factor in the accident, the plaintiff cannot recover her losses from the defendant, the person being sued. For example, if a jury found that plaintiff Ann Forrester had contributed to her own injuries by failing to look both ways before crossing the highway, she would be barred from any recovery, even if defendant Mr. Hart was found to be primarily responsible for the accident. The harshness of this rule explains why it has been abolished in many states. Assume that contributory negligence is not the law in Columbia unless your instructor indicates otherwise.

4. *Last clear chance.* This doctrine permits recovery of damages by parties who normally could not recover because of their contributory negligence. In that sense it is a defense to the defense of contributory negligence. It applies when the plaintiff, through her own negligence, is placed in the defendant's path so that the defendant has the last clear chance to avoid an accident. If the defendant does not react as a reasonable person should (is negligent), causing injury to the plaintiff, the plaintiff may recover regardless of her initial contributing negligence. For example, assume Ann Forrester carelessly ran across the ice on the road, slipped and fell, leaving her directly in the path of Mr. Hart's van. Also assume that Mr. Hart had a last clear chance to avoid the accident. If he was inattentive and did not avoid the accident, Ms. Forrester could still recover damages, in spite of her own negligence.

INTENTIONAL TORT

INTRODUCTION

All intentional torts have three common elements:

1. An offensive act

2. Intent to commit the act

3. The infringement of a victim's lawfully protected right.

The act must be purposeful and not part of a chain caused by a third party. For example, if X pushes you into Y, your act of falling into Y is not the requisite act for liability. The requisite act must also infringe on the victim's legally protected right. For example an *assault* (threat of harm) invades one's sense of well-being and security, although no discernible physical injury occurs. Because that sense of personal well-being and security has been infringed, liability attaches absent physical damage.

The requisite *intent* is the conscious decision to commit the wrongful act knowing it has harmful consequences. Intent is proven by a person's statement of intent or by circumstantial evidence. Whether the wrongdoer is a child, intends to hit A but hits B, or the harm is greater than intended makes no difference.

INTENTIONAL TORTS AGAINST PERSONS

Assault is the intentional and immediate threat or attempt to inflict injury on the victim while apparently possessing the ability to do so. No physical injury or actual contact is necessary, but generally, the tort victim must be in fear or in apprehension of harm. Words are generally an insufficient threat, but this could depend on the circumstances.

Battery is intentional physical contact on another person to cause or result in bodily injury or offensive touching. Wrongdoer A does not have to personally touch victim B—A can throw a stone that strikes B, or A can touch B's clothing or an item being carried. If A so threatens B that it is a substantial likelihood that B will be struck—and B is struck—A is liable for battery even though A intended only to threaten B. Even a physician may be held liable for battery if an operation goes beyond that which is contemplated and necessary, or causes harm from risks that were not adequately explained to the patient.

False imprisonment is the unlawful and deliberate restraining of the liberty of another. Generally the victim must be aware of the restraint or be injured by it, but the length of confinement is irrelevant. One may be unlawfully restrained by threats as well as by walls. One can be falsely imprisoned if one is at a place voluntarily and then is deliberately prevented from leaving, or no practical way to leave is provided when released, that is, the failure to unlock the door knowing X is ready to leave. Once the plaintiff proves the intentional confinement, it remains for the defendant to prove any justification or lawful authority.

Since shoplifting has become such a national problem, and its in-store investigation so vulnerable to actions for false imprisonment, most states have passed laws giving shopkeepers the right to detain persons reasonably suspected of shoplifting for a reasonable investigative period.

False arrest is a component of false imprisonment. It is the intentional abuse of the power to arrest. It occurs when a person is arrested on knowingly trumped-up charges or is detained beyond a reasonable period for investigation and interrogation. Usually, citizens can make arrests only if they have a reasonable belief the person to be detained is the perpetrator of a felony.

Intentional infliction of emotional distress is an outrageous and extreme act that is intended to cause or recklessly causes the victim to suffer severe emotional distress. A person who secretly exhumed the body of X's husband and placed it in X's house for her to discover when she arrived home would likely be guilty of this tort. In this tort the conduct must be truly abhorrent and the distress must go well beyond normal humiliation or brief depression. There is no need to prove physical injury, but the distress should normally be manifested over a significant period of time. The need for extended psychological or psychiatric care would be such evidence.

Invasion of privacy concerns a series of rights including the right to be left alone (intrusion), the right to exclusive use of one's name and image, the right not to be placed in a false light in the public eye, and the right against unreasonable publicity of private facts [RESTATEMENT (SECOND) § 652A]. Generally the award is for mental suffering, shame, or humiliation as gauged by a person's ordinary sensibilities.

May a business conglomerate try to silence an effective critic by tapping the critic's phone, threatening him, and hiring women to entice him and place him in a compromising light? If it does, it is liable for the tort of intrusion. [See *Nader v. General Motors Corporation*, 298 N.Y.S.2d 137 (1969).] Intrusion is one of four torts under the umbrella phrase invasion of privacy.

Intrusion can consist of entry of another's dwelling, an illegal series of persistent phone calls or intrusive appearances, unauthorized blood tests, and the like.

The right to exclusive use of one's name and image prevents advertisers, for example, from misappropriating an actor's name in an embarrassing or humiliating way. Under such a theory, talk-show host Johnny Carson successfully sued a toilet company for using "Here's Johnny" to advertise its company and product [*Carson v. Here's Johnny Portable Toilets*, 698 F.2d 831 (1983)].

The right not to be placed in a false, and usually humiliating, light places liability on a person for, for example, taking a photo of a public official stepping out of a thunderstorm to shelter under the entrance of a triple-X-rated peep show and publishing it with a caption that suggests the official is a frequent customer of the show.

The fourth area of privacy addresses the *intentional and unreasonable publicity of private facts* and protects persons from the unwarranted publicity of personal or private matters. The matters could include financial concerns, revelation of embarrassing diseases, intimate relations, and similar kinds of things. The publication normally involves newspapers, television, the Internet, and other media where the revelation serves little public purpose and is normally embarrassing and humiliating. Truth, which is a defense to libel and defamation (to be discussed), is not a defense to this tort.

These torts and the entire area of the right of privacy are being reinforced by laws that secure aspects of the right of privacy. These laws give persons the right to live together as consenting, unmarried adults, the right to an abortion, the right against tampering with mail, the right against electronic eavesdropping, and others.

Fraud is the intentional deceit of another for the purpose of depriving the person of property or some other right. The tort of fraud consists of four elements:

1. a false material statement about a past or current fact known by the perpetrator to be false or in reckless disregard of the truth

2. with the intent of securing the victim's reliance on the statement

3. causing the victim to reasonably rely on the statement

4. resulting in loss or harm to the victim.

Tort actions for fraud generally arise in the context of business dealings. Typical fraud is the sale of used cars whose odometers have been turned back or other misrepresentations concerning quality of performance. Fraud does not generally encompass statements of opinion such as, "This is the best value on the market," (puffing in advertising or salesmanship) or statements made from lack of information. In one of the most celebrated fraud cases, Sears was held liable for providing false information to the inventor of quick-release socket wrenches that led the inventor to believe his invention was worth far less than it was. Sears paid $10,000 in royalties for the device that brought in close to $50 million for Sears. Eventually the inventor was awarded several million dollars [*Roberts v. Sears, Roebuck & Co.*, 573 F.2d 976 (1978)].

Defamation is the intentional publishing of false information about a person that injures the person's reputation, respect, or goodwill, or which holds the person out to ridicule, scorn, or contempt. Its origin may lie in the admonition, "Thou shalt not bear false witness against thy neighbor," and its justification stems from the fact that good reputations take years to build but can be dashed on the rocks with one lie. Defamation has become a complex area of law, especially in the struggle of values between a person's right to his or her reputation and the belief in freedom of the press.

First, a party suing for damages must show that the information communicated is false and defamatory. Second, the plaintiff must show that the information was in fact communicated to others—in other words, published. *Publication* can occur in two basic ways. The first is by *slander,* which is the oral communication of the lie, but may include gestures in some circumstances. It involves stating the lie to a third person. The other form of publication, called *libel,* is the writing or printing of the lie in a manner that will communicate the information to at least one third party. Because of the greater permanency of something written, libel is considered the more serious of the two defamation torts. Printing can include pictures or signs or even a message posted on the Internet. When oral statements are recorded or preserved in a way that the danger of dissemination and repetition are similar to written words, then such oral statements are treated as libel rather than as slander.

In addition to the statement being a defamatory lie and being published in some form, the perpetrator must have intended to communicate the statement and there must exist a special harm or a statement that is actionable in and of itself regardless of any special harm.

Some of the principles or rules of defamation law are:

1. There is no action in tort if the person defamed is dead.

2. Individuals, corporations, and groups can sue for defamation if the targets are reasonably identifiable.

3. A statement is not defamatory if said in jest or humor.

4. There is no tort if only a small segment of the community would or does find the statement to be offensive.

5. The plaintiff must be able to show that he or she is the target of the statement.

6. Bookstores and libraries are not liable for libel if they are not aware the book is defamatory.

7. When newspapers and radio stations report a defamatory statement made by another, they are held liable as the primary publisher.

8. Generally the plaintiff must be able to show damages. Special damages are monetary losses such as loss of a job, loss of a promotion, loss of a business deal, or loss of sales.

9. Damages cannot be for emotional harms such as humiliation, stress, or anger.

10. No special damages need to be shown if a slanderous statement

    a. defames a person's business, business outlook, or professional qualifications,

    b. says a person committed an immoral crime (moral turpitude),

    c. says a person has a horrible and humiliating disease (venereal disease), or

    d. impugns the chastity of a woman.

11. Special damages may not have to be shown in libel cases if it is *libel on its face* (obvious). Special damages may need to be shown, however, where the statement is *libel per quod* (where other information is needed). For example, if it was published that X just married Y, that is not libelous on its face. If the community knows that X is already married to Z, however, then we have a problem.

12. To defame a public figure (movie actor, athlete, or other person of voluntary celebrity) or public official (mayor, judge), it must be shown that the publication was reckless as to the truth, malicious (with a desire to hurt the victim), or knowingly false. For ordinary persons and persons involuntarily thrust into the limelight (by being party to a lawsuit), the standard is simply negligence as to the truth.

Several defenses are unique and specific to defamation. They are as follows:

1. The victim's consent to publish.

2. The statement is true (but not if incomplete and thus misleading).

3. The publisher has an absolute privilege—participants in a trial and related procedures, legislators and public officials during the course of their official duties, and spouse to spouse.

4. The publisher has a qualified privilege—news reporter reporting false statements of another made in judicial or legislative hearing, critics of the arts but not the personal life of the artist, and statements made to public officials to facilitate their duties. An example of the latter would be reporting criminal behavior to a police officer or an employee reporting suspected theft by another employee to the manager. If these reports are made with malice then the limited privilege evaporates.

VICARIOUS LIABILITY

The doctrine of vicarious liability imposes liability on persons who, because of a relationship, are held responsible for the torts committed by others. Thus an employer is held responsible for the torts of an employee if the employee at the time of the tort is in the course of employment or doing something on behalf of the employer. It is the doctrine of *respondeat superior*. If the job requires some use of force, such as in the case of a police officer or a private security officer, the employer is liable for excessive force. Normally, however, employers are not liable for intentional torts beyond the control of the employee. Likewise, one partner is responsible for the actions of another partner if the person was acting on behalf of the partnership. And a parent is liable for the torts of a child, but only if the child is acting on behalf of the parent. Vicarious liability has expanded in some states to include the owner of a bar for the unlawful service of minors, and for the tortious acts of patrons who have become intoxicated at a bar even if the owner was not present at the bar. The negligence of the operator of a vehicle can be applied to the owner of the vehicle if the person was driving on behalf of the owner. Vicarious liability does not extend from the independent contractor to the person employing the independent contractor.

CONTRIBUTION AND INDEMNITY

Contribution permits an injured party to sue two or more parties when the wrongdoers have indivisibly contributed to the injuries or if they have acted in agreement. The plaintiff may sue one or both for the entire amount. If one is sued for the entire amount, that defendant may in turn sue the joint tort feasor for an appropriate share of the damages.

In *indemnity* one party either has or assumes the legal obligation to pay for one or more kinds of tortious acts of the other. Contracts frequently state that one party indemnifies the other party for any damages arising from the indemnifier's actions.

EMPLOYER'S LIABILITY TO EMPLOYEES

Today most employers are covered by *workers' compensation* insurance. Thus, an employee's injury is compensated at legislated rates from an insurance fund to which the employer contributes. Negligence or fault is no longer an issue in such cases. If the employer intentionally or recklessly subjects an employee to an unreasonable risk, however, then the employee has an action in tort.

STRICT LIABILITY

Strict liability is an area of tort law that for reasons of public policy attaches liability to certain kinds of hazardous and other activities regardless of fault. Workers' compensation, discussed previously, is one area that has been statutorily made into a strict liability matter. Traditionally, however, it is the more dangerous activities that incur strict liability. An owner of animals is generally strictly liable for the injuries and trespasses caused by the animals. There are some exceptions for dogs and cats and livestock in certain circumstances. Owners of wild animals are strictly liable for injuries caused by the animals. Otherwise, any use of land or other activity that is unnatural and particularly hazardous incurs strict liability. Persons using explosives, hauling gasoline, and storing toxic waste are held to a strict liability standard. The key in strict liability is that no fault must be shown if the person engaging in the dangerous activity is aware of the risk that is being created.

PRODUCT LIABILITY

When a person is injured by a dangerous product, several theories under the broad term *product liability* may provide a remedy for the injury.

Negligence: Product liability negligence requires proof of the same basic elements required in any negligence action: duty, breach of the duty, injury, and breach being the actual and proximate cause of the injury. Negligence might occur in the design, manufacture, testing, or packaging of the product. If the product is dangerous and its danger is not obvious, the failure to place adequate warnings may provide the basis for a negligence suit. The person harmed can be anyone likely to use the product, and the manufacturer, supplier of a part in the final product, seller, and distributor might all be liable.

Breach of warranty: An area of commercial law (Uniform Commercial Code) stemming from the old law of torts provides a remedy for physical harms caused by defective or unfit products. *Express warranties* are promises of quality on which a buyer relies when purchasing a product. A defective product that causes injury is a breach of the promise and is actionable. Express warranties are voluntarily assumed by the manufacturer to help sell the product.

Implied warranties are warranties required by law and follow the goods. Manufacturers and sellers can avoid such warranties by expressly disclaiming them, but such a waiver is deemed unconscionable as applied to physical harm [U.C.C. § 2-719(3)]. The implied *warranty of merchantability* promises that the product is reasonably safe, is of a certain standard of quality, and is fit for its ordinary use. The implied *warranty of fitness* arises when the buyer relies on the seller's knowledge that the product is fit for a specific purpose. Breach of these warranties imposes strict liability unless the seller has expressly limited or disclaimed the warranty.

Strict tort liability: In most jurisdictions today, the manufacturers and sellers of goods are strictly liable for any defective or unfit product that is unusually dangerous and which causes physical harm. Automobiles must withstand certain standards of "crashworthiness" and cannot, for example, have a gas tank that is likely to explode in a typical rear-end collision. Defenses include assumption of risk and improper use of the product.

GLOSSARY

Active data: Active data is the information stored on the hard drive or network.

Additur: A post-trial motion in which the plaintiff requests the court to increase a jury award.

Adjudication on the merits: A judgment by the court deciding the issues of an action, precluding that action from being brought again.

Admissible evidence: Evidence that may be presented in court because it complies with the rules of evidence that it must be relevant.

Affiant: The person who signs an affidavit.

Affidavit: A written, sworn statement.

Affirmative defense: Defense showing that the defendant is not liable even if the plaintiff's claim is assumed to be true and for which the defendant bears the burden of proof.

Alienage jurisdiction: A diversity jurisdiction involving foreign states and their citizens or subjects.

Alternative dispute resolution (ADR): Any means of settling disputes outside of a courtroom or without litigation.

Answer: A formal pleading filed in response to the complaint; identifies the issues to be contested and contains a statement of what the defendant admits and denies and what defenses to the claim, if any, will be presented.

Appellant: The person bringing an appeal.

Appellee: The person defending against an appeal.

Arbitration: An alternative dispute resolution process consisting of the submission of a dispute to a neutral decision maker.

Argumentative denials: Denials that state facts suggesting a defense, but in fact are not really defenses.

Associates: Attorneys who are salaried in a law firm.

Attorney's work product (trial preparation materials): The attorney's mental impressions, conclusions, opinions, or legal theories concerning a case; not discoverable.

Backup data: Backup data is that data that duplicates information as a protective method.

Best evidence rule: Rule that allows only the original document or item to be admitted (exceptions are allowed for practical reasons).

Bill of particulars: A request for the opponent to make an ambiguous pleading more definite and certain.

Billable hours: The time spent on a client's case that can be billed to the client.

Brief: A document stating the relevant legal authority and how it should be applied to the issues and facts of a case.

Burden of proof: The obligation to prove the allegations; usually falls to the accuser.

BYOD—bring-your-own-device: Personal electronic device used for work purposes.

Capacity: Requirements of age, competency, and so on, for a party to be allowed to sue or be sued.

Cause of action: Statement of the claim upon which relief may be granted in an action.

Certificate of service: Certification that a document has been served on the opposing party.

Chain of custody: The chronological record tracing a piece of evidence to the event that has resulted in the action, proving that it is the item in question.

Challenge for cause: The attorney's request to remove a potential juror on the grounds of bias or other reason.

Circumstantial evidence: Evidence that suggests the existence of some other occurrence or thing.

Civil litigation: The process whereby one person sues another person in a court of law to enforce a right or to seek a remedy such as financial compensation.

Class action: Lawsuit filed by individuals with a common interest.

Clawback agreement: An agreement that sets forth the procedures the parties will follow when inadvertent privileged or work product information is disclosed in response to a discovery request.

Clear and convincing evidence: A higher standard of proof than preponderance of the evidence; requires that the matter be shown to be highly probable.

Closing arguments: Summation given by the parties at the end of a trial.

CM/ECF-Case Management/Electronic Case Filing system: Electronic filing system used in the federal court system.

COPE—Company owned personally enabled device: Electronic device issued by employer and used exclusively for work purposes only.

Complaint: The formal document used to commence a lawsuit; tolls the statute of limitations, identifies parties, and states the cause of action the plaintiff alleges against the defendant.

Concurrent jurisdiction: Two courts having the ability to hear the same type of case.

Constructive service: Service of process other than direct service, such as through a newspaper of general circulation.

Contingent fee: Legal fee for representation based on a percentage of the award won by the plaintiff and allowing for no fee if the plaintiff does not win.

Counterclaim: A claim asserted by the defendant against the plaintiff, often included in or with the answer.

Court reporter: Individual who records and transcribes verbatim testimony or court proceedings, such as depositions, by stenography.

Cross-claim: A claim by one party against a co-party in the same action.

Declarant: The person making the statement.

Default judgment: Judgment rendered against the defendant for the damages specified in the claim without the case going to trial, based on the defendant's failure to respond to the complaint within the time limit.

Defendant: The party being sued for an alleged wrong.

Defendant's rebuttal (rejoinder): Last opportunity for defendant to challenge the fact that plaintiff has not proven the case.

Demonstrative evidence: Depiction or representation of something such as a photograph of a scar or a diagram of the accident scene.

Demurrer: A document used in some states to dispute the sufficiency of the complaint or other pleading.

Deponent: A witness or party giving testimony under oath and recorded before trial.

Deposition: A discovery device permitting a party's attorney to question a witness or party spontaneously and under oath before trial, and to record the testimony.

Direct evidence: Evidence that is directly observable and proves the truth asserted.

Direct examination: The initial questioning of the plaintiff's or party who called that particular witness.

Disclosure: The procedure automatically triggered early in a case requiring a party to give to the opponent a broad spectrum of information relevant to the case.

Discovery: The process in a lawsuit involving the exchange of information, exhibits, and documents between parties according to specific rules of procedure.

Diversity of citizenship: Jurisdictional requirement for U.S. District Court that parties of a lawsuit be citizens of different states.

Documentary evidence: Paper evidence such as letters, contracts, or medical records.

Domicile: A person's true, permanent home.

Due process of law: Fair, prescribed judicial proceedings that must be followed before a person may be deprived of life, liberty, or property; guaranteed by the Constitution.

Duty: In tort law, due care owed by one person to another.

E-filing: A court-approved, Internet-based system for filing, serving, and accessing legal documents.

Electronic billing (e-billing): The posting of billing information by the law office to a secure electronic host site for instant client access.

Electronic discovery or e-discovery: Process in civil litigation that deals with electronic formats and information.

Electronically stored information (ESI): Information stored within any electronic device.

Embedded data: Another term for metadata.

Execution: The process of carrying out or enforcing a judgment.

Exemplary (punitive) damages: Damages awarded to a plaintiff beyond actual loss as punishment for conduct of the defendant that is particularly aggravated; also called punitive damages.

Exemplified: Authenticated as a true copy, as an official transcript to be used as evidence.

Fact pleading: The requirement that the body of a pleading state in detail the facts in support of each element of the rule of law or claim.

Federal magistrate judge: Judge appointed under 28 U.S.C.§631 to assist U.S. District Court judges in conducting routine matters in the federal trial courts.

Federal questions: All civil actions arising under the Constitution, laws, or treaties of the United States.

Findings of fact and conclusions of law: The document that contains the court's judgment summarizing the key evidence on the elements of the cause of action and the judge's conclusions that form the basis of the judgment.

Garnishee: The third party who is directed to surrender property owed to the judgment debtor to satisfy the judgment.

Garnishment: The process of trying to reach the assets of a judgment debtor that are in the possession of a third party in order to satisfy the judgment.

General damages: Damages that are a natural and direct result of the defendant's wrong, such as pain and suffering, humiliation, and loss of enjoyment of life.

General jurisdiction: Ability of court to hear all types of cases.

General verdict: Pronouncement of the result, whether finding for the plaintiff or the defendant, with any damages associated with that result.

General verdict with interrogatories: Requires jurors to answer questions relating to the verdict.

Guardian ad litem: Representative for a party who lacks the legal capacity to sue or be sued; serves for the duration of the action.

Habit: The semiautomatic, repeated response to a specific situation.

Harmless error: An error found to have occurred at the trial court by the appellate court, but insufficient to substantially affect the verdict of the case, and therefore, insufficient to overturn the verdict.

In forma pauperis: "In the manner of a pauper"; permission given to an indigent person to sue without liability for costs.

In rem action: An action involving the attachment of property to resolve claims to the property.

In rem jurisdiction: Jurisdiction over property.

Interpleader: The joining of those parties that have the same claim against a third party; done to limit the liability of the third party.

Interrogatories: A discovery device consisting of written questions submitted to another party and answered by that party in writing and under oath.

Joinder of parties: The uniting of parties making claims or defending against an action as co-plaintiffs or co-defendants.

Judgment creditor: The winner in civil cases in which money has been awarded.

Judgment debtor: The loser in civil cases in which money has been awarded.

Judgment proof: Description of a party who has no assets with which to pay a judgment.

Judgment: Formal finding by judge.

Judicial notice: Admission of evidence without authentication, either a fact commonly known in the territorial jurisdiction of the court or a fact readily verifiable through undisputed sources.

Jurisdiction: The power or authority of a court to hear and decide the questions of law or fact (or both) presented by a lawsuit.

Jurisdictional amount (amount in controversy): Specific dollar amount that must be claimed in an action to meet jurisdictional minimum of a given court.

Jury selection: Process of questioning prospective jurors by a judge, or sometimes the attorneys, to choose an impartial jury.

Kill switch: Device that permits a judge to shut down monitors or displays with the click of the switch; used when admissibility of evidence is questioned.

Lawsuit: Formal complaint filed by a wronged party.

Leading question: Question phrased in such a manner as to suggest the desired answer (e.g., "It was raining that night, wasn't it?").

Legal advice: Independent professional judgment based on knowledge of the law and given for the benefit of a particular client.

Levy: To seize and sell property of the judgment debtor as specified by the court to satisfy the judgment.

Lis pendens: Record to notify potential buyers that the plaintiff has asserted a claim against property in a lawsuit.

Litigation system: A detailed procedure manual that is a chronological collection of the guidelines, forms, correspondence, checklists, procedures, and pertinent law for all steps in the litigation process.

Long-arm statutes: Statutes that identify circumstances where a person from another jurisdiction can be held accountable in that jurisdiction.

Malpractice: Legal negligence that causes harm to a client for which an attorney or law firm may be sued.

Mandatory injunction: Requirement that the defendant perform conduct specified by the court.

Material: Of consequence to the determination of the action.

Med-arb: A combination of mediation and arbitration; the matter is first mediated, then any unresolved issue is decided by the same or a different person who serves as an arbitrator.

Mediation: An alternative dispute resolution process incorporating a neutral person (the mediator) who facilitates a mutual resolution of the dispute.

Memorandum of law (memorandum of points and authorities): A document, normally shorter and less formal than a brief, stating the relevant legal authority and how it should be applied to the issues and facts of a case.

Metadata: Data that explains other data.

Motion: A request for a court order granting relief to the moving party.

Motion in limine: A motion filed for protection against prejudicial questions and statements at trial.

Multijurisdictional practice: The provision of legal services in states other than the one for which the attorney is licensed.

Non-waiver agreement: Another term for clawback agreement.

Notary public: Individual who is authorized to administer oaths and attest or certify signatures for their authenticity.

Notice pleading: Abbreviated form of pleading authorized by the Federal Rules of Civil Procedure and parallel state rules.

Opening statement: Introductory remarks by the opposing attorneys on the case and what they will be proving during the trial.

Order: A directive from a judge requiring some act or restraint from some act in a lawsuit.

Partner: Attorney owners of the law firm who share in profits.

Peremptory challenge: The authority of an attorney to strike the name of a potential juror without having to express any reason for the strike; limited in number.

Personal jurisdiction: Courts' power to hear a case against a person.

Physical evidence: Tangible articles; evidence that can be seen, touched, or heard.

Plaintiff: The party bringing the lawsuit.

Pleadings: Formal documents filed in a lawsuit that inform all parties of the basis for and defenses to the lawsuit; normally include the complaint, answer, counterclaim and reply, answer to cross-claim, and third-party complaint and answer.

Plaintiff's rebuttal: Last chance for plaintiff to discredit the evidence admitted during the defense's case.

Postjudgment interrogatory: A method to discover the assets of the judgment debtor through written questions to be answered under oath.

Post-trial deposition: Device used to discover the assets of the judgment debtor through oral examination under oath.

Post-trial request for production of documents: Method to obtain documents that will help in locating the assets of the judgment debtor.

Preponderance of the evidence: Evidence that is more convincing to the trier than the opposing evidence; meets the requirement for the burden of proof in civil cases.

Preservation letter: A letter sent to the opposing party requesting preservation of evidence.

Presumption: A mechanism that allows a jury to presume a fact is true based on indirect evidence if it might be awkward or difficult to prove by direct evidence. For example, mailing a letter creates the presumption it was received. A presumption stands unless it is rebutted.

Prima facie case: The minimum evidence sufficient to prove a case, prior to any rebuttal by the defense.

Pro bono: Free legal services provided to those unable to afford representation.

Pro hace vice: Application by licensed attorneys to practice for a limited purpose in another jurisdiction where they are not licensed.

Probative value of evidence: The degree to which evidence tends to prove or actually proves something.

Procedural law: Law that defines the rules and steps that must be followed in a lawsuit.

Professional ethics: For attorneys, the rules of conduct that govern the practice of law.

Prohibitory injunction: Order that informs a defendant to refrain from a specific course of conduct.

Proof beyond a reasonable doubt: Proof that is so strong it excludes any other reasonable hypothesis or explanation—almost a certainty.

Proximate cause: In tort law, the cause-and-effect relationship that must be established to prove that the conduct in question was the substantial cause of the injury in question.

Quasi in rem action: An action in which the court uses the property of a defendant over whom it does not have personal jurisdiction to pay a judgment against the defendant entered in an action unrelated to the property.

Question of fact: A point decided on evidence; for example, whether the traffic light was red.

Question of law: A point requiring the application or interpretation of statutes and case law, to be decided by a judge; for example, whether a statute is constitutional.

Quick Peek Agreement: An agreement between parties where one party is given access to all, or substantially all, of an opposing party's ESI with the understanding that any disclosure of privileged information is not a waiver of privilege.

Real evidence: The thing itself, physically present as opposed to being described, such as a scar, implement, or live view of the accident scene.

Real party in interest: The one who has the right to sue by law—for example, the injured party or legal representative of that party.

Receivership: Placement of the assets of a business or an individual under the control of a court-appointed receiver who will protect those assets to pay a debt.

Recuse: To disqualify oneself from hearing a case to avoid a potential conflict of interest.

Redaction: The process of editing out irrelevant or privileged information from the text of a document.

Release: A document executed by the plaintiff or claimant that frees the defendant from any further obligations or liability stemming from the incident causing the damages in return for consideration (money).

Relevant: Admissible in court, of consequence to the determination of the action, and tending to prove or refute a fact of consequence.

Remittitur: A post-trial motion in which the defendant requests the court to reduce a jury award because of an error in determining the award or because the award is unreasonably excessive.

Residual data: Residual data is the fragmented data that is from deleted or corrupted files. Also known as latent or ambient data.

Res gestae statements: Statements that are present sense impressions, excited utterances, or about then-existing mental, emotional, or physical conditions.

Routine (custom): The equivalent of "habit" for organizations.

Sanctions: Court imposed remedy that can include dismissal of the lawsuit, imposition of attorney's fees and expenses, contempt orders, and adverse jury instructions.

Service of process: Delivery to the defendant of official notification of the lawsuit and of his or her need to respond; delivery of a copy of the summons, complaint, writs, and other documents to another party.

Settlement: The process whereby both sides review strengths and weaknesses of a case and reach a mutual agreement on how to dispose of the case.

Settlement agreement: A contract between the parties setting all the terms, conditions, and obligations of the parties, including how the action will be dismissed.

Settlement conference: A meeting between the parties to discuss settlement of the case.

Settlement précis: A brief presentation of the client's case designed to persuade the opposing party to settle the case on terms satisfactory to the client.

Special damages: Damages that are incurred because of the defendant's wrong and the actual result of the injury, but not the necessary result, such as medical bills, lost wages, or property loss.

Special verdict: Requests jurors to respond to specific questions relating to the case.

Specific performance: In breach of contract cases, the requirement of the offending party to fulfill specific terms of the contract regarding a unique piece of property.

Spoliation: The destruction or loss of evidence, including the failure to preserve it.

Standard of review: Focuses on the deference an appellate court gives to a lower court decision or jury verdict.

Standing to sue: Requirement that only plaintiffs who suffer or will suffer real or direct injury may sue.

Statute of limitations: Law stating the time limit in which an action must be filed. If the time limit is not met, the defendant has a defense to the action, and the case will be dismissed.

Stipulation: Formal agreement between opposing parties to a lawsuit regarding matters pertinent to the lawsuit, such as to admit certain evidence without testimony.

Subject matter jurisdiction: Jurisdiction defined by nature or subject of the type of lawsuit handled by a court.

Subpoena duces tecum: A document pursuant to a court order that commands a person to appear with certain books, documents, electronically stored information, or tangible things.

Subpoena: A document that commands or orders a person to appear in court or a designated place, which may include a request for documents.

Substantive law: Law that defines the duties owed by one person to another.

Substituted service: Any type of service of process other than actual, personal service, such as through mail, waiver, publication, or legal representative.

Summary trial: A nonbinding, abbreviated trial before a summary jury to see whether either side's case merits a real trial; encourages settlement of especially large cases.

Summons: A document issued by the court that informs the defendant of the action and requires the defendant to respond or appear by or at a designated time; when served, gives the court personal jurisdiction over the defendant.

Supersedeas bond: Bond filed by the judgment debtor to secure the amount of the judgment while the execution of that judgment is stayed pending post-trial motions.

Supplemental jurisdiction (formerly pendant jurisdiction): The power of federal courts already having jurisdiction over a federal claim to hear a state claim and add parties if that claim is based on essentially the same facts as the federal claim.

Supplementary proceedings: The methods used to acquire information about the judgment debtor to enforce a judgment; for example, the post-trial deposition.

Testimonial evidence: Spoken or signed, elicited from a witness.

Third-party practice (impleader): The filing of a third-party complaint by the original defendant against a person not yet named a party to the lawsuit, alleging that the third party is or may be liable for all or a part of any damages won by the original plaintiff against the original defendant.

Tickler system: Calendaring system for deadlines used in a law office.

Trial court: Court where initial lawsuit is filed.

Trustee: Person appointed by the court to represent the debtor's estate in a bankruptcy case.

Unbundling legal services: The mutually agreed limitation of legal representation to one distinct step in a legal matter or process that may have numerous steps.

Venire member: Pool of people that can be called to be on a jury.

Venue: "Neighborhood"; the geographical area in which a court with jurisdiction can hear a case; distinct from jurisdiction.

Verdict: The final decision of the jury regarding the questions of fact submitted to it by the judge.

Voir dire: The questioning of potential jurors by the judge (and attorneys in state some courts) to reveal disqualifying information in the process of selecting an impartial jury.

With prejudice: In the dismissal of a case, the understanding that the action may not be brought again.

Without prejudice: In the dismissal of a case, the understanding that the action may be brought again.

Writ of certiorari: A discretionary writ that allows the U.S. Supreme Court to take only cases that, in its opinion, have sufficient national significance to warrant its attention.

INDEX